Ernie Bushmiller (1905–1982) was an American cartoonist best known for creating the daily comic strip *Nancy*, which has remained in print since 1938. After completing the eighth grade, Bushmiller dropped out of school and began working as a copy boy at the *New York World*. There, he ran errands, observed his cartoonist colleagues, and eventually picked up illustration assignments such as lettering speech balloons and designing crossword puzzles. In 1925, he was given the chance to take over Larry Whittington's comic strip *Fritzi Ritz*, which evolved into *Nancy*.

Denis Kitchen is a cartoonist, writer, and publisher. In 1969, after the success of his self-published *Mom's Homemade Comics*, Kitchen launched Kitchen Sink Press to publish his own work and the work of other underground cartoonists. In its thirty-year run, Kitchen Sink published work by both new and older cartoonists, including R. Crumb, Aline Kominsky-Crumb, Will Eisner, Milton Caniff, Charles Burns, Alan Moore, M. K. Brown, and Ernie Bushmiller. A monograph of Kitchen's own work, *The Oddly Compelling Art of Denis Kitchen*, was published in 2010 by Dark Horse Comics and was nominated for Harvey and Eisner awards. Originally from Wisconsin, he now lives in Western Massachusetts.

THIS IS A NEW YORK REVIEW COMIC
PUBLISHED BY THE NEW YORK REVIEW OF BOOKS
207 East 32nd Street
New York, NY 10016
www.nyrb.com/comics

Cover design by Brian McMullen

A catalog record for this book is available from the Library of Congress.

ISBN: 978-1-68137-836-7

Printed in China

10 9 8 7 6 5 4 3 2 1

NANCY & SLUGGO'S
GUIDE
TO LIFE

Comics about Money,
Food and Other Essentials

Ernie Bushmiller

Foreword by Denis Kitchen

NEW YORK REVIEW COMICS · NEW YORK

THE OBSESSIVE FASCINATION WITH *NANCY* ONLY GROWS

For thirty years (1969–99) my publishing company Kitchen Sink Press produced numerous underground comix and then, increasingly, graphic novels and classic comics reprints. Among the classics, beginning in the early '70s, were scores of comics, magazines, and books collecting Will Eisner's *The Spirit*; nearly thirty volumes of Al Capp's *Li'l Abner*, alongside almost as many editions of Milton Caniff's *Steve Canyon*; Alex Raymond's *Flash Gordon*; V. T. Hamlin's *Alley Oop*; George Herriman's *Krazy Kat*; Cliff Sterrett's highly underrated *Polly and Her Pals*; several books by Harvey Kurtzman; and plenty more.

I was generally lauded by all segments of the comics industry for bringing back into circulation beloved comic strips of earlier generations. That is, until I began publishing topical volumes of a certain strip by Ernie Bushmiller in the late 1980s.

Reactions were swift: The co-publishers of Fantagraphics thought I had lost my marbles. Ardent fans of *The Spirit* and *Flash Gordon* recoiled at Kitchen Sink also publishing "dumb" *Nancy* strips. Retailers who stocked all our other titles expressed hesitancy to display *Nancy Eats Food* or *How Sluggo Survives!* The mere thought of adding *Bums, Beatniks and Hippies* to their otherwise respectable comics libraries evidently gave shivers to some collectors.

Oblivious to the opinions of industry philistines, I followed my own instincts, publishing five volumes of Bushmiller's *Nancy*. Despite resistance in the core comic shop market, they sold in the mass market. Further evidence of having no conventional marketing sense, I also produced Italian-made silk Nancy & Sluggo neckties, with matching tie tacks, directed to an audience whose idea of dressing up was a *clean* T-shirt.

Flash forward a few decades. The world has changed in countless ways, but nowhere so profound or dramatic as the views toward *Nancy*. A few years back, the owner of la Galerie du 9ème Art, a prestigious Parisian gallery, called me. He asked if I would consign portions of my vast Bushmiller art collection for an exhibition. "Bernard," I said, "I didn't know you were such a Bushmiller fan." "Eet ees not me," he replied. "Eet ees ze young women who work at my gallery: they love zees *Nancy*!" Young women in Paris love *Nancy*?

Who *knew*?

I still table occasionally at shows like New York Comic Con, The Small Press Expo, and Cartoon Crossroads Columbus. Whenever I do, any back stock of *Nancy* books, Nancy pins, and other Bushmiller esoterica always sells very quickly, usually to young women, many of them sporting variations of bootlegged *Nancy* shirts, others with Nancy or Sluggo tattoos. Some years back, at an Eisner Awards ceremony in San Diego, I was wearing a black suit and a Nancy tie when I saw gazillion-selling author Raina Telgemeier. She stared covetously at my tie, and practically tore it off my neck when I told her she could have it. Young women in America love *Nancy*? Who *knew*?

Fantagraphics, which had earlier derided Kitchen Sink's *Nancy* volumes, eventually published its own versions, along with Paul Karasik and Mark Newgarden's remarkable *How to Read Nancy*, an elaborate dissection and analysis of a single Bushmiller daily. Cartoonist Bill Griffith, who for many years inserted sly *Nancy* references into his syndicated *Zippy the Pinhead* strip, has authored an exceptional graphic biography of Bushmiller for Abrams. Meanwhile the esteemed *Atlantic* magazine just ran an article extolling the virtues of *Nancy*. Intellectuals love *Nancy*? Who *knew*?

I've learned there is a secret Bushmiller Society, with members expressing almost worshipful adoration of Bushmiller and his most famous creation. It is an organization with cells scattered across North America and portions of Europe. The Billy Ireland Cartoon Library & Museum—part of the Ohio State University, in Columbus—has announced a Nancy festival for 2024: an entire event devoted to our favorite character. An esoteric cult that runs so deep? Who *knew*?

Well, the astute editors at New York Review Comics knew. And thus, herein, you have a "best of" collection of those early Kitchen Sink *Nancy* volumes, *Nancy Loves Food* and *Dreams and Schemes*, along with a large numbers of freshly curated never-before-reprinted *Nancy* strips about money. Who knew there was money to be made on *Nancy*? Oh, *some* people knew.

— DENIS KITCHEN

MONEY

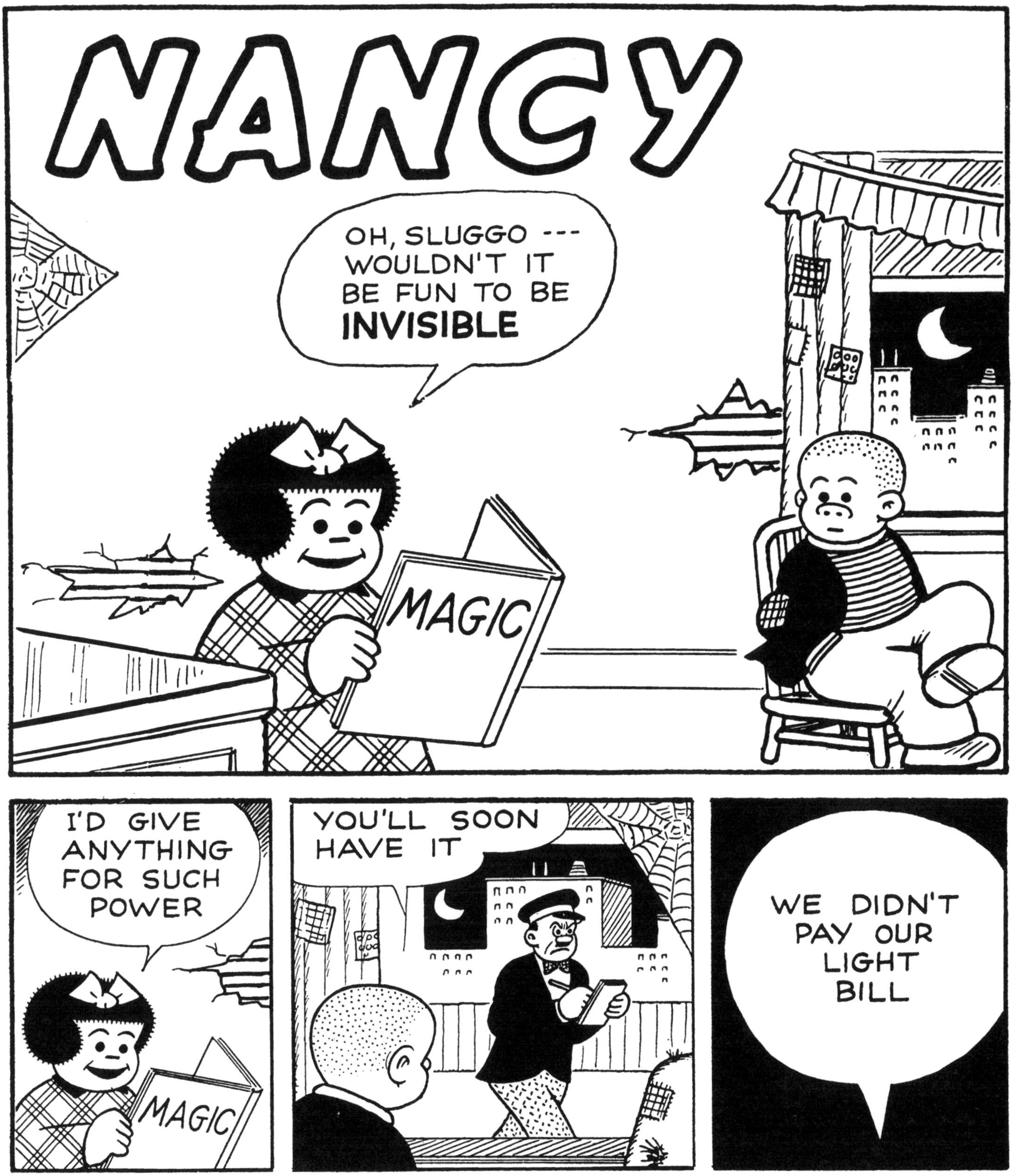
NANCY
OH, SLUGGO --- WOULDN'T IT BE FUN TO BE INVISIBLE
MAGIC
I'D GIVE ANYTHING FOR SUCH POWER
MAGIC
YOU'LL SOON HAVE IT
WE DIDN'T PAY OUR LIGHT BILL

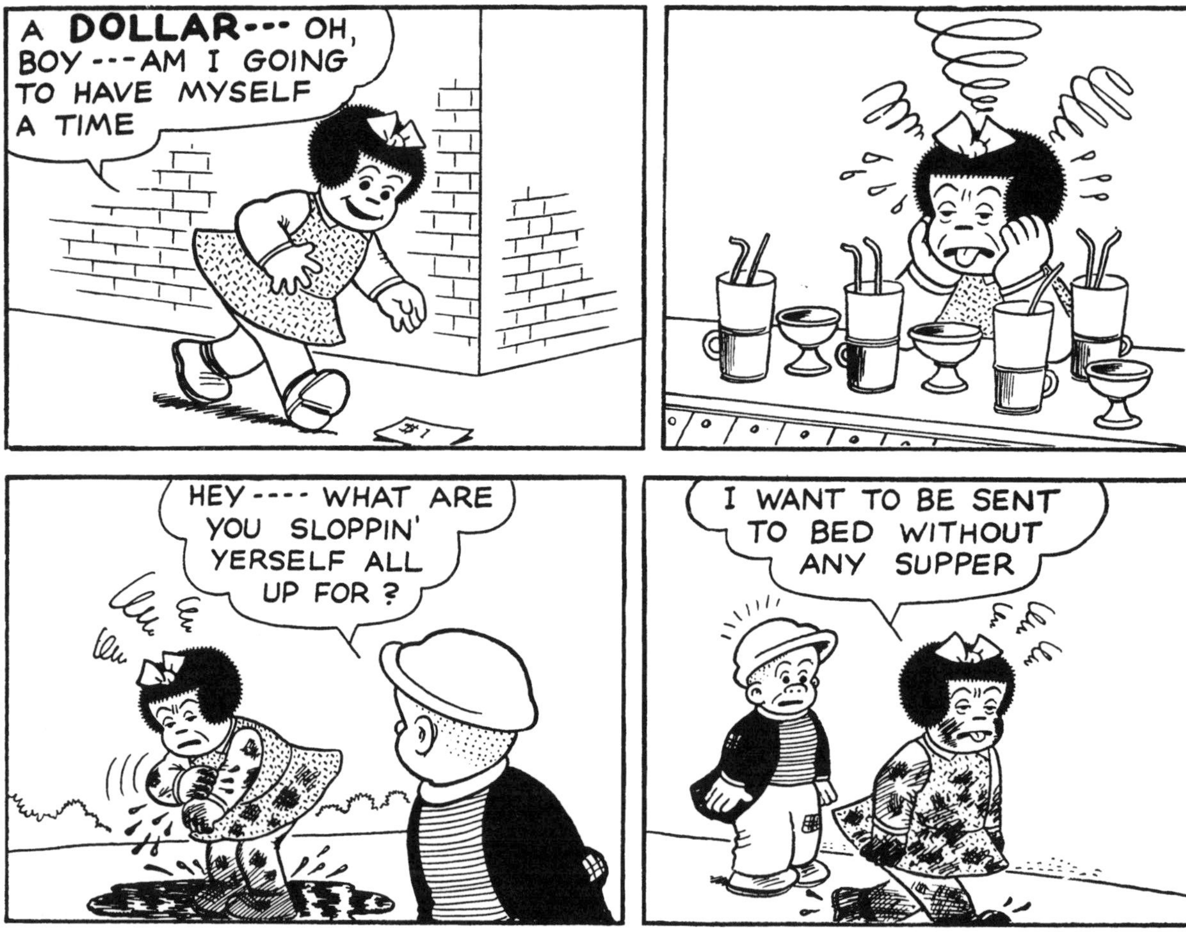
A **DOLLAR**--- OH, BOY---AM I GOING TO HAVE MYSELF A TIME
HEY---- WHAT ARE YOU SLOPPIN' YERSELF ALL UP FOR ?
I WANT TO BE SENT TO BED WITHOUT ANY SUPPER

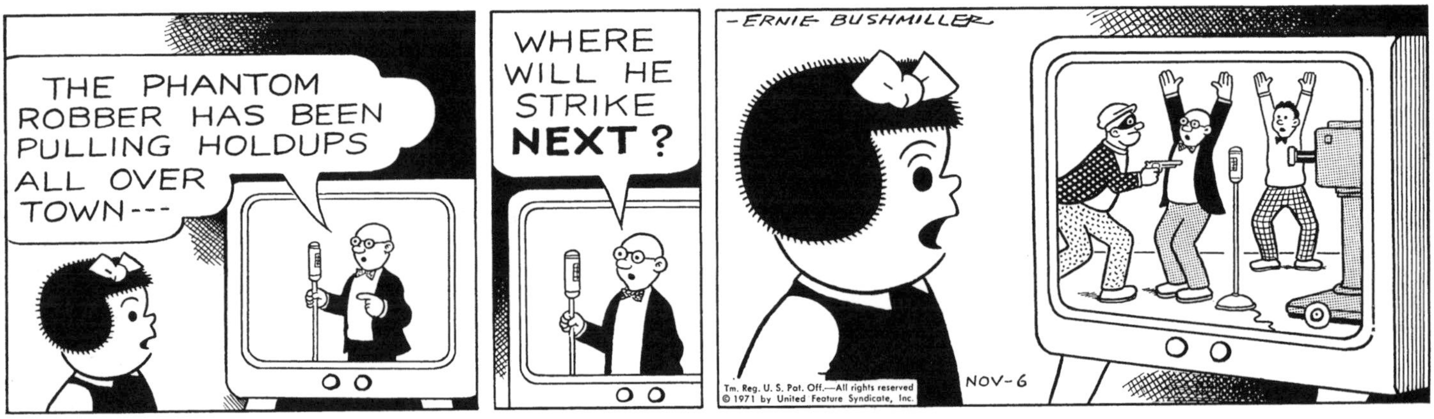
THE PHANTOM ROBBER HAS BEEN PULLING HOLDUPS ALL OVER TOWN---
WHERE WILL HE STRIKE **NEXT** ?
-ERNIE BUSHMILLER
Tm. Reg. U. S. Pat. Off.—All rights reserved © 1971 by United Feature Syndicate, Inc.
NOV-6

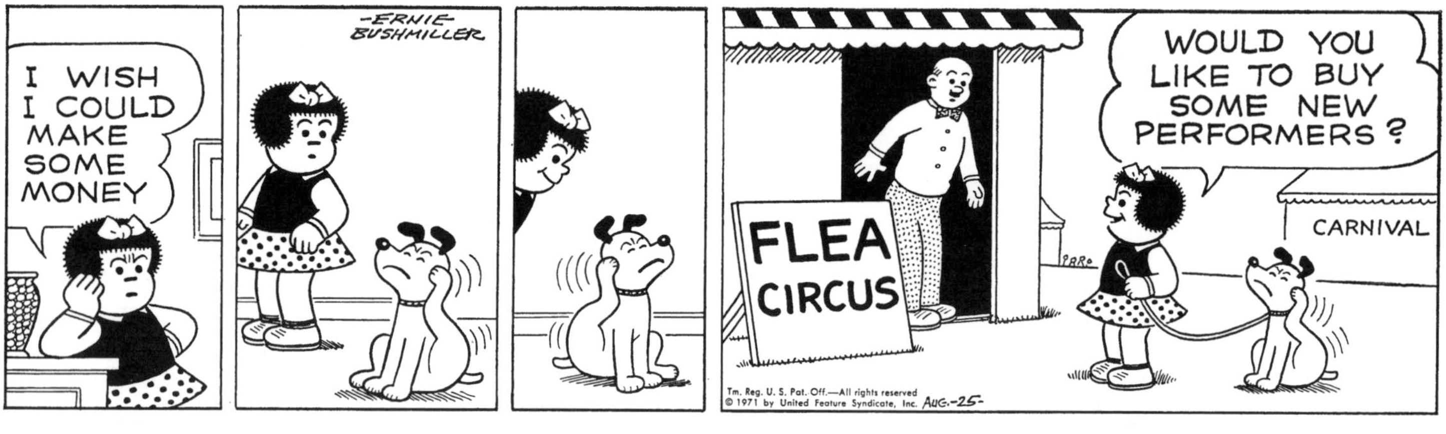
I WISH I COULD MAKE SOME MONEY
-ERNIE BUSHMILLER
FLEA CIRCUS
WOULD YOU LIKE TO BUY SOME NEW PERFORMERS ?
CARNIVAL
Tm. Reg. U. S. Pat. Off.—All rights reserved © 1971 by United Feature Syndicate, Inc.
AUG.-25-

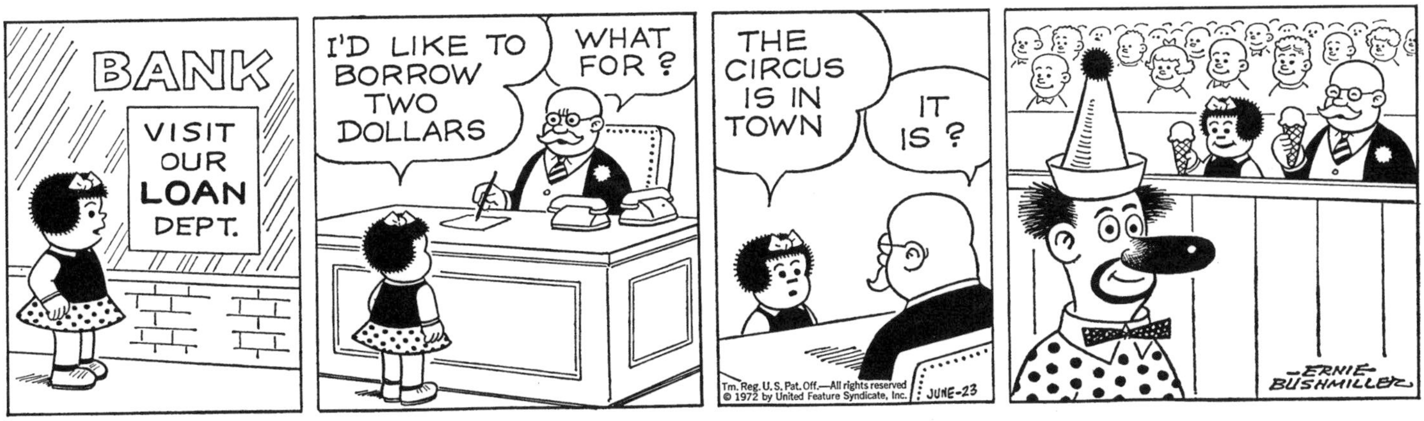
BANK
VISIT OUR LOAN DEPT.
I'D LIKE TO BORROW TWO DOLLARS
WHAT FOR ?
THE CIRCUS IS IN TOWN
IT IS ?
Tm. Reg. U. S. Pat. Off.—All rights reserved © 1972 by United Feature Syndicate, Inc.
JUNE-23
ERNIE BUSHMILLER

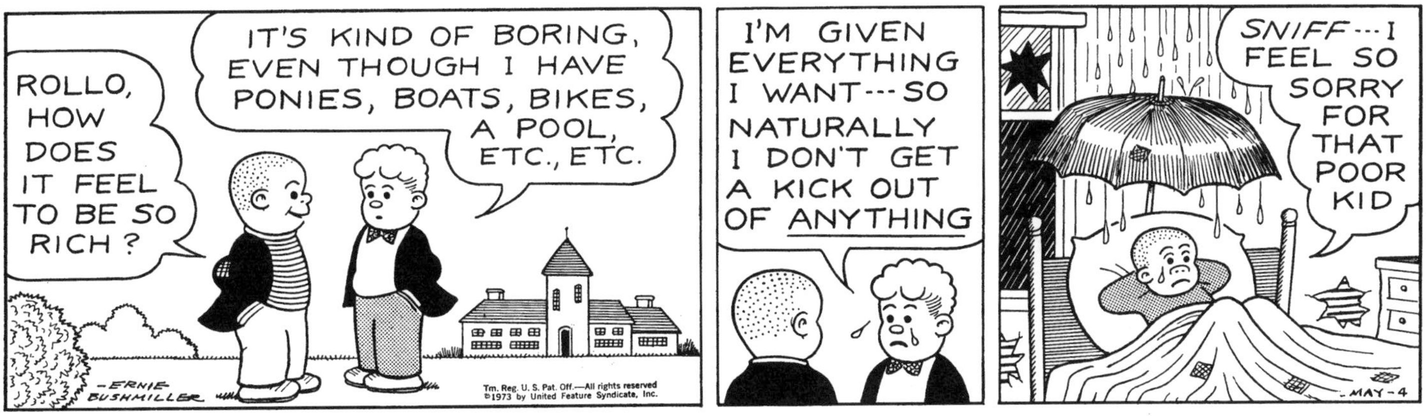
ROLLO, HOW DOES IT FEEL TO BE SO RICH ?
IT'S KIND OF BORING, EVEN THOUGH I HAVE PONIES, BOATS, BIKES, A POOL, ETC., ETC.
ERNIE BUSHMILLER
Tm. Reg. U. S. Pat. Off.—All rights reserved ©1973 by United Feature Syndicate, Inc.
I'M GIVEN EVERYTHING I WANT--- SO NATURALLY I DON'T GET A KICK OUT OF ANYTHING
SNIFF--- I FEEL SO SORRY FOR THAT POOR KID
MAY-4

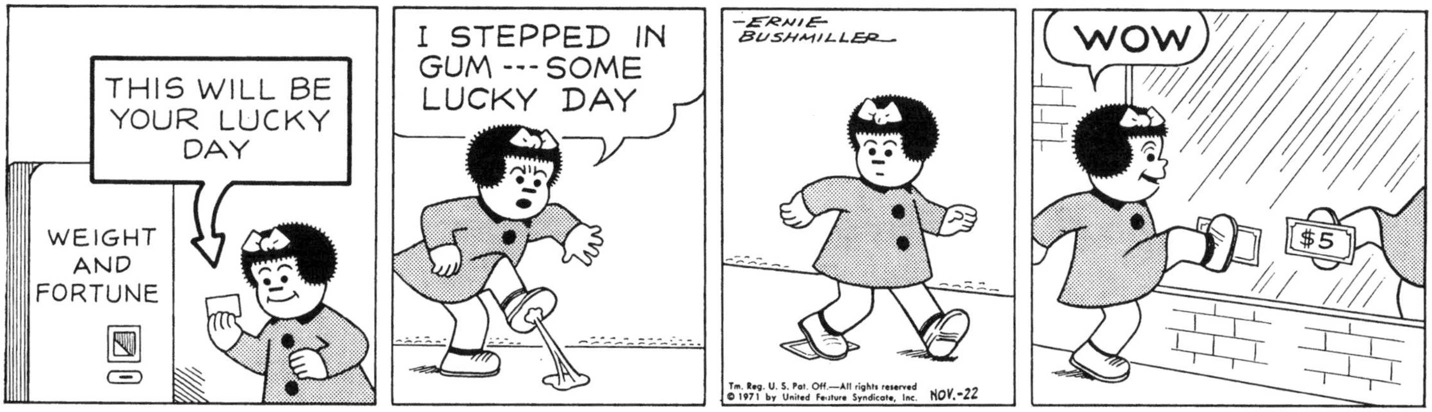
THIS WILL BE YOUR LUCKY DAY
WEIGHT AND FORTUNE
I STEPPED IN GUM --- SOME LUCKY DAY
ERNIE BUSHMILLER
Tm. Reg. U. S. Pat. Off.—All rights reserved © 1971 by United Feature Syndicate, Inc.
NOV.-22
WOW
$5

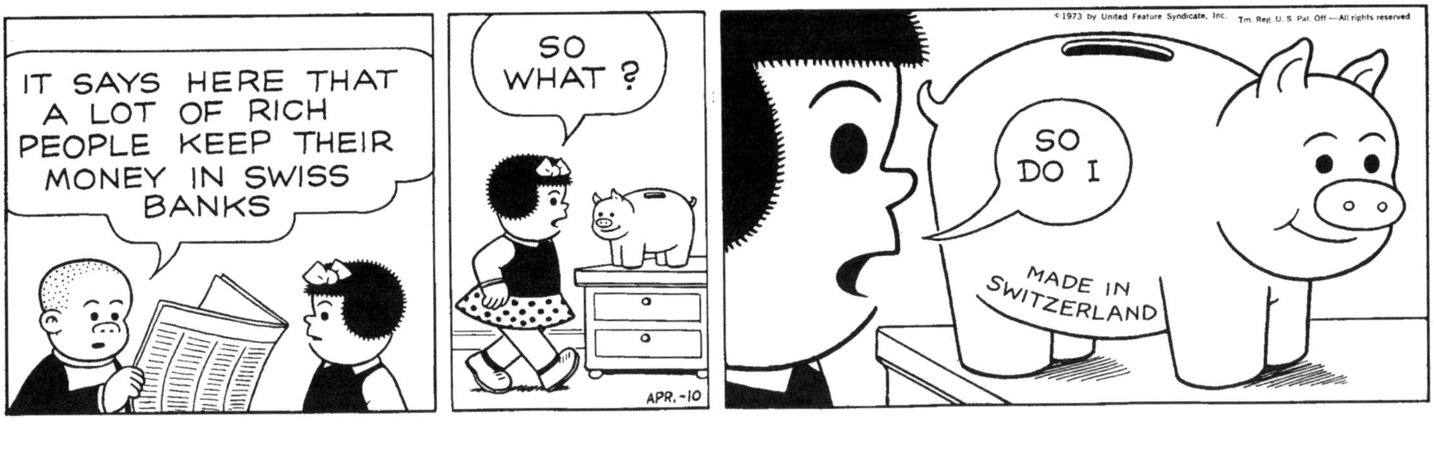
IT SAYS HERE THAT A LOT OF RICH PEOPLE KEEP THEIR MONEY IN SWISS BANKS
SO WHAT ?
APR.-10
© 1973 by United Feature Syndicate, Inc.
Tm. Reg. U. S. Pat. Off.—All rights reserved
SO DO I
MADE IN SWITZERLAND

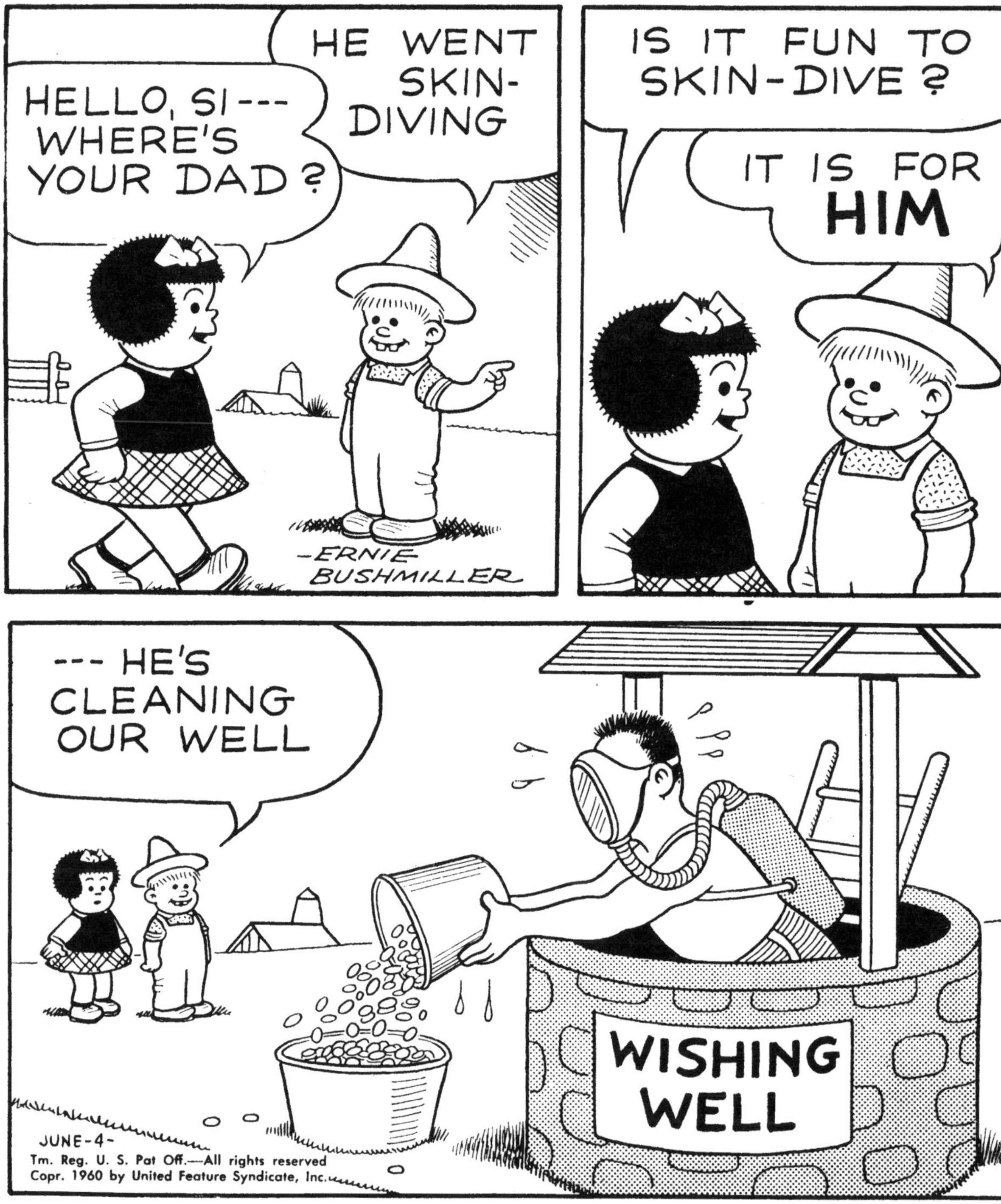
HELLO, SI--- WHERE'S YOUR DAD?
HE WENT SKIN-DIVING
-ERNIE BUSHMILLER
IS IT FUN TO SKIN-DIVE?
IT IS FOR **HIM**
--- HE'S CLEANING OUR WELL
WISHING WELL
JUNE-4-
Tm. Reg. U. S. Pat Off.—All rights reserved
Copr. 1960 by United Feature Syndicate, Inc.

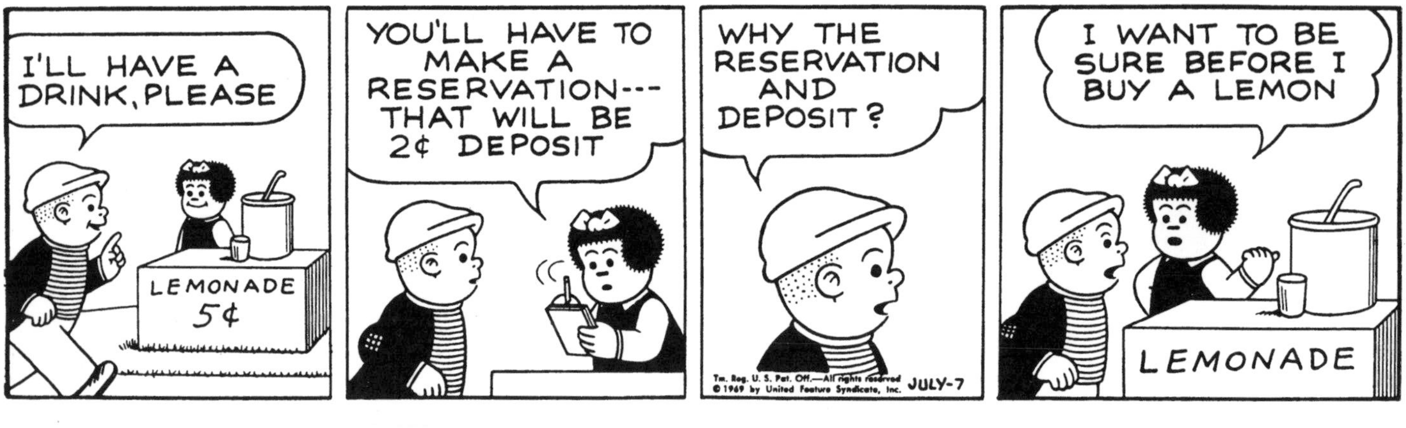
I'LL HAVE A DRINK, PLEASE
LEMONADE 5¢
YOU'LL HAVE TO MAKE A RESERVATION--- THAT WILL BE 2¢ DEPOSIT
WHY THE RESERVATION AND DEPOSIT?
Tm. Reg. U. S. Pat. Off.—All rights reserved © 1969 by United Feature Syndicate, Inc.
JULY-7
I WANT TO BE SURE BEFORE I BUY A LEMON
LEMONADE

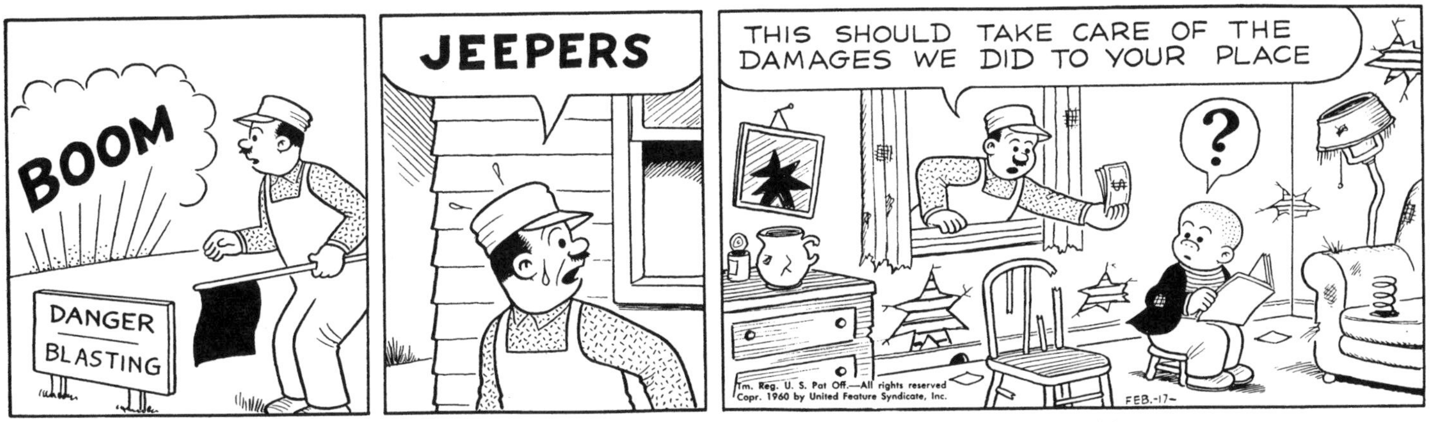
BOOM
DANGER BLASTING
JEEPERS
THIS SHOULD TAKE CARE OF THE DAMAGES WE DID TO YOUR PLACE
?
Tm. Reg. U. S. Pat Off.—All rights reserved Copr. 1960 by United Feature Syndicate, Inc.
FEB.-17-

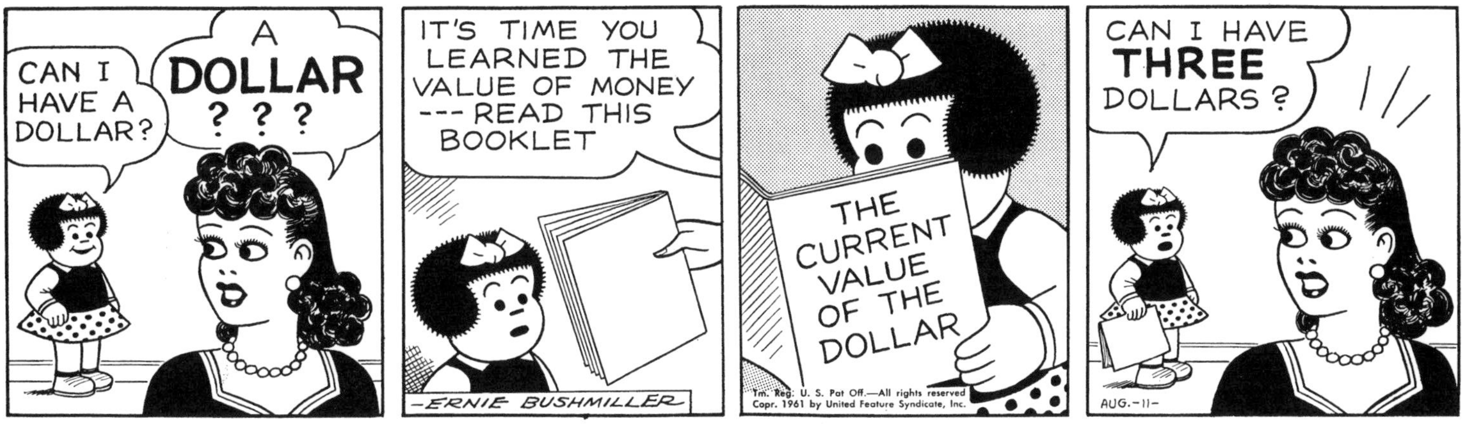
CAN I HAVE A DOLLAR?
A DOLLAR ? ? ?
IT'S TIME YOU LEARNED THE VALUE OF MONEY --- READ THIS BOOKLET
-ERNIE BUSHMILLER
THE CURRENT VALUE OF THE DOLLAR
Tm. Reg. U. S. Pat Off.—All rights reserved Copr. 1961 by United Feature Syndicate, Inc.
CAN I HAVE THREE DOLLARS ?
AUG.-11-

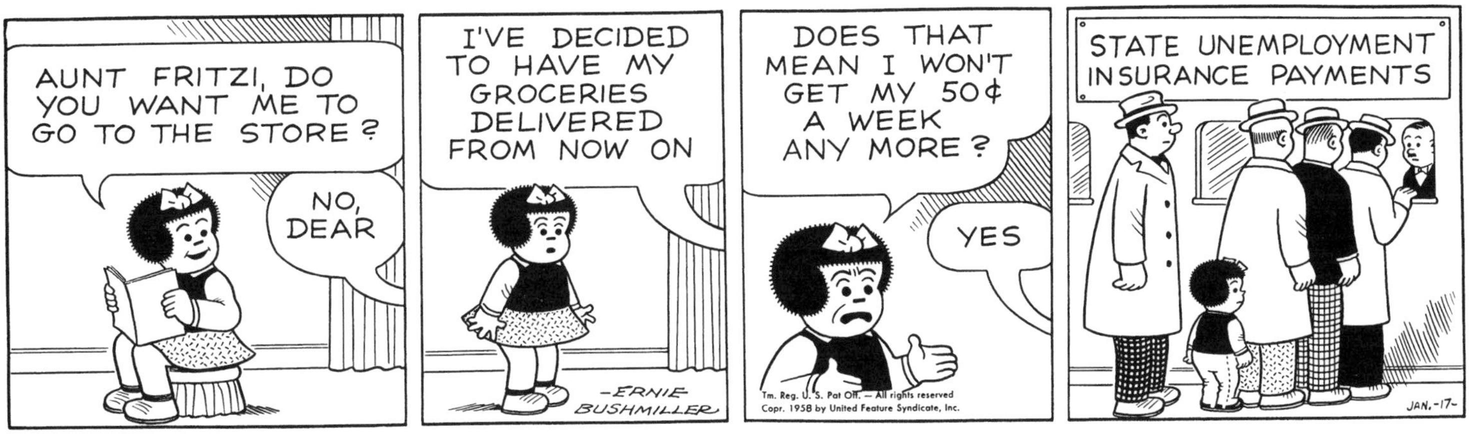
AUNT FRITZI, DO YOU WANT ME TO GO TO THE STORE ?
NO, DEAR
I'VE DECIDED TO HAVE MY GROCERIES DELIVERED FROM NOW ON
-ERNIE BUSHMILLER
DOES THAT MEAN I WON'T GET MY 50¢ A WEEK ANY MORE ?
YES
Tm. Reg. U. S. Pat Off. — All rights reserved Copr. 1958 by United Feature Syndicate, Inc.
STATE UNEMPLOYMENT INSURANCE PAYMENTS
JAN.-17-

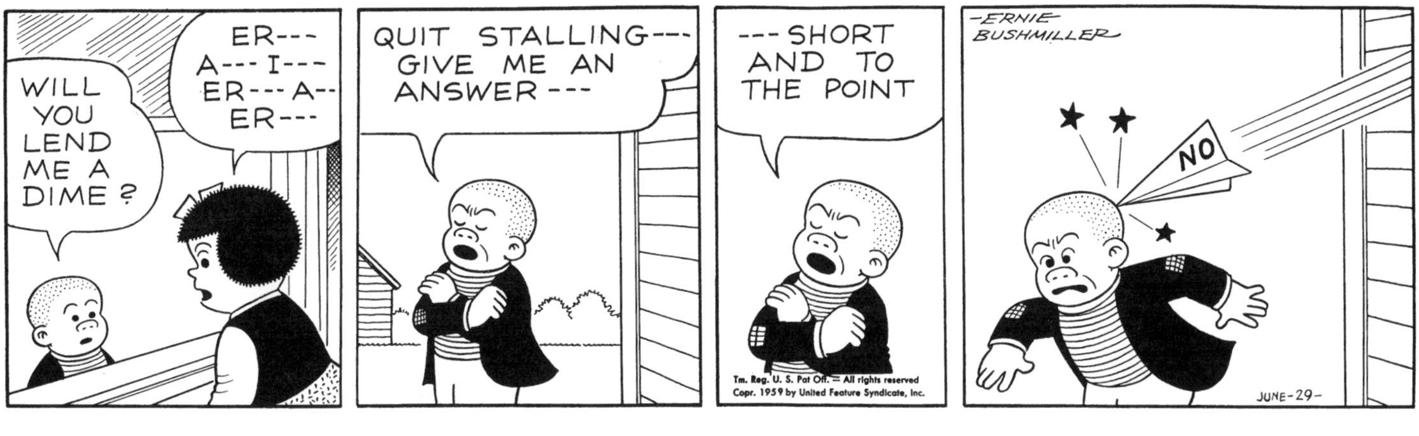
WILL YOU LEND ME A DIME ?
ER--- A--- I--- ER--- A-- ER---
QUIT STALLING--- GIVE ME AN ANSWER ---
--- SHORT AND TO THE POINT
Tm. Reg. U. S. Pat Off. — All rights reserved Copr. 1959 by United Feature Syndicate, Inc.
-ERNIE BUSHMILLER
NO
JUNE-29-

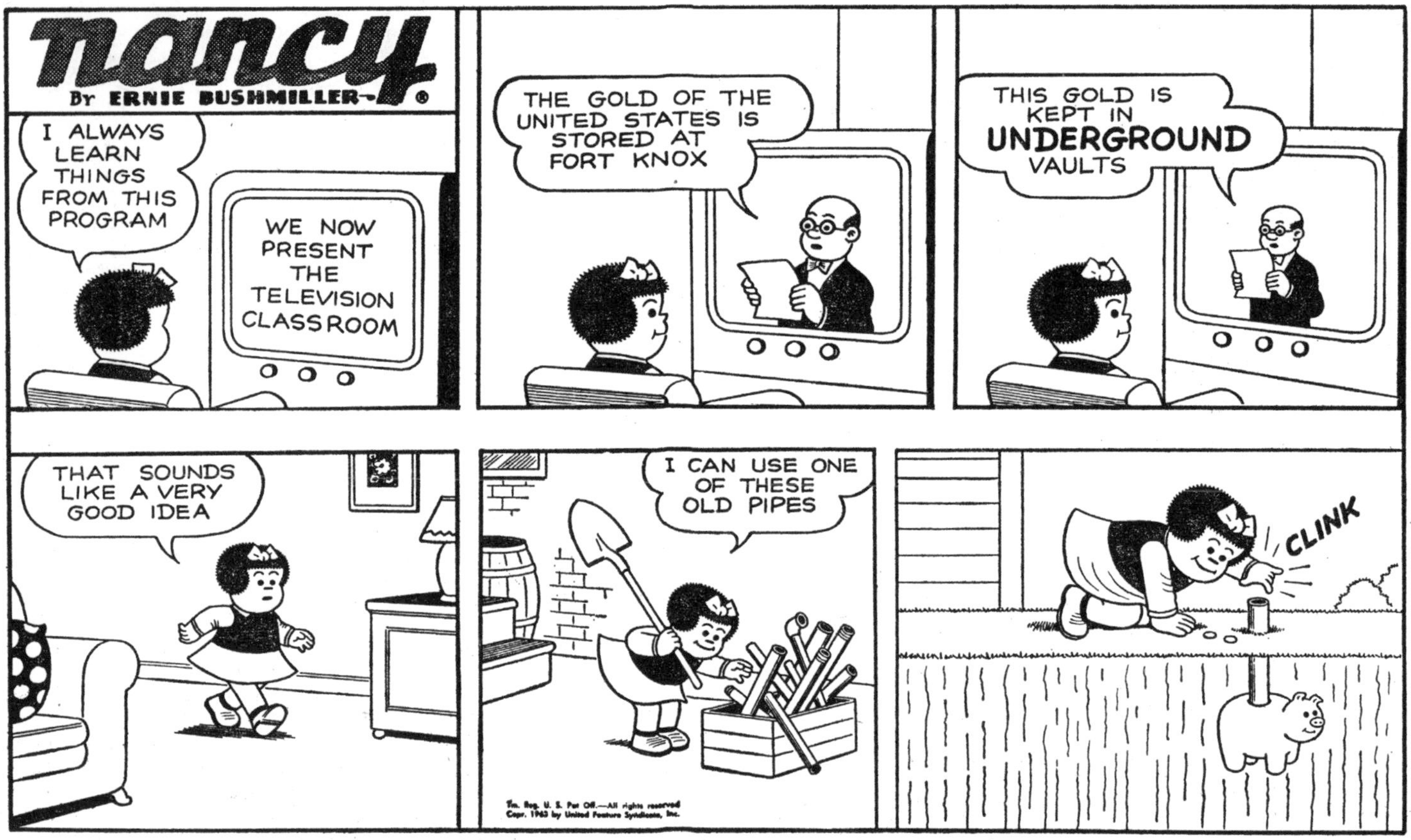
nancy
By ERNIE BUSHMILLER
I ALWAYS LEARN THINGS FROM THIS PROGRAM
WE NOW PRESENT THE TELEVISION CLASSROOM
THE GOLD OF THE UNITED STATES IS STORED AT FORT KNOX
THIS GOLD IS KEPT IN UNDERGROUND VAULTS
THAT SOUNDS LIKE A VERY GOOD IDEA
I CAN USE ONE OF THESE OLD PIPES
Tm. Reg. U. S. Pat. Off.—All rights reserved Copr. 1963 by United Feature Syndicate, Inc.
CLINK

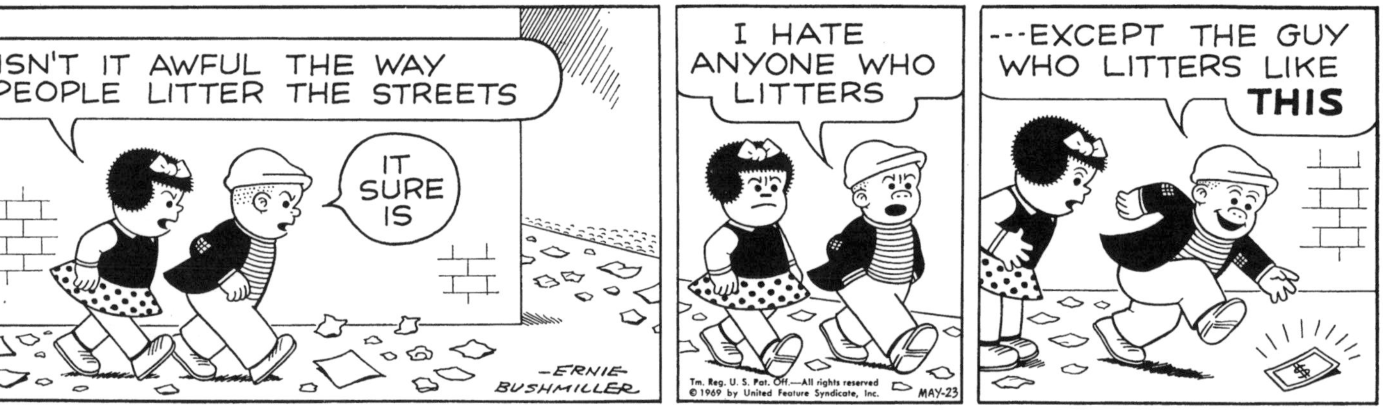
ISN'T IT AWFUL THE WAY PEOPLE LITTER THE STREETS
IT SURE IS
-ERNIE- BUSHMILLER
I HATE ANYONE WHO LITTERS
Tm. Reg. U. S. Pat. Off.—All rights reserved © 1969 by United Feature Syndicate, Inc.
MAY-23
---EXCEPT THE GUY WHO LITTERS LIKE THIS

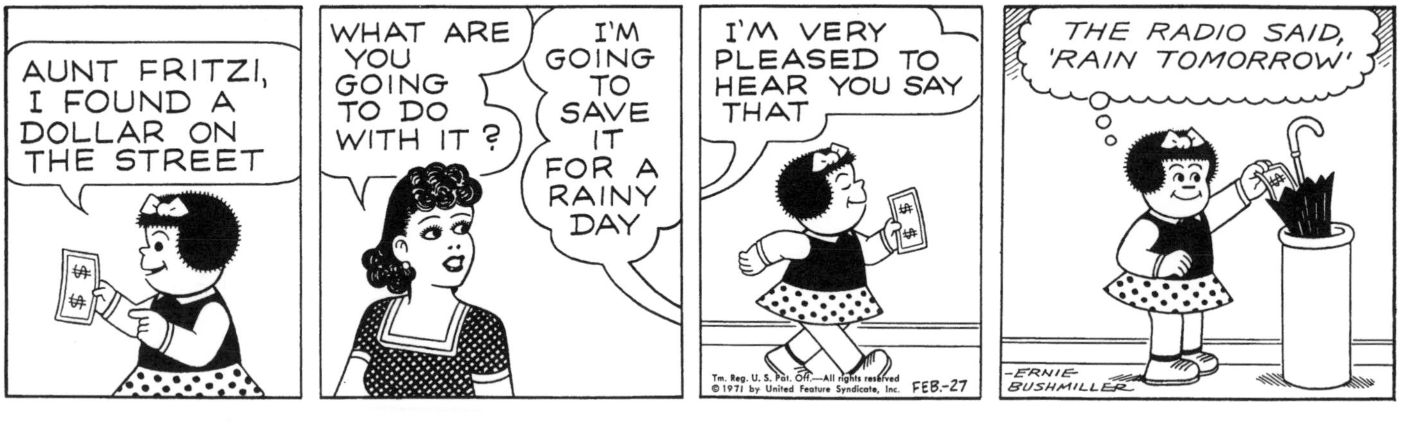
AUNT FRITZI, I FOUND A DOLLAR ON THE STREET
WHAT ARE YOU GOING TO DO WITH IT ?
I'M GOING TO SAVE IT FOR A RAINY DAY
I'M VERY PLEASED TO HEAR YOU SAY THAT
Tm. Reg. U. S. Pat. Off.—All rights reserved © 1971 by United Feature Syndicate, Inc.
FEB.-27
THE RADIO SAID, 'RAIN TOMORROW'
-ERNIE- BUSHMILLER

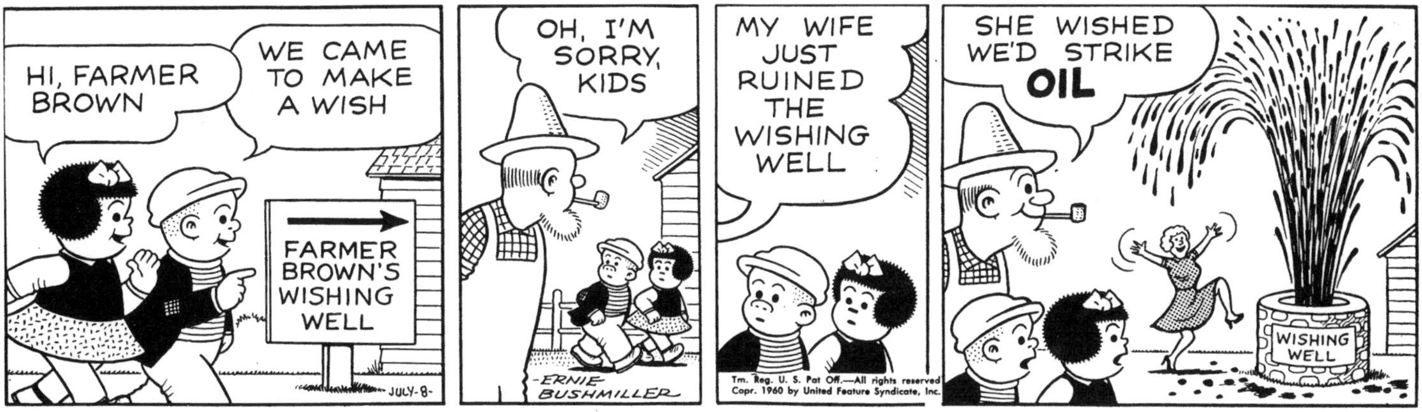
HI, FARMER BROWN
WE CAME TO MAKE A WISH
FARMER BROWN'S WISHING WELL
JULY-8-
OH, I'M SORRY, KIDS
-ERNIE BUSHMILLER
MY WIFE JUST RUINED THE WISHING WELL
Tm. Reg. U. S. Pat Off.—All rights reserved Copr. 1960 by United Feature Syndicate, Inc.
SHE WISHED WE'D STRIKE OIL
WISHING WELL

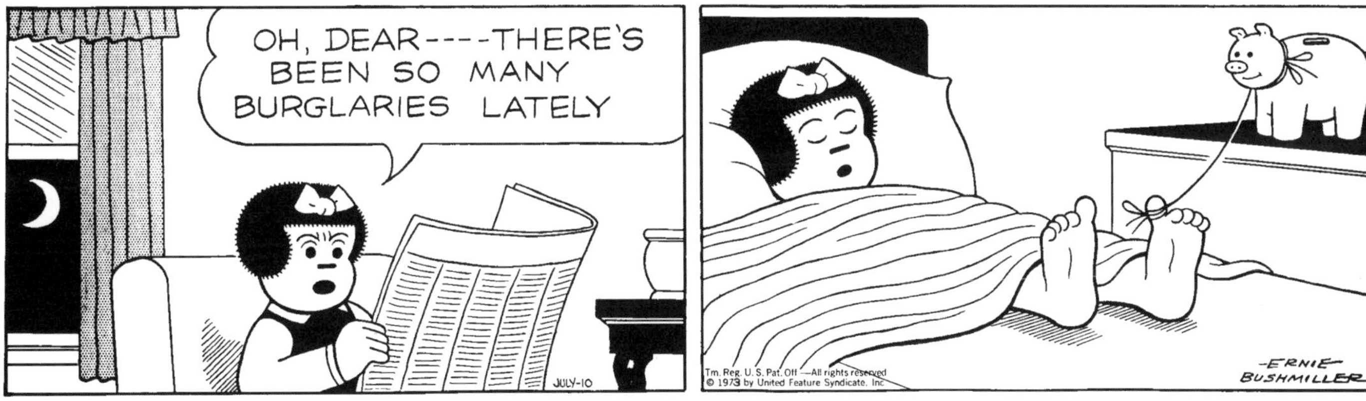
OH, DEAR----THERE'S BEEN SO MANY BURGLARIES LATELY
JULY-10
Tm. Reg. U. S. Pat. Off.—All rights reserved © 1973 by United Feature Syndicate, Inc.
-ERNIE BUSHMILLER

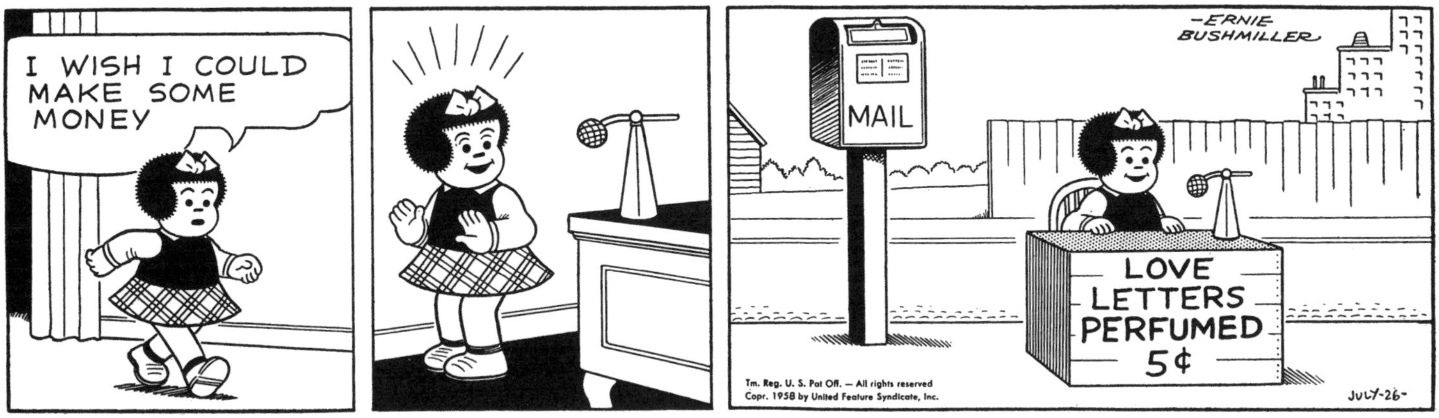
I WISH I COULD MAKE SOME MONEY
-ERNIE BUSHMILLER
MAIL
LOVE LETTERS PERFUMED 5¢
Tm. Reg. U. S. Pat Off. — All rights reserved Copr. 1958 by United Feature Syndicate, Inc.
JULY-26-

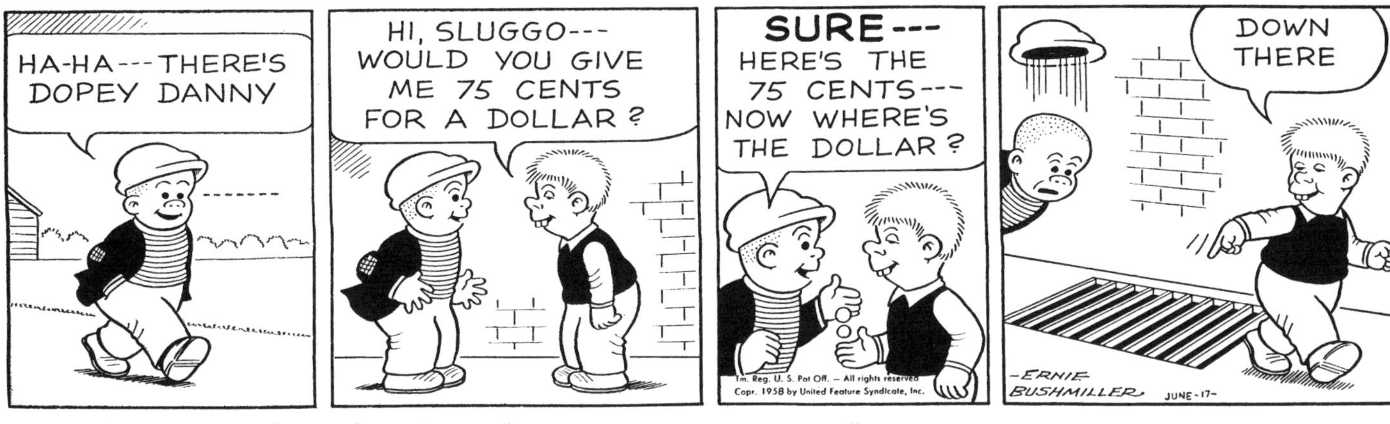
HA-HA---THERE'S DOPEY DANNY
HI, SLUGGO--- WOULD YOU GIVE ME 75 CENTS FOR A DOLLAR?
SURE--- HERE'S THE 75 CENTS--- NOW WHERE'S THE DOLLAR?
Tm. Reg. U. S. Pat Off. — All rights reserved Copr. 1958 by United Feature Syndicate, Inc.
DOWN THERE
-ERNIE BUSHMILLER
JUNE-17-

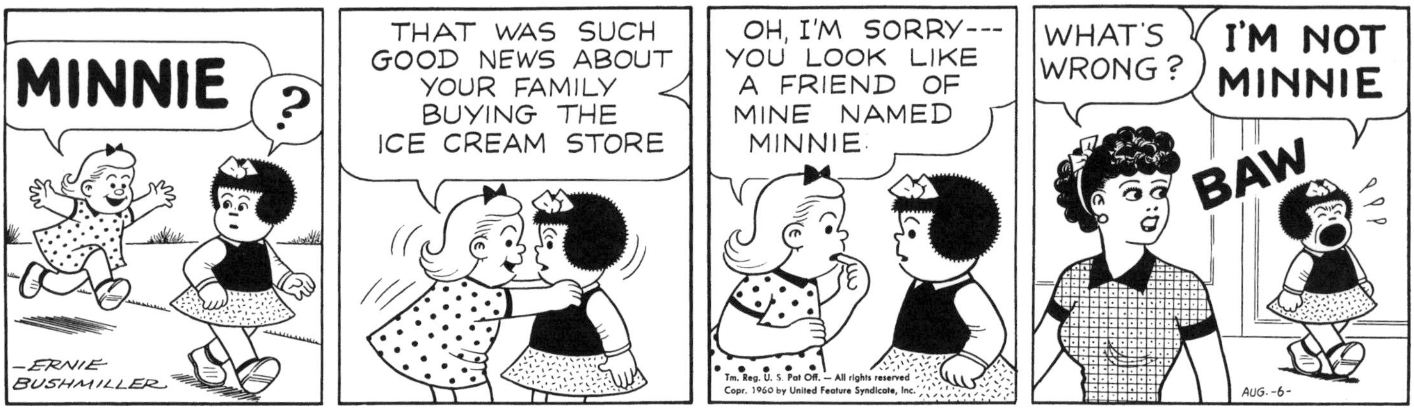
MINNIE
?
-ERNIE BUSHMILLER
THAT WAS SUCH GOOD NEWS ABOUT YOUR FAMILY BUYING THE ICE CREAM STORE
OH, I'M SORRY--- YOU LOOK LIKE A FRIEND OF MINE NAMED MINNIE.
Tm. Reg. U. S. Pat Off. — All rights reserved
Copr. 1960 by United Feature Syndicate, Inc.
WHAT'S WRONG?
I'M NOT MINNIE
BAW
AUG.-6-

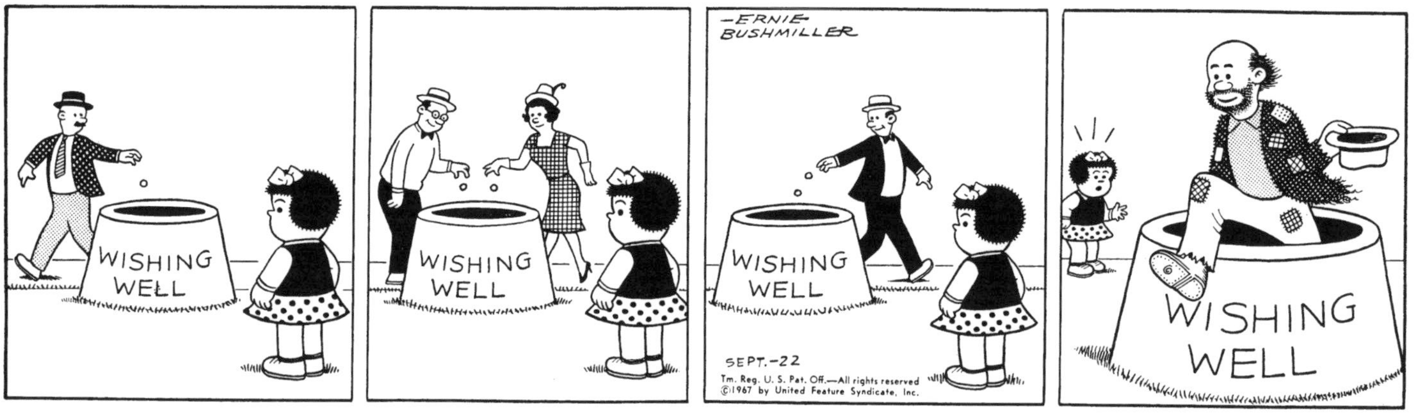
WISHING WELL
WISHING WELL
-ERNIE BUSHMILLER
WISHING WELL
SEPT.-22
Tm. Reg. U. S. Pat. Off.—All rights reserved
©1967 by United Feature Syndicate, Inc.
WISHING WELL

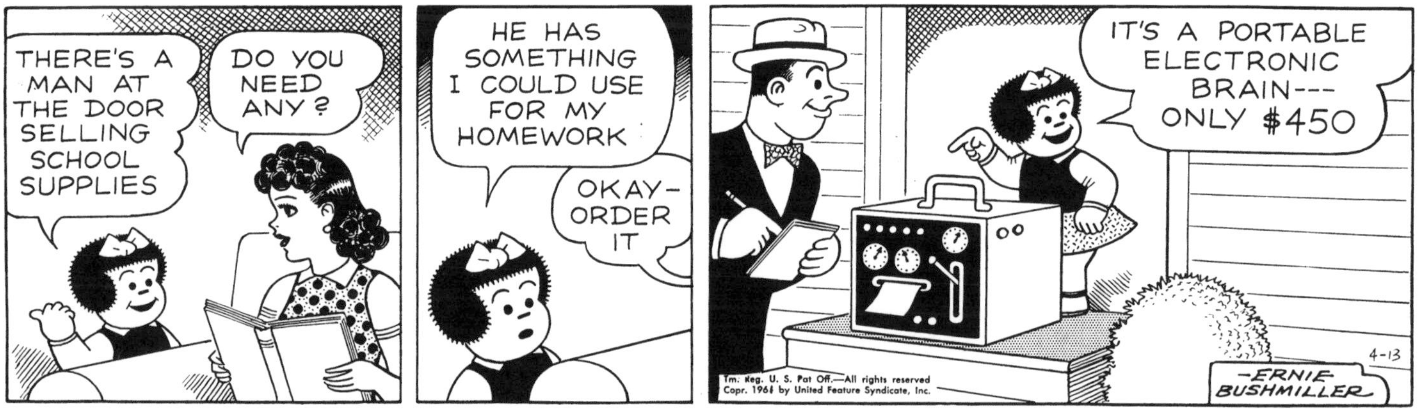
THERE'S A MAN AT THE DOOR SELLING SCHOOL SUPPLIES
DO YOU NEED ANY?
HE HAS SOMETHING I COULD USE FOR MY HOMEWORK
OKAY- ORDER IT
IT'S A PORTABLE ELECTRONIC BRAIN--- ONLY $450
Tm. Reg. U. S. Pat Off.—All rights reserved
4-13
-ERNIE BUSHMILLER

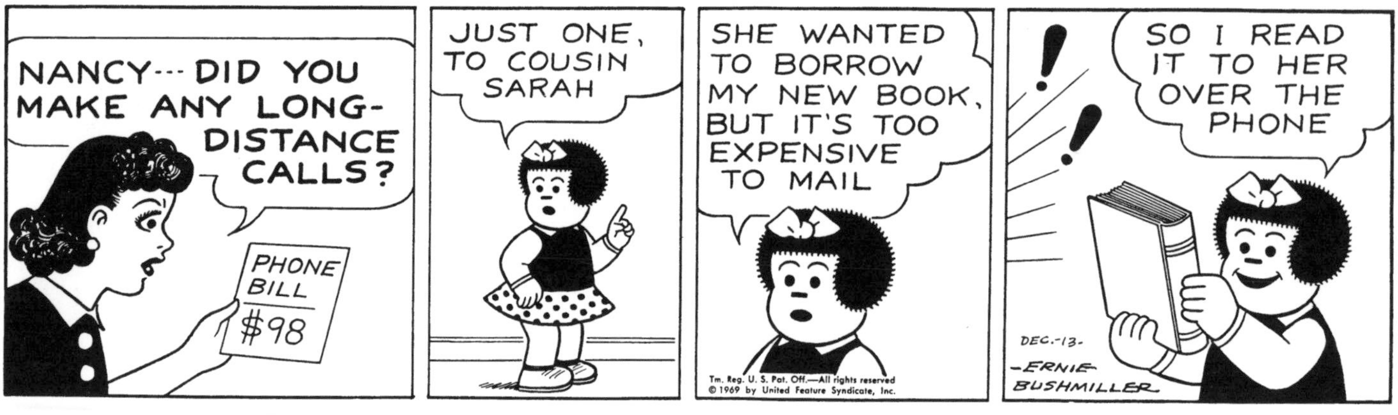
NANCY--- DID YOU MAKE ANY LONG-DISTANCE CALLS?
PHONE BILL $98
JUST ONE, TO COUSIN SARAH
SHE WANTED TO BORROW MY NEW BOOK, BUT IT'S TOO EXPENSIVE TO MAIL
Tm. Reg. U. S. Pat. Off.—All rights reserved
© 1969 by United Feature Syndicate, Inc.
!
!
SO I READ IT TO HER OVER THE PHONE
DEC.-13-
-ERNIE BUSHMILLER

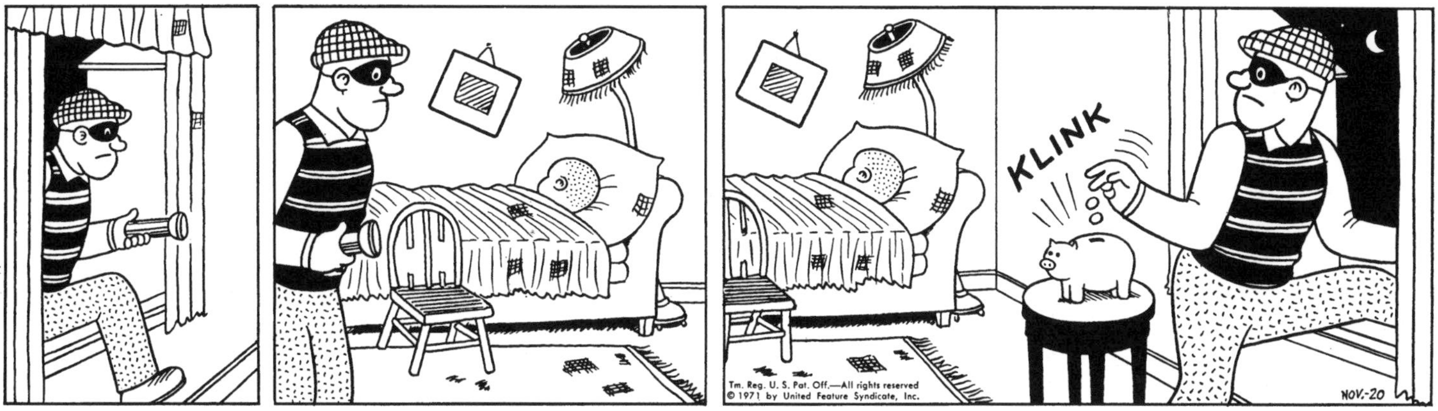

KLINK
Tm. Reg. U. S. Pat. Off.—All rights reserved
© 1971 by United Feature Syndicate, Inc.
NOV.-20

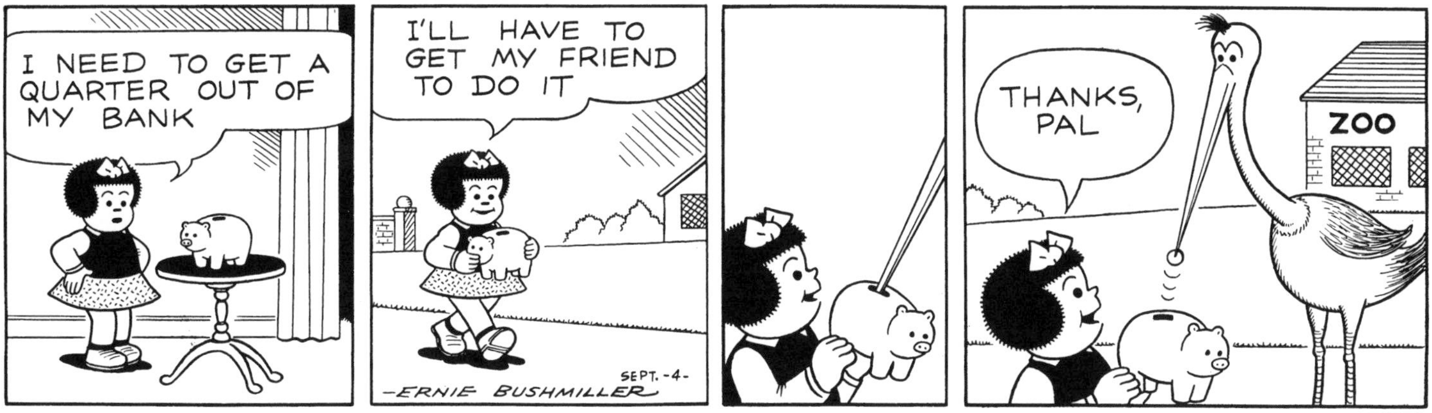

I NEED TO GET A QUARTER OUT OF MY BANK
I'LL HAVE TO GET MY FRIEND TO DO IT
SEPT.-4-
-ERNIE BUSHMILLER
THANKS, PAL
ZOO

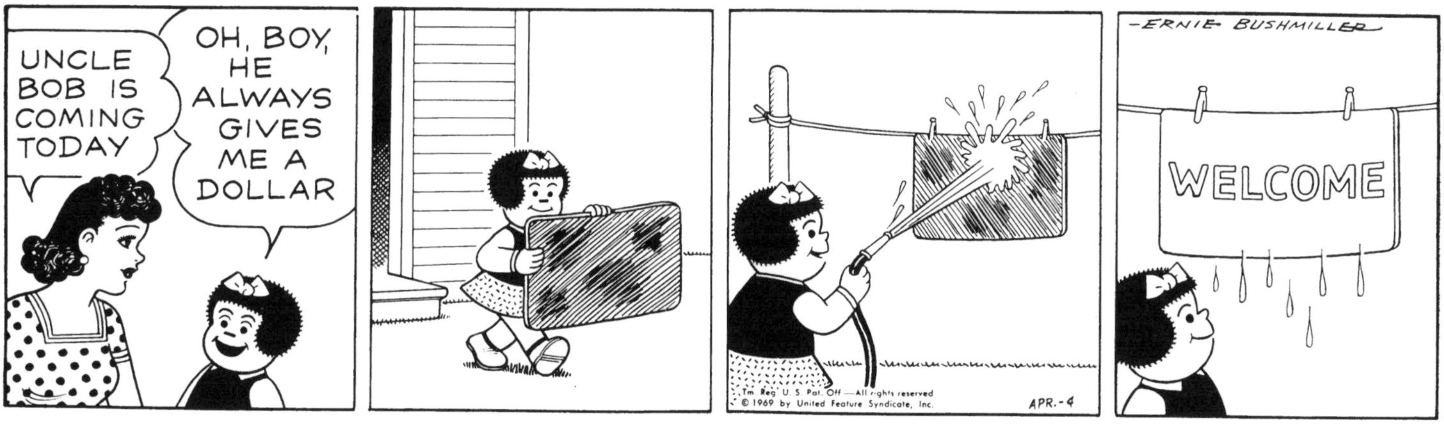

UNCLE BOB IS COMING TODAY
OH, BOY, HE ALWAYS GIVES ME A DOLLAR
Tm. Reg. U. S. Pat. Off.—All rights reserved
© 1969 by United Feature Syndicate, Inc.
APR.-4
-ERNIE BUSHMILLER
WELCOME

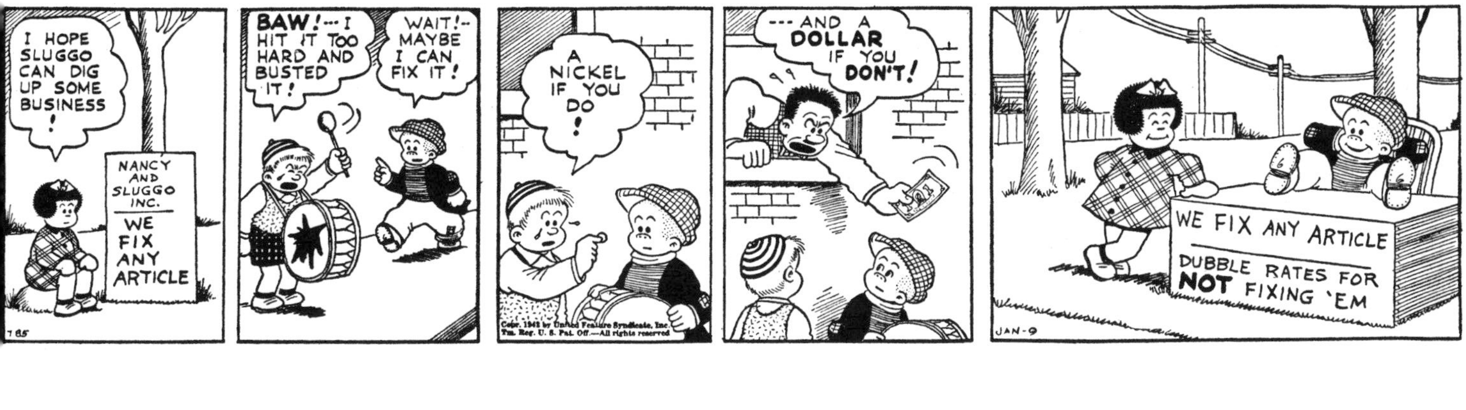

I HOPE SLUGGO CAN DIG UP SOME BUSINESS !
NANCY AND SLUGGO INC.
WE FIX ANY ARTICLE
BAW!--- I HIT IT TOO HARD AND BUSTED IT!
WAIT!-- MAYBE I CAN FIX IT!
A NICKEL IF YOU DO !
Tm. Reg. U. S. Pat. Off.—All rights reserved
--- AND A DOLLAR IF YOU DON'T!
WE FIX ANY ARTICLE
DUBBLE RATES FOR NOT FIXING 'EM
JAN-9

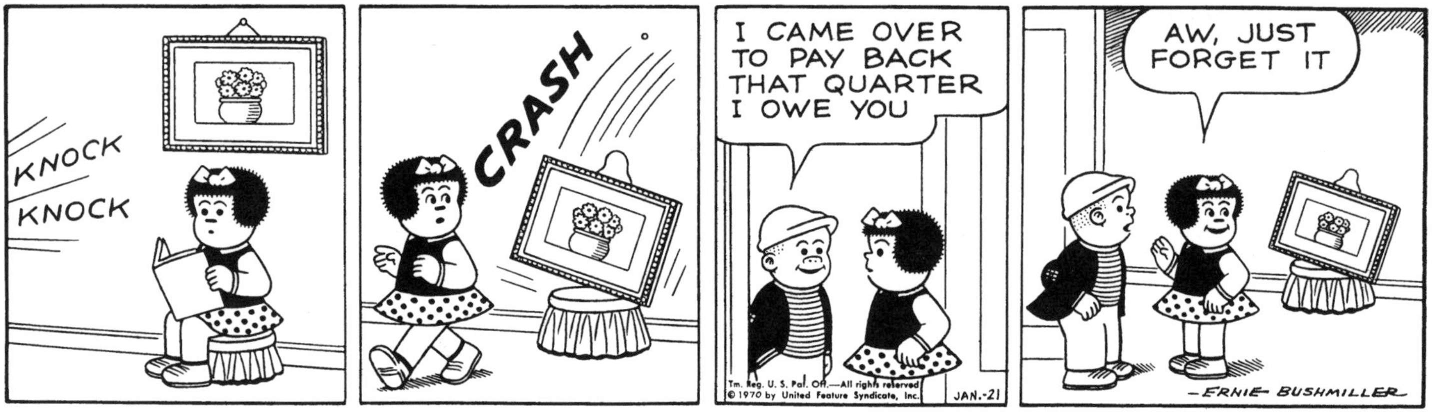
KNOCK
KNOCK
CRASH
I CAME OVER TO PAY BACK THAT QUARTER I OWE YOU
Tm. Reg. U. S. Pat. Off.—All rights reserved © 1970 by United Feature Syndicate, Inc.
JAN.-21
AW, JUST FORGET IT
-ERNIE BUSHMILLER

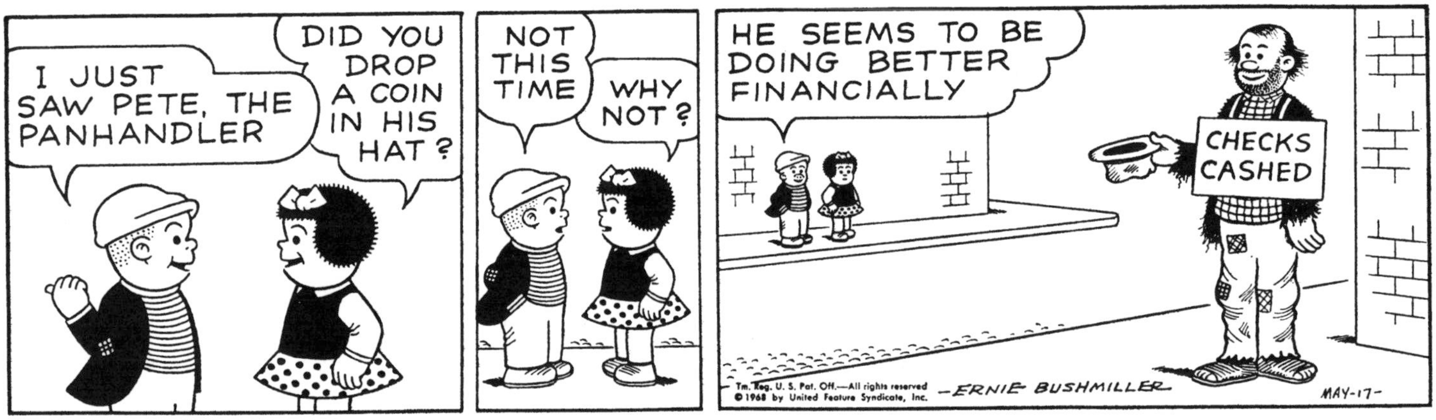
I JUST SAW PETE, THE PANHANDLER
DID YOU DROP A COIN IN HIS HAT?
NOT THIS TIME
WHY NOT?
HE SEEMS TO BE DOING BETTER FINANCIALLY
CHECKS CASHED
Tm. Reg. U. S. Pat. Off.—All rights reserved © 1968 by United Feature Syndicate, Inc.
-ERNIE BUSHMILLER
MAY-17-

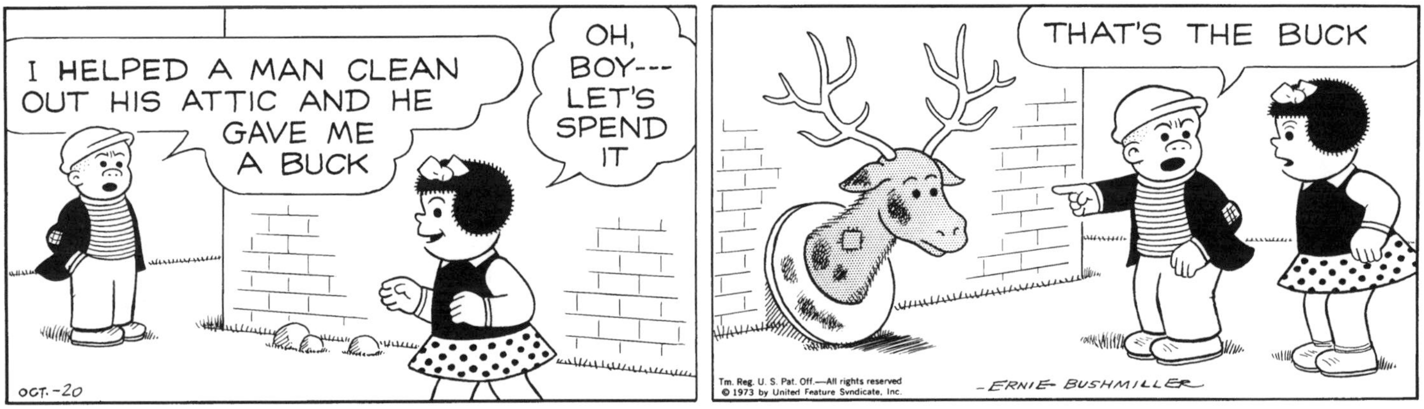
I HELPED A MAN CLEAN OUT HIS ATTIC AND HE GAVE ME A BUCK
OH, BOY--- LET'S SPEND IT
OCT.-20
THAT'S THE BUCK
Tm. Reg. U. S. Pat. Off.—All rights reserved © 1973 by United Feature Syndicate, Inc.
-ERNIE BUSHMILLER

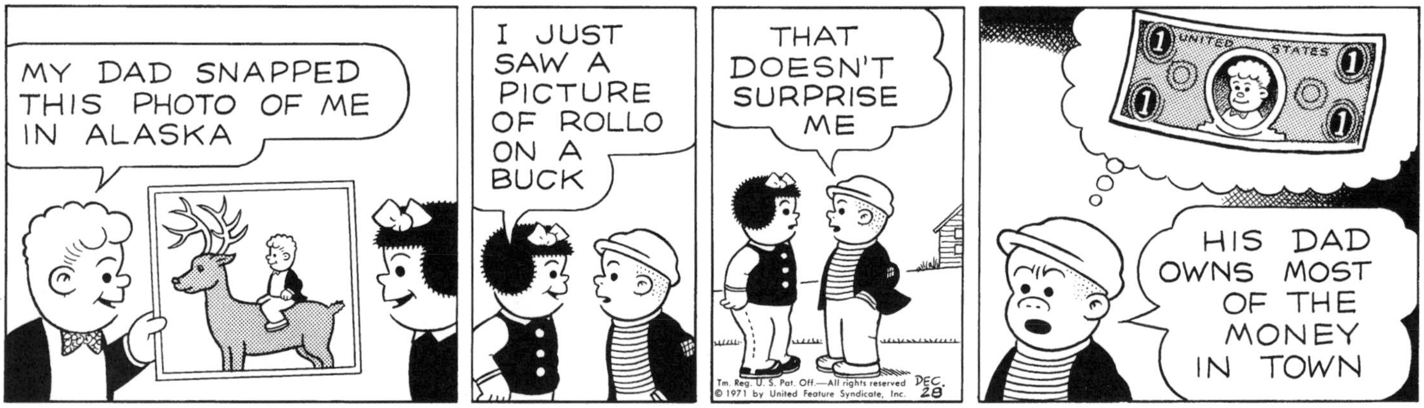
MY DAD SNAPPED THIS PHOTO OF ME IN ALASKA
I JUST SAW A PICTURE OF ROLLO ON A BUCK
THAT DOESN'T SURPRISE ME
Tm. Reg. U. S. Pat. Off.—All rights reserved © 1971 by United Feature Syndicate, Inc.
DEC. 28
UNITED STATES
HIS DAD OWNS MOST OF THE MONEY IN TOWN

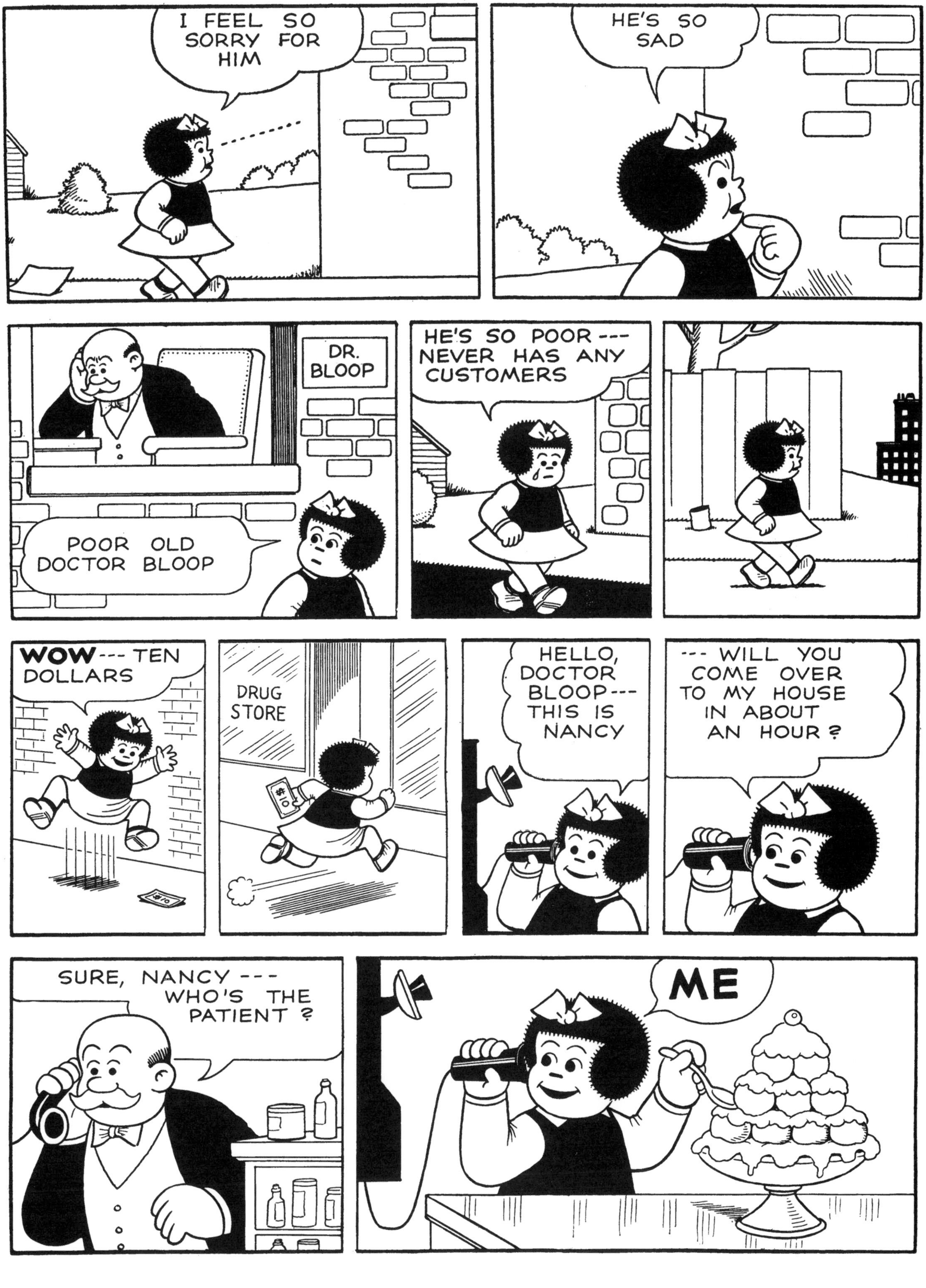
I FEEL SO SORRY FOR HIM
HE'S SO SAD
DR. BLOOP
POOR OLD DOCTOR BLOOP
HE'S SO POOR --- NEVER HAS ANY CUSTOMERS
WOW --- TEN DOLLARS
DRUG STORE
HELLO, DOCTOR BLOOP --- THIS IS NANCY
--- WILL YOU COME OVER TO MY HOUSE IN ABOUT AN HOUR ?
SURE, NANCY --- WHO'S THE PATIENT ?
ME

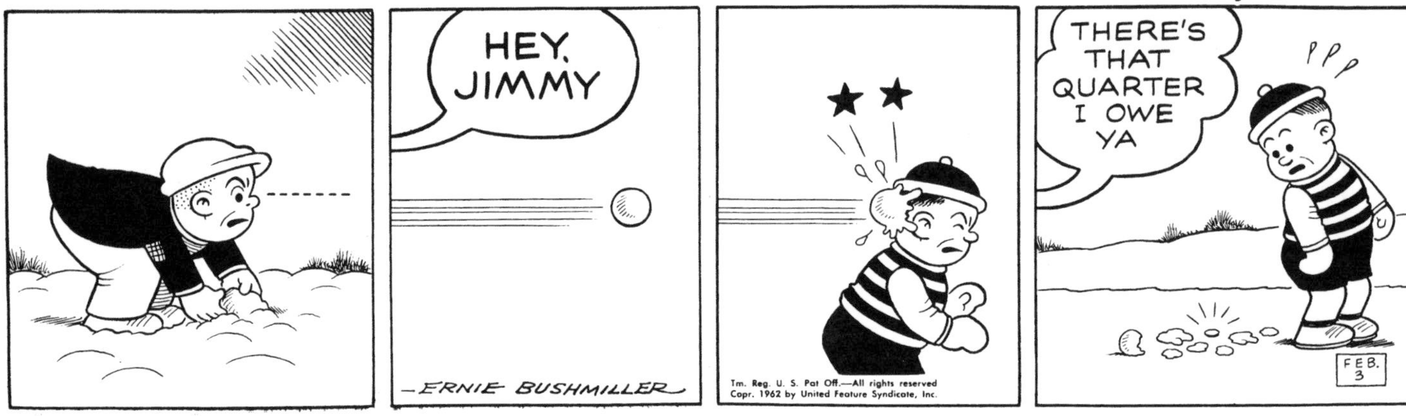
HEY, JIMMY
ERNIE BUSHMILLER
Tm. Reg. U. S. Pat Off.—All rights reserved
Copr. 1962 by United Feature Syndicate, Inc.
THERE'S THAT QUARTER I OWE YA
FEB. 3

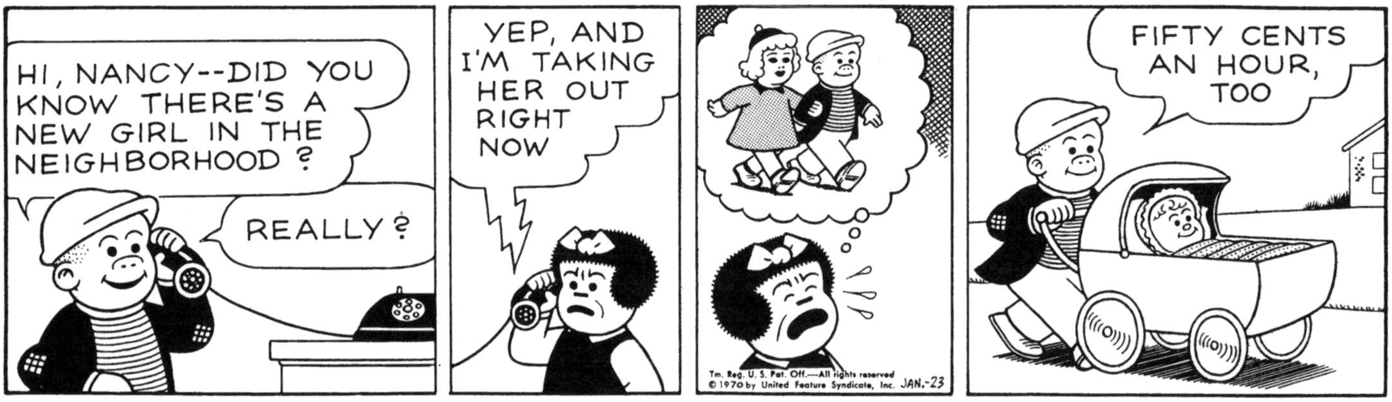
HI, NANCY--DID YOU KNOW THERE'S A NEW GIRL IN THE NEIGHBORHOOD ?
REALLY ?
YEP, AND I'M TAKING HER OUT RIGHT NOW
Tm. Reg. U. S. Pat. Off.—All rights reserved
© 1970 by United Feature Syndicate, Inc. JAN.-23
FIFTY CENTS AN HOUR, TOO

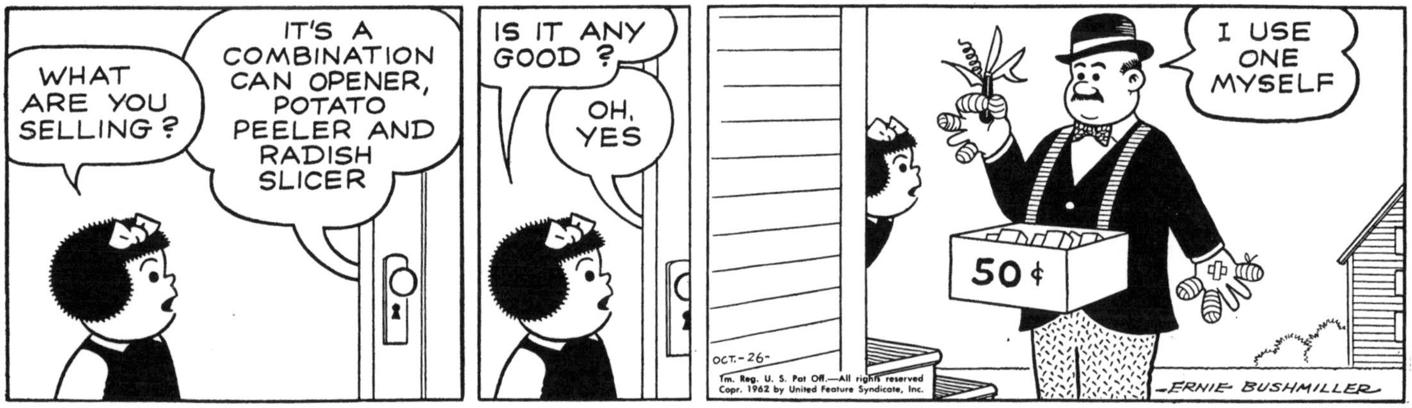
WHAT ARE YOU SELLING ?
IT'S A COMBINATION CAN OPENER, POTATO PEELER AND RADISH SLICER
IS IT ANY GOOD ?
OH, YES
I USE ONE MYSELF
50¢
OCT.-26-
Tm. Reg. U. S. Pat Off.—All rights reserved
Copr. 1962 by United Feature Syndicate, Inc.
ERNIE BUSHMILLER

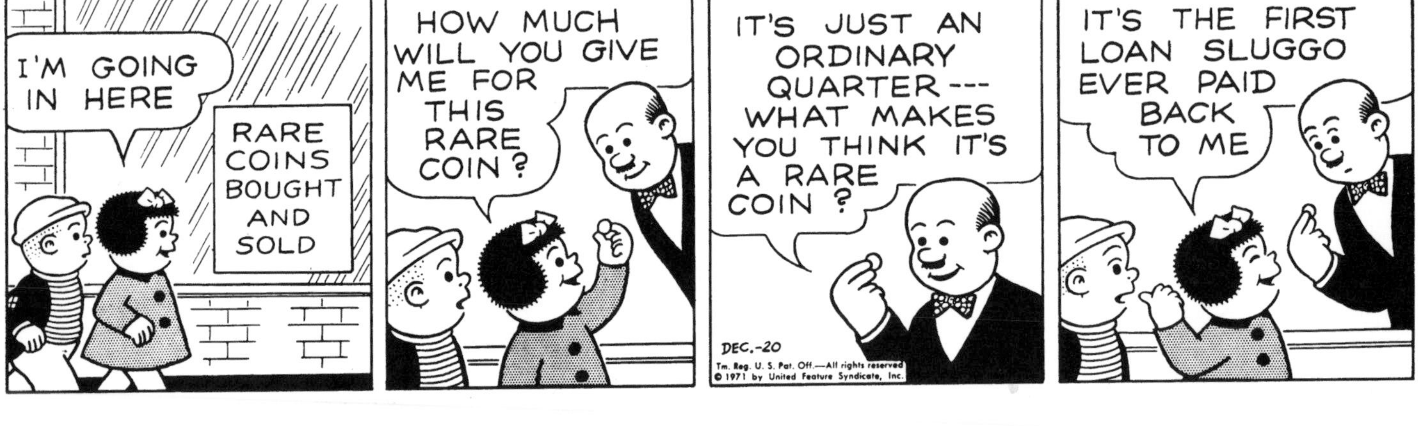
I'M GOING IN HERE
RARE COINS BOUGHT AND SOLD
HOW MUCH WILL YOU GIVE ME FOR THIS RARE COIN ?
IT'S JUST AN ORDINARY QUARTER--- WHAT MAKES YOU THINK IT'S A RARE COIN ?
DEC.-20
Tm. Reg. U. S. Pat. Off.—All rights reserved
© 1971 by United Feature Syndicate, Inc.
IT'S THE FIRST LOAN SLUGGO EVER PAID BACK TO ME

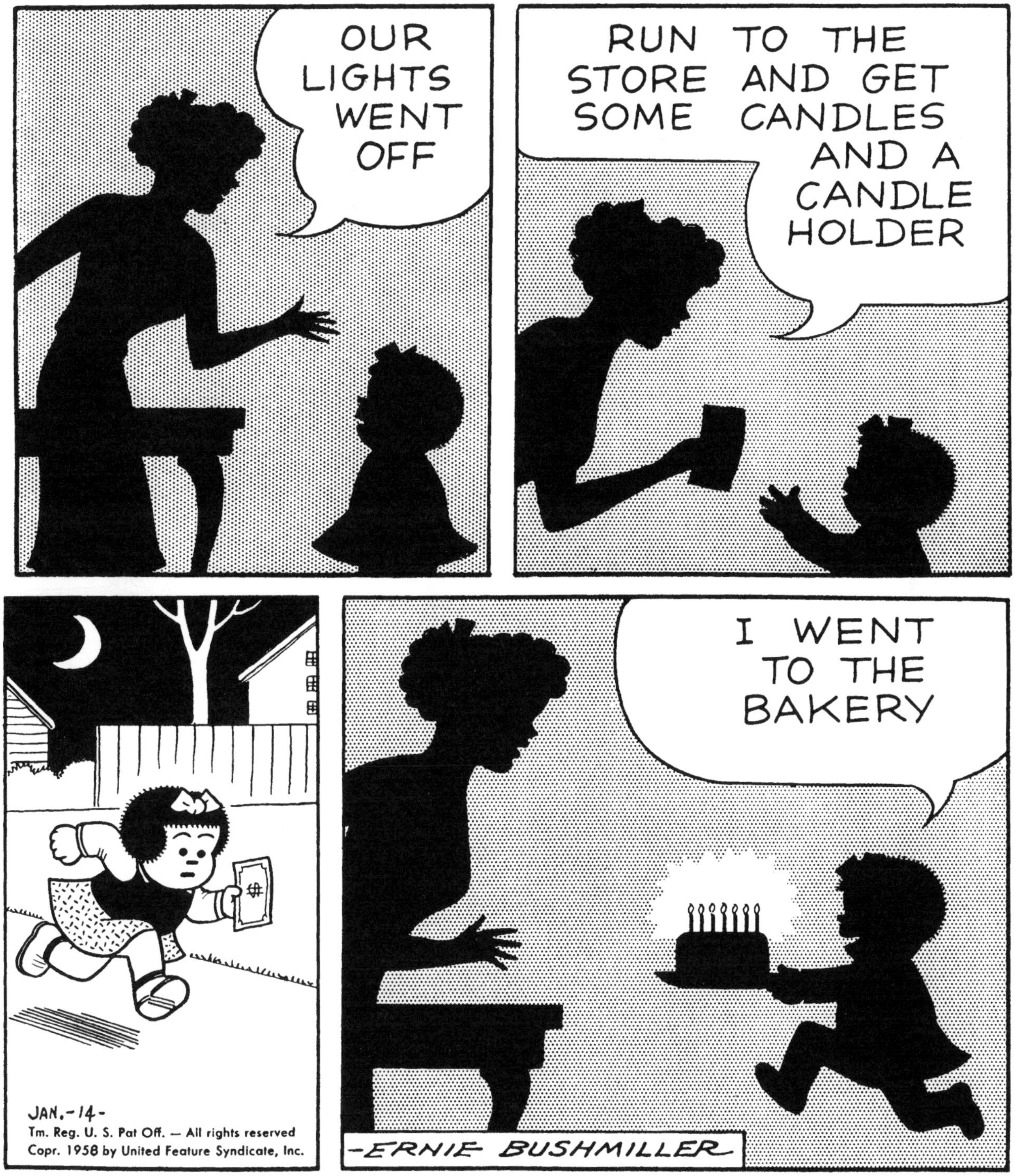

OUR LIGHTS WENT OFF
RUN TO THE STORE AND GET SOME CANDLES AND A CANDLE HOLDER
JAN.-14-
Tm. Reg. U. S. Pat Off. — All rights reserved
Copr. 1958 by United Feature Syndicate, Inc.
I WENT TO THE BAKERY
-ERNIE BUSHMILLER

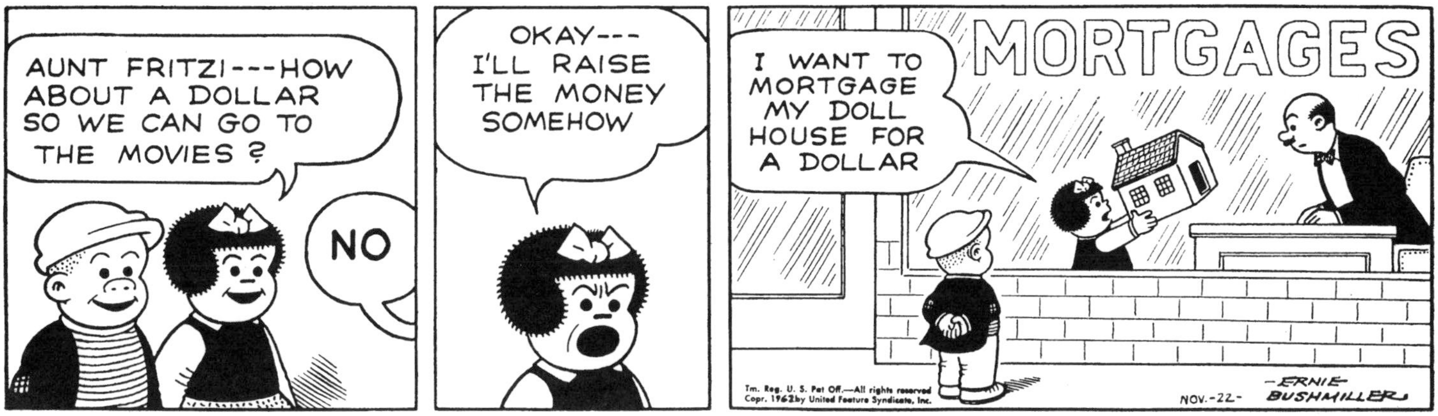

AUNT FRITZI---HOW ABOUT A DOLLAR SO WE CAN GO TO THE MOVIES ?
NO
OKAY--- I'LL RAISE THE MONEY SOMEHOW
MORTGAGES
I WANT TO MORTGAGE MY DOLL HOUSE FOR A DOLLAR
Tm. Reg. U. S. Pat Off.—All rights reserved
Copr. 1962 by United Feature Syndicate, Inc.
NOV.-22-
-ERNIE BUSHMILLER

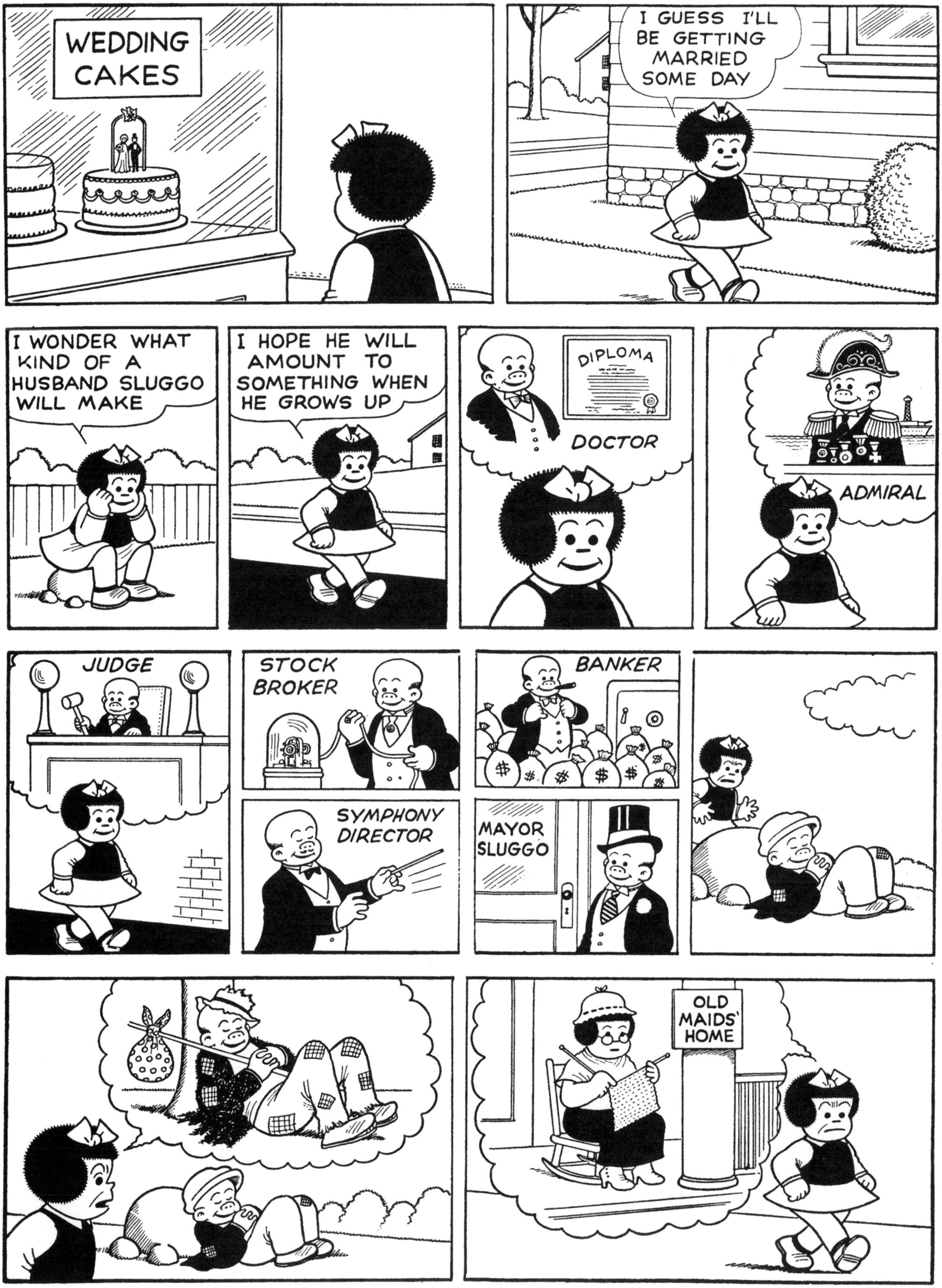
WEDDING CAKES
I GUESS I'LL BE GETTING MARRIED SOME DAY
I WONDER WHAT KIND OF A HUSBAND SLUGGO WILL MAKE
I HOPE HE WILL AMOUNT TO SOMETHING WHEN HE GROWS UP
DIPLOMA
DOCTOR
ADMIRAL
JUDGE
STOCK BROKER
BANKER
SYMPHONY DIRECTOR
MAYOR SLUGGO
OLD MAIDS' HOME

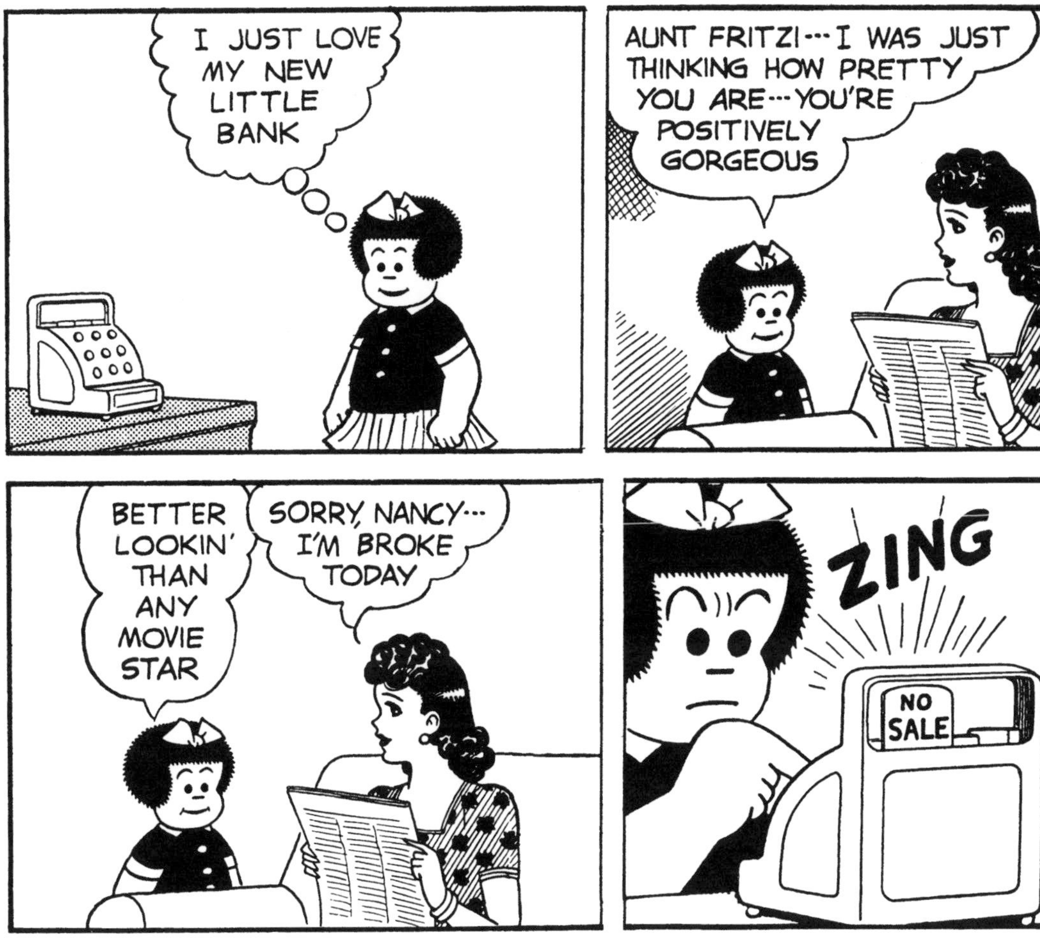
I JUST LOVE MY NEW LITTLE BANK
AUNT FRITZI--- I WAS JUST THINKING HOW PRETTY YOU ARE--- YOU'RE POSITIVELY GORGEOUS
BETTER LOOKIN' THAN ANY MOVIE STAR
SORRY, NANCY--- I'M BROKE TODAY
ZING
NO SALE

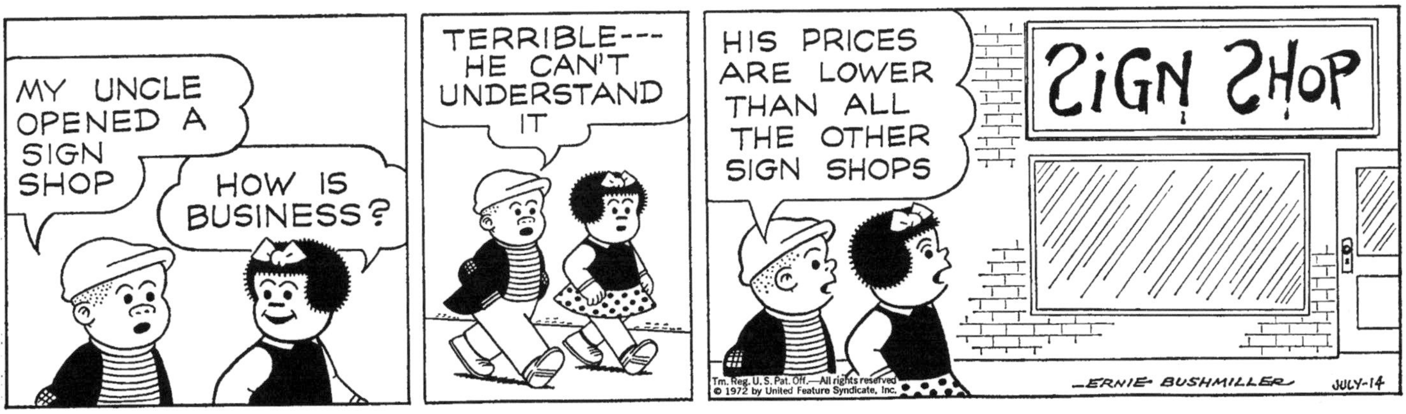
MY UNCLE OPENED A SIGN SHOP
HOW IS BUSINESS?
TERRIBLE--- HE CAN'T UNDERSTAND IT
HIS PRICES ARE LOWER THAN ALL THE OTHER SIGN SHOPS
SiGN SHOP
Tm. Reg. U. S. Pat. Off.—All rights reserved © 1972 by United Feature Syndicate, Inc.
ERNIE BUSHMILLER
JULY-14

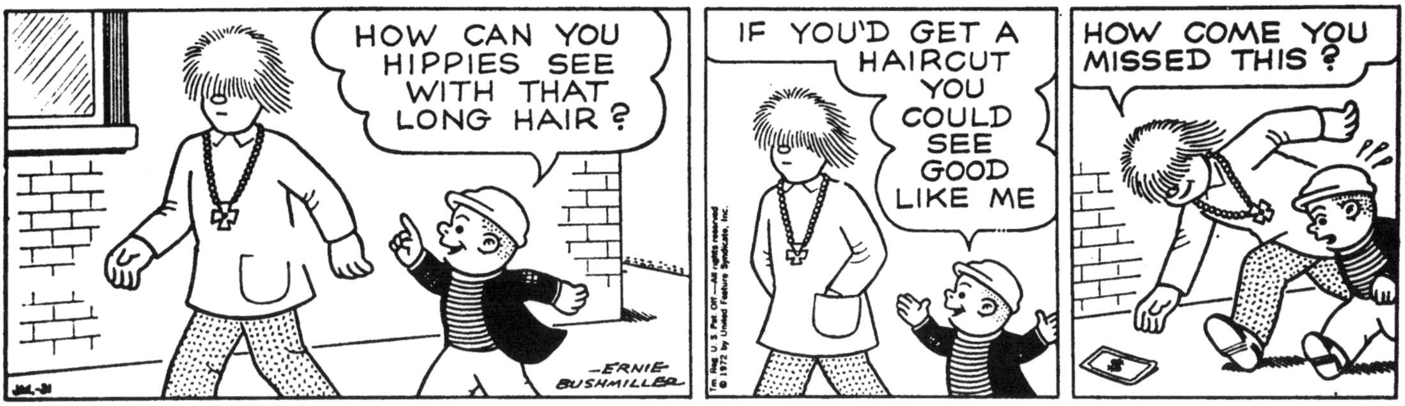
HOW CAN YOU HIPPIES SEE WITH THAT LONG HAIR?
ERNIE BUSHMILLER
IF YOU'D GET A HAIRCUT YOU COULD SEE GOOD LIKE ME
Tm Reg U S Pat Off—All rights reserved © 1972 by United Feature Syndicate, Inc.
HOW COME YOU MISSED THIS?

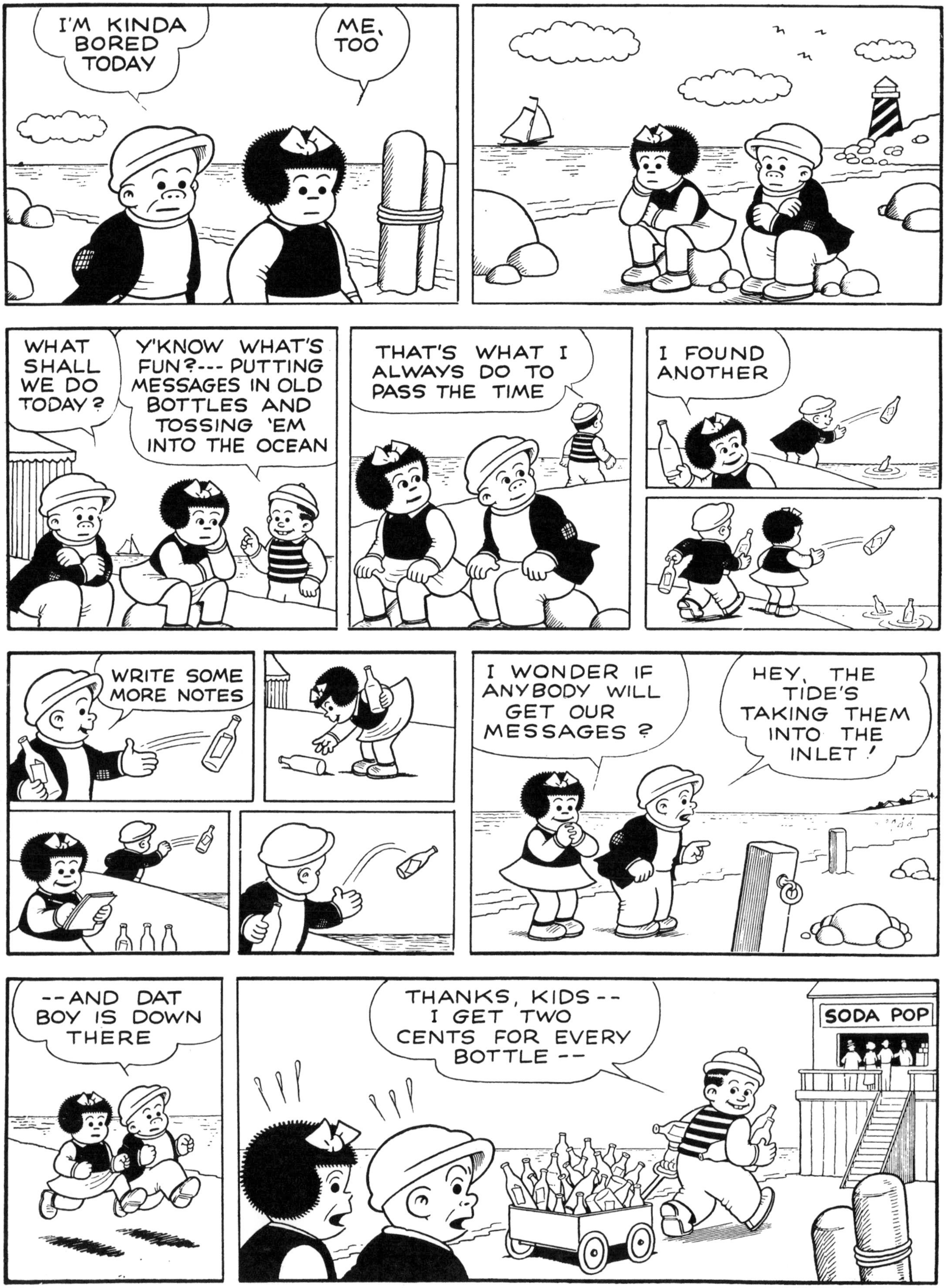
I'M KINDA BORED TODAY
ME, TOO
WHAT SHALL WE DO TODAY?
Y'KNOW WHAT'S FUN?--- PUTTING MESSAGES IN OLD BOTTLES AND TOSSING 'EM INTO THE OCEAN
THAT'S WHAT I ALWAYS DO TO PASS THE TIME
I FOUND ANOTHER
WRITE SOME MORE NOTES
I WONDER IF ANYBODY WILL GET OUR MESSAGES?
HEY, THE TIDE'S TAKING THEM INTO THE INLET!
--AND DAT BOY IS DOWN THERE
THANKS, KIDS -- I GET TWO CENTS FOR EVERY BOTTLE --
SODA POP

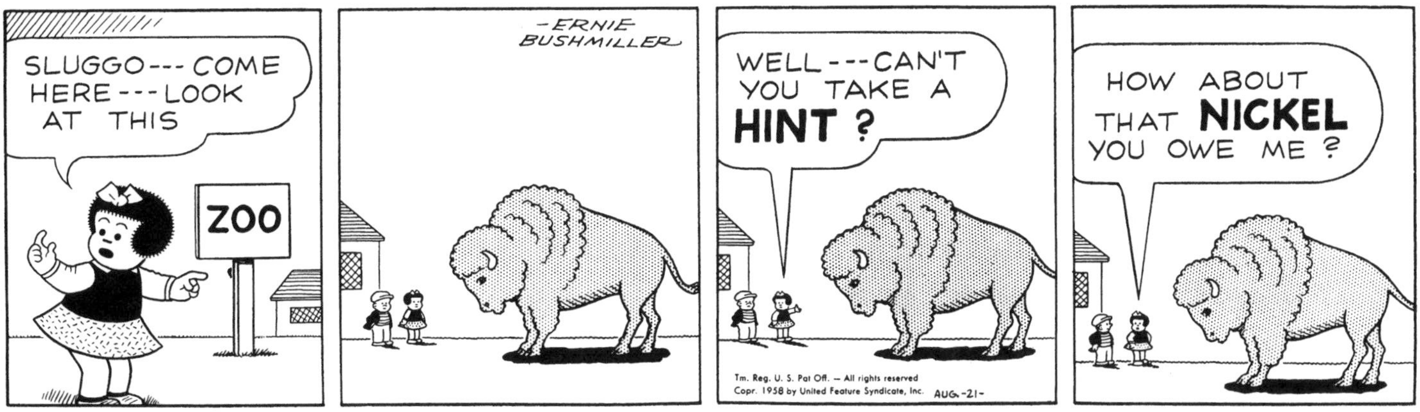
SLUGGO---COME HERE---LOOK AT THIS
ZOO
-ERNIE BUSHMILLER
WELL---CAN'T YOU TAKE A HINT ?
Tm. Reg. U. S. Pat Off. — All rights reserved
Copr. 1958 by United Feature Syndicate, Inc. AUG.-21-
HOW ABOUT THAT NICKEL YOU OWE ME ?

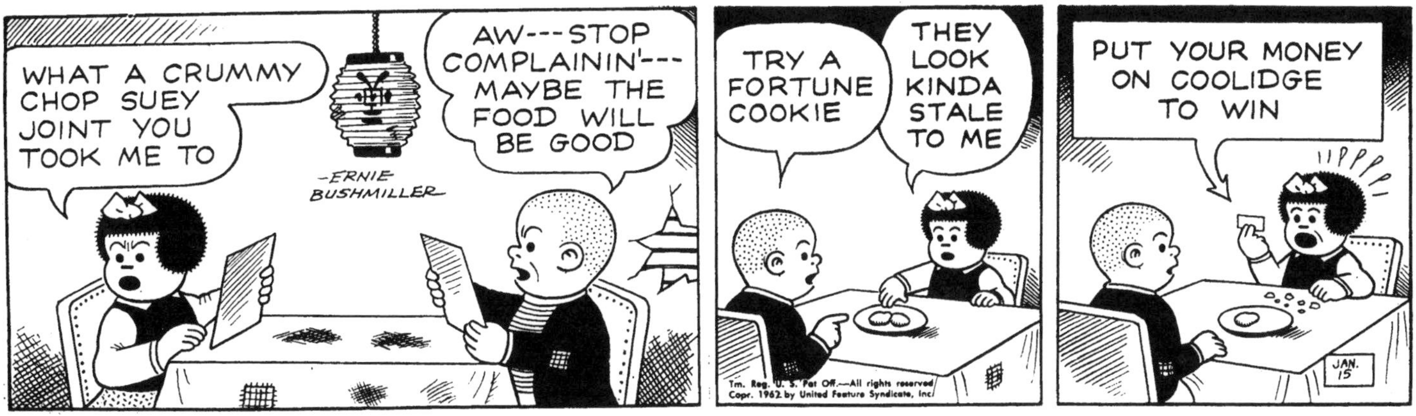
WHAT A CRUMMY CHOP SUEY JOINT YOU TOOK ME TO
AW---STOP COMPLAININ'---MAYBE THE FOOD WILL BE GOOD
-ERNIE BUSHMILLER
TRY A FORTUNE COOKIE
THEY LOOK KINDA STALE TO ME
Tm. Reg. U. S. Pat Off.—All rights reserved
Copr. 1962 by United Feature Syndicate, Inc.
PUT YOUR MONEY ON COOLIDGE TO WIN
JAN. 15

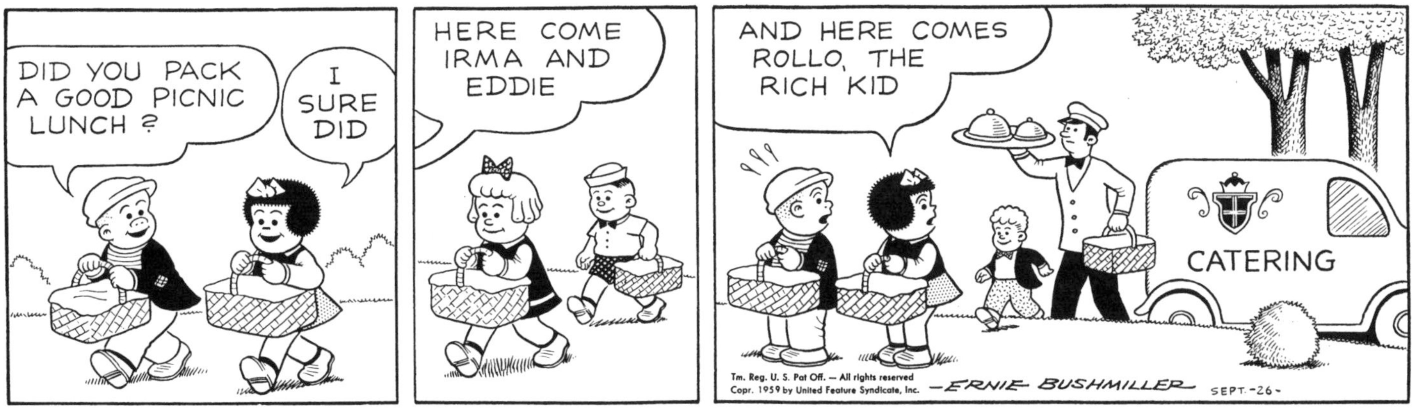
DID YOU PACK A GOOD PICNIC LUNCH ?
I SURE DID
HERE COME IRMA AND EDDIE
AND HERE COMES ROLLO, THE RICH KID
CATERING
Tm. Reg. U. S. Pat Off. — All rights reserved
Copr. 1959 by United Feature Syndicate, Inc.
-ERNIE BUSHMILLER SEPT.-26-

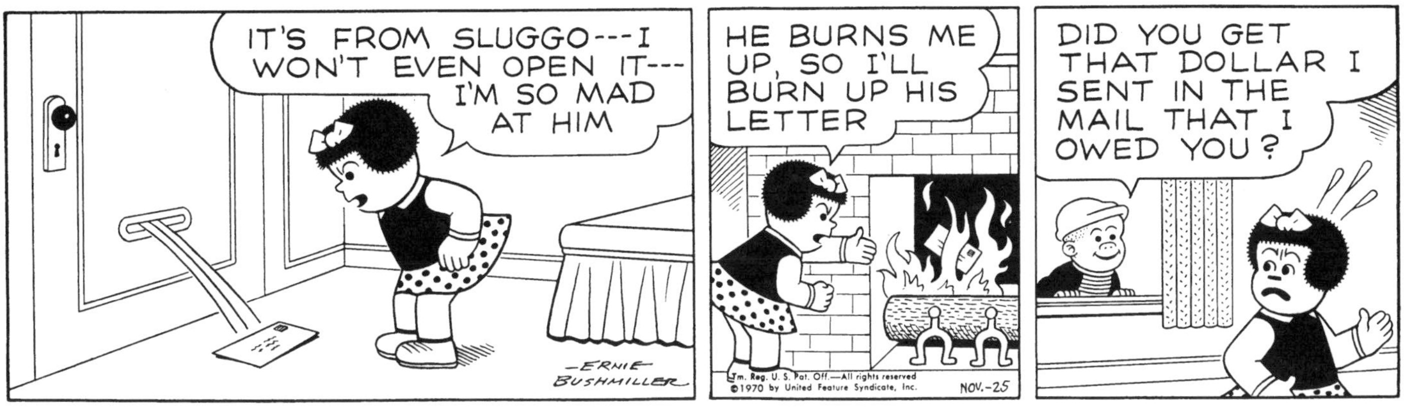
IT'S FROM SLUGGO---I WON'T EVEN OPEN IT---I'M SO MAD AT HIM
-ERNIE BUSHMILLER
HE BURNS ME UP, SO I'LL BURN UP HIS LETTER
Tm. Reg. U. S. Pat. Off.—All rights reserved
©1970 by United Feature Syndicate, Inc. NOV.-25
DID YOU GET THAT DOLLAR I SENT IN THE MAIL THAT I OWED YOU ?

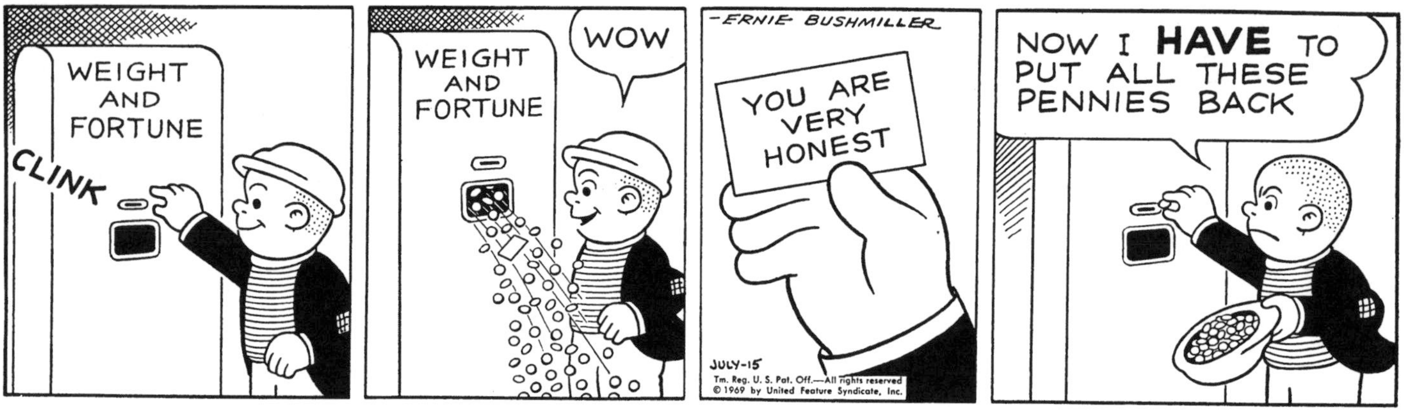
WEIGHT AND FORTUNE
CLINK
WEIGHT AND FORTUNE
WOW
-ERNIE BUSHMILLER
YOU ARE VERY HONEST
JULY-15
Tm. Reg. U. S. Pat. Off.—All rights reserved © 1969 by United Feature Syndicate, Inc.
NOW I **HAVE** TO PUT ALL THESE PENNIES BACK

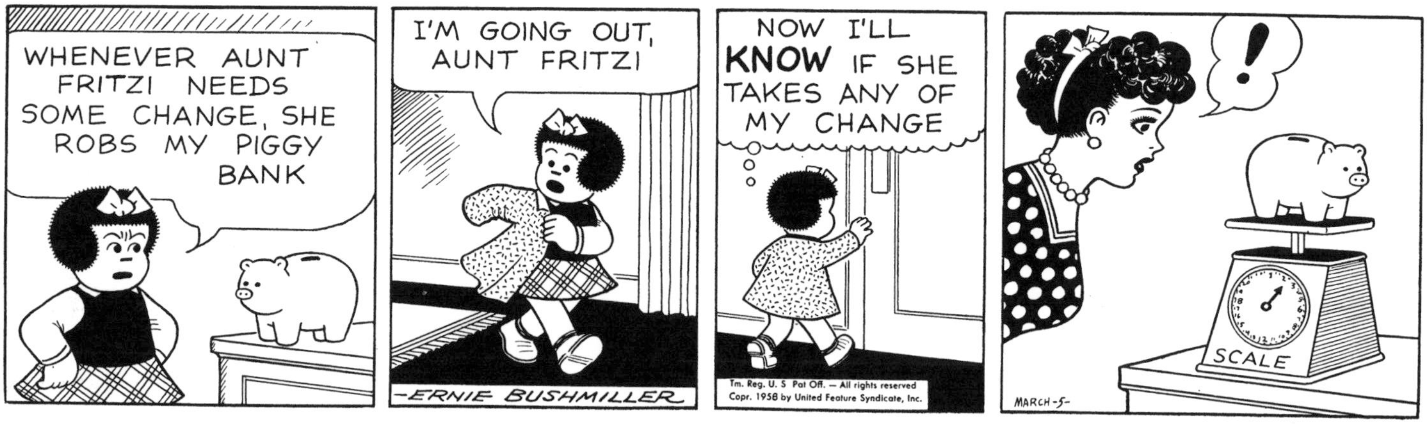
WHENEVER AUNT FRITZI NEEDS SOME CHANGE, SHE ROBS MY PIGGY BANK
I'M GOING OUT, AUNT FRITZI
-ERNIE BUSHMILLER
NOW I'LL **KNOW** IF SHE TAKES ANY OF MY CHANGE
Tm. Reg. U. S Pat Off. — All rights reserved Copr. 1958 by United Feature Syndicate, Inc.
!
SCALE
MARCH-5-

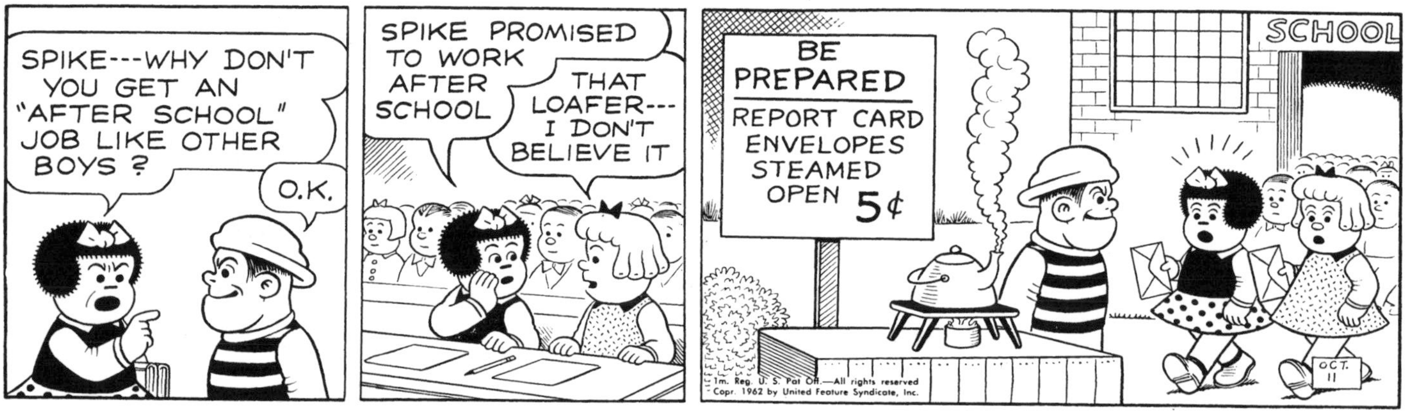
SPIKE---WHY DON'T YOU GET AN "AFTER SCHOOL" JOB LIKE OTHER BOYS ?
O.K.
SPIKE PROMISED TO WORK AFTER SCHOOL
THAT LOAFER--- I DON'T BELIEVE IT
BE PREPARED
REPORT CARD ENVELOPES STEAMED OPEN 5¢
SCHOOL
Tm. Reg. U. S. Pat Off.—All rights reserved Copr. 1962 by United Feature Syndicate, Inc.
OCT. 11

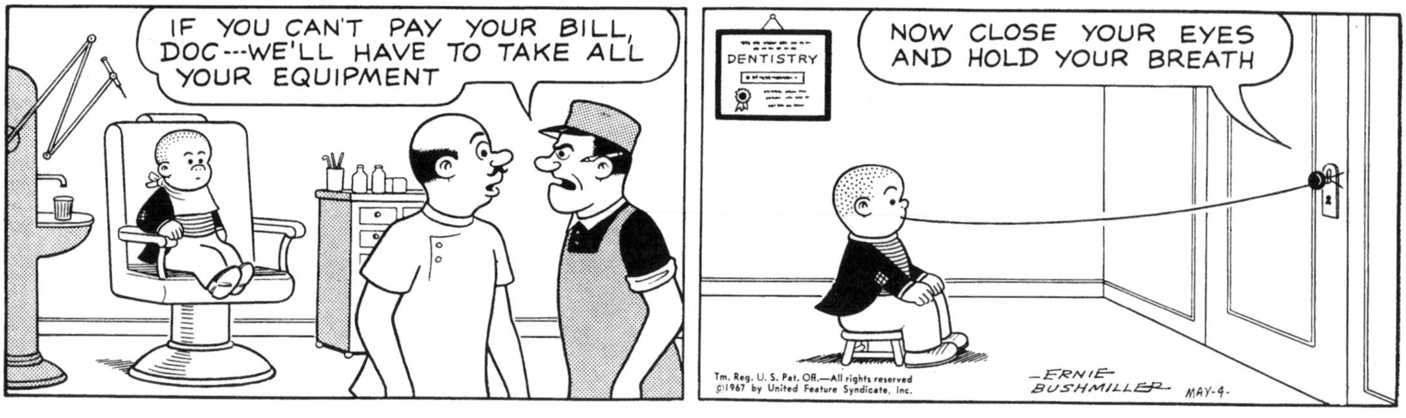
IF YOU CAN'T PAY YOUR BILL, DOC---WE'LL HAVE TO TAKE ALL YOUR EQUIPMENT
DENTISTRY
NOW CLOSE YOUR EYES AND HOLD YOUR BREATH
Tm. Reg. U. S. Pat. Off.—All rights reserved ©1967 by United Feature Syndicate, Inc.
-ERNIE BUSHMILLER
MAY-4-

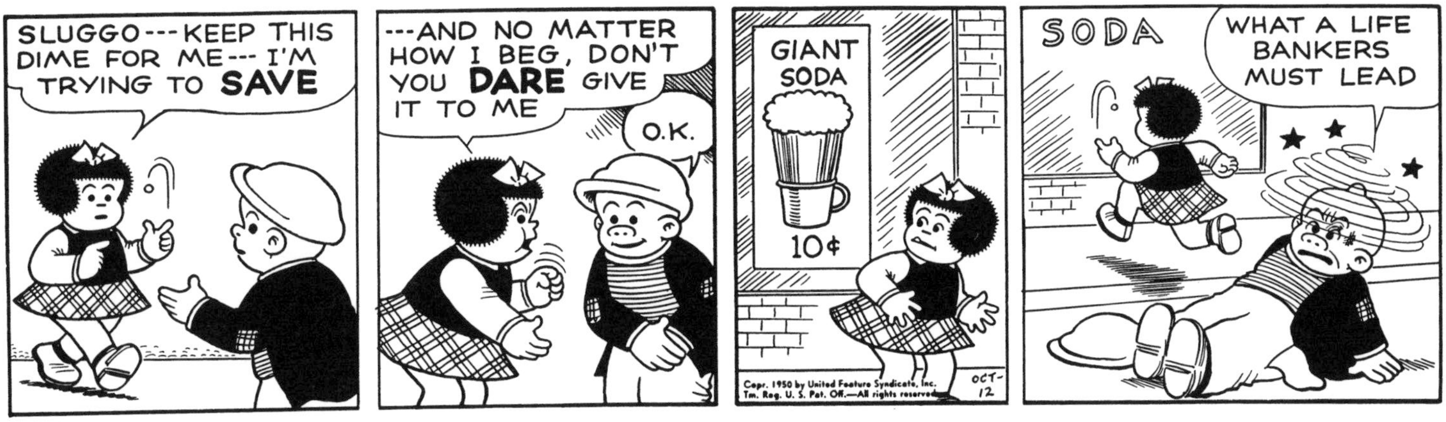
SLUGGO---KEEP THIS DIME FOR ME---I'M TRYING TO SAVE
---AND NO MATTER HOW I BEG, DON'T YOU DARE GIVE IT TO ME
O.K.
GIANT SODA
10¢
Copr. 1950 by United Feature Syndicate, Inc. Tm. Reg. U. S. Pat. Off.—All rights reserved
OCT-12
SODA
WHAT A LIFE BANKERS MUST LEAD

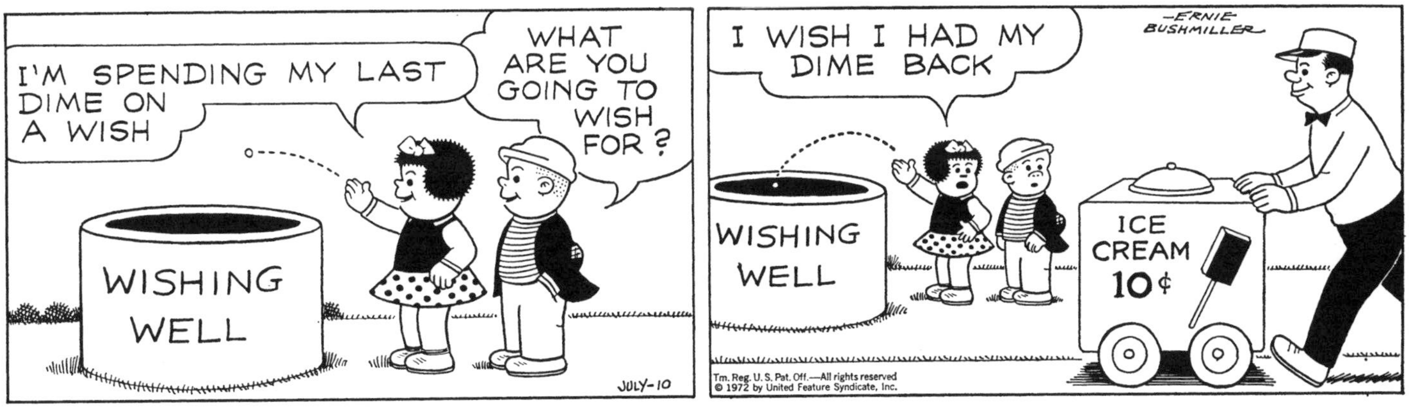
I'M SPENDING MY LAST DIME ON A WISH
WHAT ARE YOU GOING TO WISH FOR ?
WISHING WELL
JULY-10
I WISH I HAD MY DIME BACK
-ERNIE BUSHMILLER
WISHING WELL
ICE CREAM 10¢
Tm. Reg. U. S. Pat. Off.—All rights reserved © 1972 by United Feature Syndicate, Inc.

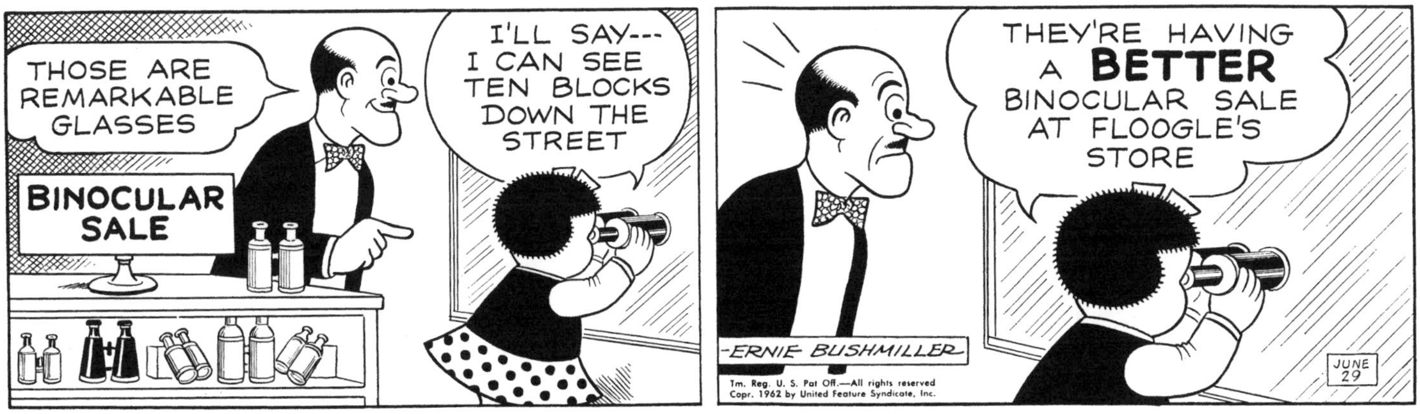
THOSE ARE REMARKABLE GLASSES
BINOCULAR SALE
I'LL SAY--- I CAN SEE TEN BLOCKS DOWN THE STREET
THEY'RE HAVING A BETTER BINOCULAR SALE AT FLOOGLE'S STORE
-ERNIE BUSHMILLER
Tm. Reg. U. S. Pat Off.—All rights reserved Copr. 1962 by United Feature Syndicate, Inc.
JUNE 29

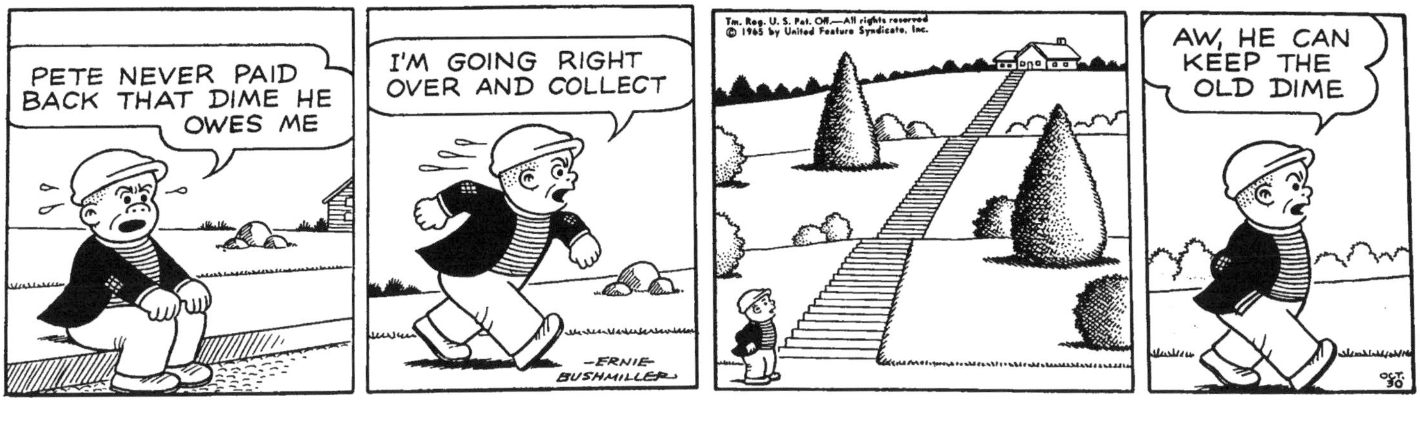
PETE NEVER PAID BACK THAT DIME HE OWES ME
I'M GOING RIGHT OVER AND COLLECT
-ERNIE BUSHMILLER
Tm. Reg. U. S. Pat. Off.—All rights reserved © 1965 by United Feature Syndicate, Inc.
AW, HE CAN KEEP THE OLD DIME
OCT. 30

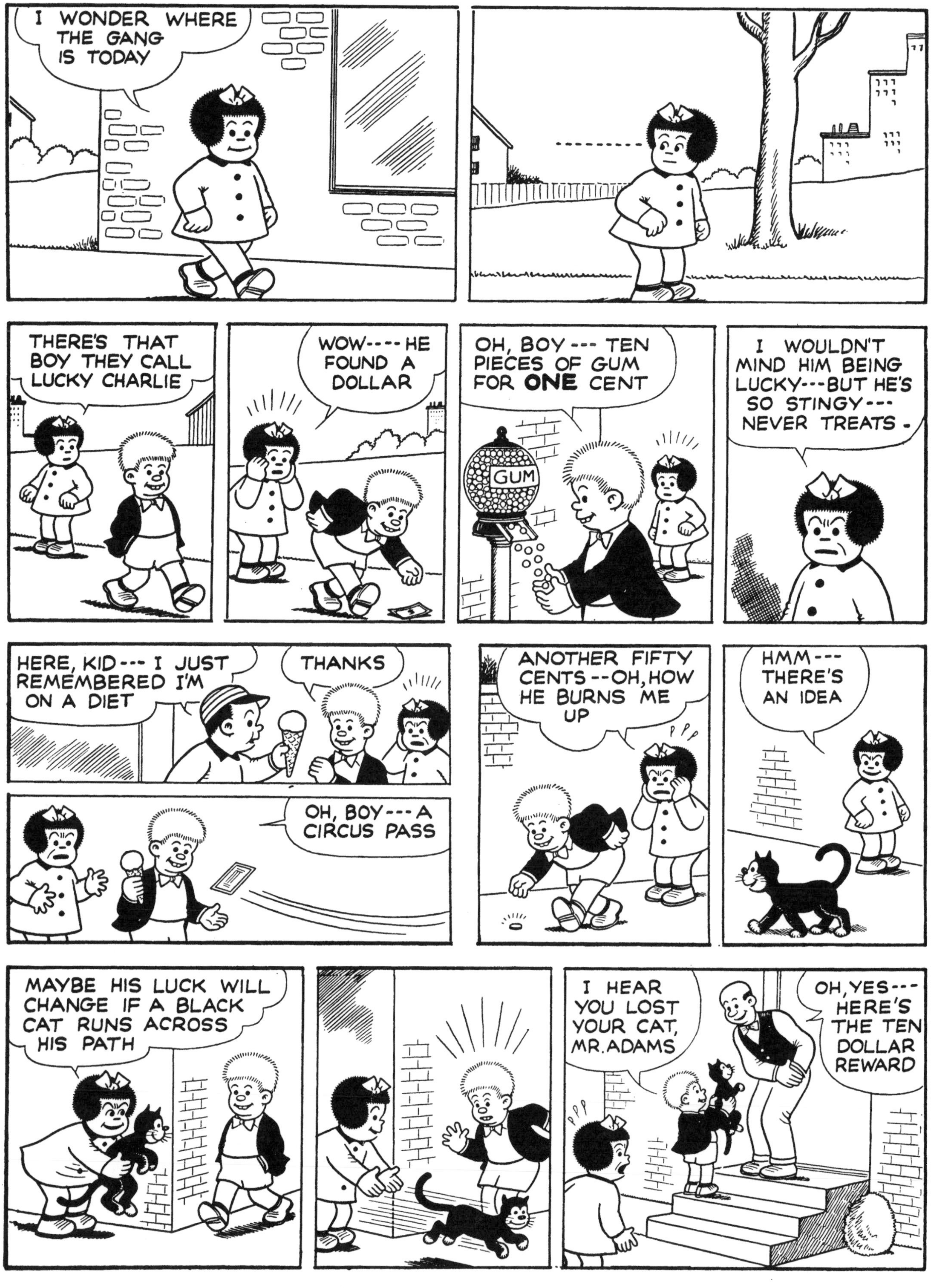
I WONDER WHERE THE GANG IS TODAY
THERE'S THAT BOY THEY CALL LUCKY CHARLIE
WOW---- HE FOUND A DOLLAR
OH, BOY --- TEN PIECES OF GUM FOR ONE CENT
GUM
I WOULDN'T MIND HIM BEING LUCKY---BUT HE'S SO STINGY--- NEVER TREATS -
HERE, KID--- I JUST REMEMBERED I'M ON A DIET
THANKS
OH, BOY --- A CIRCUS PASS
ANOTHER FIFTY CENTS --OH, HOW HE BURNS ME UP
HMM--- THERE'S AN IDEA
MAYBE HIS LUCK WILL CHANGE IF A BLACK CAT RUNS ACROSS HIS PATH
I HEAR YOU LOST YOUR CAT, MR. ADAMS
OH, YES--- HERE'S THE TEN DOLLAR REWARD

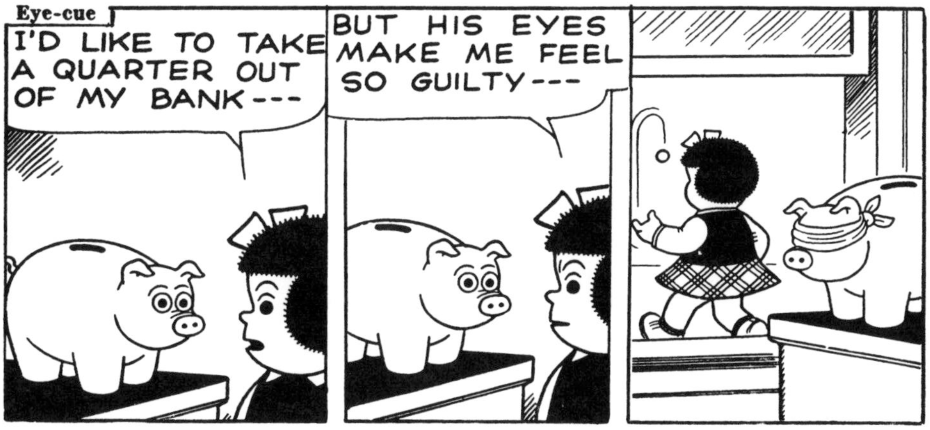
Eye-cue
I'D LIKE TO TAKE A QUARTER OUT OF MY BANK---
BUT HIS EYES MAKE ME FEEL SO GUILTY---

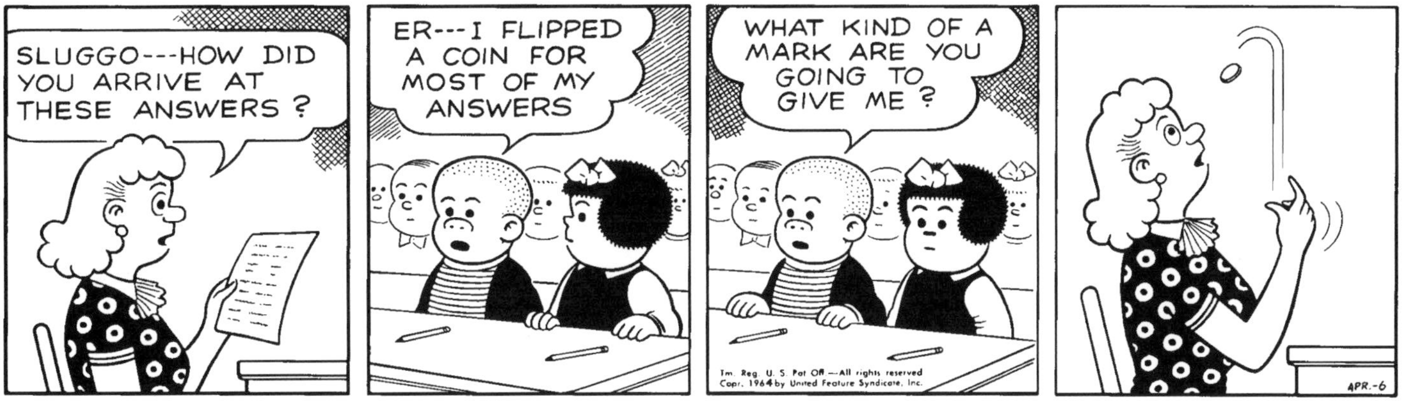
SLUGGO---HOW DID YOU ARRIVE AT THESE ANSWERS ?
ER---I FLIPPED A COIN FOR MOST OF MY ANSWERS
WHAT KIND OF A MARK ARE YOU GOING TO GIVE ME ?
Tm. Reg. U. S. Pat Off.—All rights reserved Copr. 1964 by United Feature Syndicate, Inc.
APR.-6

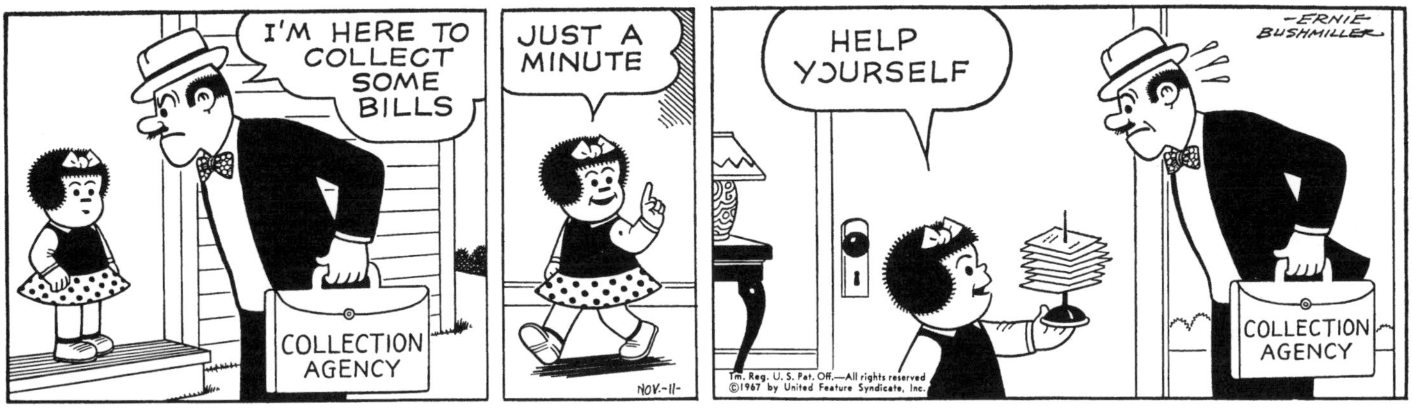
I'M HERE TO COLLECT SOME BILLS
COLLECTION AGENCY
JUST A MINUTE
NOV.-11-
HELP YOURSELF
-ERNIE BUSHMILLER
COLLECTION AGENCY
Tm. Reg. U. S. Pat. Off.—All rights reserved ©1967 by United Feature Syndicate, Inc.

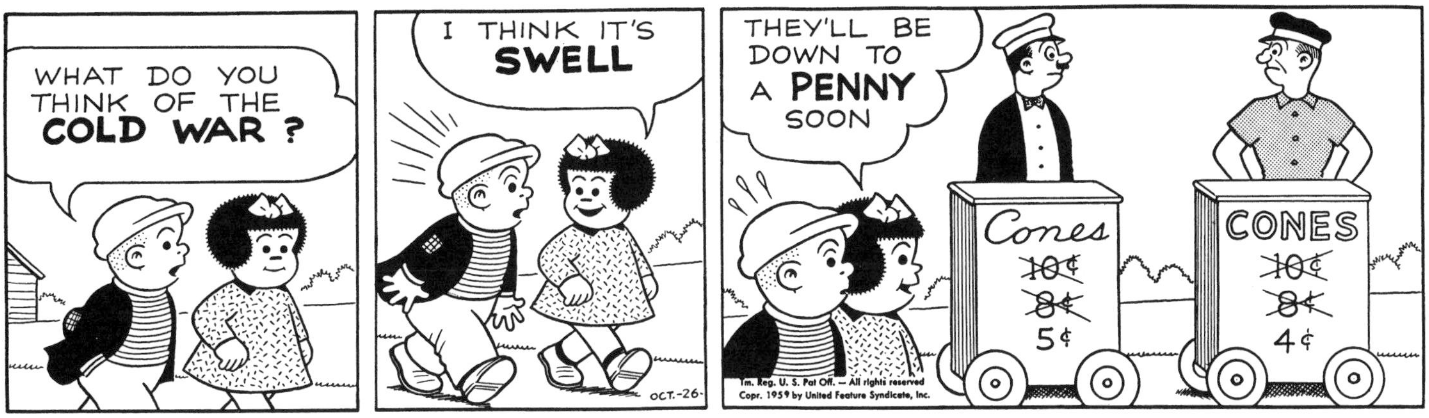
WHAT DO YOU THINK OF THE **COLD WAR** ?
I THINK IT'S **SWELL**
OCT.-26-
THEY'LL BE DOWN TO A **PENNY** SOON
Cones
10¢
8¢
5¢
CONES
10¢
8¢
4¢
Tm. Reg. U. S. Pat Off. — All rights reserved Copr. 1959 by United Feature Syndicate, Inc.

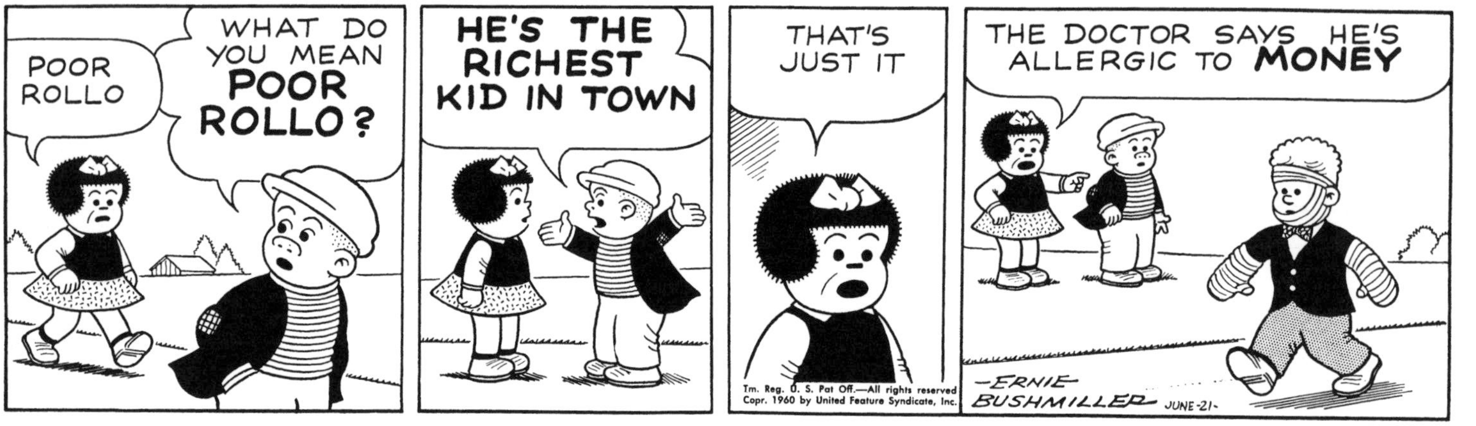
POOR ROLLO
WHAT DO YOU MEAN POOR ROLLO?
HE'S THE RICHEST KID IN TOWN
THAT'S JUST IT
THE DOCTOR SAYS HE'S ALLERGIC TO MONEY
Tm. Reg. U. S. Pat. Off.—All rights reserved Copr. 1960 by United Feature Syndicate, Inc.
—ERNIE— BUSHMILLER JUNE-21-

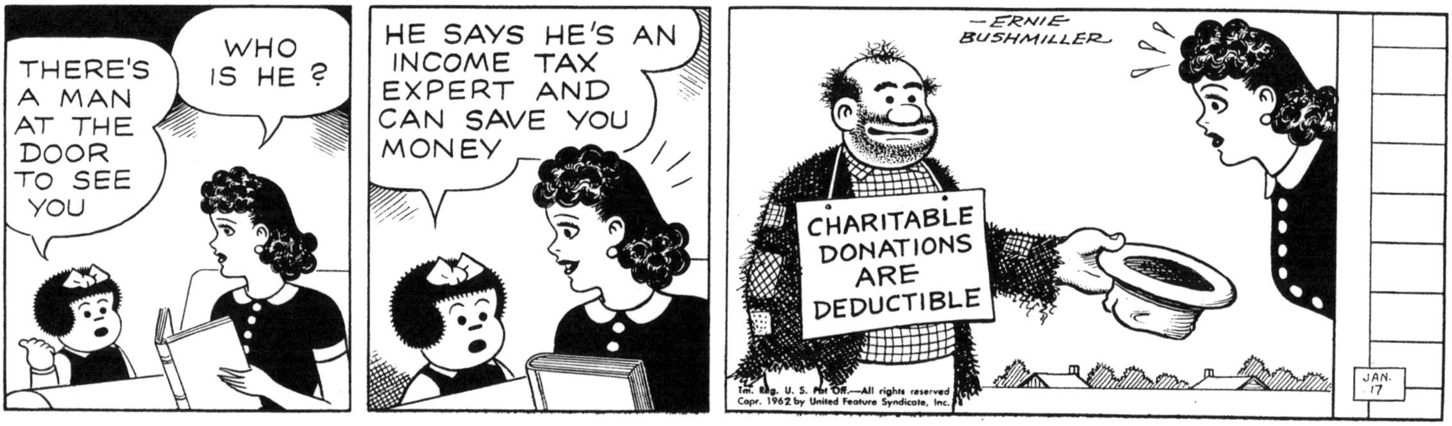
THERE'S A MAN AT THE DOOR TO SEE YOU
WHO IS HE ?
HE SAYS HE'S AN INCOME TAX EXPERT AND CAN SAVE YOU MONEY
—ERNIE— BUSHMILLER
CHARITABLE DONATIONS ARE DEDUCTIBLE
Tm. Reg. U. S. Pat. Off.—All rights reserved Copr. 1962 by United Feature Syndicate, Inc.
JAN. 17

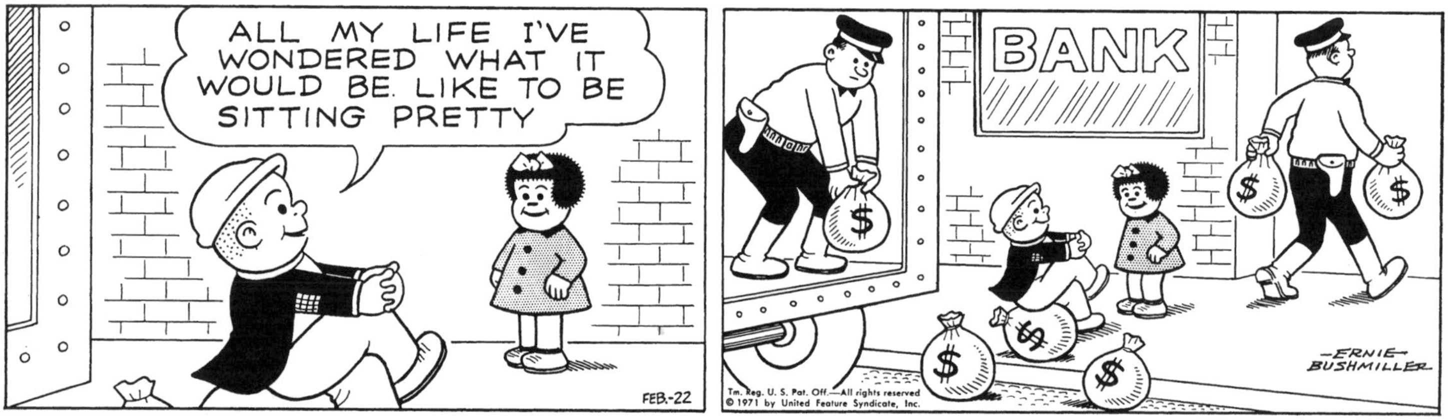
ALL MY LIFE I'VE WONDERED WHAT IT WOULD BE LIKE TO BE SITTING PRETTY
FEB.-22
BANK
$
—ERNIE— BUSHMILLER
Tm. Reg. U. S. Pat. Off.—All rights reserved © 1971 by United Feature Syndicate, Inc.

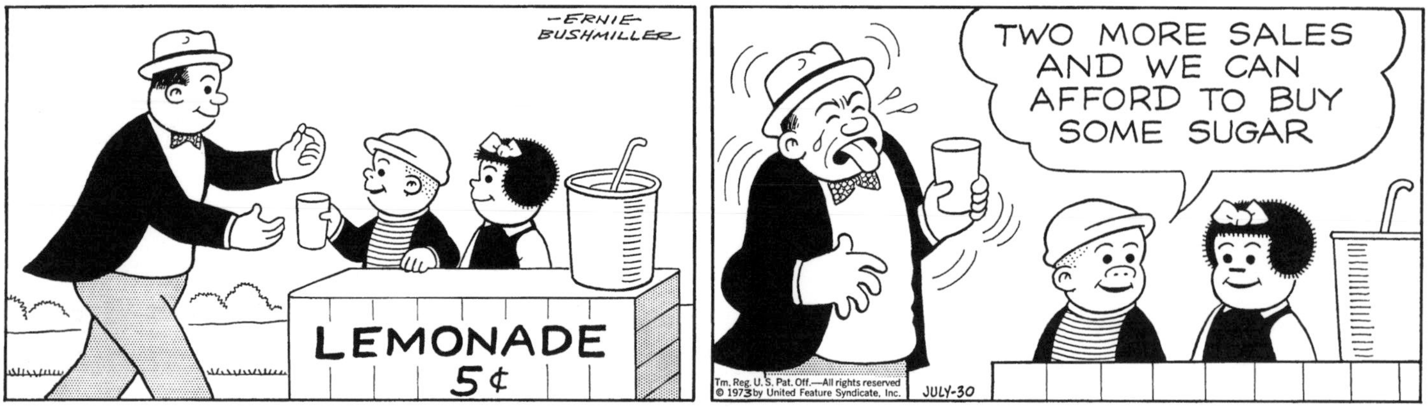
—ERNIE— BUSHMILLER
LEMONADE 5¢
TWO MORE SALES AND WE CAN AFFORD TO BUY SOME SUGAR
Tm. Reg. U. S. Pat. Off.—All rights reserved © 1973 by United Feature Syndicate, Inc.
JULY-30

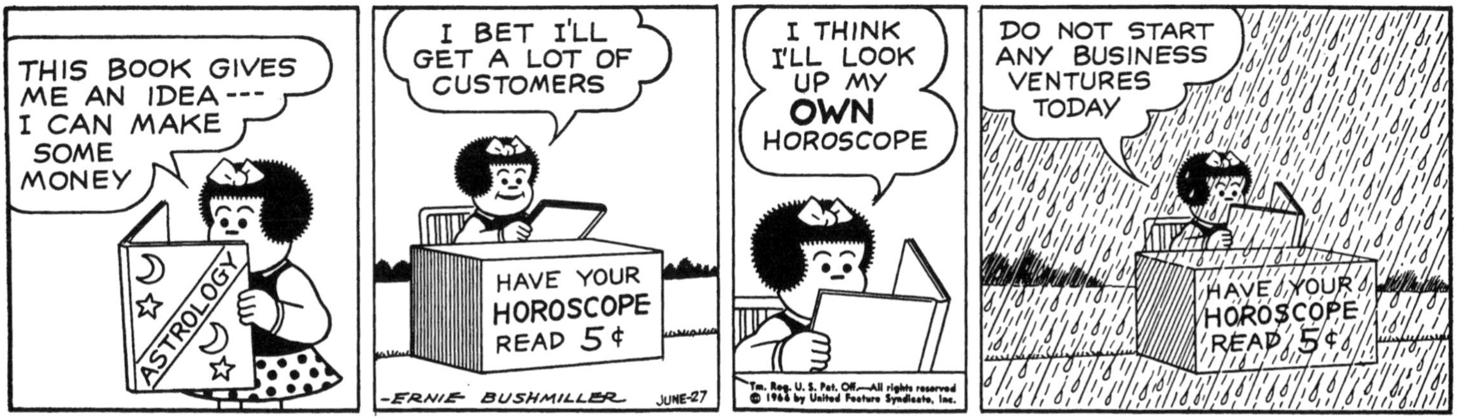
THIS BOOK GIVES ME AN IDEA--- I CAN MAKE SOME MONEY
ASTROLOGY
I BET I'LL GET A LOT OF CUSTOMERS
HAVE YOUR HOROSCOPE READ 5¢
-ERNIE BUSHMILLER
JUNE-27
I THINK I'LL LOOK UP MY **OWN** HOROSCOPE
Tm. Reg. U. S. Pat. Off.—All rights reserved © 1966 by United Feature Syndicate, Inc.
DO NOT START ANY BUSINESS VENTURES TODAY
HAVE YOUR HOROSCOPE READ 5¢

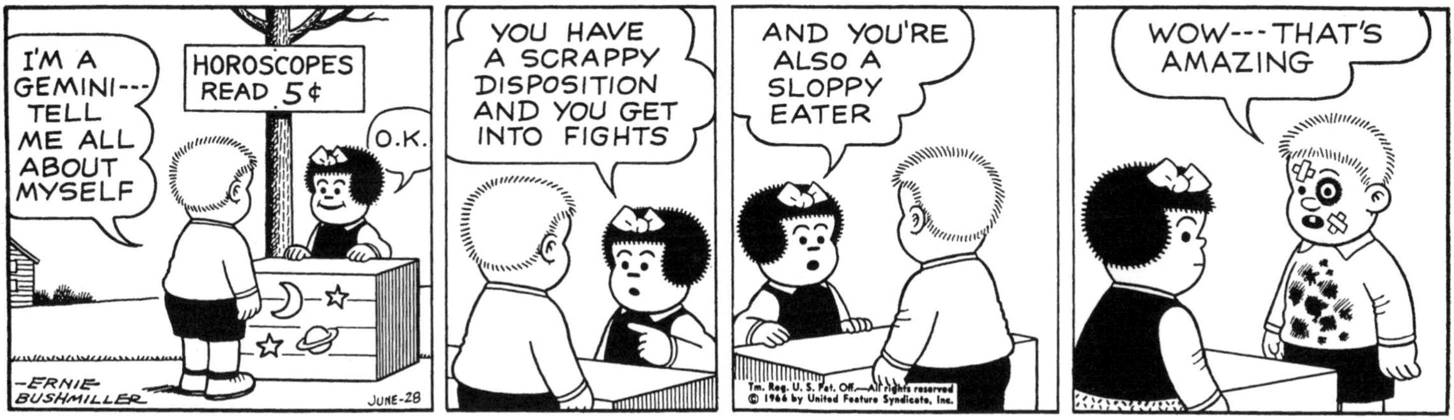
I'M A GEMINI--- TELL ME ALL ABOUT MYSELF
HOROSCOPES READ 5¢
O.K.
-ERNIE BUSHMILLER
JUNE-28
YOU HAVE A SCRAPPY DISPOSITION AND YOU GET INTO FIGHTS
AND YOU'RE ALSO A SLOPPY EATER
Tm. Reg. U. S. Pat. Off.—All rights reserved © 1966 by United Feature Syndicate, Inc.
WOW---THAT'S AMAZING

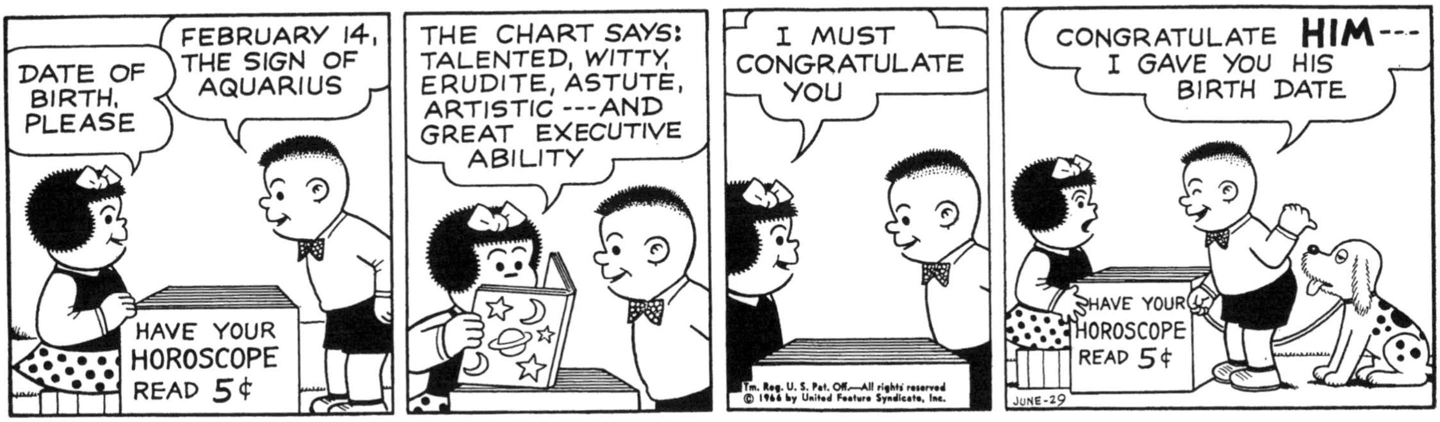
DATE OF BIRTH, PLEASE
FEBRUARY 14, THE SIGN OF AQUARIUS
HAVE YOUR HOROSCOPE READ 5¢
THE CHART SAYS: TALENTED, WITTY, ERUDITE, ASTUTE, ARTISTIC ---AND GREAT EXECUTIVE ABILITY
I MUST CONGRATULATE YOU
Tm. Reg. U. S. Pat. Off.—All rights reserved © 1966 by United Feature Syndicate, Inc.
CONGRATULATE **HIM**--- I GAVE YOU HIS BIRTH DATE
HAVE YOUR HOROSCOPE READ 5¢
JUNE-29

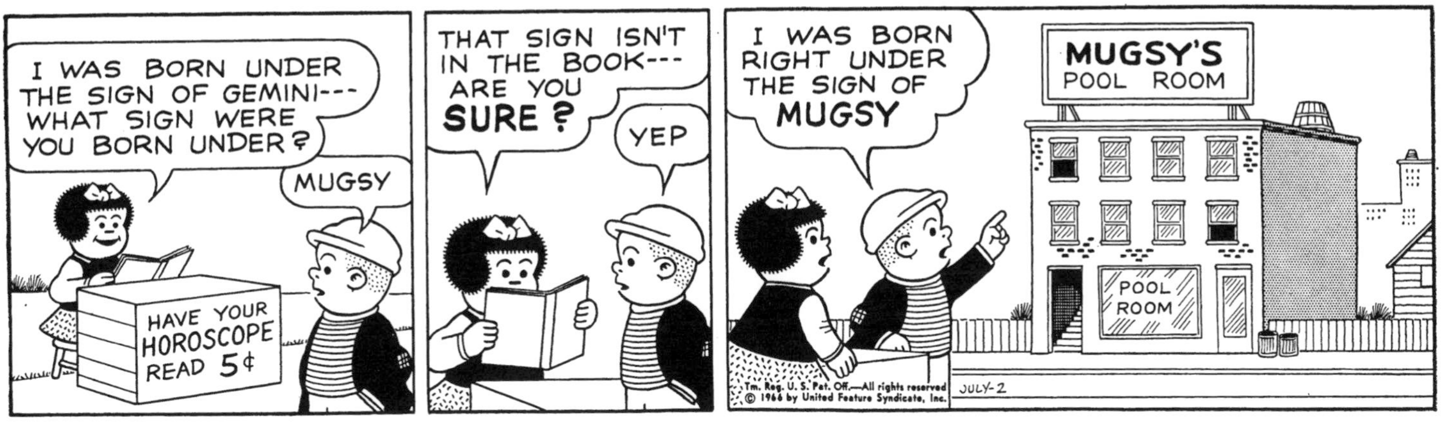
I WAS BORN UNDER THE SIGN OF GEMINI--- WHAT SIGN WERE YOU BORN UNDER?
MUGSY
HAVE YOUR HOROSCOPE READ 5¢
THAT SIGN ISN'T IN THE BOOK--- ARE YOU **SURE?**
YEP
I WAS BORN RIGHT UNDER THE SIGN OF **MUGSY**
MUGSY'S POOL ROOM
POOL ROOM
Tm. Reg. U. S. Pat. Off.—All rights reserved © 1966 by United Feature Syndicate, Inc.
JULY-2

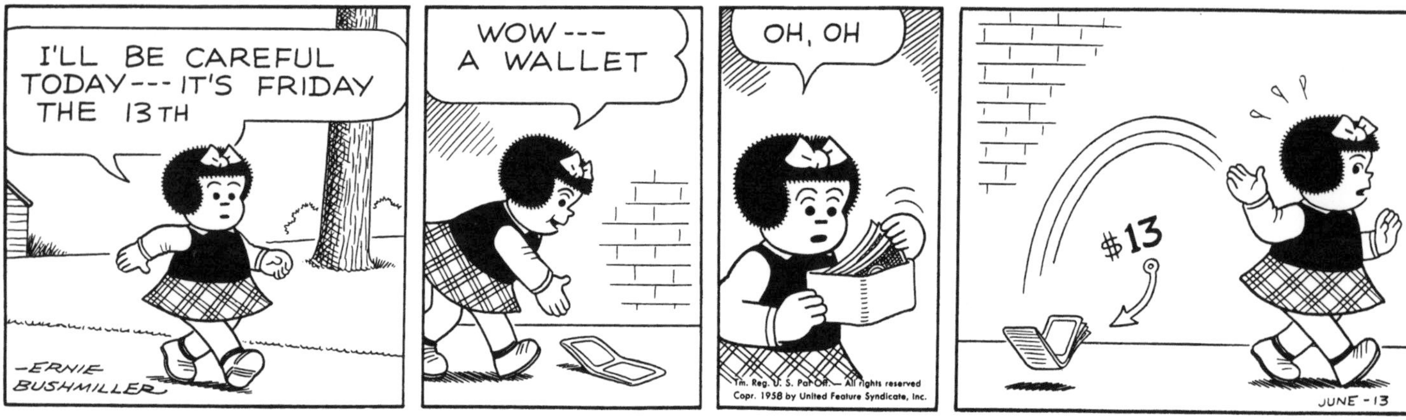
I'LL BE CAREFUL TODAY--- IT'S FRIDAY THE 13TH
-ERNIE BUSHMILLER
WOW--- A WALLET
OH, OH
Tm. Reg. U. S. Pat Off. — All rights reserved Copr. 1958 by United Feature Syndicate, Inc.
$13
JUNE-13

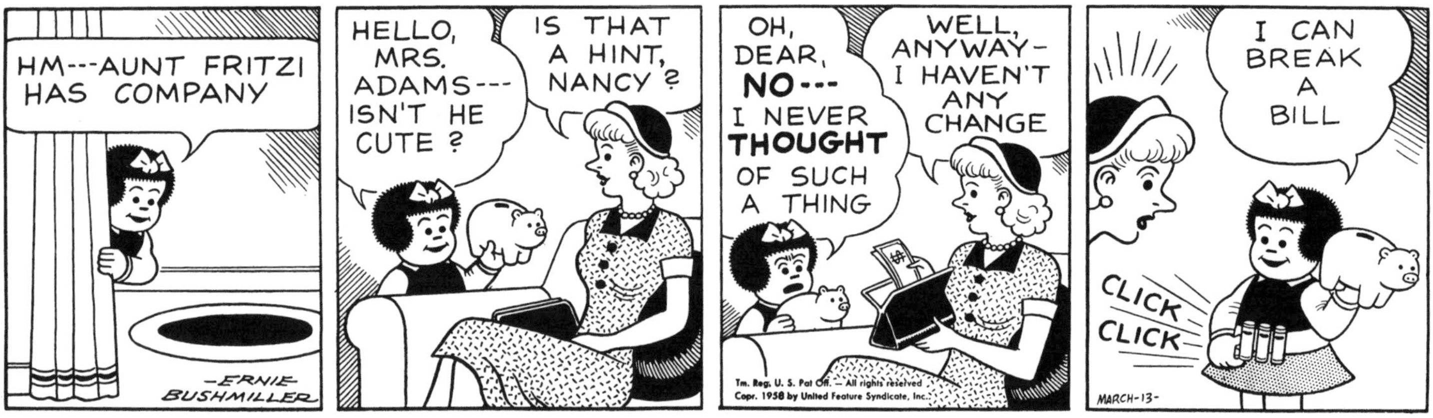
HM---AUNT FRITZI HAS COMPANY
-ERNIE BUSHMILLER
HELLO, MRS. ADAMS--- ISN'T HE CUTE ?
IS THAT A HINT, NANCY ?
OH, DEAR, NO--- I NEVER THOUGHT OF SUCH A THING
WELL, ANYWAY- I HAVEN'T ANY CHANGE
Tm. Reg. U. S. Pat Off. — All rights reserved Copr. 1958 by United Feature Syndicate, Inc.
I CAN BREAK A BILL
CLICK
CLICK
MARCH-13-

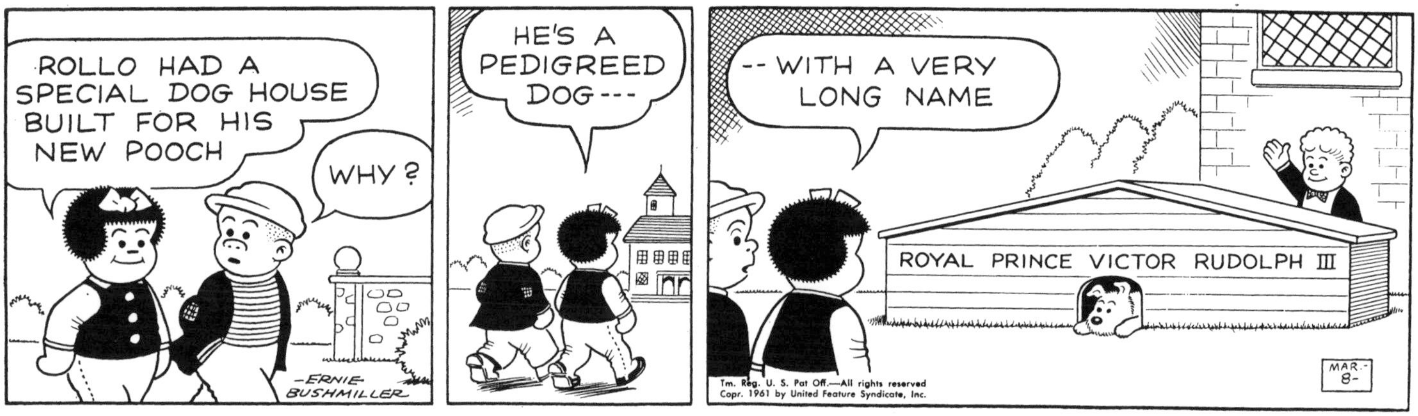
ROLLO HAD A SPECIAL DOG HOUSE BUILT FOR HIS NEW POOCH
WHY ?
-ERNIE BUSHMILLER
HE'S A PEDIGREED DOG---
-- WITH A VERY LONG NAME
ROYAL PRINCE VICTOR RUDOLPH III
Tm. Reg. U. S. Pat Off.—All rights reserved Copr. 1961 by United Feature Syndicate, Inc.
MAR.-8-

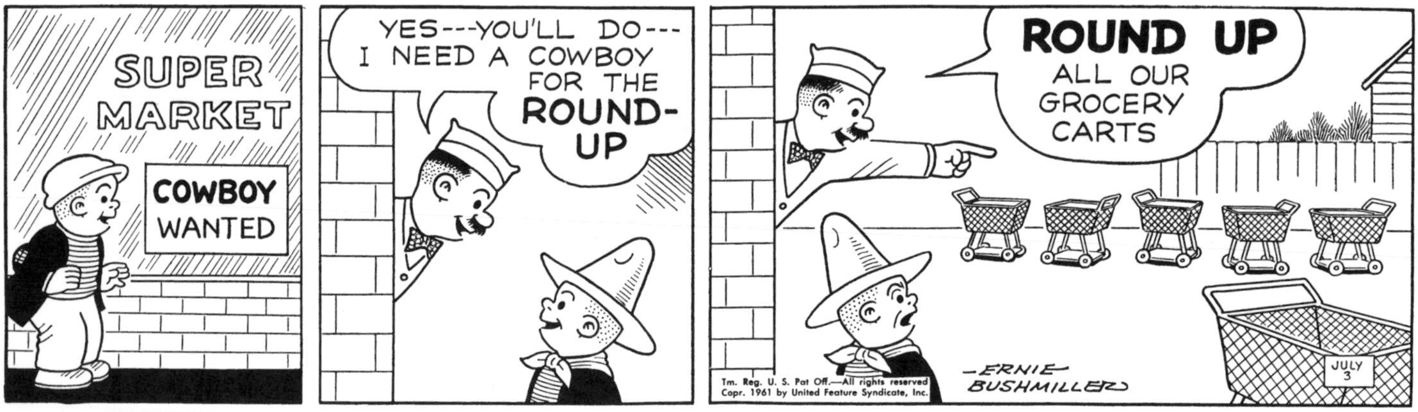
SUPER MARKET
COWBOY WANTED
YES---YOU'LL DO--- I NEED A COWBOY FOR THE ROUND-UP
ROUND UP ALL OUR GROCERY CARTS
Tm. Reg. U. S. Pat Off.—All rights reserved Copr. 1961 by United Feature Syndicate, Inc.
-ERNIE BUSHMILLER
JULY 3

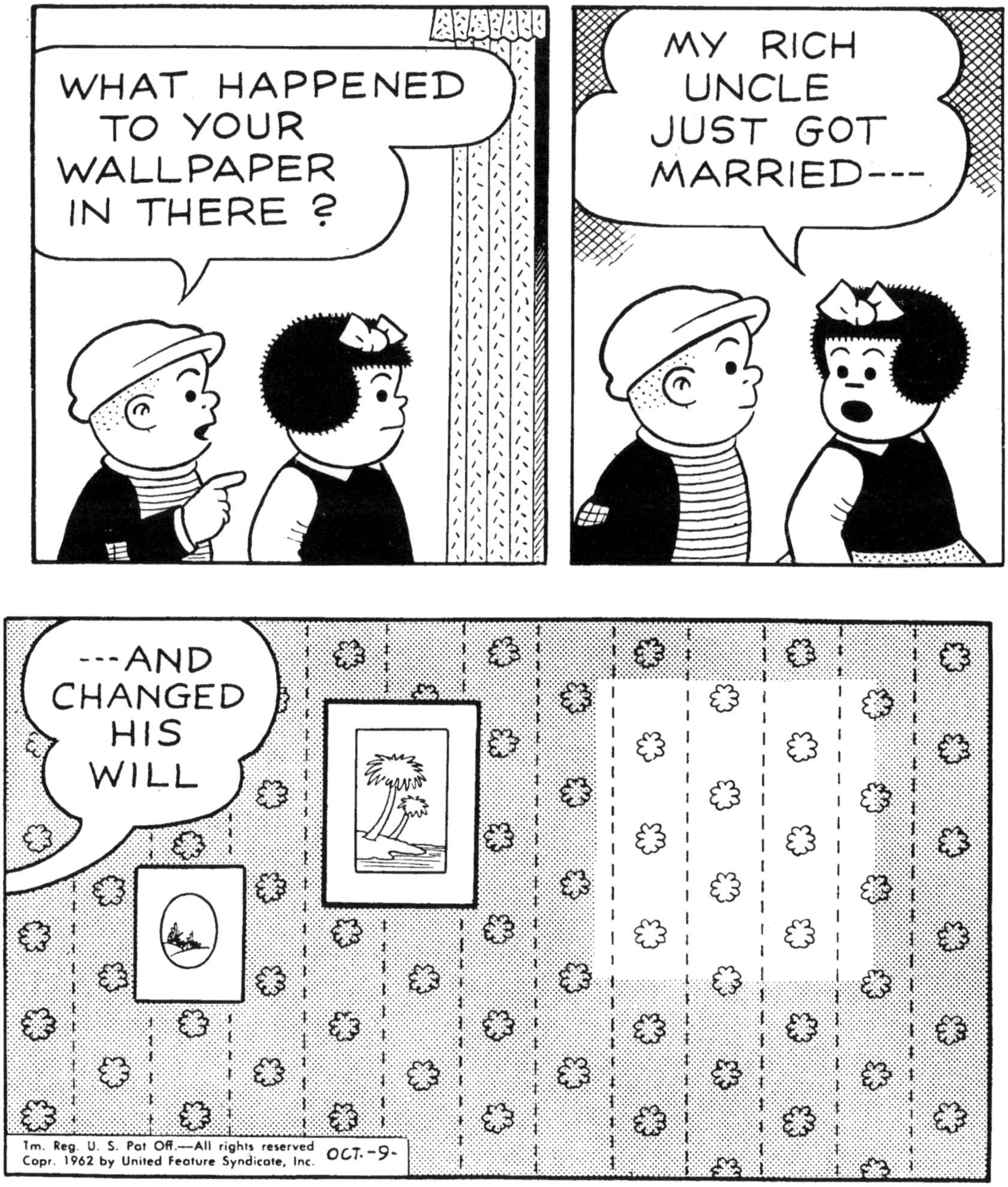

WHAT HAPPENED TO YOUR WALLPAPER IN THERE ?
MY RICH UNCLE JUST GOT MARRIED---
---AND CHANGED HIS WILL
Tm. Reg. U. S. Pat Off.—All rights reserved Copr. 1962 by United Feature Syndicate, Inc.
OCT.-9-

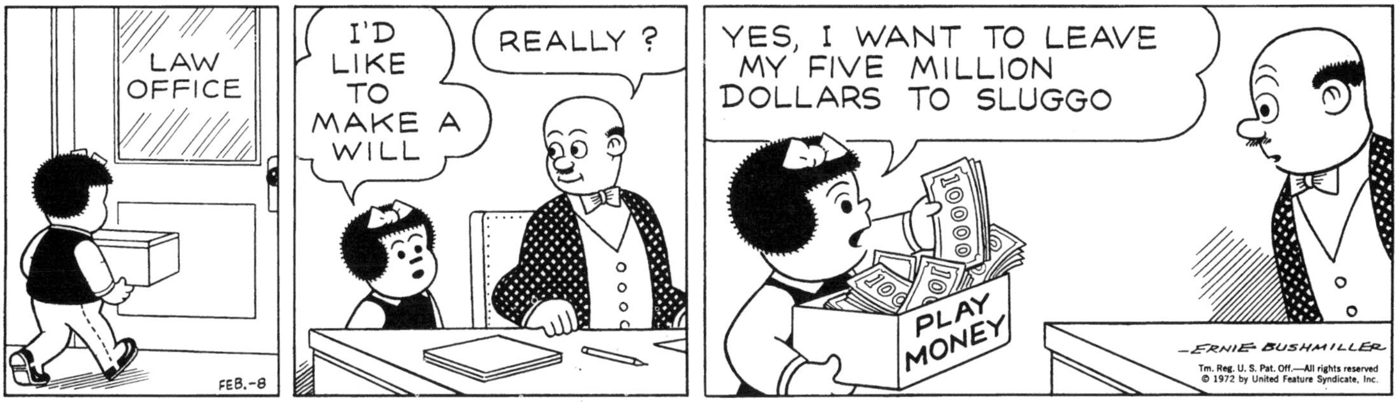

LAW OFFICE
FEB.-8
I'D LIKE TO MAKE A WILL
REALLY ?
YES, I WANT TO LEAVE MY FIVE MILLION DOLLARS TO SLUGGO
PLAY MONEY
-ERNIE BUSHMILLER
Tm. Reg. U. S. Pat. Off.—All rights reserved © 1972 by United Feature Syndicate, Inc.

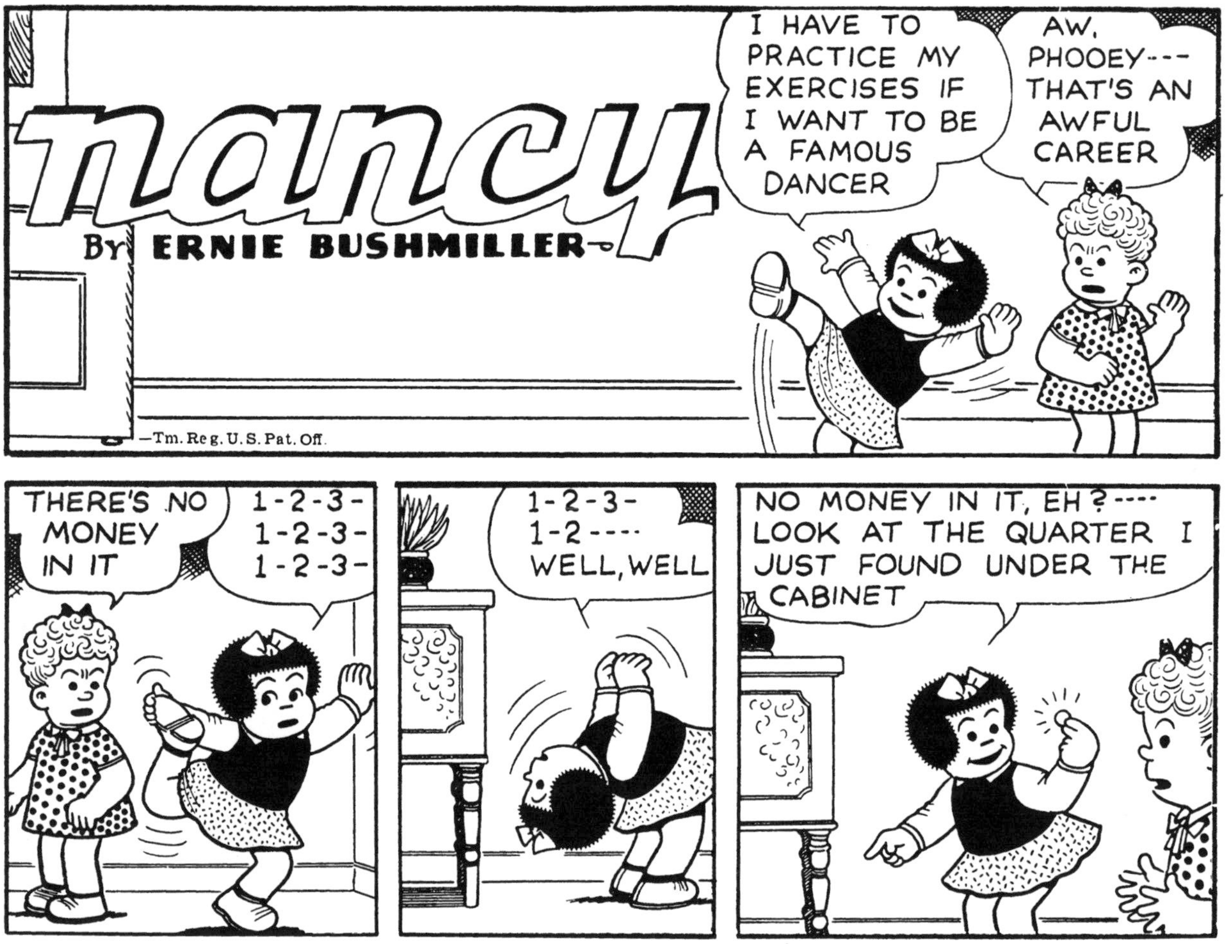
nancy
By ERNIE BUSHMILLER
—Tm. Reg. U. S. Pat. Off.
I HAVE TO PRACTICE MY EXERCISES IF I WANT TO BE A FAMOUS DANCER
AW, PHOOEY--- THAT'S AN AWFUL CAREER
THERE'S NO MONEY IN IT
1-2-3- 1-2-3- 1-2-3-
1-2-3- 1-2---- WELL, WELL
NO MONEY IN IT, EH?---- LOOK AT THE QUARTER I JUST FOUND UNDER THE CABINET

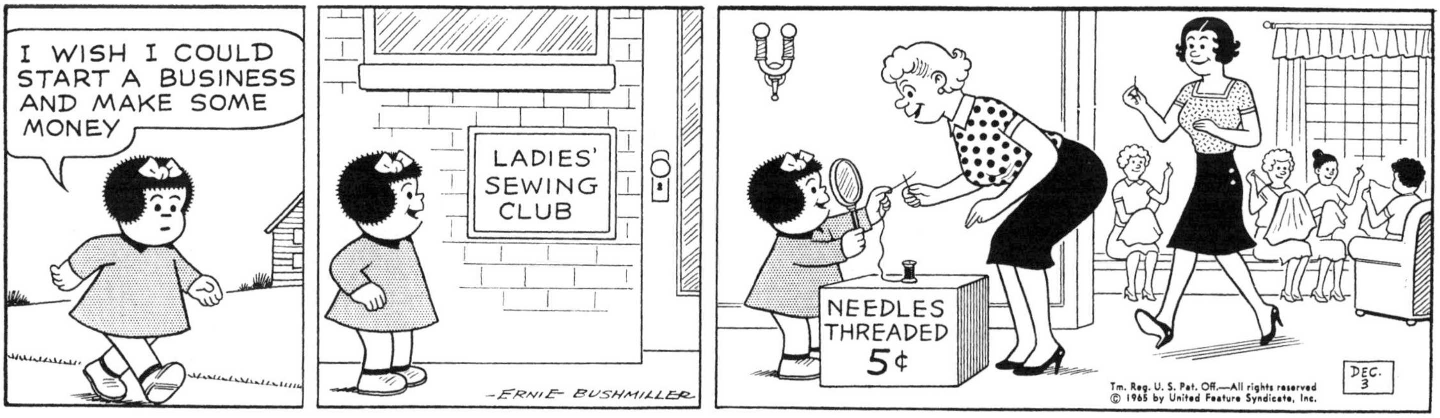
I WISH I COULD START A BUSINESS AND MAKE SOME MONEY
LADIES' SEWING CLUB
-ERNIE BUSHMILLER
NEEDLES THREADED 5¢
Tm. Reg. U. S. Pat. Off.—All rights reserved © 1965 by United Feature Syndicate, Inc.
DEC. 3

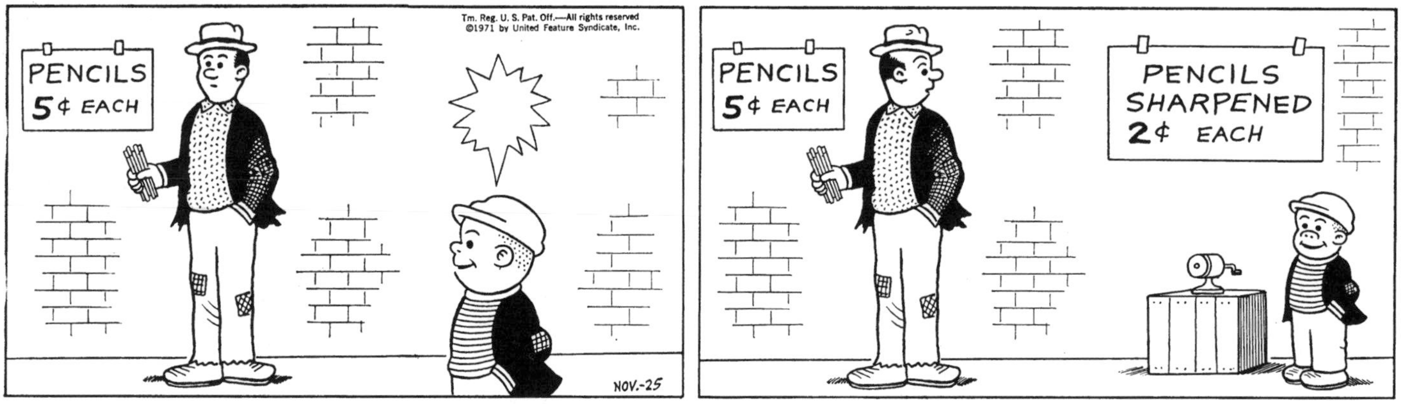
PENCILS 5¢ EACH
Tm. Reg. U. S. Pat. Off.—All rights reserved ©1971 by United Feature Syndicate, Inc.
NOV.-25
PENCILS 5¢ EACH
PENCILS SHARPENED 2¢ EACH

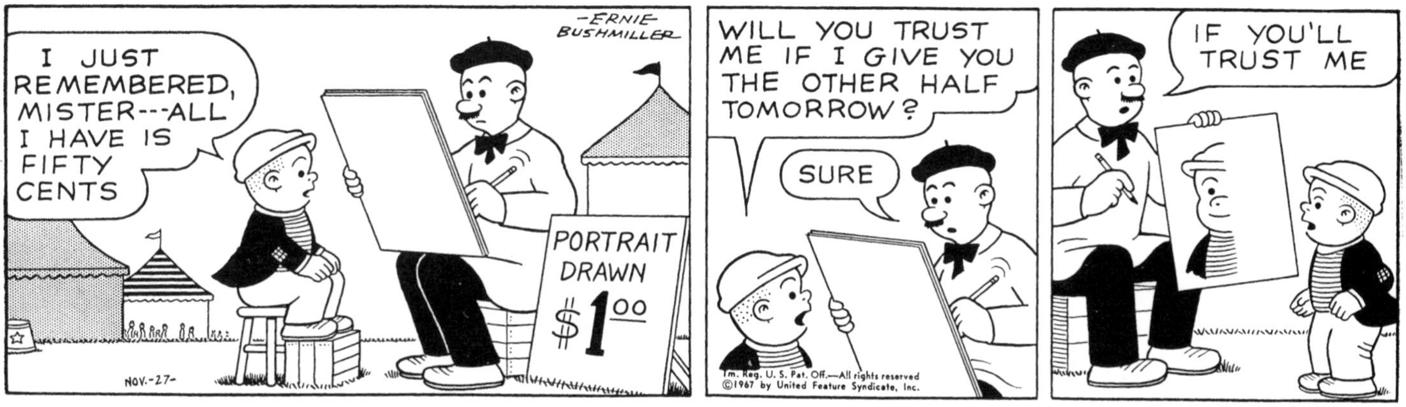
-ERNIE BUSHMILLER
I JUST REMEMBERED, MISTER---ALL I HAVE IS FIFTY CENTS
PORTRAIT DRAWN $1.00
NOV.-27-
WILL YOU TRUST ME IF I GIVE YOU THE OTHER HALF TOMORROW?
SURE
Tm. Reg. U. S. Pat. Off.—All rights reserved ©1967 by United Feature Syndicate, Inc.
IF YOU'LL TRUST ME

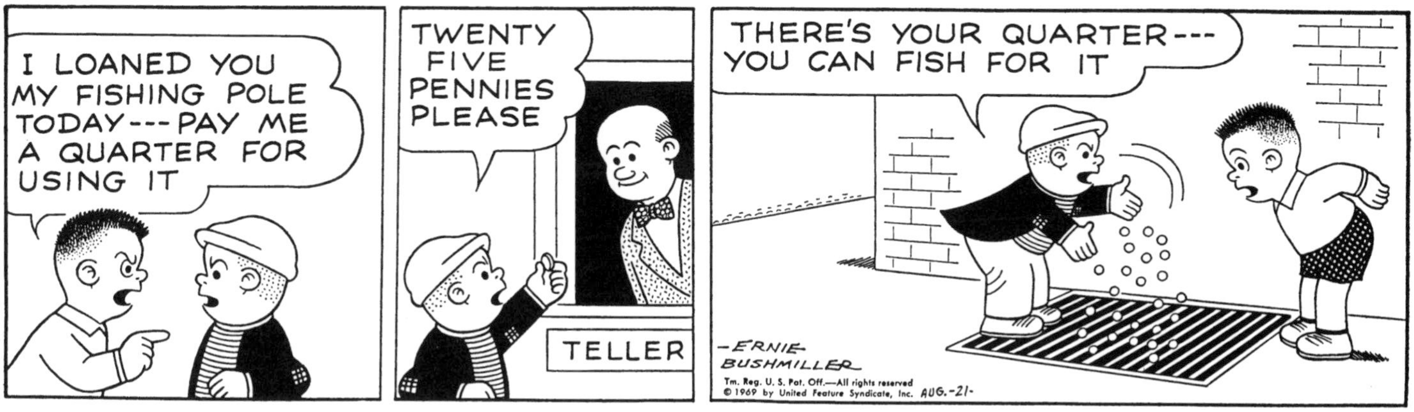
I LOANED YOU MY FISHING POLE TODAY---PAY ME A QUARTER FOR USING IT
TWENTY FIVE PENNIES PLEASE
TELLER
THERE'S YOUR QUARTER--- YOU CAN FISH FOR IT
-ERNIE BUSHMILLER
Tm. Reg. U. S. Pat. Off.—All rights reserved © 1969 by United Feature Syndicate, Inc. AUG.-21-

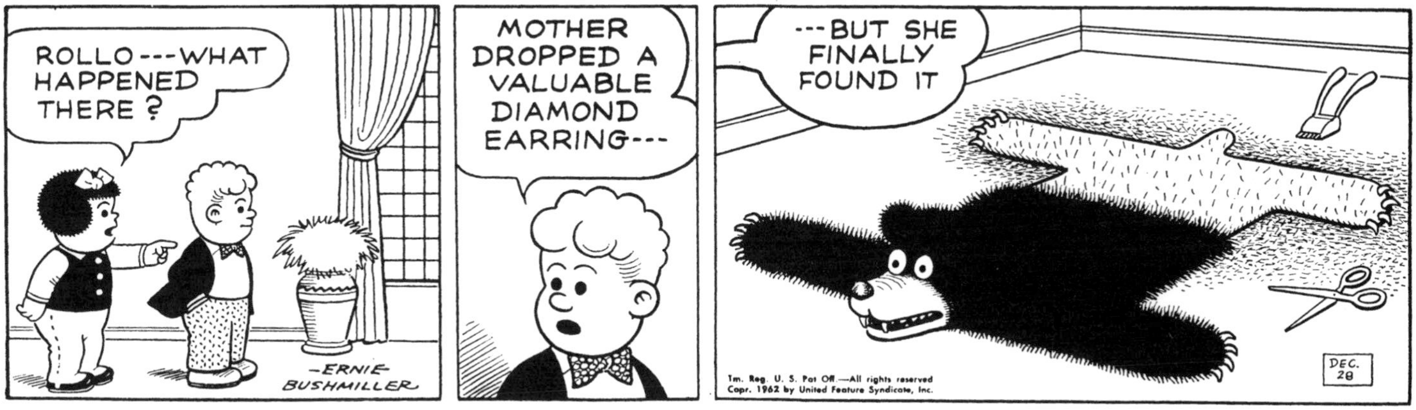
ROLLO---WHAT HAPPENED THERE?
-ERNIE BUSHMILLER
MOTHER DROPPED A VALUABLE DIAMOND EARRING---
---BUT SHE FINALLY FOUND IT
Tm. Reg. U. S. Pat Off.—All rights reserved Copr. 1962 by United Feature Syndicate, Inc.
DEC. 28

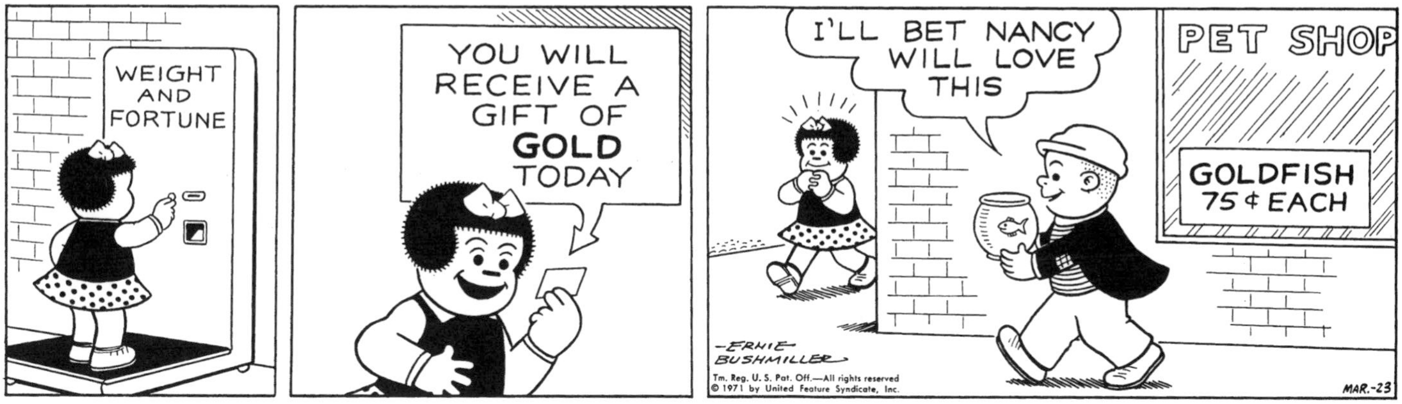
WEIGHT AND FORTUNE
YOU WILL RECEIVE A GIFT OF GOLD TODAY
I'LL BET NANCY WILL LOVE THIS
PET SHOP
GOLDFISH 75¢ EACH
-ERNIE BUSHMILLER
Tm. Reg. U. S. Pat. Off.—All rights reserved © 1971 by United Feature Syndicate, Inc.
MAR.-23

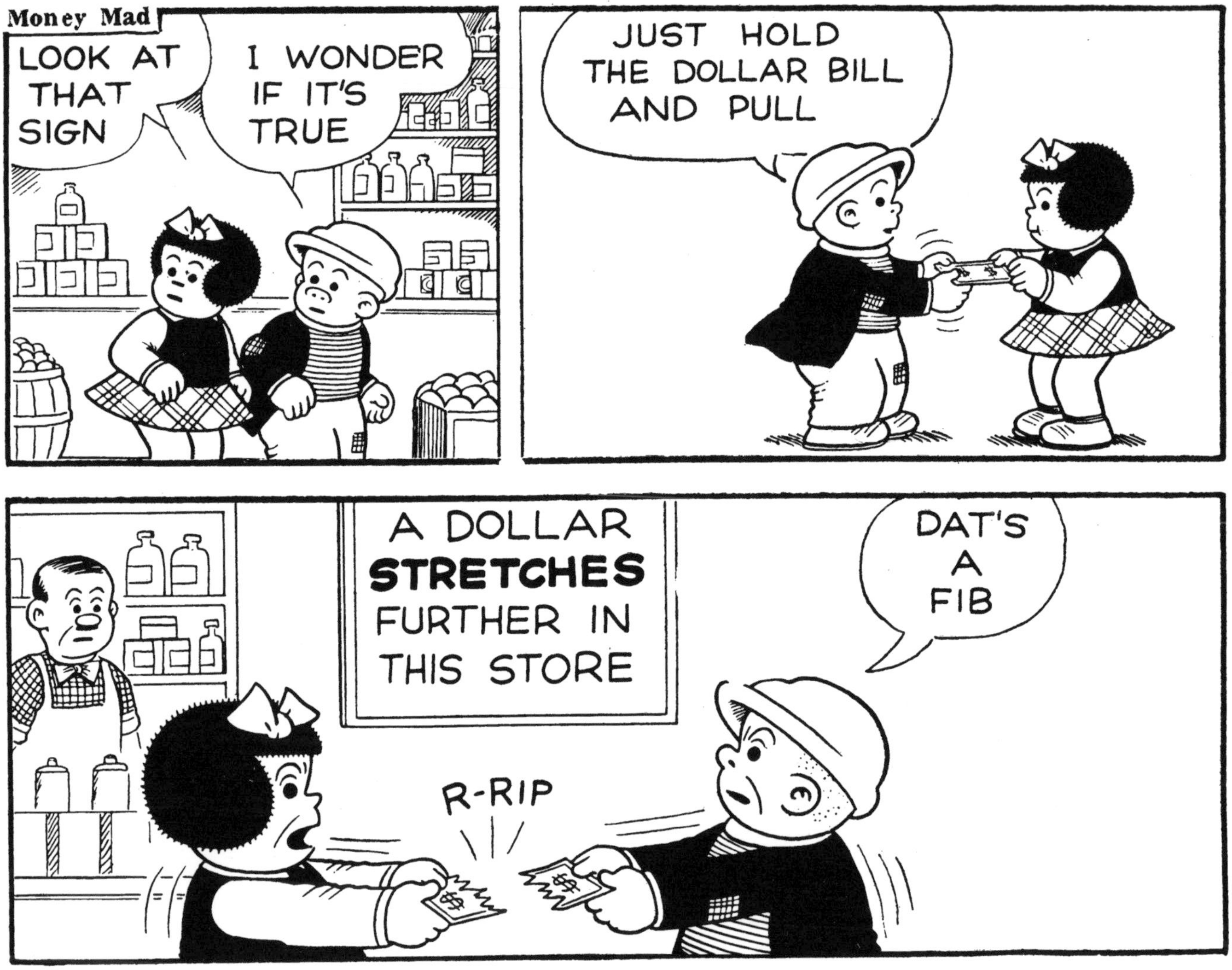
Money Mad
LOOK AT THAT SIGN
I WONDER IF IT'S TRUE
JUST HOLD THE DOLLAR BILL AND PULL
A DOLLAR STRETCHES FURTHER IN THIS STORE
DAT'S A FIB
R-RIP

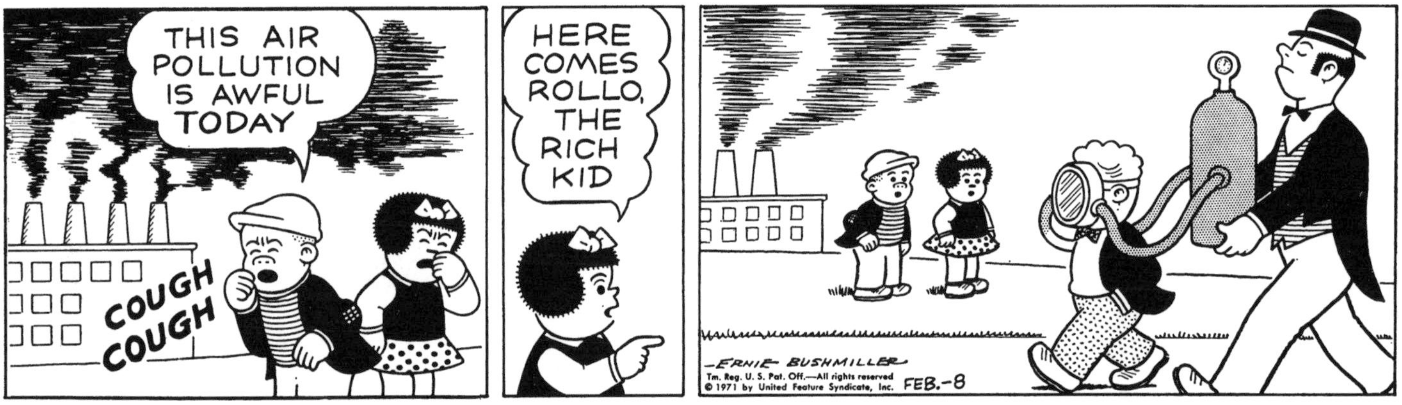
THIS AIR POLLUTION IS AWFUL TODAY
COUGH COUGH
HERE COMES ROLLO, THE RICH KID
-ERNIE BUSHMILLER
Tm. Reg. U. S. Pat. Off.—All rights reserved © 1971 by United Feature Syndicate, Inc. FEB.-8

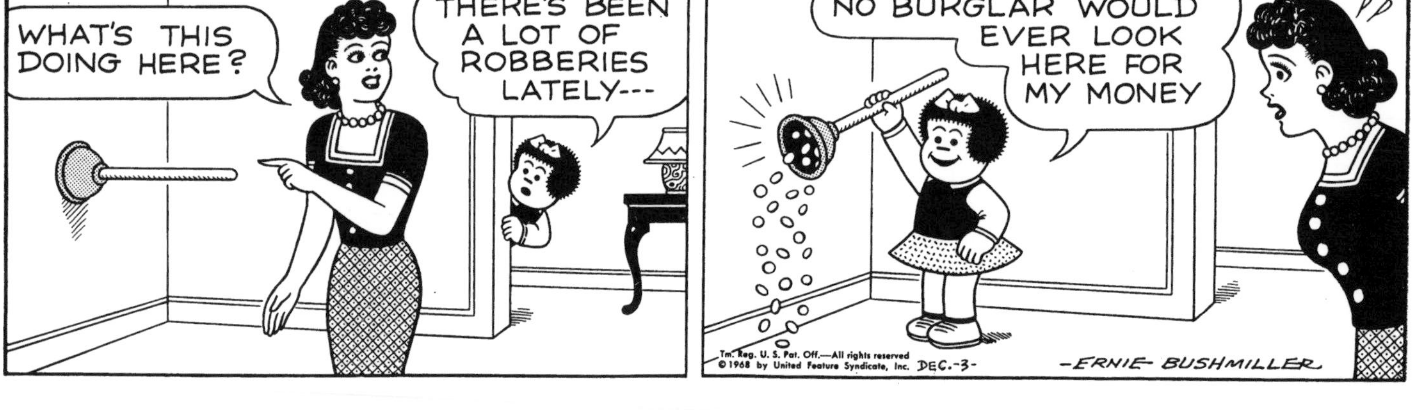
WHAT'S THIS DOING HERE?
THERE'S BEEN A LOT OF ROBBERIES LATELY---
NO BURGLAR WOULD EVER LOOK HERE FOR MY MONEY
Tm. Reg. U. S. Pat. Off.—All rights reserved © 1968 by United Feature Syndicate, Inc. DEC.-3-
-ERNIE BUSHMILLER

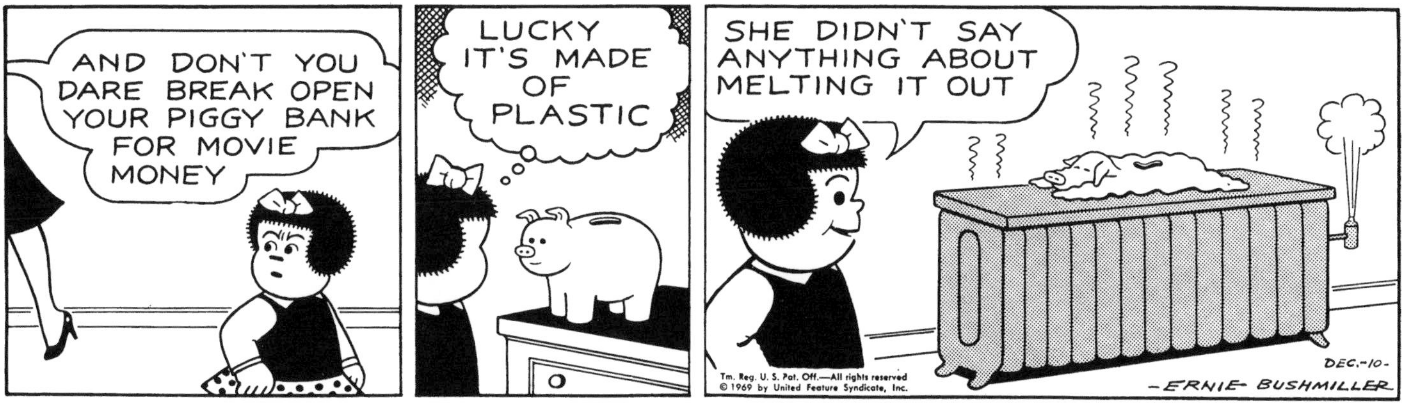
AND DON'T YOU DARE BREAK OPEN YOUR PIGGY BANK FOR MOVIE MONEY
LUCKY IT'S MADE OF PLASTIC
SHE DIDN'T SAY ANYTHING ABOUT MELTING IT OUT
Tm. Reg. U. S. Pat. Off.—All rights reserved © 1969 by United Feature Syndicate, Inc.
DEC.-10-
-ERNIE BUSHMILLER

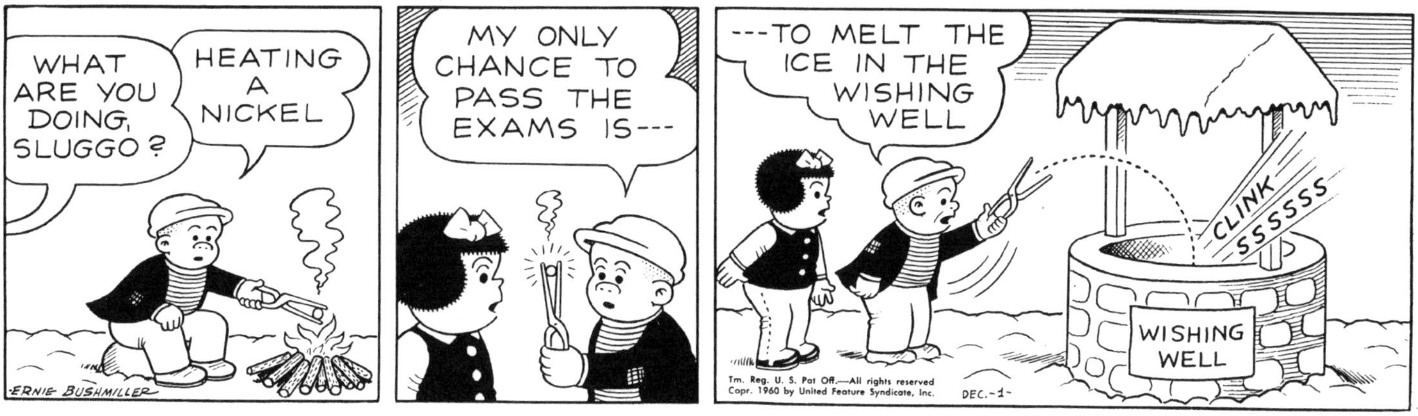
WHAT ARE YOU DOING, SLUGGO?
HEATING A NICKEL
-ERNIE BUSHMILLER
MY ONLY CHANCE TO PASS THE EXAMS IS---
---TO MELT THE ICE IN THE WISHING WELL
CLINK
SSSSSS
WISHING WELL
Tm. Reg. U. S. Pat. Off.—All rights reserved Copr. 1960 by United Feature Syndicate, Inc.
DEC.-1-

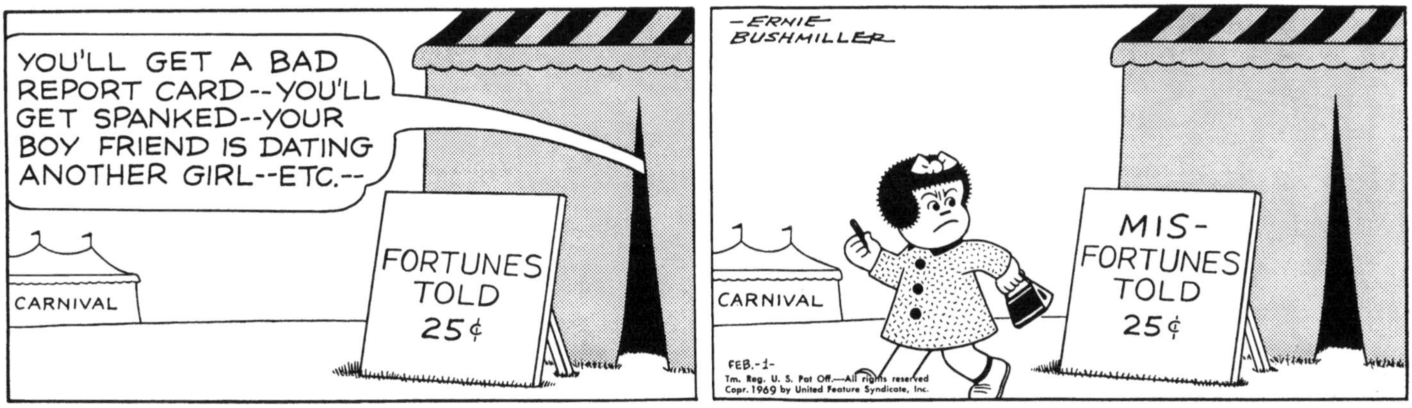
YOU'LL GET A BAD REPORT CARD--YOU'LL GET SPANKED--YOUR BOY FRIEND IS DATING ANOTHER GIRL--ETC.--
CARNIVAL
FORTUNES TOLD 25¢
-ERNIE BUSHMILLER
CARNIVAL
MIS-FORTUNES TOLD 25¢
FEB.-1-
Tm. Reg. U. S. Pat Off.—All rights reserved Copr. 1969 by United Feature Syndicate, Inc.

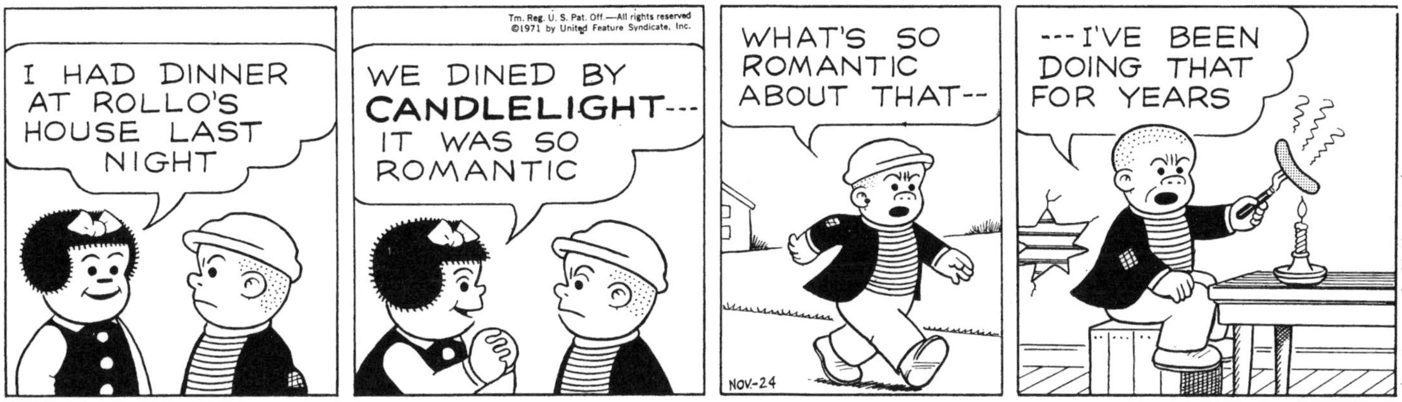
I HAD DINNER AT ROLLO'S HOUSE LAST NIGHT
Tm. Reg. U. S. Pat. Off.—All rights reserved ©1971 by United Feature Syndicate, Inc.
WE DINED BY CANDLELIGHT--- IT WAS SO ROMANTIC
WHAT'S SO ROMANTIC ABOUT THAT--
NOV-24
---I'VE BEEN DOING THAT FOR YEARS

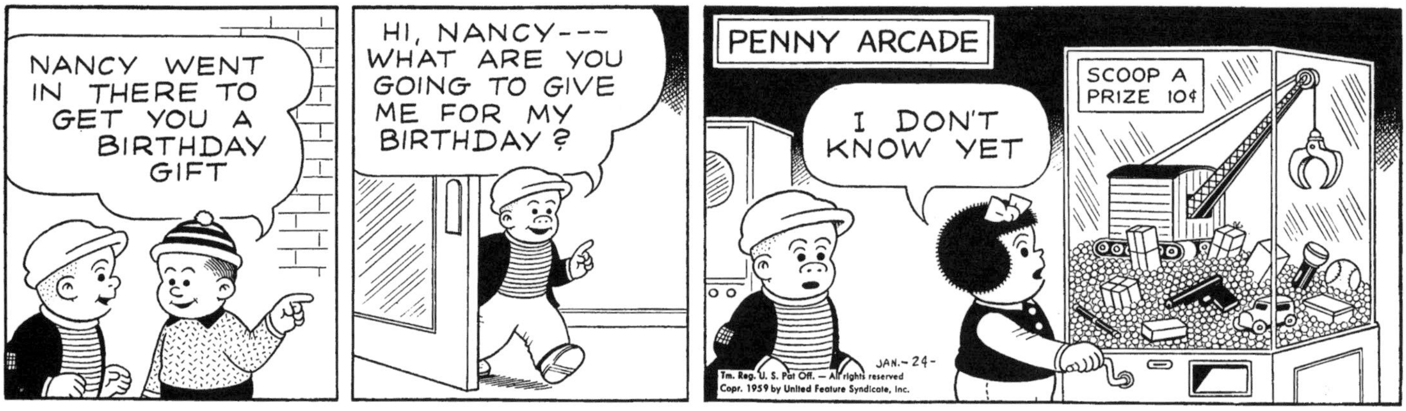
NANCY WENT IN THERE TO GET YOU A BIRTHDAY GIFT
HI, NANCY--- WHAT ARE YOU GOING TO GIVE ME FOR MY BIRTHDAY ?
PENNY ARCADE
I DON'T KNOW YET
SCOOP A PRIZE 10¢
JAN.-24-
Tm. Reg. U. S. Pat. Off. — All rights reserved
Copr. 1959 by United Feature Syndicate, Inc.

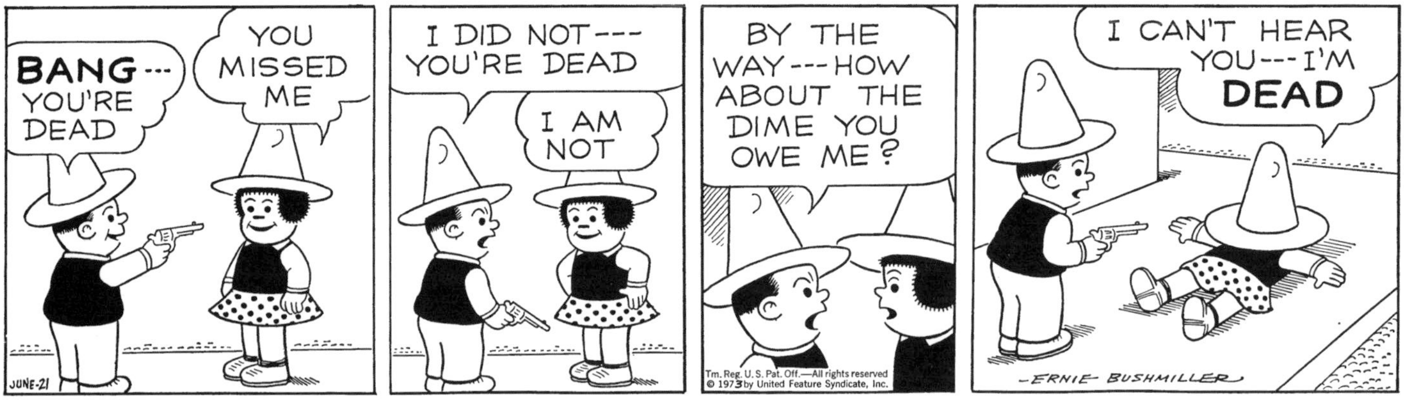
BANG--- YOU'RE DEAD
YOU MISSED ME
JUNE-21
I DID NOT--- YOU'RE DEAD
I AM NOT
BY THE WAY---HOW ABOUT THE DIME YOU OWE ME ?
Tm. Reg. U. S. Pat. Off.—All rights reserved
© 1973 by United Feature Syndicate, Inc.
I CAN'T HEAR YOU---I'M DEAD
-ERNIE BUSHMILLER

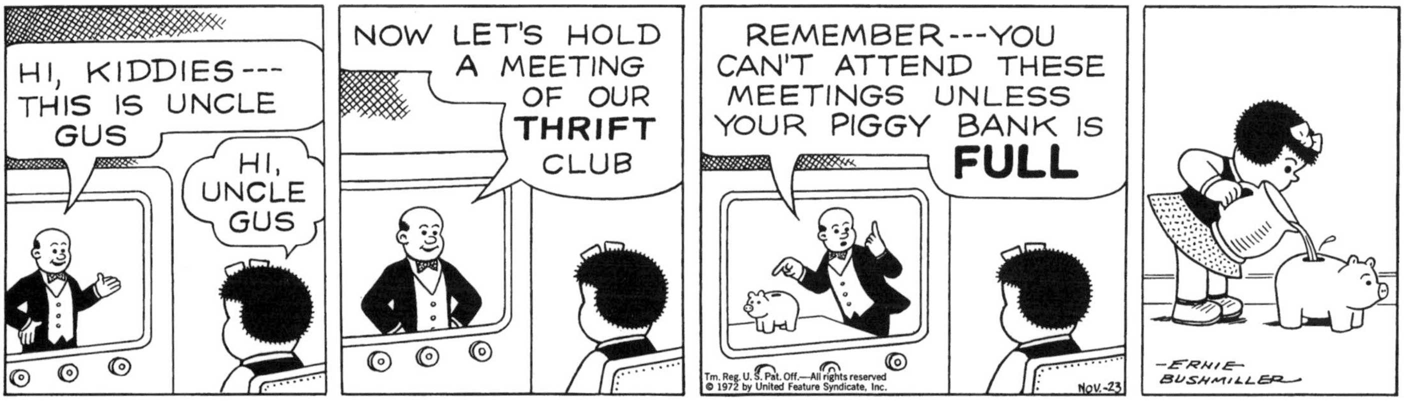
HI, KIDDIES--- THIS IS UNCLE GUS
HI, UNCLE GUS
NOW LET'S HOLD A MEETING OF OUR THRIFT CLUB
REMEMBER---YOU CAN'T ATTEND THESE MEETINGS UNLESS YOUR PIGGY BANK IS FULL
Tm. Reg. U. S. Pat. Off.—All rights reserved
© 1972 by United Feature Syndicate, Inc.
NOV.-23
-ERNIE BUSHMILLER

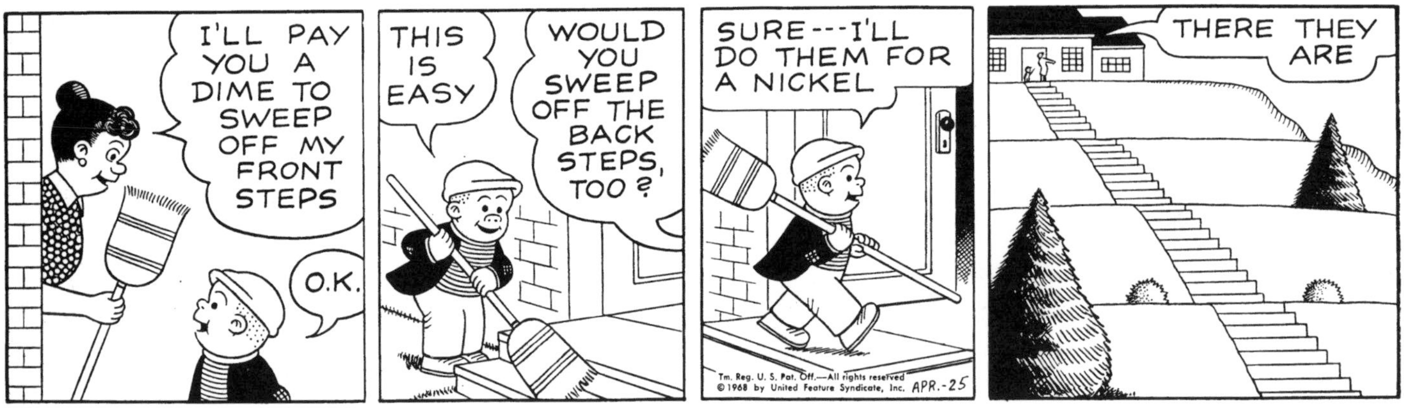
I'LL PAY YOU A DIME TO SWEEP OFF MY FRONT STEPS
O.K.
THIS IS EASY
WOULD YOU SWEEP OFF THE BACK STEPS, TOO ?
SURE---I'LL DO THEM FOR A NICKEL
Tm. Reg. U. S. Pat. Off.—All rights reserved
© 1968 by United Feature Syndicate, Inc. APR.-25
THERE THEY ARE

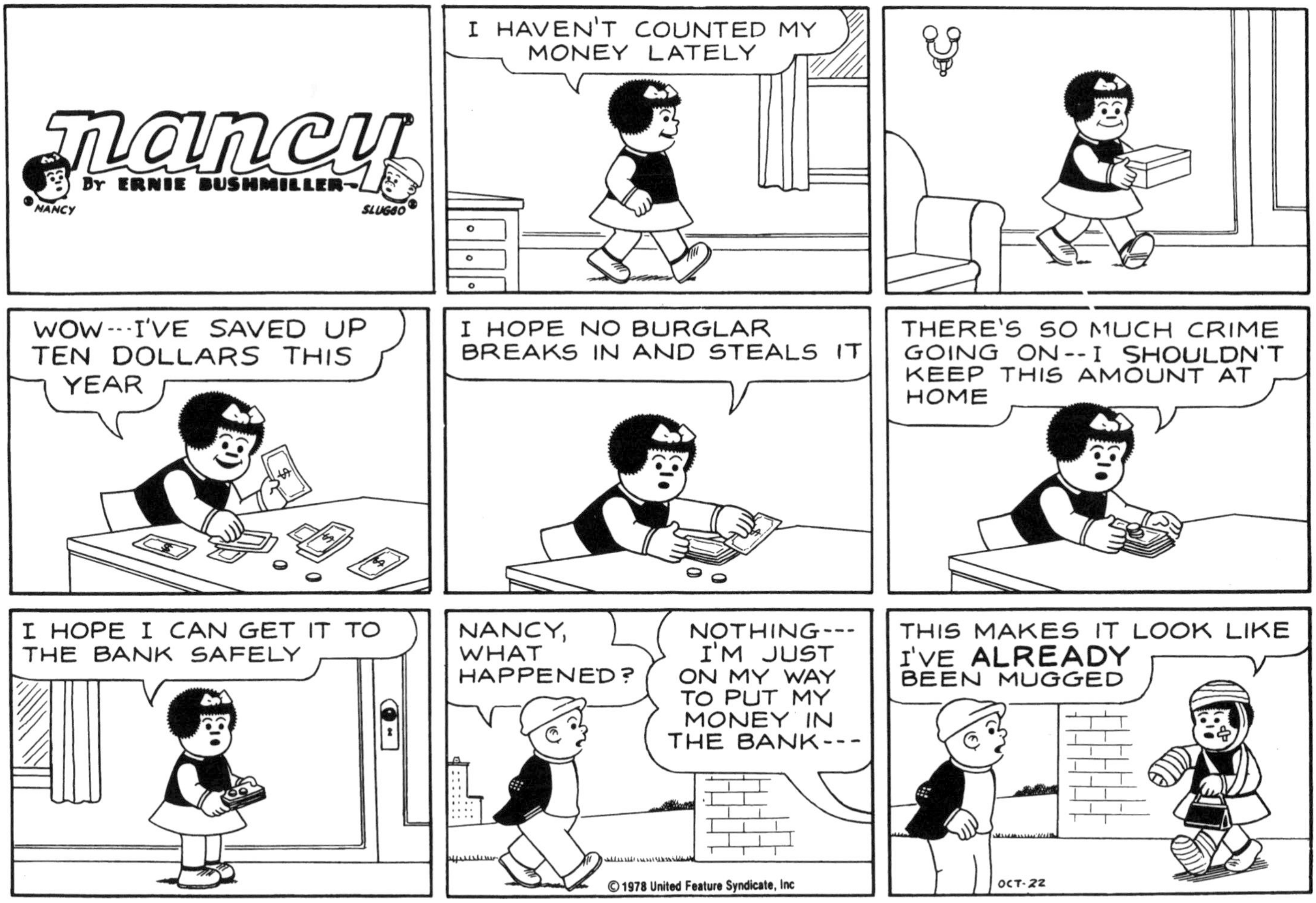
nancy
BY ERNIE BUSHMILLER
NANCY
SLUGGO
I HAVEN'T COUNTED MY MONEY LATELY
WOW---I'VE SAVED UP TEN DOLLARS THIS YEAR
I HOPE NO BURGLAR BREAKS IN AND STEALS IT
THERE'S SO MUCH CRIME GOING ON--I SHOULDN'T KEEP THIS AMOUNT AT HOME
I HOPE I CAN GET IT TO THE BANK SAFELY
NANCY, WHAT HAPPENED?
NOTHING--- I'M JUST ON MY WAY TO PUT MY MONEY IN THE BANK---
© 1978 United Feature Syndicate, Inc
THIS MAKES IT LOOK LIKE I'VE **ALREADY** BEEN MUGGED
OCT-22

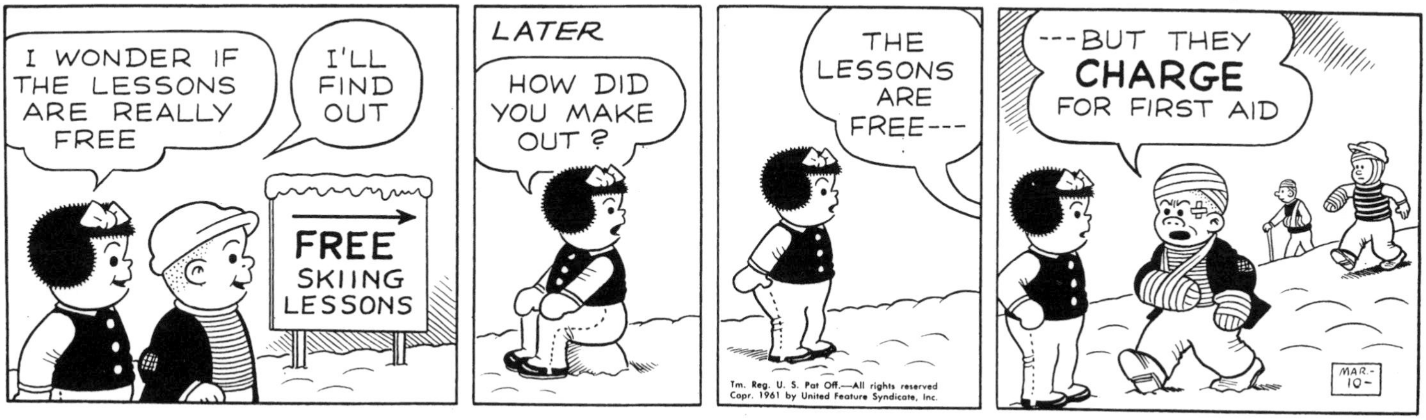
I WONDER IF THE LESSONS ARE REALLY FREE
I'LL FIND OUT
FREE SKIING LESSONS
LATER
HOW DID YOU MAKE OUT?
THE LESSONS ARE FREE---
Tm. Reg. U. S. Pat Off.—All rights reserved Copr. 1961 by United Feature Syndicate, Inc.
---BUT THEY **CHARGE** FOR FIRST AID
MAR.-10-

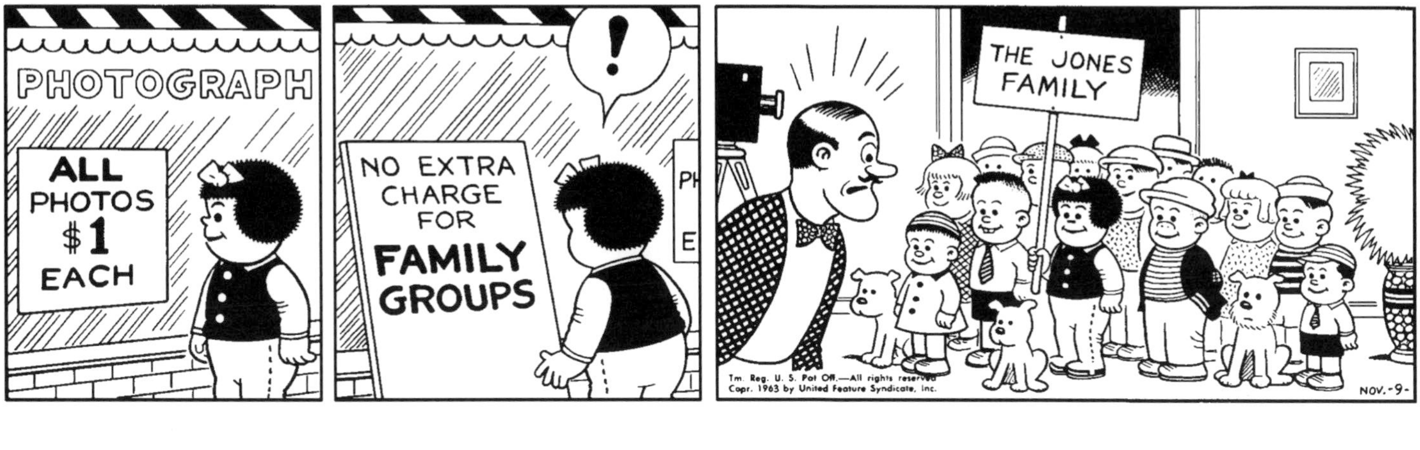
PHOTOGRAPH
ALL PHOTOS $1 EACH
!
NO EXTRA CHARGE FOR FAMILY GROUPS
THE JONES FAMILY
Tm. Reg. U. S. Pat Off.—All rights reserved Copr. 1963 by United Feature Syndicate, Inc.
NOV.-9-

That's One Way

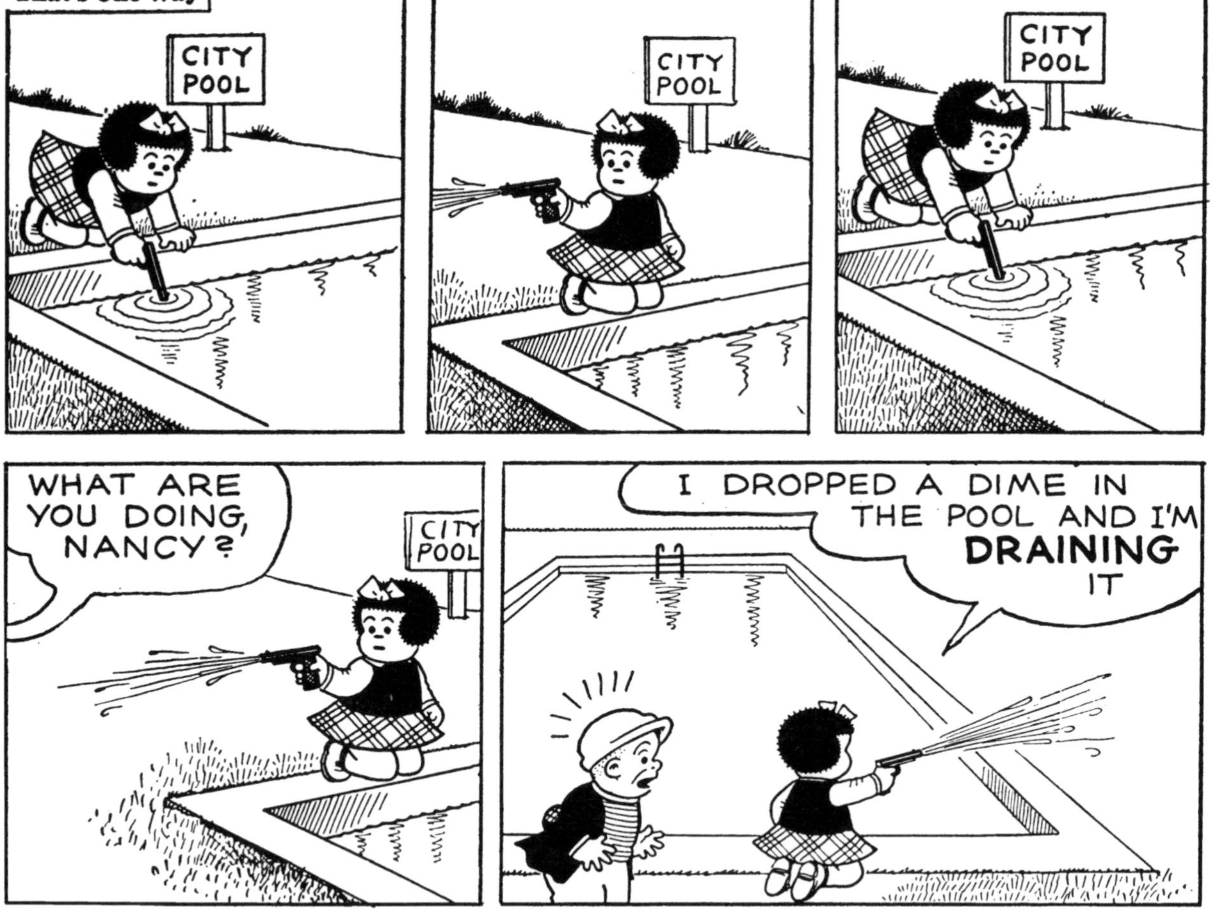
CITY POOL
CITY POOL
CITY POOL
WHAT ARE YOU DOING, NANCY?
CITY POOL
I DROPPED A DIME IN THE POOL AND I'M **DRAINING** IT

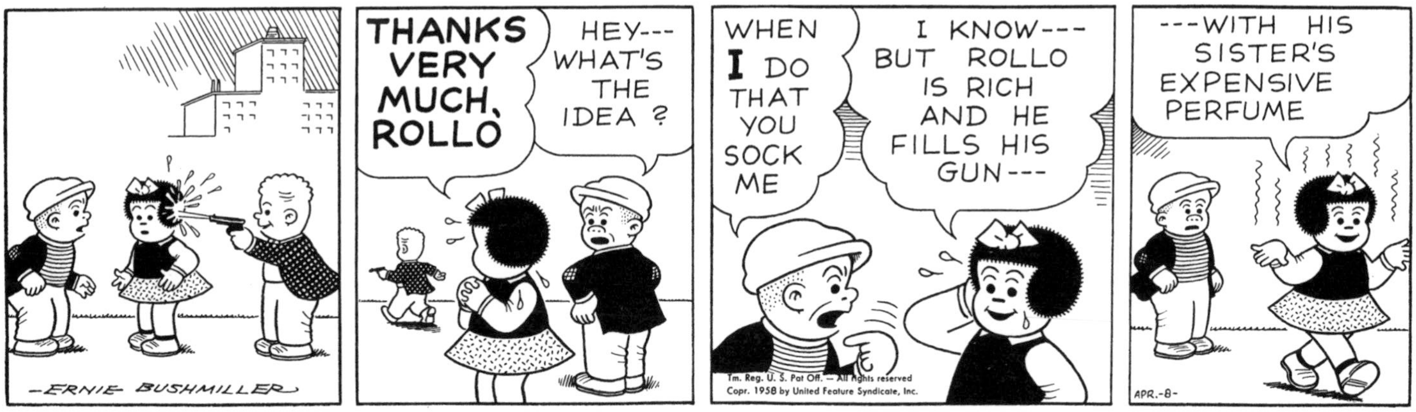
-ERNIE BUSHMILLER
THANKS VERY MUCH, ROLLO
HEY--- WHAT'S THE IDEA?
WHEN **I** DO THAT YOU SOCK ME
I KNOW--- BUT ROLLO IS RICH AND HE FILLS HIS GUN---
Tm. Reg. U. S. Pat Off. — All rights reserved
Copr. 1958 by United Feature Syndicate, Inc.
---WITH HIS SISTER'S EXPENSIVE PERFUME
APR.-8-

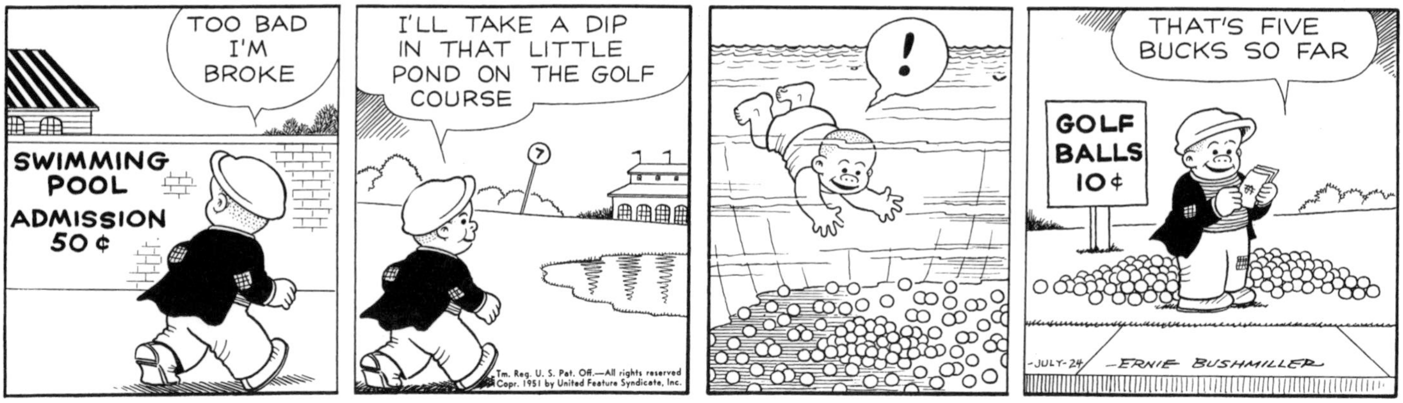
TOO BAD I'M BROKE
SWIMMING POOL
ADMISSION 50¢
I'LL TAKE A DIP IN THAT LITTLE POND ON THE GOLF COURSE
7
Tm. Reg. U. S. Pat. Off.—All rights reserved
Copr. 1951 by United Feature Syndicate, Inc.
!
THAT'S FIVE BUCKS SO FAR
GOLF BALLS 10¢
-JULY-24-
-ERNIE BUSHMILLER

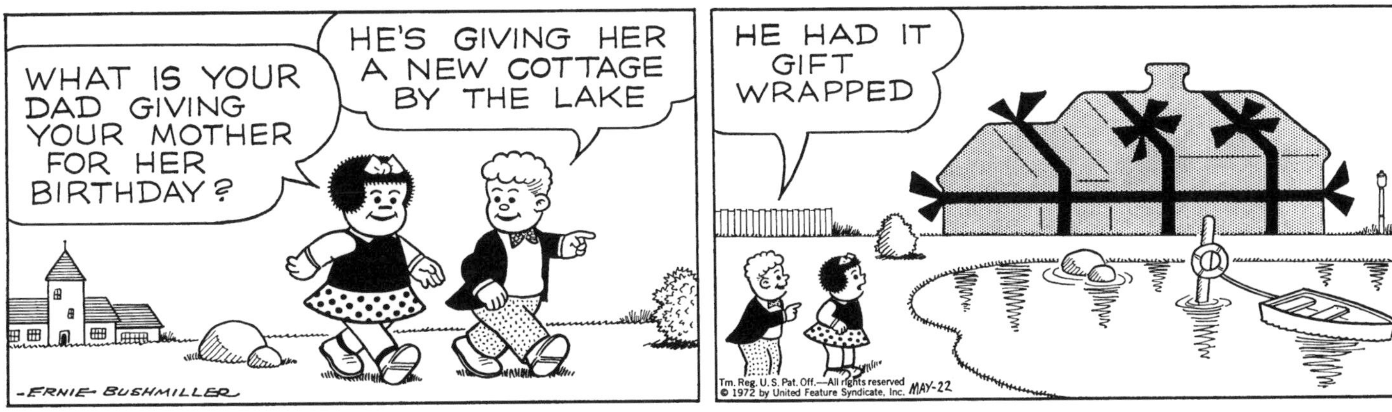
WHAT IS YOUR DAD GIVING YOUR MOTHER FOR HER BIRTHDAY?
HE'S GIVING HER A NEW COTTAGE BY THE LAKE
-ERNIE BUSHMILLER
HE HAD IT GIFT WRAPPED
Tm. Reg. U. S. Pat. Off.—All rights reserved © 1972 by United Feature Syndicate, Inc. MAY-22

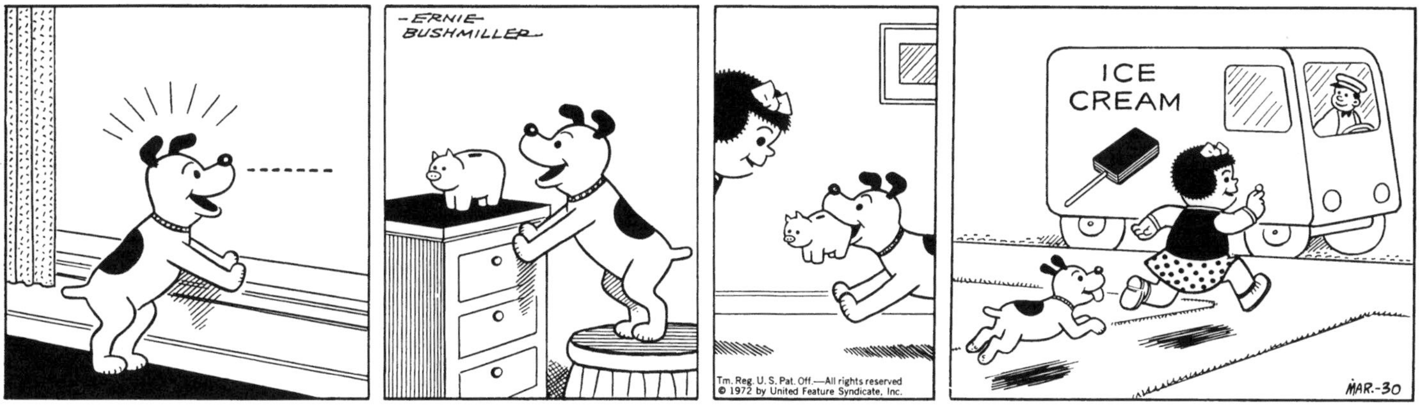
-ERNIE BUSHMILLER
Tm. Reg. U. S. Pat. Off.—All rights reserved © 1972 by United Feature Syndicate, Inc.
ICE CREAM
MAR.-30

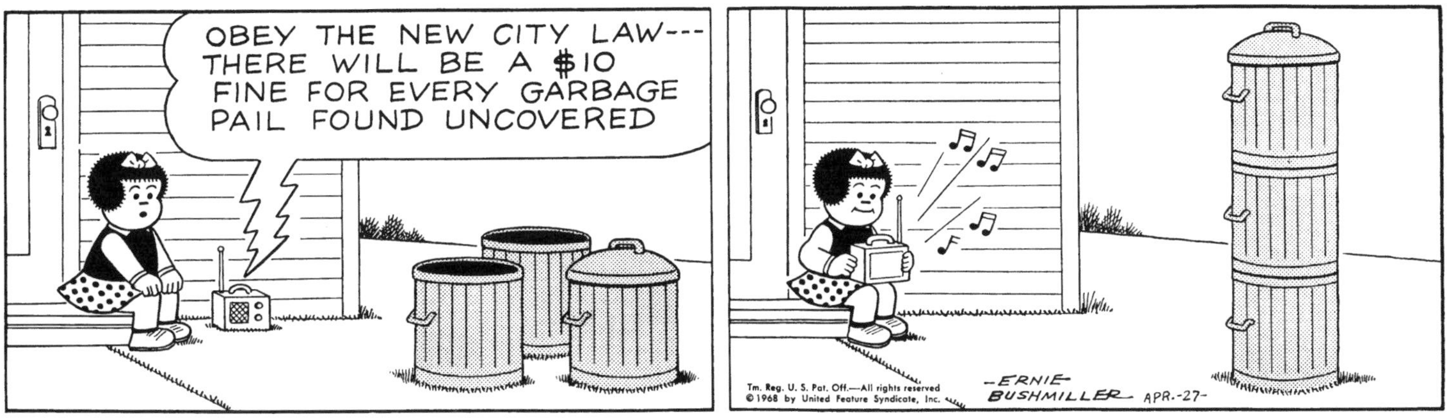
OBEY THE NEW CITY LAW--- THERE WILL BE A $10 FINE FOR EVERY GARBAGE PAIL FOUND UNCOVERED
Tm. Reg. U. S. Pat. Off.—All rights reserved ©1968 by United Feature Syndicate, Inc.
-ERNIE BUSHMILLER APR.-27-

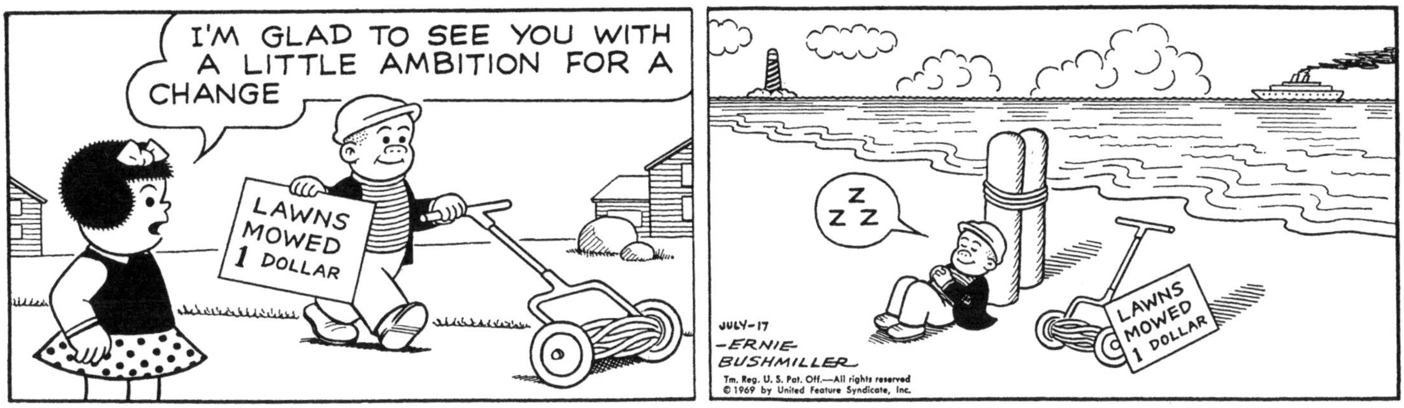
I'M GLAD TO SEE YOU WITH A LITTLE AMBITION FOR A CHANGE
LAWNS MOWED 1 DOLLAR
Z Z Z
LAWNS MOWED 1 DOLLAR
JULY-17
-ERNIE BUSHMILLER
Tm. Reg. U. S. Pat. Off.—All rights reserved ©1969 by United Feature Syndicate, Inc.

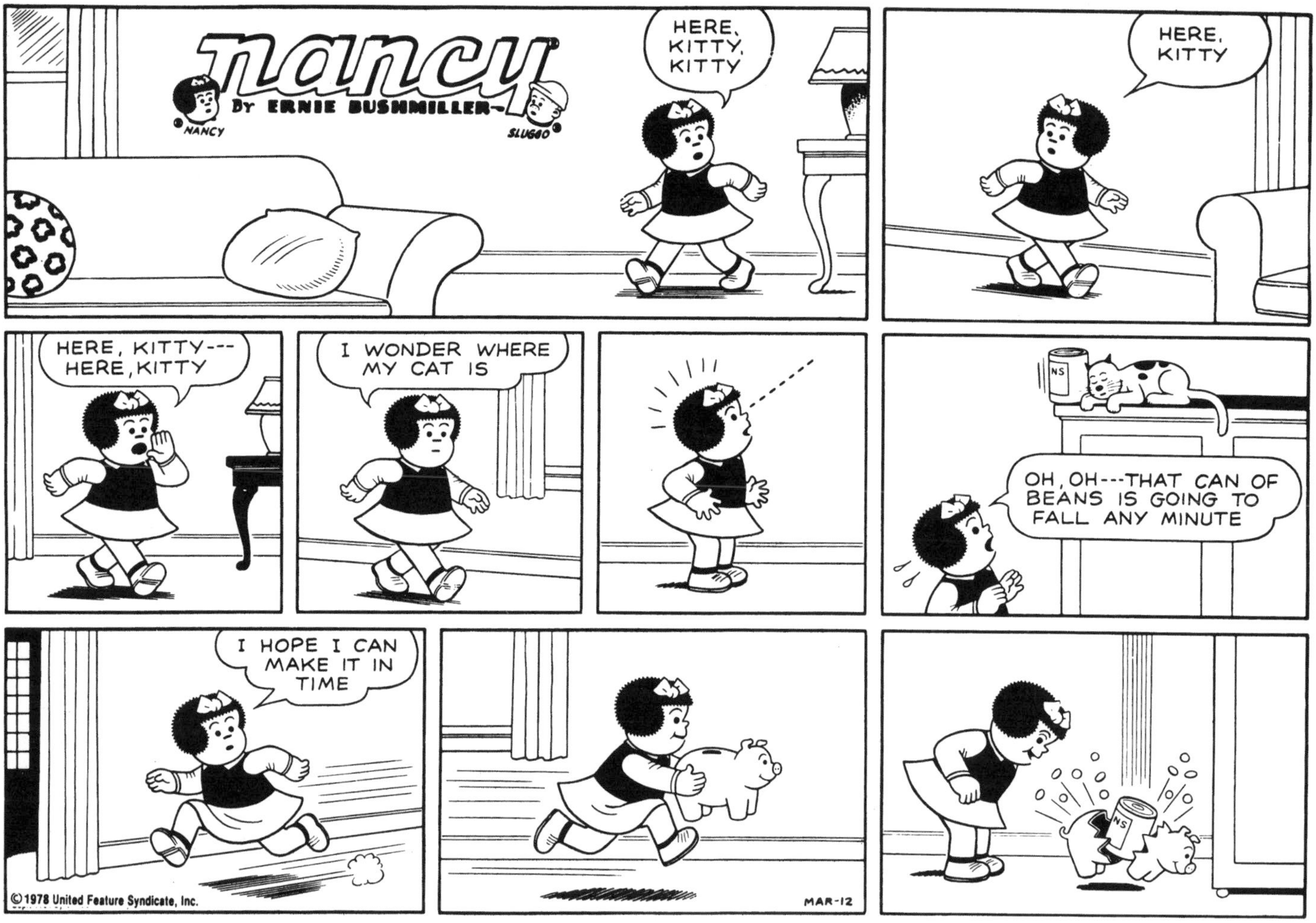
nancy
BY ERNIE BUSHMILLER
NANCY
SLUGGO
HERE, KITTY, KITTY
HERE, KITTY
HERE, KITTY--- HERE, KITTY
I WONDER WHERE MY CAT IS
NS
OH, OH---THAT CAN OF BEANS IS GOING TO FALL ANY MINUTE
I HOPE I CAN MAKE IT IN TIME
NS
© 1978 United Feature Syndicate, Inc.
MAR-12

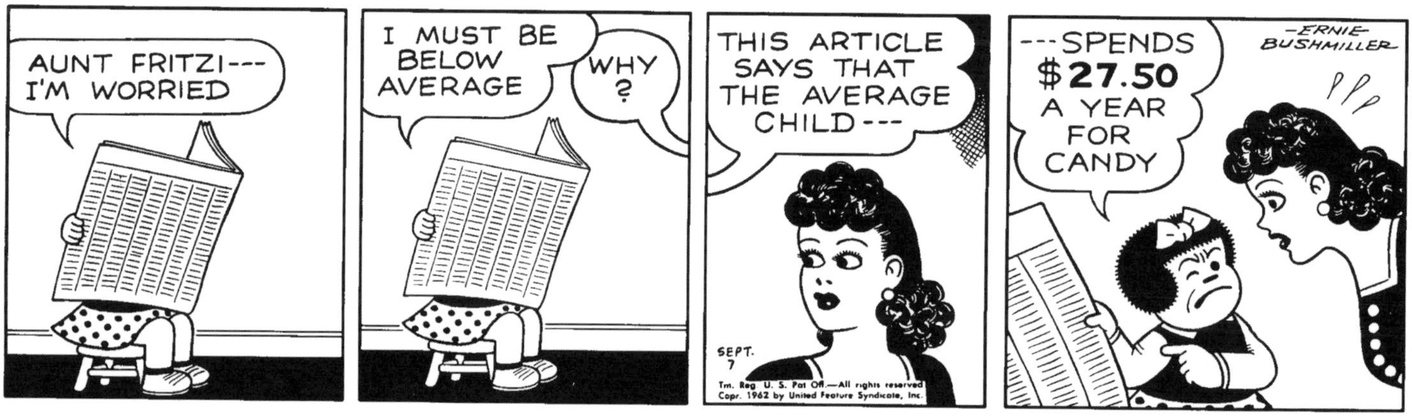
AUNT FRITZI--- I'M WORRIED
I MUST BE BELOW AVERAGE
WHY ?
THIS ARTICLE SAYS THAT THE AVERAGE CHILD---
SEPT. 7
Tm. Reg. U. S. Pat. Off.—All rights reserved Copr. 1962 by United Feature Syndicate, Inc.
---SPENDS $27.50 A YEAR FOR CANDY
-ERNIE BUSHMILLER

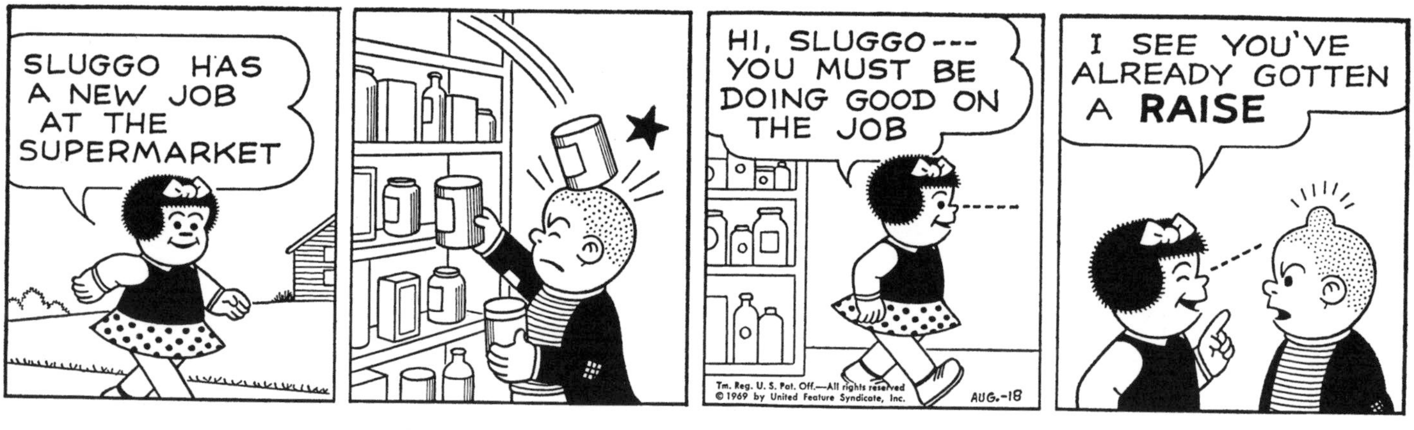
SLUGGO HAS A NEW JOB AT THE SUPERMARKET
HI, SLUGGO--- YOU MUST BE DOING GOOD ON THE JOB
Tm. Reg. U. S. Pat. Off.—All rights reserved © 1969 by United Feature Syndicate, Inc.
AUG.-18
I SEE YOU'VE ALREADY GOTTEN A RAISE

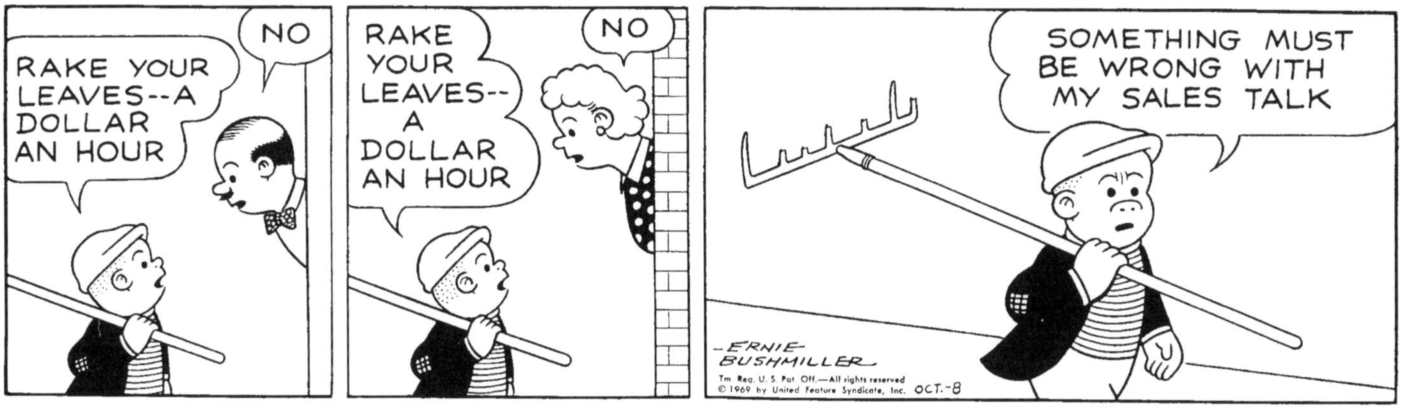
RAKE YOUR LEAVES--A DOLLAR AN HOUR
NO
RAKE YOUR LEAVES-- A DOLLAR AN HOUR
NO
SOMETHING MUST BE WRONG WITH MY SALES TALK
-ERNIE BUSHMILLER
Tm Reg. U.S. Pat. Off.—All rights reserved © 1969 by United Feature Syndicate, Inc.
OCT.-8

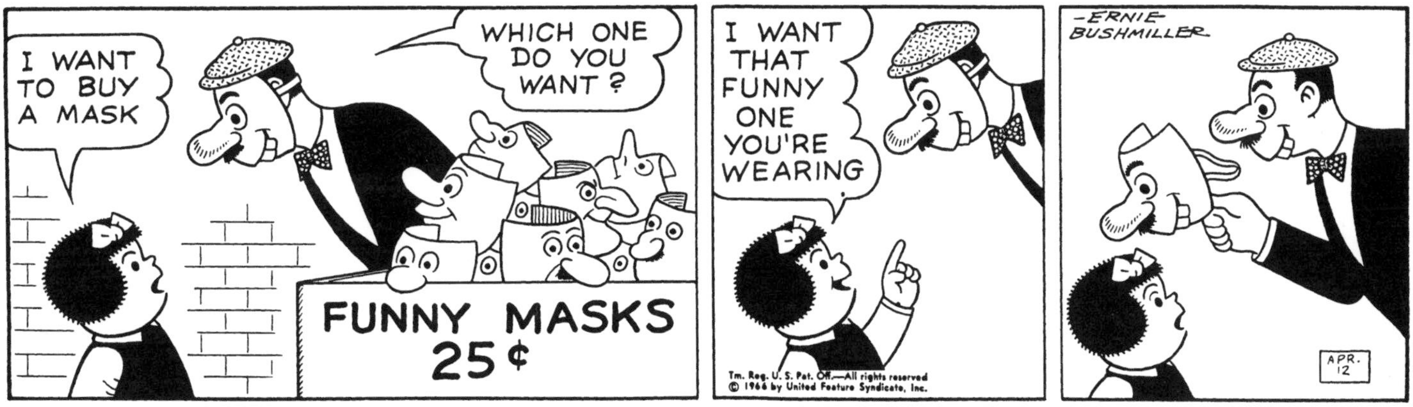
I WANT TO BUY A MASK
WHICH ONE DO YOU WANT ?
FUNNY MASKS 25¢
I WANT THAT FUNNY ONE YOU'RE WEARING
Tm. Reg. U.S. Pat. Off.—All rights reserved © 1966 by United Feature Syndicate, Inc.
-ERNIE BUSHMILLER
APR. 12

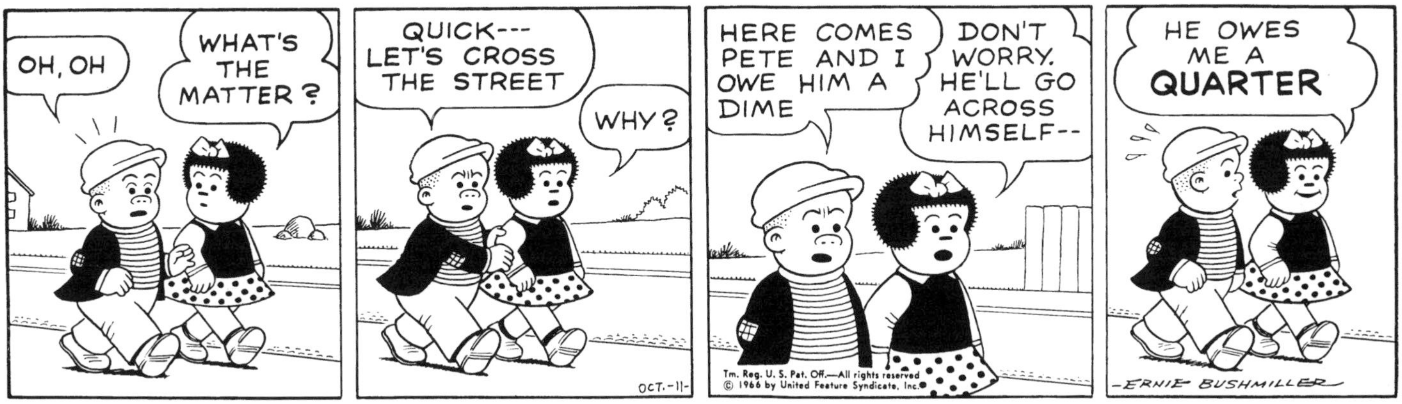
OH, OH
WHAT'S THE MATTER ?
QUICK--- LET'S CROSS THE STREET
WHY ?
OCT.-11-
HERE COMES PETE AND I OWE HIM A DIME
DON'T WORRY. HE'LL GO ACROSS HIMSELF--
Tm. Reg. U.S. Pat. Off.—All rights reserved © 1966 by United Feature Syndicate, Inc.
HE OWES ME A QUARTER
-ERNIE BUSHMILLER

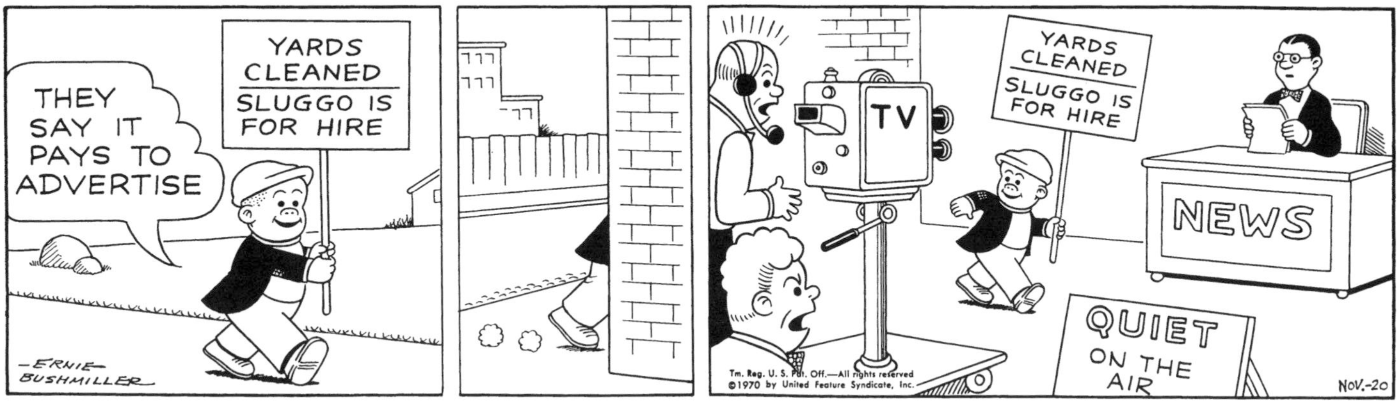
THEY SAY IT PAYS TO ADVERTISE
YARDS CLEANED
SLUGGO IS FOR HIRE
-ERNIE BUSHMILLER
TV
YARDS CLEANED
SLUGGO IS FOR HIRE
NEWS
QUIET ON THE AIR
Tm. Reg. U.S. Pat. Off.—All rights reserved ©1970 by United Feature Syndicate, Inc.
NOV.-20

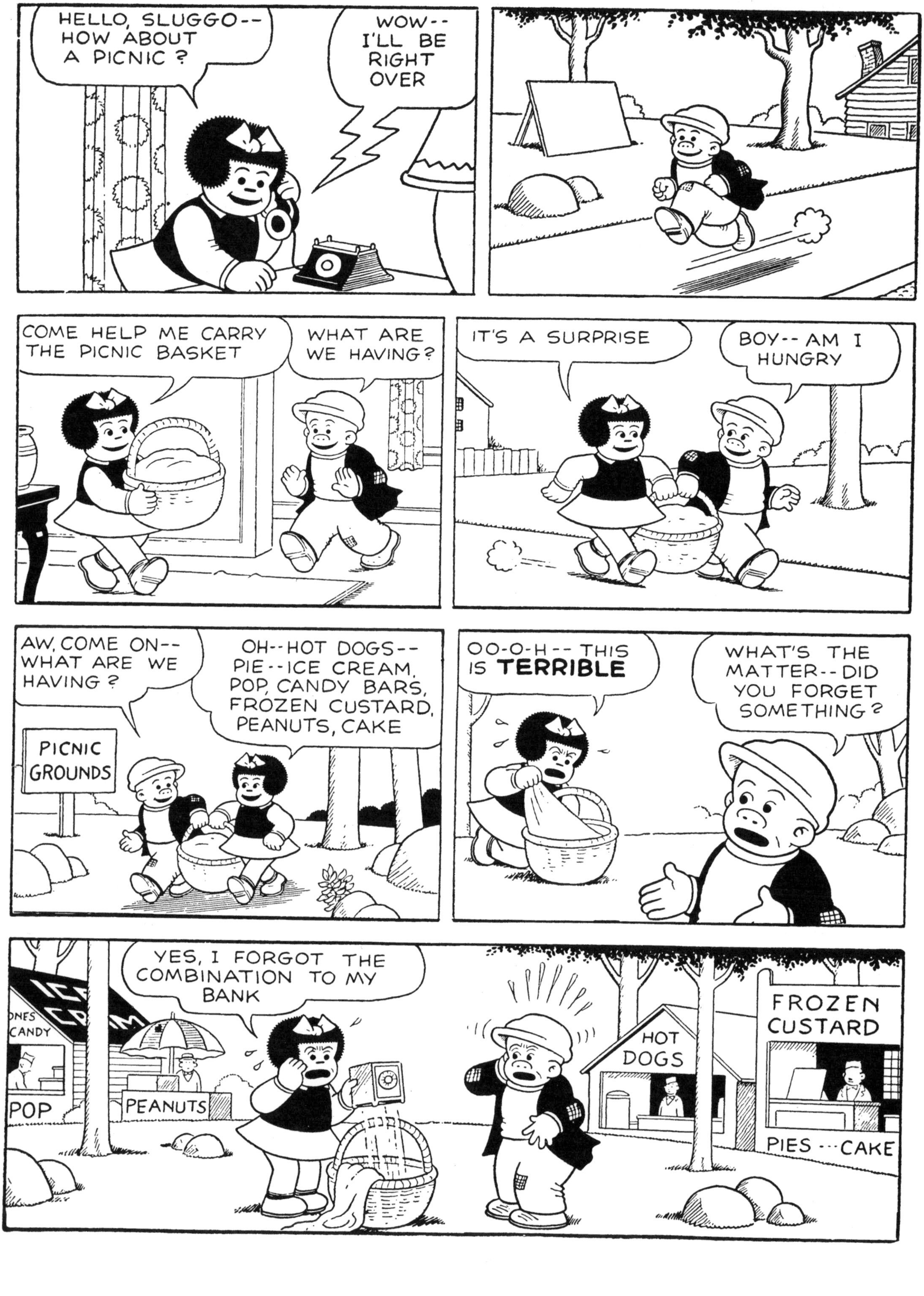
HELLO, SLUGGO-- HOW ABOUT A PICNIC ?
WOW-- I'LL BE RIGHT OVER
COME HELP ME CARRY THE PICNIC BASKET
WHAT ARE WE HAVING?
IT'S A SURPRISE
BOY-- AM I HUNGRY
AW, COME ON-- WHAT ARE WE HAVING ?
OH--HOT DOGS-- PIE--ICE CREAM, POP, CANDY BARS, FROZEN CUSTARD, PEANUTS, CAKE
PICNIC GROUNDS
OO-O-H -- THIS IS **TERRIBLE**
WHAT'S THE MATTER--DID YOU FORGET SOMETHING ?
YES, I FORGOT THE COMBINATION TO MY BANK
CANDY
POP
PEANUTS
HOT DOGS
FROZEN CUSTARD
PIES ---CAKE

One for the Book

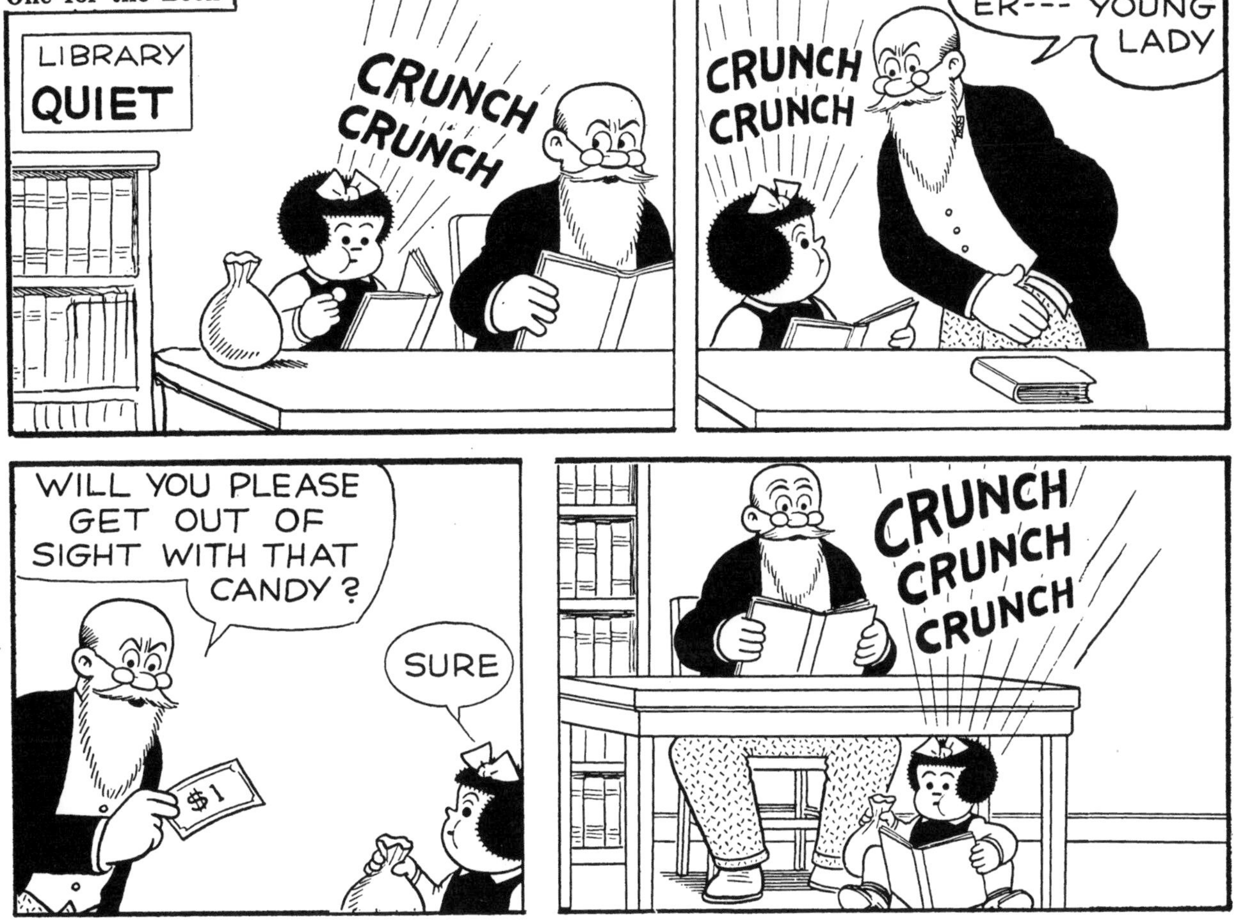
LIBRARY
QUIET
CRUNCH CRUNCH
CRUNCH CRUNCH
ER--- YOUNG LADY
WILL YOU PLEASE GET OUT OF SIGHT WITH THAT CANDY?
$1
SURE
CRUNCH CRUNCH CRUNCH

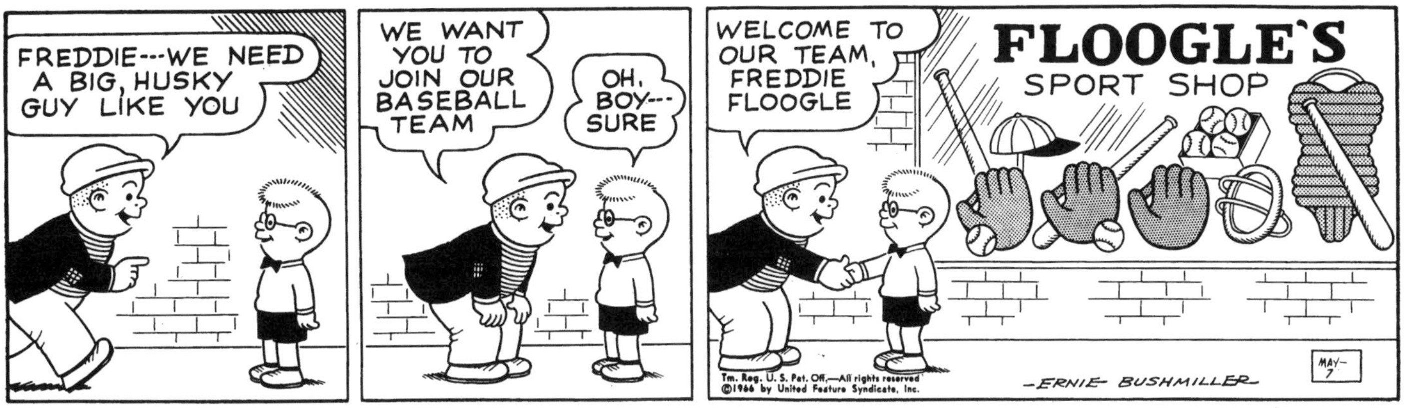
FREDDIE---WE NEED A BIG, HUSKY GUY LIKE YOU
WE WANT YOU TO JOIN OUR BASEBALL TEAM
OH, BOY--- SURE
WELCOME TO OUR TEAM, FREDDIE FLOOGLE
FLOOGLE'S
SPORT SHOP
Tm. Reg. U. S. Pat. Off.—All rights reserved ©1966 by United Feature Syndicate, Inc.
-ERNIE BUSHMILLER-
MAY-7

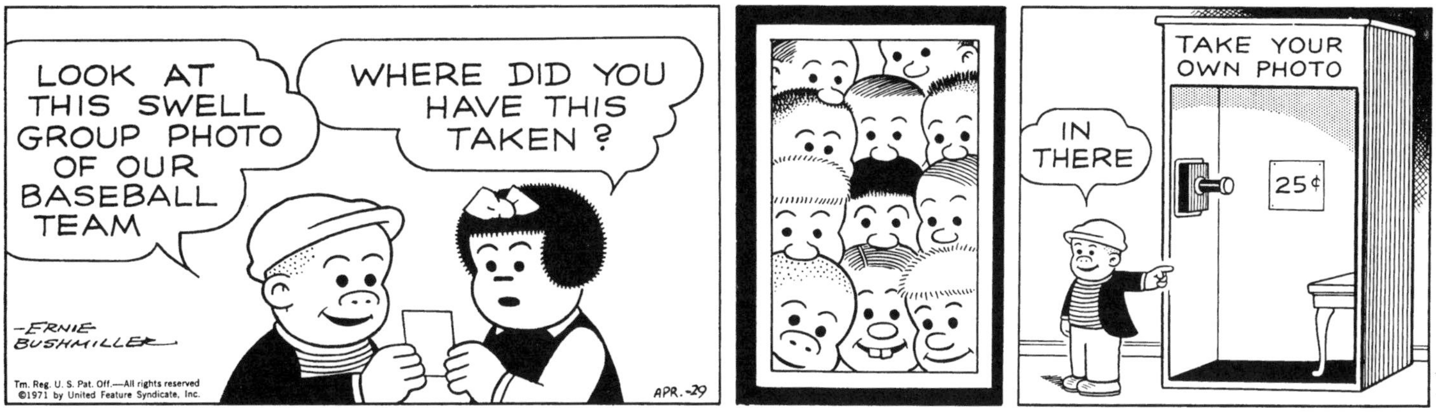
LOOK AT THIS SWELL GROUP PHOTO OF OUR BASEBALL TEAM
WHERE DID YOU HAVE THIS TAKEN?
-ERNIE BUSHMILLER-
Tm. Reg. U. S. Pat. Off.—All rights reserved ©1971 by United Feature Syndicate, Inc.
APR.-29
TAKE YOUR OWN PHOTO
IN THERE
25¢

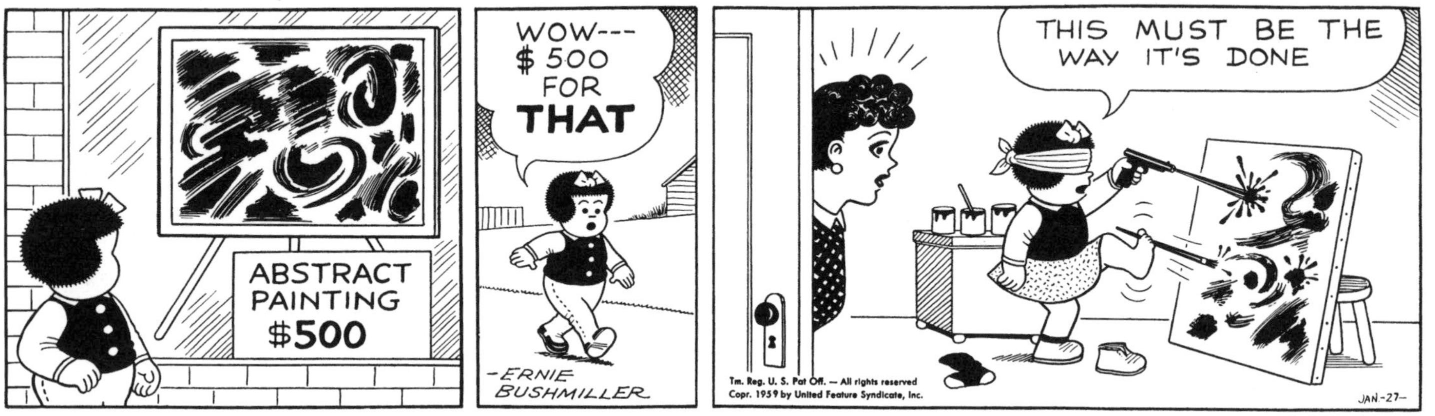
ABSTRACT PAINTING $500
WOW--- $500 FOR THAT
-ERNIE BUSHMILLER
THIS MUST BE THE WAY IT'S DONE
Tm. Reg. U. S. Pat Off. — All rights reserved Copr. 1959 by United Feature Syndicate, Inc.
JAN-27-

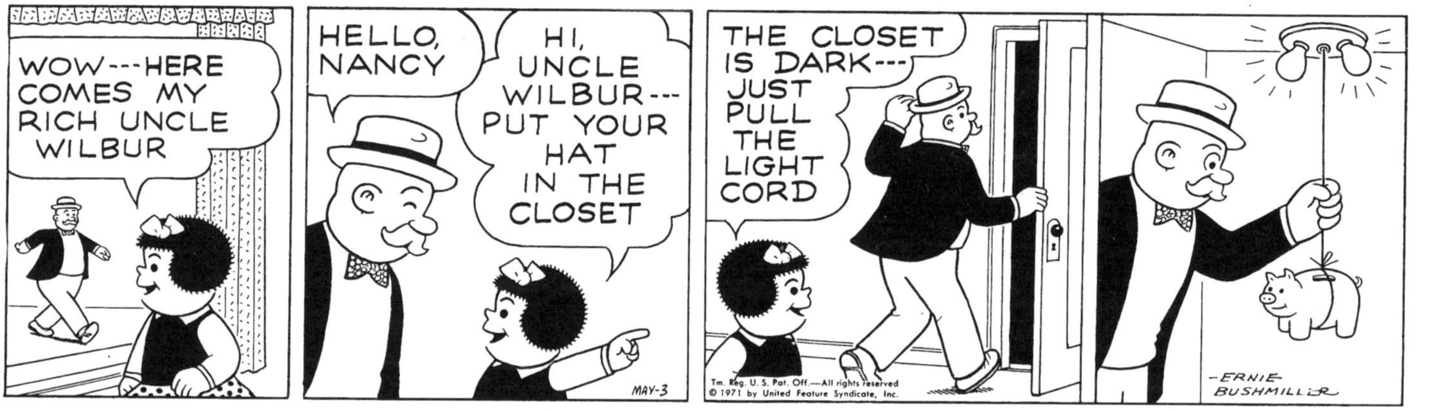
WOW---HERE COMES MY RICH UNCLE WILBUR
HELLO, NANCY
HI, UNCLE WILBUR--- PUT YOUR HAT IN THE CLOSET
MAY-3
THE CLOSET IS DARK--- JUST PULL THE LIGHT CORD
Tm. Reg. U. S. Pat. Off.—All rights reserved © 1971 by United Feature Syndicate, Inc.
-ERNIE BUSHMILLER

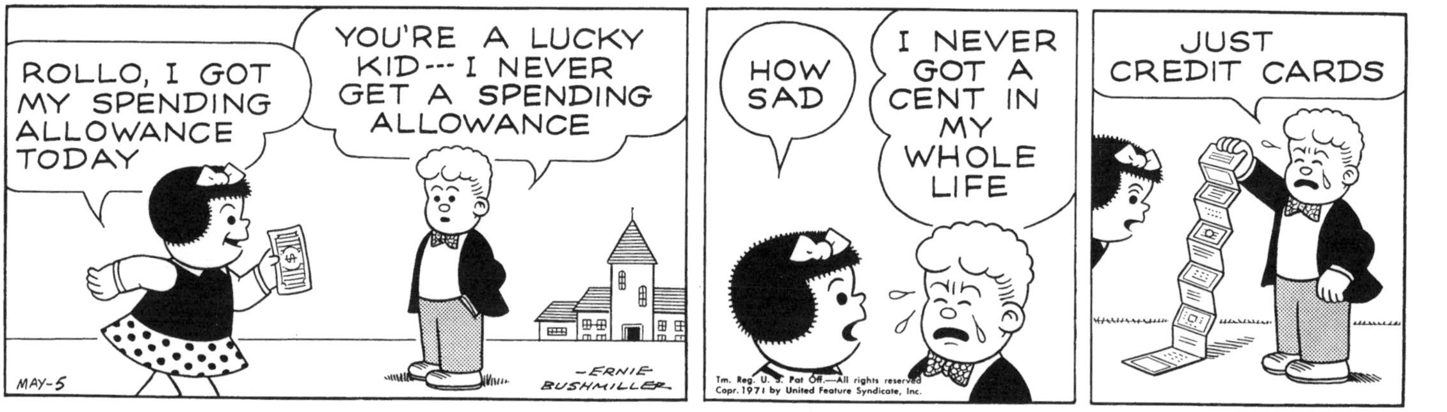
ROLLO, I GOT MY SPENDING ALLOWANCE TODAY
YOU'RE A LUCKY KID--- I NEVER GET A SPENDING ALLOWANCE
MAY-5
-ERNIE BUSHMILLER
HOW SAD
I NEVER GOT A CENT IN MY WHOLE LIFE
Tm. Reg. U. S. Pat Off.—All rights reserved Copr. 1971 by United Feature Syndicate, Inc.
JUST CREDIT CARDS

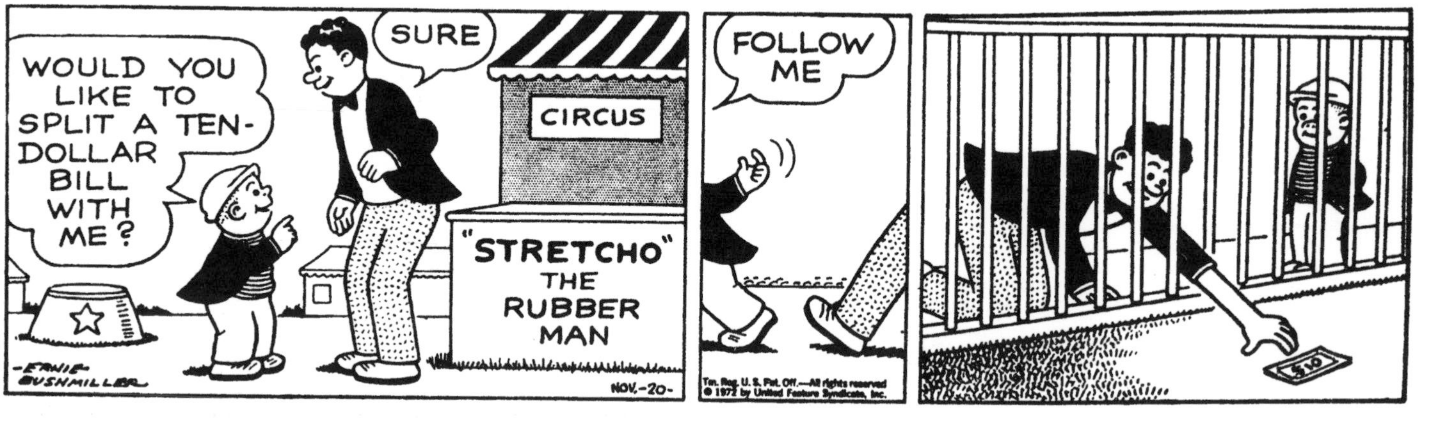
WOULD YOU LIKE TO SPLIT A TEN-DOLLAR BILL WITH ME?
SURE
CIRCUS
"STRETCHO" THE RUBBER MAN
-ERNIE BUSHMILLER
NOV.-20-
FOLLOW ME
Tm. Reg. U. S. Pat. Off.—All rights reserved © 1972 by United Feature Syndicate, Inc.
$10

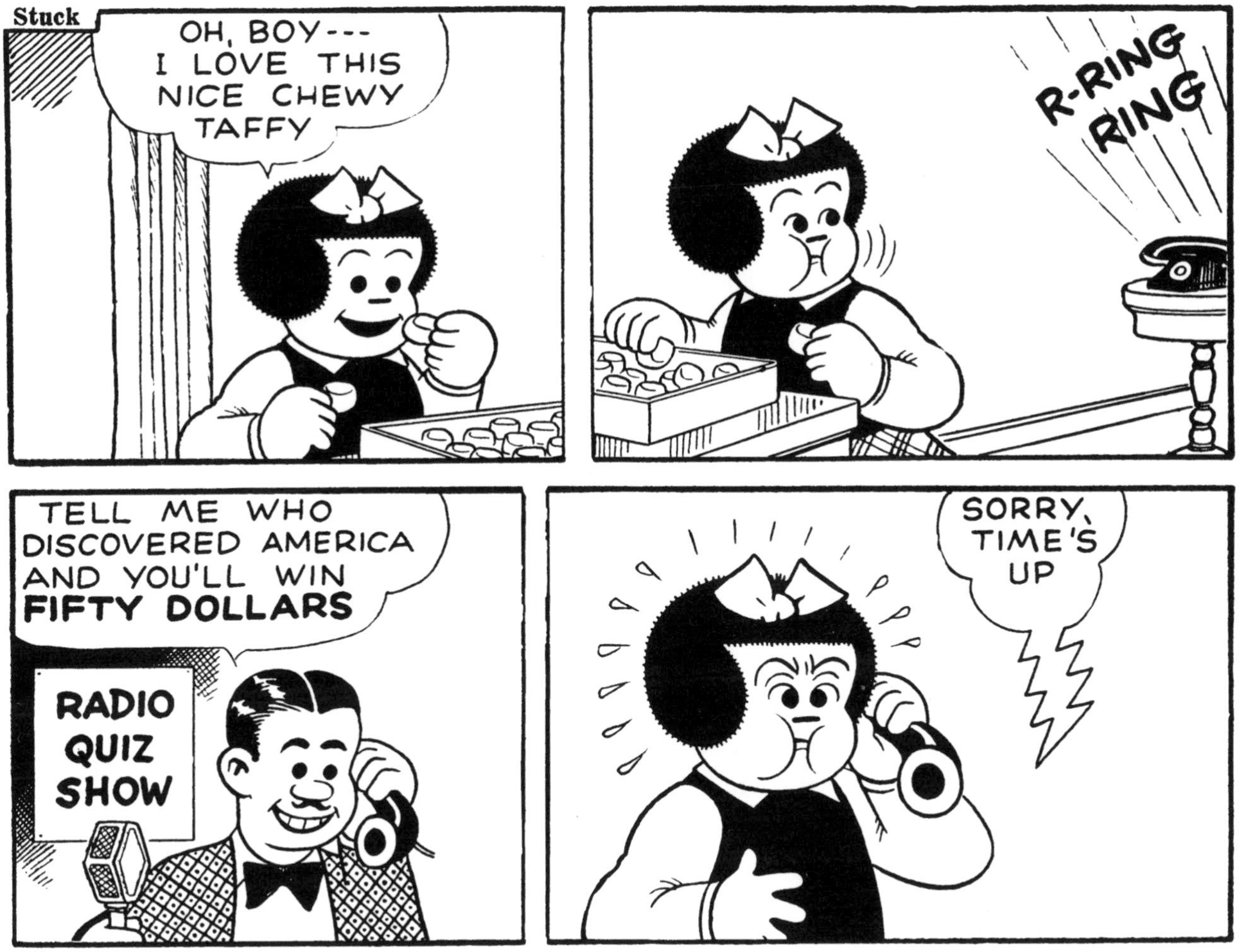
Stuck
OH, BOY--- I LOVE THIS NICE CHEWY TAFFY
R-RING RING
TELL ME WHO DISCOVERED AMERICA AND YOU'LL WIN FIFTY DOLLARS
RADIO QUIZ SHOW
SORRY, TIME'S UP

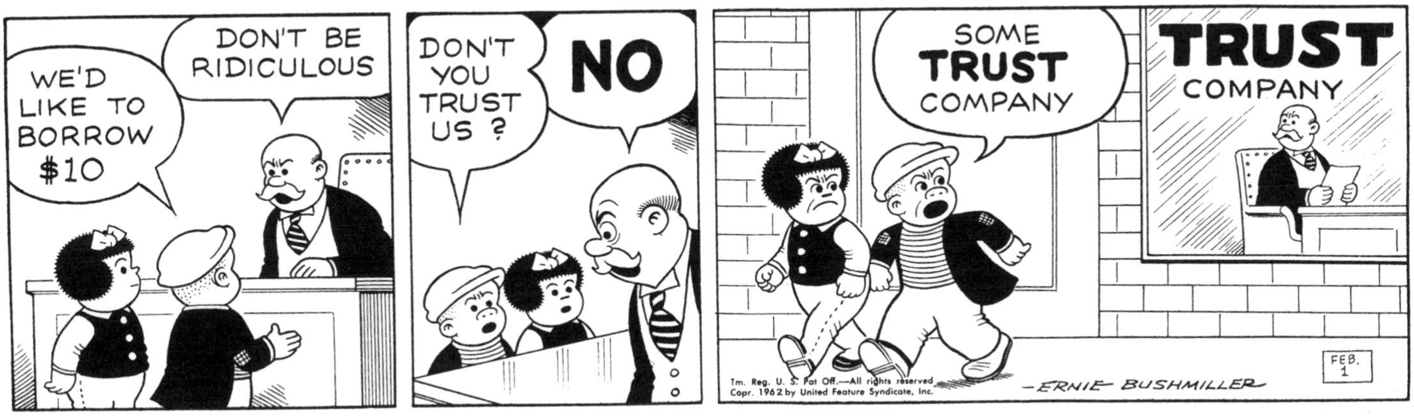
WE'D LIKE TO BORROW $10
DON'T BE RIDICULOUS
DON'T YOU TRUST US ?
NO
SOME TRUST COMPANY
TRUST COMPANY
Tm. Reg. U. S. Pat Off.—All rights reserved Copr. 1962 by United Feature Syndicate, Inc.
-ERNIE BUSHMILLER
FEB. 1

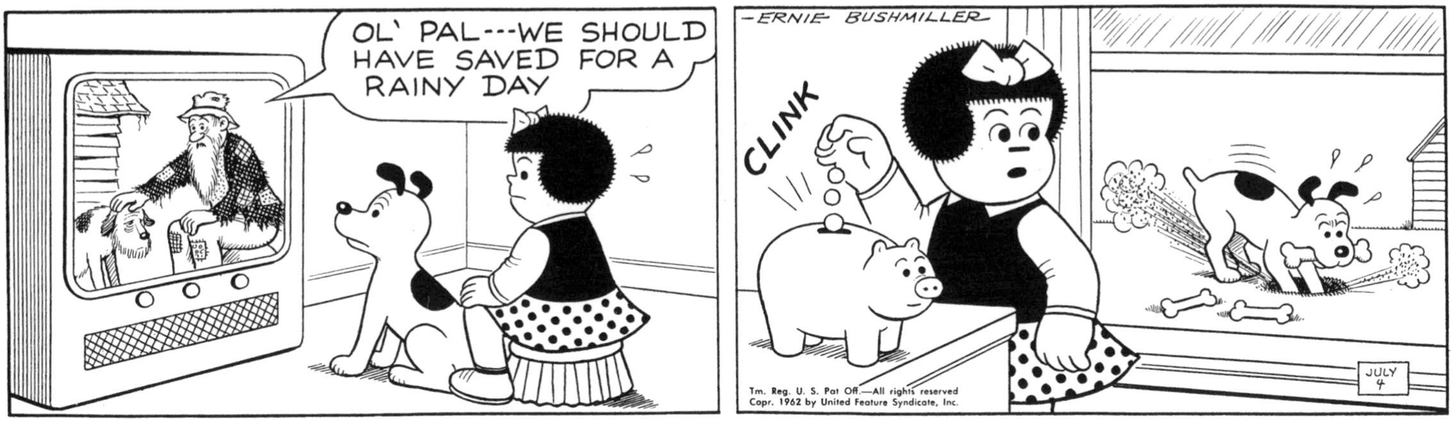
OL' PAL---WE SHOULD HAVE SAVED FOR A RAINY DAY
-ERNIE BUSHMILLER
CLINK
Tm. Reg. U. S. Pat Off.—All rights reserved Copr. 1962 by United Feature Syndicate, Inc.
JULY 4

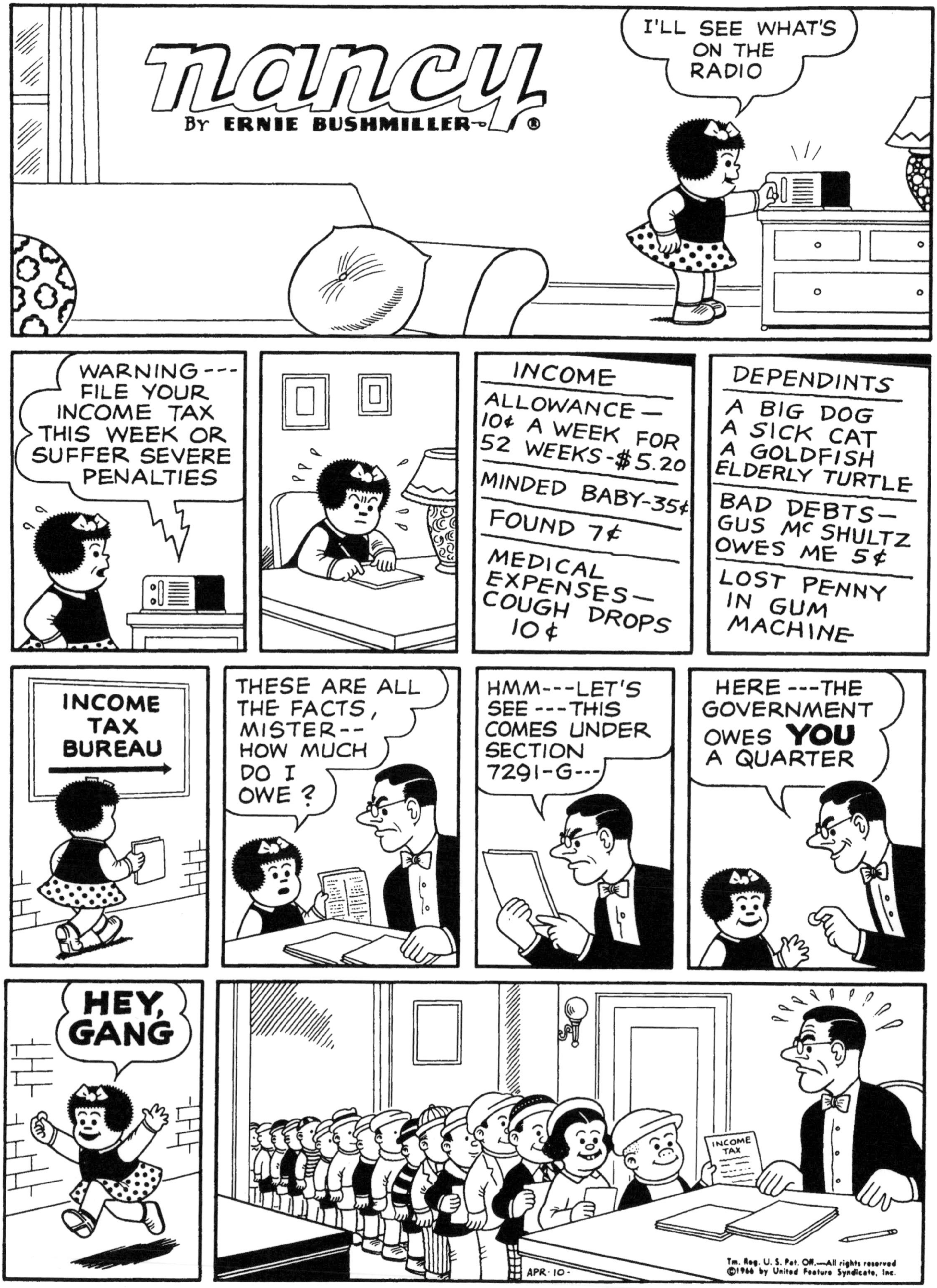
nancy
By ERNIE BUSHMILLER ®
I'LL SEE WHAT'S ON THE RADIO
WARNING--- FILE YOUR INCOME TAX THIS WEEK OR SUFFER SEVERE PENALTIES
INCOME
ALLOWANCE— 10¢ A WEEK FOR 52 WEEKS-$5.20
MINDED BABY-35¢
FOUND 7¢
MEDICAL EXPENSES— COUGH DROPS 10¢
DEPENDINTS
A BIG DOG
A SICK CAT
A GOLDFISH
ELDERLY TURTLE
BAD DEBTS— GUS Mc SHULTZ OWES ME 5¢
LOST PENNY IN GUM MACHINE
INCOME TAX BUREAU
THESE ARE ALL THE FACTS, MISTER-- HOW MUCH DO I OWE ?
HMM---LET'S SEE---THIS COMES UNDER SECTION 7291-G---
HERE---THE GOVERNMENT OWES **YOU** A QUARTER
HEY, GANG
INCOME TAX
APR-10-
Tm. Reg. U. S. Pat. Off.—All rights reserved
©1966 by United Feature Syndicate, Inc.

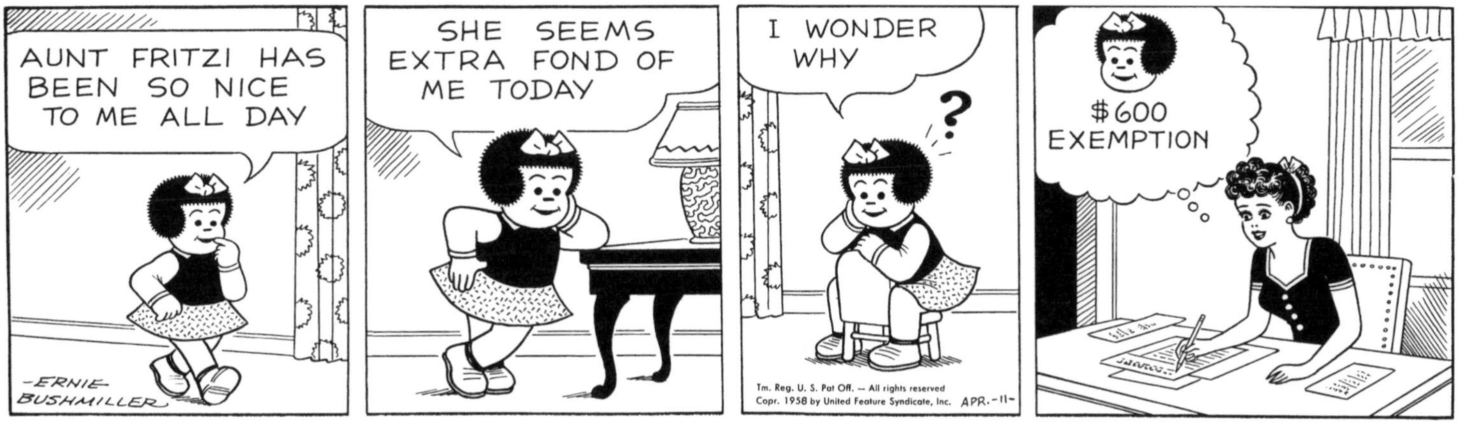
AUNT FRITZI HAS BEEN SO NICE TO ME ALL DAY
-ERNIE BUSHMILLER
SHE SEEMS EXTRA FOND OF ME TODAY
I WONDER WHY
?
Tm. Reg. U. S. Pat Off. — All rights reserved Copr. 1958 by United Feature Syndicate, Inc. APR.-11-
$600 EXEMPTION

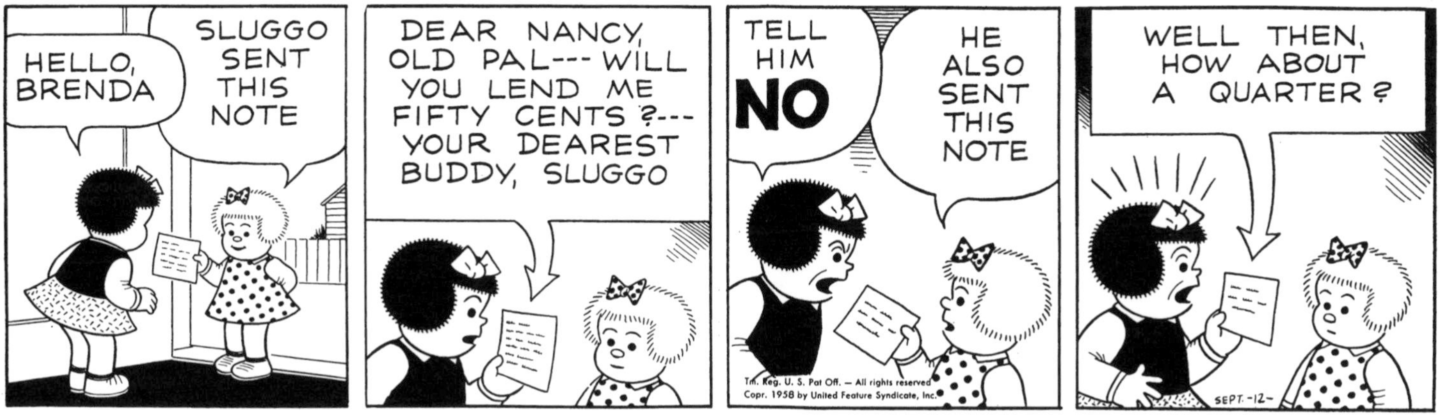
HELLO, BRENDA
SLUGGO SENT THIS NOTE
DEAR NANCY, OLD PAL--- WILL YOU LEND ME FIFTY CENTS ?--- YOUR DEAREST BUDDY, SLUGGO
TELL HIM NO
HE ALSO SENT THIS NOTE
Tm. Reg. U. S. Pat Off. — All rights reserved Copr. 1958 by United Feature Syndicate, Inc.
WELL THEN, HOW ABOUT A QUARTER ?
SEPT.-12-

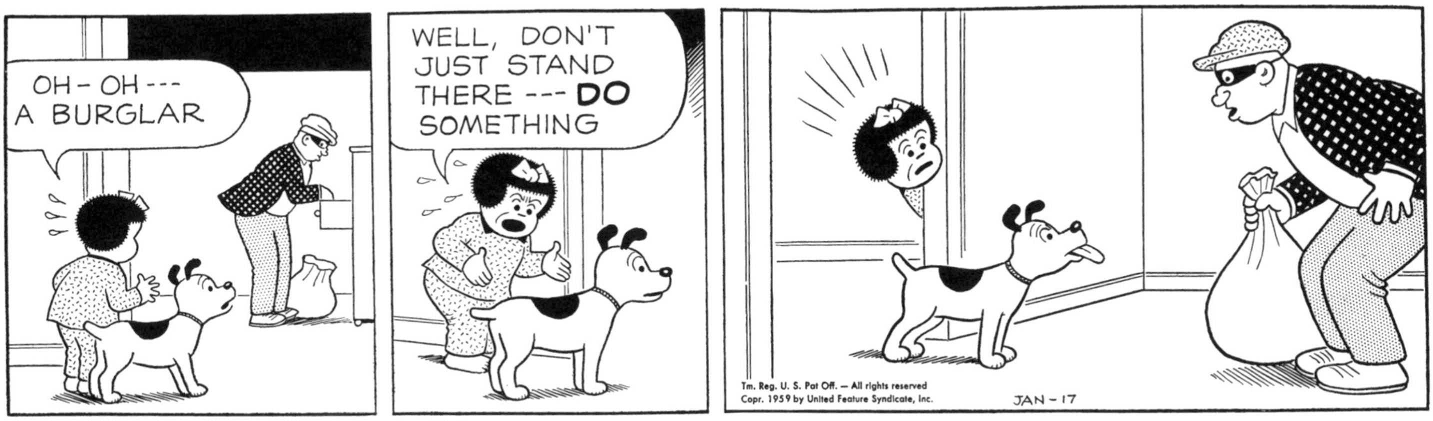
OH-OH --- A BURGLAR
WELL, DON'T JUST STAND THERE --- DO SOMETHING
Tm. Reg. U. S. Pat Off. — All rights reserved Copr. 1959 by United Feature Syndicate, Inc.
JAN-17

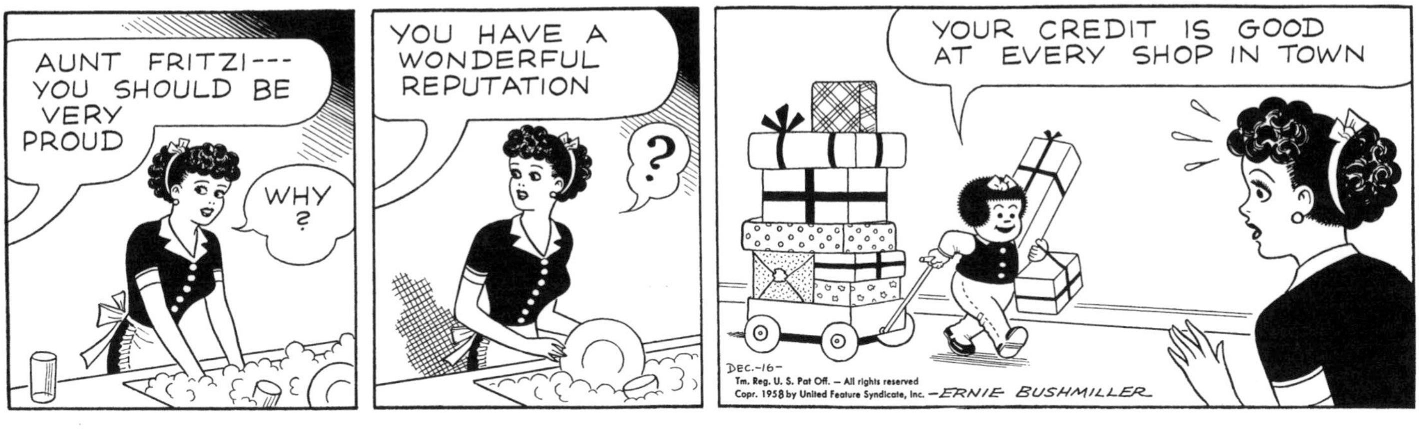
AUNT FRITZI--- YOU SHOULD BE VERY PROUD
WHY ?
YOU HAVE A WONDERFUL REPUTATION
?
YOUR CREDIT IS GOOD AT EVERY SHOP IN TOWN
DEC.-16-
Tm. Reg. U. S. Pat Off. — All rights reserved Copr. 1958 by United Feature Syndicate, Inc. —ERNIE BUSHMILLER

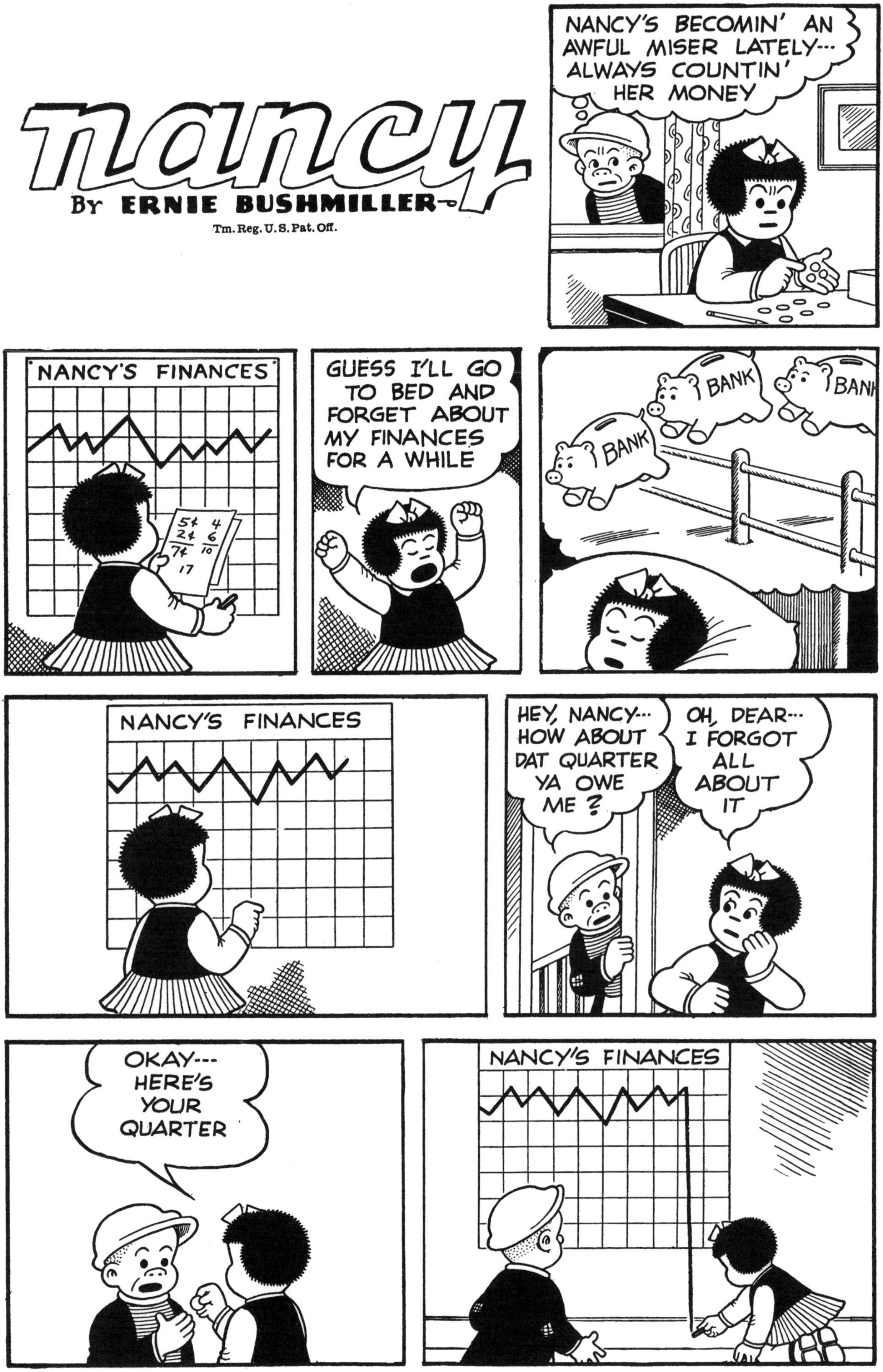
nancy
By ERNIE BUSHMILLER
Tm. Reg. U. S. Pat. Off.
NANCY'S BECOMIN' AN AWFUL MISER LATELY--- ALWAYS COUNTIN' HER MONEY
NANCY'S FINANCES
5¢ 4
2¢ 6
7¢ 10
17
GUESS I'LL GO TO BED AND FORGET ABOUT MY FINANCES FOR A WHILE
BANK
BANK
BANK
NANCY'S FINANCES
HEY, NANCY--- HOW ABOUT DAT QUARTER YA OWE ME ?
OH, DEAR--- I FORGOT ALL ABOUT IT
OKAY--- HERE'S YOUR QUARTER
NANCY'S FINANCES

Market Quotation

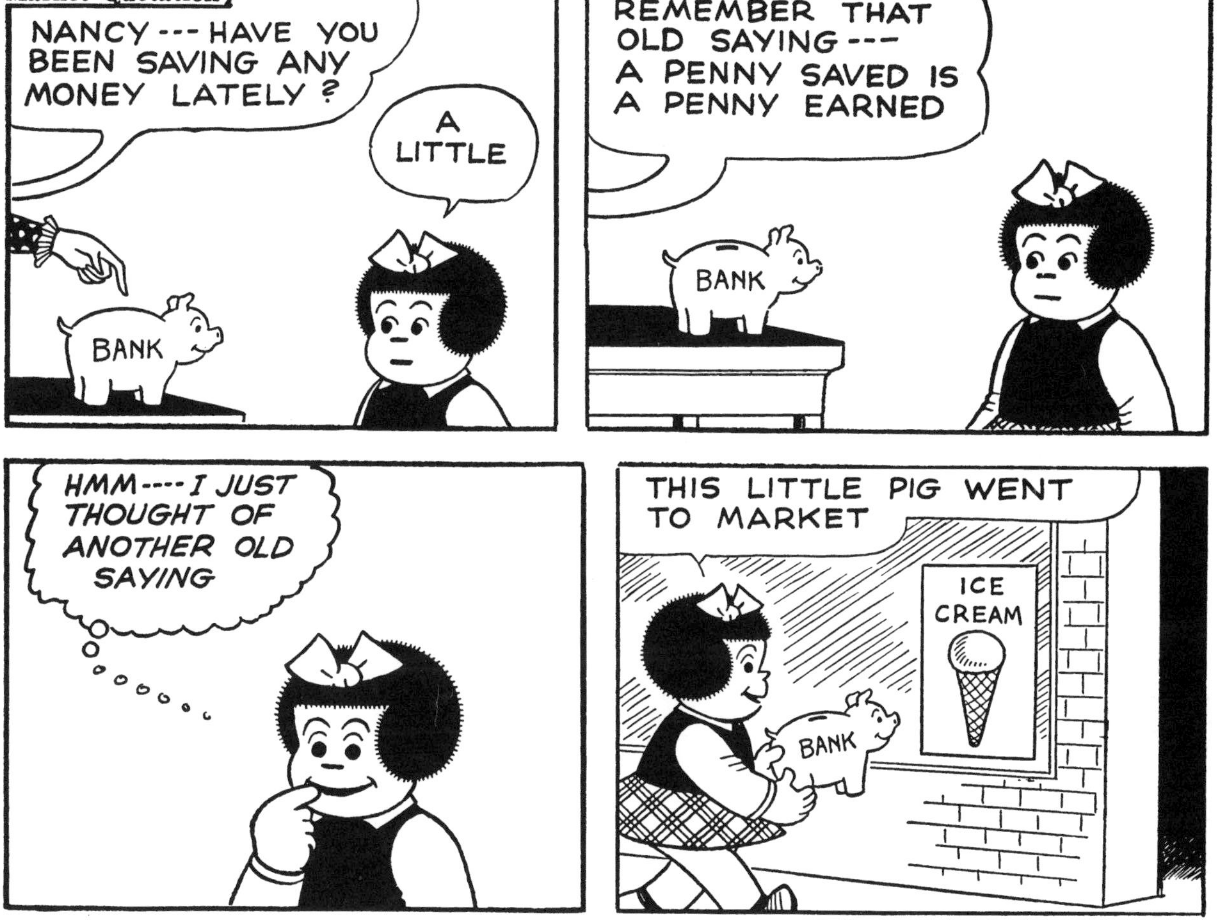

NANCY --- HAVE YOU BEEN SAVING ANY MONEY LATELY ?
A LITTLE
BANK
REMEMBER THAT OLD SAYING --- A PENNY SAVED IS A PENNY EARNED
BANK
HMM ---- I JUST THOUGHT OF ANOTHER OLD SAYING
THIS LITTLE PIG WENT TO MARKET
ICE CREAM
BANK

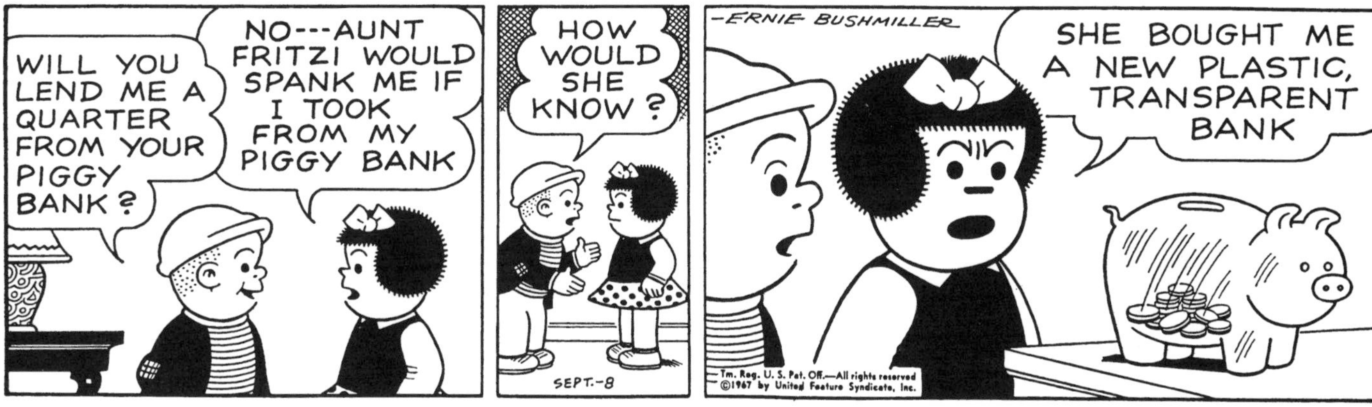

WILL YOU LEND ME A QUARTER FROM YOUR PIGGY BANK ?
NO---AUNT FRITZI WOULD SPANK ME IF I TOOK FROM MY PIGGY BANK
HOW WOULD SHE KNOW ?
SEPT.-8
-ERNIE BUSHMILLER
SHE BOUGHT ME A NEW PLASTIC, TRANSPARENT BANK
Tm. Reg. U. S. Pat. Off.—All rights reserved ©1967 by United Feature Syndicate, Inc.

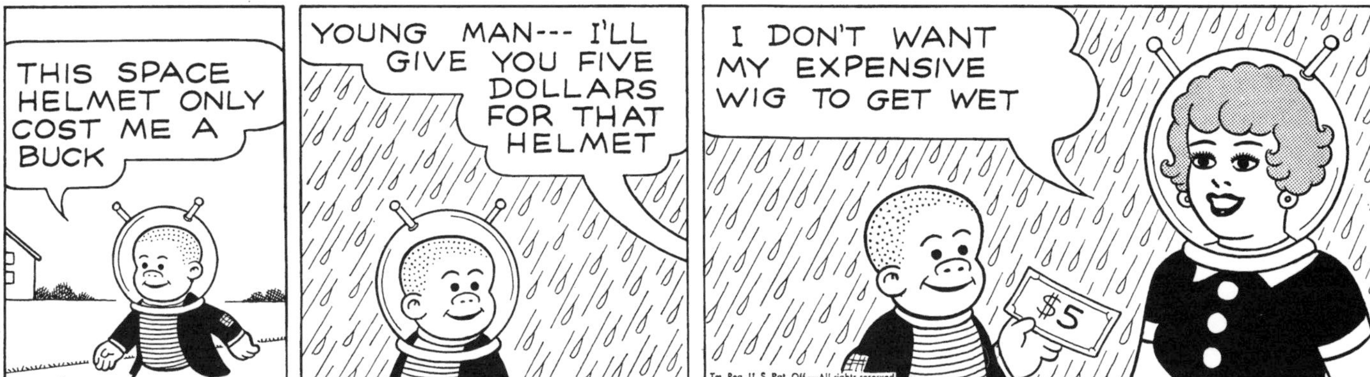

THIS SPACE HELMET ONLY COST ME A BUCK
MAR.-25
YOUNG MAN--- I'LL GIVE YOU FIVE DOLLARS FOR THAT HELMET
I DON'T WANT MY EXPENSIVE WIG TO GET WET
$5
Tm. Reg. U. S. Pat. Off.—All rights reserved © 1971 by United Feature Syndicate, Inc.

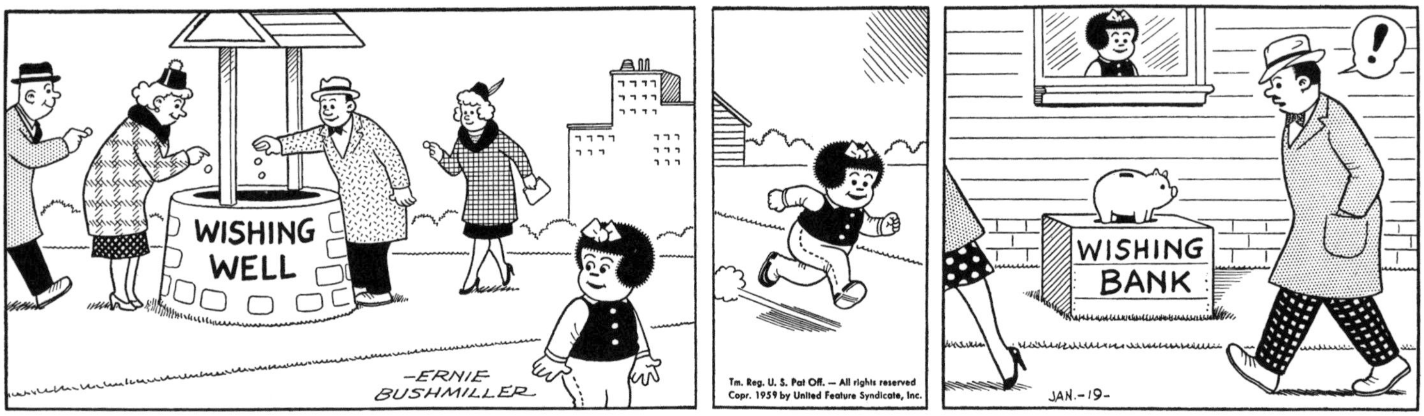
WISHING WELL
-ERNIE BUSHMILLER
Tm. Reg. U. S. Pat Off. — All rights reserved
Copr. 1959 by United Feature Syndicate, Inc.
!
WISHING BANK
JAN.-19-

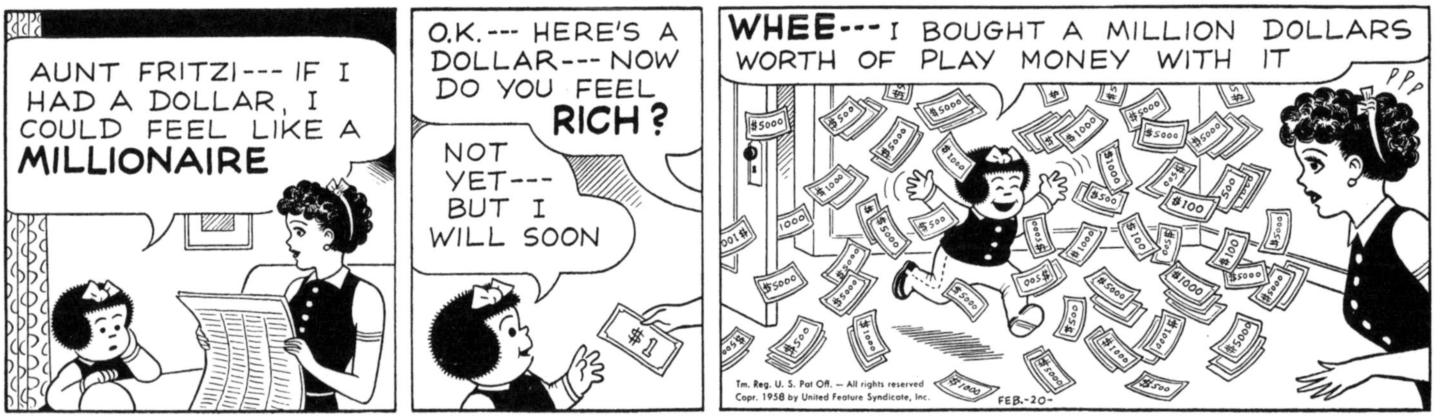
AUNT FRITZI--- IF I HAD A DOLLAR, I COULD FEEL LIKE A MILLIONAIRE
O.K.--- HERE'S A DOLLAR--- NOW DO YOU FEEL RICH?
NOT YET--- BUT I WILL SOON
$1
WHEE--- I BOUGHT A MILLION DOLLARS WORTH OF PLAY MONEY WITH IT
Tm. Reg. U. S. Pat Off. — All rights reserved
Copr. 1958 by United Feature Syndicate, Inc.
FEB.-20-

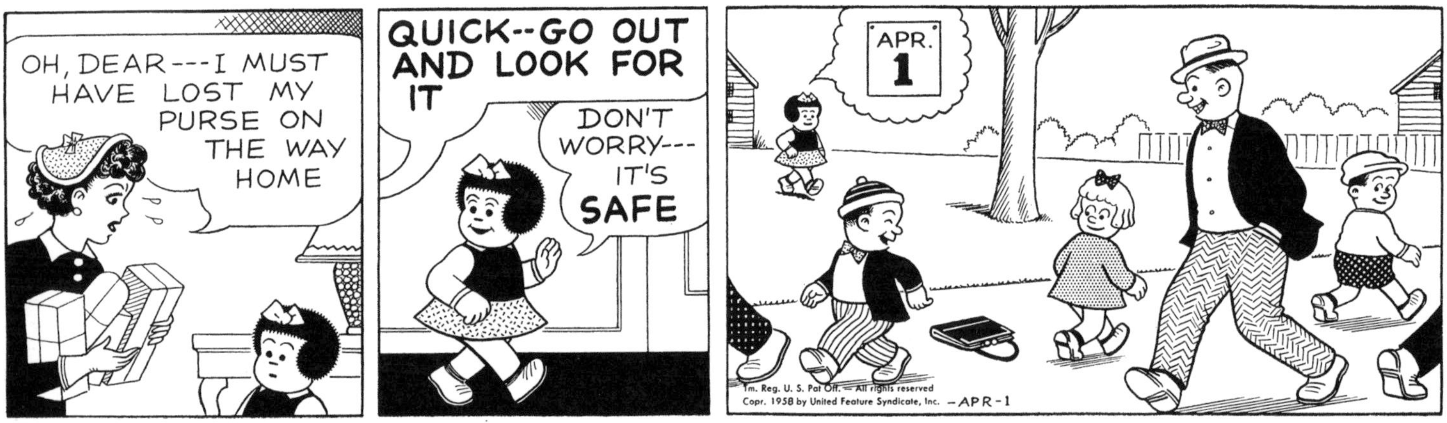
OH, DEAR---I MUST HAVE LOST MY PURSE ON THE WAY HOME
QUICK--GO OUT AND LOOK FOR IT
DON'T WORRY--- IT'S SAFE
APR. 1
Tm. Reg. U. S. Pat Off. — All rights reserved
Copr. 1958 by United Feature Syndicate, Inc.
-APR-1

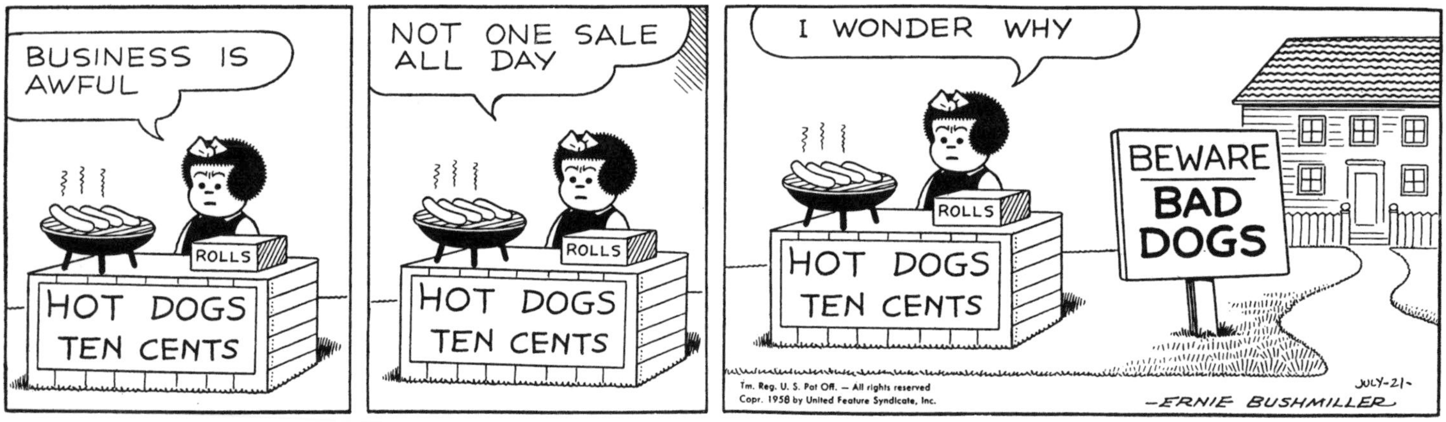
BUSINESS IS AWFUL
ROLLS
HOT DOGS TEN CENTS
NOT ONE SALE ALL DAY
ROLLS
HOT DOGS TEN CENTS
I WONDER WHY
ROLLS
HOT DOGS TEN CENTS
BEWARE BAD DOGS
Tm. Reg. U. S. Pat Off. — All rights reserved
Copr. 1958 by United Feature Syndicate, Inc.
JULY-21-
-ERNIE BUSHMILLER

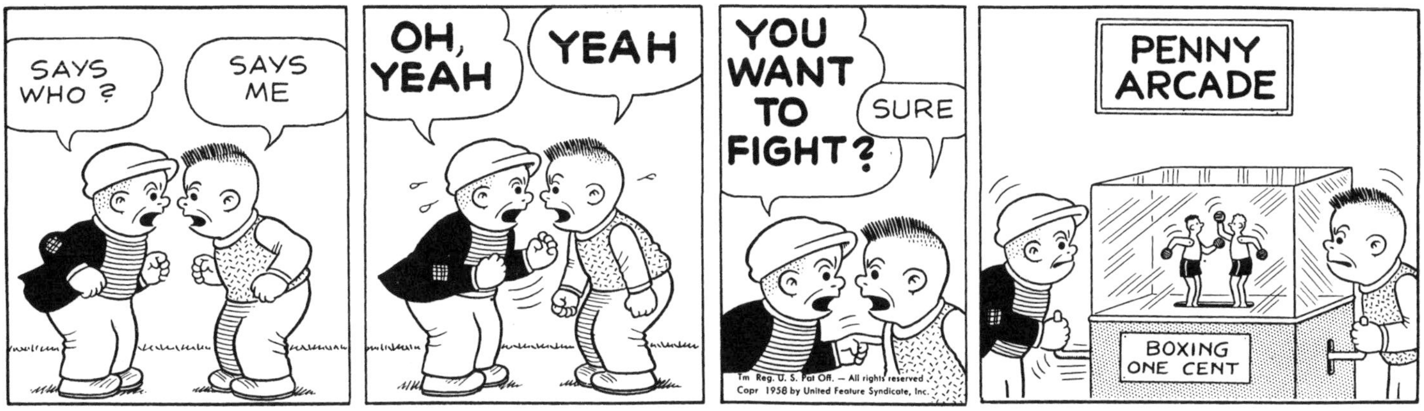
SAYS WHO?
SAYS ME
OH, YEAH
YEAH
YOU WANT TO FIGHT?
SURE
Tm Reg. U. S. Pat Off. — All rights reserved
Copr 1958 by United Feature Syndicate, Inc.
PENNY ARCADE
BOXING ONE CENT

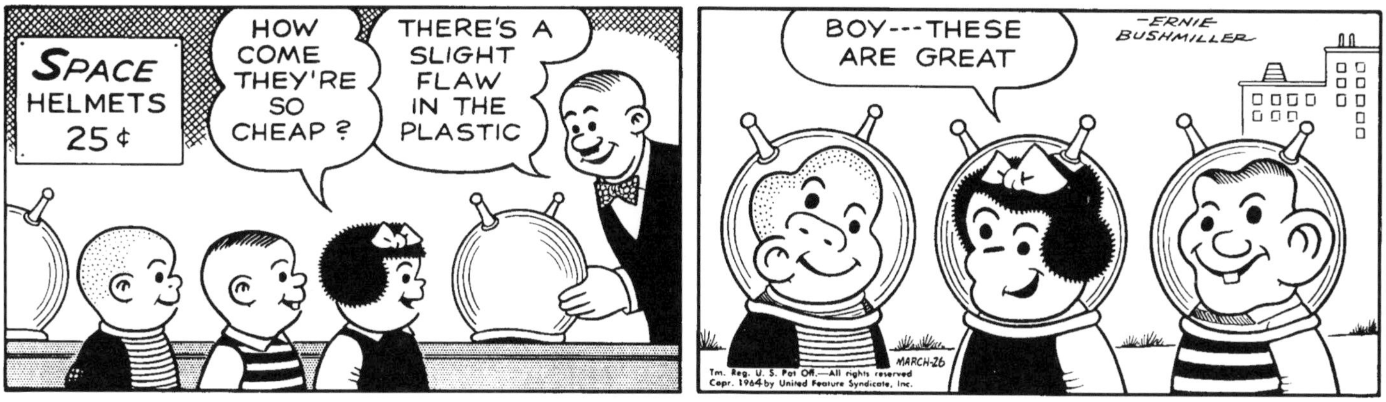
SPACE HELMETS 25¢
HOW COME THEY'RE SO CHEAP?
THERE'S A SLIGHT FLAW IN THE PLASTIC
BOY---THESE ARE GREAT
-ERNIE BUSHMILLER
MARCH-26
Tm. Reg. U. S. Pat Off.—All rights reserved
Copr. 1964 by United Feature Syndicate, Inc.

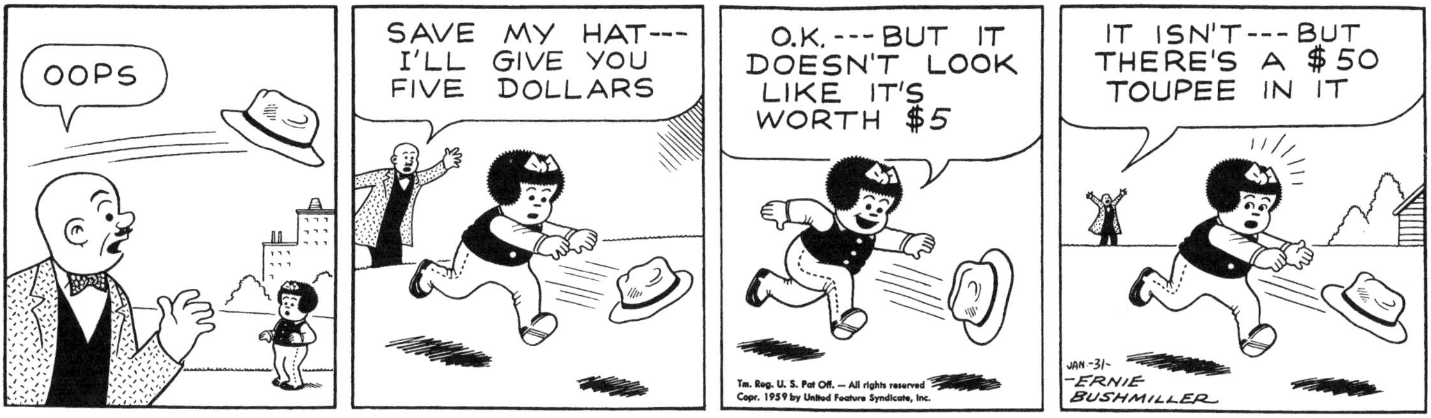
OOPS
SAVE MY HAT--- I'LL GIVE YOU FIVE DOLLARS
O.K.---BUT IT DOESN'T LOOK LIKE IT'S WORTH $5
Tm. Reg. U. S. Pat Off. — All rights reserved
Copr. 1959 by United Feature Syndicate, Inc.
IT ISN'T---BUT THERE'S A $50 TOUPEE IN IT
JAN-31-
-ERNIE BUSHMILLER

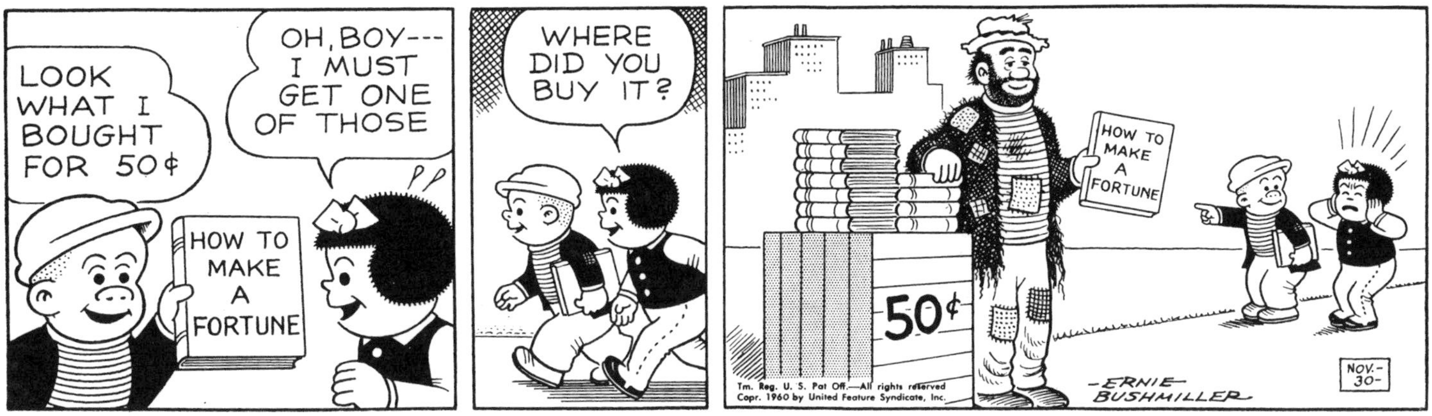
LOOK WHAT I BOUGHT FOR 50¢
OH, BOY--- I MUST GET ONE OF THOSE
HOW TO MAKE A FORTUNE
WHERE DID YOU BUY IT?
HOW TO MAKE A FORTUNE
50¢
Tm. Reg. U. S. Pat Off.—All rights reserved
Copr. 1960 by United Feature Syndicate, Inc.
-ERNIE BUSHMILLER
NOV.-30-

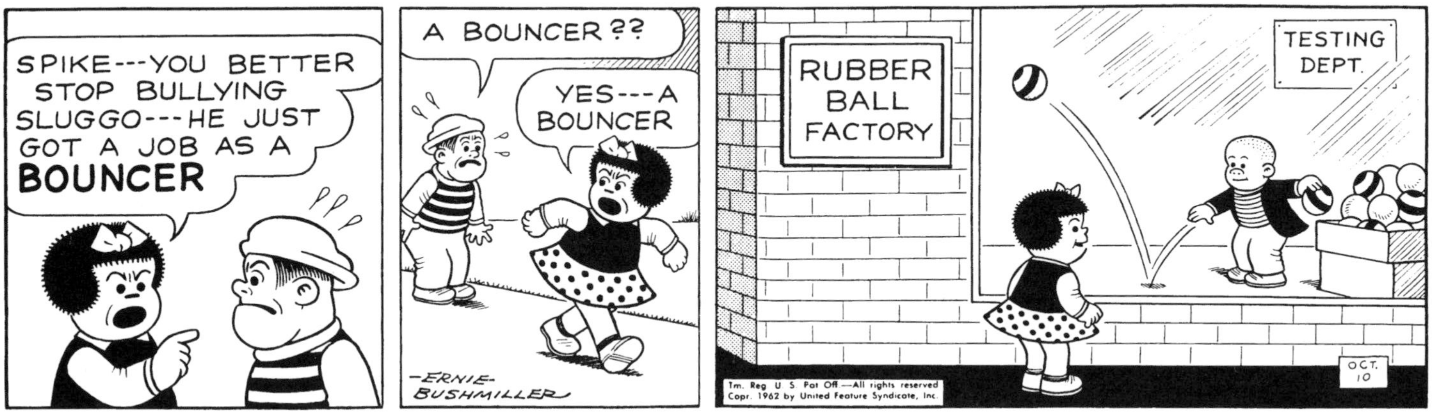

SPIKE---YOU BETTER STOP BULLYING SLUGGO---HE JUST GOT A JOB AS A BOUNCER
A BOUNCER??
YES---A BOUNCER
-ERNIE- BUSHMILLER
RUBBER BALL FACTORY
TESTING DEPT.
OCT. 10
Tm. Reg U S Pat Off.---All rights reserved
Copr. 1962 by United Feature Syndicate, Inc

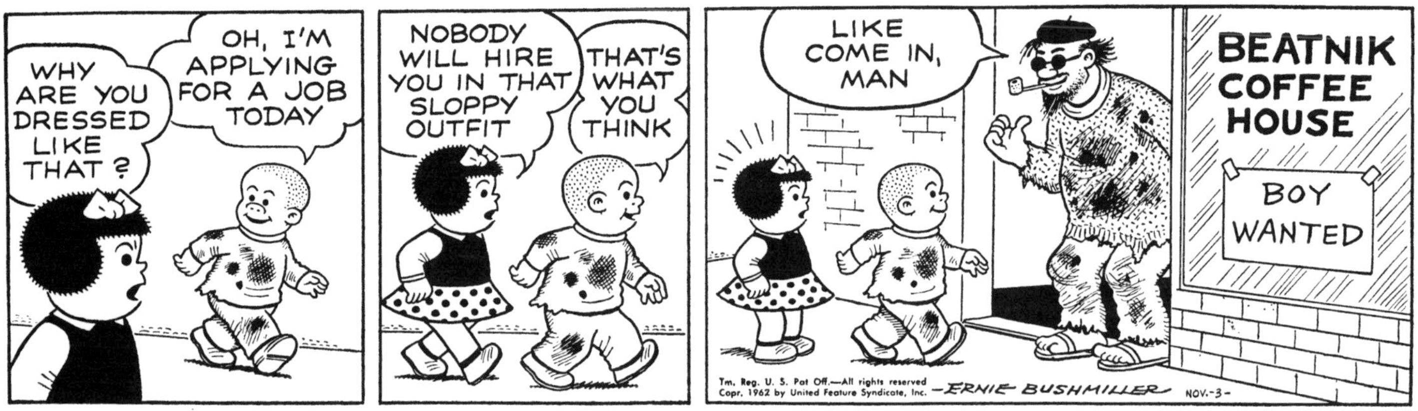

WHY ARE YOU DRESSED LIKE THAT?
OH, I'M APPLYING FOR A JOB TODAY
NOBODY WILL HIRE YOU IN THAT SLOPPY OUTFIT
THAT'S WHAT YOU THINK
LIKE COME IN, MAN
BEATNIK COFFEE HOUSE
BOY WANTED
Tm. Reg. U. S. Pat Off.—All rights reserved
Copr. 1962 by United Feature Syndicate, Inc.
-ERNIE- BUSHMILLER
NOV.-3-

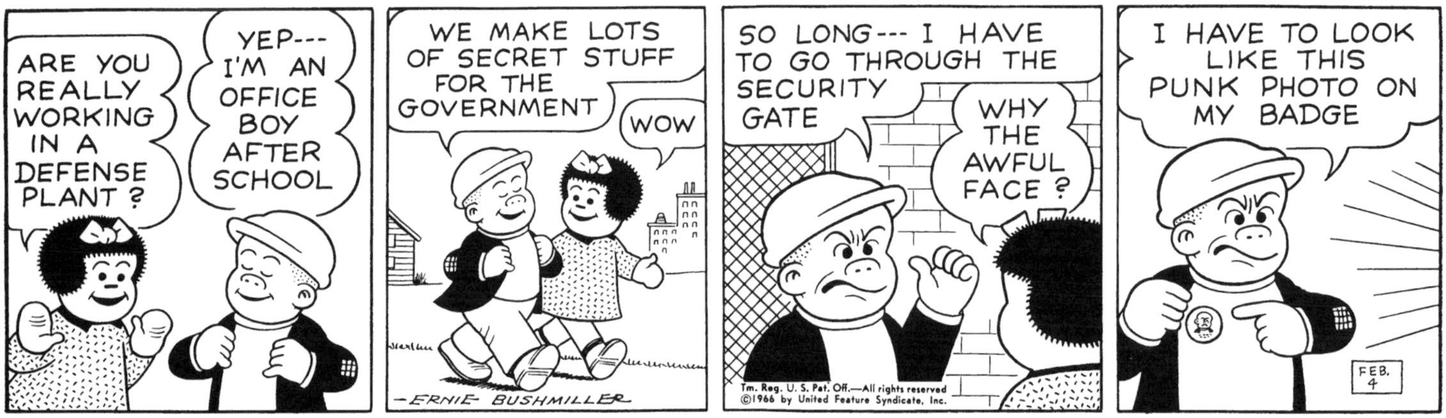

ARE YOU REALLY WORKING IN A DEFENSE PLANT?
YEP--- I'M AN OFFICE BOY AFTER SCHOOL
WE MAKE LOTS OF SECRET STUFF FOR THE GOVERNMENT
WOW
-ERNIE- BUSHMILLER
SO LONG--- I HAVE TO GO THROUGH THE SECURITY GATE
WHY THE AWFUL FACE?
Tm. Reg. U. S. Pat. Off.—All rights reserved
©1966 by United Feature Syndicate, Inc.
I HAVE TO LOOK LIKE THIS PUNK PHOTO ON MY BADGE
FEB. 4

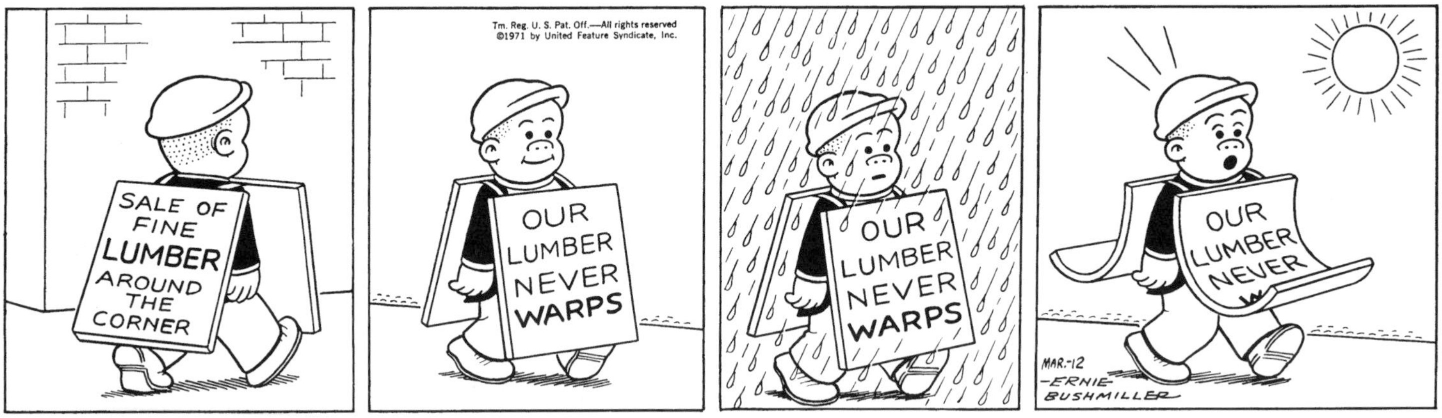

SALE OF FINE LUMBER AROUND THE CORNER
Tm. Reg. U. S. Pat. Off.—All rights reserved
©1971 by United Feature Syndicate, Inc.
OUR LUMBER NEVER WARPS
OUR LUMBER NEVER WARPS
OUR LUMBER NEVER
MAR.-12
-ERNIE- BUSHMILLER

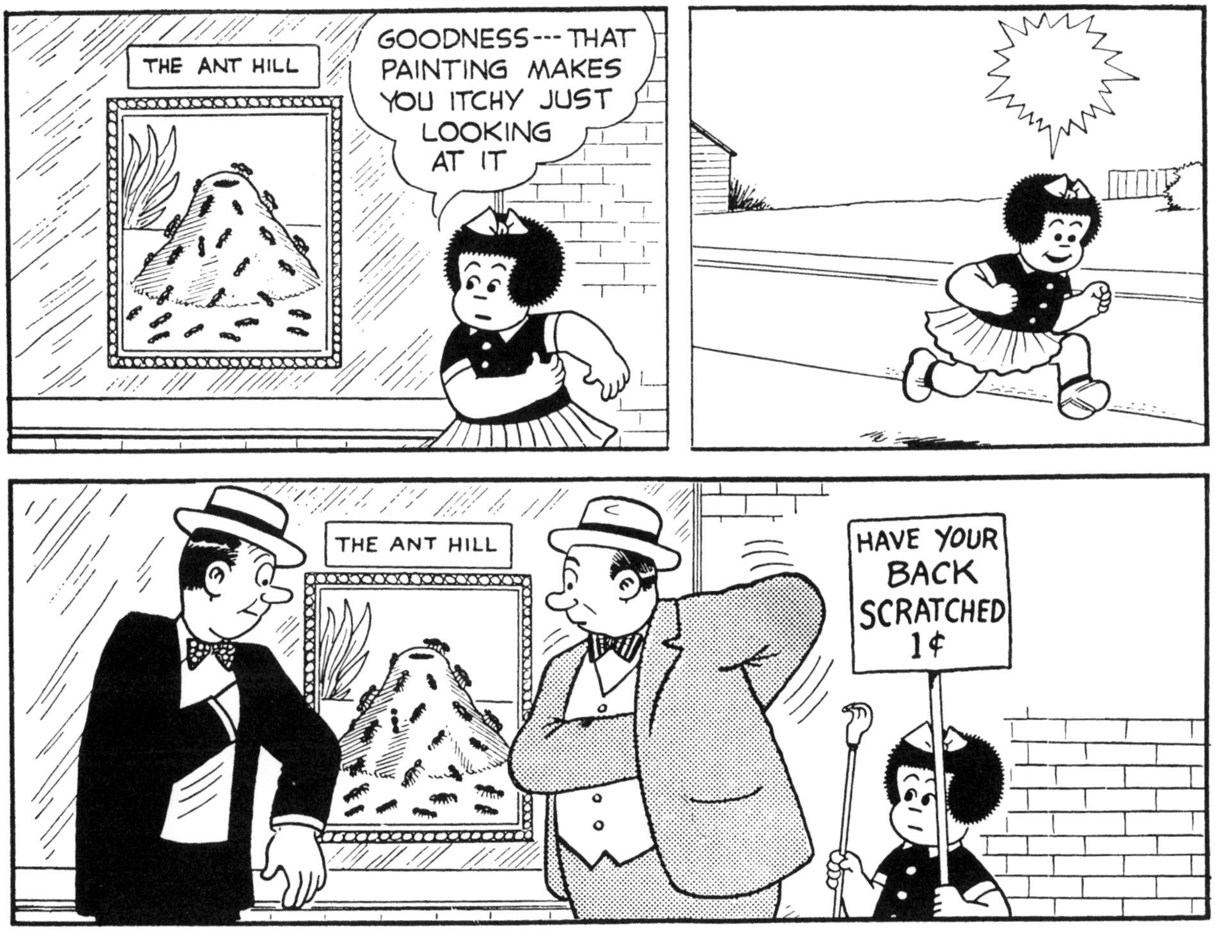
THE ANT HILL
GOODNESS --- THAT PAINTING MAKES YOU ITCHY JUST LOOKING AT IT
THE ANT HILL
HAVE YOUR BACK SCRATCHED 1¢

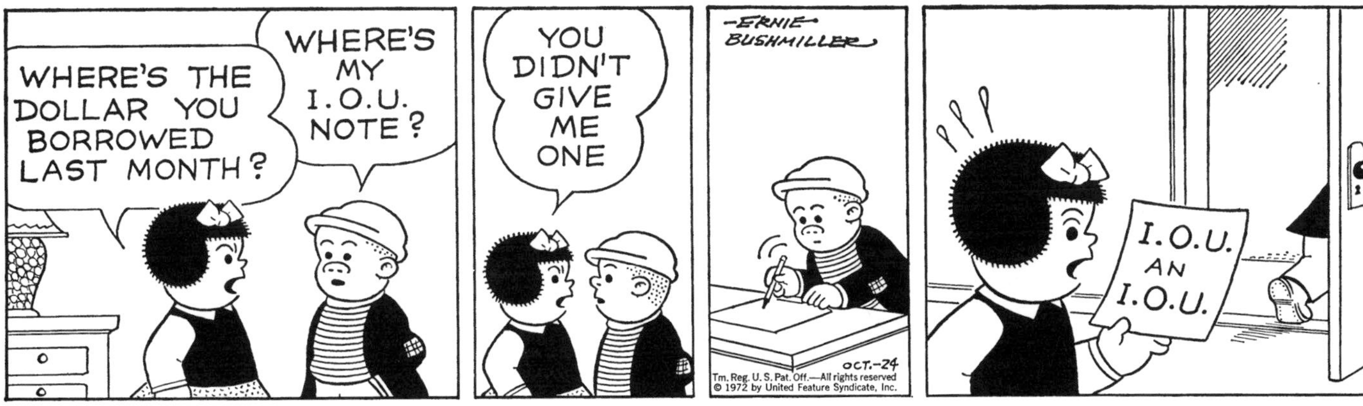
WHERE'S THE DOLLAR YOU BORROWED LAST MONTH?
WHERE'S MY I.O.U. NOTE?
YOU DIDN'T GIVE ME ONE
ERNIE BUSHMILLER
OCT.-24
Tm. Reg. U. S. Pat. Off.—All rights reserved © 1972 by United Feature Syndicate, Inc.
I.O.U. AN I.O.U.

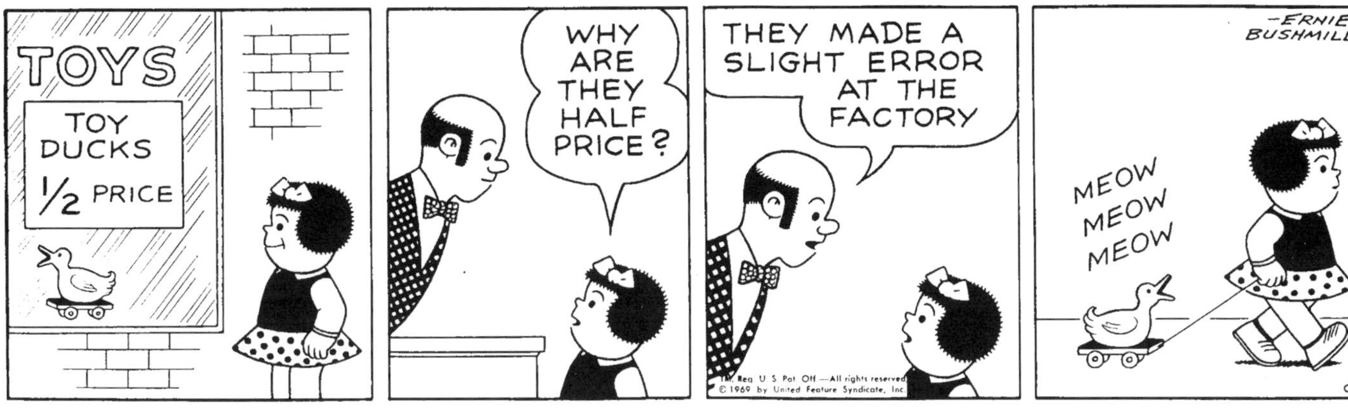
TOYS
TOY DUCKS 1/2 PRICE
WHY ARE THEY HALF PRICE?
THEY MADE A SLIGHT ERROR AT THE FACTORY
Tm. Reg. U. S. Pat. Off.—All rights reserved © 1969 by United Feature Syndicate, Inc.
ERNIE BUSHMILLER
MEOW MEOW MEOW
OCT.-6

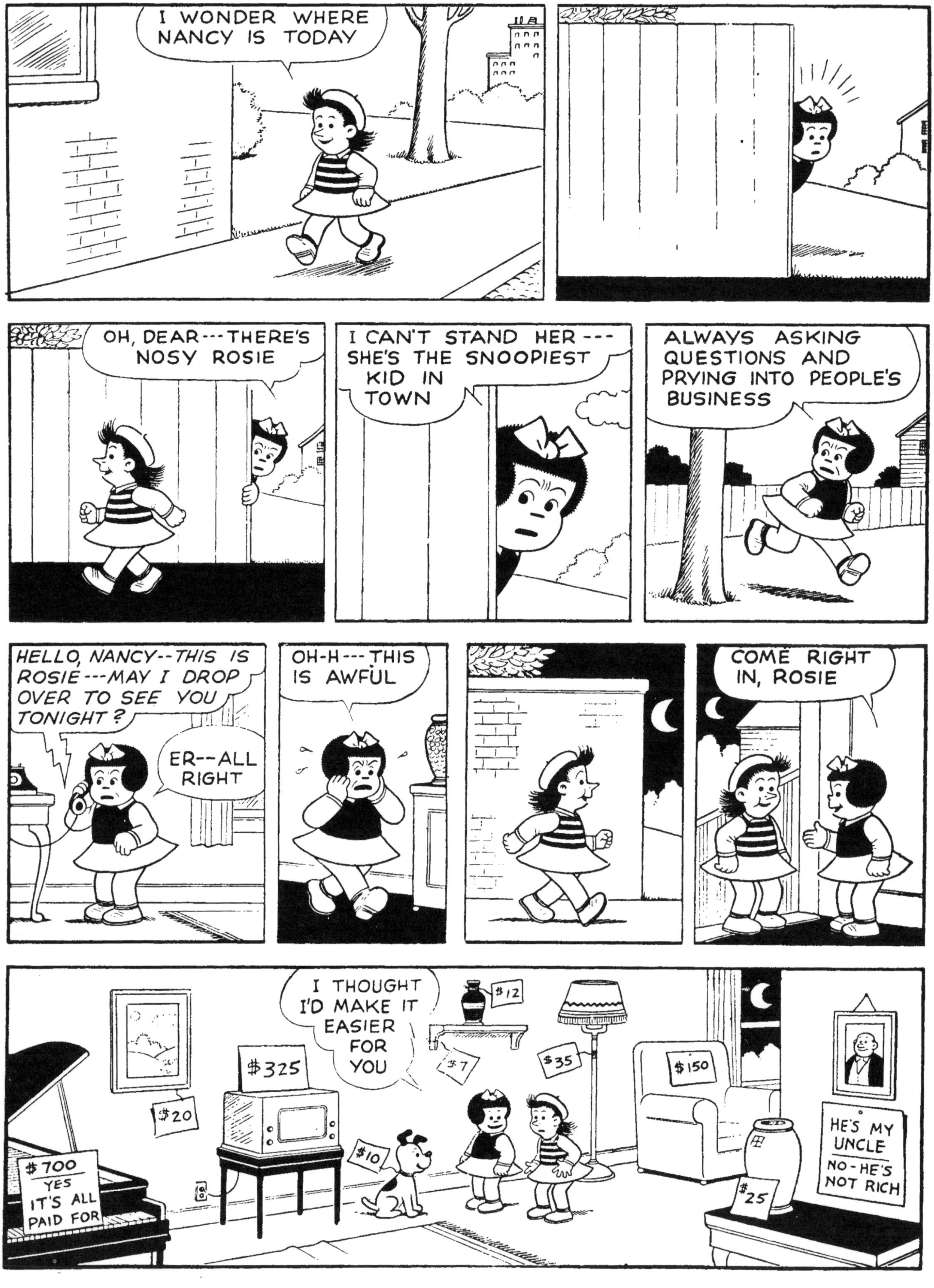
I WONDER WHERE NANCY IS TODAY
OH, DEAR---THERE'S NOSY ROSIE
I CAN'T STAND HER--- SHE'S THE SNOOPIEST KID IN TOWN
ALWAYS ASKING QUESTIONS AND PRYING INTO PEOPLE'S BUSINESS
HELLO, NANCY--THIS IS ROSIE---MAY I DROP OVER TO SEE YOU TONIGHT ?
ER--ALL RIGHT
OH-H---THIS IS AWFUL
COME RIGHT IN, ROSIE
I THOUGHT I'D MAKE IT EASIER FOR YOU
$700
YES
IT'S ALL PAID FOR
$20
$325
$10
$12
$7
$35
$150
HE'S MY UNCLE
NO-HE'S NOT RICH
$25

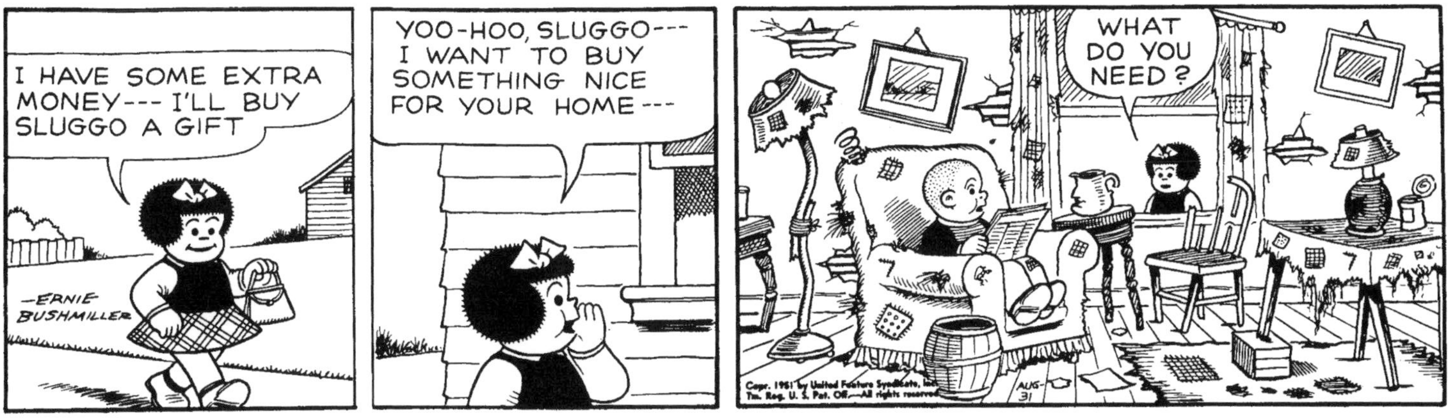

I HAVE SOME EXTRA MONEY--- I'LL BUY SLUGGO A GIFT
-ERNIE BUSHMILLER
YOO-HOO, SLUGGO--- I WANT TO BUY SOMETHING NICE FOR YOUR HOME---
WHAT DO YOU NEED?
Copr. 1961 by United Feature Syndicate, Inc.
Tm. Reg. U. S. Pat. Off.—All rights reserved
AUG-31

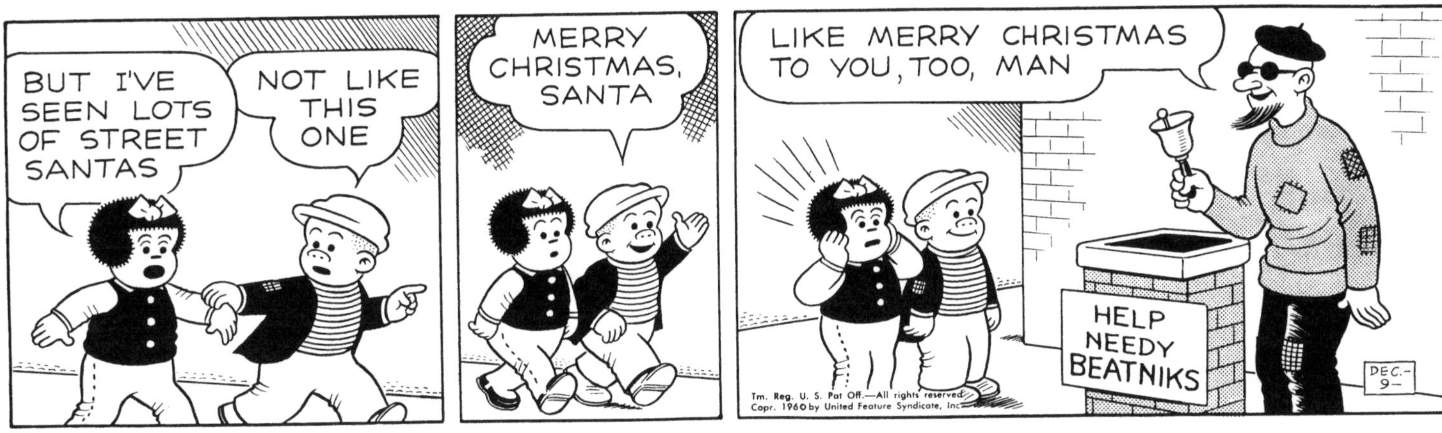

BUT I'VE SEEN LOTS OF STREET SANTAS
NOT LIKE THIS ONE
MERRY CHRISTMAS, SANTA
LIKE MERRY CHRISTMAS TO YOU, TOO, MAN
HELP NEEDY BEATNIKS
Tm. Reg. U. S. Pat Off.—All rights reserved
Copr. 1960 by United Feature Syndicate, Inc.
DEC.-9-

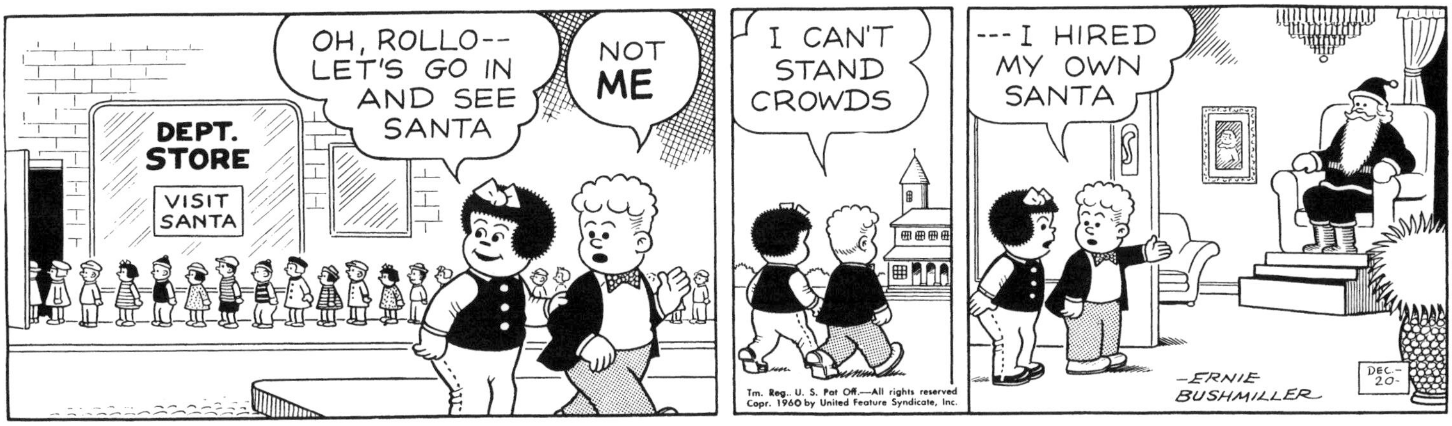

DEPT. STORE
VISIT SANTA
OH, ROLLO-- LET'S GO IN AND SEE SANTA
NOT ME
I CAN'T STAND CROWDS
---I HIRED MY OWN SANTA
Tm. Reg.. U. S. Pat Off.—All rights reserved
Copr. 1960 by United Feature Syndicate, Inc.
-ERNIE BUSHMILLER
DEC.-20-

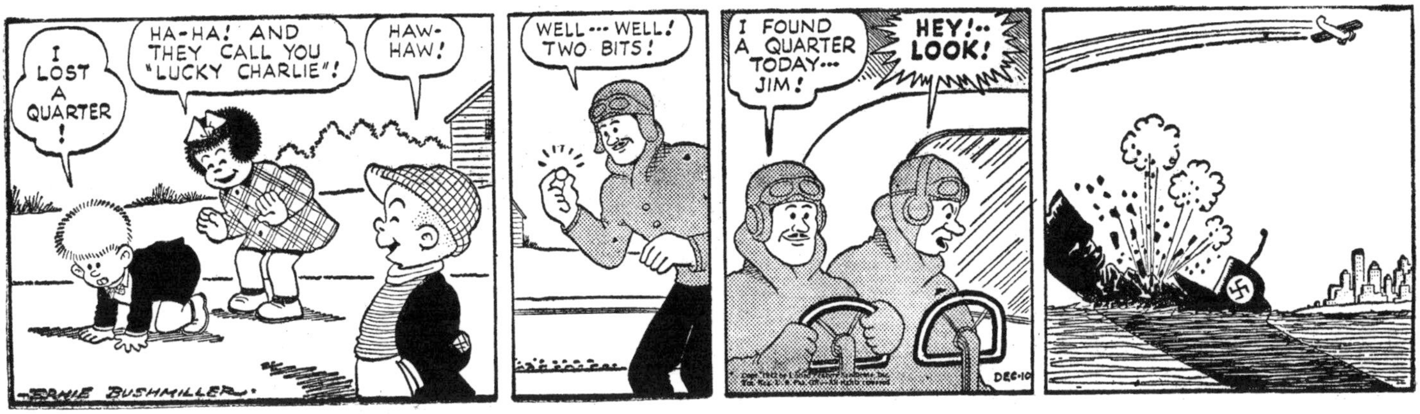

I LOST A QUARTER!
HA-HA! AND THEY CALL YOU "LUCKY CHARLIE"!
HAW-HAW!
-ERNIE BUSHMILLER-
WELL---WELL! TWO BITS!
I FOUND A QUARTER TODAY--- JIM!
HEY!-- LOOK!
DEC-10

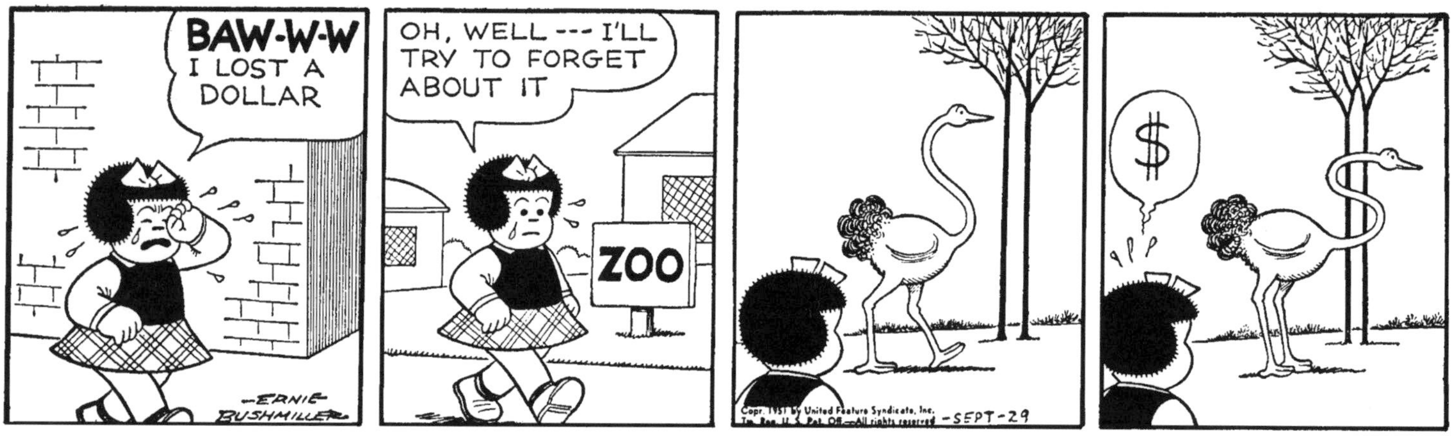
BAW-W-W I LOST A DOLLAR
-ERNIE BUSHMILLER
OH, WELL --- I'LL TRY TO FORGET ABOUT IT
ZOO
Copr. 1951 by United Feature Syndicate, Inc.
Tm. Reg. U. S. Pat. Off.—All rights reserved
-SEPT-29
$

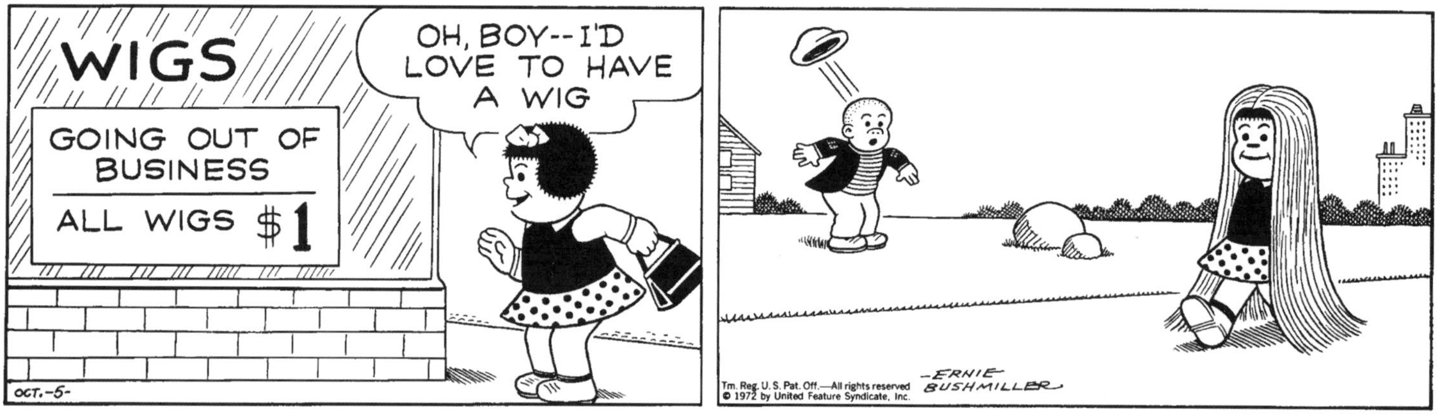
WIGS
GOING OUT OF BUSINESS
ALL WIGS $1
OH, BOY--I'D LOVE TO HAVE A WIG
OCT.-5-
Tm. Reg. U.S. Pat. Off.—All rights reserved
© 1972 by United Feature Syndicate, Inc.
-ERNIE BUSHMILLER

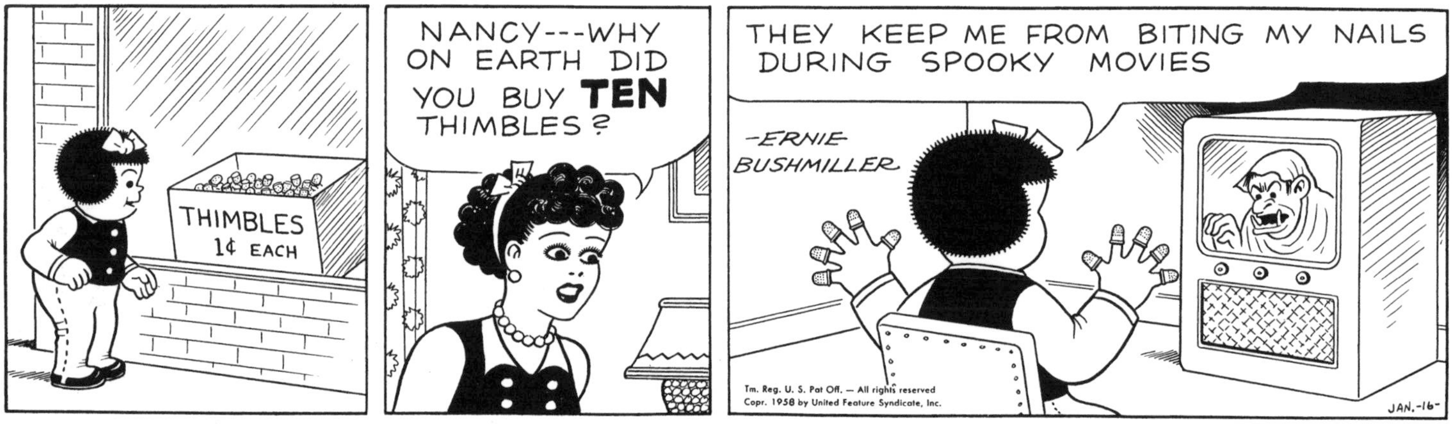
THIMBLES 1¢ EACH
NANCY---WHY ON EARTH DID YOU BUY TEN THIMBLES?
THEY KEEP ME FROM BITING MY NAILS DURING SPOOKY MOVIES
-ERNIE BUSHMILLER
Tm. Reg. U. S. Pat Off. — All rights reserved
Copr. 1958 by United Feature Syndicate, Inc.
JAN.-16-

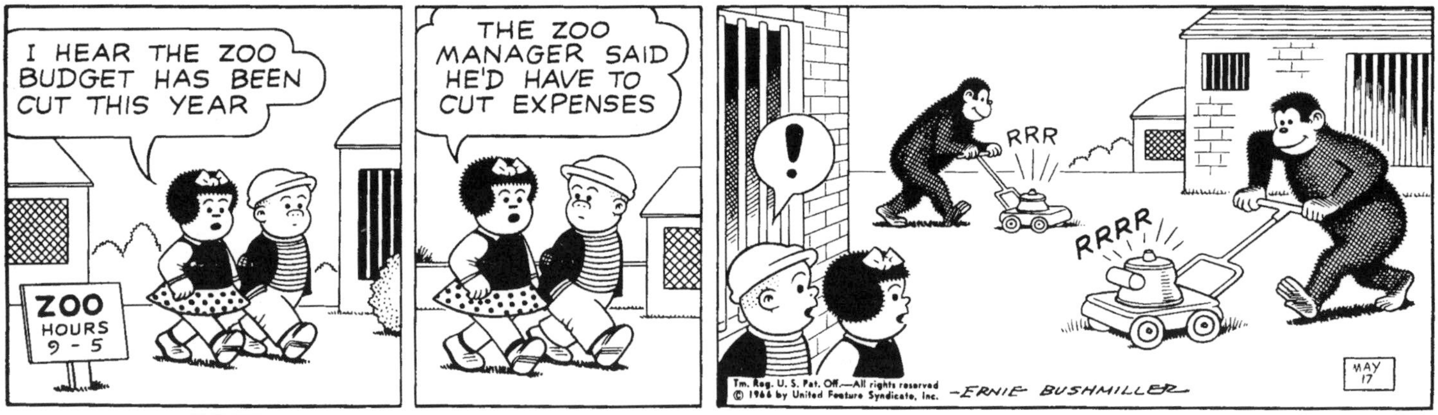
I HEAR THE ZOO BUDGET HAS BEEN CUT THIS YEAR
ZOO HOURS 9 - 5
THE ZOO MANAGER SAID HE'D HAVE TO CUT EXPENSES
!
RRR
RRRR
MAY 17
Tm. Reg. U. S. Pat. Off.—All rights reserved
© 1966 by United Feature Syndicate, Inc.
-ERNIE BUSHMILLER

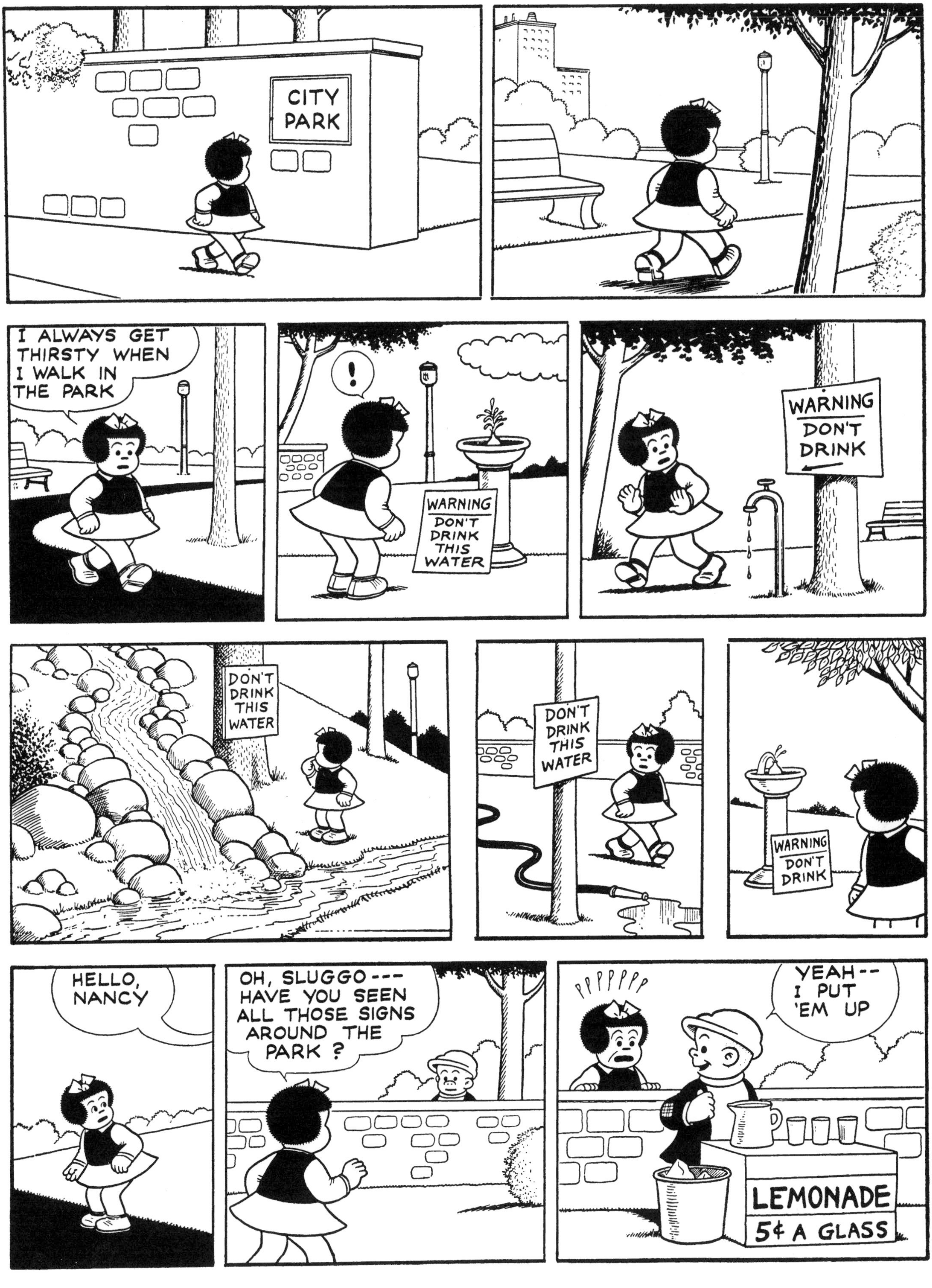
CITY PARK
I ALWAYS GET THIRSTY WHEN I WALK IN THE PARK
!
WARNING DON'T DRINK THIS WATER
WARNING DON'T DRINK
DON'T DRINK THIS WATER
DON'T DRINK THIS WATER
WARNING DON'T DRINK
HELLO, NANCY
OH, SLUGGO --- HAVE YOU SEEN ALL THOSE SIGNS AROUND THE PARK ?
YEAH -- I PUT 'EM UP
LEMONADE
5¢ A GLASS

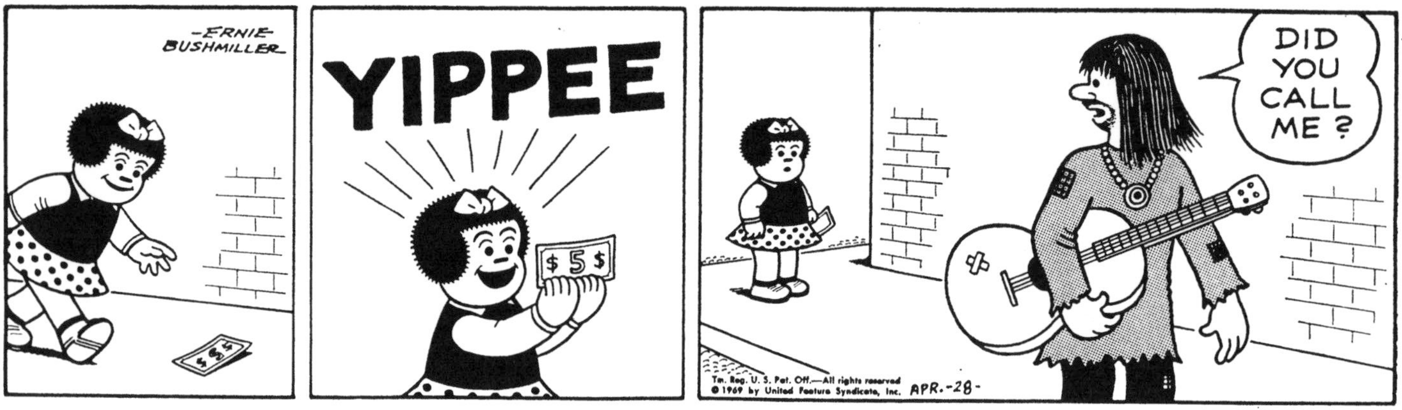
-ERNIE BUSHMILLER
YIPPEE
$ 5 $
DID YOU CALL ME ?
Tm. Reg. U. S. Pat. Off.—All rights reserved © 1969 by United Feature Syndicate, Inc.
APR.-28-

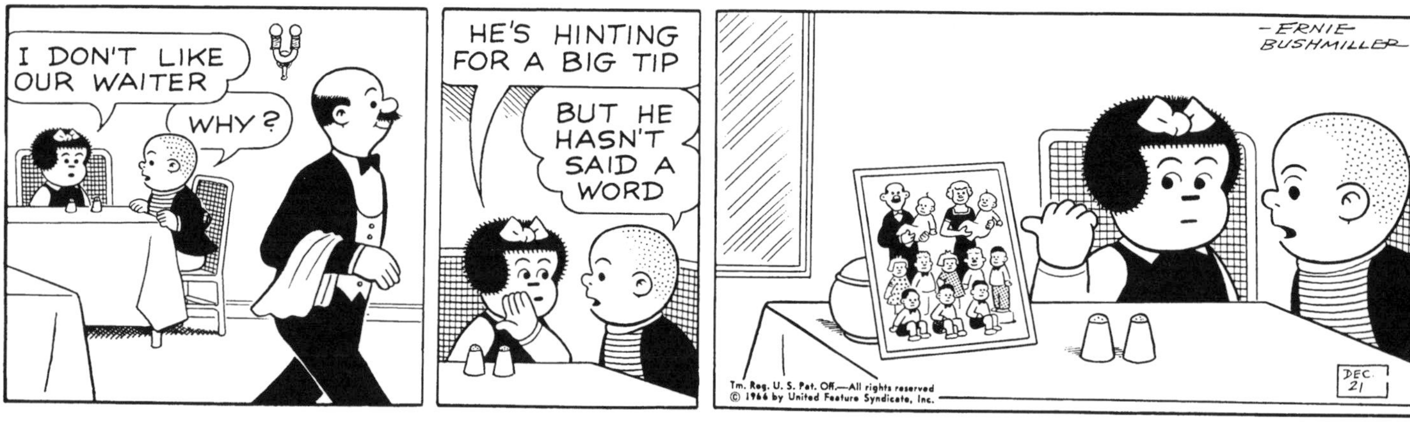
I DON'T LIKE OUR WAITER
WHY ?
HE'S HINTING FOR A BIG TIP
BUT HE HASN'T SAID A WORD
-ERNIE BUSHMILLER
Tm. Reg. U. S. Pat. Off.—All rights reserved © 1966 by United Feature Syndicate, Inc.
DEC. 21

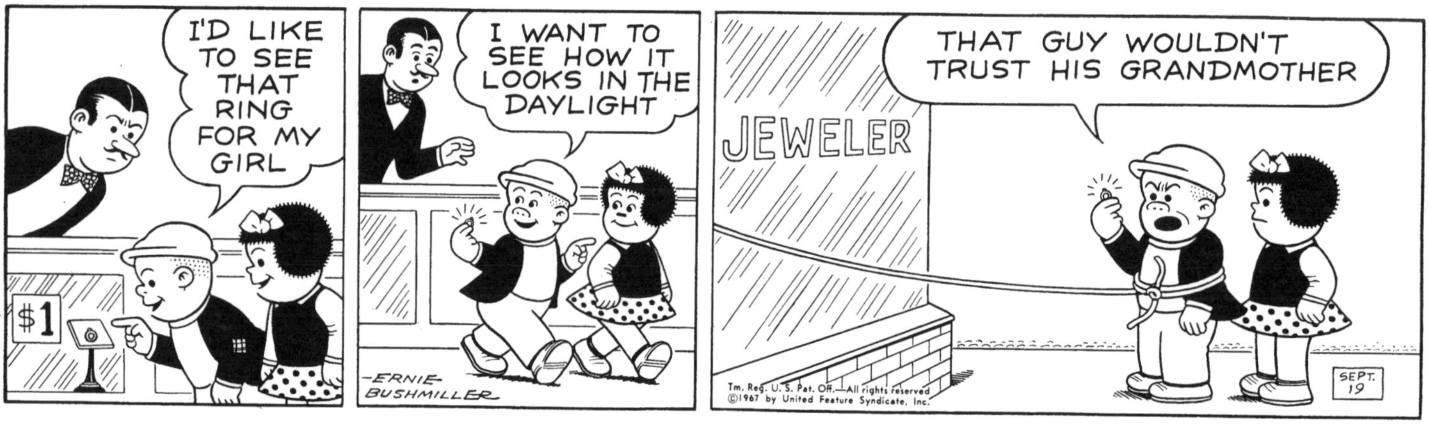
I'D LIKE TO SEE THAT RING FOR MY GIRL
$1
I WANT TO SEE HOW IT LOOKS IN THE DAYLIGHT
-ERNIE BUSHMILLER
THAT GUY WOULDN'T TRUST HIS GRANDMOTHER
JEWELER
Tm. Reg. U. S. Pat. Off.—All rights reserved ©1967 by United Feature Syndicate, Inc.
SEPT. 19

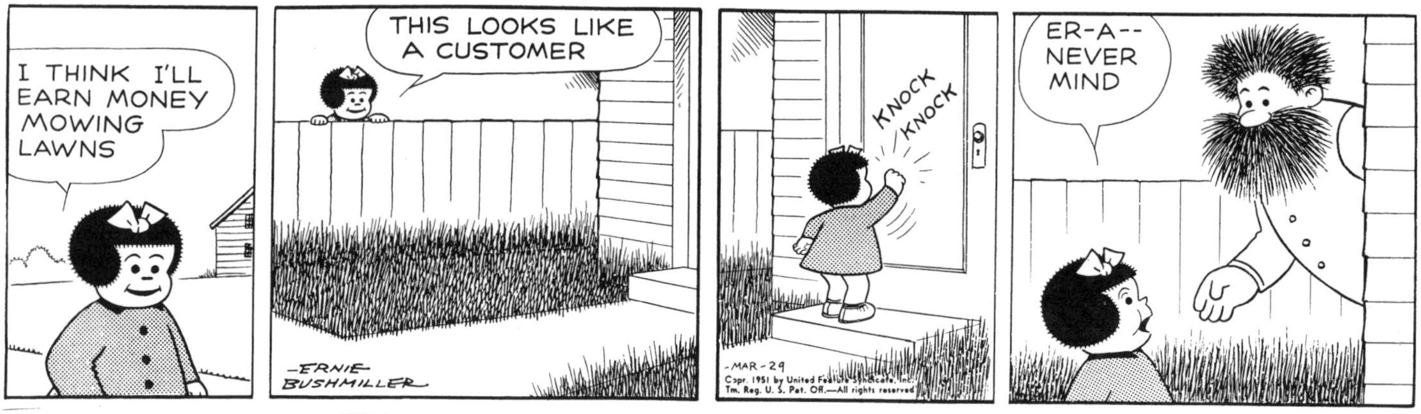
I THINK I'LL EARN MONEY MOWING LAWNS
THIS LOOKS LIKE A CUSTOMER
-ERNIE BUSHMILLER
KNOCK KNOCK
-MAR-29
Copr. 1951 by United Feature Syndicate, Inc. Tm. Reg. U. S. Pat. Off.—All rights reserved
ER-A-- NEVER MIND

FOOD

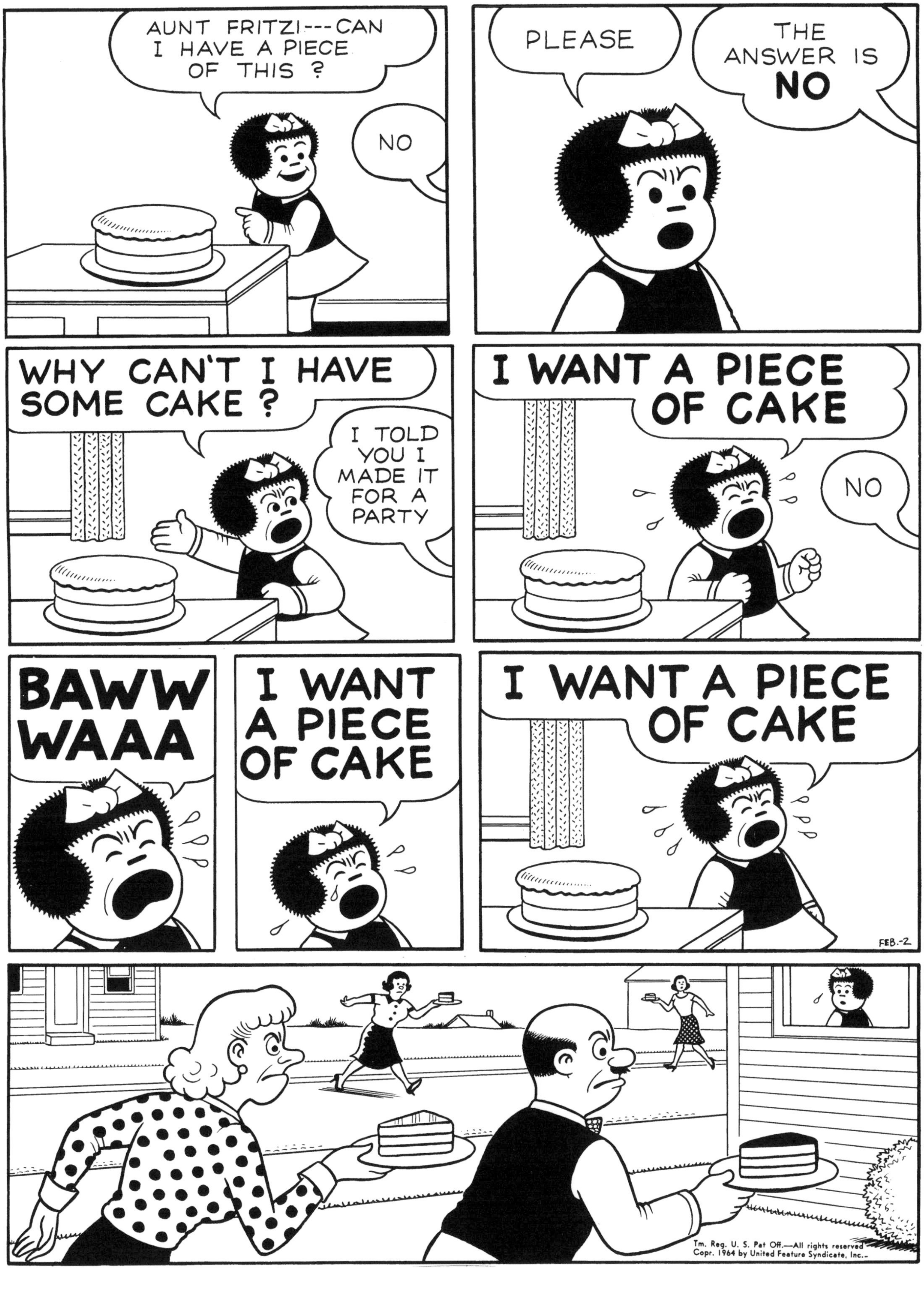
AUNT FRITZI---CAN I HAVE A PIECE OF THIS ?
NO
PLEASE
THE ANSWER IS NO
WHY CAN'T I HAVE SOME CAKE ?
I TOLD YOU I MADE IT FOR A PARTY
I WANT A PIECE OF CAKE
NO
BAWW WAAA
I WANT A PIECE OF CAKE
I WANT A PIECE OF CAKE
FEB.-2
Tm. Reg. U. S. Pat Off.—All rights reserved
Copr. 1964 by United Feature Syndicate, Inc.

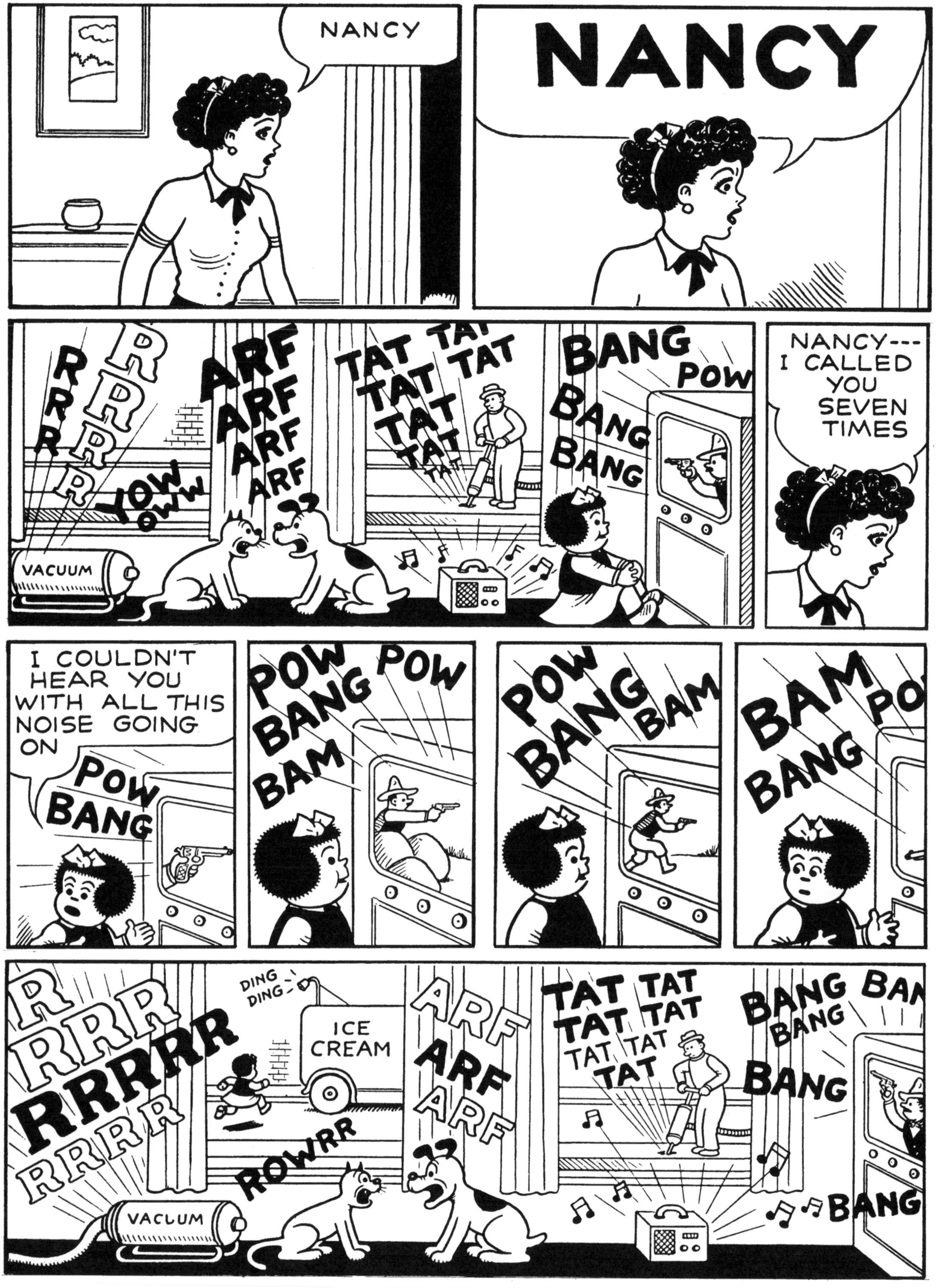
NANCY
NANCY
R R R R
R R R R
ARF ARF ARF ARF
YOW OWW
TAT TAT TAT TAT TAT TAT TAT
BANG POW BANG BANG
VACUUM
NANCY--- I CALLED YOU SEVEN TIMES
I COULDN'T HEAR YOU WITH ALL THIS NOISE GOING ON
POW BANG
POW BANG POW BAM
POW BANG BAM
BAM BANG
R RRR RRRRR RRRRR RRRR
DING DING
ICE CREAM
ARF ARF ARF
ROWRR
TAT TAT TAT TAT TAT TAT TAT
BANG BANG BANG BANG
BANG
VACUUM

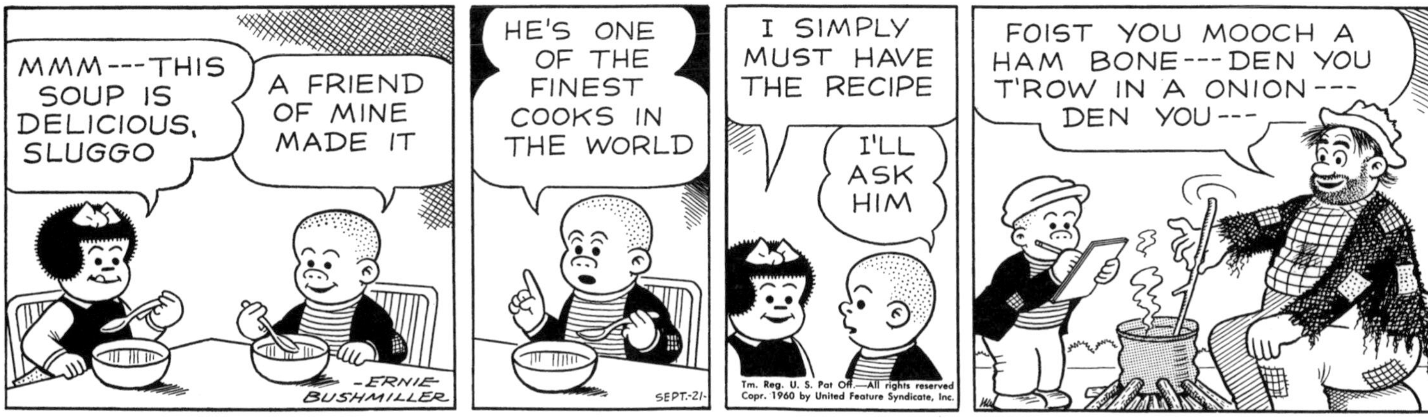
MMM---THIS SOUP IS DELICIOUS, SLUGGO
A FRIEND OF MINE MADE IT
-ERNIE BUSHMILLER
HE'S ONE OF THE FINEST COOKS IN THE WORLD
SEPT.-21-
I SIMPLY MUST HAVE THE RECIPE
I'LL ASK HIM
Tm. Reg. U. S. Pat. Off.—All rights reserved Copr. 1960 by United Feature Syndicate, Inc.
FOIST YOU MOOCH A HAM BONE---DEN YOU T'ROW IN A ONION---DEN YOU---

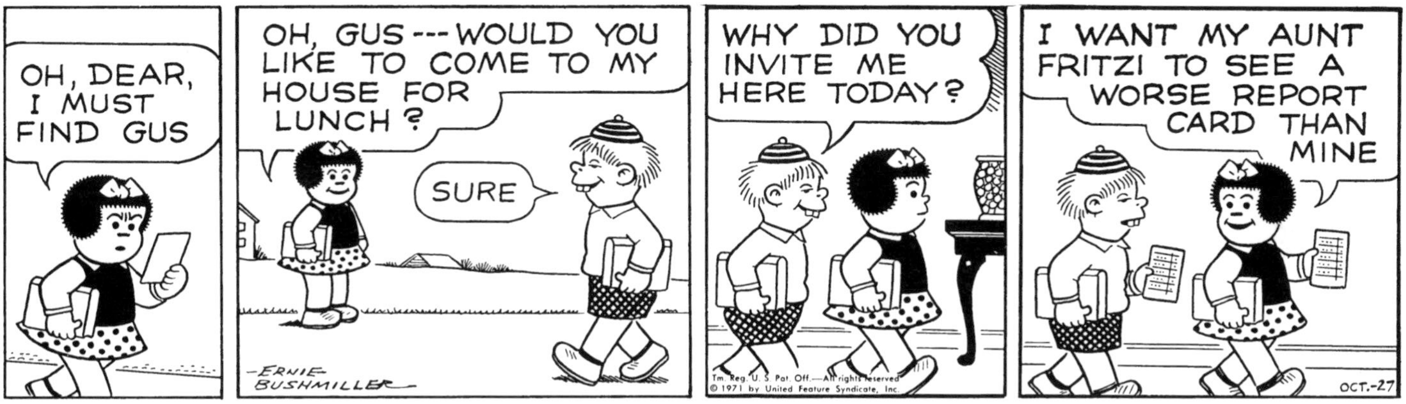
OH, DEAR, I MUST FIND GUS
OH, GUS---WOULD YOU LIKE TO COME TO MY HOUSE FOR LUNCH?
SURE
-ERNIE BUSHMILLER
WHY DID YOU INVITE ME HERE TODAY?
Tm. Reg. U. S. Pat. Off.—All rights reserved © 1971 by United Feature Syndicate, Inc.
I WANT MY AUNT FRITZI TO SEE A WORSE REPORT CARD THAN MINE
OCT.-27

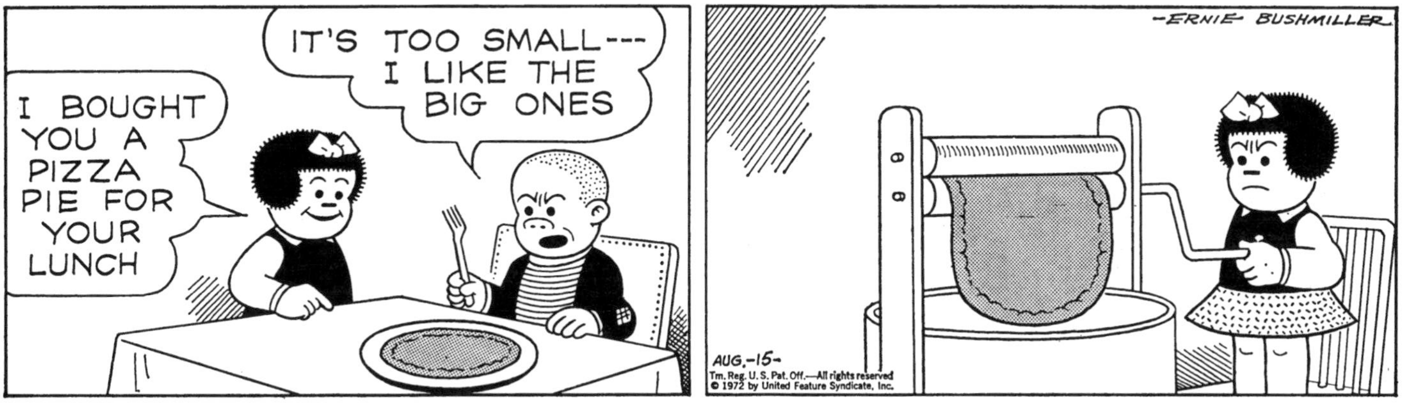
I BOUGHT YOU A PIZZA PIE FOR YOUR LUNCH
IT'S TOO SMALL--- I LIKE THE BIG ONES
-ERNIE BUSHMILLER
AUG.-15-
Tm. Reg. U. S. Pat. Off.—All rights reserved © 1972 by United Feature Syndicate, Inc.

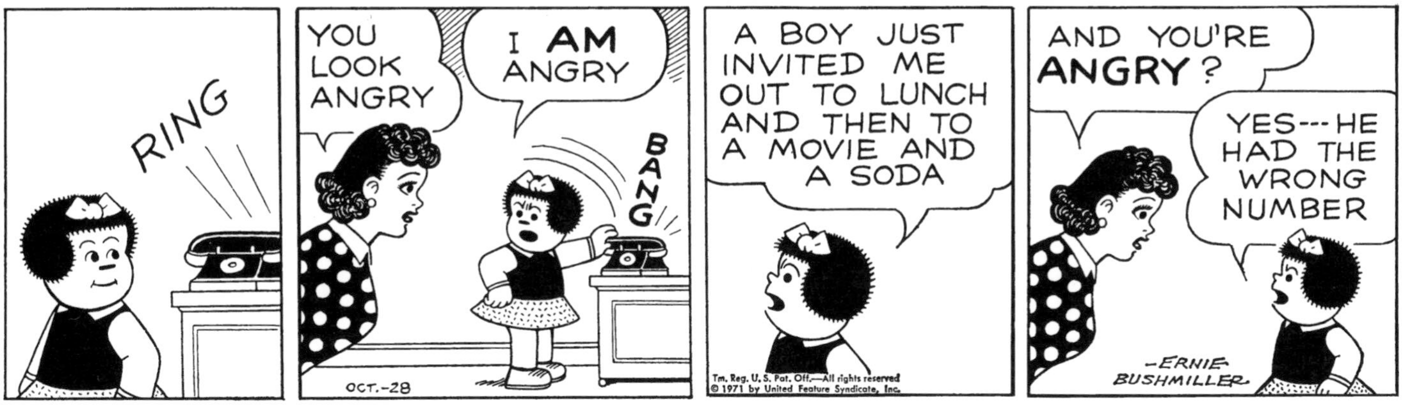
RING
YOU LOOK ANGRY
I AM ANGRY
BANG
OCT.-28
A BOY JUST INVITED ME OUT TO LUNCH AND THEN TO A MOVIE AND A SODA
Tm. Reg. U. S. Pat. Off.—All rights reserved © 1971 by United Feature Syndicate, Inc.
AND YOU'RE ANGRY?
YES---HE HAD THE WRONG NUMBER
-ERNIE BUSHMILLER

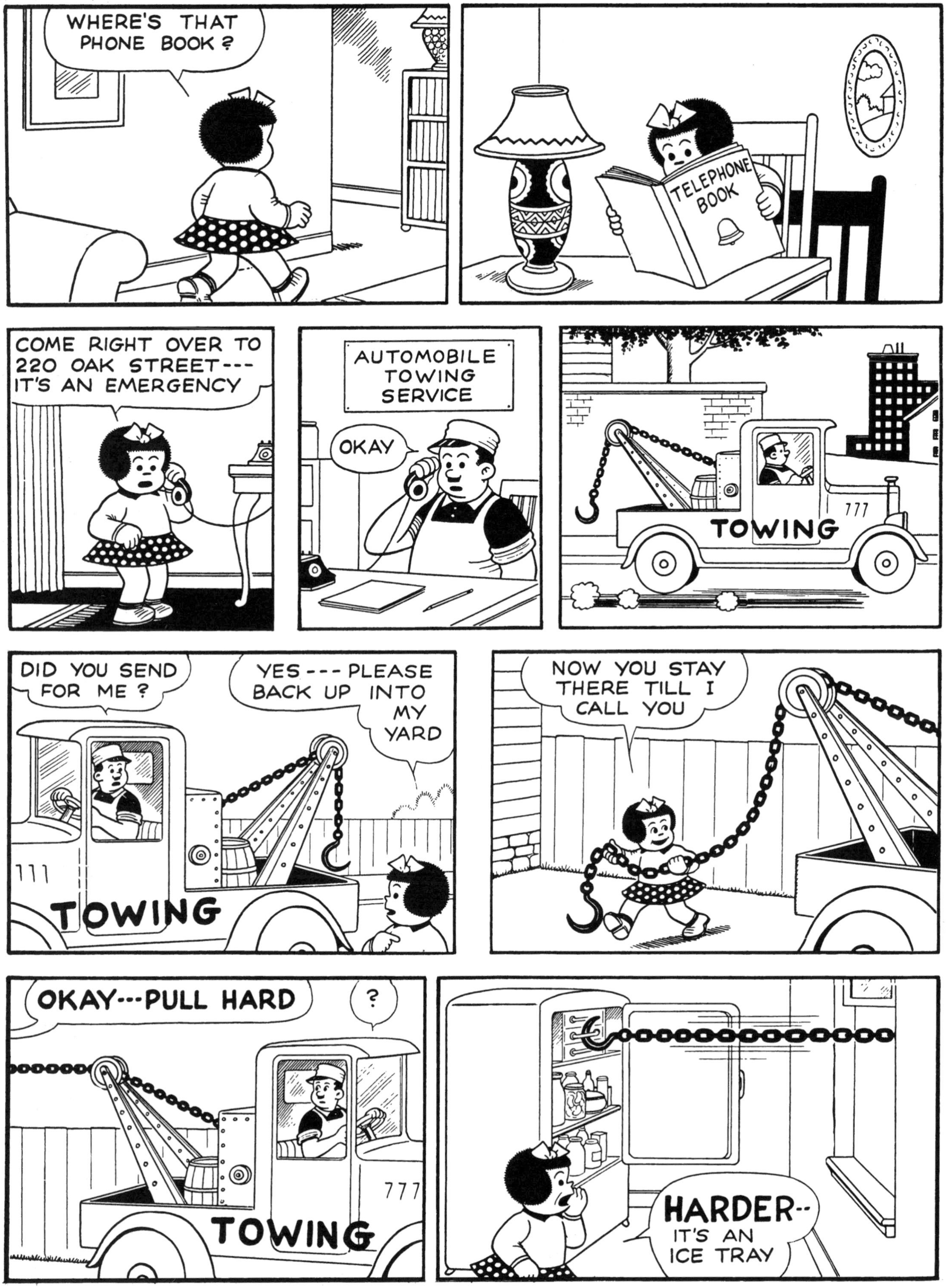

WHERE'S THAT PHONE BOOK?
TELEPHONE BOOK
COME RIGHT OVER TO 220 OAK STREET--- IT'S AN EMERGENCY
AUTOMOBILE TOWING SERVICE
OKAY
777
TOWING
DID YOU SEND FOR ME?
YES --- PLEASE BACK UP INTO MY YARD
777
TOWING
NOW YOU STAY THERE TILL I CALL YOU
OKAY---PULL HARD
?
777
TOWING
HARDER-- IT'S AN ICE TRAY

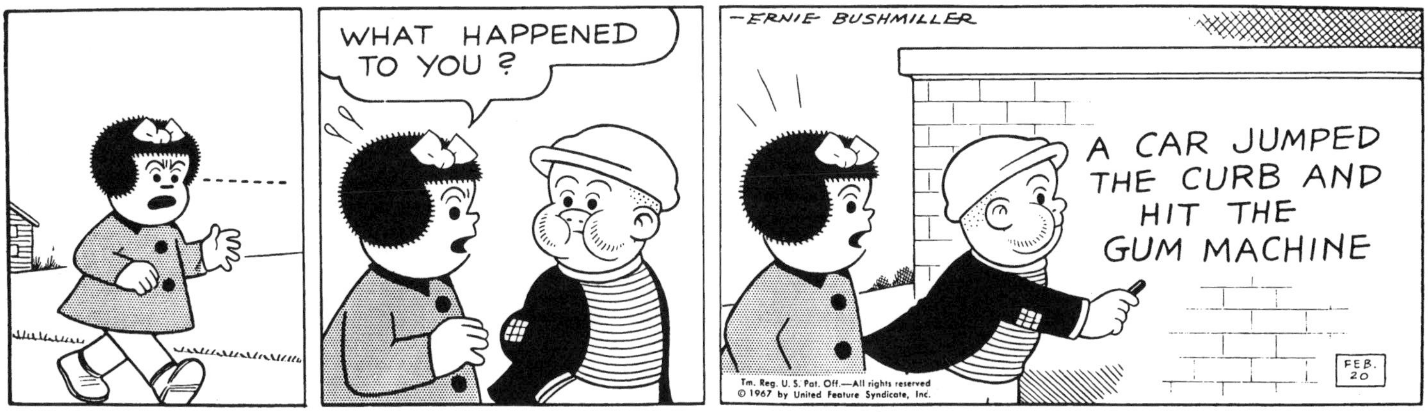
WHAT HAPPENED TO YOU ?
-ERNIE BUSHMILLER
A CAR JUMPED THE CURB AND HIT THE GUM MACHINE
FEB. 20
Tm. Reg. U. S. Pat. Off.—All rights reserved © 1967 by United Feature Syndicate, Inc.

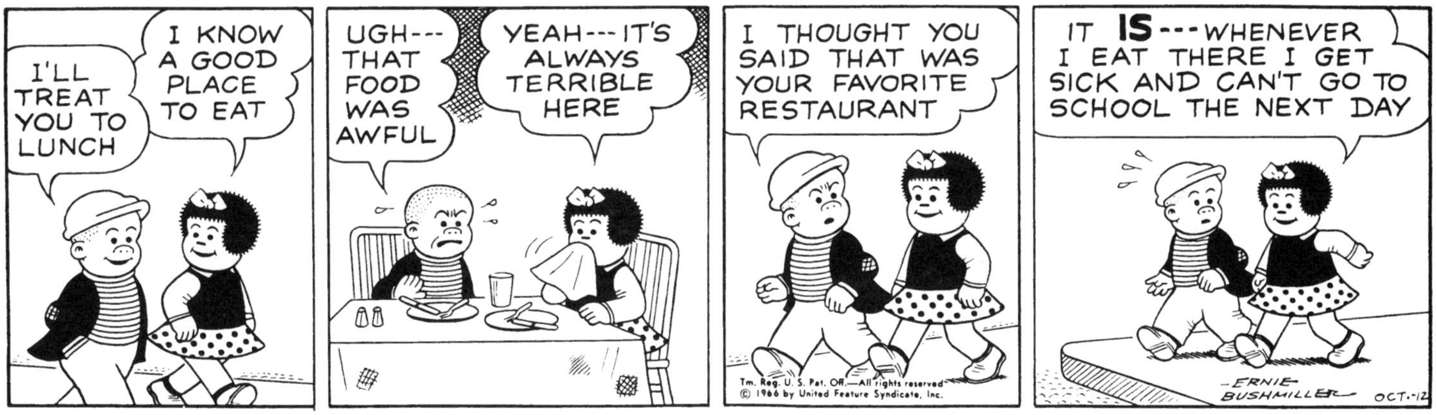
I'LL TREAT YOU TO LUNCH
I KNOW A GOOD PLACE TO EAT
UGH--- THAT FOOD WAS AWFUL
YEAH--- IT'S ALWAYS TERRIBLE HERE
I THOUGHT YOU SAID THAT WAS YOUR FAVORITE RESTAURANT
Tm. Reg. U. S. Pat. Off.—All rights reserved © 1966 by United Feature Syndicate, Inc.
IT IS--- WHENEVER I EAT THERE I GET SICK AND CAN'T GO TO SCHOOL THE NEXT DAY
-ERNIE BUSHMILLER
OCT.-12

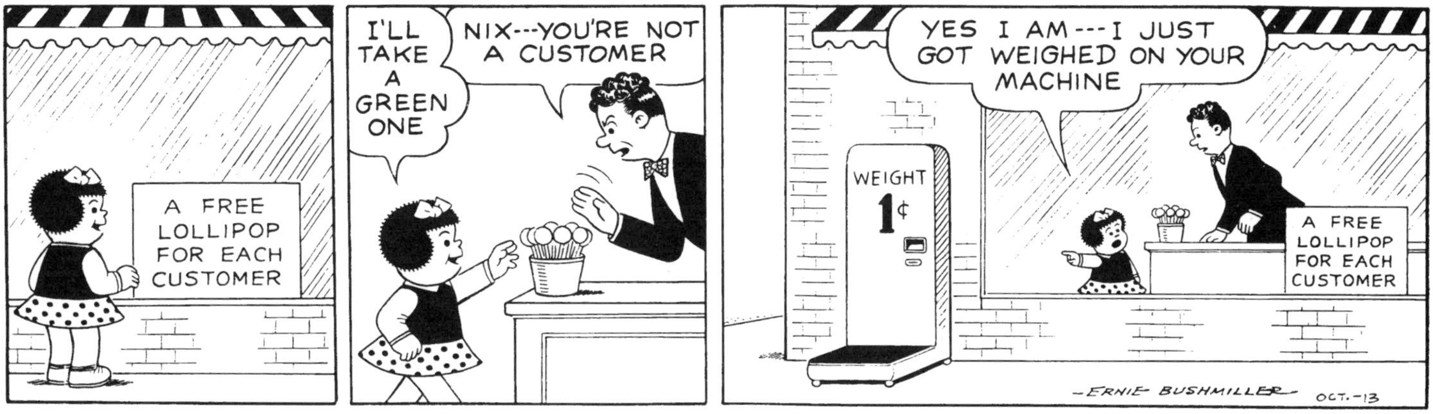
A FREE LOLLIPOP FOR EACH CUSTOMER
I'LL TAKE A GREEN ONE
NIX---YOU'RE NOT A CUSTOMER
YES I AM --- I JUST GOT WEIGHED ON YOUR MACHINE
WEIGHT 1¢
A FREE LOLLIPOP FOR EACH CUSTOMER
-ERNIE BUSHMILLER
OCT.-13

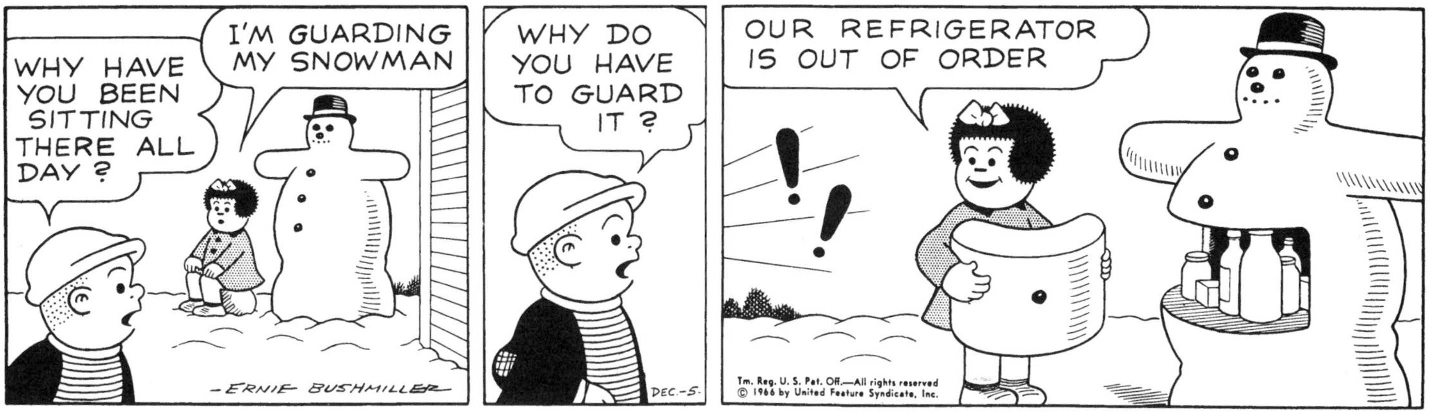
WHY HAVE YOU BEEN SITTING THERE ALL DAY ?
I'M GUARDING MY SNOWMAN
-ERNIE BUSHMILLER
WHY DO YOU HAVE TO GUARD IT ?
DEC.-5.
OUR REFRIGERATOR IS OUT OF ORDER
Tm. Reg. U. S. Pat. Off.—All rights reserved © 1966 by United Feature Syndicate, Inc.

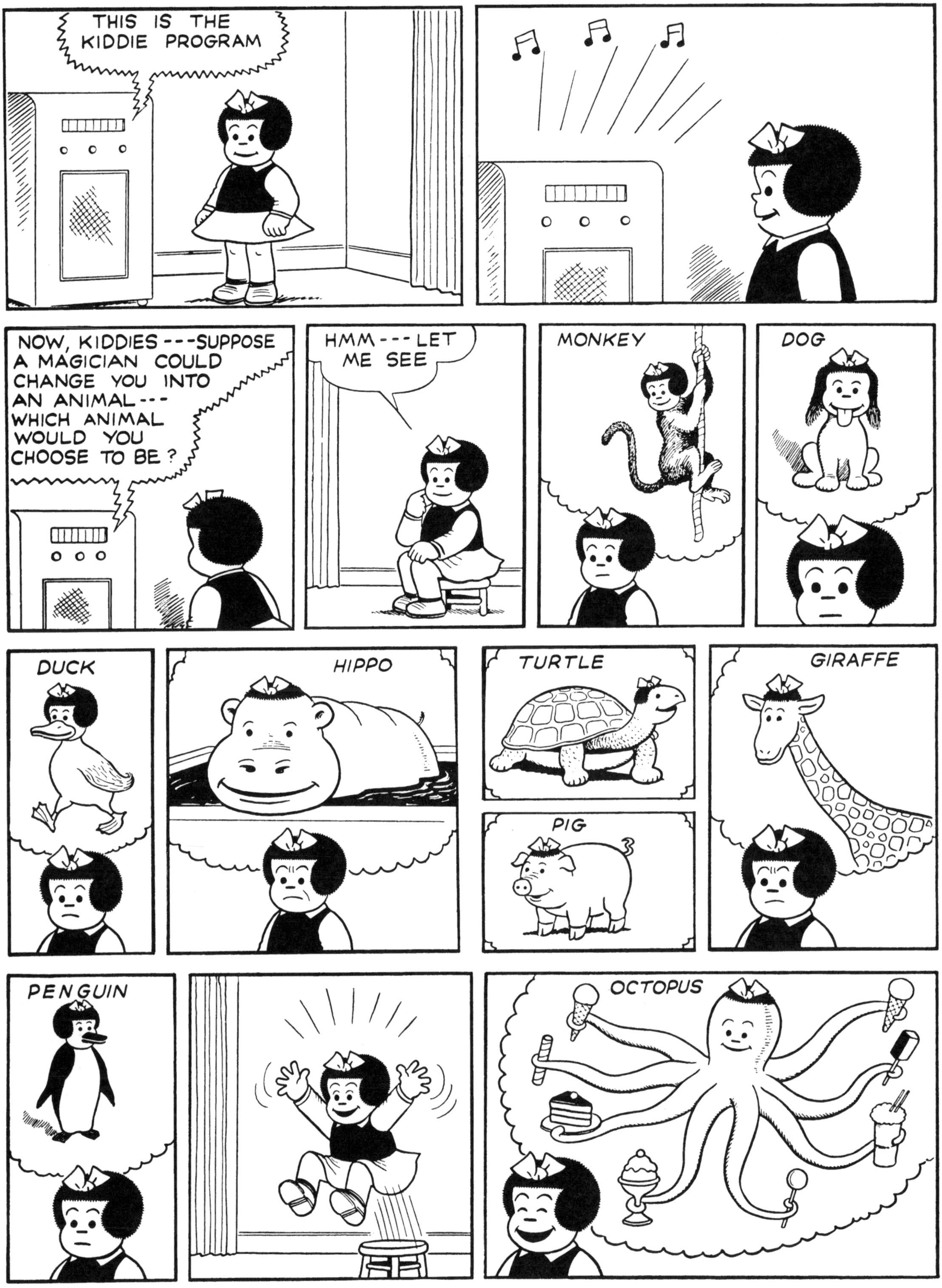
THIS IS THE KIDDIE PROGRAM
NOW, KIDDIES---SUPPOSE A MAGICIAN COULD CHANGE YOU INTO AN ANIMAL--- WHICH ANIMAL WOULD YOU CHOOSE TO BE?
HMM---LET ME SEE
MONKEY
DOG
DUCK
HIPPO
TURTLE
PIG
GIRAFFE
PENGUIN
OCTOPUS

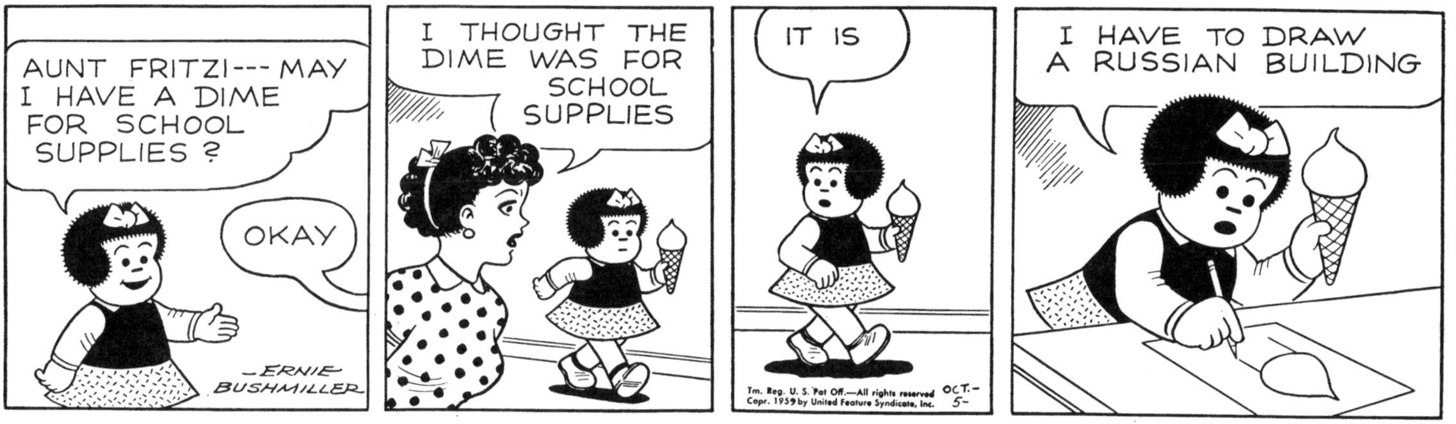
AUNT FRITZI---MAY I HAVE A DIME FOR SCHOOL SUPPLIES ?
OKAY
ERNIE BUSHMILLER
I THOUGHT THE DIME WAS FOR SCHOOL SUPPLIES
IT IS
Tm. Reg. U. S. Pat Off.—All rights reserved Copr. 1959 by United Feature Syndicate, Inc.
OCT.-5-
I HAVE TO DRAW A RUSSIAN BUILDING

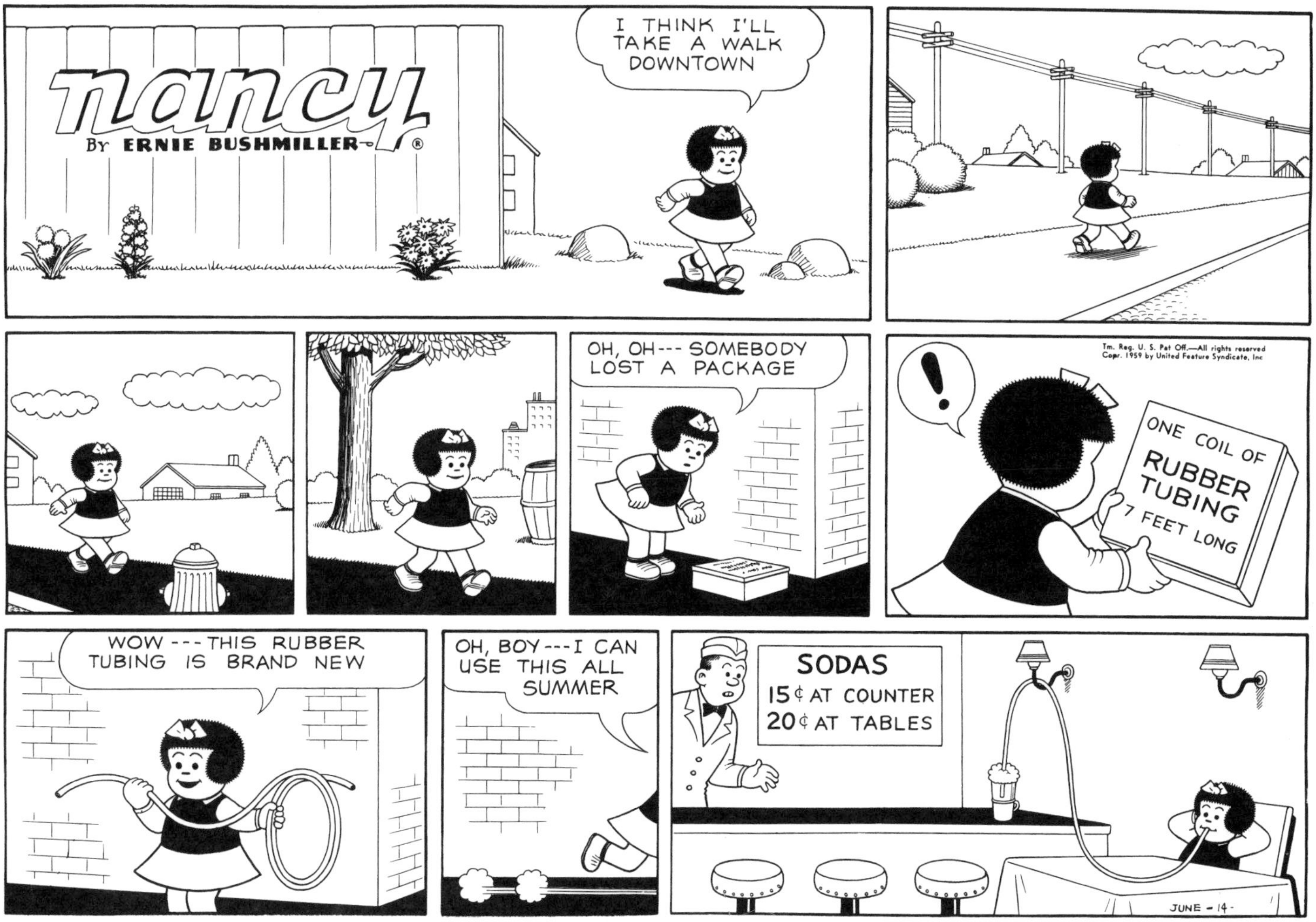
nancy
By ERNIE BUSHMILLER ®
I THINK I'LL TAKE A WALK DOWNTOWN
OH, OH--- SOMEBODY LOST A PACKAGE
!
Tm. Reg. U. S. Pat Off.—All rights reserved Copr. 1959 by United Feature Syndicate, Inc
ONE COIL OF RUBBER TUBING 7 FEET LONG
WOW---THIS RUBBER TUBING IS BRAND NEW
OH, BOY---I CAN USE THIS ALL SUMMER
SODAS
15¢ AT COUNTER
20¢ AT TABLES
JUNE-14-

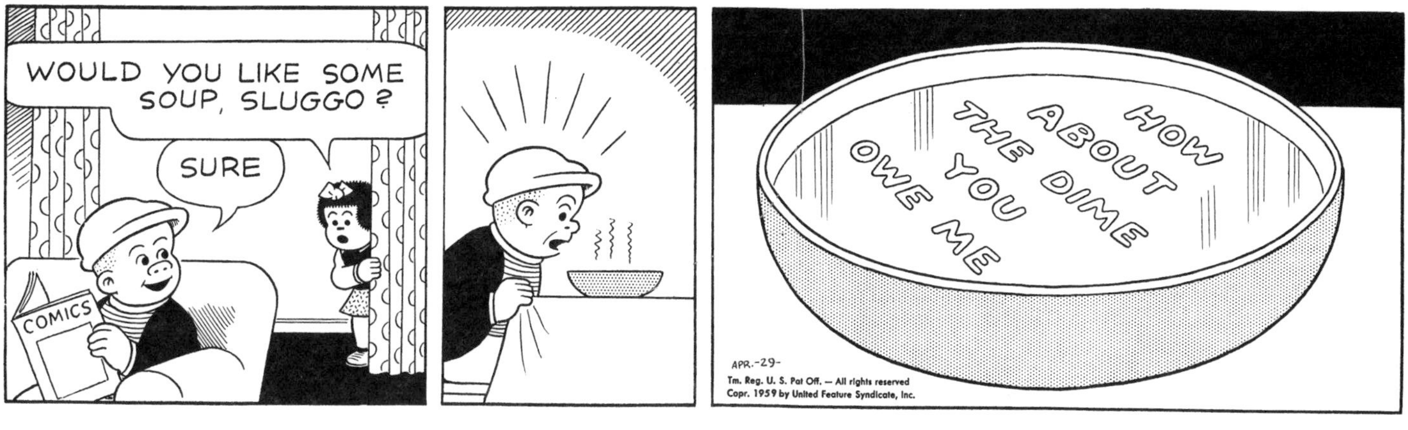
WOULD YOU LIKE SOME SOUP, SLUGGO ?
SURE
COMICS
HOW ABOUT THE DIME YOU OWE ME
APR.-29-
Tm. Reg. U. S. Pat Off. — All rights reserved Copr. 1959 by United Feature Syndicate, Inc.

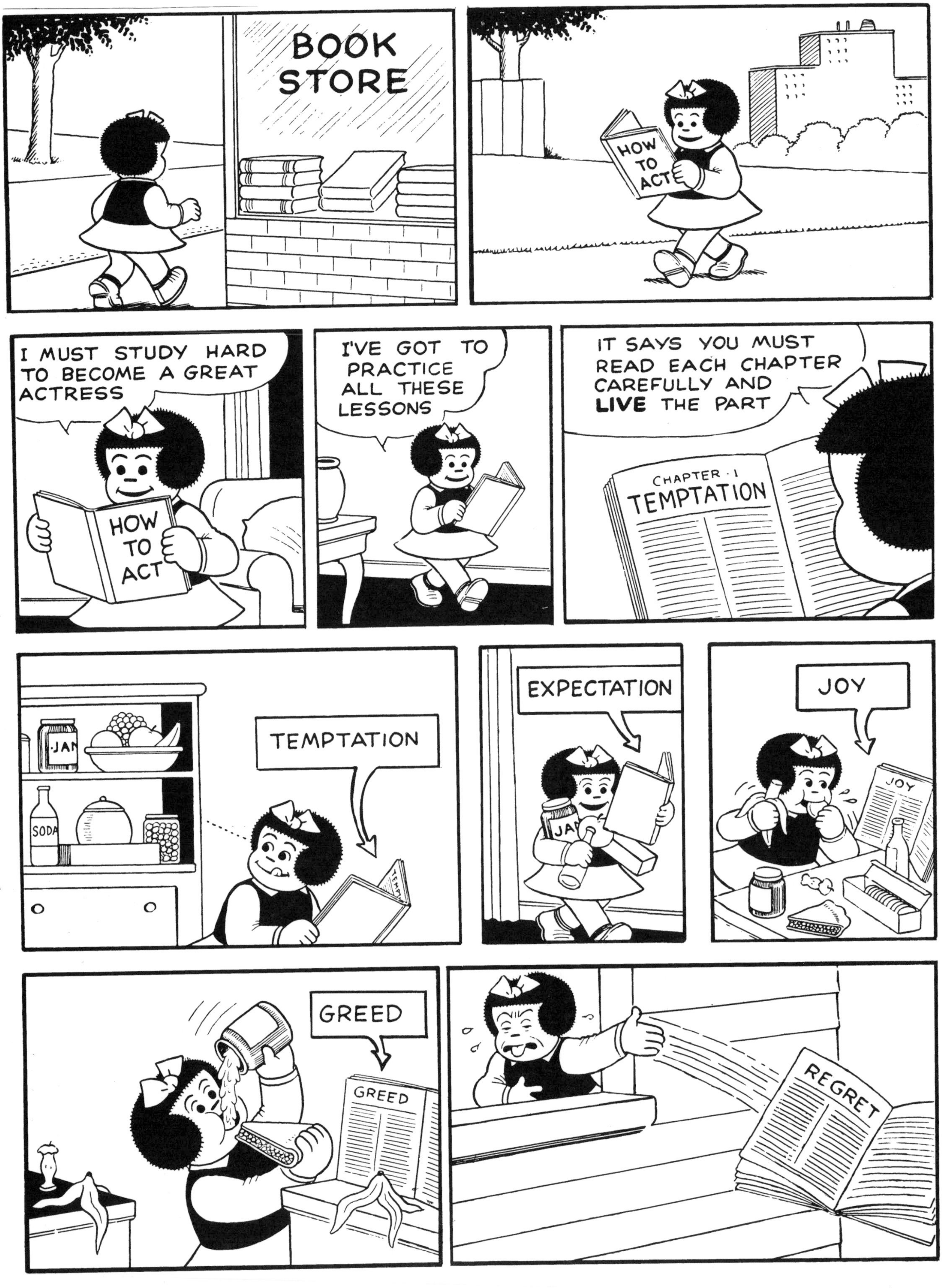

BOOK STORE
HOW TO ACT
I MUST STUDY HARD TO BECOME A GREAT ACTRESS
HOW TO ACT
I'VE GOT TO PRACTICE ALL THESE LESSONS
IT SAYS YOU MUST READ EACH CHAPTER CAREFULLY AND **LIVE** THE PART
CHAPTER · I
TEMPTATION
JAM
SODA
TEMPTATION
EXPECTATION
JOY
JOY
GREED
GREED
REGRET

Dis-stink-ly Unpopular

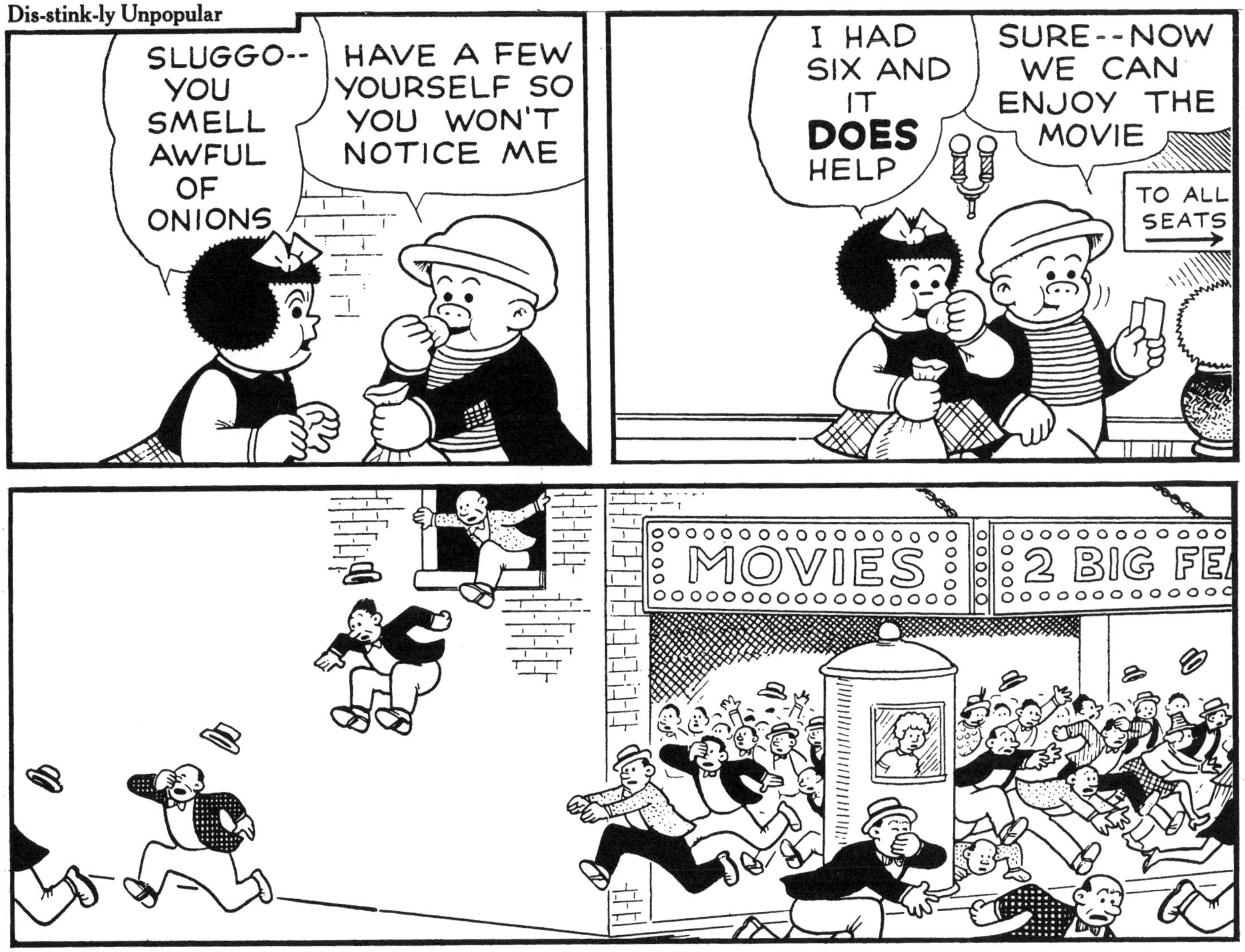

SLUGGO-- YOU SMELL AWFUL OF ONIONS
HAVE A FEW YOURSELF SO YOU WON'T NOTICE ME
I HAD SIX AND IT **DOES** HELP
SURE--NOW WE CAN ENJOY THE MOVIE
TO ALL SEATS
MOVIES
2 BIG FE

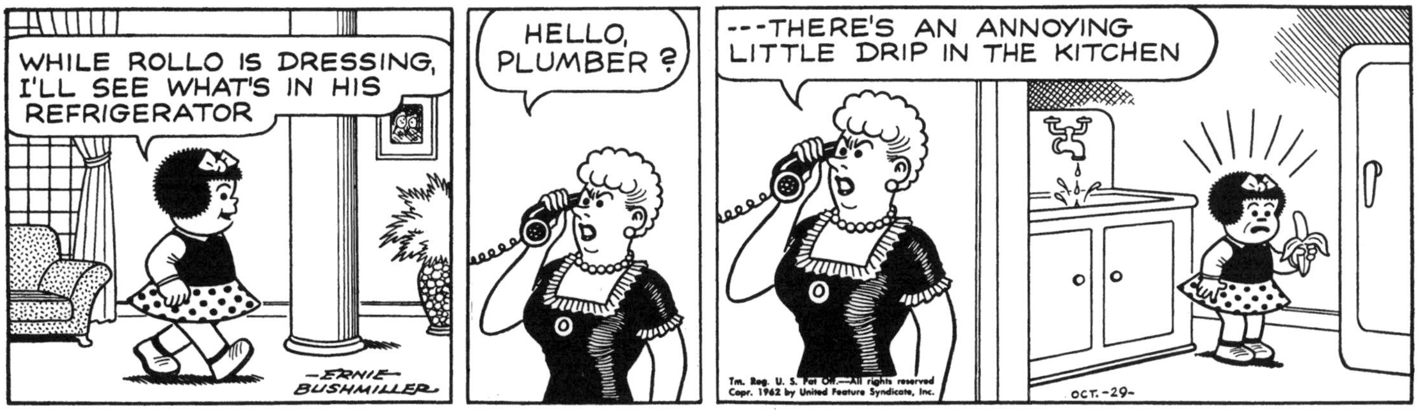

WHILE ROLLO IS DRESSING, I'LL SEE WHAT'S IN HIS REFRIGERATOR
-ERNIE- BUSHMILLER
HELLO, PLUMBER ?
---THERE'S AN ANNOYING LITTLE DRIP IN THE KITCHEN
Tm. Reg. U. S. Pat Off.—All rights reserved Copr. 1962 by United Feature Syndicate, Inc.
OCT.-29-

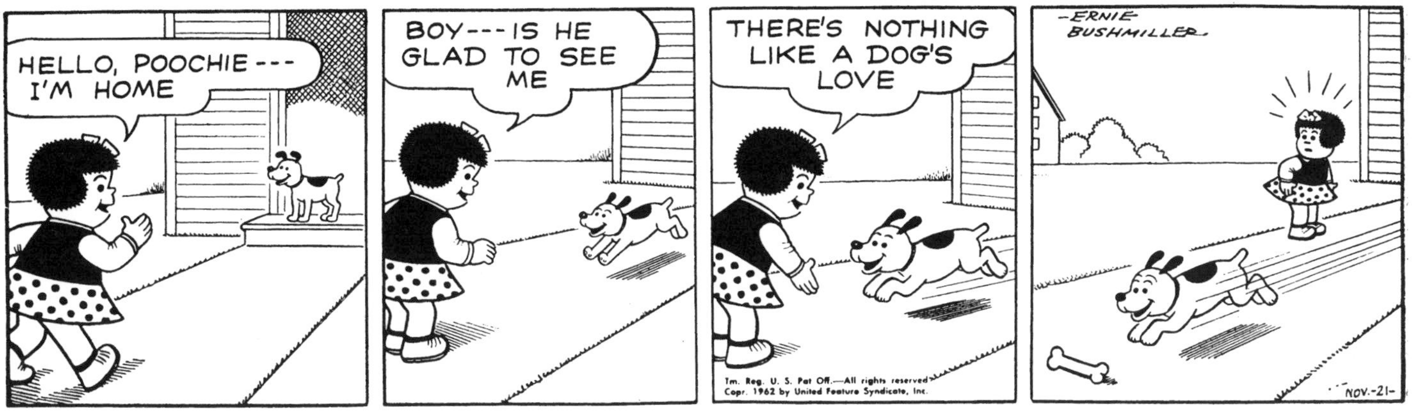

HELLO, POOCHIE--- I'M HOME
BOY---IS HE GLAD TO SEE ME
THERE'S NOTHING LIKE A DOG'S LOVE
Tm. Reg. U. S. Pat Off.—All rights reserved Copr. 1962 by United Feature Syndicate, Inc.
-ERNIE- BUSHMILLER
NOV.-21-

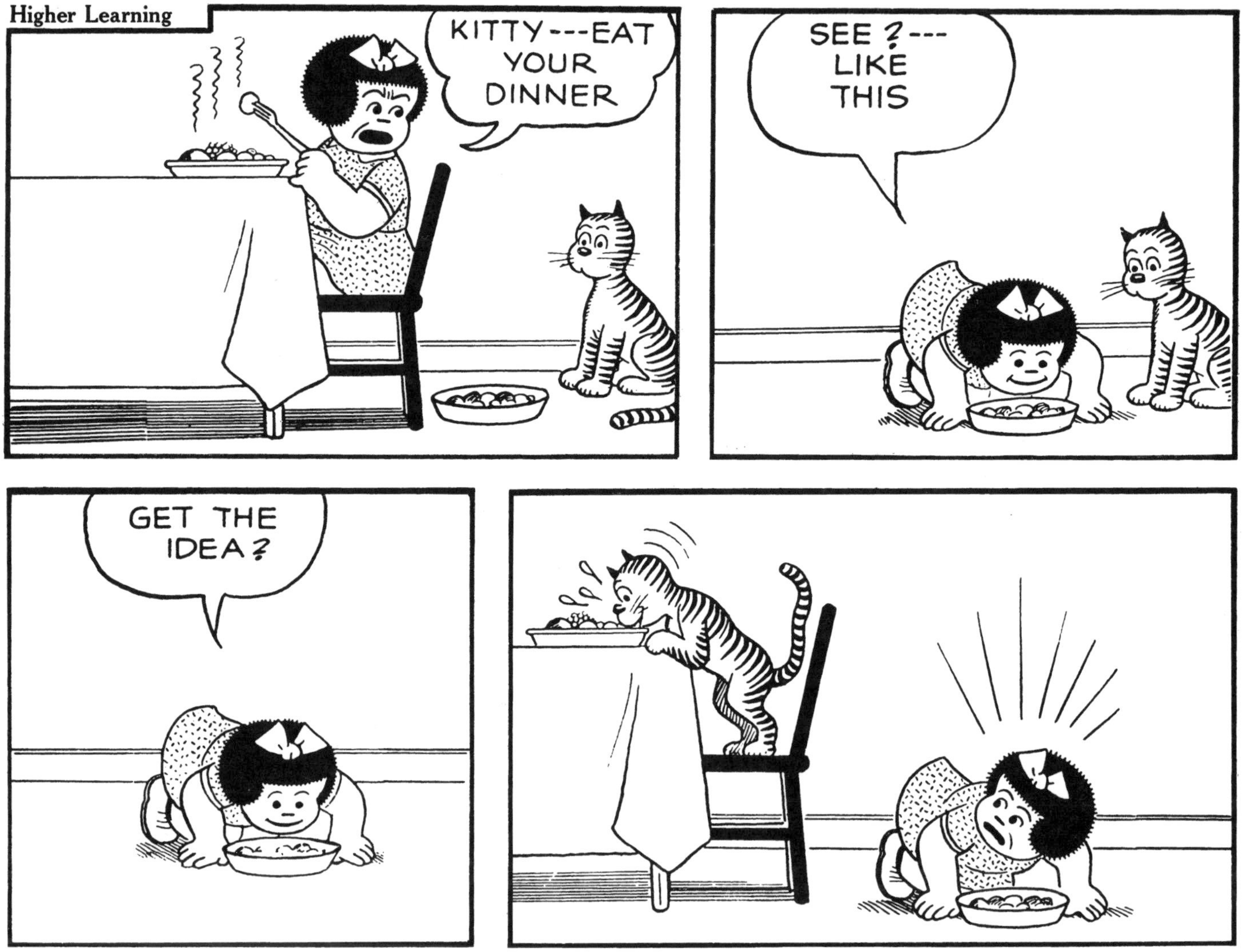
KITTY---EAT YOUR DINNER
SEE ?--- LIKE THIS
GET THE IDEA ?

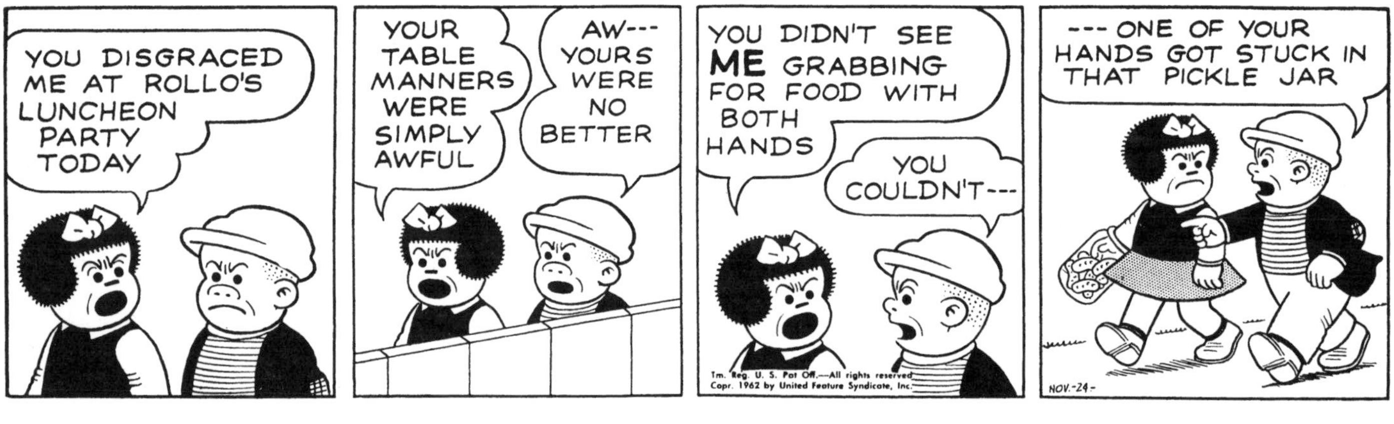
YOU DISGRACED ME AT ROLLO'S LUNCHEON PARTY TODAY
YOUR TABLE MANNERS WERE SIMPLY AWFUL
AW--- YOURS WERE NO BETTER
YOU DIDN'T SEE **ME** GRABBING FOR FOOD WITH BOTH HANDS
YOU COULDN'T---
--- ONE OF YOUR HANDS GOT STUCK IN THAT PICKLE JAR
Tm. Reg. U. S. Pat. Off.—All rights reserved Copr. 1962 by United Feature Syndicate, Inc.
NOV.-24-

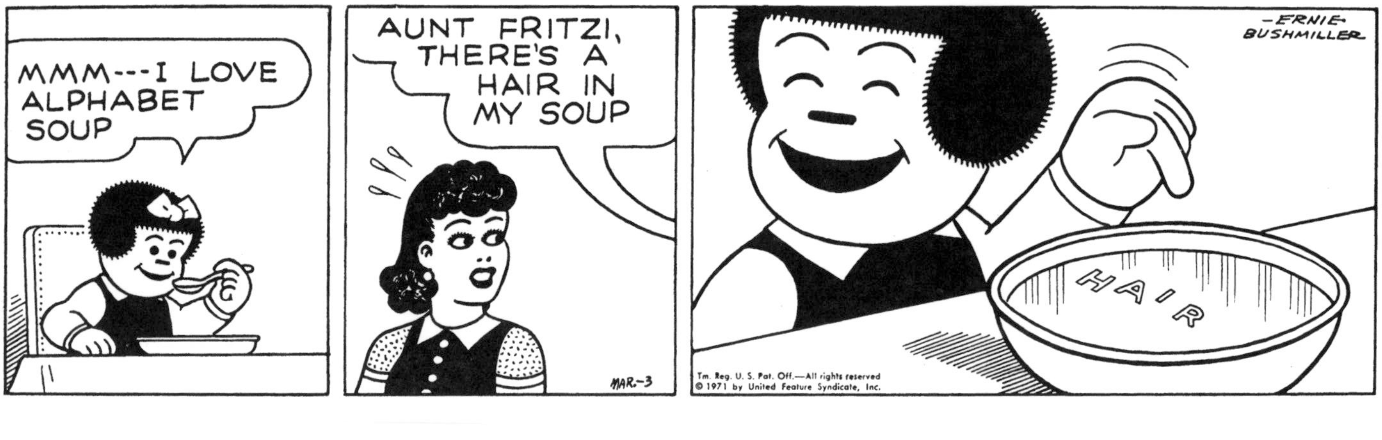
MMM---I LOVE ALPHABET SOUP
AUNT FRITZI, THERE'S A HAIR IN MY SOUP
MAR.-3
-ERNIE- BUSHMILLER
HAIR
Tm. Reg. U. S. Pat. Off.—All rights reserved © 1971 by United Feature Syndicate, Inc.

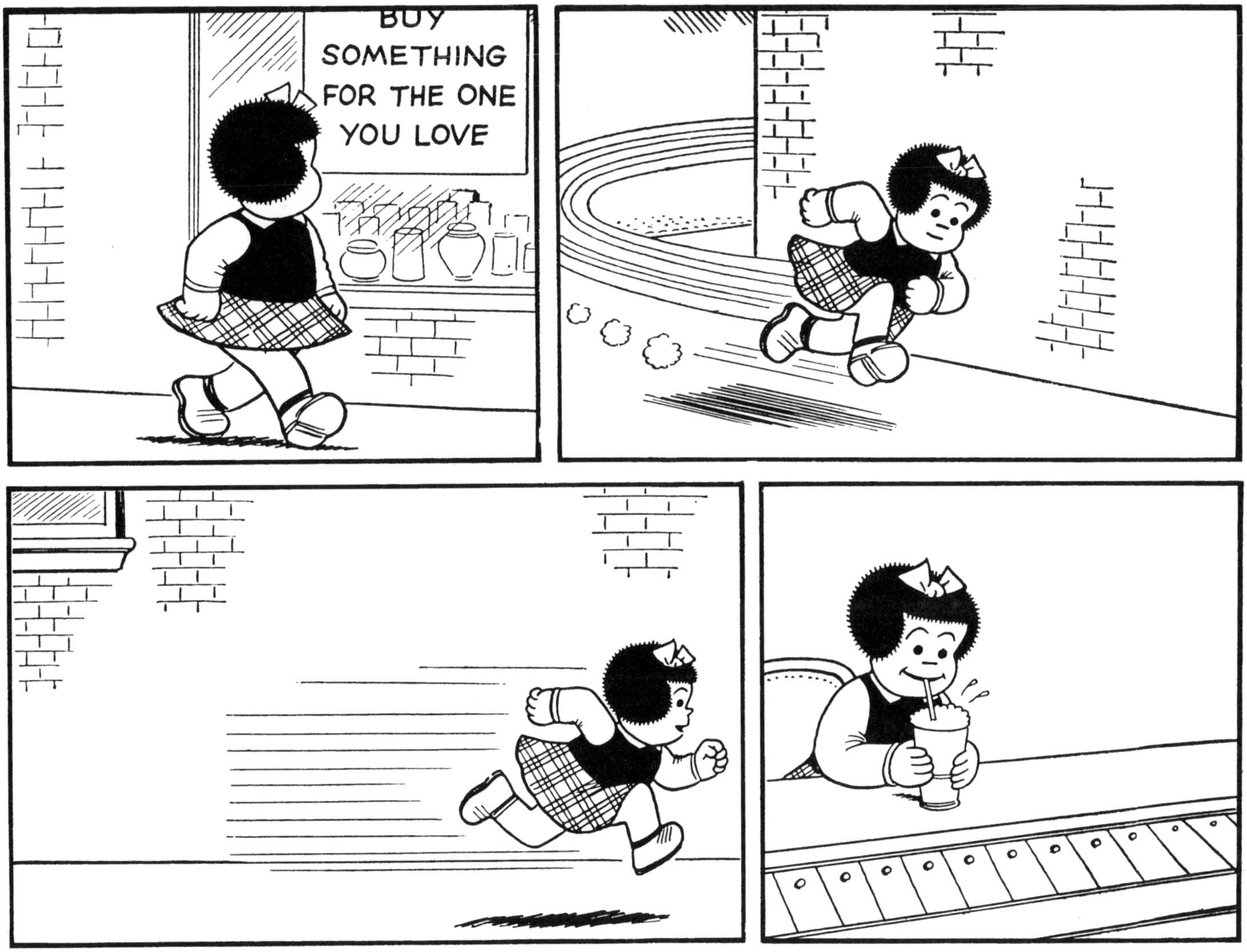
BUY SOMETHING FOR THE ONE YOU LOVE

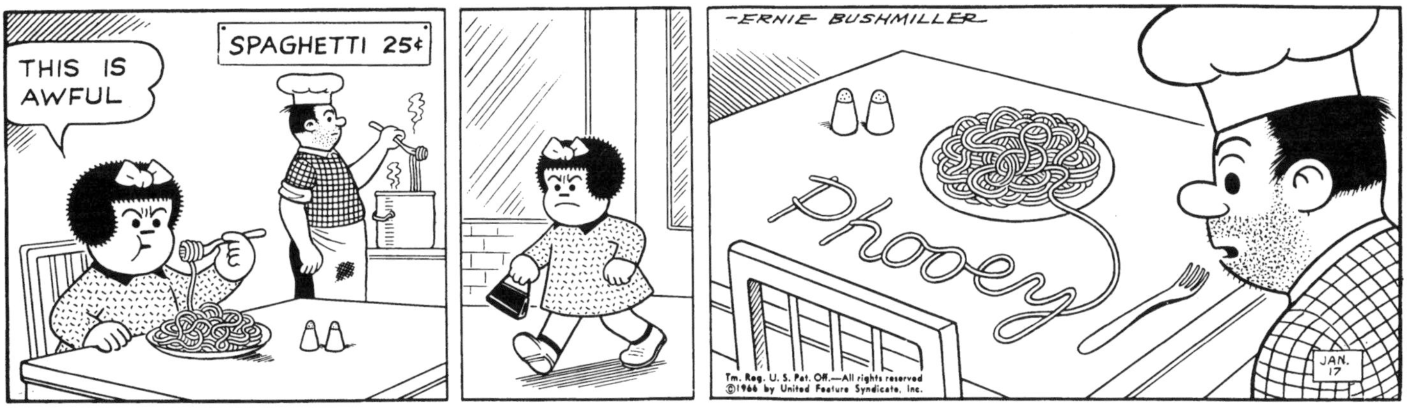
THIS IS AWFUL
SPAGHETTI 25¢
-ERNIE BUSHMILLER
Phooey
Tm. Reg. U. S. Pat. Off.—All rights reserved ©1966 by United Feature Syndicate, Inc.
JAN. 17

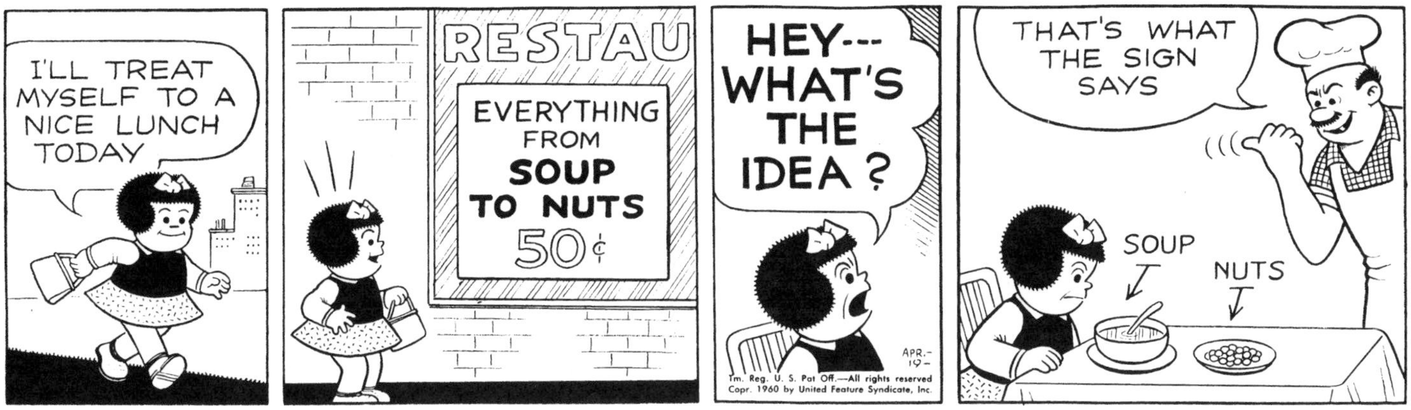
I'LL TREAT MYSELF TO A NICE LUNCH TODAY
RESTAU
EVERYTHING FROM SOUP TO NUTS 50¢
HEY--- WHAT'S THE IDEA?
APR. 19
Tm. Reg. U. S. Pat. Off.—All rights reserved Copr. 1960 by United Feature Syndicate, Inc.
THAT'S WHAT THE SIGN SAYS
SOUP
NUTS

Bass Wishes!

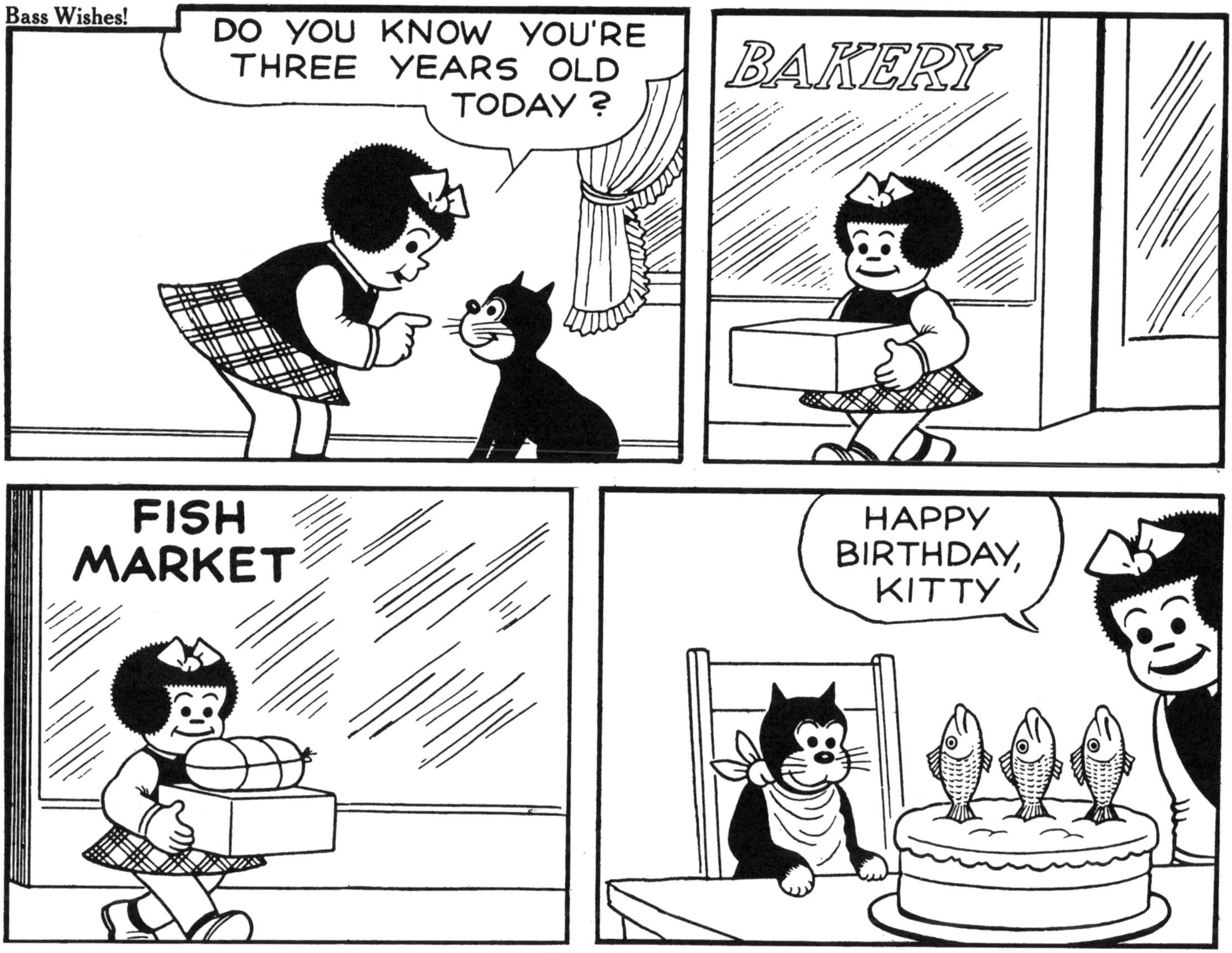

DO YOU KNOW YOU'RE THREE YEARS OLD TODAY ?
BAKERY
FISH MARKET
HAPPY BIRTHDAY, KITTY

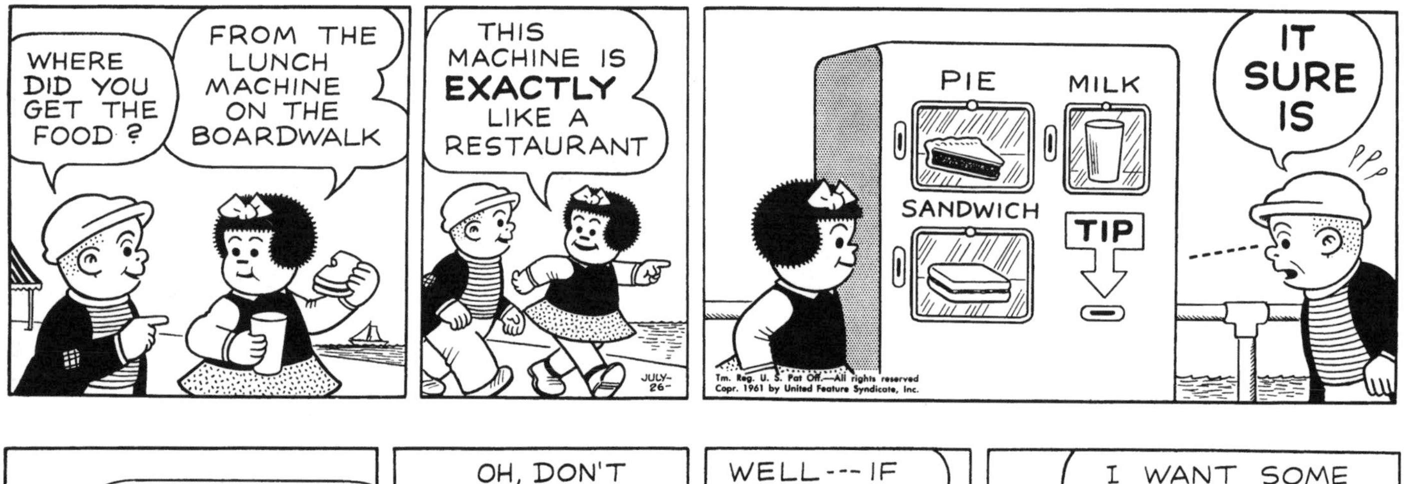

WHERE DID YOU GET THE FOOD ?
FROM THE LUNCH MACHINE ON THE BOARDWALK
THIS MACHINE IS **EXACTLY** LIKE A RESTAURANT
JULY-26-
PIE
MILK
SANDWICH
TIP
IT SURE IS
Tm. Reg. U. S. Pat Off.—All rights reserved
Copr. 1961 by United Feature Syndicate, Inc.

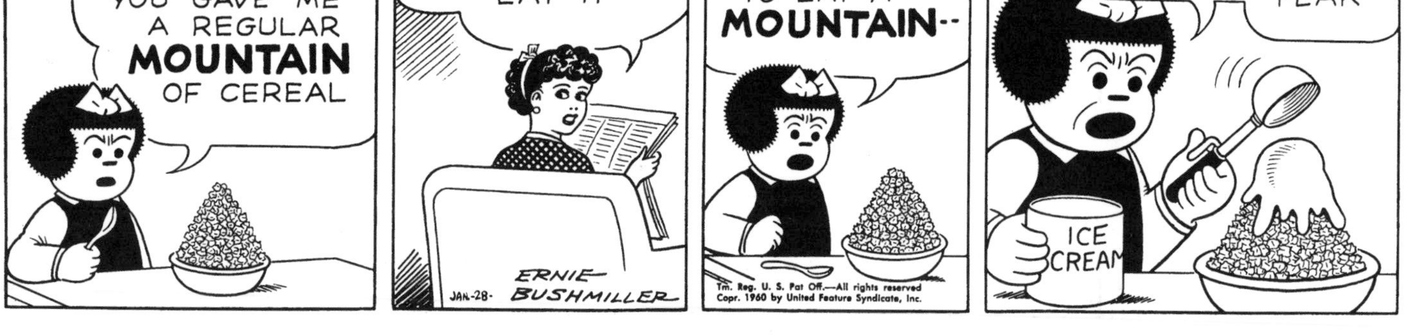

AUNT FRITZI--- YOU GAVE ME A REGULAR **MOUNTAIN** OF CEREAL
OH, DON'T EXAGGERATE--- EAT IT
JAN.-28-
ERNIE BUSHMILLER
WELL---IF I'M GOING TO EAT A **MOUNTAIN**--
Tm. Reg. U. S. Pat Off.—All rights reserved
Copr. 1960 by United Feature Syndicate, Inc.
I WANT SOME SNOW ON THE PEAK
ICE CREAM

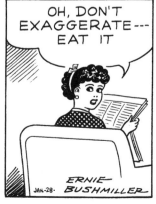

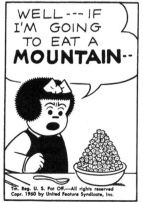

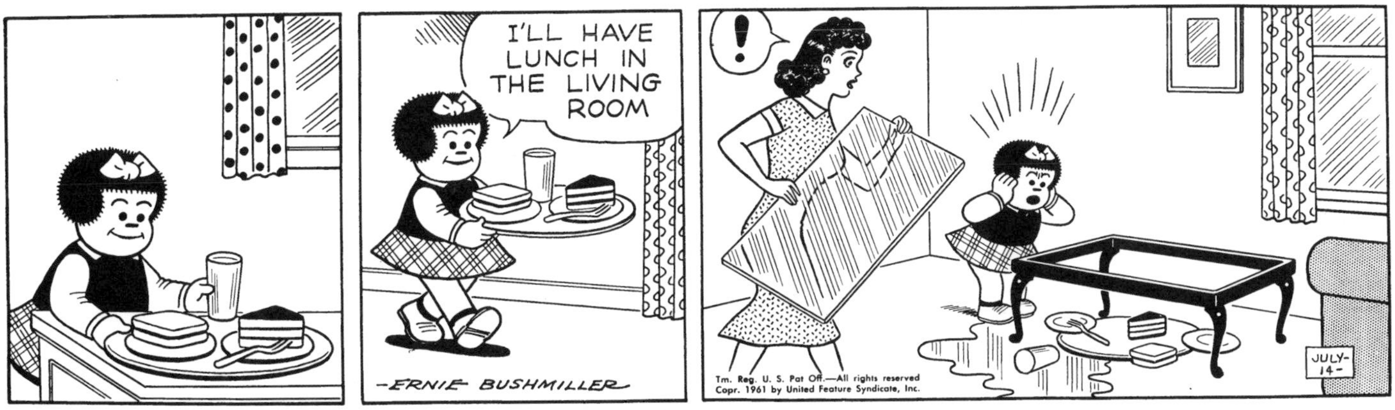
I'LL HAVE LUNCH IN THE LIVING ROOM
-ERNIE BUSHMILLER
!
Tm. Reg. U. S. Pat Off.—All rights reserved
Copr. 1961 by United Feature Syndicate, Inc.
JULY-14-

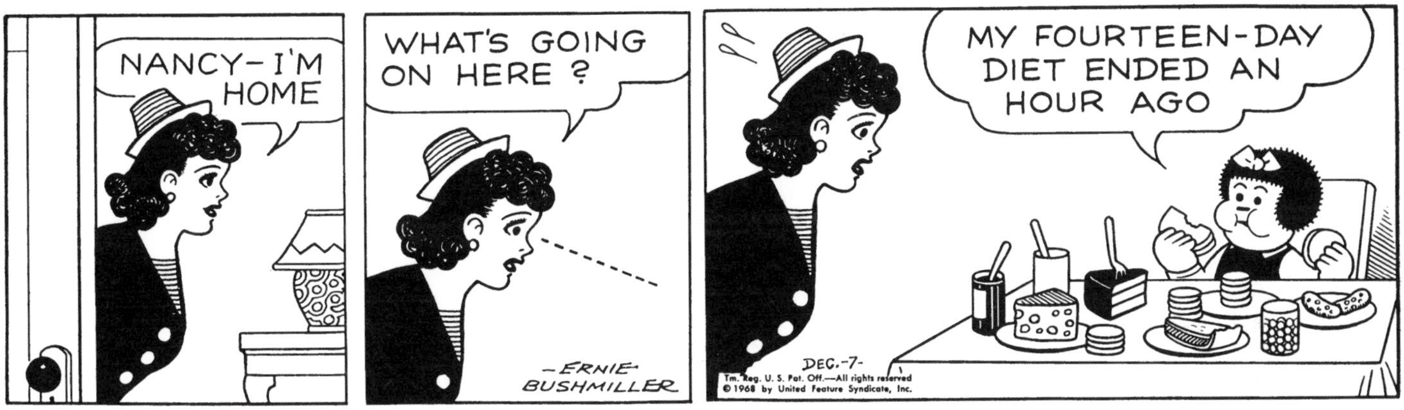
NANCY-I'M HOME
WHAT'S GOING ON HERE ?
-ERNIE BUSHMILLER
MY FOURTEEN-DAY DIET ENDED AN HOUR AGO
DEC.-7-
Tm. Reg. U. S. Pat. Off.—All rights reserved
© 1968 by United Feature Syndicate, Inc.

Washing Soda

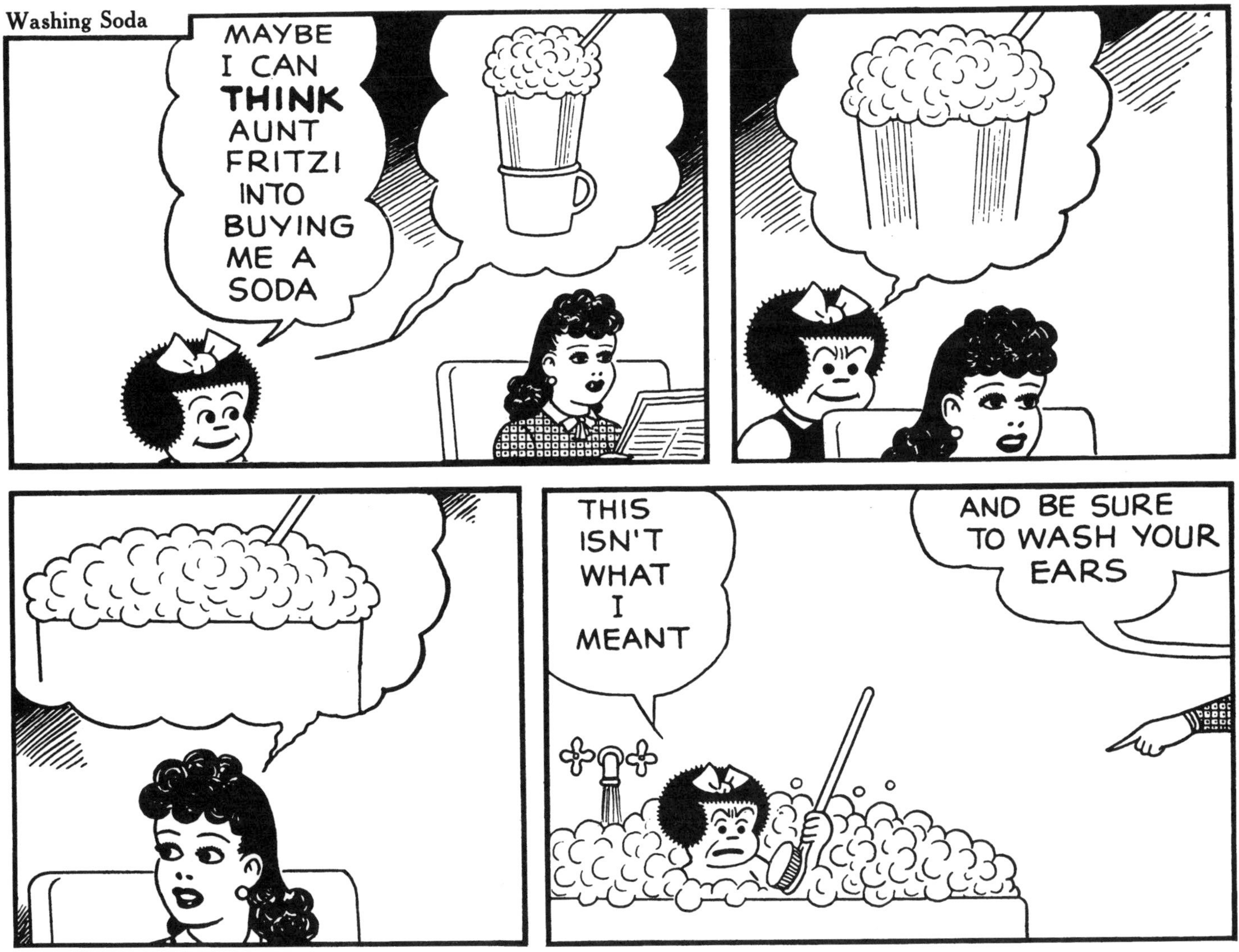
MAYBE I CAN **THINK** AUNT FRITZI INTO BUYING ME A SODA
THIS ISN'T WHAT I MEANT
AND BE SURE TO WASH YOUR EARS

Sweet Competition

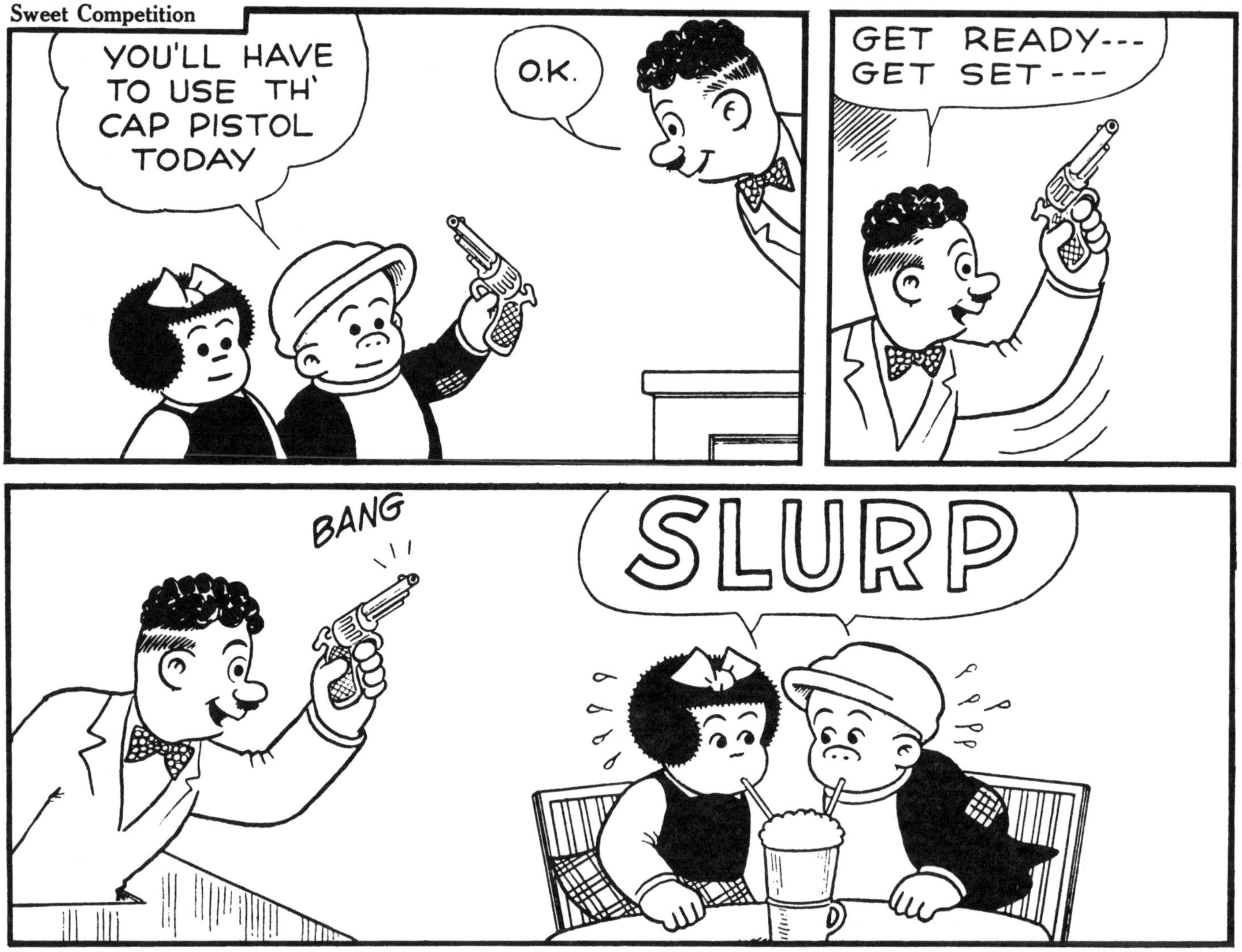

YOU'LL HAVE TO USE TH' CAP PISTOL TODAY
O.K.
GET READY--- GET SET---
BANG
SLURP

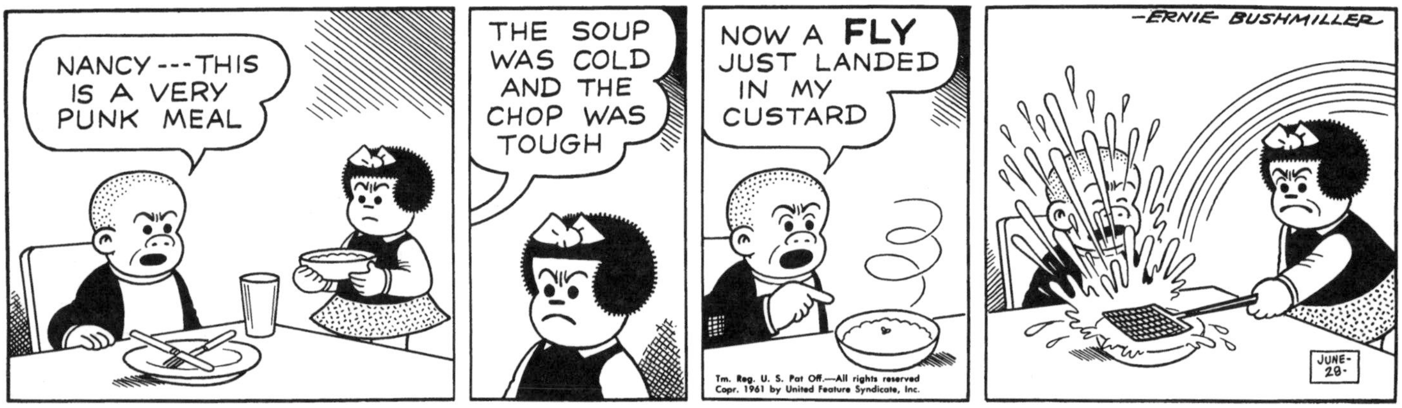

NANCY---THIS IS A VERY PUNK MEAL
THE SOUP WAS COLD AND THE CHOP WAS TOUGH
NOW A FLY JUST LANDED IN MY CUSTARD
Tm. Reg. U. S. Pat Off.—All rights reserved
Copr. 1961 by United Feature Syndicate, Inc.
-ERNIE BUSHMILLER
JUNE-28-

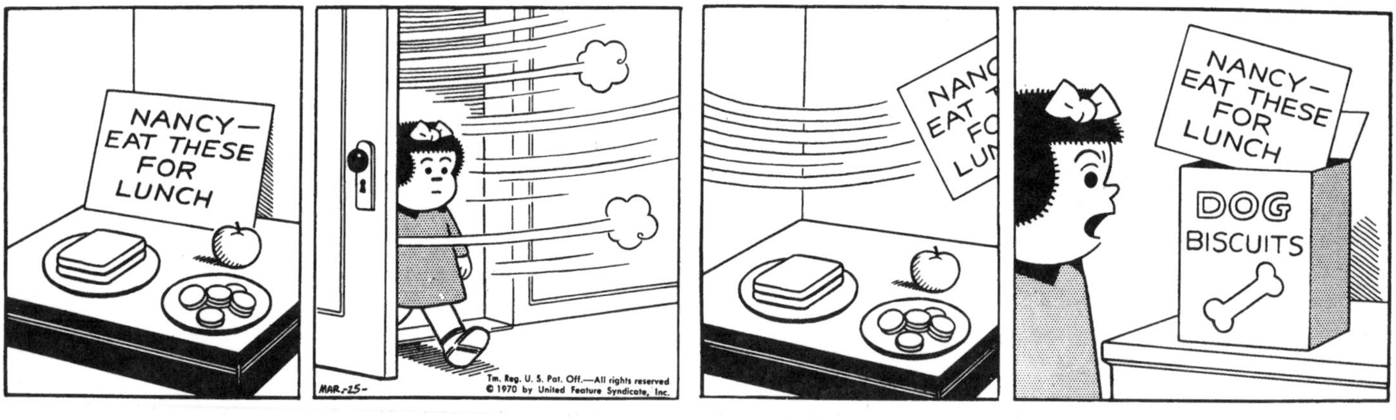

NANCY— EAT THESE FOR LUNCH
MAR-25-
Tm. Reg. U. S. Pat. Off.—All rights reserved
© 1970 by United Feature Syndicate, Inc.
NANCY— EAT THESE FOR LUNCH
DOG BISCUITS

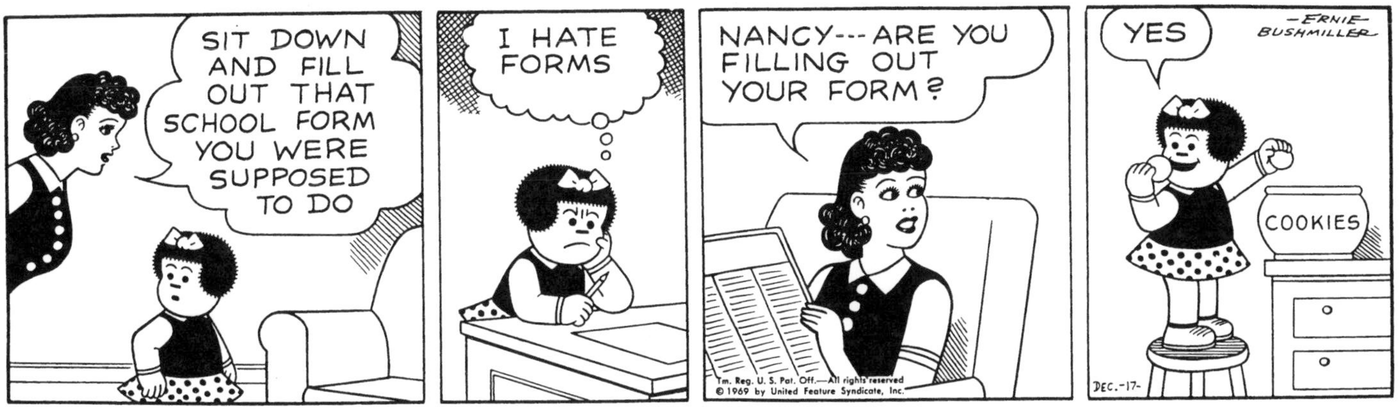
SIT DOWN AND FILL OUT THAT SCHOOL FORM YOU WERE SUPPOSED TO DO
I HATE FORMS
NANCY--- ARE YOU FILLING OUT YOUR FORM?
Tm. Reg. U. S. Pat. Off.—All rights reserved © 1969 by United Feature Syndicate, Inc.
YES
—ERNIE BUSHMILLER
COOKIES
DEC.-17-

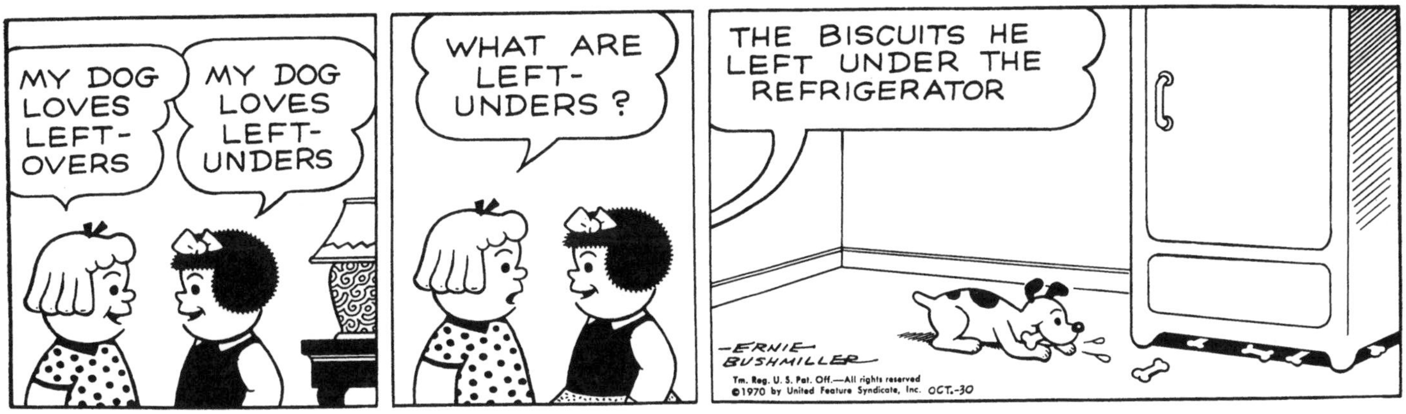
MY DOG LOVES LEFT-OVERS
MY DOG LOVES LEFT-UNDERS
WHAT ARE LEFT-UNDERS?
THE BISCUITS HE LEFT UNDER THE REFRIGERATOR
—ERNIE BUSHMILLER
Tm. Reg. U. S. Pat. Off.—All rights reserved ©1970 by United Feature Syndicate, Inc. OCT.-30

The Little Dipper

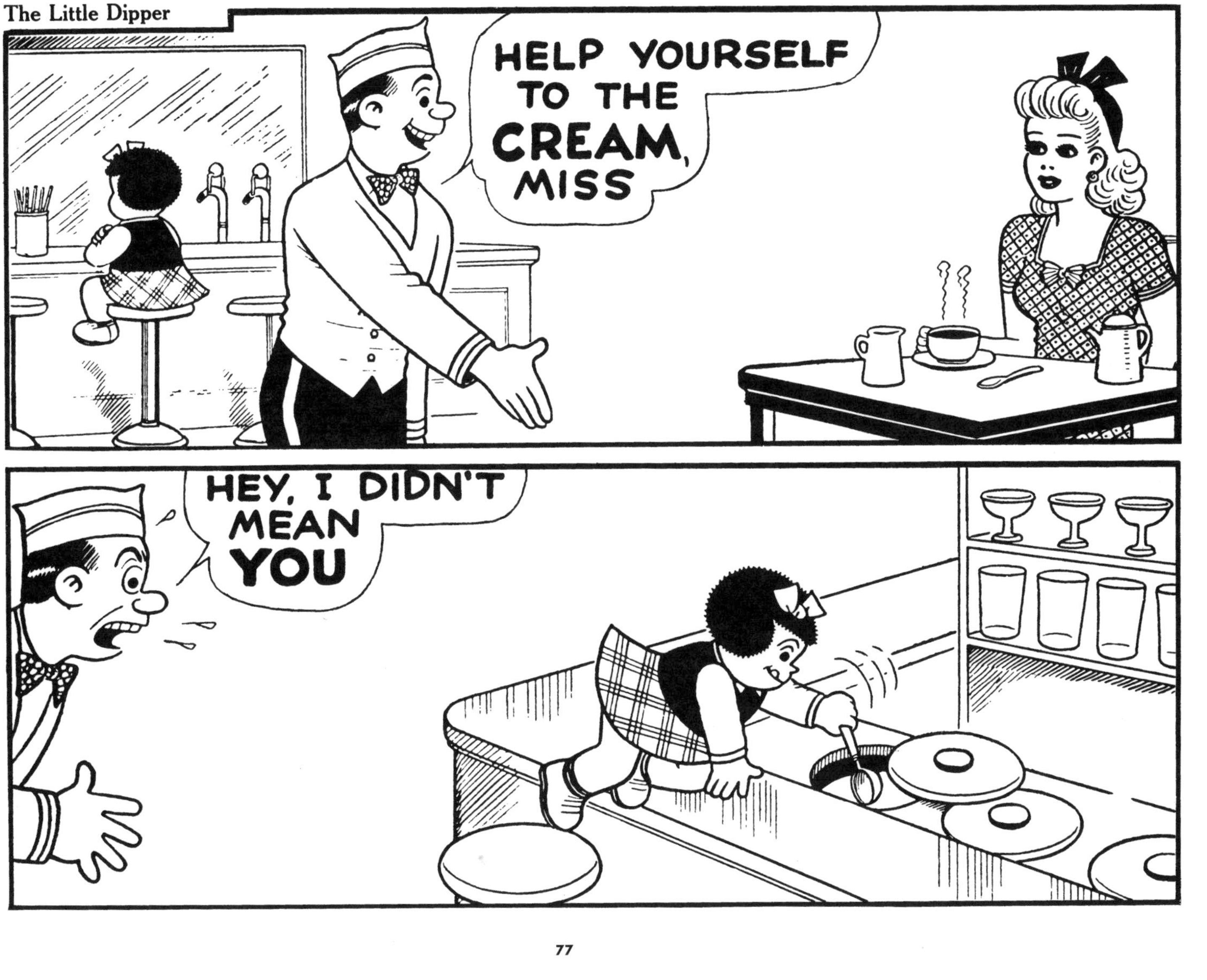
HELP YOURSELF TO THE CREAM, MISS
HEY, I DIDN'T MEAN YOU

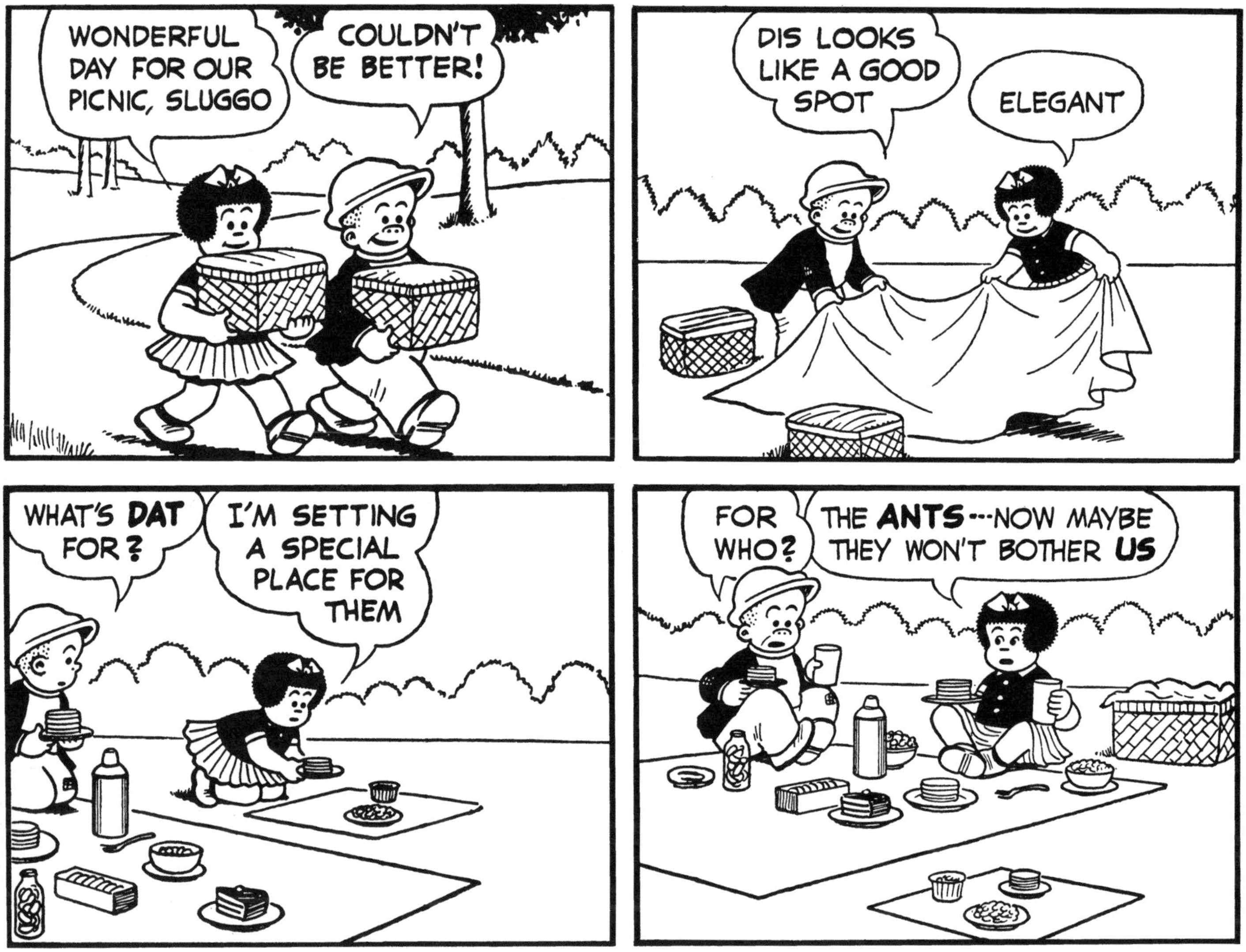
WONDERFUL DAY FOR OUR PICNIC, SLUGGO
COULDN'T BE BETTER!
DIS LOOKS LIKE A GOOD SPOT
ELEGANT
WHAT'S **DAT** FOR?
I'M SETTING A SPECIAL PLACE FOR THEM
FOR WHO?
THE **ANTS**---NOW MAYBE THEY WON'T BOTHER **US**

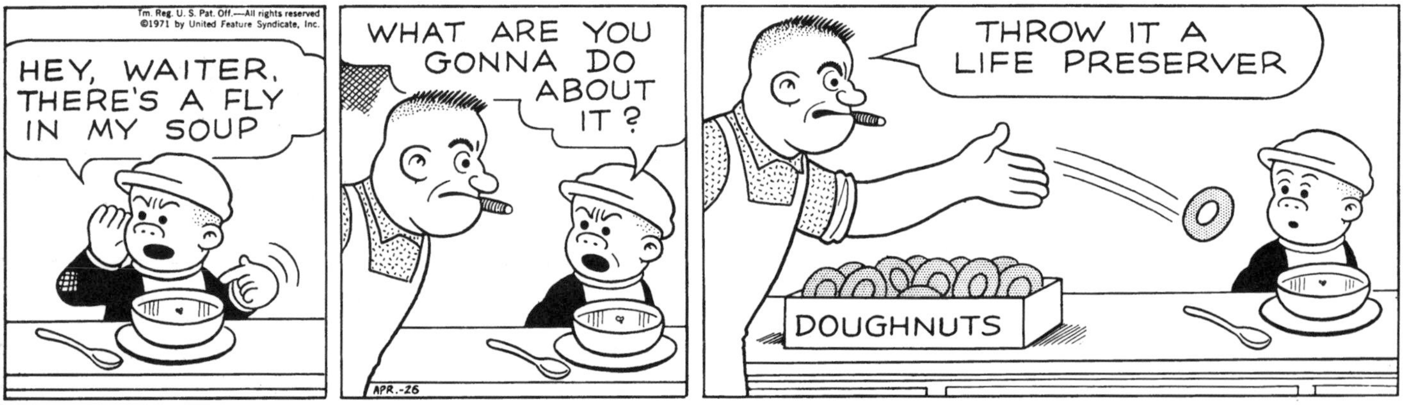
Tm. Reg. U. S. Pat. Off.—All rights reserved ©1971 by United Feature Syndicate, Inc.
HEY, WAITER, THERE'S A FLY IN MY SOUP
WHAT ARE YOU GONNA DO ABOUT IT?
APR.-26
THROW IT A LIFE PRESERVER
DOUGHNUTS

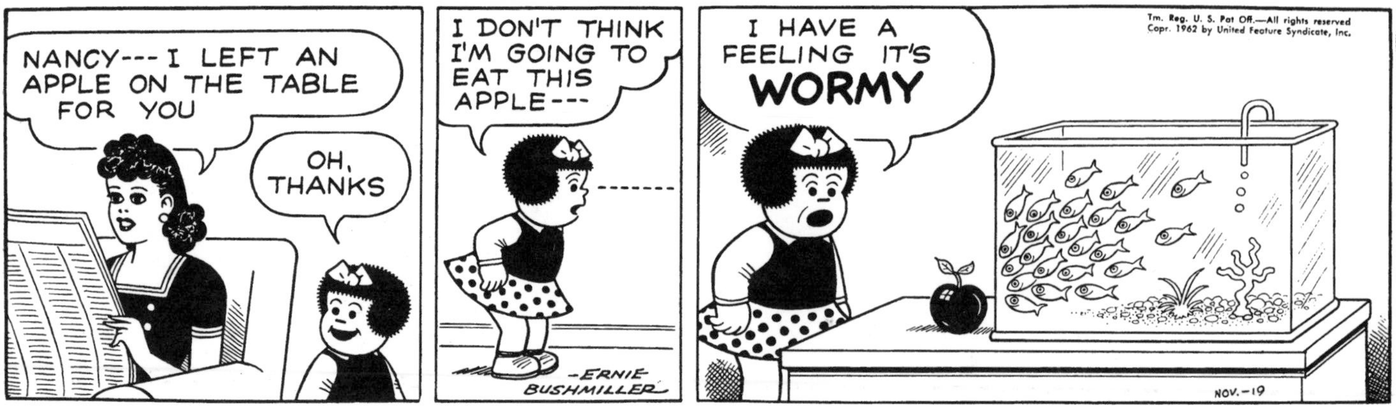
NANCY---I LEFT AN APPLE ON THE TABLE FOR YOU
OH, THANKS
I DON'T THINK I'M GOING TO EAT THIS APPLE---
-ERNIE BUSHMILLER
I HAVE A FEELING IT'S **WORMY**
Tm. Reg. U. S. Pat Off.—All rights reserved Copr. 1962 by United Feature Syndicate, Inc.
NOV.-19

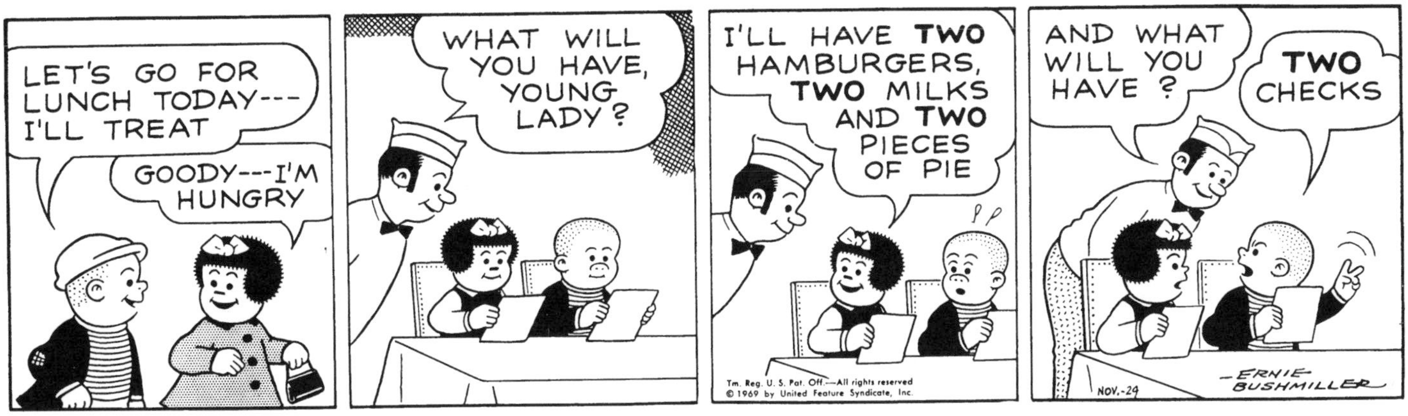
LET'S GO FOR LUNCH TODAY--- I'LL TREAT
GOODY---I'M HUNGRY
WHAT WILL YOU HAVE, YOUNG LADY ?
I'LL HAVE **TWO** HAMBURGERS, **TWO** MILKS AND **TWO** PIECES OF PIE
Tm. Reg. U. S. Pat. Off.—All rights reserved © 1969 by United Feature Syndicate, Inc.
AND WHAT WILL YOU HAVE ?
TWO CHECKS
NOV.-24
-ERNIE BUSHMILLER

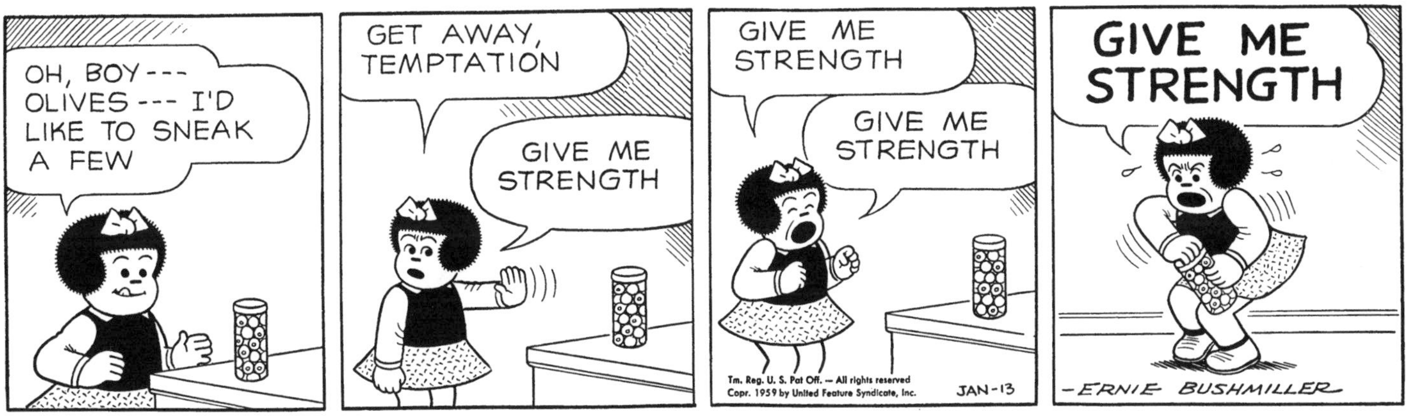
OH, BOY--- OLIVES--- I'D LIKE TO SNEAK A FEW
GET AWAY, TEMPTATION
GIVE ME STRENGTH
GIVE ME STRENGTH
GIVE ME STRENGTH
Tm. Reg. U. S. Pat Off.—All rights reserved Copr. 1959 by United Feature Syndicate, Inc.
JAN-13
GIVE ME STRENGTH
-ERNIE BUSHMILLER

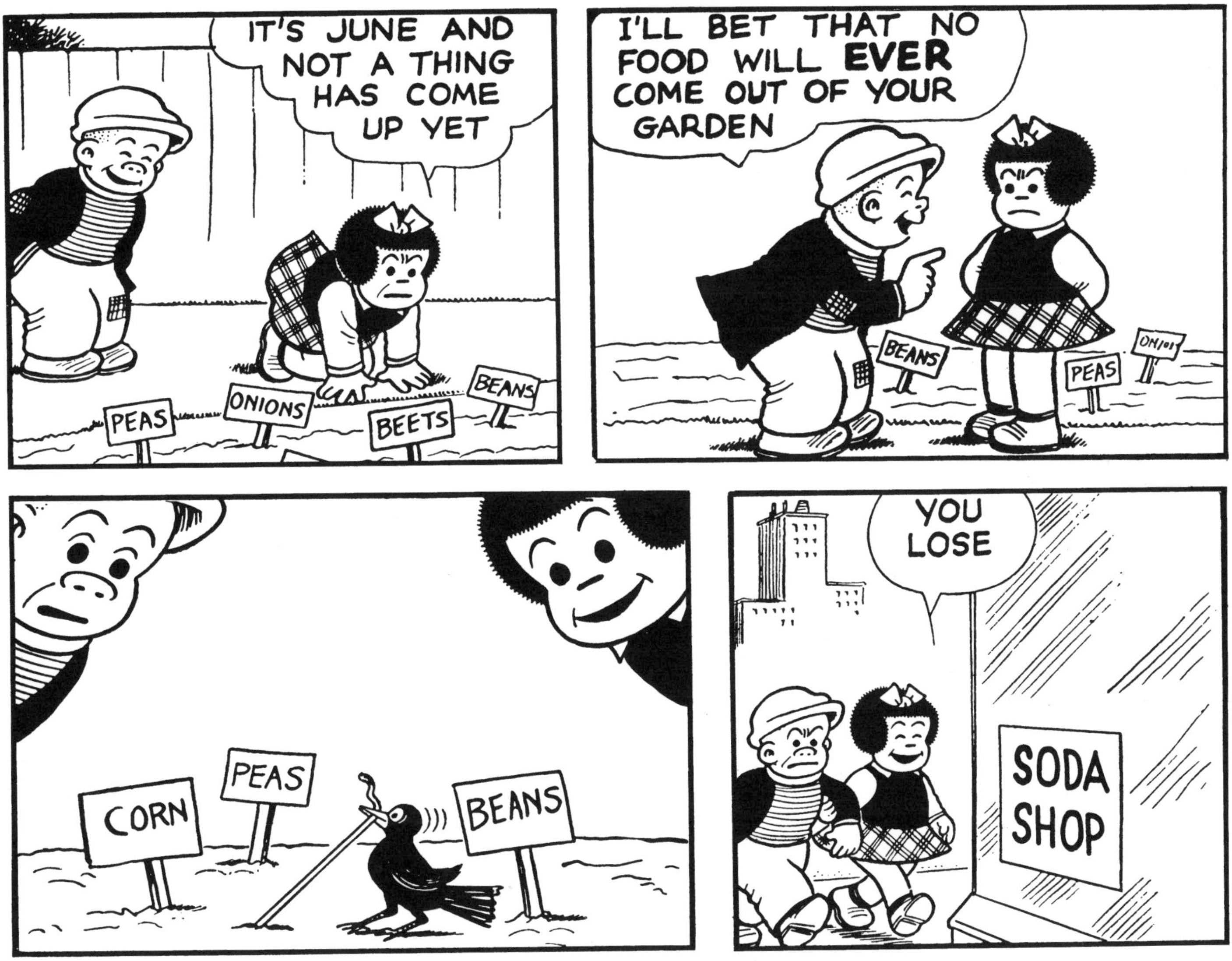
IT'S JUNE AND NOT A THING HAS COME UP YET
PEAS
ONIONS
BEETS
BEANS
I'LL BET THAT NO FOOD WILL **EVER** COME OUT OF YOUR GARDEN
BEANS
PEAS
ONIONS
CORN
PEAS
BEANS
YOU LOSE
SODA SHOP

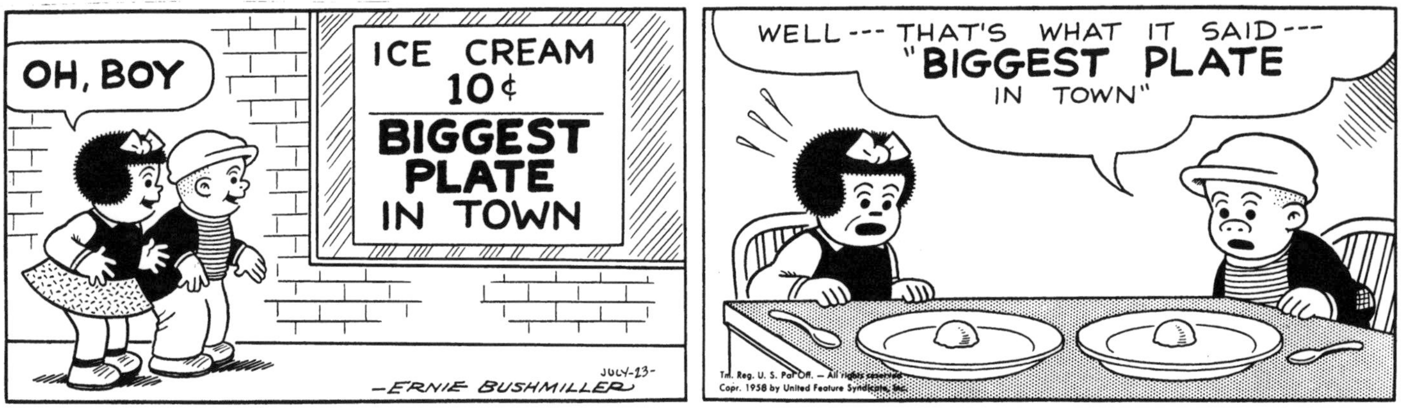
OH, BOY
ICE CREAM 10¢
BIGGEST PLATE IN TOWN
JULY-23-
-ERNIE BUSHMILLER
WELL --- THAT'S WHAT IT SAID--- "BIGGEST PLATE IN TOWN"
Tm. Reg. U. S. Pat. Off. — All rights reserved
Copr. 1958 by United Feature Syndicate, Inc.

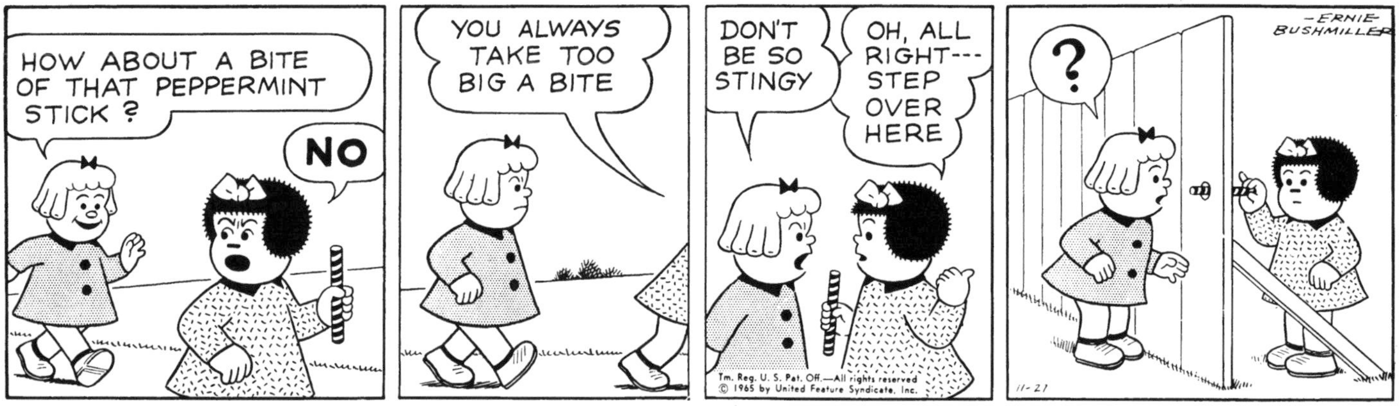
HOW ABOUT A BITE OF THAT PEPPERMINT STICK ?
NO
YOU ALWAYS TAKE TOO BIG A BITE
DON'T BE SO STINGY
OH, ALL RIGHT--- STEP OVER HERE
Tm. Reg. U. S. Pat. Off.—All rights reserved
© 1965 by United Feature Syndicate, Inc.
-ERNIE BUSHMILLER
?
11-27

It Beats the Band

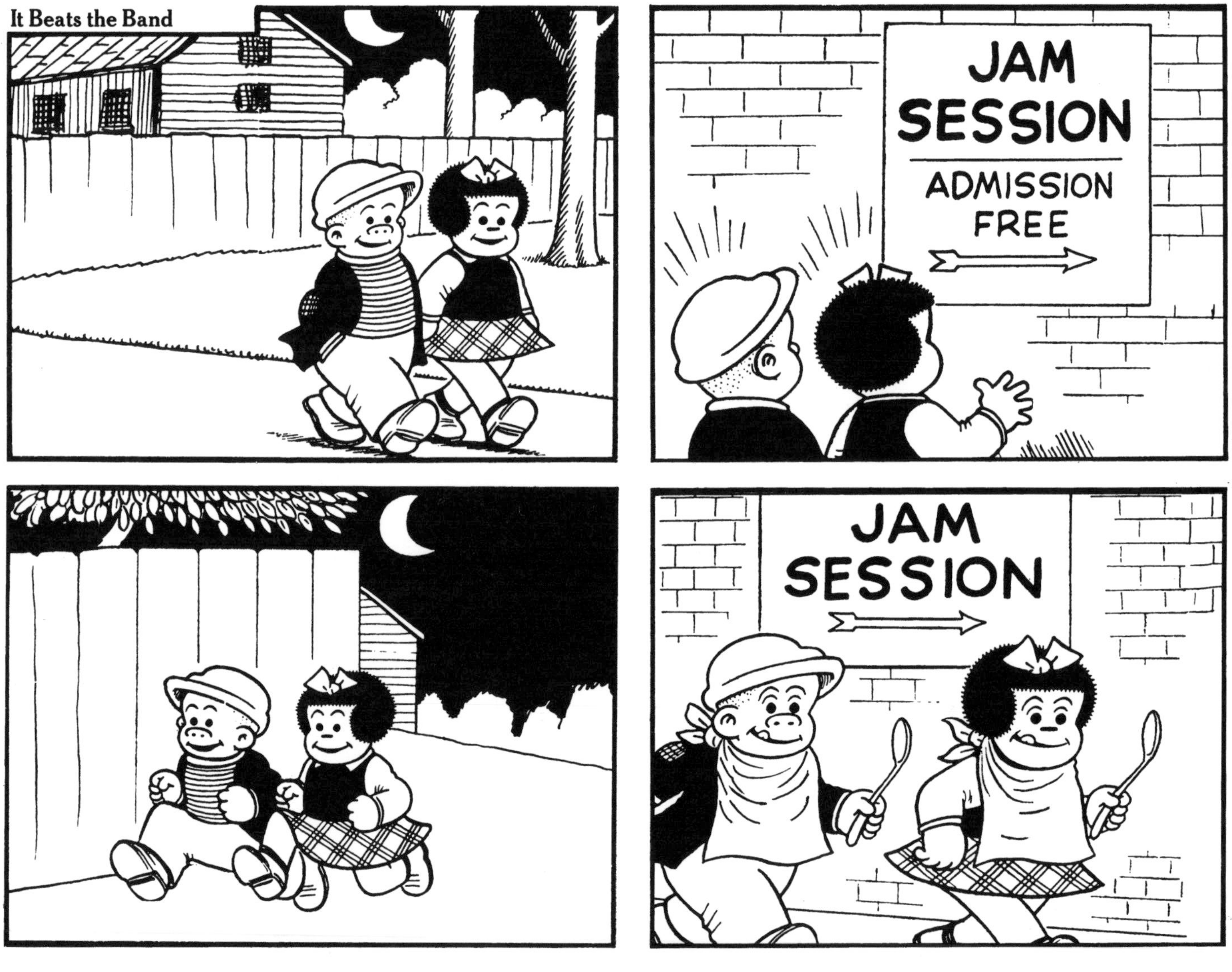
JAM SESSION
ADMISSION FREE
JAM SESSION

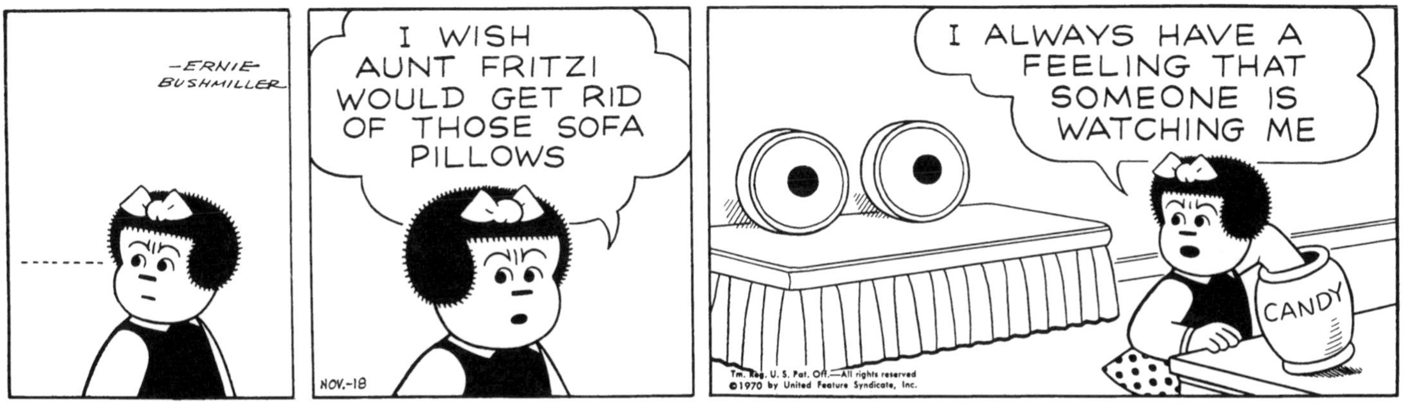
-ERNIE-
BUSHMILLER
I WISH AUNT FRITZI WOULD GET RID OF THOSE SOFA PILLOWS
NOV.-18
I ALWAYS HAVE A FEELING THAT SOMEONE IS WATCHING ME
CANDY
Tm. Reg. U. S. Pat. Off.—All rights reserved
©1970 by United Feature Syndicate, Inc.

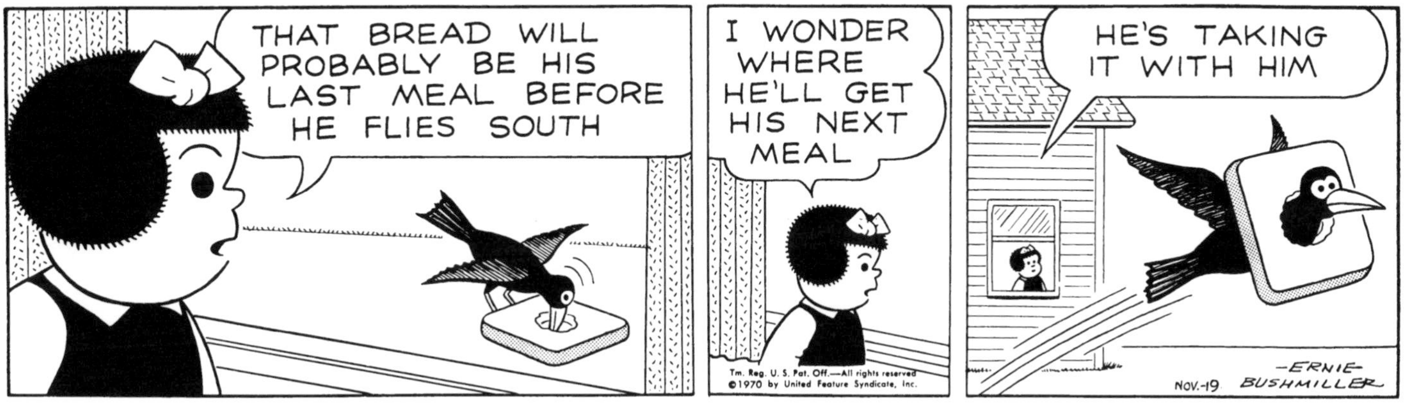
THAT BREAD WILL PROBABLY BE HIS LAST MEAL BEFORE HE FLIES SOUTH
I WONDER WHERE HE'LL GET HIS NEXT MEAL
Tm. Reg. U. S. Pat. Off.—All rights reserved
©1970 by United Feature Syndicate, Inc.
HE'S TAKING IT WITH HIM
NOV.-19
-ERNIE-
BUSHMILLER

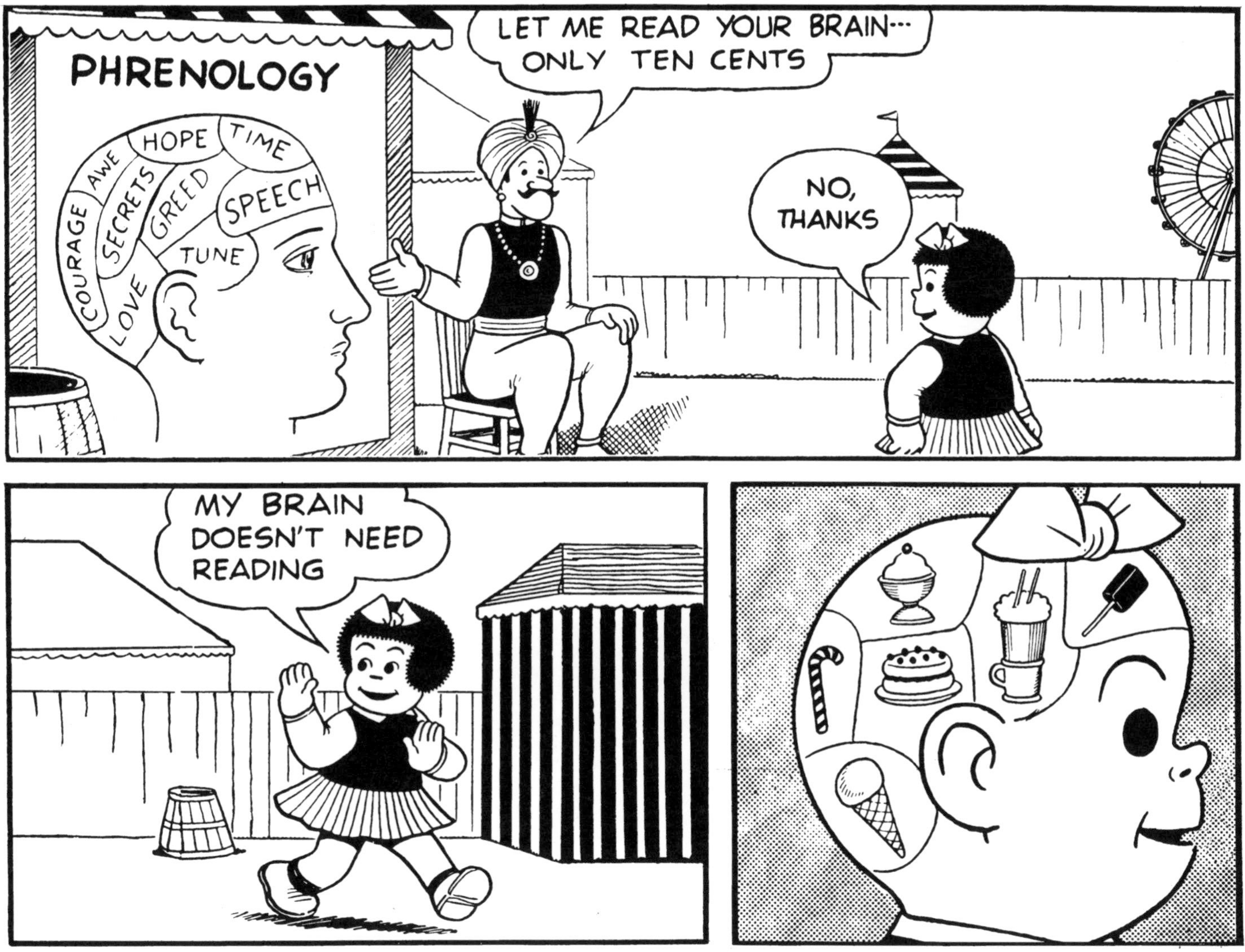
PHRENOLOGY
HOPE
TIME
AWE
SECRETS
GREED
SPEECH
COURAGE
TUNE
LOVE
LET ME READ YOUR BRAIN··· ONLY TEN CENTS
NO, THANKS
MY BRAIN DOESN'T NEED READING

Psychological Flavor

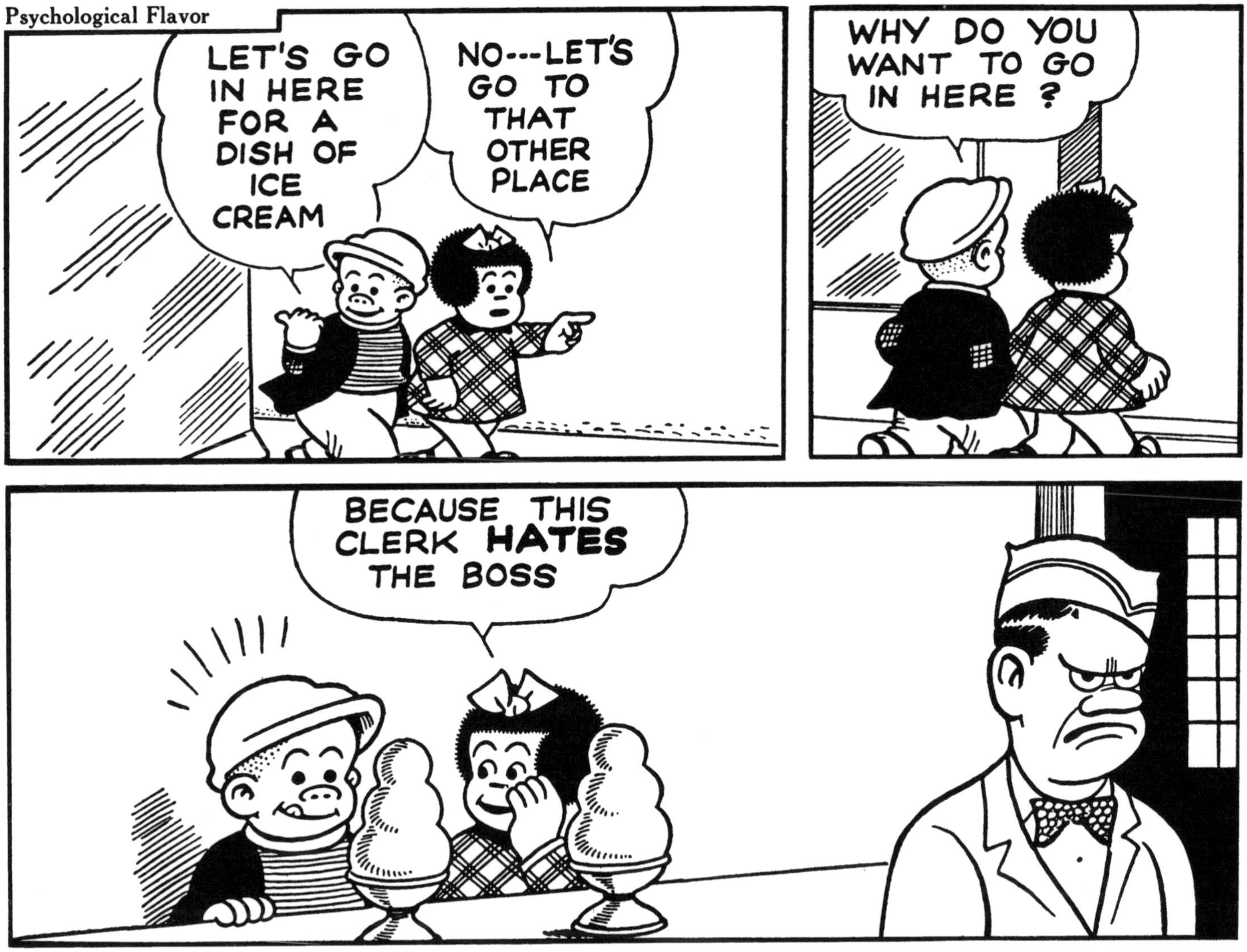
LET'S GO IN HERE FOR A DISH OF ICE CREAM
NO---LET'S GO TO THAT OTHER PLACE
WHY DO YOU WANT TO GO IN HERE ?
BECAUSE THIS CLERK HATES THE BOSS

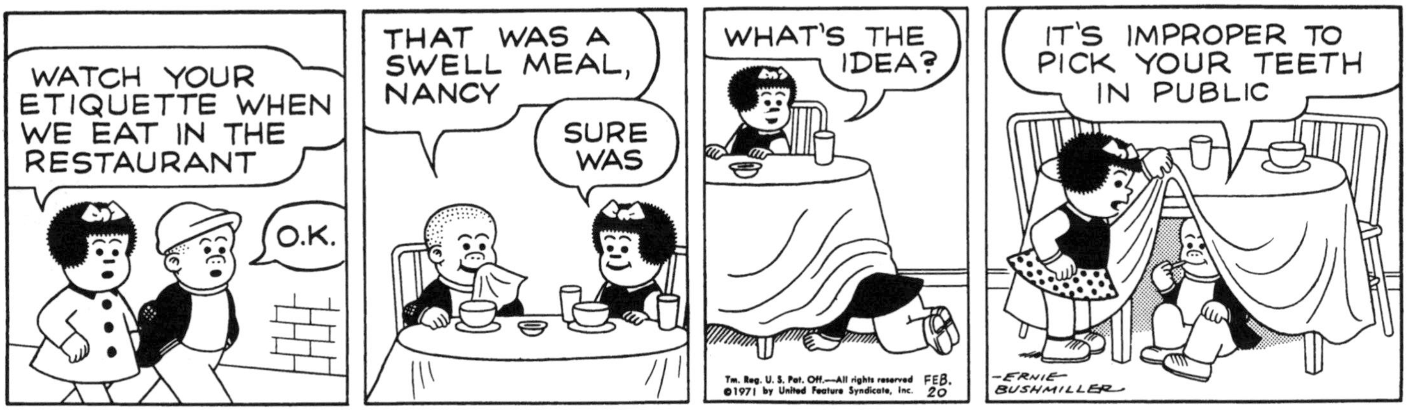
WATCH YOUR ETIQUETTE WHEN WE EAT IN THE RESTAURANT
O.K.
THAT WAS A SWELL MEAL, NANCY
SURE WAS
WHAT'S THE IDEA?
Tm. Reg. U. S. Pat. Off.—All rights reserved ©1971 by United Feature Syndicate, Inc.
FEB. 20
IT'S IMPROPER TO PICK YOUR TEETH IN PUBLIC
-ERNIE BUSHMILLER

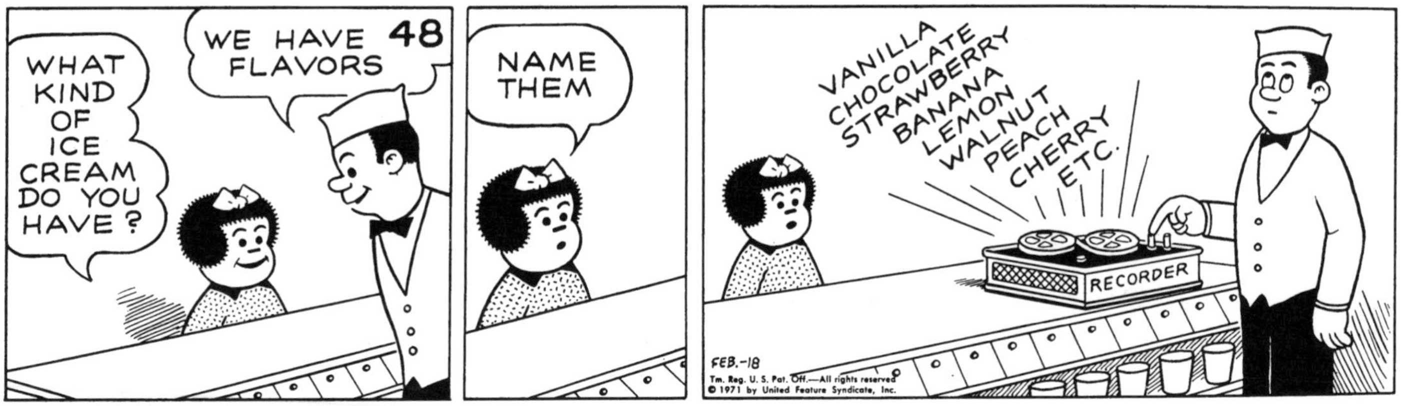
WHAT KIND OF ICE CREAM DO YOU HAVE ?
WE HAVE 48 FLAVORS
NAME THEM
VANILLA
CHOCOLATE
STRAWBERRY
BANANA
LEMON
WALNUT
PEACH
CHERRY
ETC.
RECORDER
FEB.-18
Tm. Reg. U. S. Pat. Off.—All rights reserved ©1971 by United Feature Syndicate, Inc.

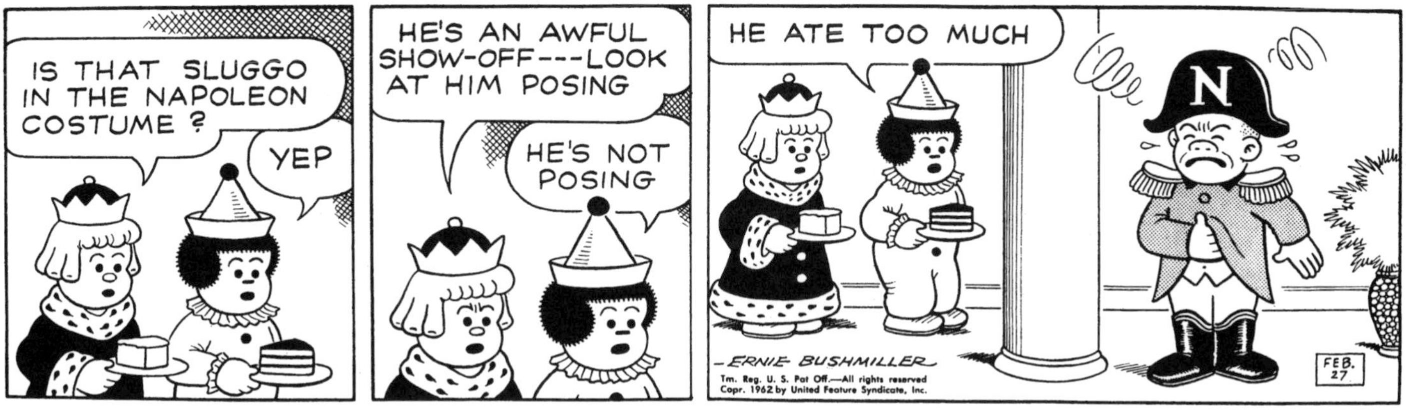

IS THAT SLUGGO IN THE NAPOLEON COSTUME ?
YEP
HE'S AN AWFUL SHOW-OFF---LOOK AT HIM POSING
HE'S NOT POSING
HE ATE TOO MUCH
N
-ERNIE BUSHMILLER
Tm. Reg. U. S. Pat Off.—All rights reserved Copr. 1962 by United Feature Syndicate, Inc.
FEB. 27

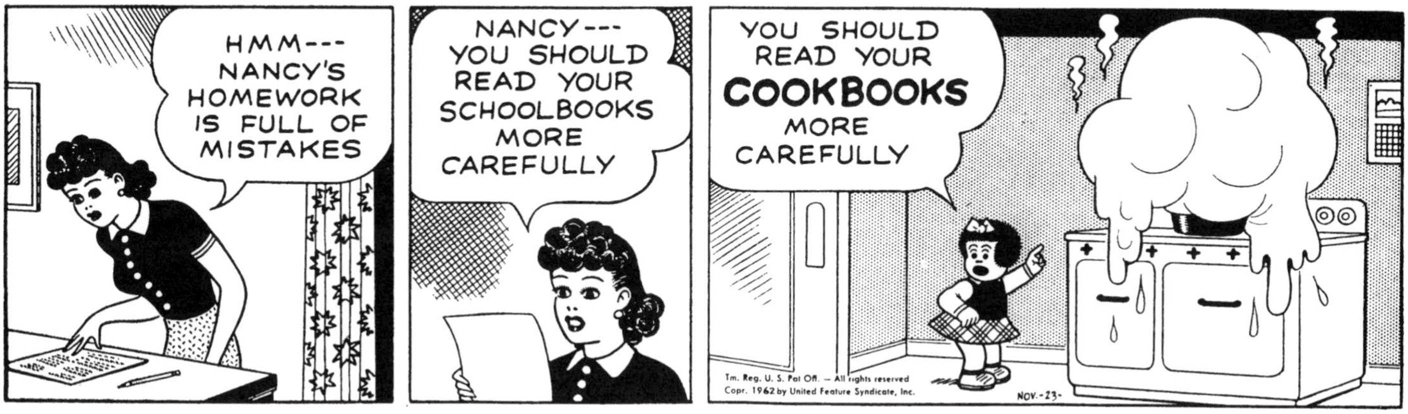

HMM--- NANCY'S HOMEWORK IS FULL OF MISTAKES
NANCY--- YOU SHOULD READ YOUR SCHOOLBOOKS MORE CAREFULLY
YOU SHOULD READ YOUR COOKBOOKS MORE CAREFULLY
Tm. Reg. U. S. Pat Off. — All rights reserved Copr. 1962 by United Feature Syndicate, Inc.
NOV.-23-

Sweet Victory

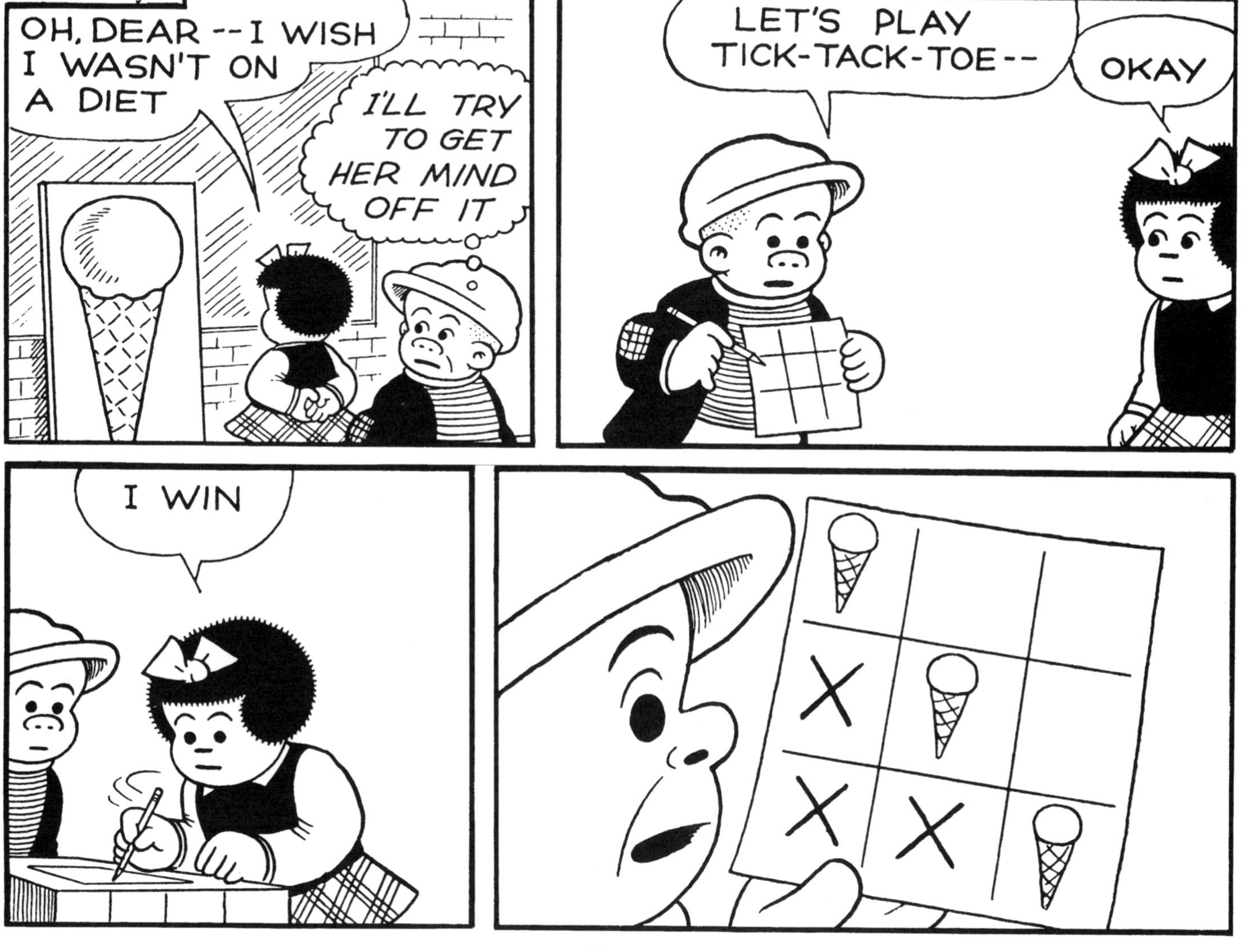

OH, DEAR --I WISH I WASN'T ON A DIET
I'LL TRY TO GET HER MIND OFF IT
LET'S PLAY TICK-TACK-TOE--
OKAY
I WIN

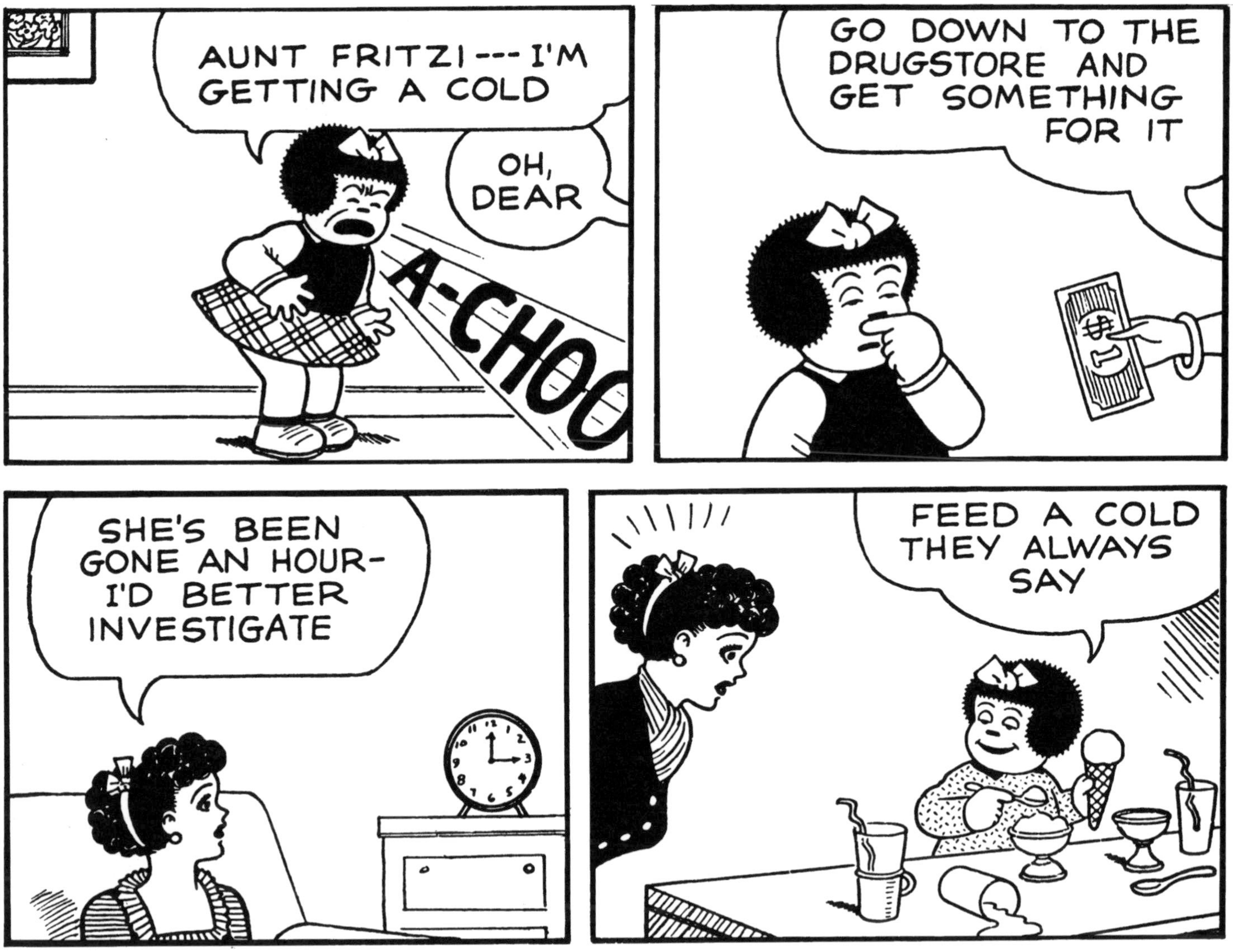
AUNT FRITZI --- I'M GETTING A COLD
OH, DEAR
A-CHOO
GO DOWN TO THE DRUGSTORE AND GET SOMETHING FOR IT
SHE'S BEEN GONE AN HOUR- I'D BETTER INVESTIGATE
FEED A COLD THEY ALWAYS SAY

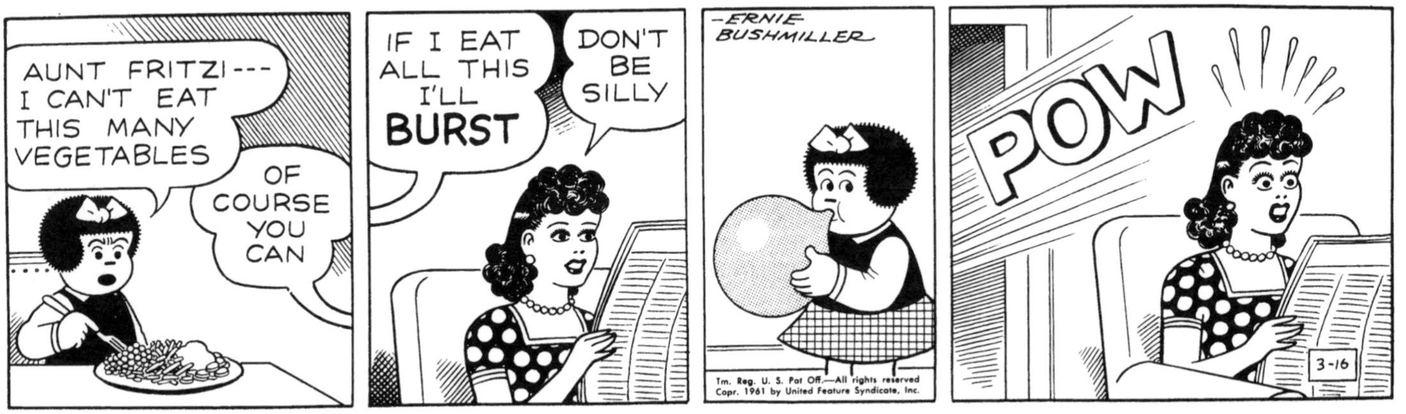
AUNT FRITZI --- I CAN'T EAT THIS MANY VEGETABLES
OF COURSE YOU CAN
IF I EAT ALL THIS I'LL **BURST**
DON'T BE SILLY
-ERNIE BUSHMILLER
Tm. Reg. U. S. Pat Off.—All rights reserved Copr. 1961 by United Feature Syndicate, Inc.
POW
3-16

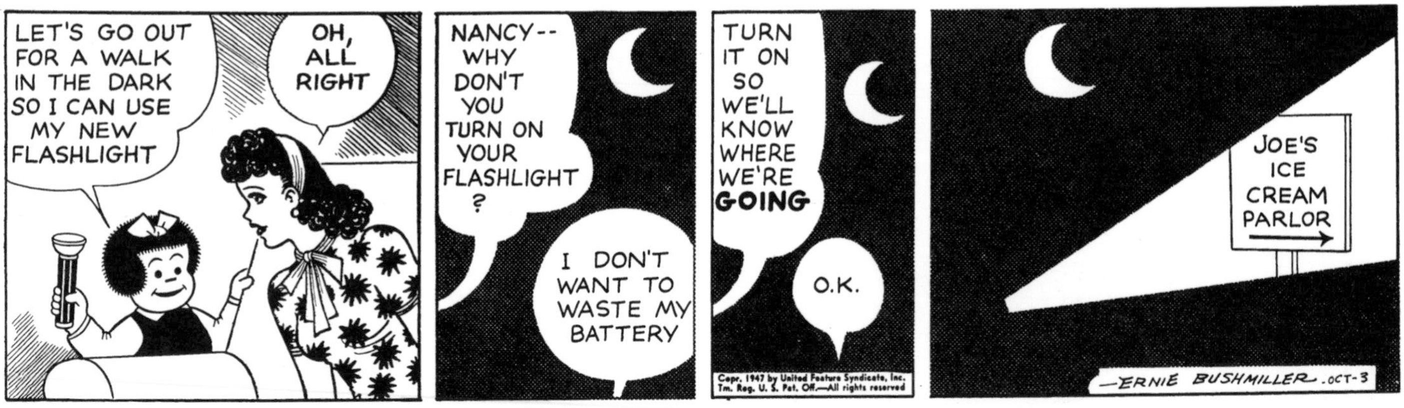
LET'S GO OUT FOR A WALK IN THE DARK SO I CAN USE MY NEW FLASHLIGHT
OH, ALL RIGHT
NANCY-- WHY DON'T YOU TURN ON YOUR FLASHLIGHT ?
I DON'T WANT TO WASTE MY BATTERY
TURN IT ON SO WE'LL KNOW WHERE WE'RE **GOING**
O.K.
Copr. 1947 by United Feature Syndicate, Inc. Tm. Reg. U. S. Pat. Off.—All rights reserved
JOE'S ICE CREAM PARLOR
-ERNIE BUSHMILLER .OCT-3

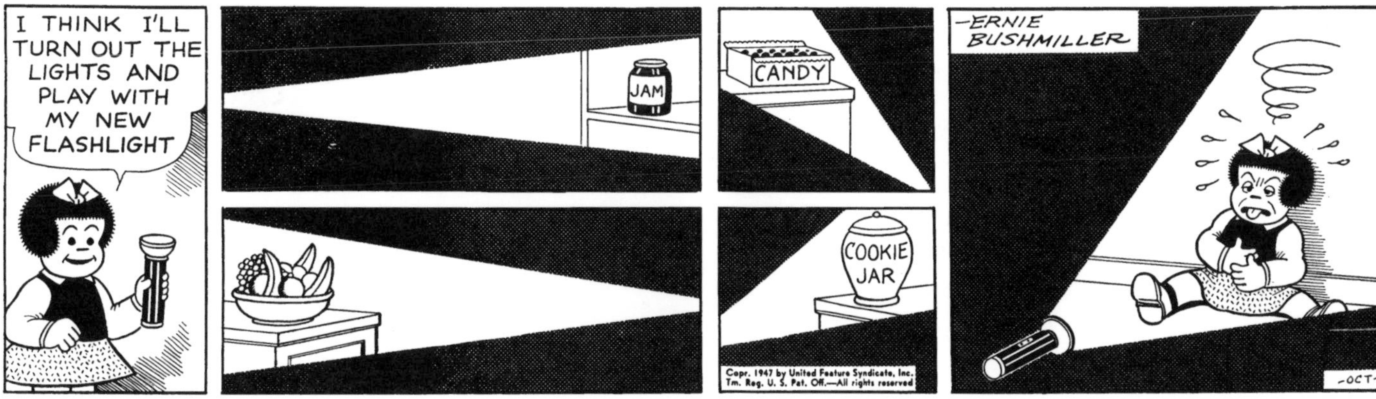
I THINK I'LL TURN OUT THE LIGHTS AND PLAY WITH MY NEW FLASHLIGHT
JAM
CANDY
COOKIE JAR
Copr. 1947 by United Feature Syndicate, Inc. Tm. Reg. U. S. Pat. Off.—All rights reserved
-ERNIE BUSHMILLER
-OCT-2

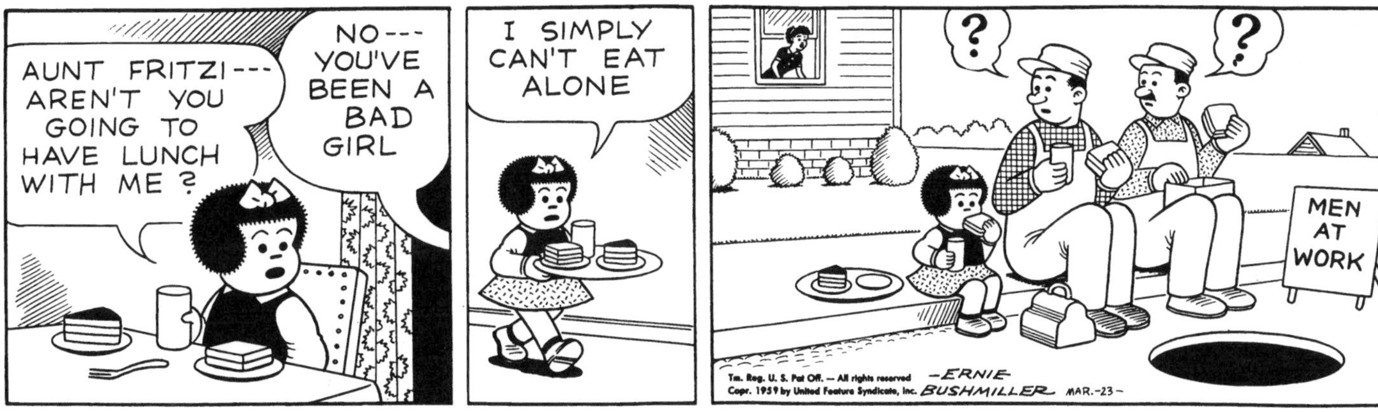
AUNT FRITZI--- AREN'T YOU GOING TO HAVE LUNCH WITH ME ?
NO--- YOU'VE BEEN A BAD GIRL
I SIMPLY CAN'T EAT ALONE
?
?
MEN AT WORK
Tm. Reg. U. S. Pat Off. — All rights reserved
Copr. 1959 by United Feature Syndicate, Inc.
-ERNIE BUSHMILLER
MAR.-23-

Cat-astrophe

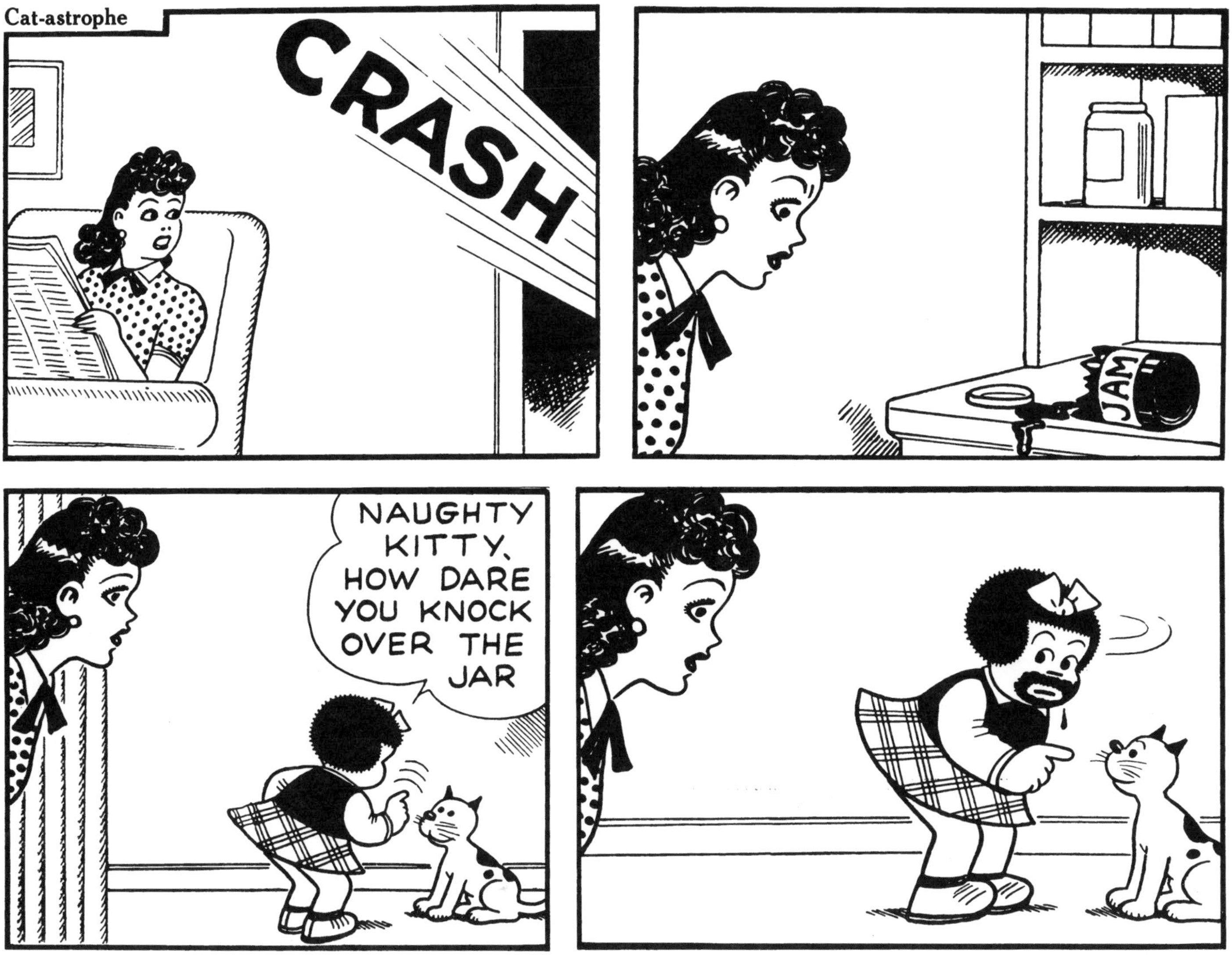
CRASH
JAM
NAUGHTY KITTY, HOW DARE YOU KNOCK OVER THE JAR

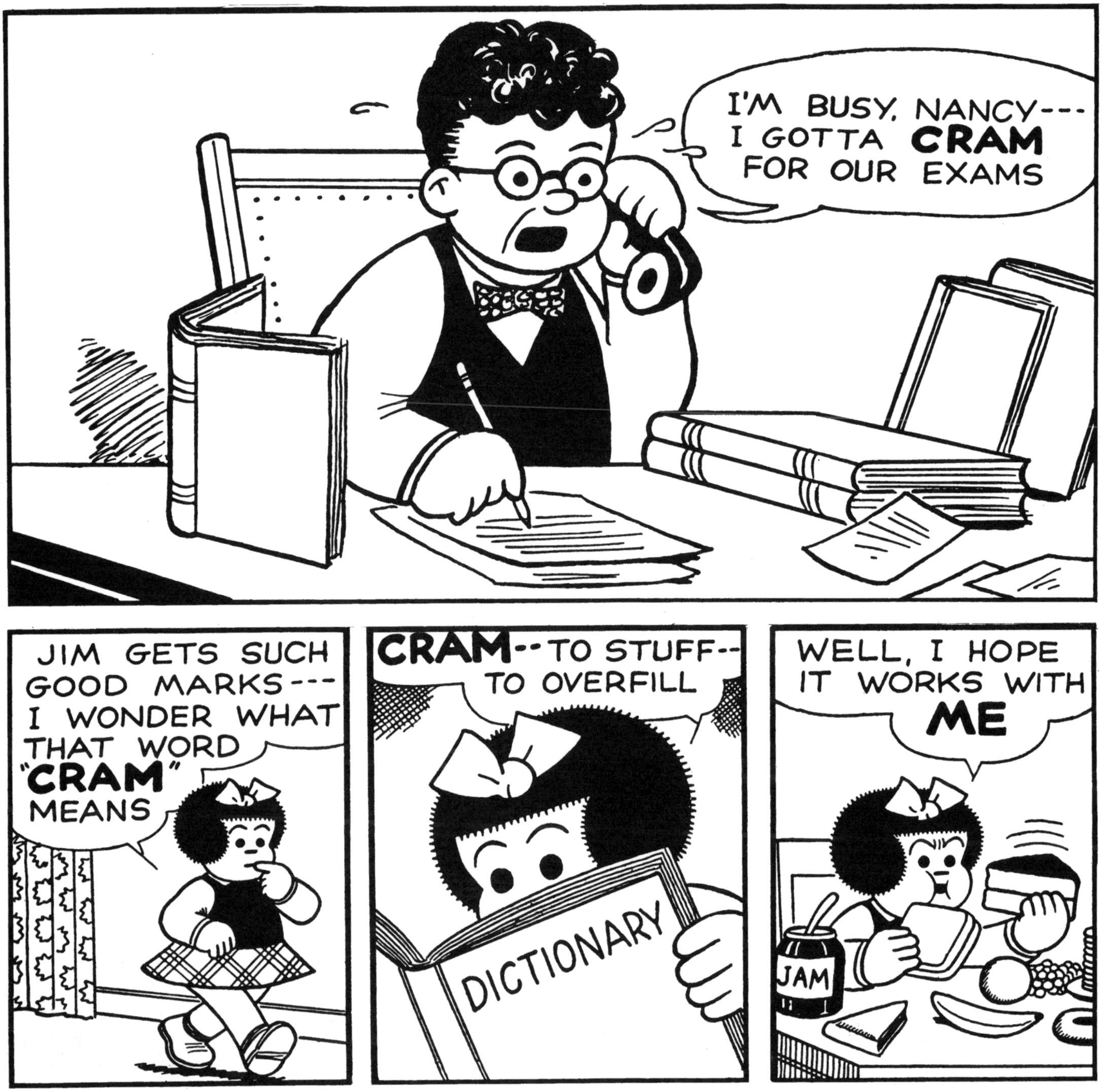
I'M BUSY, NANCY---
I GOTTA CRAM
FOR OUR EXAMS
JIM GETS SUCH GOOD MARKS--- I WONDER WHAT THAT WORD "CRAM" MEANS
CRAM--TO STUFF--TO OVERFILL
DICTIONARY
WELL, I HOPE IT WORKS WITH ME
JAM

Munch Ado About Nothing

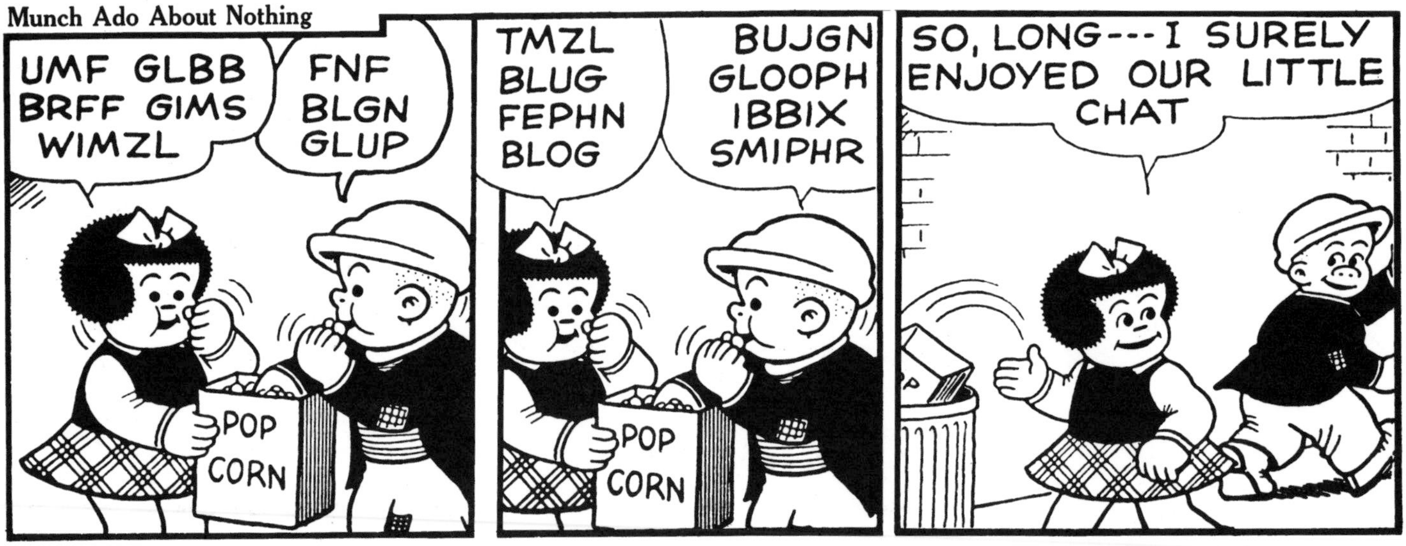
UMF GLBB BRFF GIMS WIMZL
FNF BLGN GLUP
POP CORN
TMZL BLUG FEPHN BLOG
BUJGN GLOOPH IBBIX SMIPHR
POP CORN
SO, LONG--- I SURELY ENJOYED OUR LITTLE CHAT

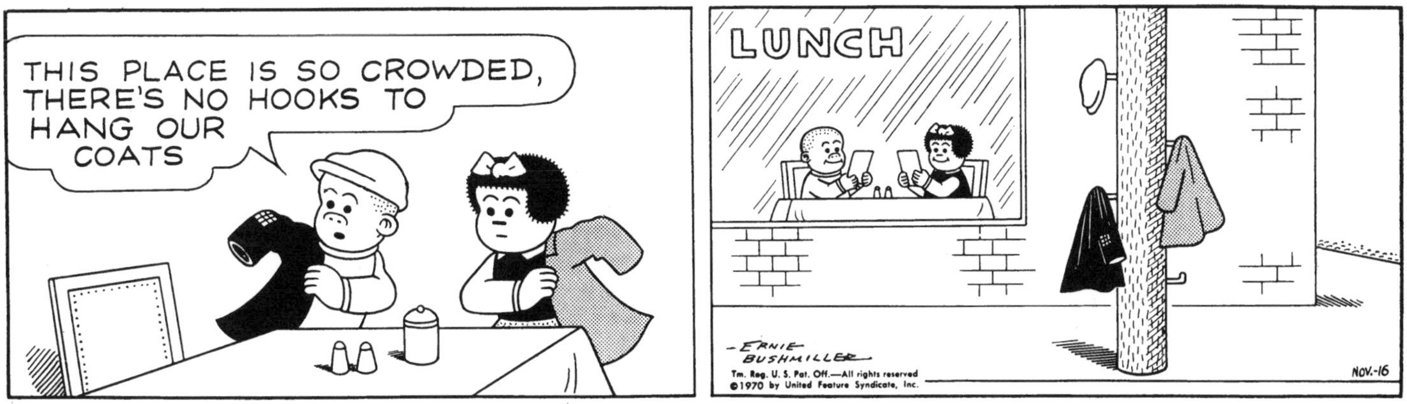
THIS PLACE IS SO CROWDED, THERE'S NO HOOKS TO HANG OUR COATS
LUNCH
-ERNIE BUSHMILLER
Tm. Reg. U. S. Pat. Off.—All rights reserved
©1970 by United Feature Syndicate, Inc.
NOV.-16

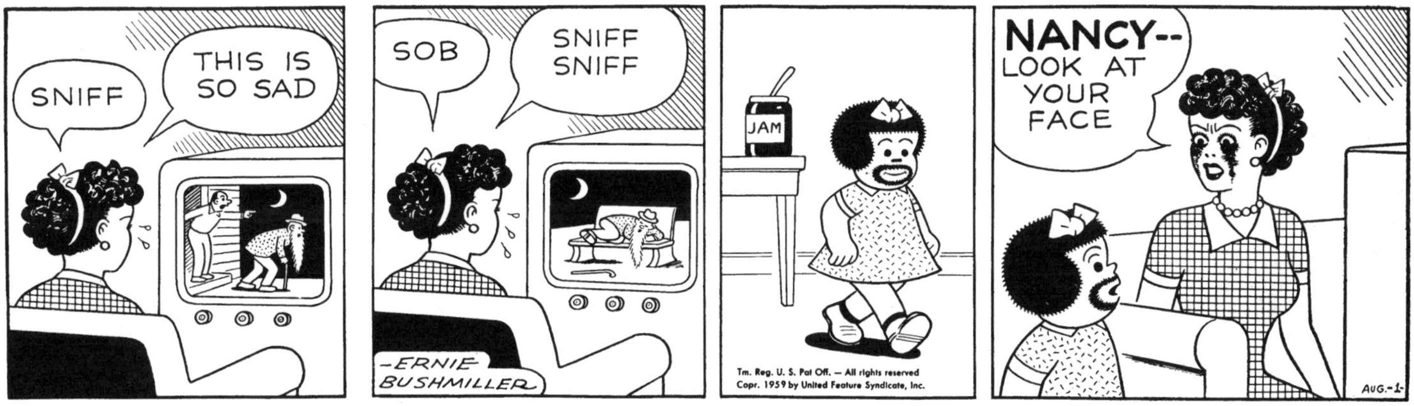
SNIFF
THIS IS SO SAD
SOB
SNIFF SNIFF
-ERNIE BUSHMILLER
JAM
Tm. Reg. U. S. Pat Off. — All rights reserved
Copr. 1959 by United Feature Syndicate, Inc.
NANCY-- LOOK AT YOUR FACE
AUG.-1-

Treat and Retreat

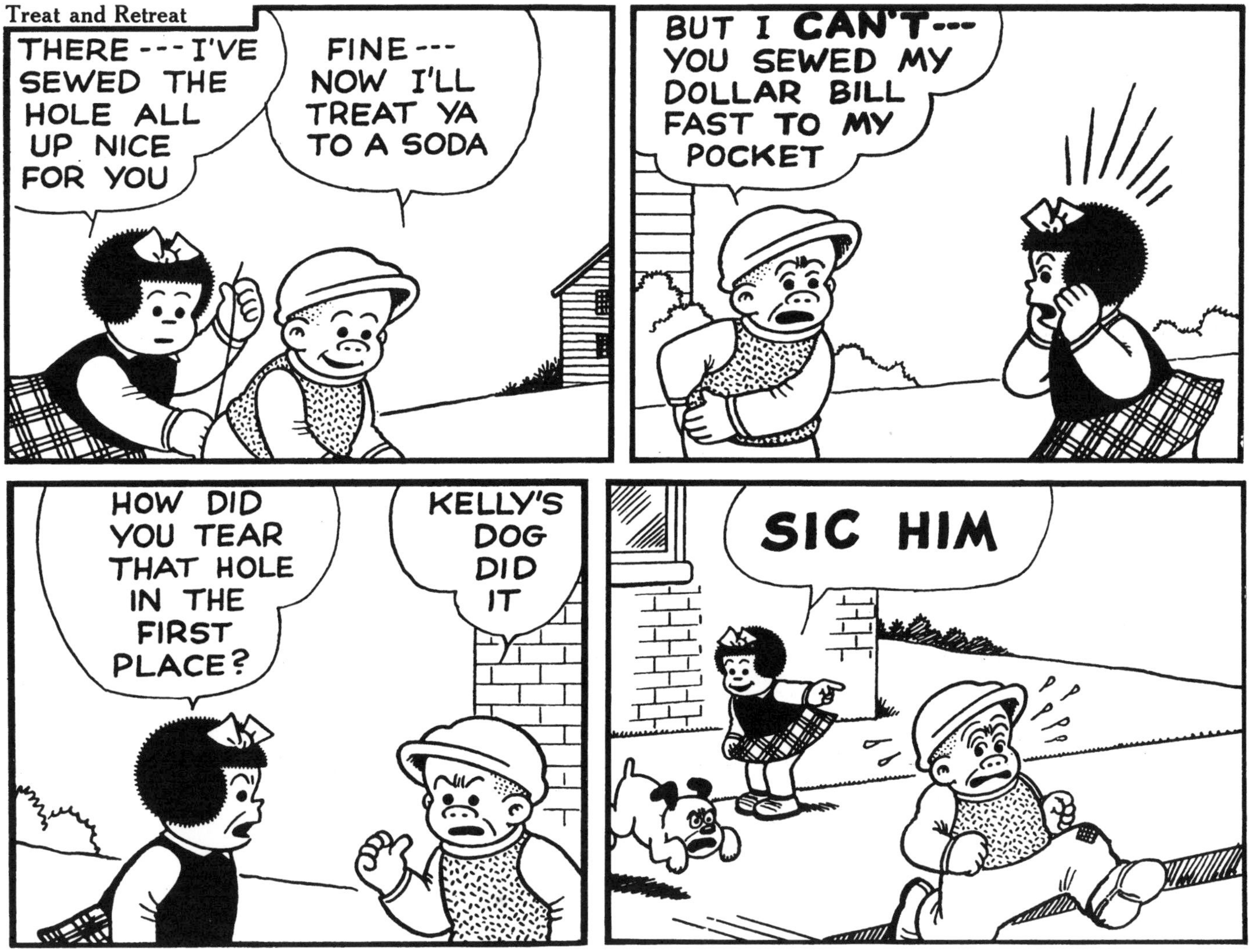
THERE---I'VE SEWED THE HOLE ALL UP NICE FOR YOU
FINE--- NOW I'LL TREAT YA TO A SODA
BUT I CAN'T--- YOU SEWED MY DOLLAR BILL FAST TO MY POCKET
HOW DID YOU TEAR THAT HOLE IN THE FIRST PLACE?
KELLY'S DOG DID IT
SIC HIM

What A Pill!

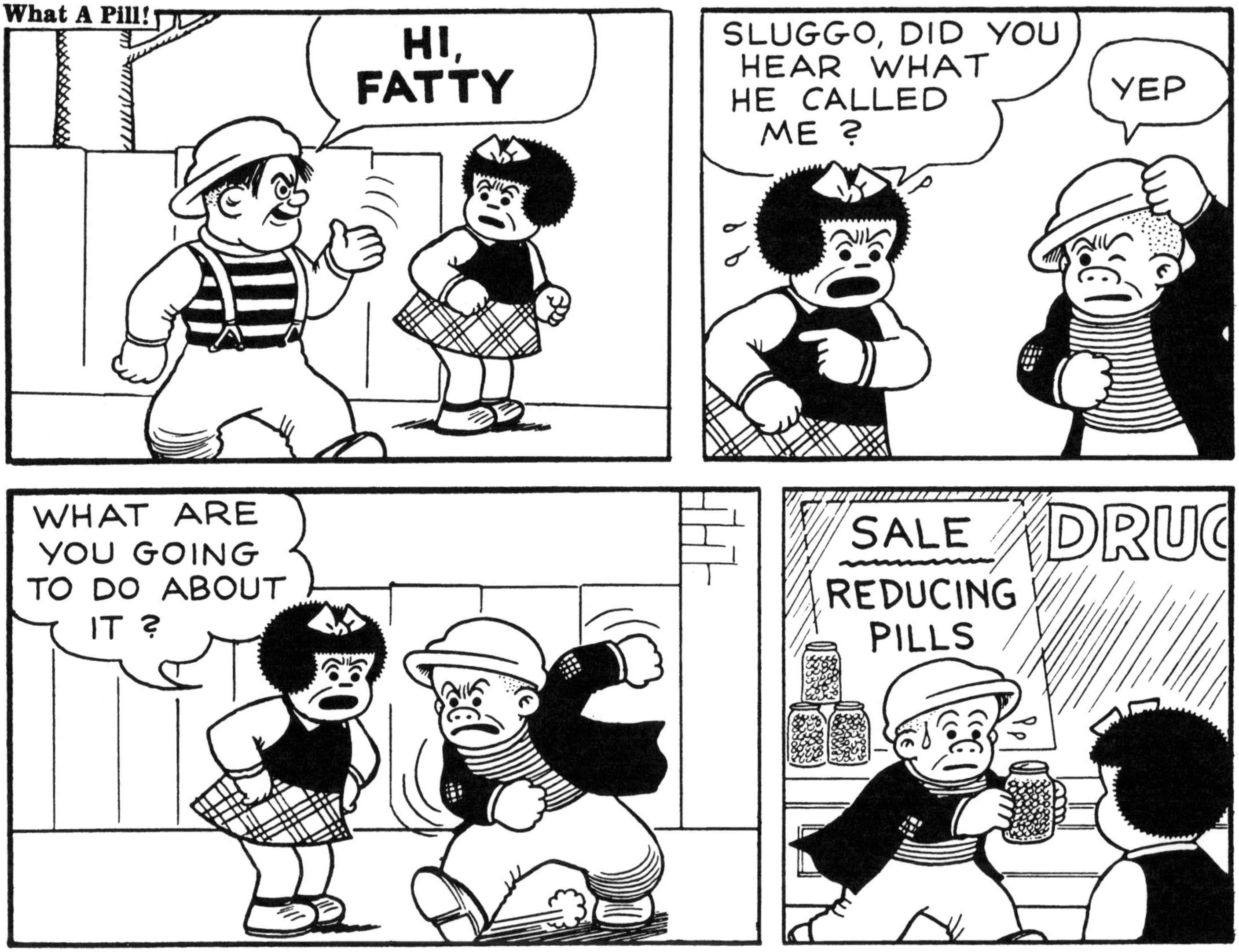

HI, FATTY
SLUGGO, DID YOU HEAR WHAT HE CALLED ME ?
YEP
WHAT ARE YOU GOING TO DO ABOUT IT ?
SALE
REDUCING PILLS
DRUG

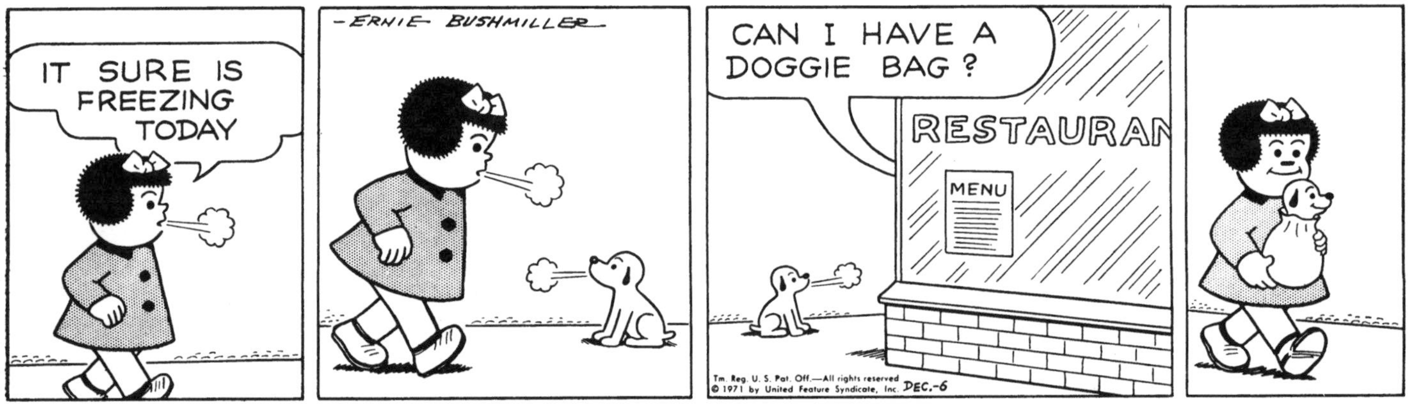

IT SURE IS FREEZING TODAY
-ERNIE BUSHMILLER
CAN I HAVE A DOGGIE BAG ?
RESTAURAN
MENU
Tm. Reg. U. S. Pat. Off.—All rights reserved © 1971 by United Feature Syndicate, Inc. DEC.-6

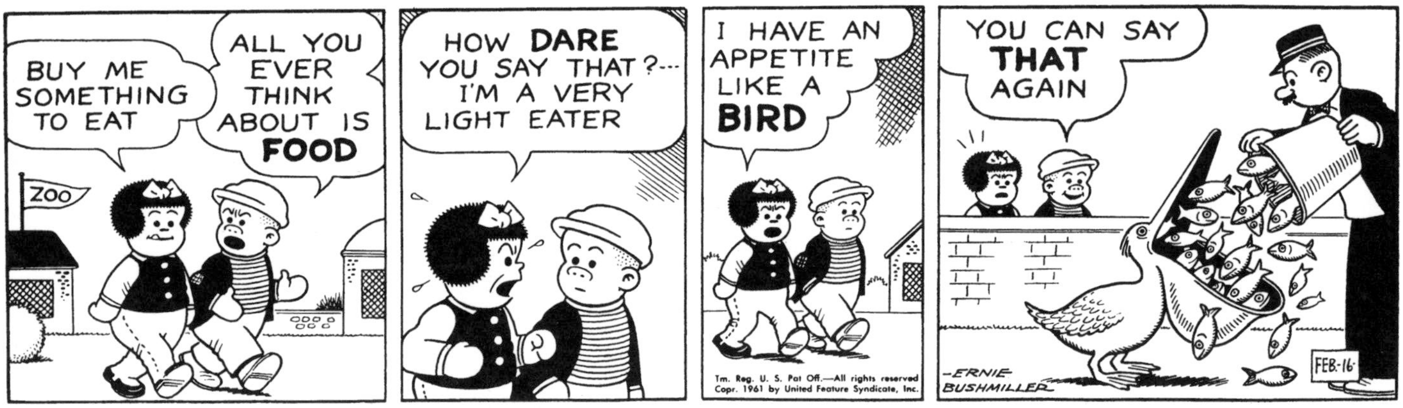

BUY ME SOMETHING TO EAT
ALL YOU EVER THINK ABOUT IS **FOOD**
ZOO
HOW **DARE** YOU SAY THAT ?--- I'M A VERY LIGHT EATER
I HAVE AN APPETITE LIKE A **BIRD**
Tm. Reg. U. S. Pat. Off.—All rights reserved Copr. 1961 by United Feature Syndicate, Inc.
YOU CAN SAY **THAT** AGAIN
-ERNIE BUSHMILLER
FEB-16

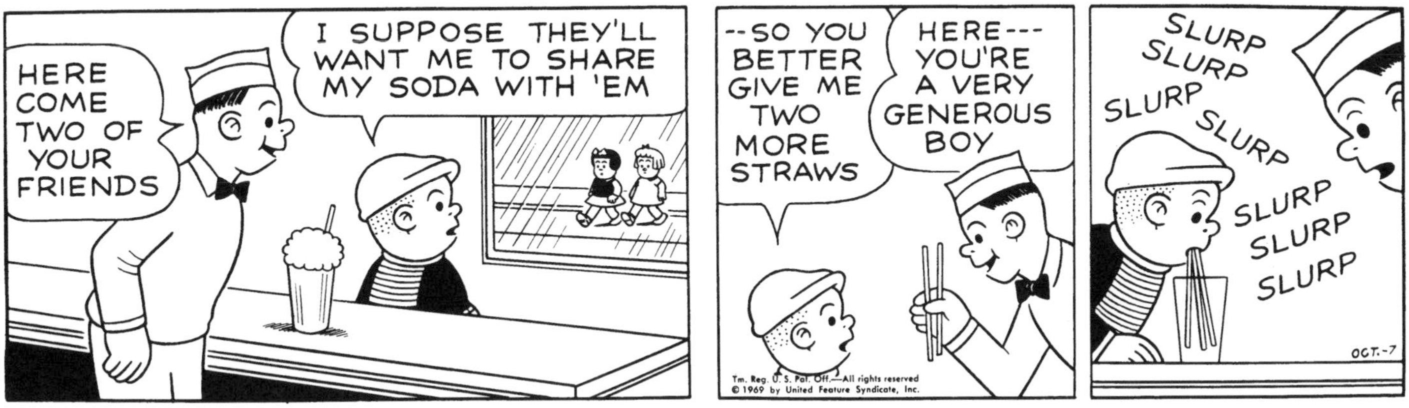
HERE COME TWO OF YOUR FRIENDS
I SUPPOSE THEY'LL WANT ME TO SHARE MY SODA WITH 'EM
--SO YOU BETTER GIVE ME TWO MORE STRAWS
HERE--- YOU'RE A VERY GENEROUS BOY
Tm. Reg. U. S. Pat. Off.—All rights reserved © 1969 by United Feature Syndicate, Inc.
SLURP SLURP SLURP SLURP SLURP SLURP SLURP
OCT.-7

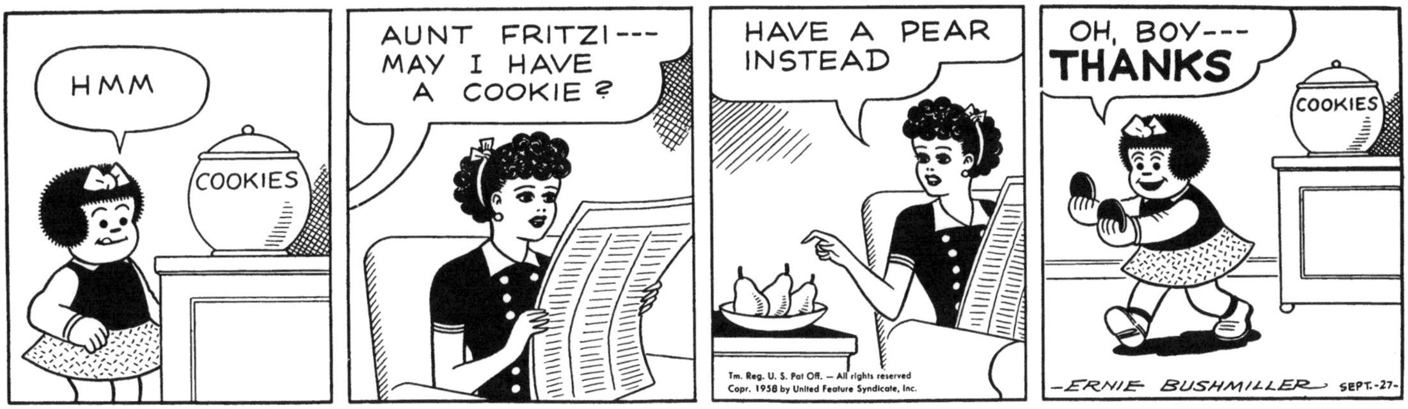
HMM
COOKIES
AUNT FRITZI--- MAY I HAVE A COOKIE?
HAVE A PEAR INSTEAD
Tm. Reg. U. S. Pat Off. — All rights reserved Copr. 1958 by United Feature Syndicate, Inc.
OH, BOY--- **THANKS**
COOKIES
-ERNIE BUSHMILLER SEPT.-27-

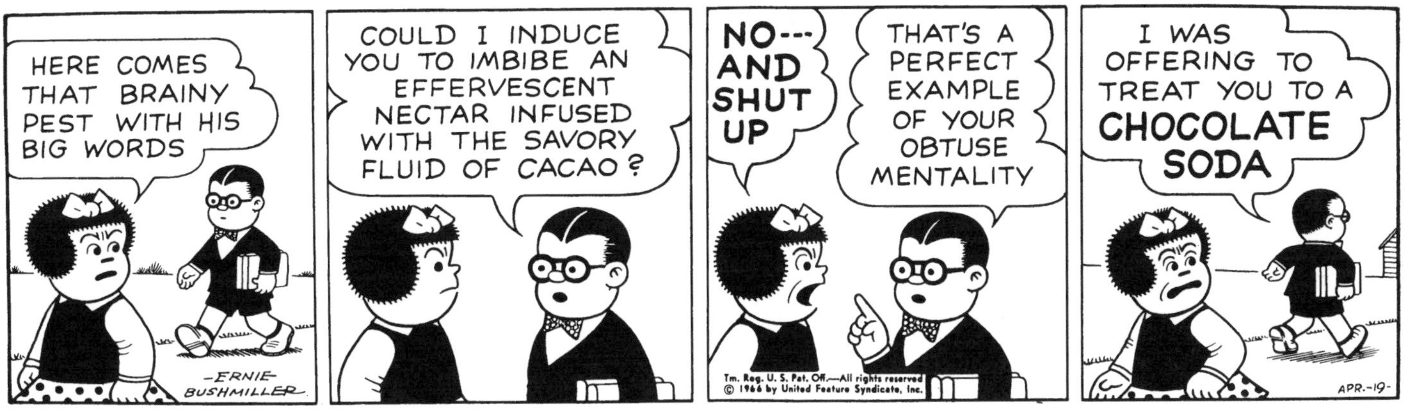
HERE COMES THAT BRAINY PEST WITH HIS BIG WORDS
-ERNIE- BUSHMILLER
COULD I INDUCE YOU TO IMBIBE AN EFFERVESCENT NECTAR INFUSED WITH THE SAVORY FLUID OF CACAO?
NO--- AND SHUT UP
THAT'S A PERFECT EXAMPLE OF YOUR OBTUSE MENTALITY
Tm. Reg. U. S. Pat. Off.—All rights reserved © 1966 by United Feature Syndicate, Inc.
I WAS OFFERING TO TREAT YOU TO A **CHOCOLATE SODA**
APR.-19-

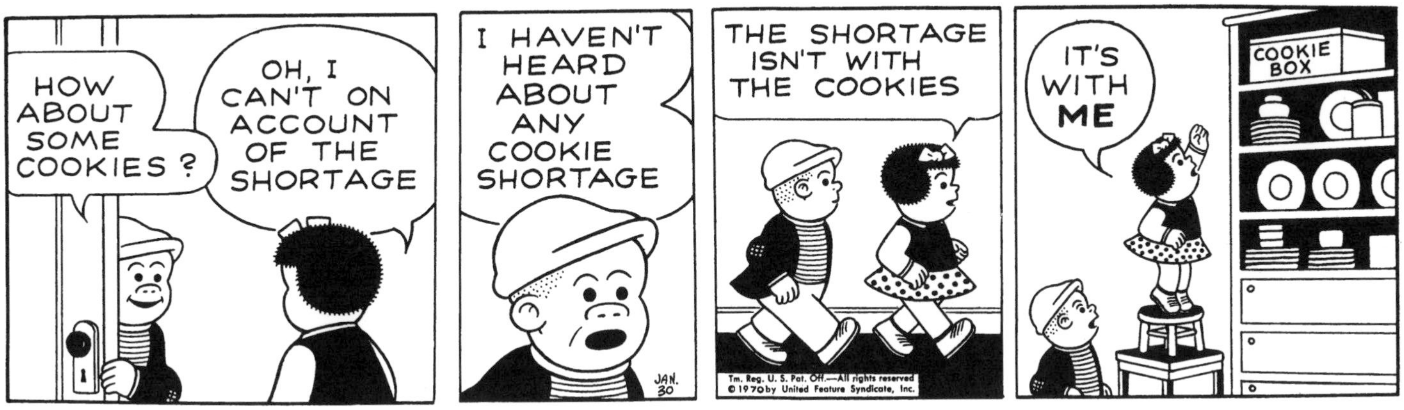
HOW ABOUT SOME COOKIES?
OH, I CAN'T ON ACCOUNT OF THE SHORTAGE
I HAVEN'T HEARD ABOUT ANY COOKIE SHORTAGE
JAN. 30
THE SHORTAGE ISN'T WITH THE COOKIES
Tm. Reg. U. S. Pat. Off.—All rights reserved © 1970 by United Feature Syndicate, Inc.
IT'S WITH **ME**
COOKIE BOX

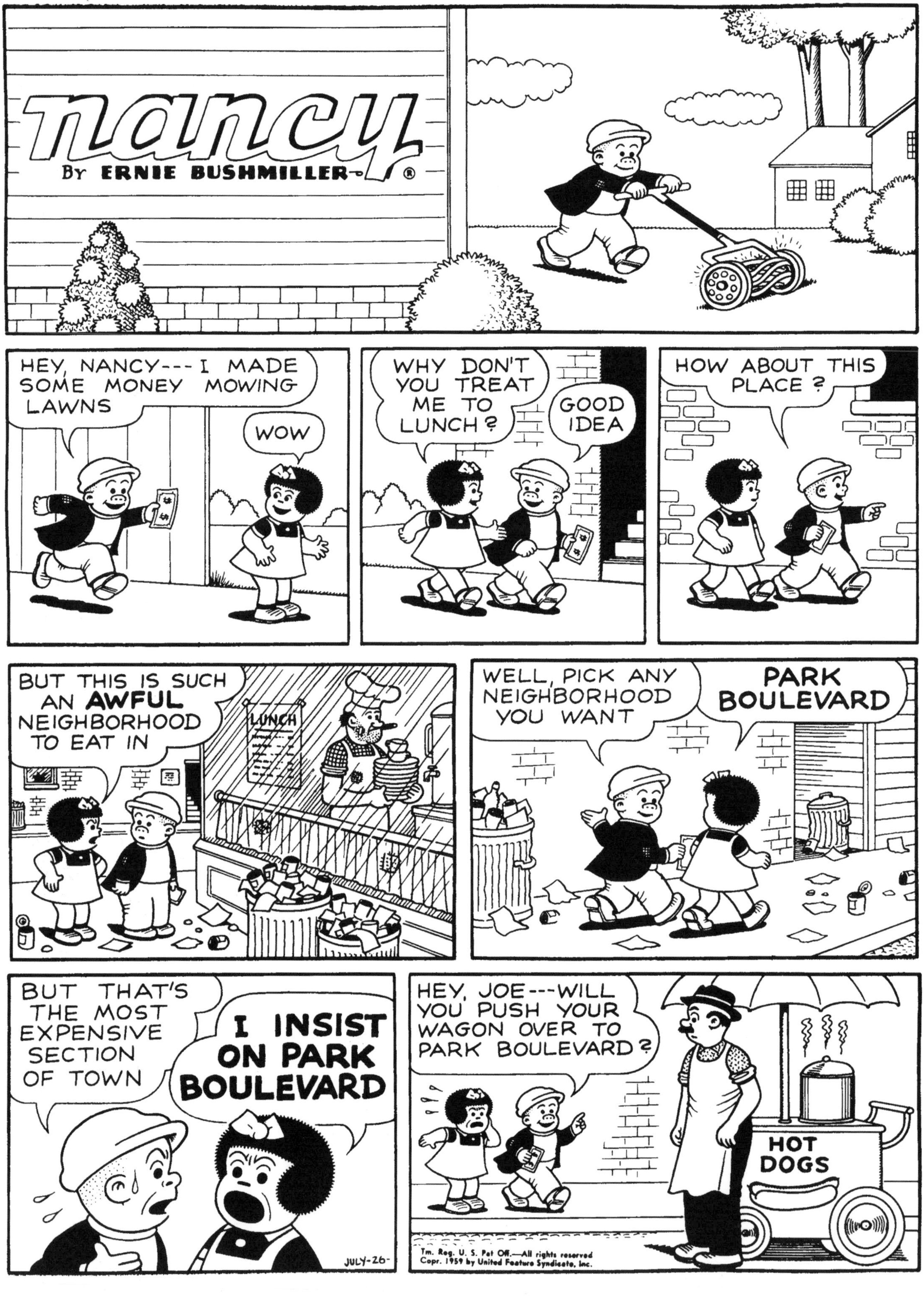
nancy
By ERNIE BUSHMILLER
HEY, NANCY--- I MADE SOME MONEY MOWING LAWNS
WOW
WHY DON'T YOU TREAT ME TO LUNCH?
GOOD IDEA
HOW ABOUT THIS PLACE?
BUT THIS IS SUCH AN AWFUL NEIGHBORHOOD TO EAT IN
LUNCH
WELL, PICK ANY NEIGHBORHOOD YOU WANT
PARK BOULEVARD
BUT THAT'S THE MOST EXPENSIVE SECTION OF TOWN
I INSIST ON PARK BOULEVARD
JULY-26-
HEY, JOE---WILL YOU PUSH YOUR WAGON OVER TO PARK BOULEVARD?
HOT DOGS
Tm. Reg. U. S. Pat Off.—All rights reserved
Copr. 1959 by United Feature Syndicate, Inc.

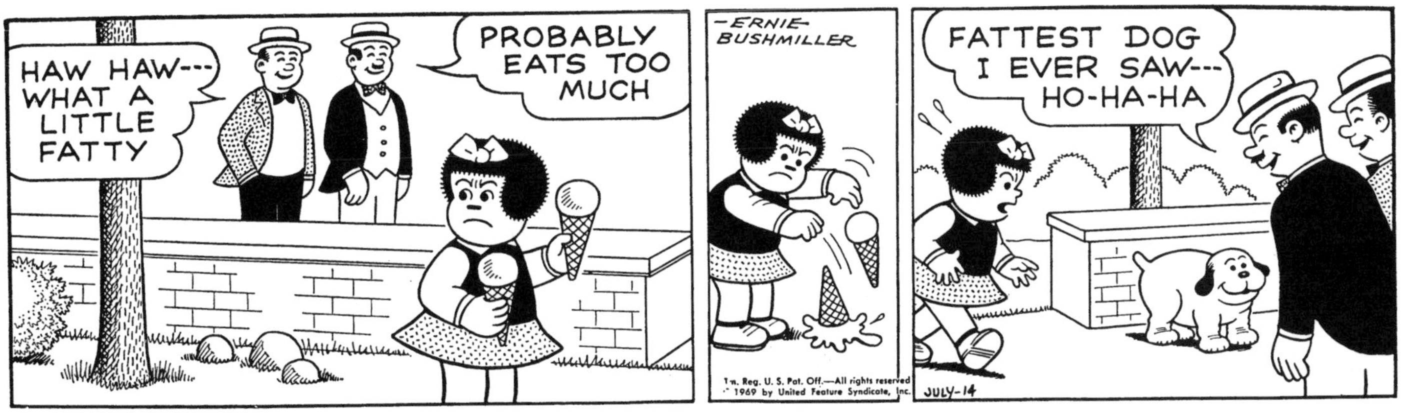
HAW HAW--- WHAT A LITTLE FATTY
PROBABLY EATS TOO MUCH
-ERNIE BUSHMILLER
Tm. Reg. U. S. Pat. Off.—All rights reserved
1969 by United Feature Syndicate, Inc.
FATTEST DOG I EVER SAW--- HO-HA-HA
JULY-14

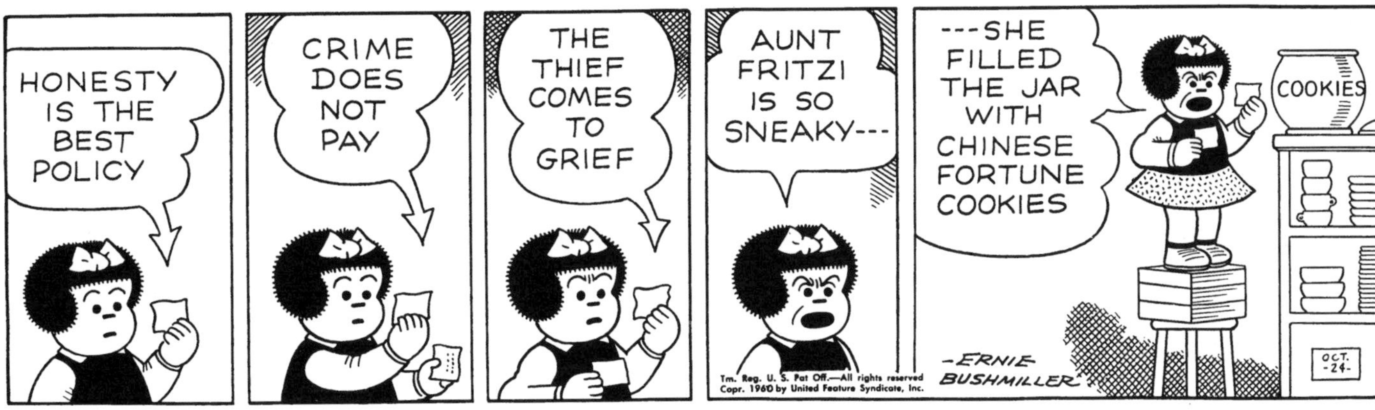
HONESTY IS THE BEST POLICY
CRIME DOES NOT PAY
THE THIEF COMES TO GRIEF
AUNT FRITZI IS SO SNEAKY---
Tm. Reg. U. S. Pat Off.—All rights reserved
Copr. 1960 by United Feature Syndicate, Inc.
---SHE FILLED THE JAR WITH CHINESE FORTUNE COOKIES
COOKIES
-ERNIE BUSHMILLER
OCT. -24-

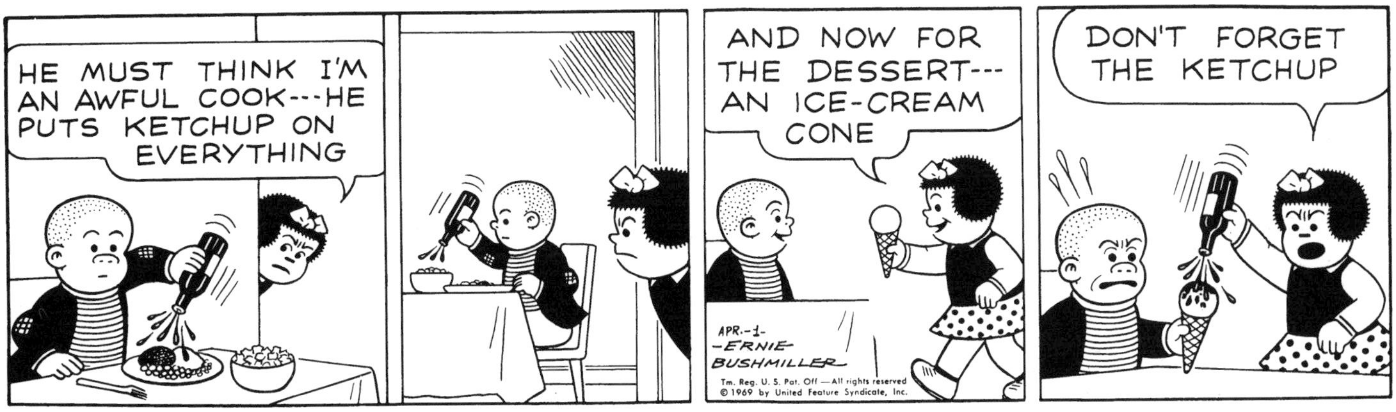
HE MUST THINK I'M AN AWFUL COOK---HE PUTS KETCHUP ON EVERYTHING
AND NOW FOR THE DESSERT--- AN ICE-CREAM CONE
APR.-1-
-ERNIE BUSHMILLER
Tm. Reg. U. S. Pat. Off —All rights reserved
© 1969 by United Feature Syndicate, Inc.
DON'T FORGET THE KETCHUP

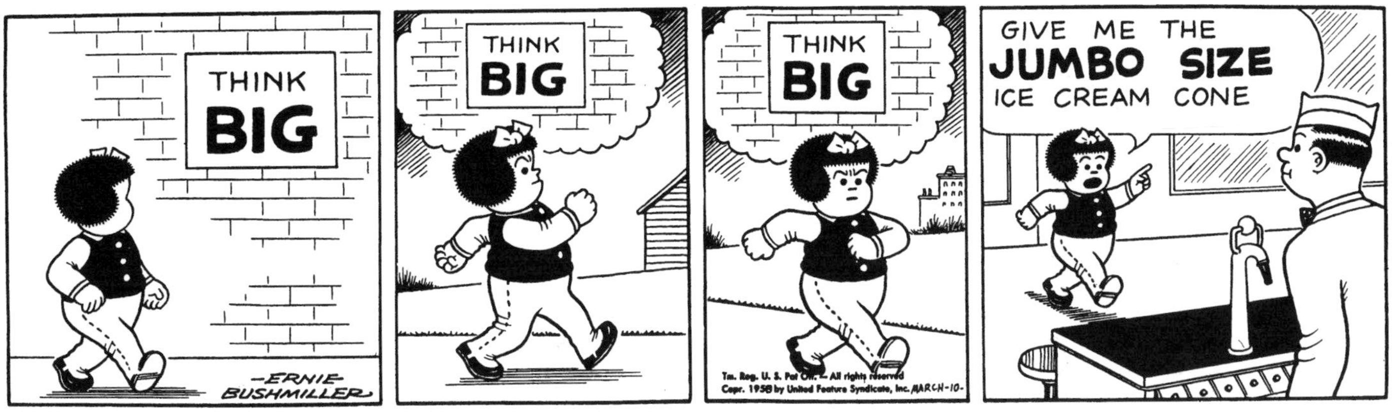
THINK BIG
-ERNIE BUSHMILLER
THINK BIG
THINK BIG
Tm. Reg. U. S. Pat Off.—All rights reserved
Copr. 1958 by United Feature Syndicate, Inc.
MARCH-10-
GIVE ME THE JUMBO SIZE ICE CREAM CONE

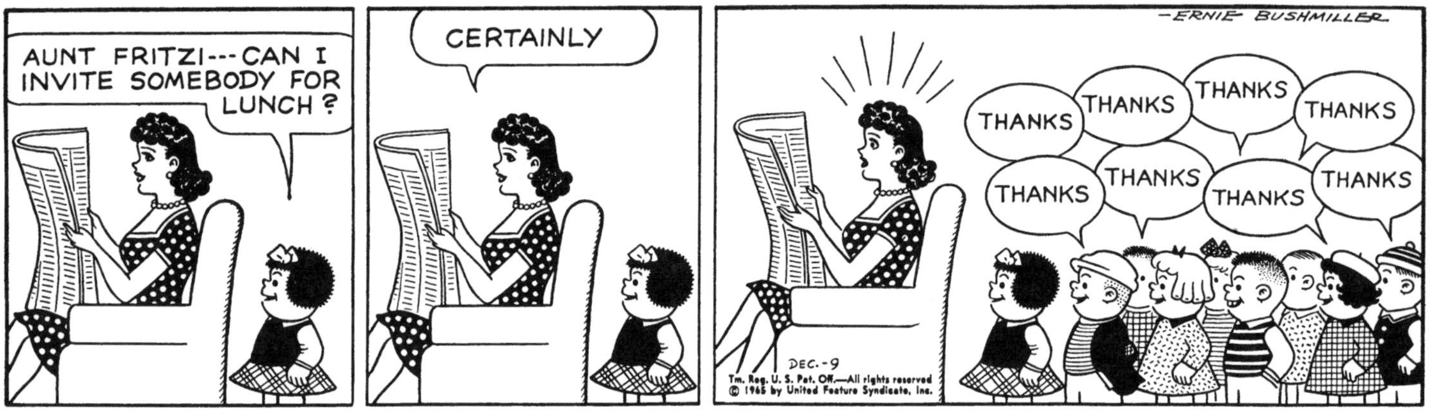
AUNT FRITZI---CAN I INVITE SOMEBODY FOR LUNCH?
CERTAINLY
-ERNIE BUSHMILLER
THANKS
THANKS
THANKS
THANKS
THANKS
THANKS
THANKS
THANKS
DEC.-9
Tm. Reg. U. S. Pat. Off.—All rights reserved © 1965 by United Feature Syndicate, Inc.

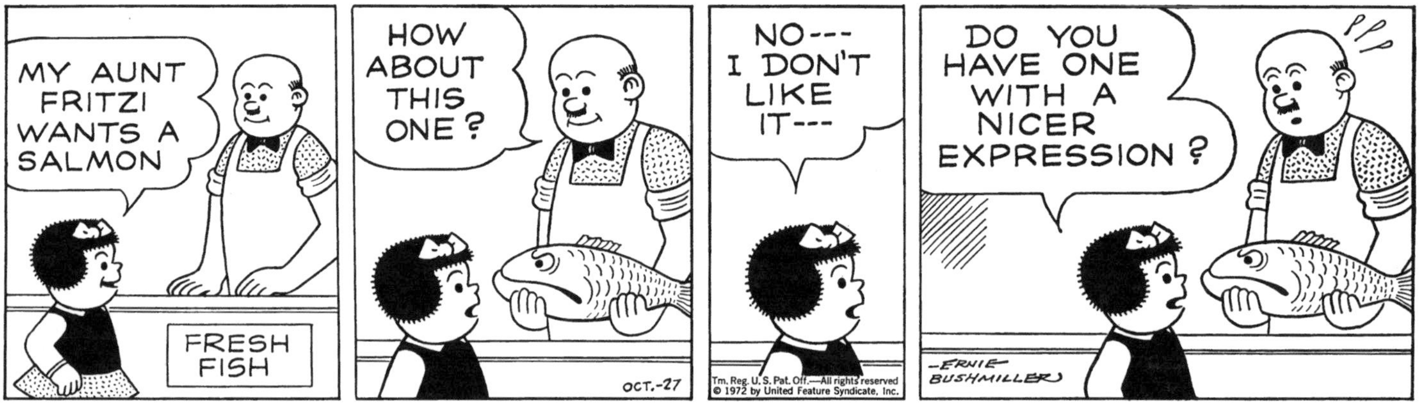
MY AUNT FRITZI WANTS A SALMON
FRESH FISH
HOW ABOUT THIS ONE?
OCT.-27
NO--- I DON'T LIKE IT---
Tm. Reg. U. S. Pat. Off.—All rights reserved © 1972 by United Feature Syndicate, Inc.
DO YOU HAVE ONE WITH A NICER EXPRESSION?
-ERNIE BUSHMILLER

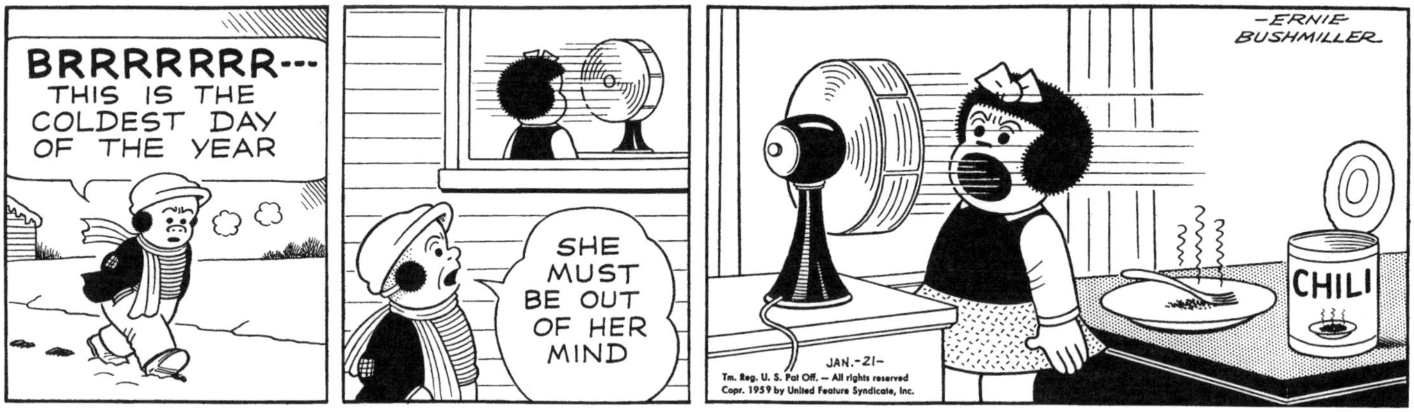
BRRRRRRR--- THIS IS THE COLDEST DAY OF THE YEAR
SHE MUST BE OUT OF HER MIND
-ERNIE BUSHMILLER
CHILI
JAN.-21-
Tm. Reg. U. S. Pat Off. — All rights reserved Copr. 1959 by United Feature Syndicate, Inc.

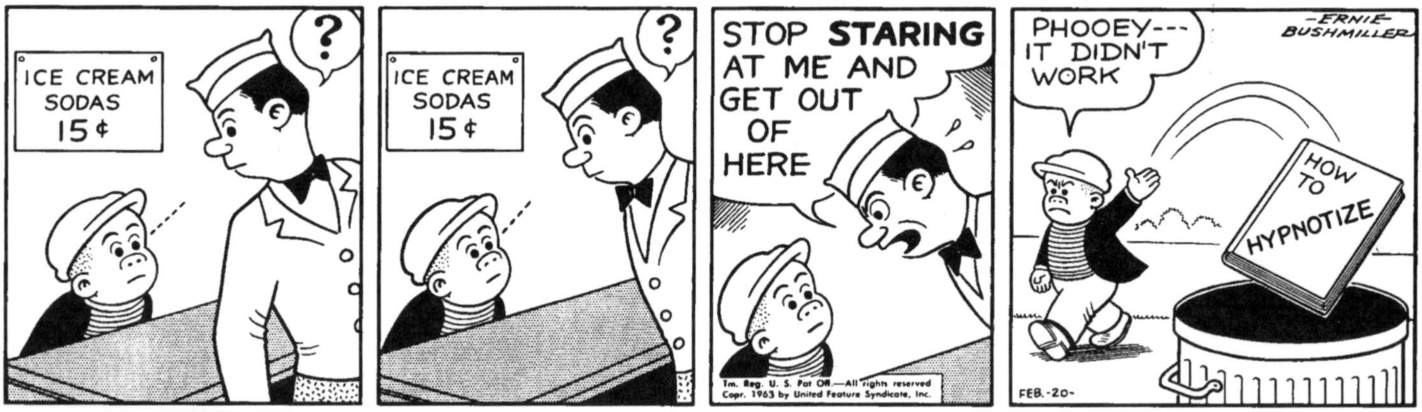
ICE CREAM SODAS 15¢
?
ICE CREAM SODAS 15¢
?
STOP **STARING** AT ME AND GET OUT OF HERE
Tm. Reg. U. S. Pat Off.—All rights reserved Copr. 1963 by United Feature Syndicate, Inc.
PHOOEY--- IT DIDN'T WORK
-ERNIE BUSHMILLER
HOW TO HYPNOTIZE
FEB.-20-

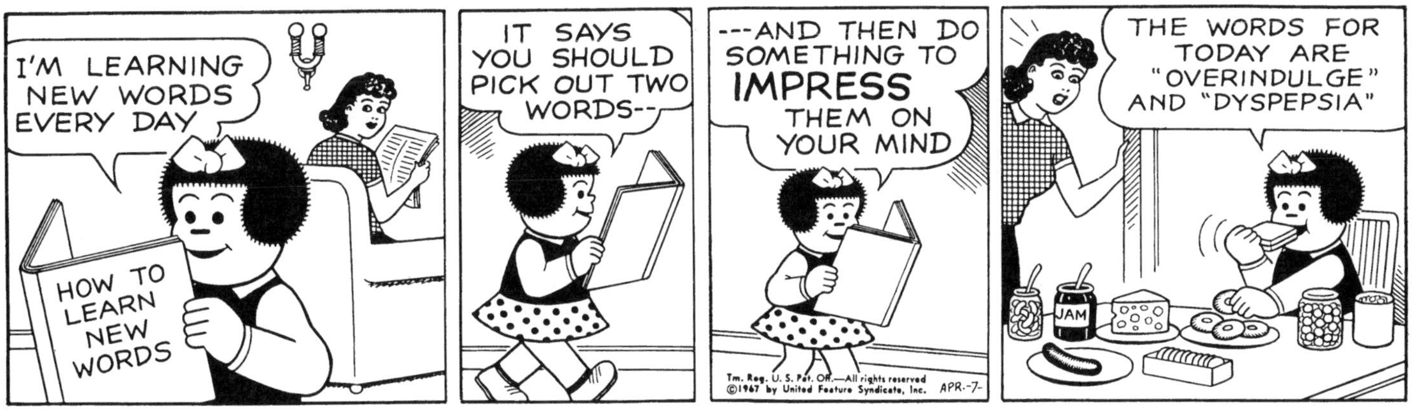
I'M LEARNING NEW WORDS EVERY DAY
HOW TO LEARN NEW WORDS
IT SAYS YOU SHOULD PICK OUT TWO WORDS--
---AND THEN DO SOMETHING TO IMPRESS THEM ON YOUR MIND
Tm. Reg. U. S. Pat. Off.—All rights reserved ©1967 by United Feature Syndicate, Inc.
APR.-7-
THE WORDS FOR TODAY ARE "OVERINDULGE" AND "DYSPEPSIA"
JAM

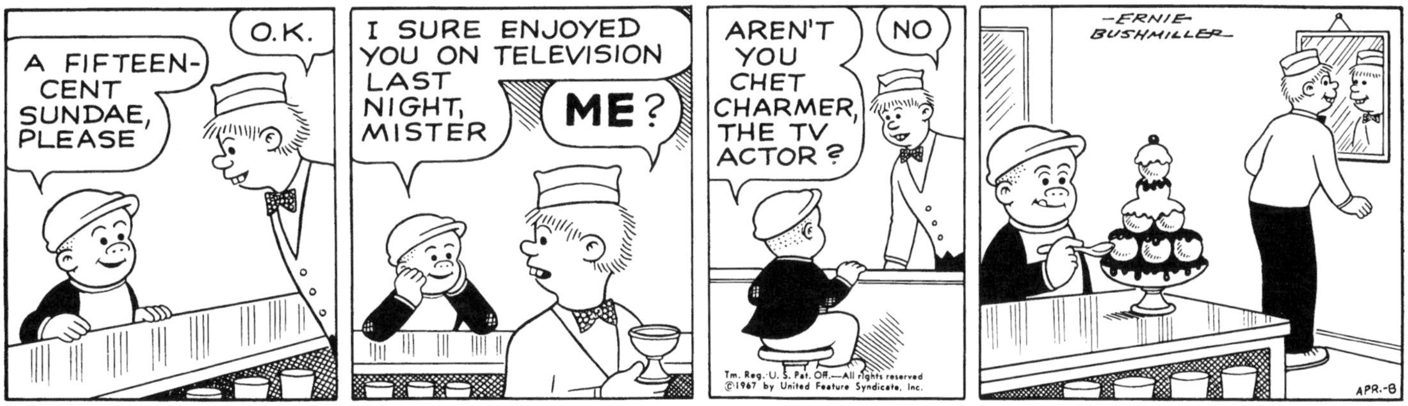
A FIFTEEN-CENT SUNDAE, PLEASE
O.K.
I SURE ENJOYED YOU ON TELEVISION LAST NIGHT, MISTER
ME?
AREN'T YOU CHET CHARMER, THE TV ACTOR?
NO
Tm. Reg. U. S. Pat. Off.—All rights reserved ©1967 by United Feature Syndicate, Inc.
-ERNIE- BUSHMILLER
APR.-8

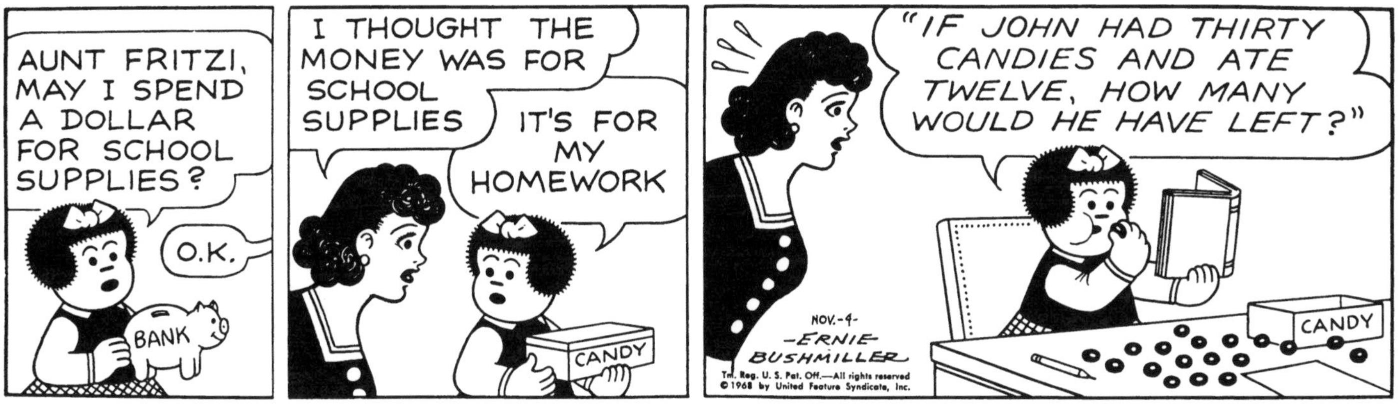
AUNT FRITZI, MAY I SPEND A DOLLAR FOR SCHOOL SUPPLIES?
O.K.
BANK
I THOUGHT THE MONEY WAS FOR SCHOOL SUPPLIES
IT'S FOR MY HOMEWORK
CANDY
"IF JOHN HAD THIRTY CANDIES AND ATE TWELVE, HOW MANY WOULD HE HAVE LEFT?"
NOV.-4-
-ERNIE- BUSHMILLER
Tm. Reg. U. S. Pat. Off.—All rights reserved ©1968 by United Feature Syndicate, Inc.
CANDY

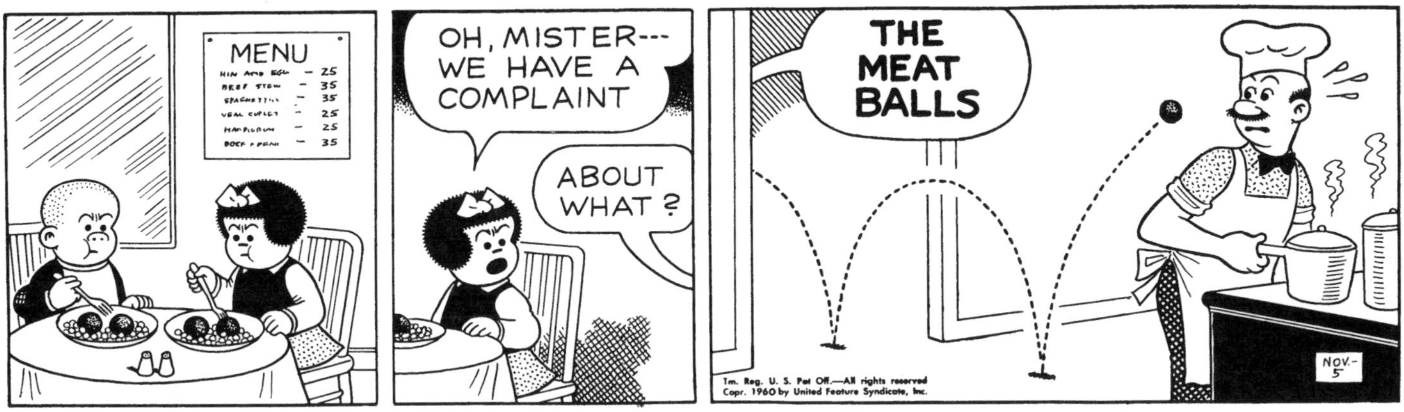
MENU
OH, MISTER--- WE HAVE A COMPLAINT
ABOUT WHAT?
THE MEAT BALLS
Tm. Reg. U. S. Pat Off.—All rights reserved Copr. 1960 by United Feature Syndicate, Inc.
NOV.-5

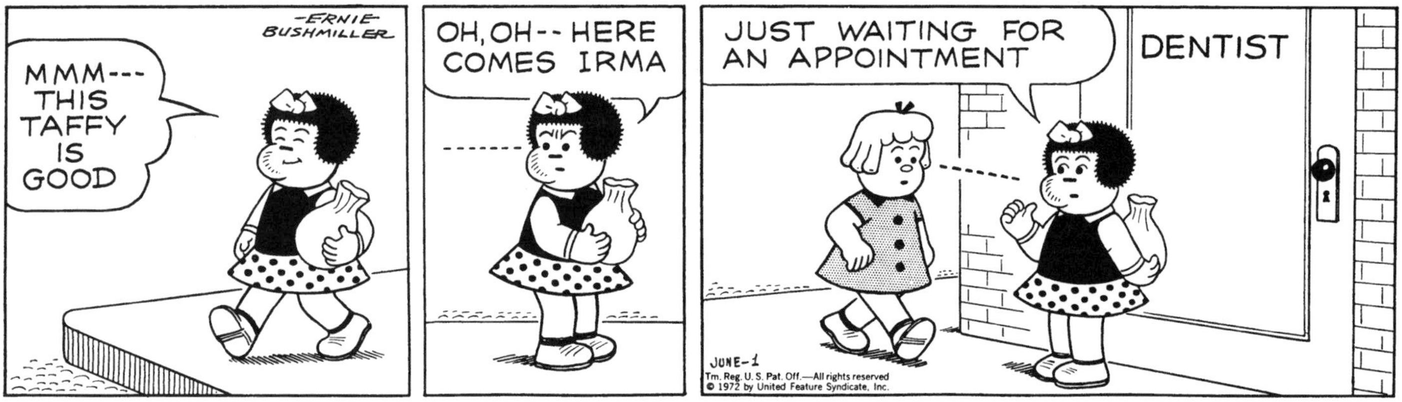
-ERNIE BUSHMILLER
MMM--- THIS TAFFY IS GOOD
OH, OH-- HERE COMES IRMA
JUST WAITING FOR AN APPOINTMENT
DENTIST
JUNE-1
Tm. Reg. U. S. Pat. Off.—All rights reserved © 1972 by United Feature Syndicate, Inc.

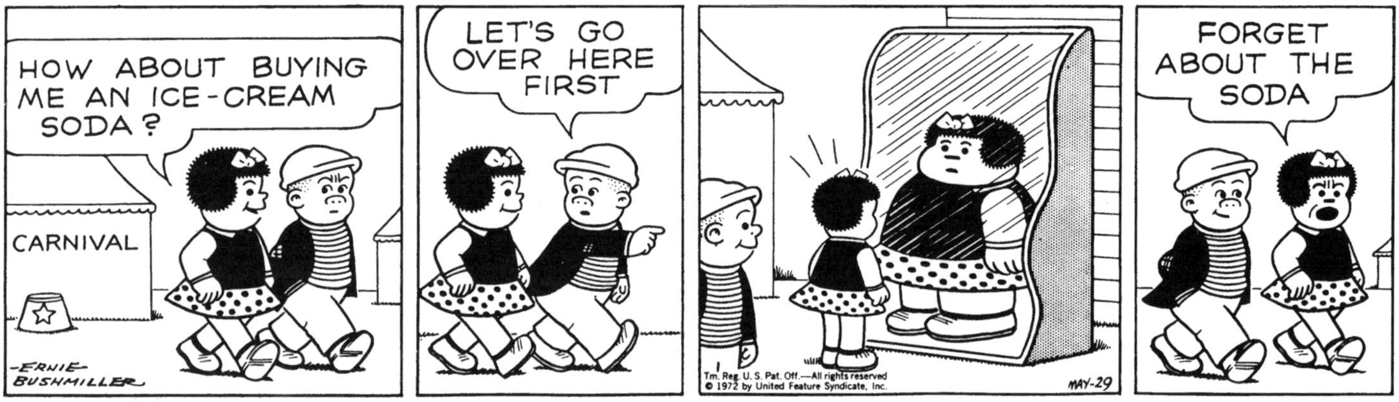
HOW ABOUT BUYING ME AN ICE-CREAM SODA?
CARNIVAL
-ERNIE BUSHMILLER
LET'S GO OVER HERE FIRST
Tm. Reg. U. S. Pat. Off.—All rights reserved © 1972 by United Feature Syndicate, Inc.
MAY-29
FORGET ABOUT THE SODA

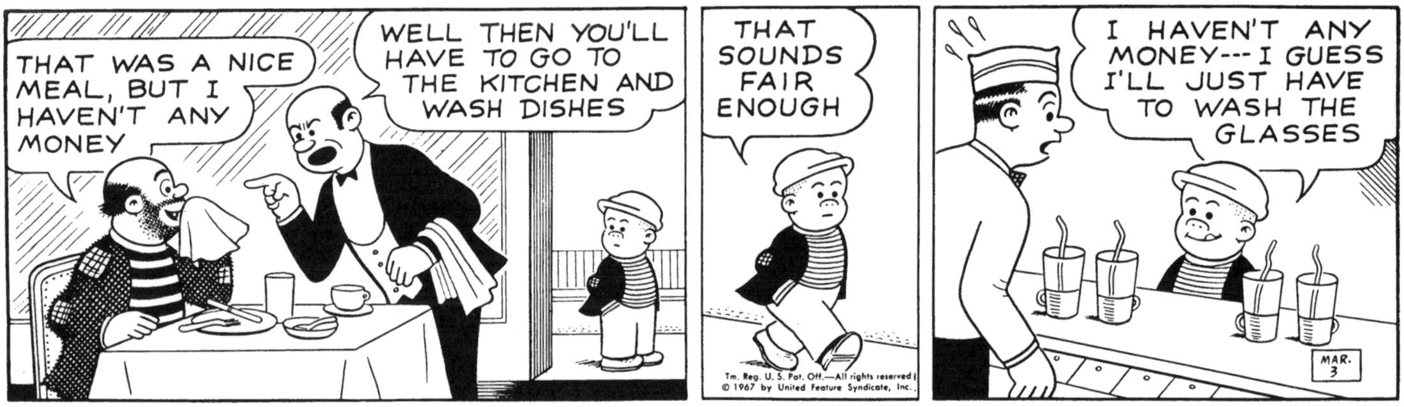
THAT WAS A NICE MEAL, BUT I HAVEN'T ANY MONEY
WELL THEN YOU'LL HAVE TO GO TO THE KITCHEN AND WASH DISHES
THAT SOUNDS FAIR ENOUGH
Tm. Reg. U. S. Pat. Off.—All rights reserved © 1967 by United Feature Syndicate, Inc.
I HAVEN'T ANY MONEY--- I GUESS I'LL JUST HAVE TO WASH THE GLASSES
MAR. 3

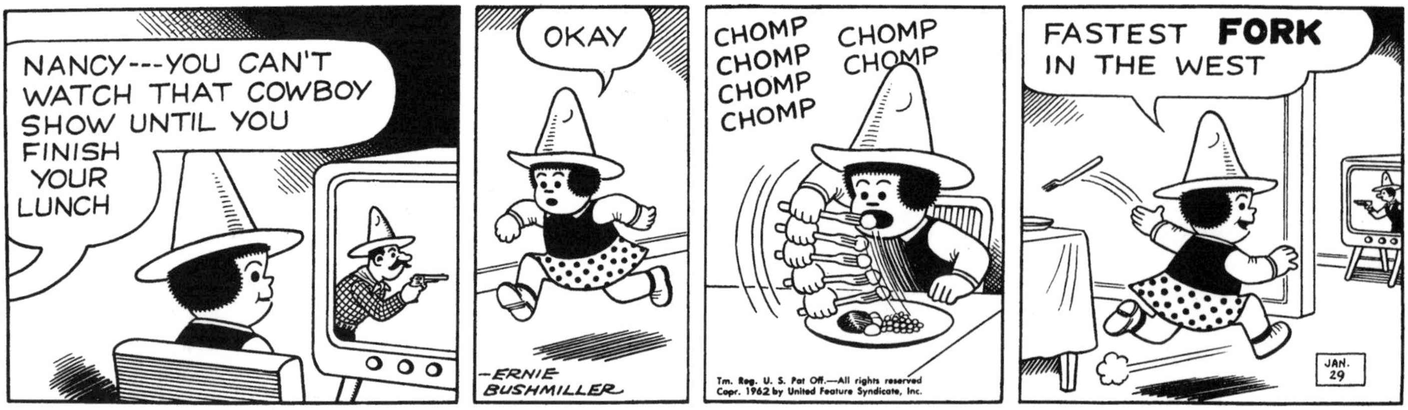
NANCY---YOU CAN'T WATCH THAT COWBOY SHOW UNTIL YOU FINISH YOUR LUNCH
OKAY
-ERNIE BUSHMILLER
CHOMP CHOMP CHOMP CHOMP
CHOMP CHOMP
Tm. Reg. U. S. Pat Off.—All rights reserved Copr. 1962 by United Feature Syndicate, Inc.
FASTEST **FORK** IN THE WEST
JAN. 29

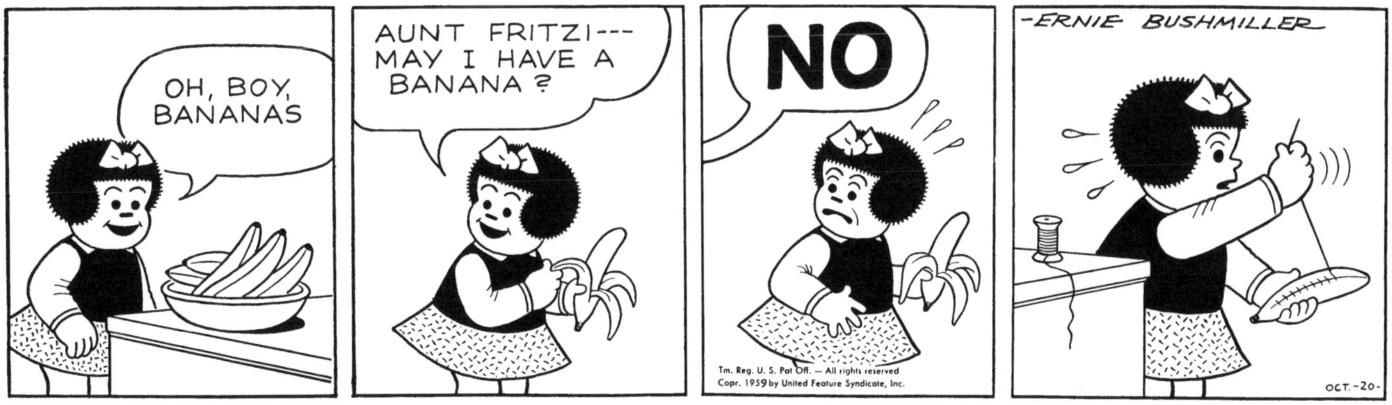
OH, BOY, BANANAS
AUNT FRITZI--- MAY I HAVE A BANANA?
NO
Tm. Reg. U. S. Pat. Off. — All rights reserved
Copr. 1959 by United Feature Syndicate, Inc.
-ERNIE BUSHMILLER
OCT.-20-

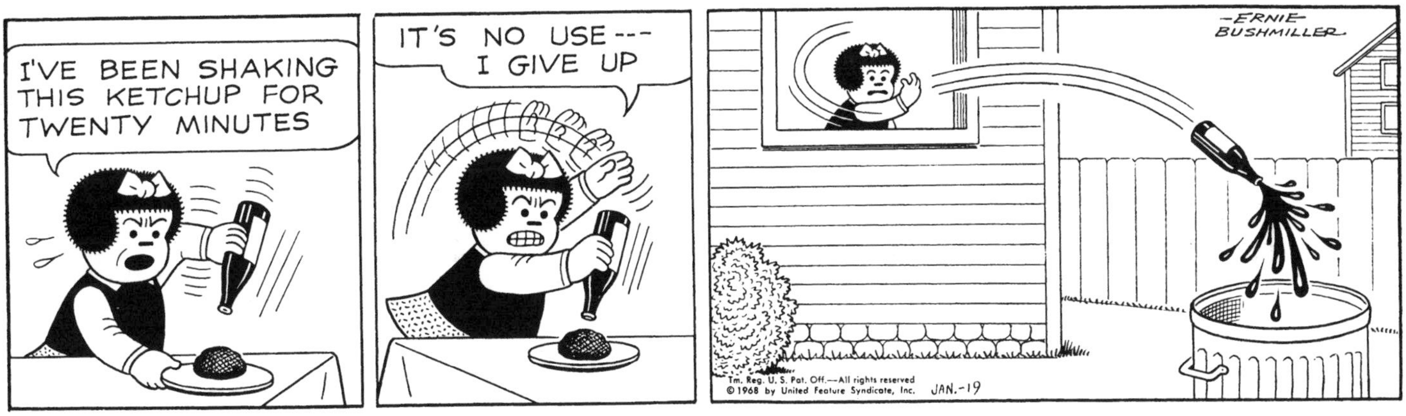
I'VE BEEN SHAKING THIS KETCHUP FOR TWENTY MINUTES
IT'S NO USE--- I GIVE UP
-ERNIE- BUSHMILLER
Tm. Reg. U. S. Pat. Off.—All rights reserved
© 1968 by United Feature Syndicate, Inc.
JAN.-19

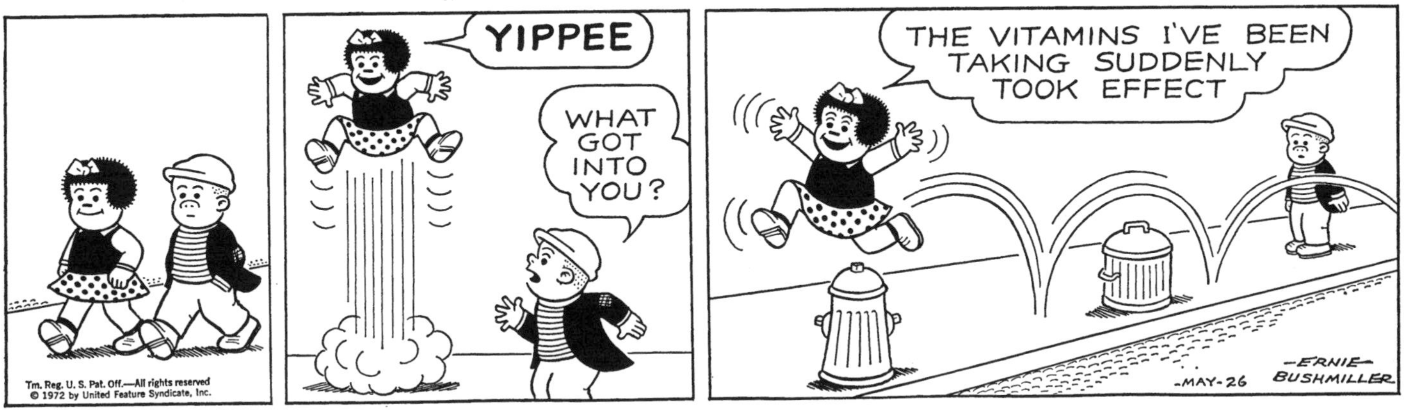
Tm. Reg. U. S. Pat. Off.—All rights reserved
© 1972 by United Feature Syndicate, Inc.
YIPPEE
WHAT GOT INTO YOU?
THE VITAMINS I'VE BEEN TAKING SUDDENLY TOOK EFFECT
-MAY-26
-ERNIE- BUSHMILLER

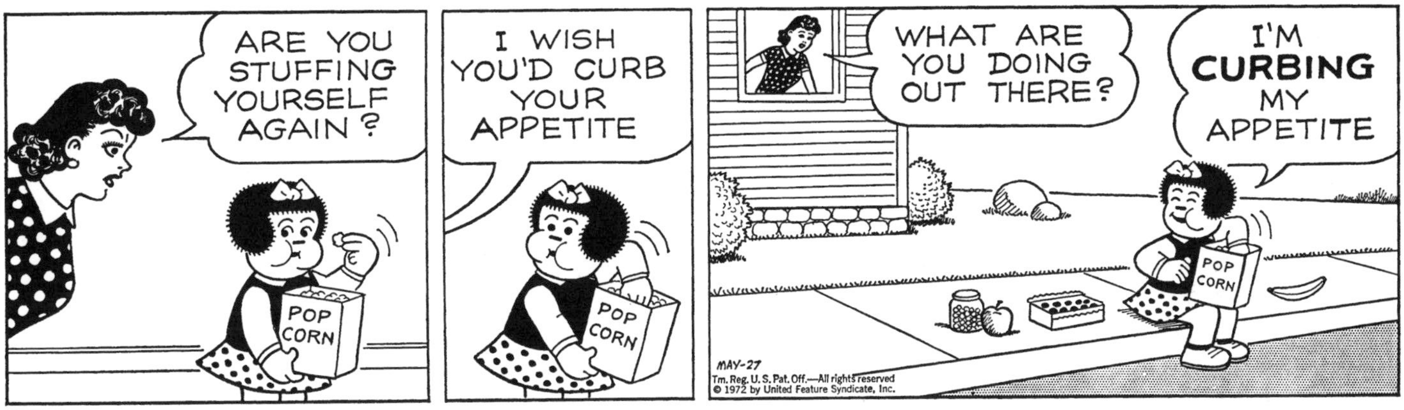
ARE YOU STUFFING YOURSELF AGAIN?
POP CORN
I WISH YOU'D CURB YOUR APPETITE
POP CORN
WHAT ARE YOU DOING OUT THERE?
I'M CURBING MY APPETITE
POP CORN
MAY-27
Tm. Reg. U. S. Pat. Off.—All rights reserved
© 1972 by United Feature Syndicate, Inc.

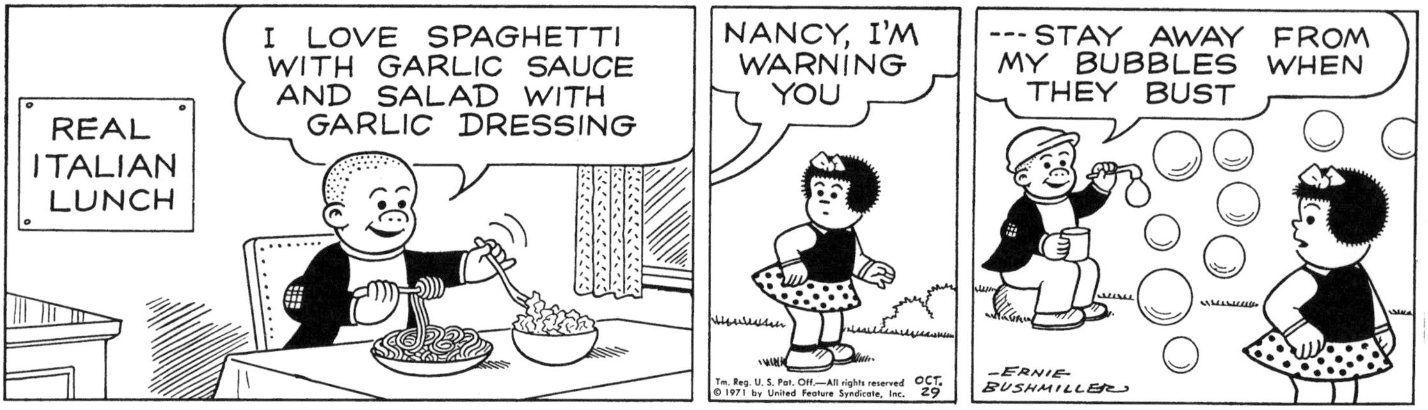
REAL ITALIAN LUNCH
I LOVE SPAGHETTI WITH GARLIC SAUCE AND SALAD WITH GARLIC DRESSING
NANCY, I'M WARNING YOU
Tm. Reg. U. S. Pat. Off.—All rights reserved © 1971 by United Feature Syndicate, Inc.
OCT. 29
---STAY AWAY FROM MY BUBBLES WHEN THEY BUST
-ERNIE BUSHMILLER

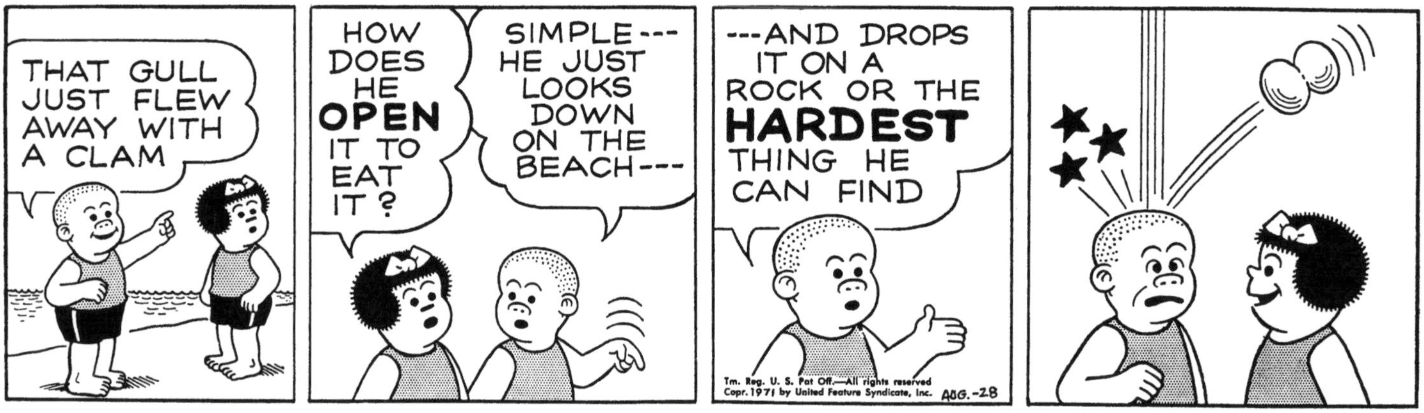
THAT GULL JUST FLEW AWAY WITH A CLAM
HOW DOES HE OPEN IT TO EAT IT ?
SIMPLE--- HE JUST LOOKS DOWN ON THE BEACH---
---AND DROPS IT ON A ROCK OR THE HARDEST THING HE CAN FIND
Tm. Reg. U. S. Pat. Off.—All rights reserved Copr. 1971 by United Feature Syndicate, Inc.
AUG.-28

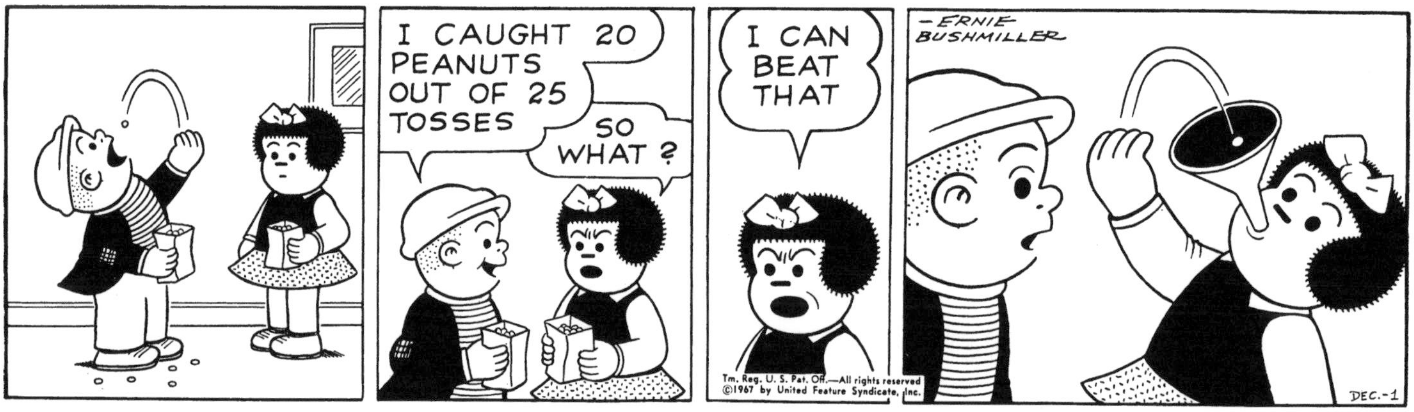
I CAUGHT 20 PEANUTS OUT OF 25 TOSSES
SO WHAT ?
I CAN BEAT THAT
Tm. Reg. U. S. Pat. Off.—All rights reserved ©1967 by United Feature Syndicate, Inc.
-ERNIE BUSHMILLER
DEC.-1

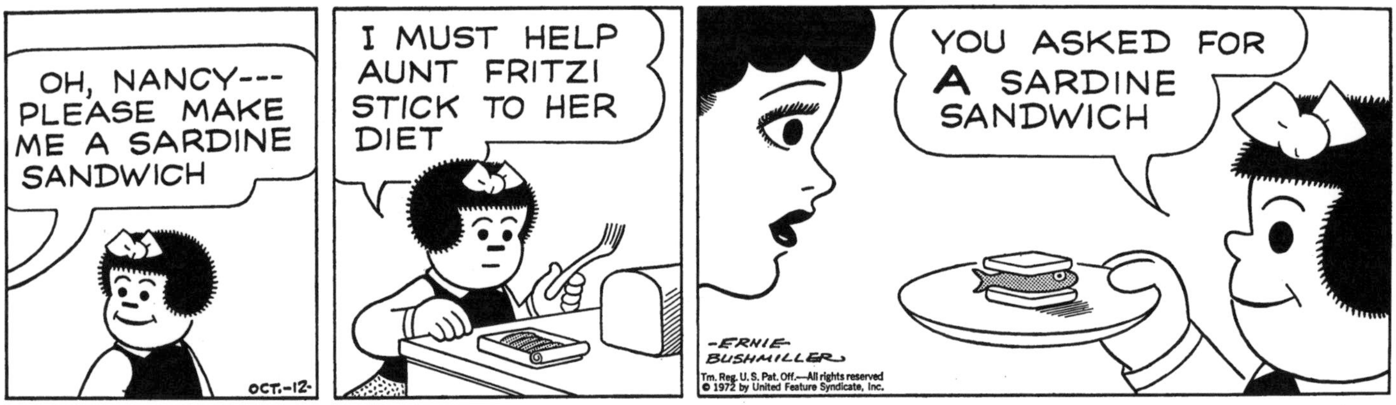
OH, NANCY--- PLEASE MAKE ME A SARDINE SANDWICH
OCT.-12-
I MUST HELP AUNT FRITZI STICK TO HER DIET
YOU ASKED FOR A SARDINE SANDWICH
-ERNIE BUSHMILLER
Tm. Reg. U. S. Pat. Off.—All rights reserved © 1972 by United Feature Syndicate, Inc.

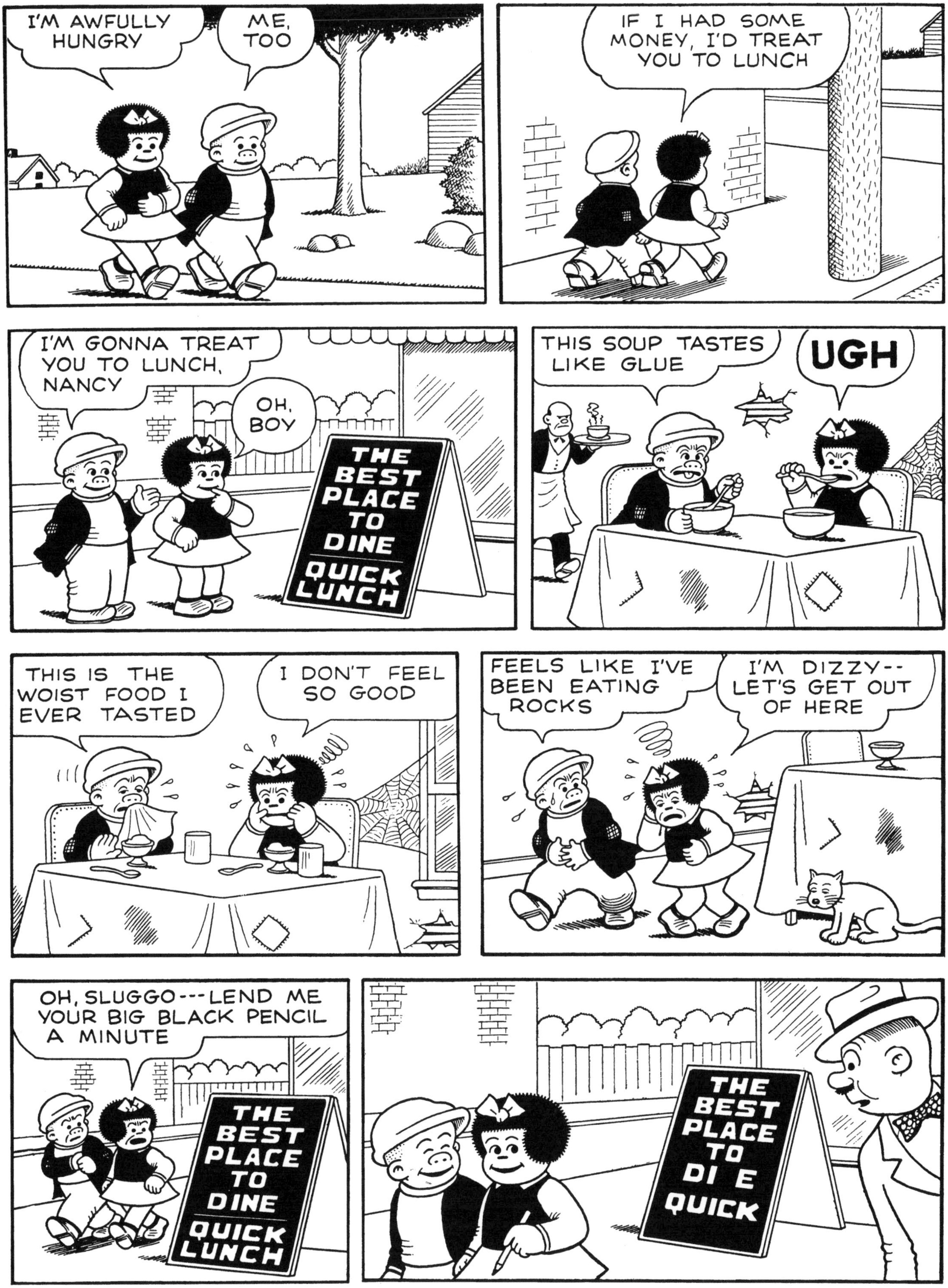
I'M AWFULLY HUNGRY
ME, TOO
IF I HAD SOME MONEY, I'D TREAT YOU TO LUNCH
I'M GONNA TREAT YOU TO LUNCH, NANCY
OH, BOY
THE BEST PLACE TO DINE
QUICK LUNCH
THIS SOUP TASTES LIKE GLUE
UGH
THIS IS THE WOIST FOOD I EVER TASTED
I DON'T FEEL SO GOOD
FEELS LIKE I'VE BEEN EATING ROCKS
I'M DIZZY-- LET'S GET OUT OF HERE
OH, SLUGGO---LEND ME YOUR BIG BLACK PENCIL A MINUTE
THE BEST PLACE TO DINE
QUICK LUNCH
THE BEST PLACE TO DI E
QUICK

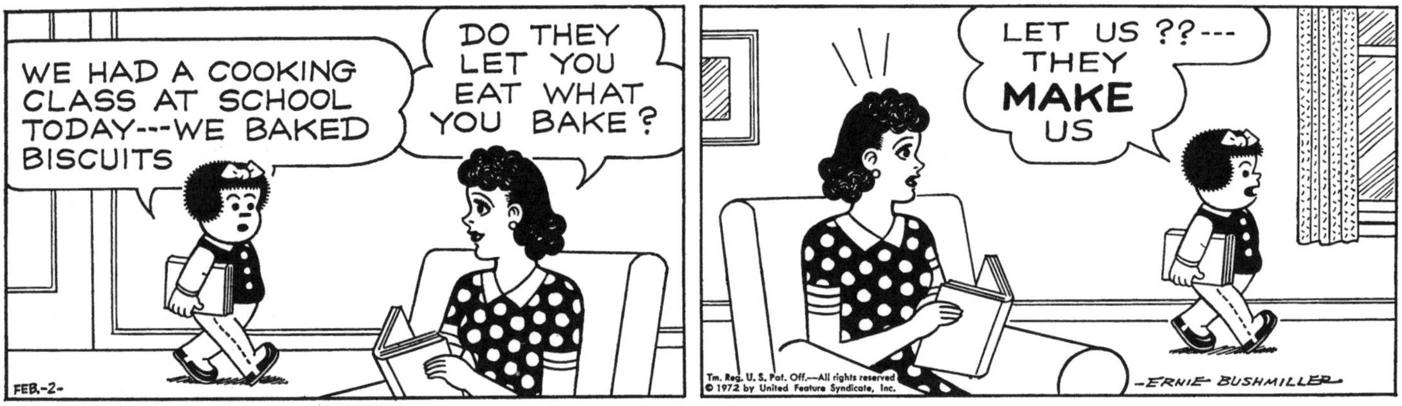
WE HAD A COOKING CLASS AT SCHOOL TODAY---WE BAKED BISCUITS
DO THEY LET YOU EAT WHAT YOU BAKE?
LET US ??--- THEY MAKE US
FEB.-2-
Tm. Reg. U. S. Pat. Off.—All rights reserved © 1972 by United Feature Syndicate, Inc.
-ERNIE BUSHMILLER

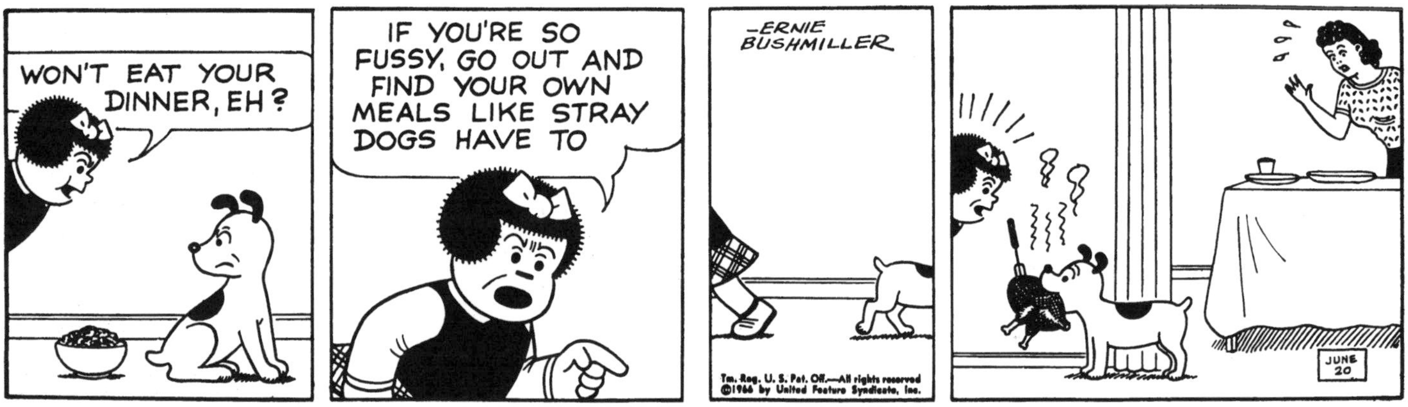
WON'T EAT YOUR DINNER, EH?
IF YOU'RE SO FUSSY, GO OUT AND FIND YOUR OWN MEALS LIKE STRAY DOGS HAVE TO
-ERNIE BUSHMILLER
Tm. Reg. U. S. Pat. Off.—All rights reserved ©1966 by United Feature Syndicate, Inc.
JUNE 20

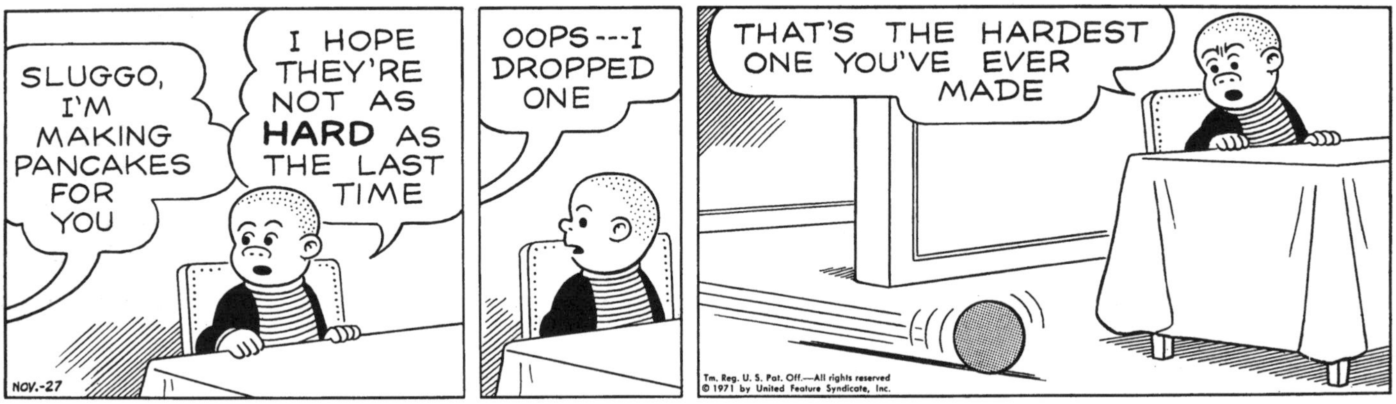
SLUGGO, I'M MAKING PANCAKES FOR YOU
I HOPE THEY'RE NOT AS HARD AS THE LAST TIME
NOV.-27
OOPS---I DROPPED ONE
THAT'S THE HARDEST ONE YOU'VE EVER MADE
Tm. Reg. U. S. Pat. Off.—All rights reserved © 1971 by United Feature Syndicate, Inc.

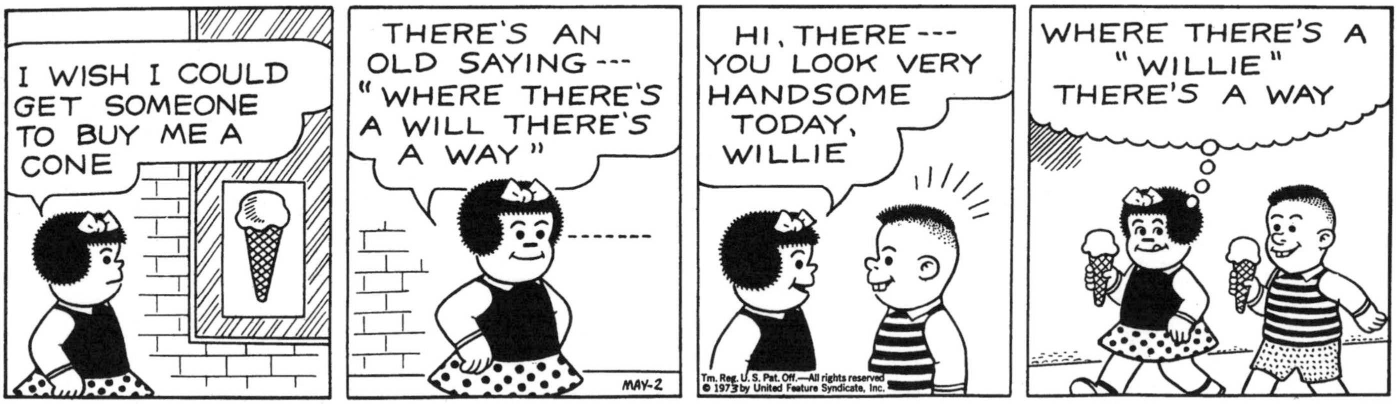
I WISH I COULD GET SOMEONE TO BUY ME A CONE
THERE'S AN OLD SAYING--- "WHERE THERE'S A WILL THERE'S A WAY"
MAY-2
HI, THERE--- YOU LOOK VERY HANDSOME TODAY, WILLIE
Tm. Reg. U. S. Pat. Off.—All rights reserved © 1973 by United Feature Syndicate, Inc.
WHERE THERE'S A "WILLIE" THERE'S A WAY

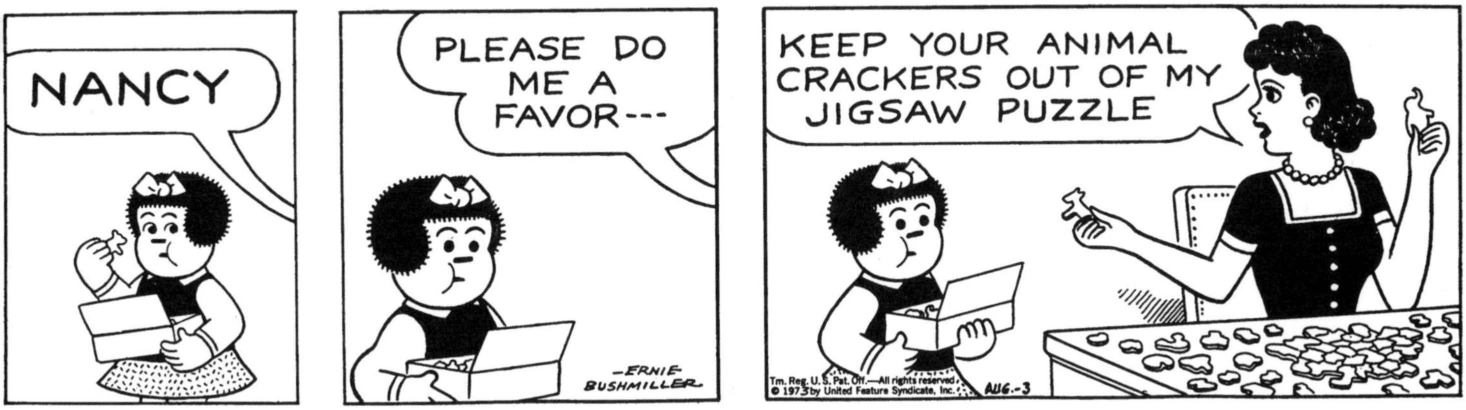
NANCY
PLEASE DO ME A FAVOR---
-ERNIE BUSHMILLER
KEEP YOUR ANIMAL CRACKERS OUT OF MY JIGSAW PUZZLE
Tm. Reg. U. S. Pat. Off.—All rights reserved © 1973 by United Feature Syndicate, Inc.
AUG.-3

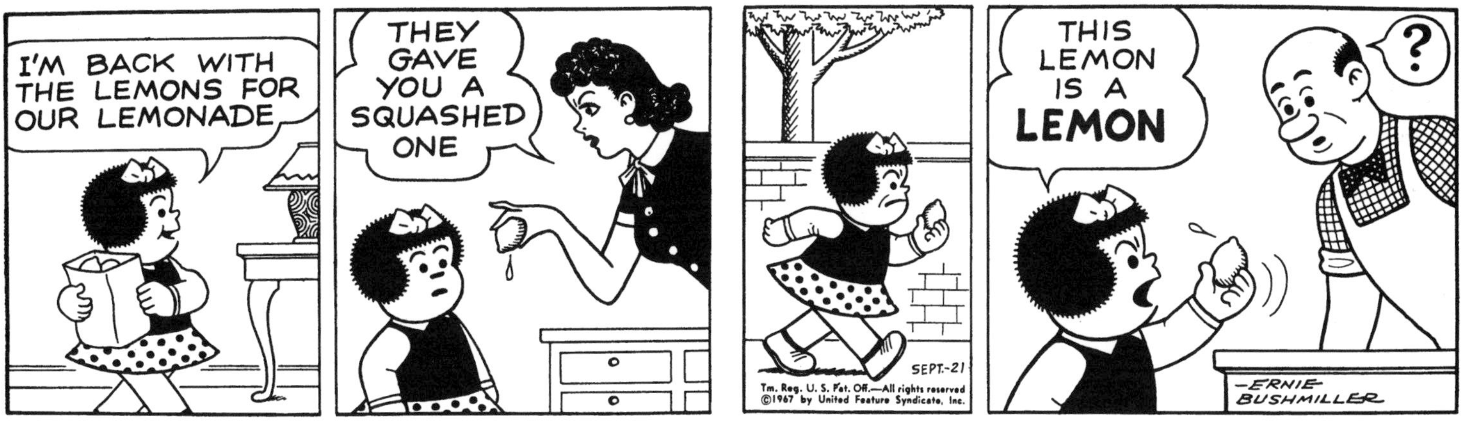
I'M BACK WITH THE LEMONS FOR OUR LEMONADE
THEY GAVE YOU A SQUASHED ONE
SEPT.-21
Tm. Reg. U. S. Pat. Off.—All rights reserved ©1967 by United Feature Syndicate, Inc.
THIS LEMON IS A **LEMON**
?
-ERNIE BUSHMILLER

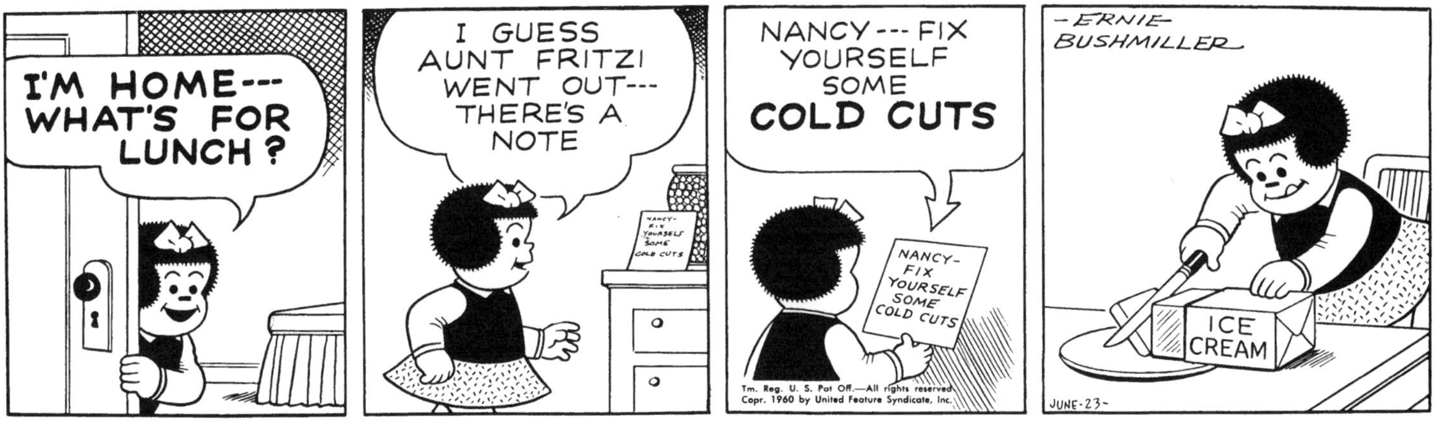
I'M HOME--- WHAT'S FOR LUNCH?
I GUESS AUNT FRITZI WENT OUT--- THERE'S A NOTE
NANCY--- FIX YOURSELF SOME **COLD CUTS**
NANCY- FIX YOURSELF SOME COLD CUTS
Tm. Reg. U. S. Pat Off.—All rights reserved Copr. 1960 by United Feature Syndicate, Inc.
-ERNIE BUSHMILLER
ICE CREAM
JUNE-23-

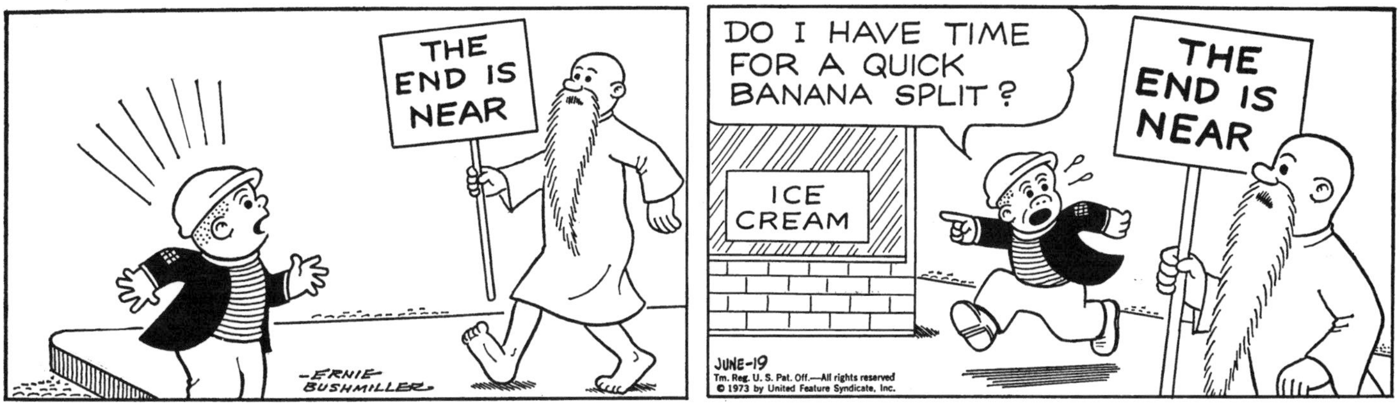
THE END IS NEAR
-ERNIE BUSHMILLER
DO I HAVE TIME FOR A QUICK BANANA SPLIT?
ICE CREAM
THE END IS NEAR
JUNE-19
Tm. Reg. U. S. Pat. Off.—All rights reserved © 1973 by United Feature Syndicate, Inc.

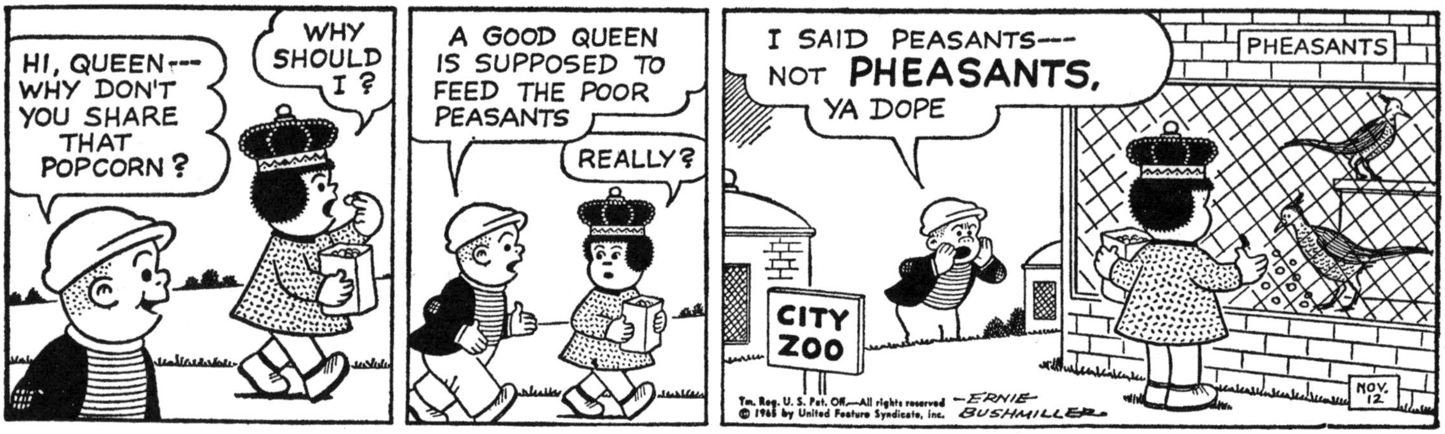
HI, QUEEN--- WHY DON'T YOU SHARE THAT POPCORN?
WHY SHOULD I?
A GOOD QUEEN IS SUPPOSED TO FEED THE POOR PEASANTS
REALLY?
I SAID PEASANTS--- NOT PHEASANTS, YA DOPE
PHEASANTS
CITY ZOO
Tm. Reg. U. S. Pat. Off.—All rights reserved © 1965 by United Feature Syndicate, Inc.
—ERNIE BUSHMILLER
NOV. 12

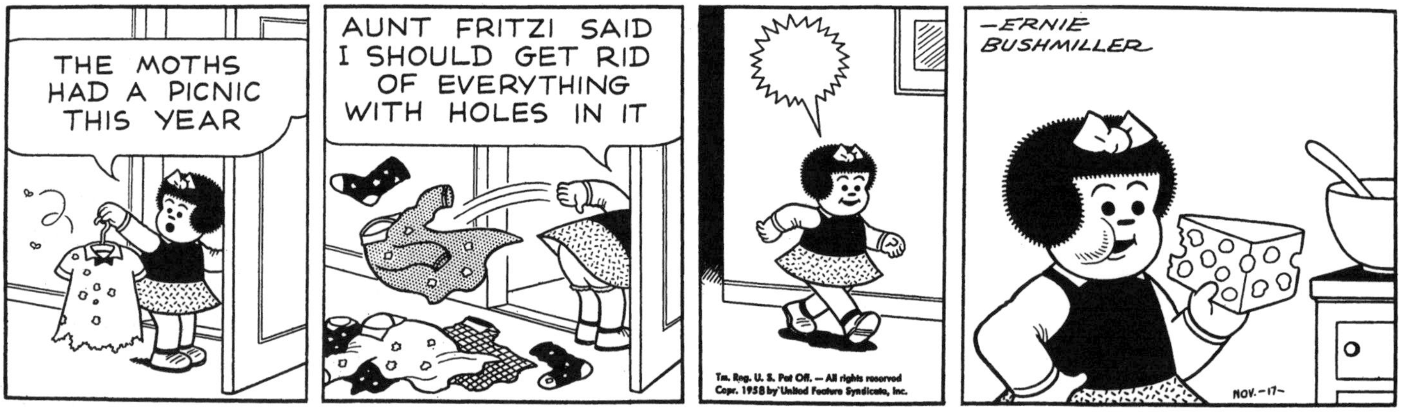
THE MOTHS HAD A PICNIC THIS YEAR
AUNT FRITZI SAID I SHOULD GET RID OF EVERYTHING WITH HOLES IN IT
Tm. Reg. U. S. Pat. Off. — All rights reserved Copr. 1958 by United Feature Syndicate, Inc.
—ERNIE BUSHMILLER
NOV.-17-

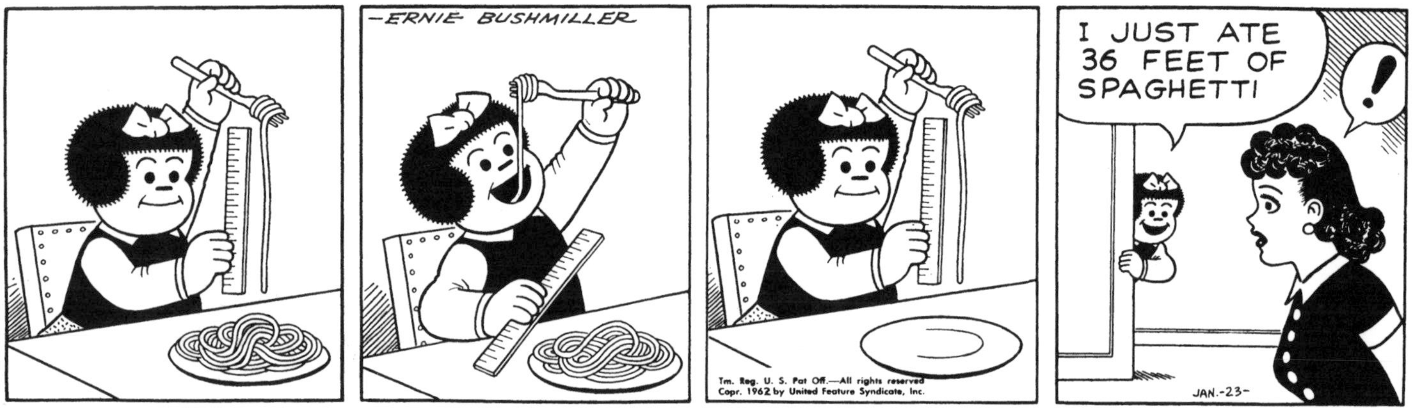
—ERNIE BUSHMILLER
Tm. Reg. U. S. Pat Off.—All rights reserved Copr. 1962 by United Feature Syndicate, Inc.
I JUST ATE 36 FEET OF SPAGHETTI
!
JAN.-23-

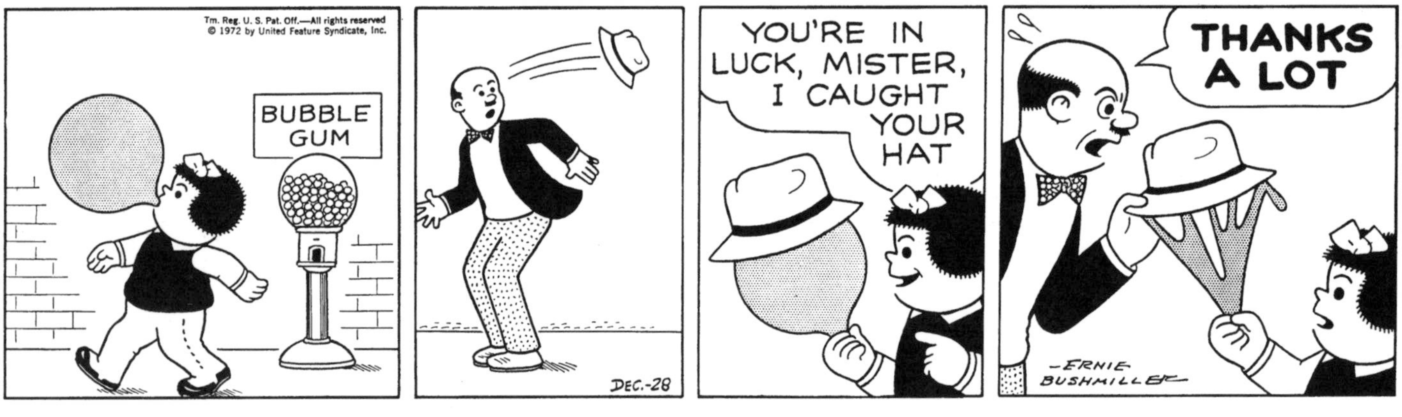
Tm. Reg. U. S. Pat. Off.—All rights reserved © 1972 by United Feature Syndicate, Inc.
BUBBLE GUM
DEC.-28
YOU'RE IN LUCK, MISTER, I CAUGHT YOUR HAT
THANKS A LOT
—ERNIE BUSHMILLER

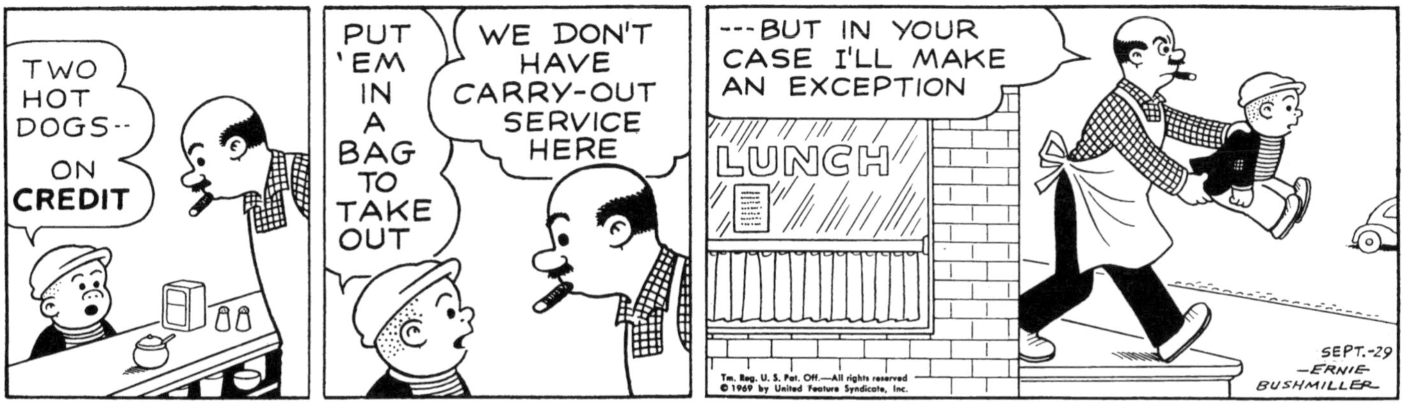
TWO HOT DOGS-- ON CREDIT
PUT 'EM IN A BAG TO TAKE OUT
WE DON'T HAVE CARRY-OUT SERVICE HERE
---BUT IN YOUR CASE I'LL MAKE AN EXCEPTION
LUNCH
Tm. Reg. U. S. Pat. Off.—All rights reserved © 1969 by United Feature Syndicate, Inc.
SEPT.-29
-ERNIE BUSHMILLER

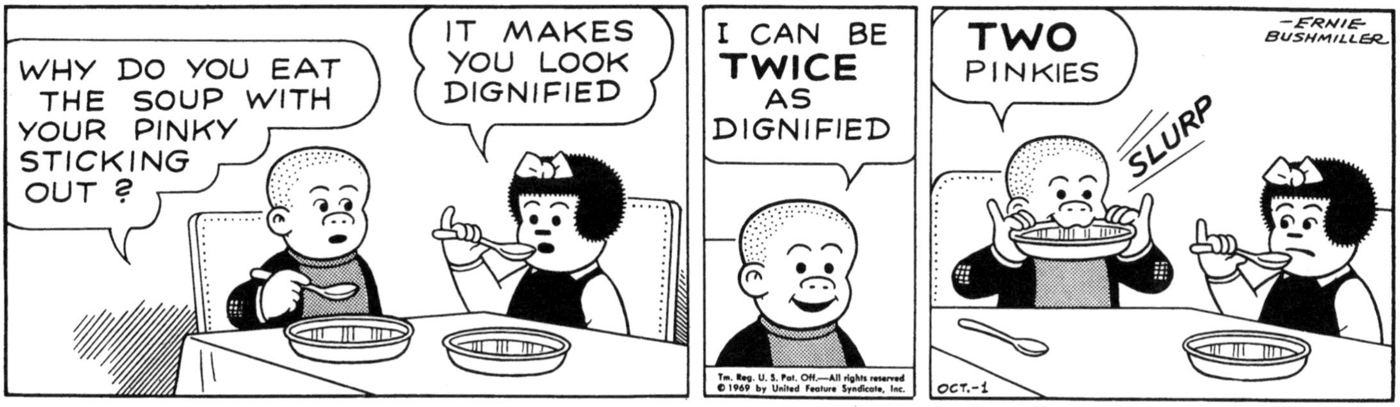
WHY DO YOU EAT THE SOUP WITH YOUR PINKY STICKING OUT ?
IT MAKES YOU LOOK DIGNIFIED
I CAN BE TWICE AS DIGNIFIED
Tm. Reg. U. S. Pat. Off.—All rights reserved © 1969 by United Feature Syndicate, Inc.
-ERNIE BUSHMILLER
TWO PINKIES
SLURP
OCT.-1

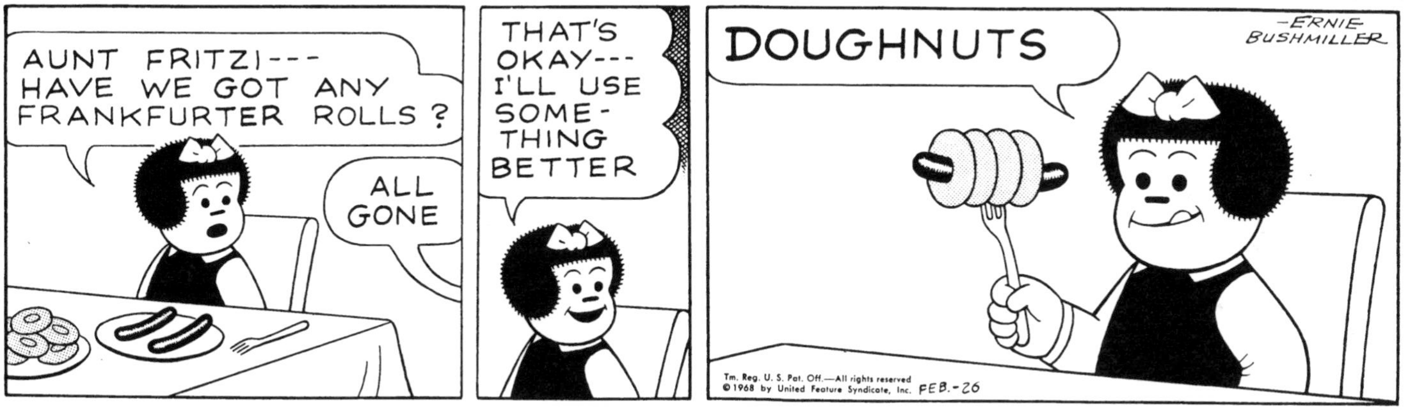
AUNT FRITZI--- HAVE WE GOT ANY FRANKFURTER ROLLS ?
ALL GONE
THAT'S OKAY--- I'LL USE SOME-THING BETTER
DOUGHNUTS
-ERNIE BUSHMILLER
Tm. Reg. U. S. Pat. Off.—All rights reserved © 1968 by United Feature Syndicate, Inc.
FEB.-26

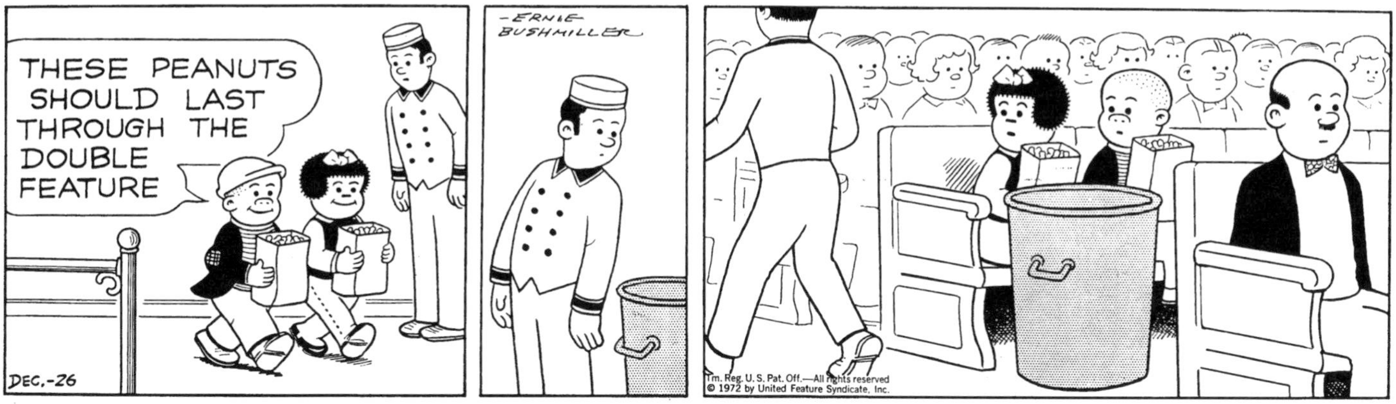
THESE PEANUTS SHOULD LAST THROUGH THE DOUBLE FEATURE
DEC.-26
-ERNIE BUSHMILLER
Tm. Reg. U. S. Pat. Off.—All rights reserved © 1972 by United Feature Syndicate, Inc.

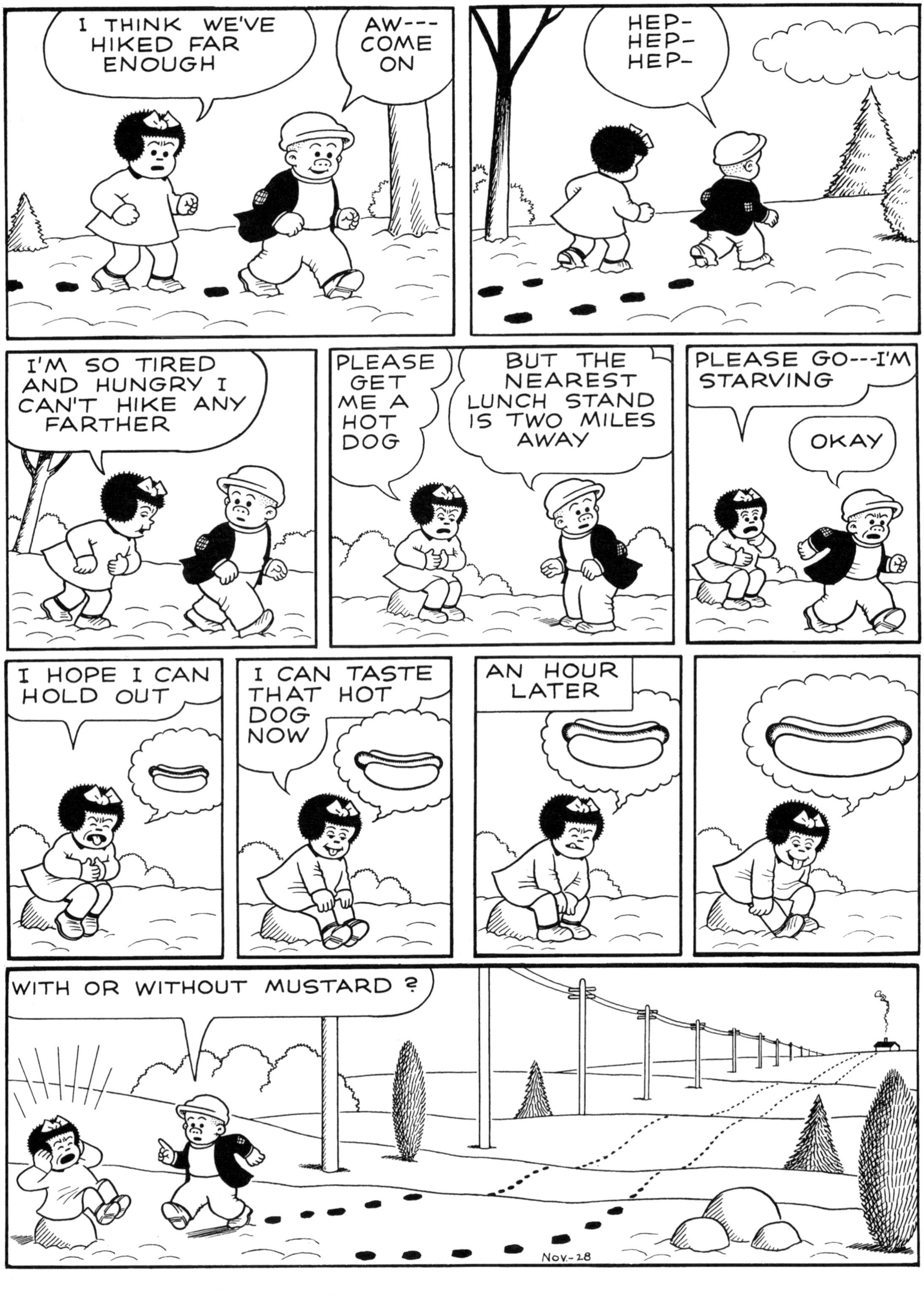

I THINK WE'VE HIKED FAR ENOUGH
AW--- COME ON
HEP- HEP- HEP-
I'M SO TIRED AND HUNGRY I CAN'T HIKE ANY FARTHER
PLEASE GET ME A HOT DOG
BUT THE NEAREST LUNCH STAND IS TWO MILES AWAY
PLEASE GO---I'M STARVING
OKAY
I HOPE I CAN HOLD OUT
I CAN TASTE THAT HOT DOG NOW
AN HOUR LATER
WITH OR WITHOUT MUSTARD ?
NOV.-28

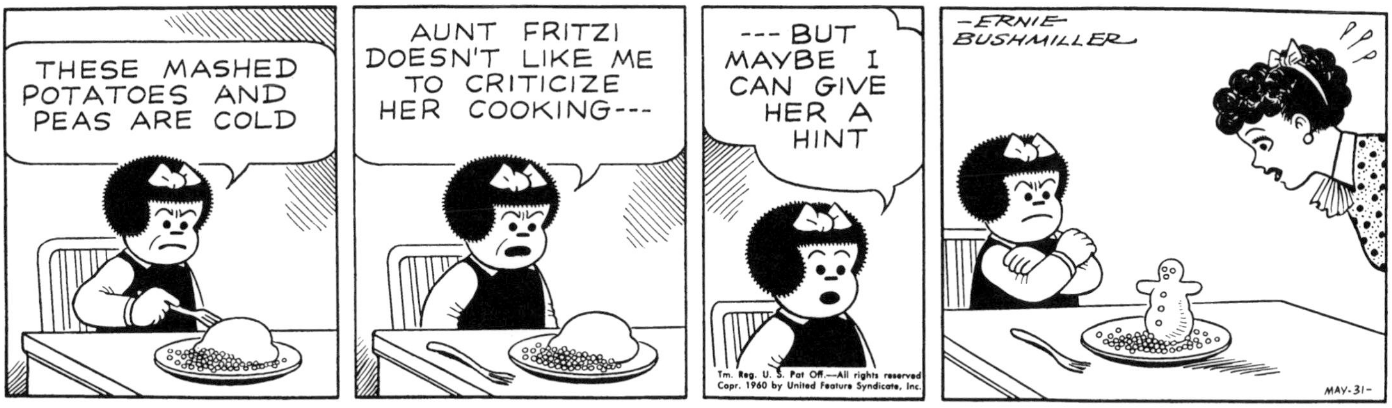
THESE MASHED POTATOES AND PEAS ARE COLD
AUNT FRITZI DOESN'T LIKE ME TO CRITICIZE HER COOKING---
---BUT MAYBE I CAN GIVE HER A HINT
Tm. Reg. U. S. Pat Off.—All rights reserved Copr. 1960 by United Feature Syndicate, Inc.
-ERNIE BUSHMILLER
MAY-31-

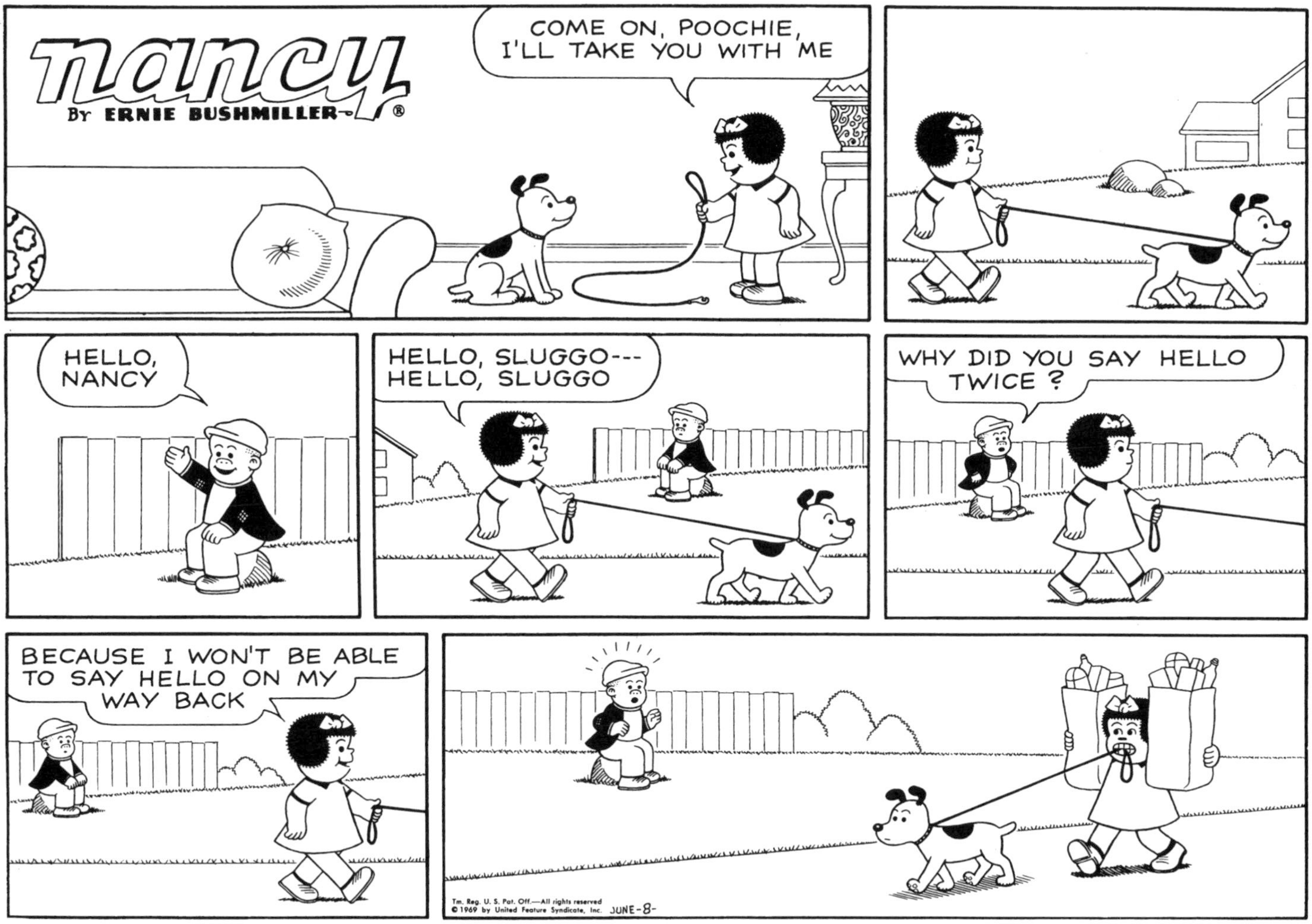
nancy
By ERNIE BUSHMILLER
COME ON, POOCHIE, I'LL TAKE YOU WITH ME
HELLO, NANCY
HELLO, SLUGGO--- HELLO, SLUGGO
WHY DID YOU SAY HELLO TWICE ?
BECAUSE I WON'T BE ABLE TO SAY HELLO ON MY WAY BACK
Tm. Reg. U. S. Pat. Off.—All rights reserved © 1969 by United Feature Syndicate, Inc.
JUNE-8-

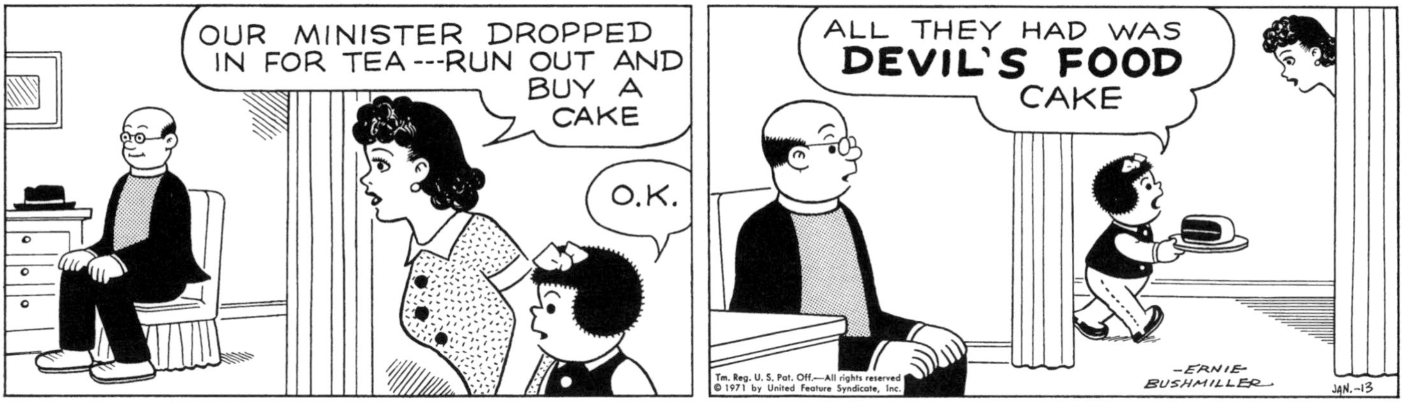
OUR MINISTER DROPPED IN FOR TEA---RUN OUT AND BUY A CAKE
O.K.
ALL THEY HAD WAS DEVIL'S FOOD CAKE
Tm. Reg. U. S. Pat. Off.—All rights reserved © 1971 by United Feature Syndicate, Inc.
-ERNIE BUSHMILLER
JAN.-13

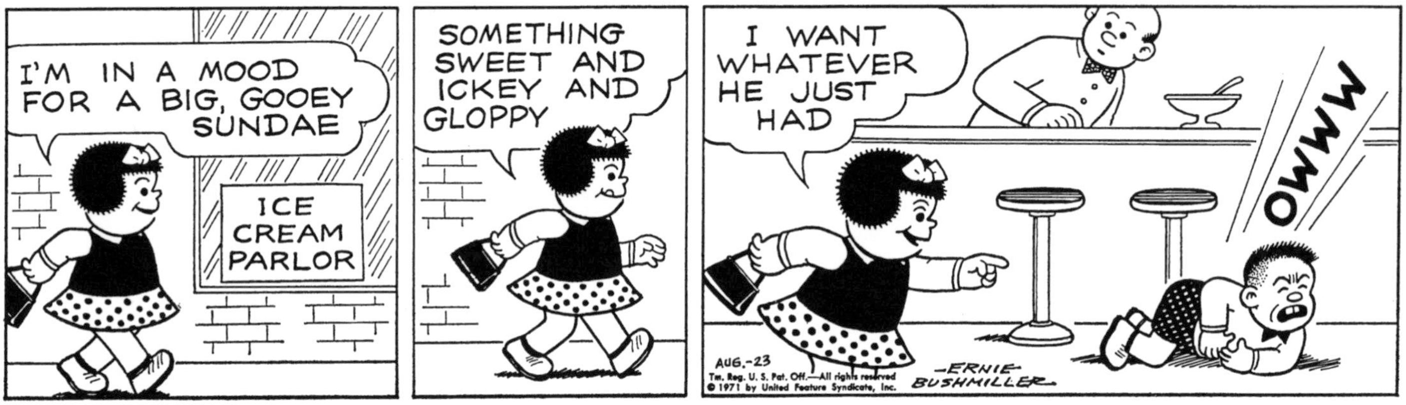
I'M IN A MOOD FOR A BIG, GOOEY SUNDAE
ICE CREAM PARLOR
SOMETHING SWEET AND ICKEY AND GLOPPY
I WANT WHATEVER HE JUST HAD
OWWW
AUG.-23
Tm. Reg. U. S. Pat. Off.—All rights reserved © 1971 by United Feature Syndicate, Inc.
ERNIE BUSHMILLER

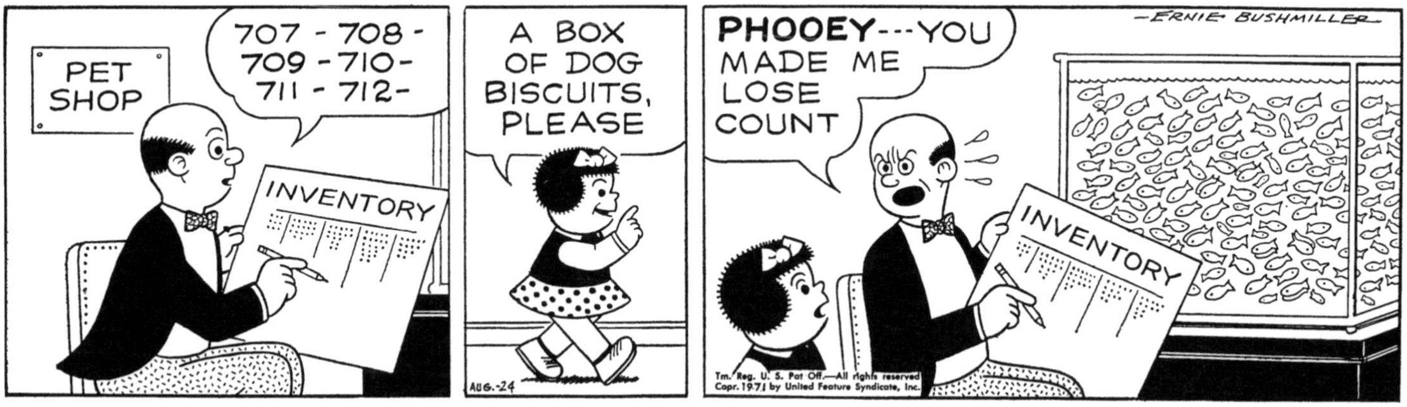
PET SHOP
707 - 708 - 709 - 710 - 711 - 712 -
INVENTORY
A BOX OF DOG BISCUITS, PLEASE
AUG.-24
PHOOEY---YOU MADE ME LOSE COUNT
ERNIE BUSHMILLER
INVENTORY
Tm. Reg. U. S. Pat. Off.—All rights reserved Copr. 1971 by United Feature Syndicate, Inc.

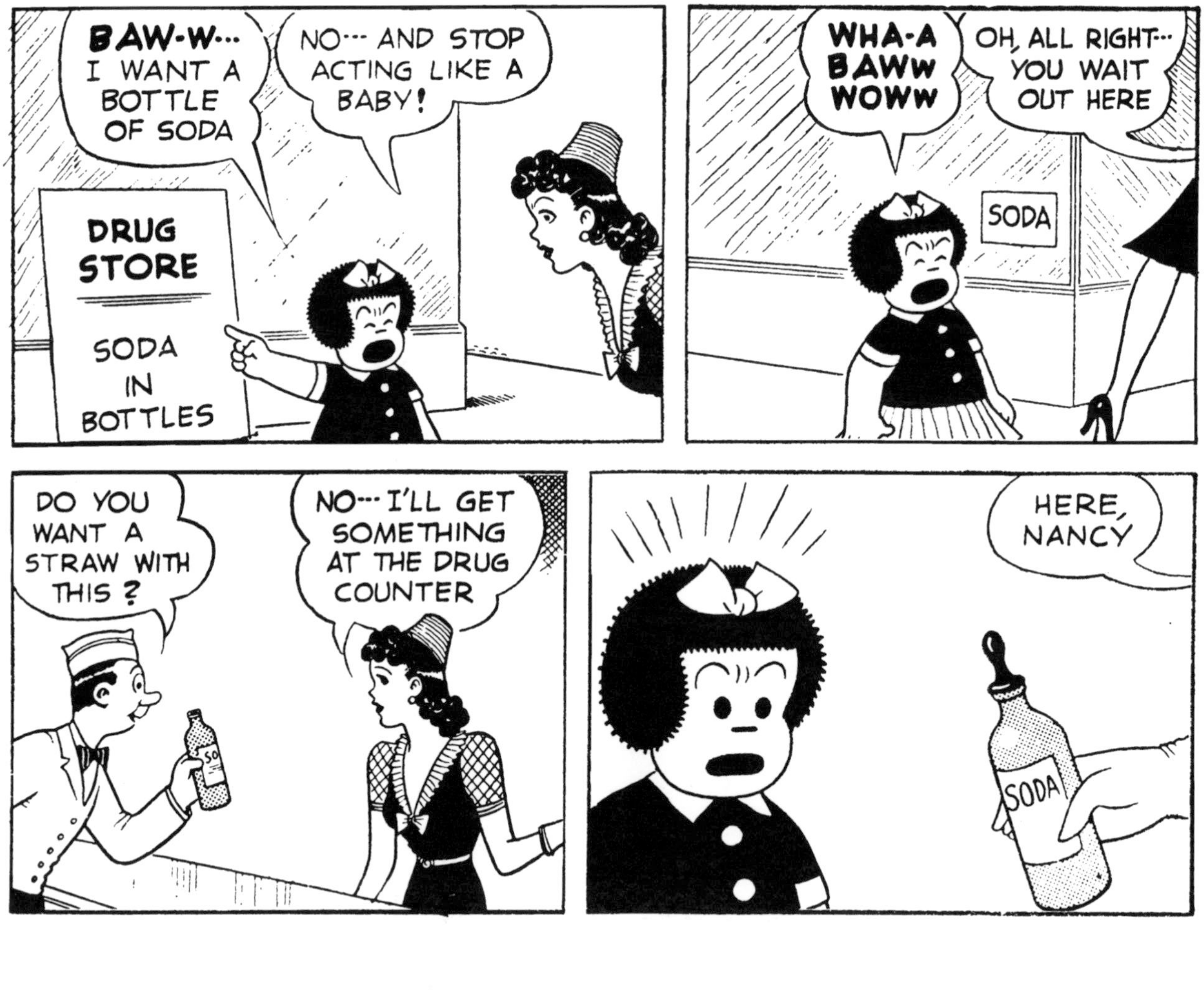
BAW-W... I WANT A BOTTLE OF SODA
NO--- AND STOP ACTING LIKE A BABY!
DRUG STORE
SODA IN BOTTLES
WHA-A BAWW WOWW
OH, ALL RIGHT--- YOU WAIT OUT HERE
SODA
DO YOU WANT A STRAW WITH THIS ?
NO--- I'LL GET SOMETHING AT THE DRUG COUNTER
HERE, NANCY
SODA

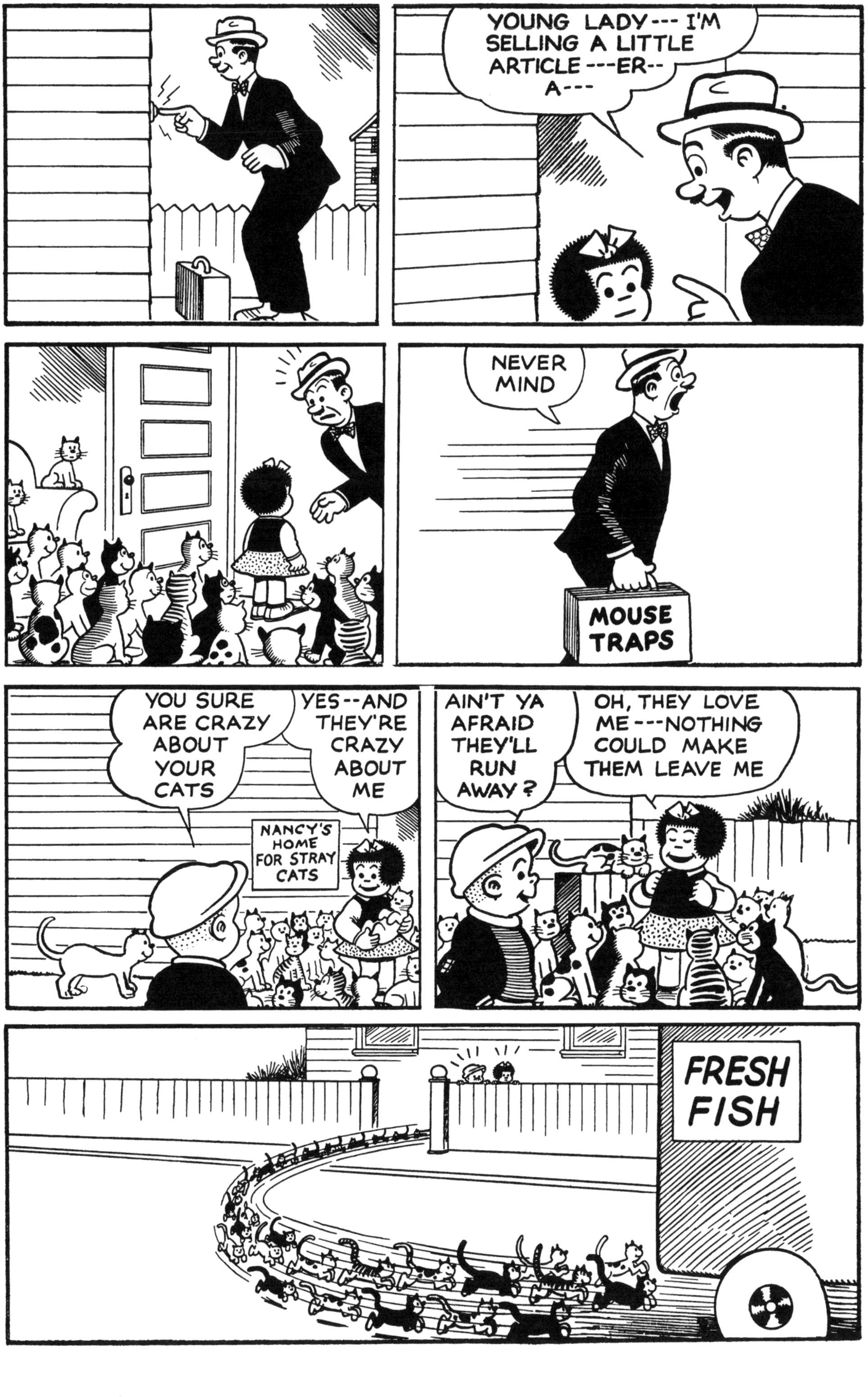
YOUNG LADY --- I'M SELLING A LITTLE ARTICLE ---ER-- A---
NEVER MIND
MOUSE TRAPS
YOU SURE ARE CRAZY ABOUT YOUR CATS
YES--AND THEY'RE CRAZY ABOUT ME
NANCY'S HOME FOR STRAY CATS
AIN'T YA AFRAID THEY'LL RUN AWAY?
OH, THEY LOVE ME---NOTHING COULD MAKE THEM LEAVE ME
FRESH FISH

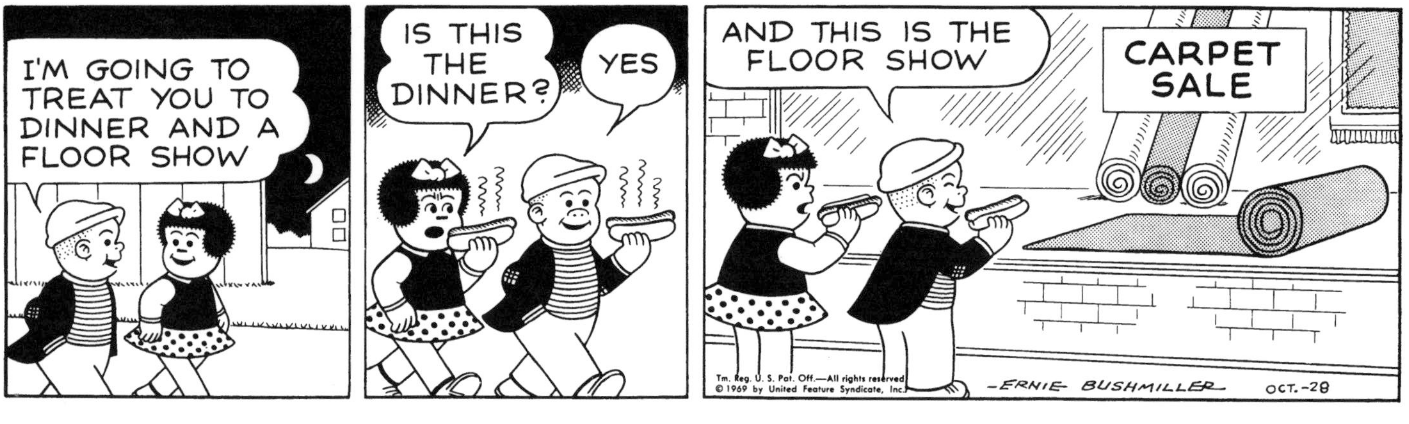
I'M GOING TO TREAT YOU TO DINNER AND A FLOOR SHOW
IS THIS THE DINNER?
YES
AND THIS IS THE FLOOR SHOW
CARPET SALE
Tm. Reg. U. S. Pat. Off.—All rights reserved © 1969 by United Feature Syndicate, Inc.
-ERNIE BUSHMILLER
OCT.-28

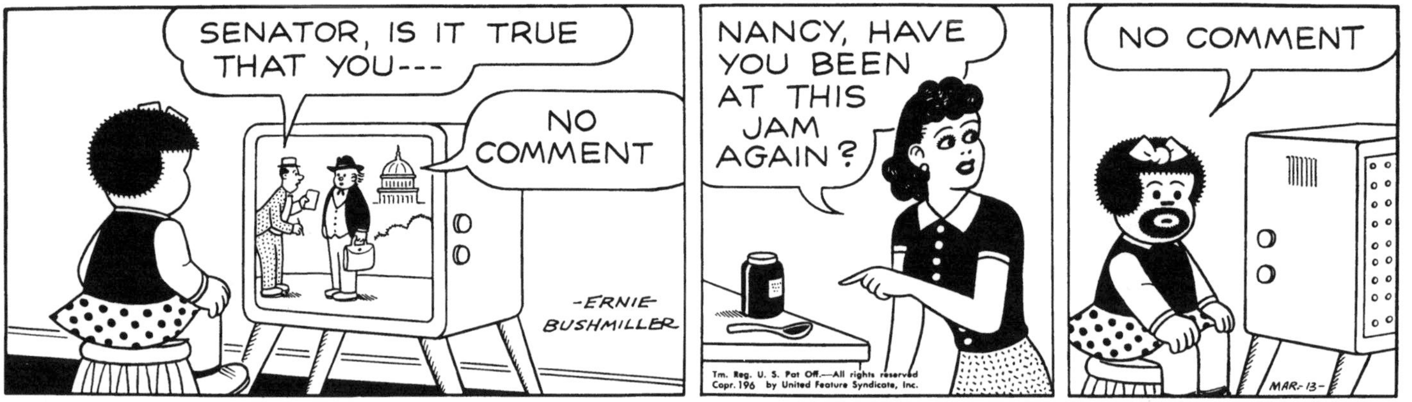
SENATOR, IS IT TRUE THAT YOU---
NO COMMENT
-ERNIE BUSHMILLER
NANCY, HAVE YOU BEEN AT THIS JAM AGAIN?
Tm. Reg. U. S. Pat. Off.—All rights reserved Copr. 196 by United Feature Syndicate, Inc.
NO COMMENT
MAR.-13-

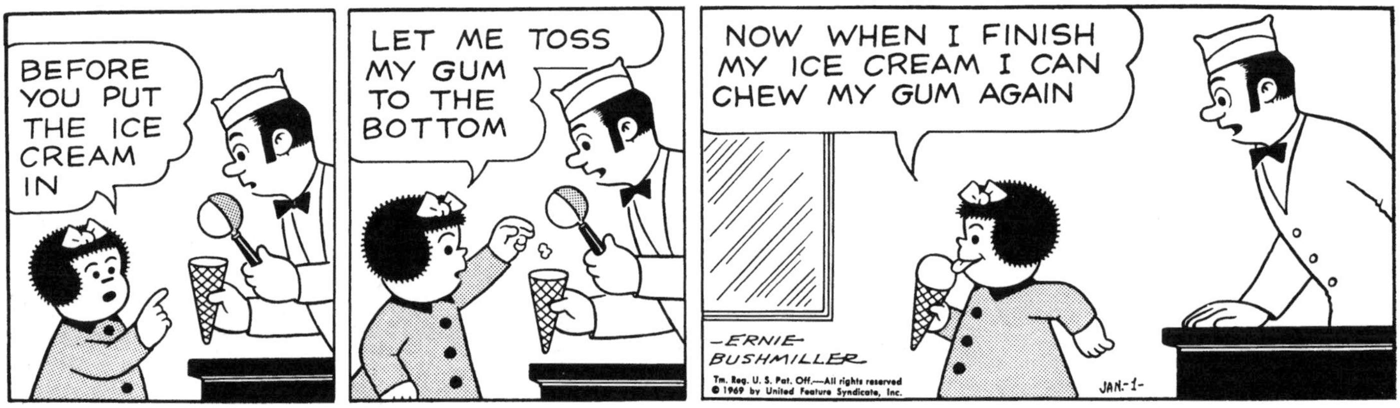
BEFORE YOU PUT THE ICE CREAM IN
LET ME TOSS MY GUM TO THE BOTTOM
NOW WHEN I FINISH MY ICE CREAM I CAN CHEW MY GUM AGAIN
-ERNIE BUSHMILLER
Tm. Reg. U. S. Pat. Off.—All rights reserved © 1969 by United Feature Syndicate, Inc.
JAN.-1-

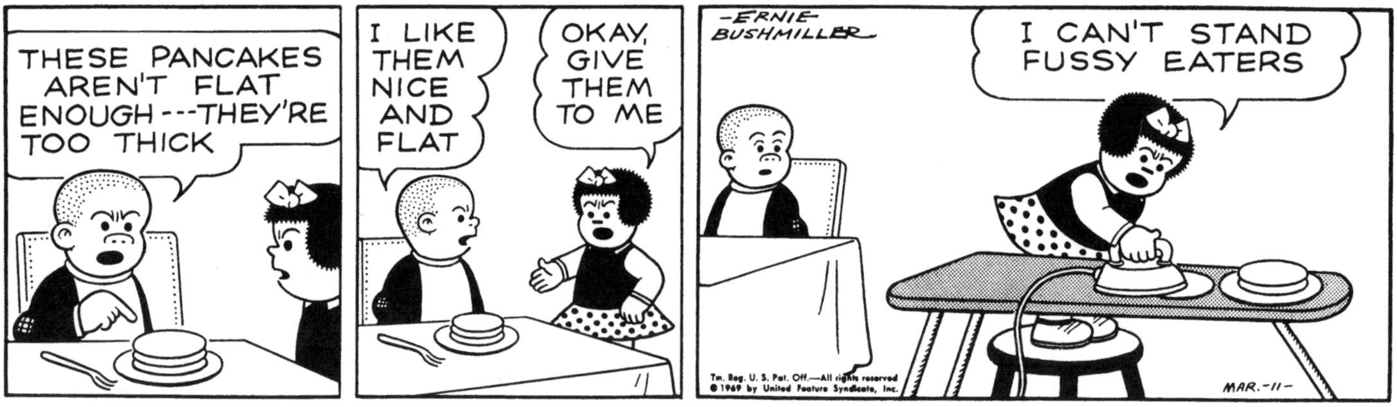
THESE PANCAKES AREN'T FLAT ENOUGH---THEY'RE TOO THICK
I LIKE THEM NICE AND FLAT
OKAY, GIVE THEM TO ME
-ERNIE BUSHMILLER
I CAN'T STAND FUSSY EATERS
Tm. Reg. U. S. Pat. Off.—All rights reserved © 1969 by United Feature Syndicate, Inc.
MAR.-11-

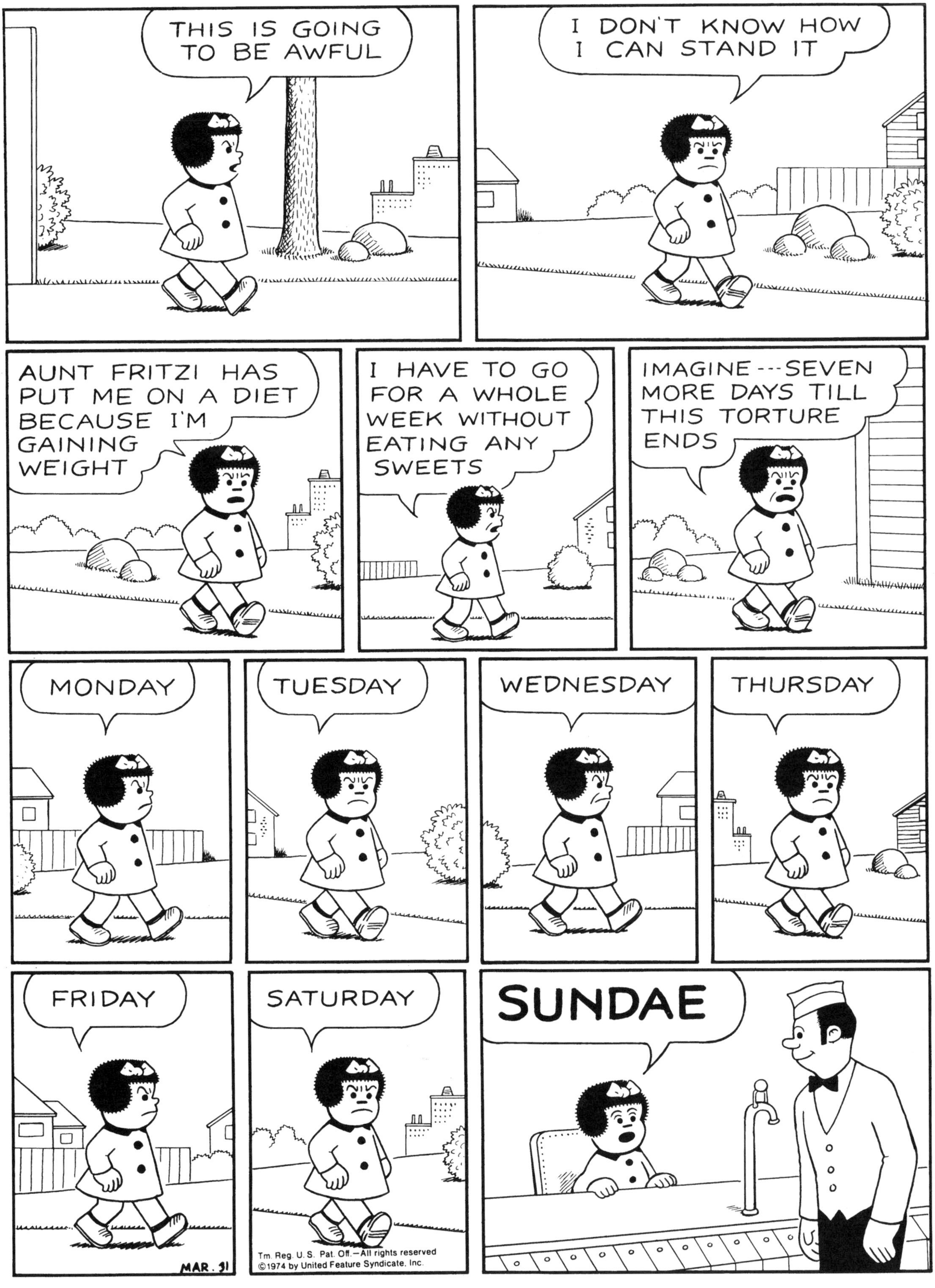
THIS IS GOING TO BE AWFUL
I DON'T KNOW HOW I CAN STAND IT
AUNT FRITZI HAS PUT ME ON A DIET BECAUSE I'M GAINING WEIGHT
I HAVE TO GO FOR A WHOLE WEEK WITHOUT EATING ANY SWEETS
IMAGINE---SEVEN MORE DAYS TILL THIS TORTURE ENDS
MONDAY
TUESDAY
WEDNESDAY
THURSDAY
FRIDAY
MAR. 31
SATURDAY
Tm. Reg. U.S. Pat. Off.—All rights reserved
©1974 by United Feature Syndicate, Inc.
SUNDAE

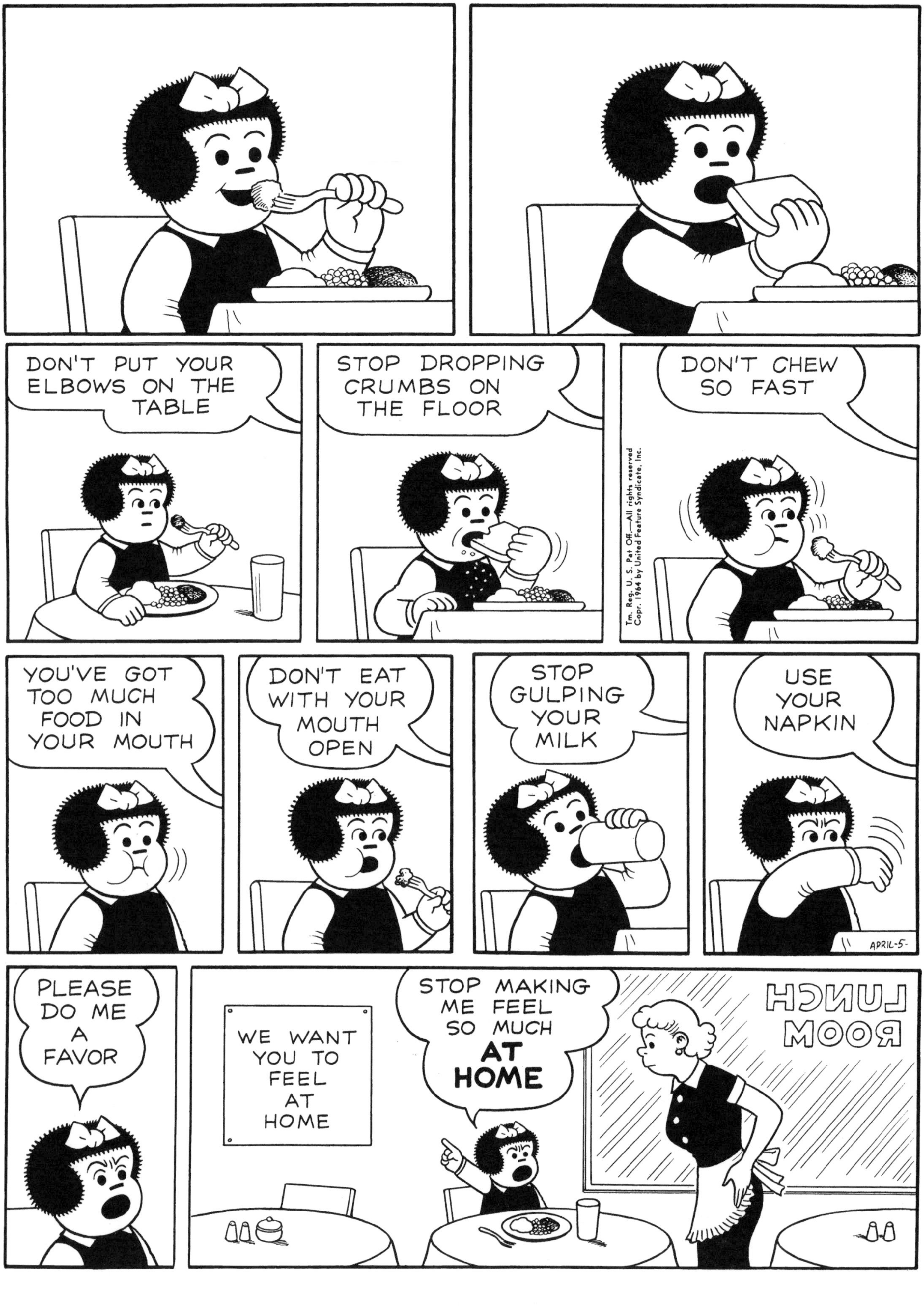
DON'T PUT YOUR ELBOWS ON THE TABLE
STOP DROPPING CRUMBS ON THE FLOOR
Tm. Reg. U. S. Pat Off.—All rights reserved
Copr. 1964 by United Feature Syndicate, Inc.
DON'T CHEW SO FAST
YOU'VE GOT TOO MUCH FOOD IN YOUR MOUTH
DON'T EAT WITH YOUR MOUTH OPEN
STOP GULPING YOUR MILK
USE YOUR NAPKIN
APRIL-5-
PLEASE DO ME A FAVOR
WE WANT YOU TO FEEL AT HOME
STOP MAKING ME FEEL SO MUCH **AT HOME**
LUNCH ROOM

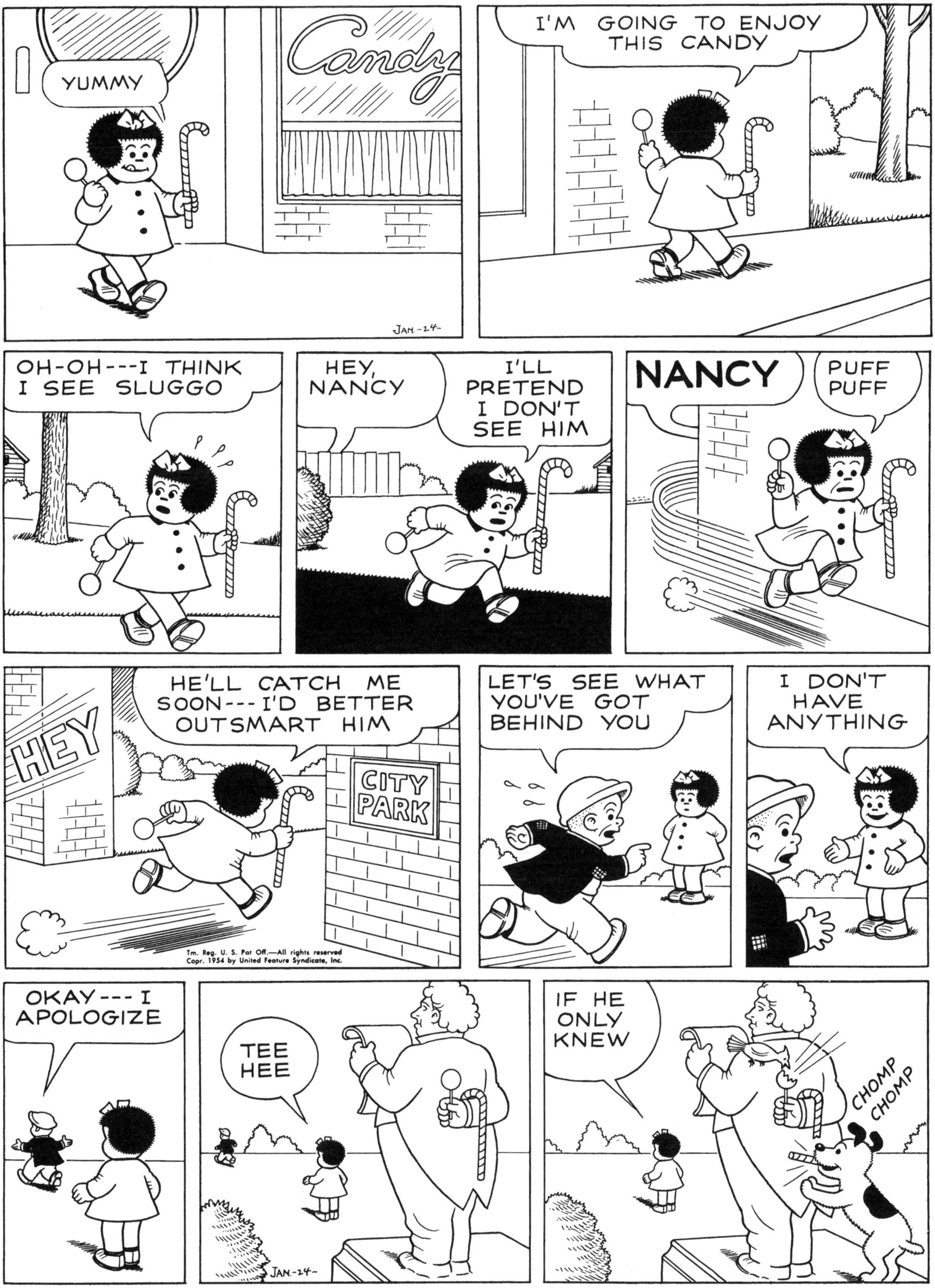
Candy
YUMMY
JAN.-24-
I'M GOING TO ENJOY THIS CANDY
OH-OH---I THINK I SEE SLUGGO
HEY, NANCY
I'LL PRETEND I DON'T SEE HIM
NANCY
PUFF PUFF
HEY
HE'LL CATCH ME SOON---I'D BETTER OUTSMART HIM
CITY PARK
Tm. Reg. U. S. Pat Off.—All rights reserved
Copr. 1954 by United Feature Syndicate, Inc.
LET'S SEE WHAT YOU'VE GOT BEHIND YOU
I DON'T HAVE ANYTHING
OKAY---I APOLOGIZE
TEE HEE
JAN.-24-
IF HE ONLY KNEW
CHOMP CHOMP

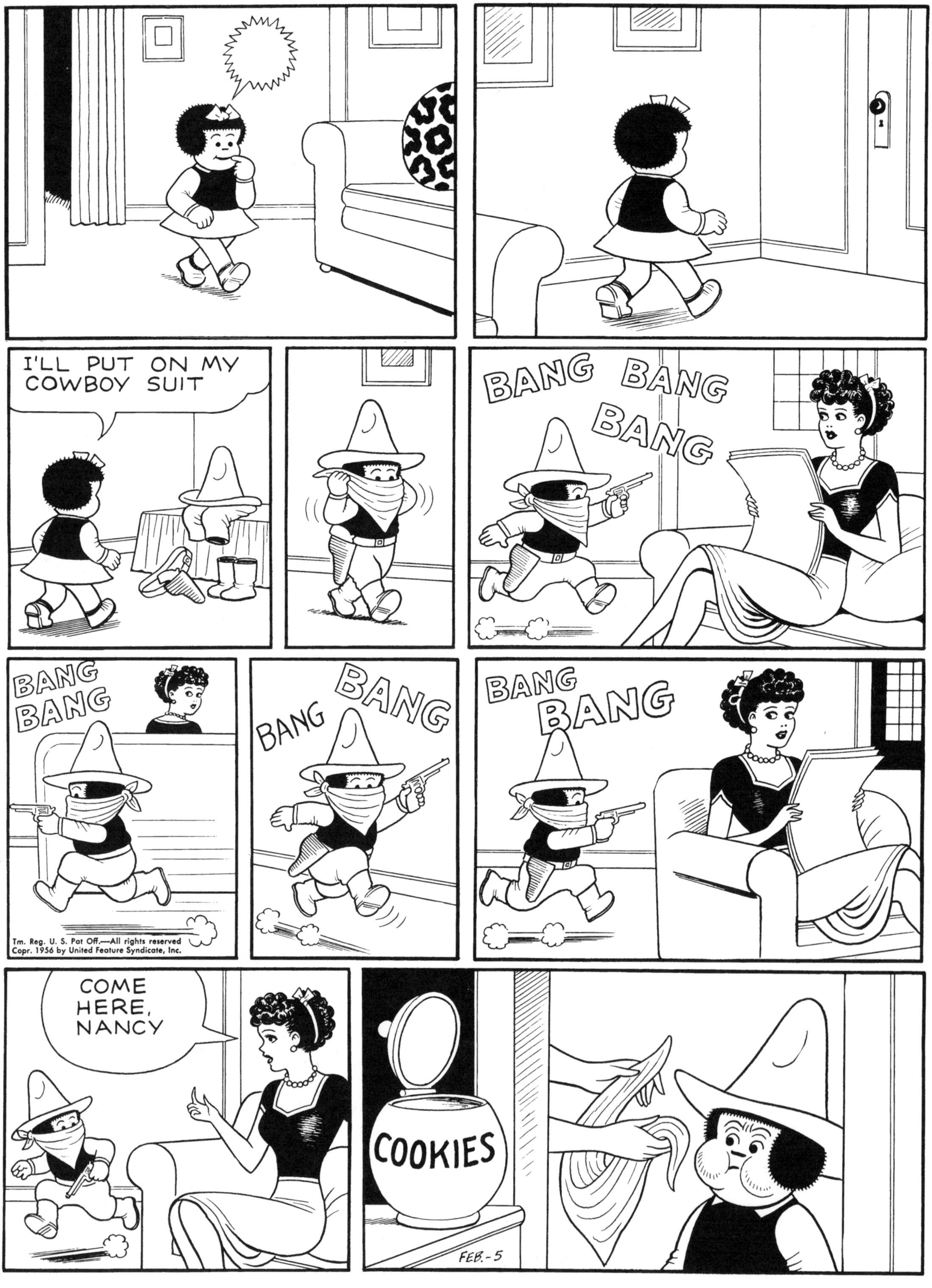
I'LL PUT ON MY COWBOY SUIT
BANG BANG BANG
BANG BANG
BANG BANG
BANG BANG
COME HERE, NANCY
COOKIES
FEB.-5

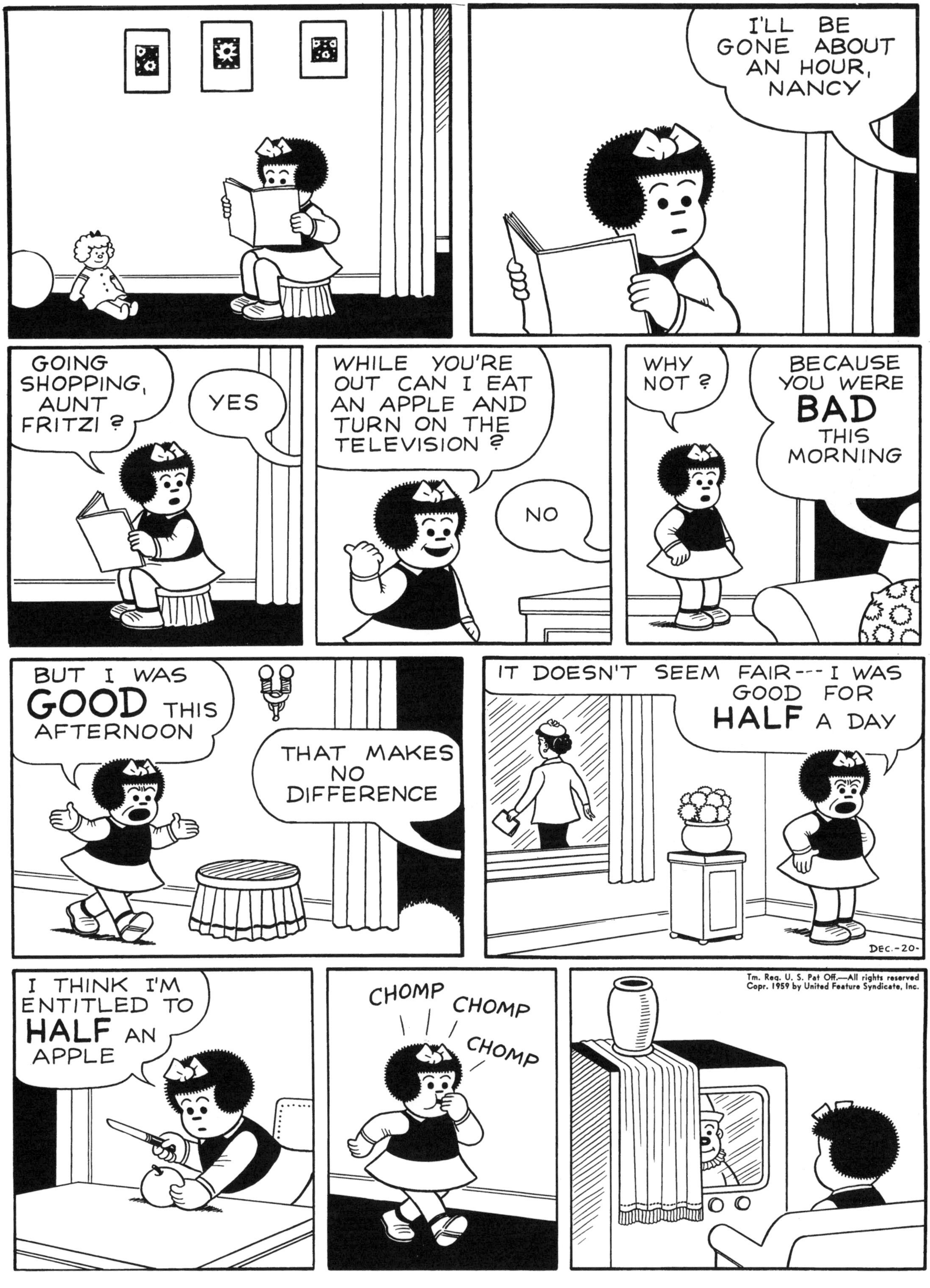
I'LL BE GONE ABOUT AN HOUR, NANCY
GOING SHOPPING, AUNT FRITZI ?
YES
WHILE YOU'RE OUT CAN I EAT AN APPLE AND TURN ON THE TELEVISION ?
NO
WHY NOT ?
BECAUSE YOU WERE BAD THIS MORNING
BUT I WAS GOOD THIS AFTERNOON
THAT MAKES NO DIFFERENCE
IT DOESN'T SEEM FAIR--- I WAS GOOD FOR HALF A DAY
DEC.-20-
I THINK I'M ENTITLED TO HALF AN APPLE
CHOMP
CHOMP
CHOMP
Tm. Reg. U. S. Pat Off.—All rights reserved
Copr. 1959 by United Feature Syndicate, Inc.

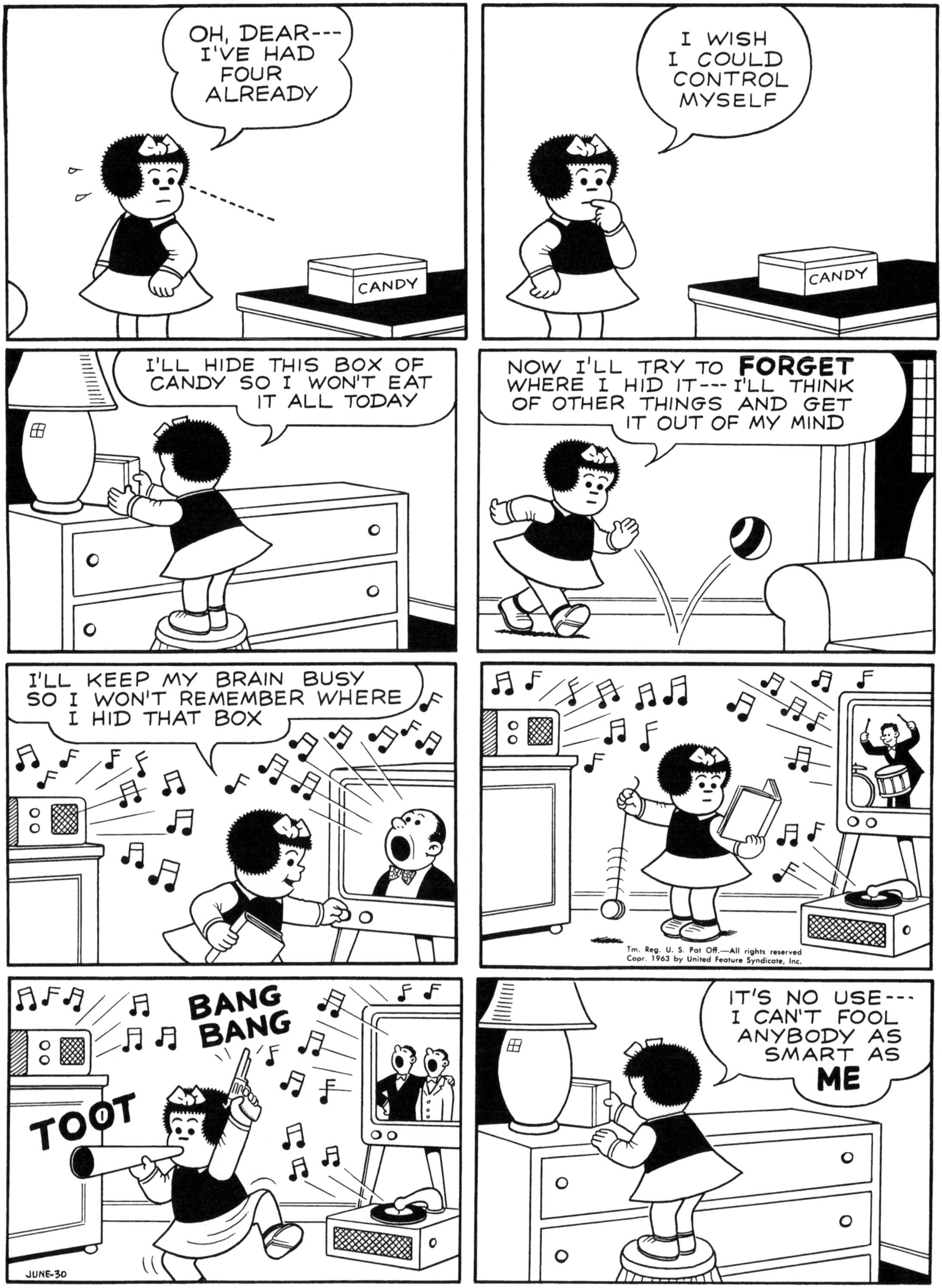
OH, DEAR--- I'VE HAD FOUR ALREADY
CANDY
I WISH I COULD CONTROL MYSELF
CANDY
I'LL HIDE THIS BOX OF CANDY SO I WON'T EAT IT ALL TODAY
NOW I'LL TRY TO **FORGET** WHERE I HID IT---I'LL THINK OF OTHER THINGS AND GET IT OUT OF MY MIND
I'LL KEEP MY BRAIN BUSY SO I WON'T REMEMBER WHERE I HID THAT BOX
Tm. Reg. U. S. Pat Off.—All rights reserved
Copr. 1963 by United Feature Syndicate, Inc.
BANG
BANG
TOOT
JUNE-30
IT'S NO USE--- I CAN'T FOOL ANYBODY AS SMART AS **ME**

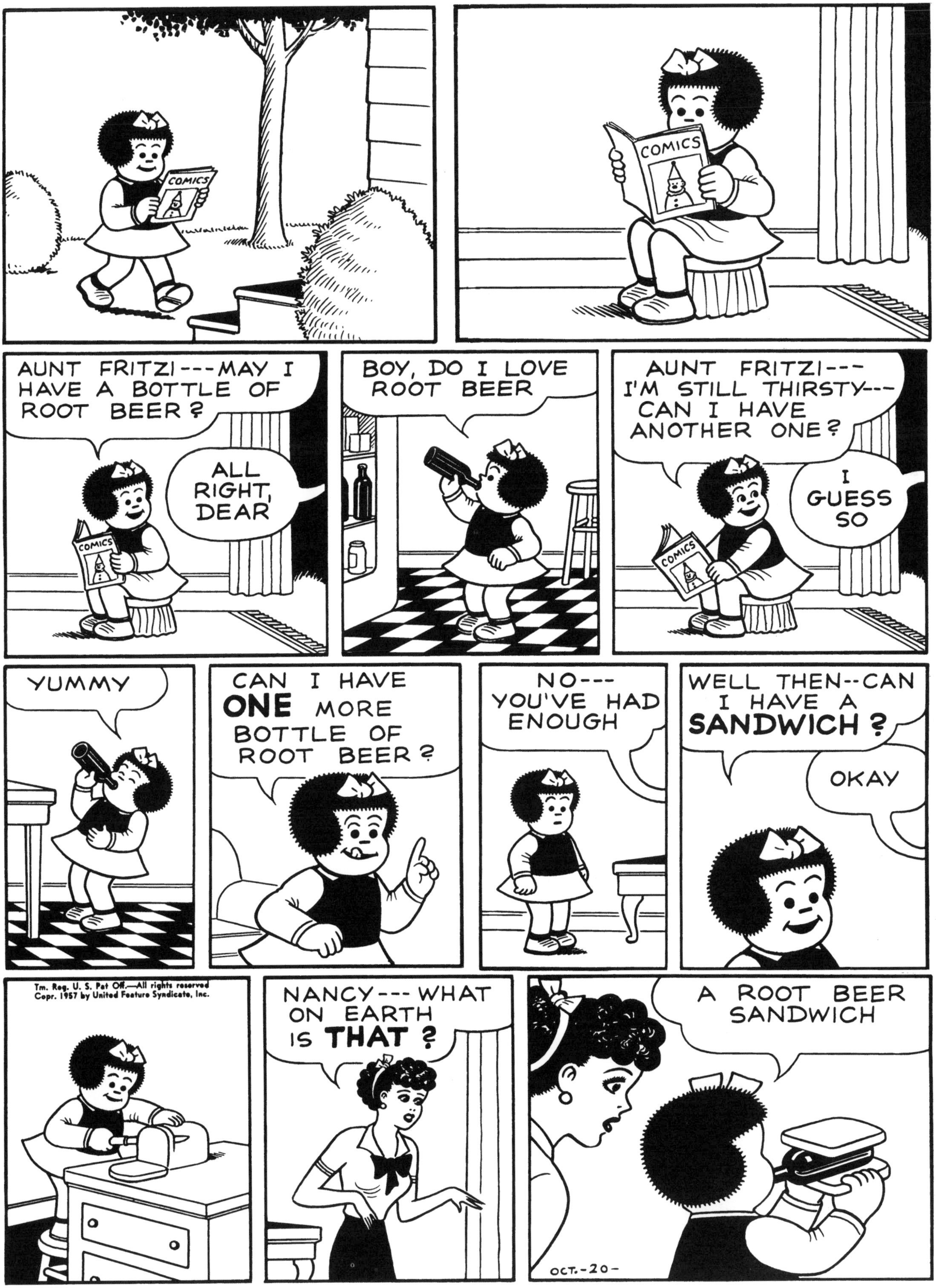

COMICS
COMICS
AUNT FRITZI---MAY I HAVE A BOTTLE OF ROOT BEER?
ALL RIGHT, DEAR
COMICS
BOY, DO I LOVE ROOT BEER
AUNT FRITZI--- I'M STILL THIRSTY--- CAN I HAVE ANOTHER ONE?
I GUESS SO
COMICS
YUMMY
CAN I HAVE ONE MORE BOTTLE OF ROOT BEER?
NO--- YOU'VE HAD ENOUGH
WELL THEN--CAN I HAVE A SANDWICH?
OKAY
Tm. Reg. U. S. Pat Off.—All rights reserved Copr. 1957 by United Feature Syndicate, Inc.
NANCY--- WHAT ON EARTH IS THAT?
A ROOT BEER SANDWICH
OCT.-20-

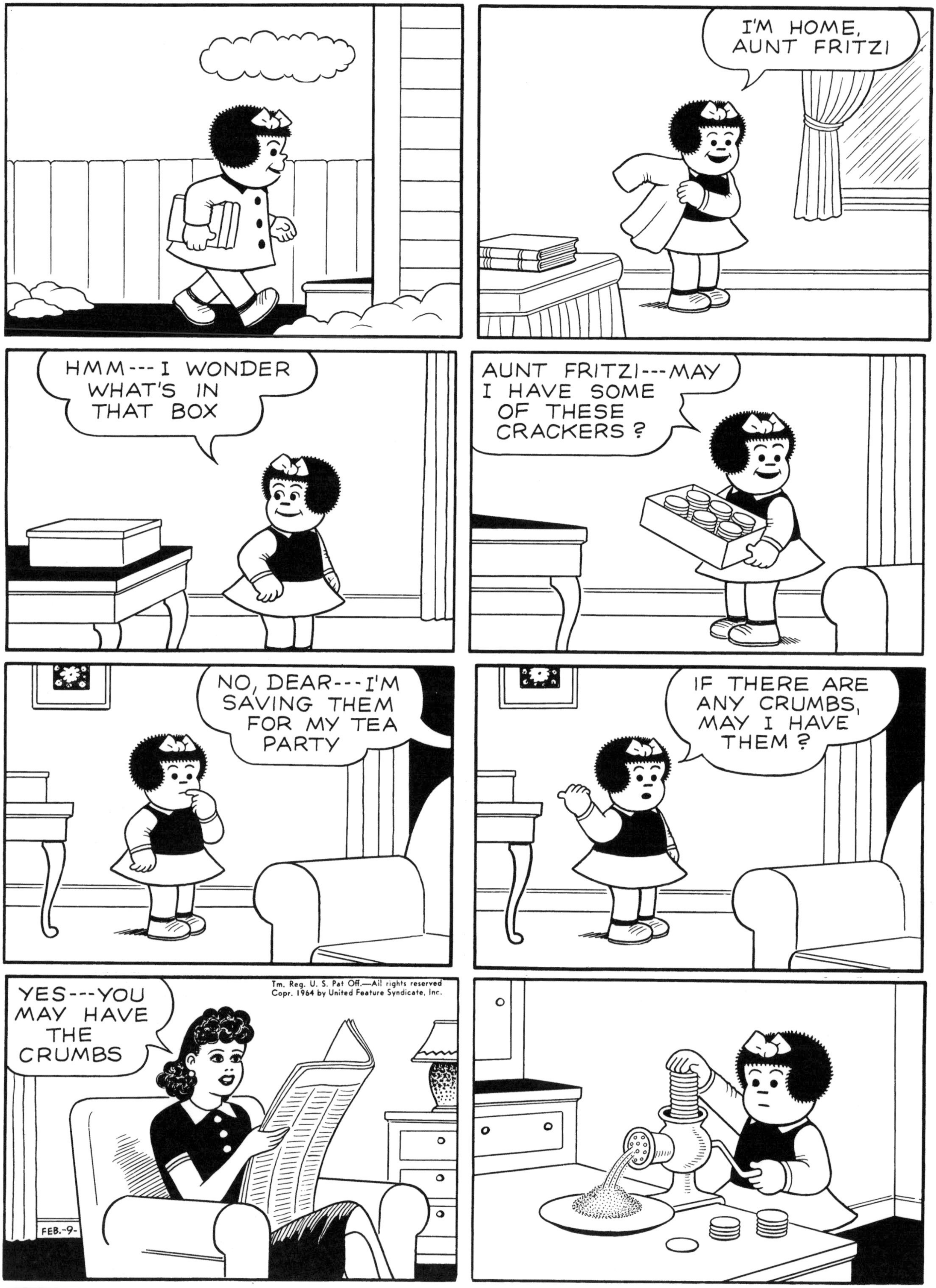
I'M HOME, AUNT FRITZI
HMM---I WONDER WHAT'S IN THAT BOX
AUNT FRITZI---MAY I HAVE SOME OF THESE CRACKERS ?
NO, DEAR---I'M SAVING THEM FOR MY TEA PARTY
IF THERE ARE ANY CRUMBS, MAY I HAVE THEM ?
YES---YOU MAY HAVE THE CRUMBS
Tm. Reg. U. S. Pat Off.—All rights reserved
Copr. 1964 by United Feature Syndicate, Inc.
FEB.-9-

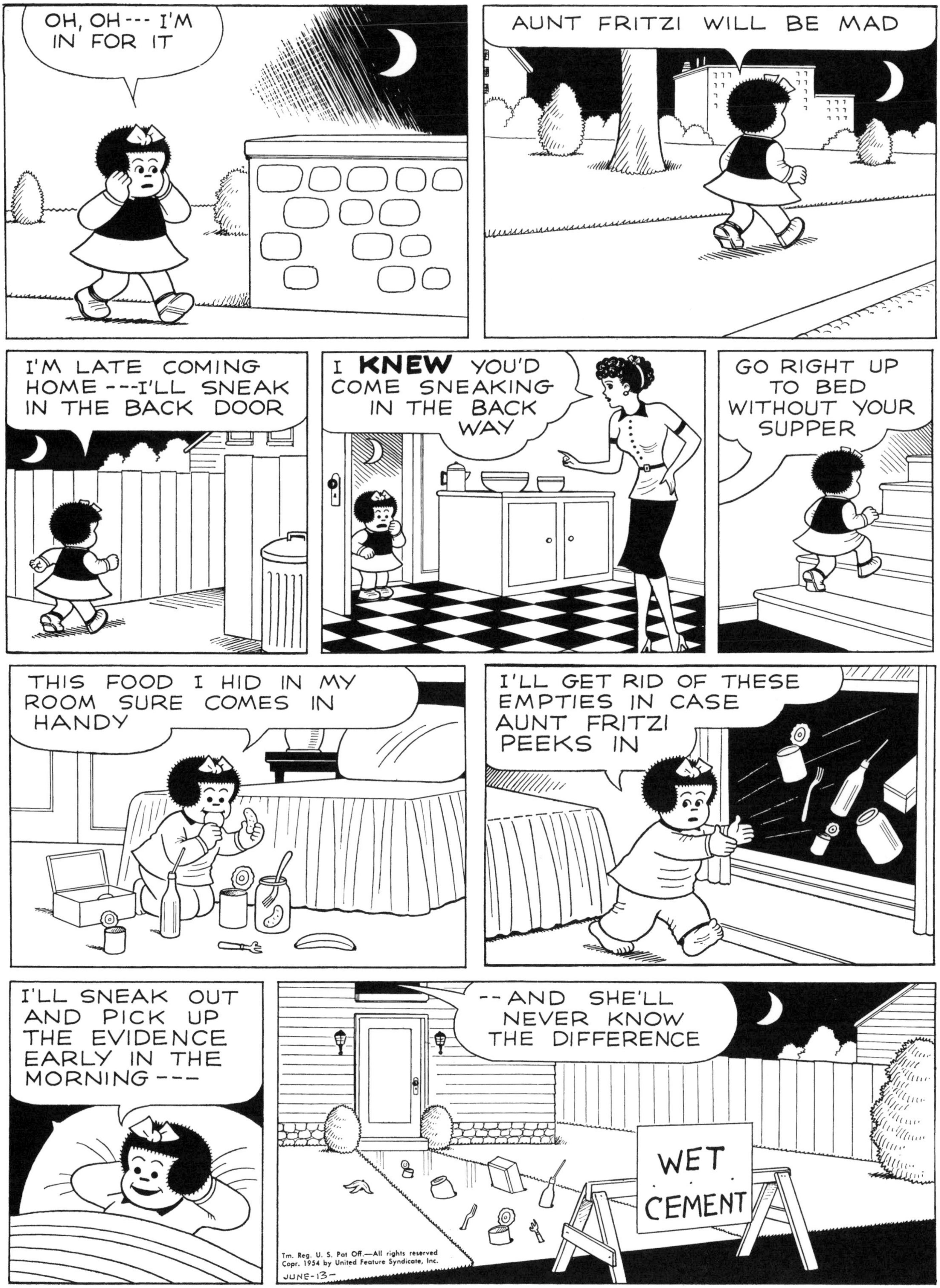

OH, OH --- I'M IN FOR IT
AUNT FRITZI WILL BE MAD
I'M LATE COMING HOME ---I'LL SNEAK IN THE BACK DOOR
I KNEW YOU'D COME SNEAKING IN THE BACK WAY
GO RIGHT UP TO BED WITHOUT YOUR SUPPER
THIS FOOD I HID IN MY ROOM SURE COMES IN HANDY
I'LL GET RID OF THESE EMPTIES IN CASE AUNT FRITZI PEEKS IN
I'LL SNEAK OUT AND PICK UP THE EVIDENCE EARLY IN THE MORNING ---
-- AND SHE'LL NEVER KNOW THE DIFFERENCE
WET CEMENT
Tm. Reg. U. S. Pat Off.—All rights reserved
Copr. 1954 by United Feature Syndicate, Inc.
JUNE-13-

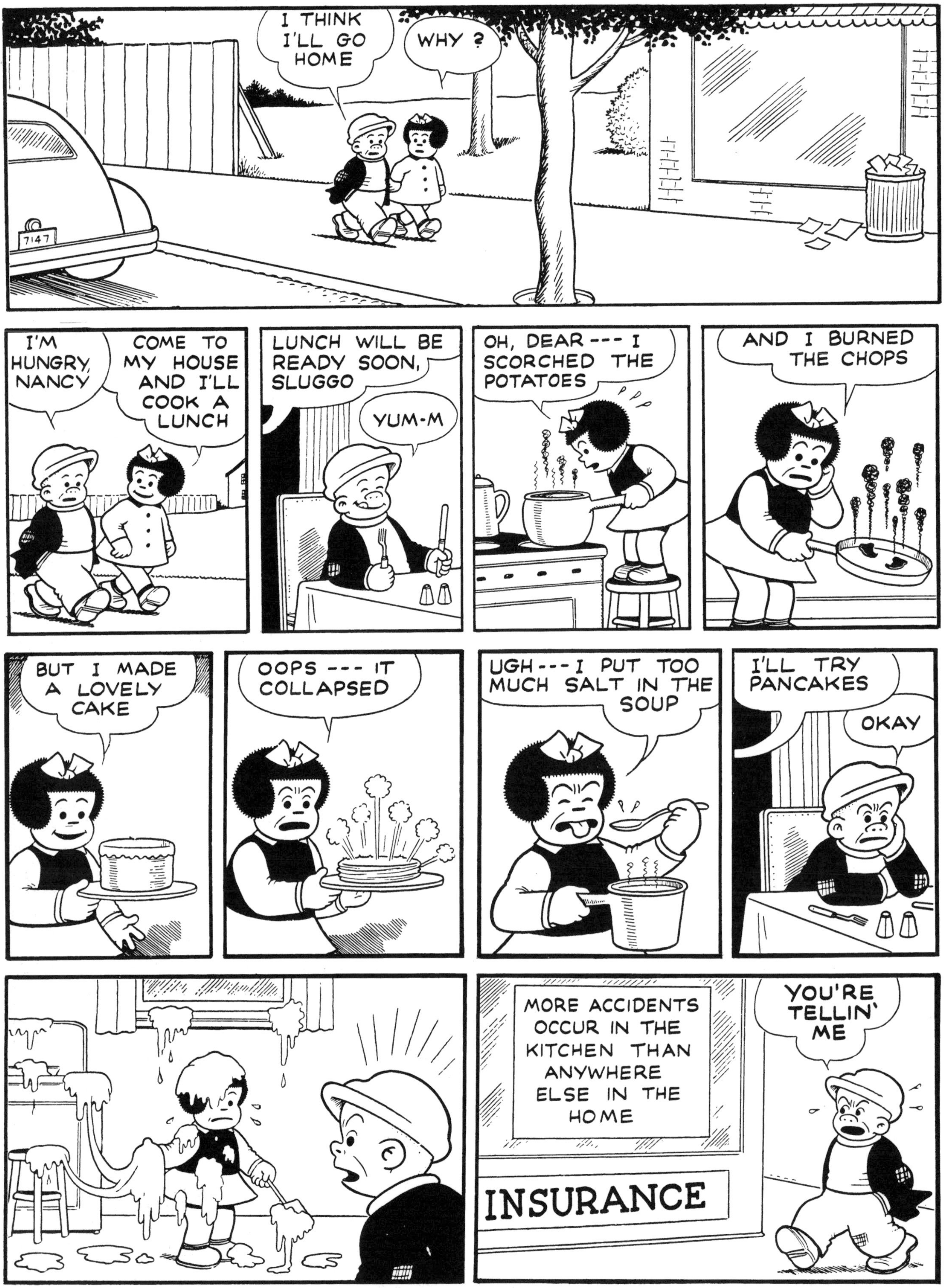
I THINK I'LL GO HOME
WHY ?
7147
I'M HUNGRY, NANCY
COME TO MY HOUSE AND I'LL COOK A LUNCH
LUNCH WILL BE READY SOON, SLUGGO
YUM-M
OH, DEAR --- I SCORCHED THE POTATOES
AND I BURNED THE CHOPS
BUT I MADE A LOVELY CAKE
OOPS --- IT COLLAPSED
UGH --- I PUT TOO MUCH SALT IN THE SOUP
I'LL TRY PANCAKES
OKAY
MORE ACCIDENTS OCCUR IN THE KITCHEN THAN ANYWHERE ELSE IN THE HOME
INSURANCE
YOU'RE TELLIN' ME

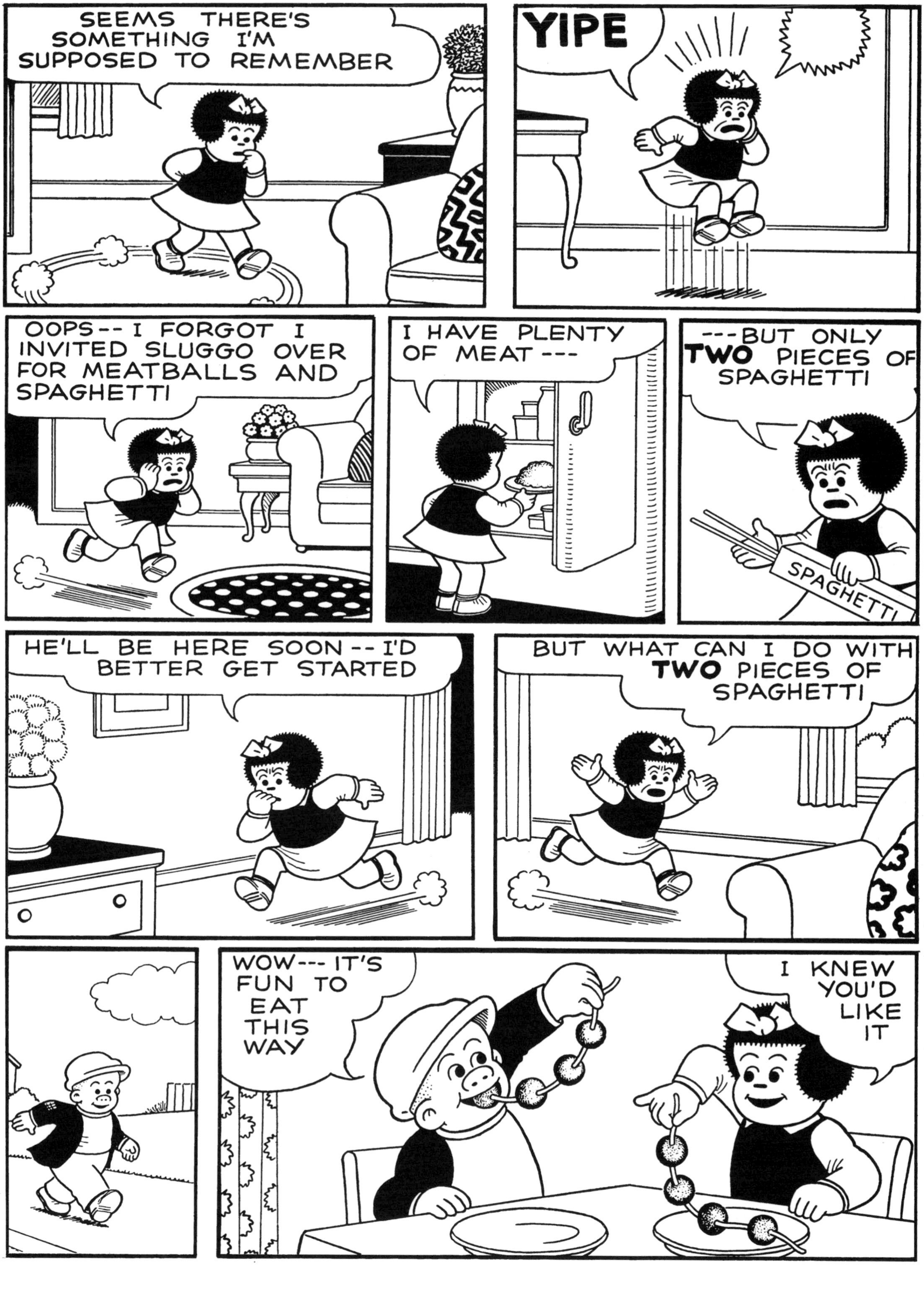
SEEMS THERE'S SOMETHING I'M SUPPOSED TO REMEMBER
YIPE
OOPS -- I FORGOT I INVITED SLUGGO OVER FOR MEATBALLS AND SPAGHETTI
I HAVE PLENTY OF MEAT ---
---BUT ONLY **TWO** PIECES OF SPAGHETTI
SPAGHETTI
HE'LL BE HERE SOON -- I'D BETTER GET STARTED
BUT WHAT CAN I DO WITH **TWO** PIECES OF SPAGHETTI
WOW--- IT'S FUN TO EAT THIS WAY
I KNEW YOU'D LIKE IT

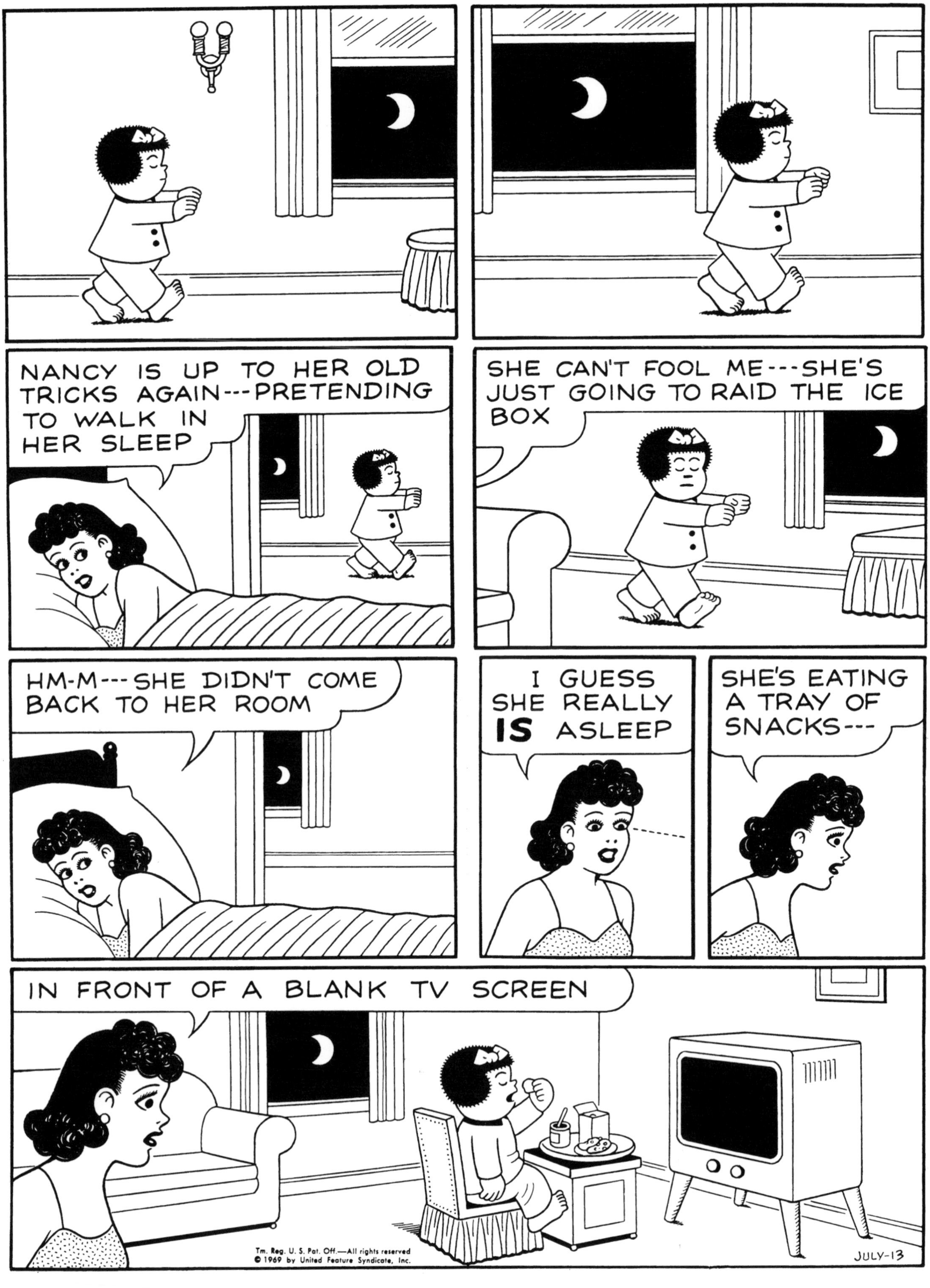
NANCY IS UP TO HER OLD TRICKS AGAIN---PRETENDING TO WALK IN HER SLEEP
SHE CAN'T FOOL ME---SHE'S JUST GOING TO RAID THE ICE BOX
HM-M---SHE DIDN'T COME BACK TO HER ROOM
I GUESS SHE REALLY **IS** ASLEEP
SHE'S EATING A TRAY OF SNACKS---
IN FRONT OF A BLANK TV SCREEN
Tm. Reg. U. S. Pat. Off.—All rights reserved
© 1969 by United Feature Syndicate, Inc.
JULY-13

SLEEP

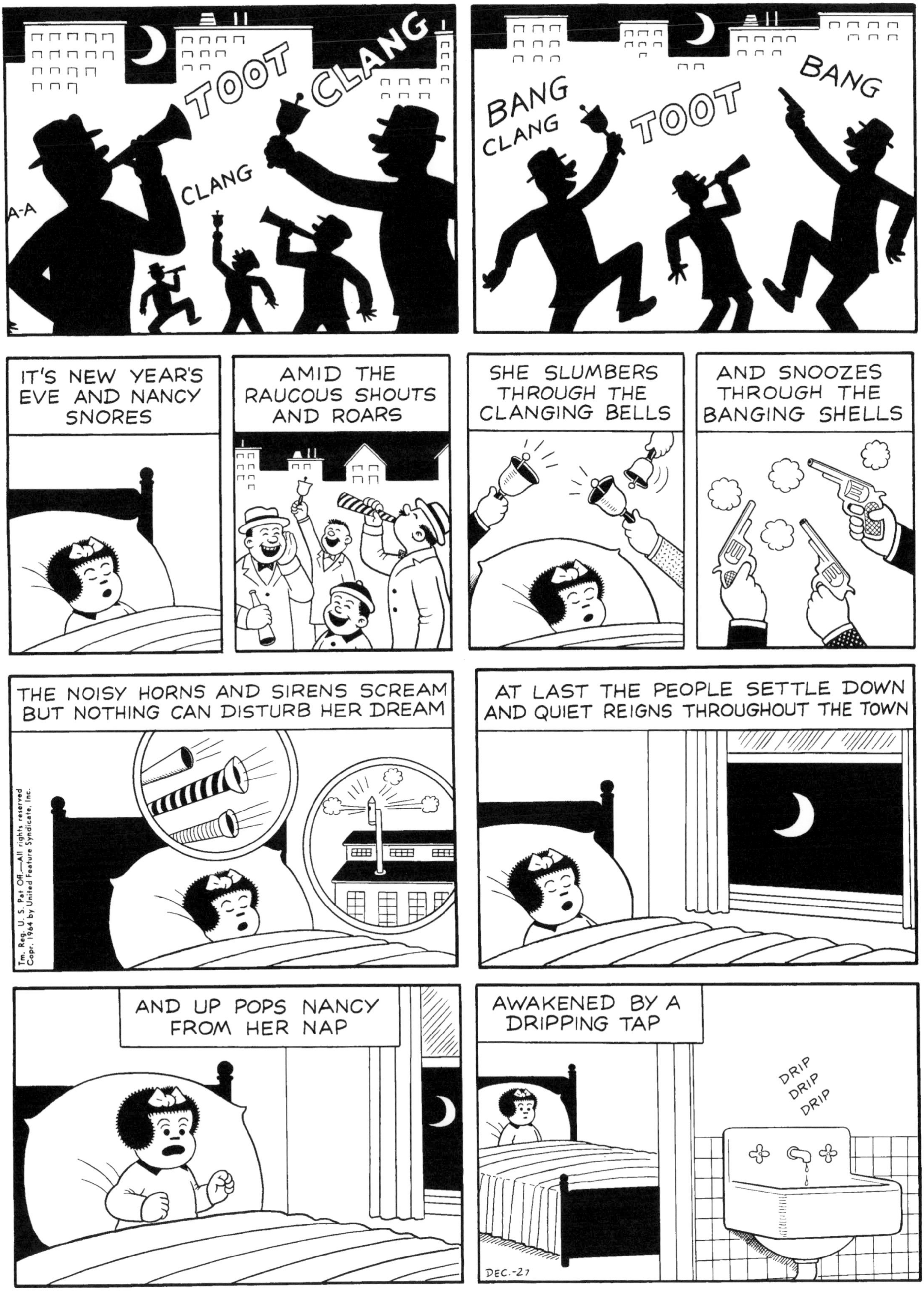
TOOT
CLANG
CLANG
A-A
BANG
CLANG
TOOT
BANG
IT'S NEW YEAR'S EVE AND NANCY SNORES
AMID THE RAUCOUS SHOUTS AND ROARS
SHE SLUMBERS THROUGH THE CLANGING BELLS
AND SNOOZES THROUGH THE BANGING SHELLS
THE NOISY HORNS AND SIRENS SCREAM BUT NOTHING CAN DISTURB HER DREAM
Tm. Reg. U. S. Pat. Off.—All rights reserved
Copr. 1964 by United Feature Syndicate, Inc.
AT LAST THE PEOPLE SETTLE DOWN AND QUIET REIGNS THROUGHOUT THE TOWN
AND UP POPS NANCY FROM HER NAP
AWAKENED BY A DRIPPING TAP
DRIP
DRIP
DRIP
DEC.-27

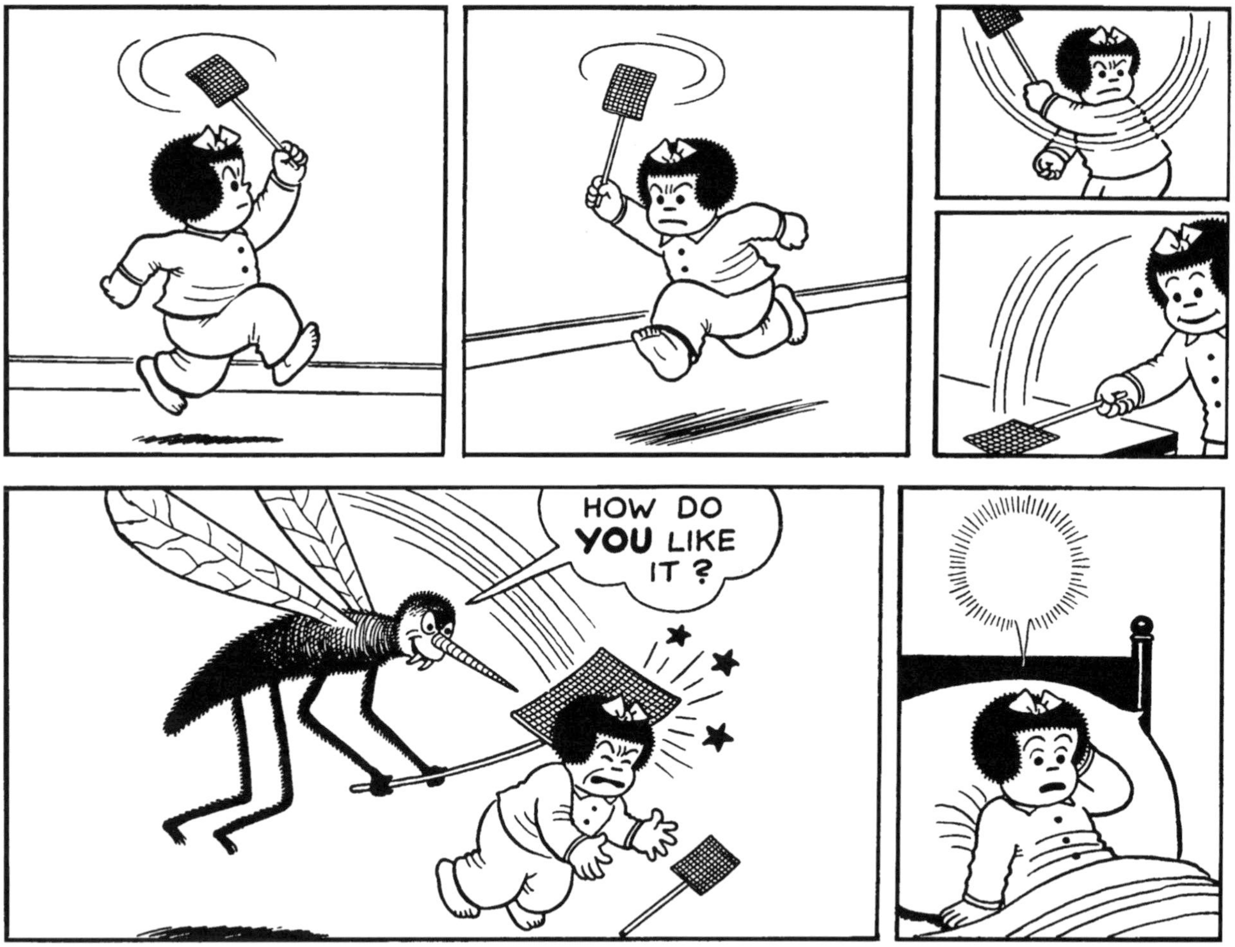
HOW DO YOU LIKE IT ?

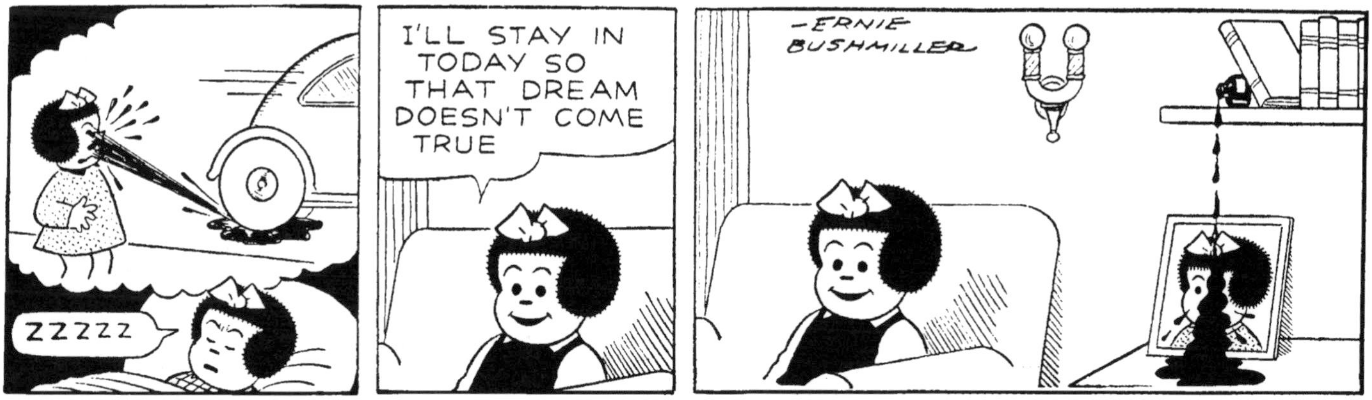
ZZZZZ
I'LL STAY IN TODAY SO THAT DREAM DOESN'T COME TRUE
-ERNIE BUSHMILLER

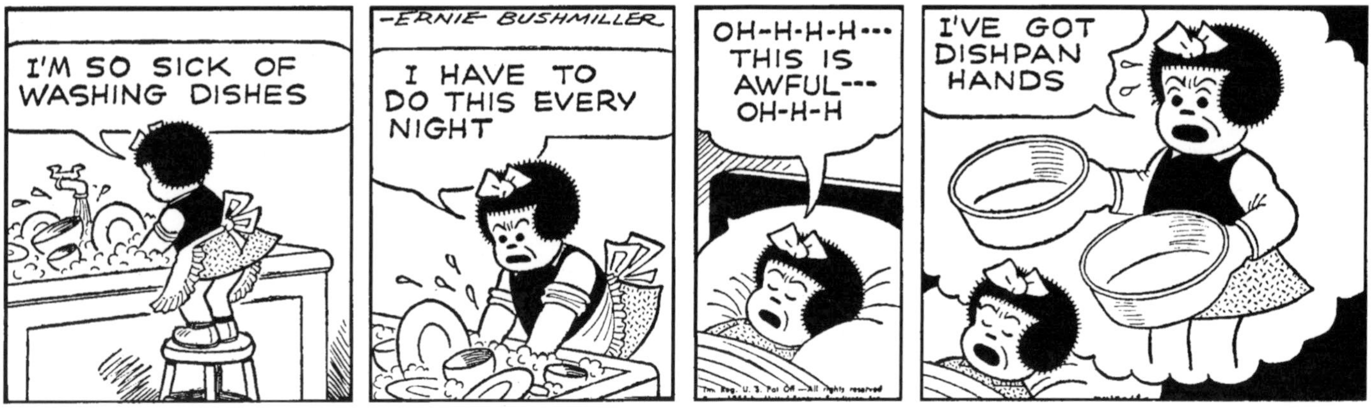
I'M SO SICK OF WASHING DISHES
-ERNIE BUSHMILLER
I HAVE TO DO THIS EVERY NIGHT
OH-H-H-H--- THIS IS AWFUL--- OH-H-H
I'VE GOT DISHPAN HANDS

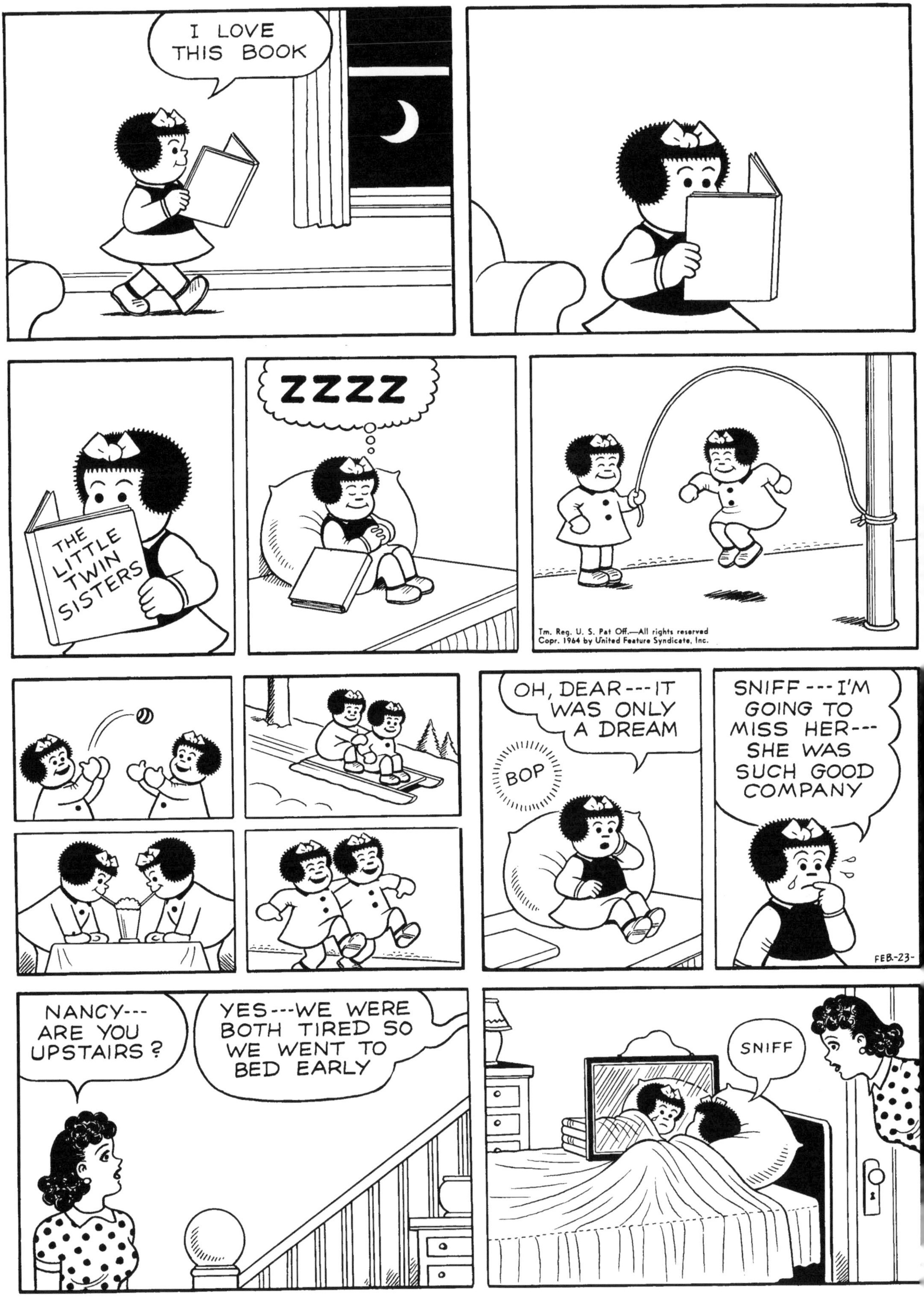
I LOVE THIS BOOK
THE LITTLE TWIN SISTERS
ZZZZ
Tm. Reg. U. S. Pat Off.—All rights reserved
Copr. 1964 by United Feature Syndicate, Inc.
OH, DEAR---IT WAS ONLY A DREAM
BOP
SNIFF---I'M GOING TO MISS HER---SHE WAS SUCH GOOD COMPANY
FEB-23-
NANCY---ARE YOU UPSTAIRS ?
YES---WE WERE BOTH TIRED SO WE WENT TO BED EARLY
SNIFF

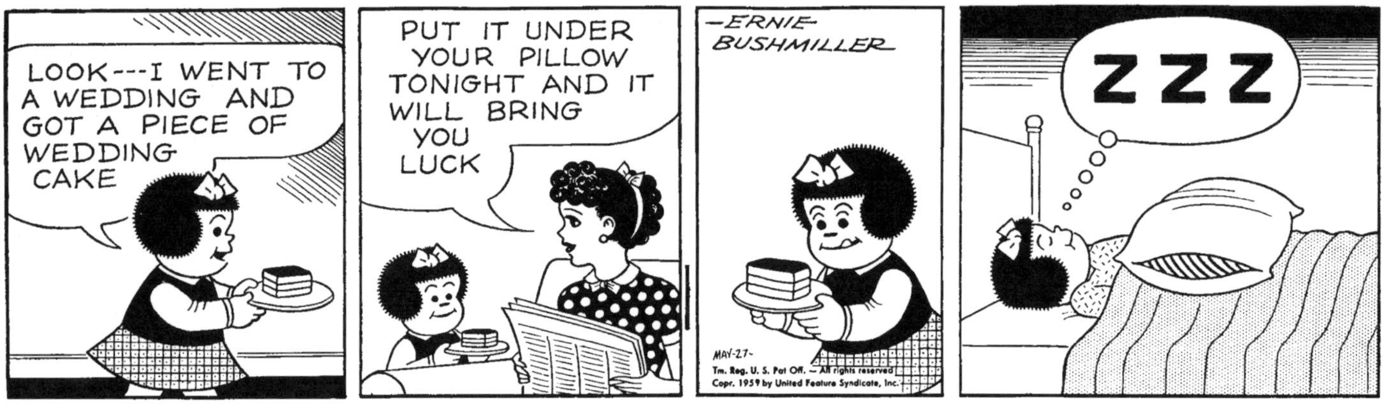
LOOK---I WENT TO A WEDDING AND GOT A PIECE OF WEDDING CAKE
PUT IT UNDER YOUR PILLOW TONIGHT AND IT WILL BRING YOU LUCK
-ERNIE-
BUSHMILLER
MAY-27-
Tm. Reg. U. S. Pat Off. — All rights reserved
Copr. 1959 by United Feature Syndicate, Inc.
ZZZ

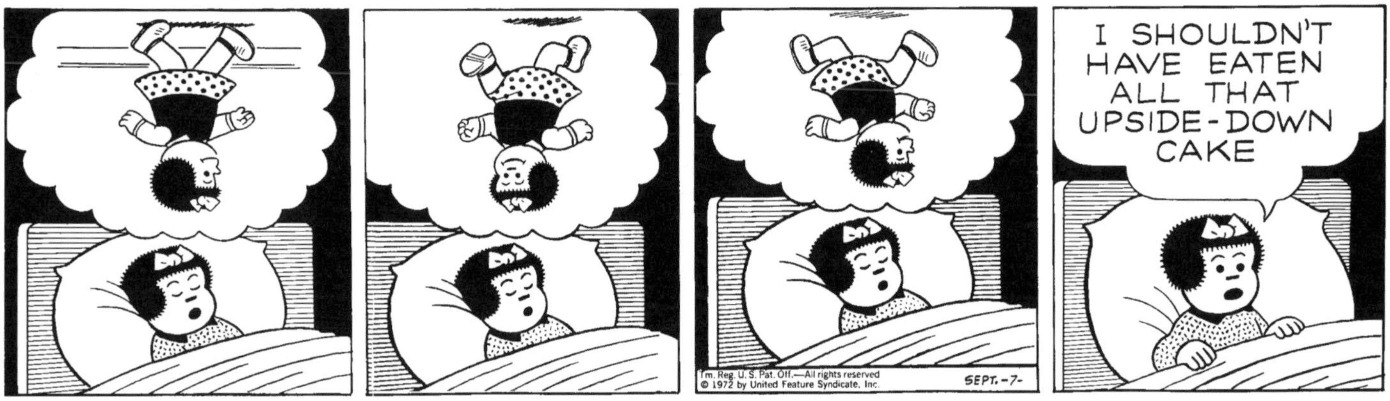
Tm. Reg. U.S. Pat. Off.—All rights reserved
© 1972 by United Feature Syndicate, Inc.
SEPT.-7-
I SHOULDN'T HAVE EATEN ALL THAT UPSIDE-DOWN CAKE

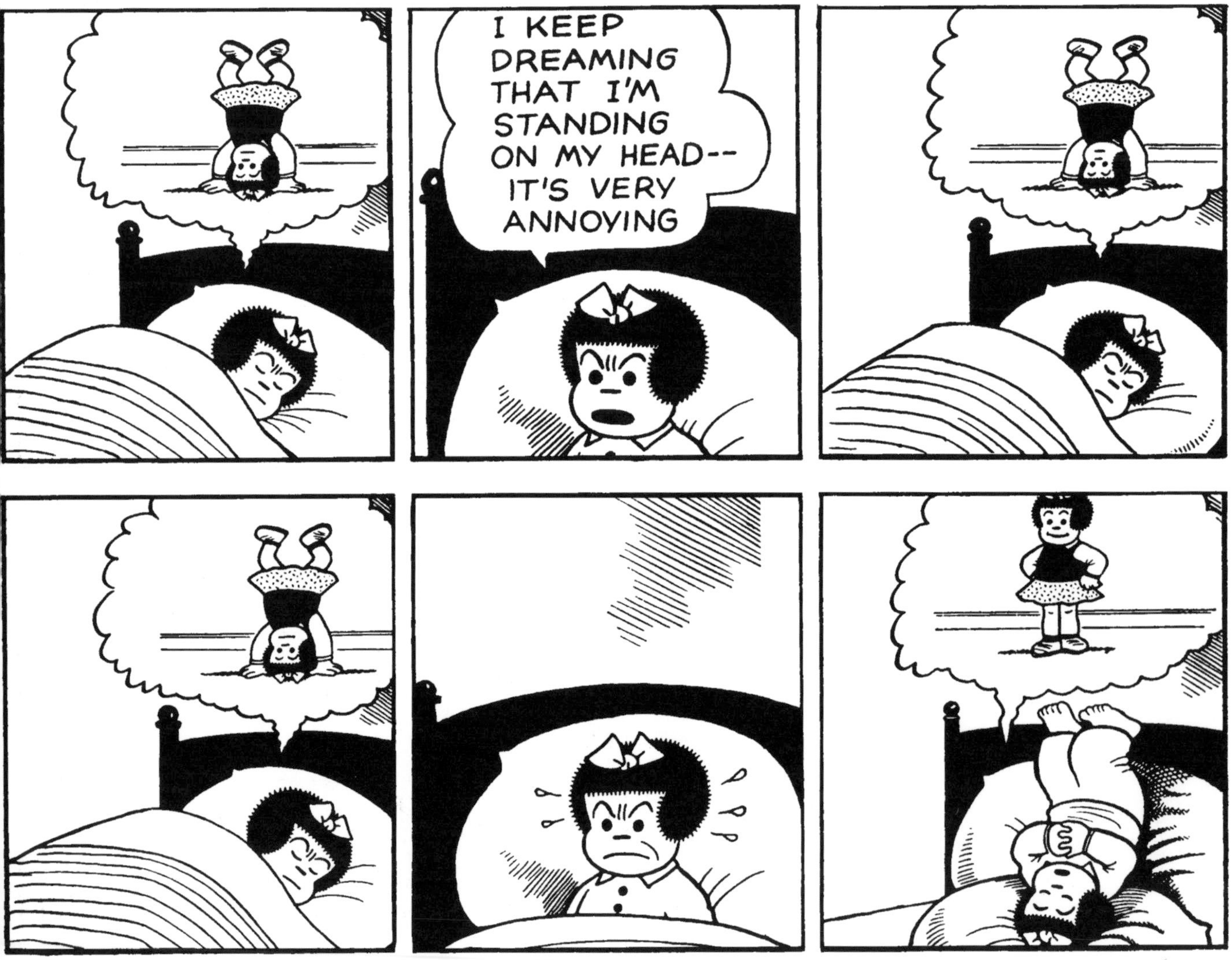
I KEEP DREAMING THAT I'M STANDING ON MY HEAD-- IT'S VERY ANNOYING

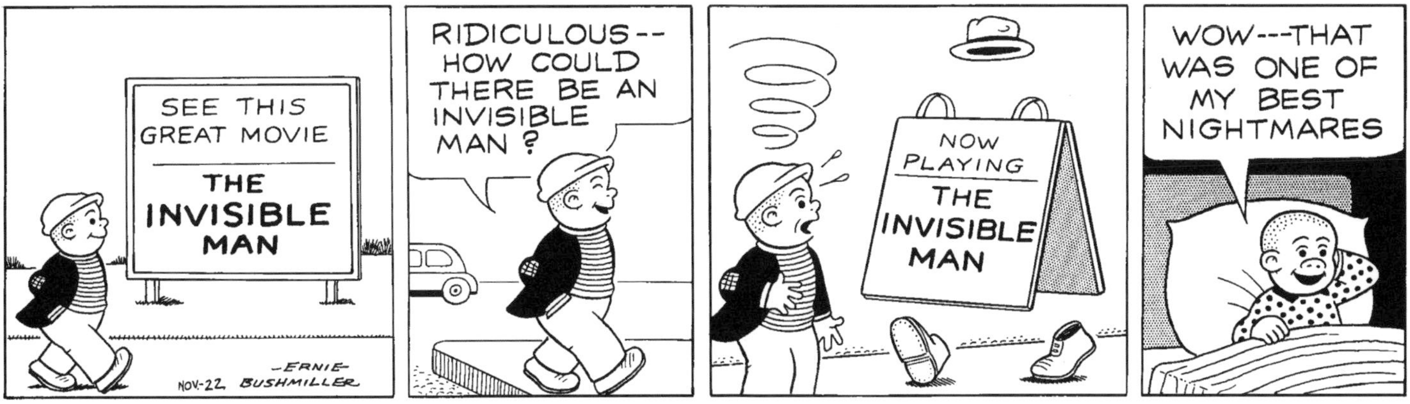
SEE THIS GREAT MOVIE
THE INVISIBLE MAN
NOV-22
-ERNIE BUSHMILLER
RIDICULOUS-- HOW COULD THERE BE AN INVISIBLE MAN ?
NOW PLAYING
THE INVISIBLE MAN
WOW---THAT WAS ONE OF MY BEST NIGHTMARES

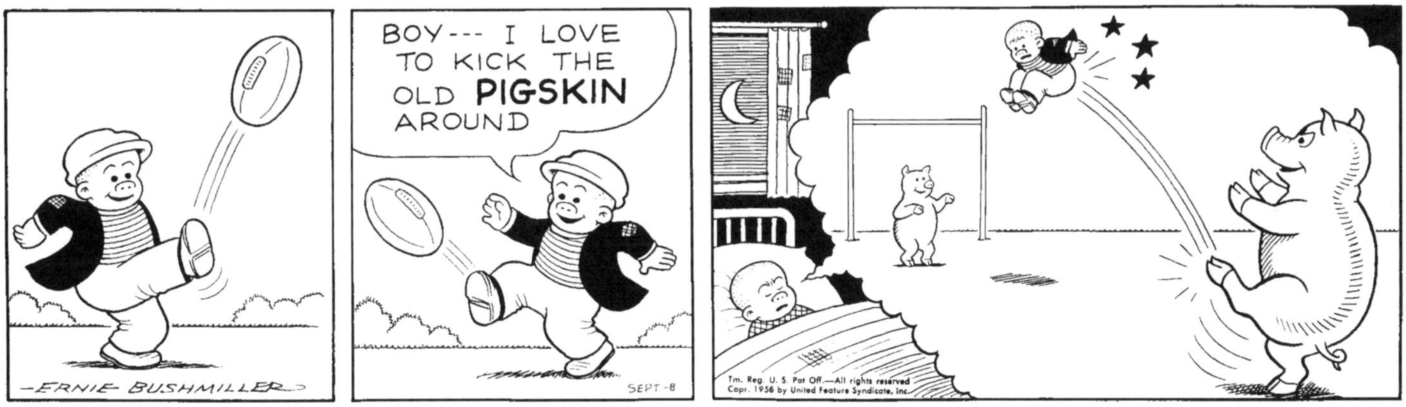
-ERNIE BUSHMILLER
BOY--- I LOVE TO KICK THE OLD PIGSKIN AROUND
SEPT-8
Tm. Reg. U. S. Pat. Off.—All rights reserved
Copr. 1956 by United Feature Syndicate, Inc.

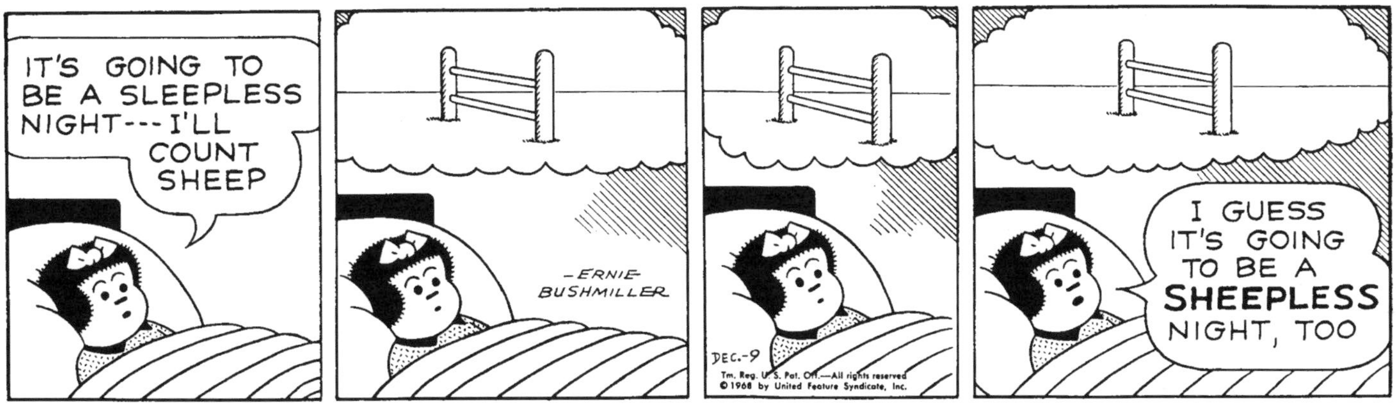
IT'S GOING TO BE A SLEEPLESS NIGHT---I'LL COUNT SHEEP
-ERNIE BUSHMILLER
DEC.-9
Tm. Reg. U. S. Pat. Off.—All rights reserved
© 1968 by United Feature Syndicate, Inc.
I GUESS IT'S GOING TO BE A SHEEPLESS NIGHT, TOO

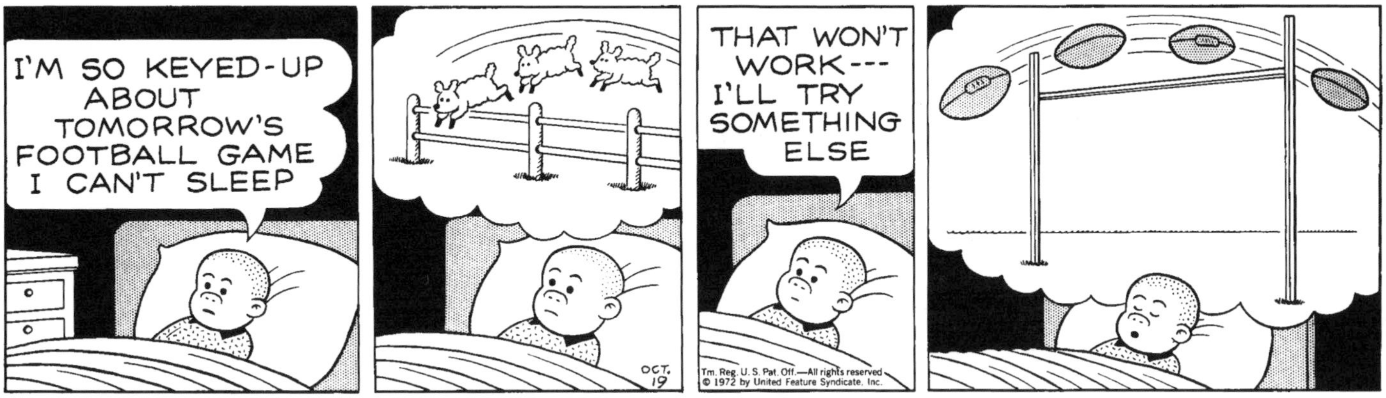
I'M SO KEYED-UP ABOUT TOMORROW'S FOOTBALL GAME I CAN'T SLEEP
OCT. 19
THAT WON'T WORK--- I'LL TRY SOMETHING ELSE
Tm. Reg. U. S. Pat. Off.—All rights reserved
© 1972 by United Feature Syndicate, Inc.

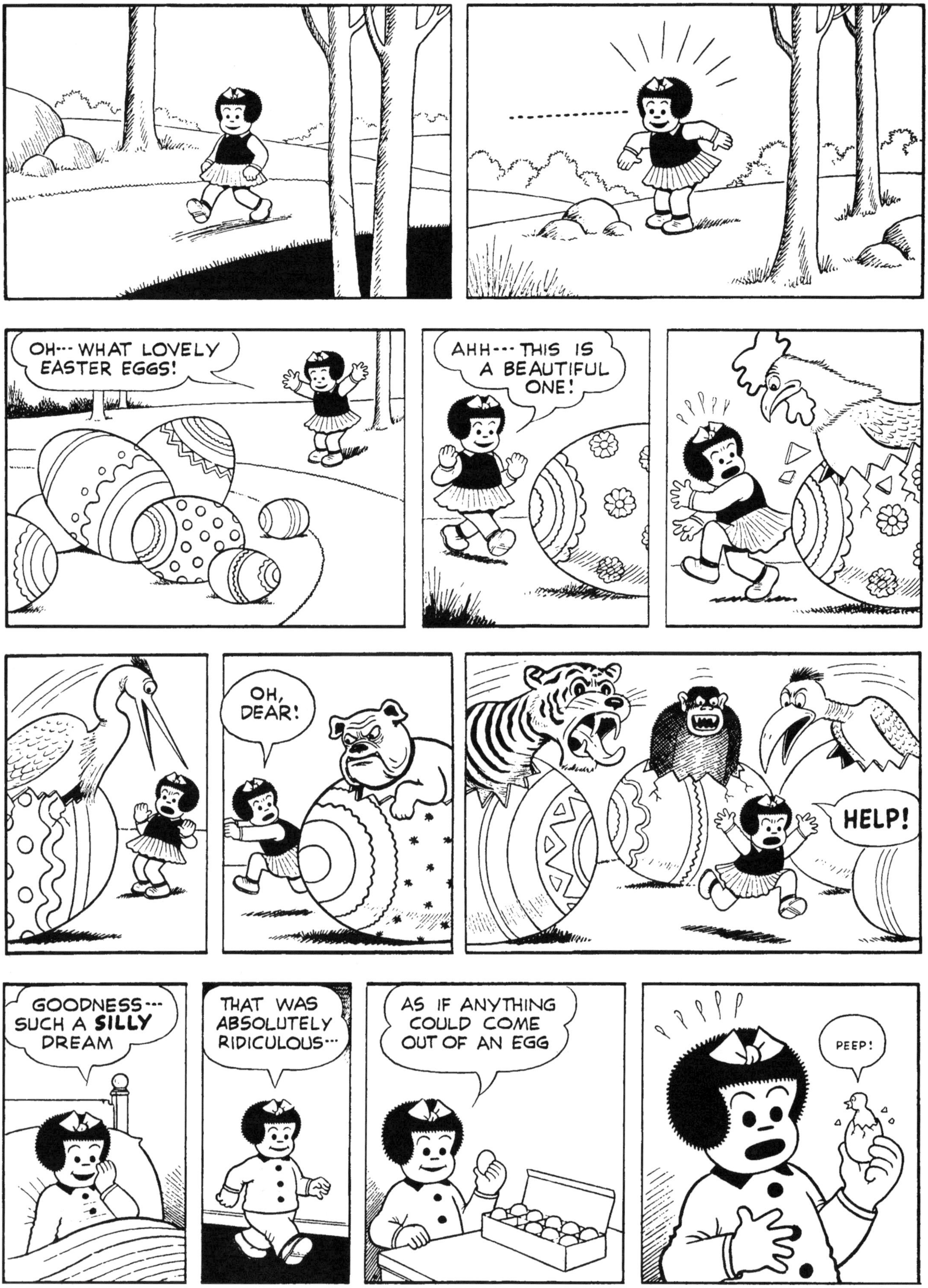
OH--- WHAT LOVELY EASTER EGGS!
AHH--- THIS IS A BEAUTIFUL ONE!
OH, DEAR!
HELP!
GOODNESS--- SUCH A **SILLY** DREAM
THAT WAS ABSOLUTELY RIDICULOUS---
AS IF ANYTHING COULD COME OUT OF AN EGG
PEEP!

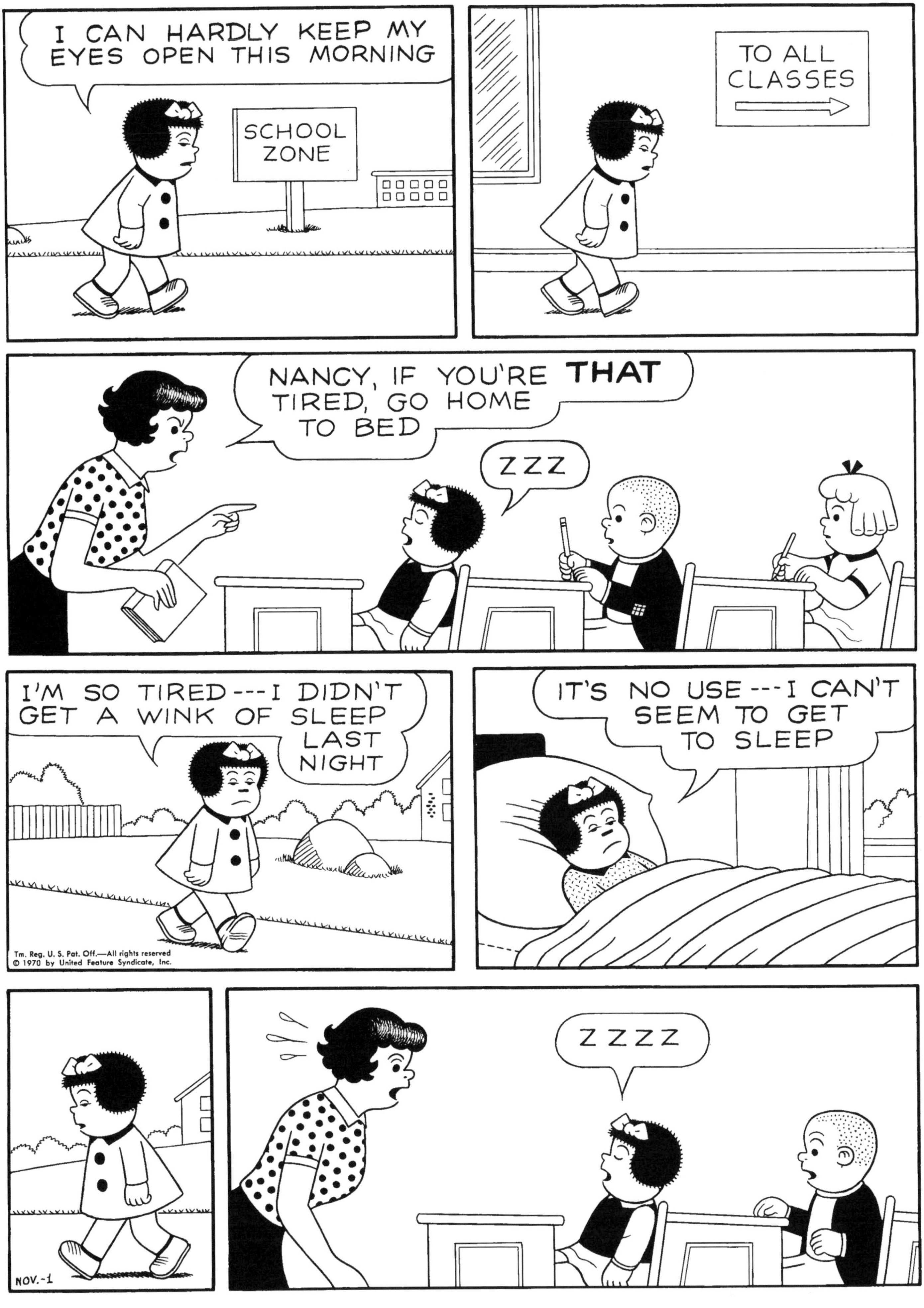
I CAN HARDLY KEEP MY EYES OPEN THIS MORNING
SCHOOL ZONE
TO ALL CLASSES
NANCY, IF YOU'RE **THAT** TIRED, GO HOME TO BED
ZZZ
I'M SO TIRED---I DIDN'T GET A WINK OF SLEEP LAST NIGHT
Tm. Reg. U. S. Pat. Off.—All rights reserved
© 1970 by United Feature Syndicate, Inc.
IT'S NO USE---I CAN'T SEEM TO GET TO SLEEP
NOV.-1
ZZZZ

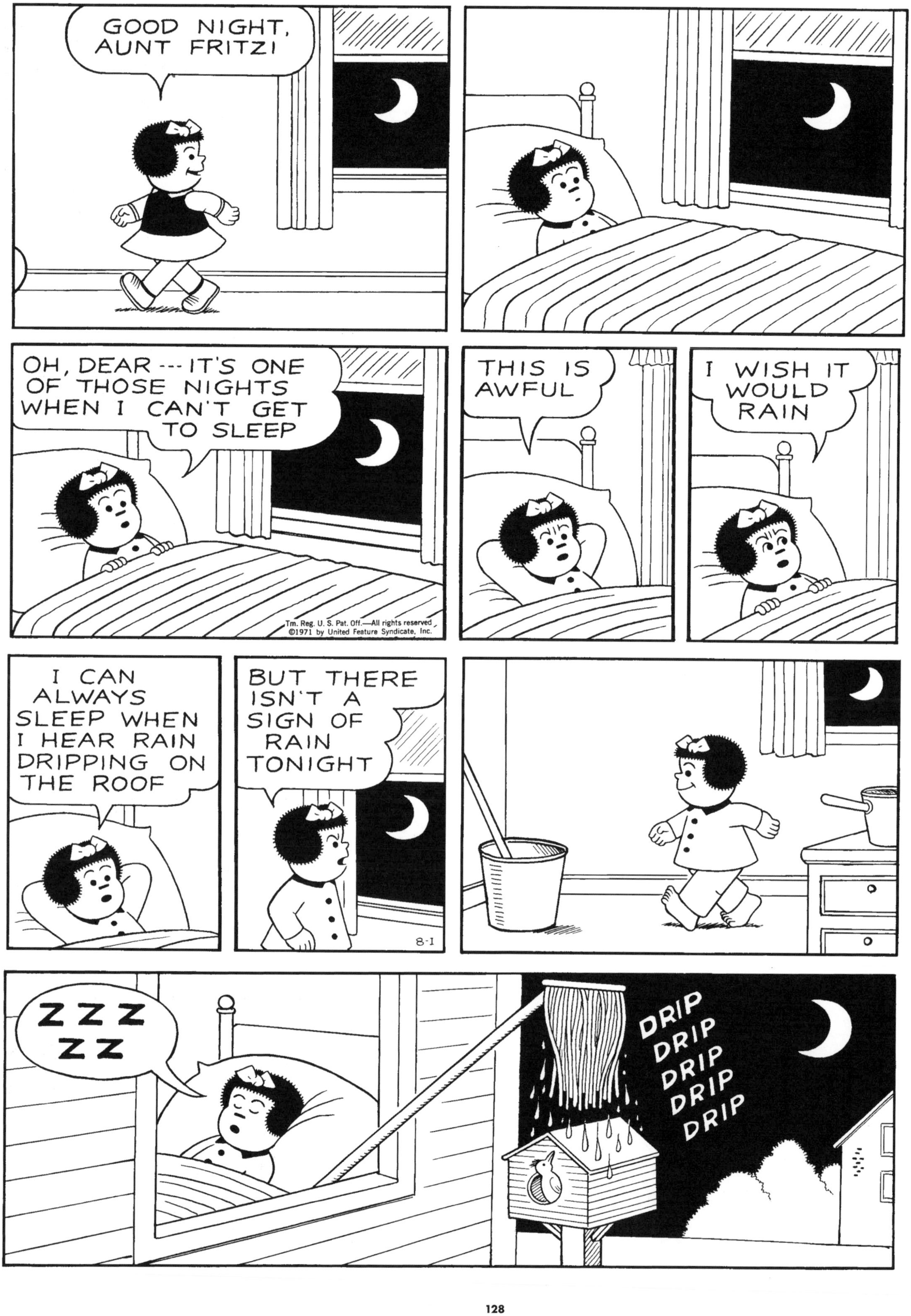

GOOD NIGHT, AUNT FRITZI
OH, DEAR --- IT'S ONE OF THOSE NIGHTS WHEN I CAN'T GET TO SLEEP
Tm. Reg. U. S. Pat. Off.—All rights reserved
©1971 by United Feature Syndicate, Inc.
THIS IS AWFUL
I WISH IT WOULD RAIN
I CAN ALWAYS SLEEP WHEN I HEAR RAIN DRIPPING ON THE ROOF
BUT THERE ISN'T A SIGN OF RAIN TONIGHT
8-1
ZZZ ZZ
DRIP DRIP DRIP DRIP DRIP

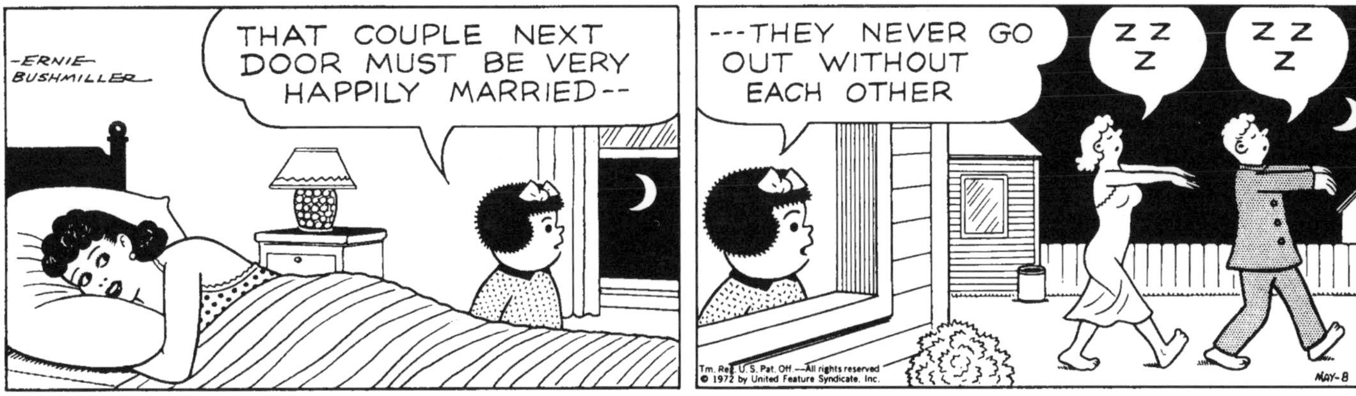
-ERNIE BUSHMILLER
THAT COUPLE NEXT DOOR MUST BE VERY HAPPILY MARRIED--
---THEY NEVER GO OUT WITHOUT EACH OTHER
Z Z Z
Z Z Z
Tm. Reg. U.S. Pat. Off.—All rights reserved © 1972 by United Feature Syndicate, Inc.
MAY-8

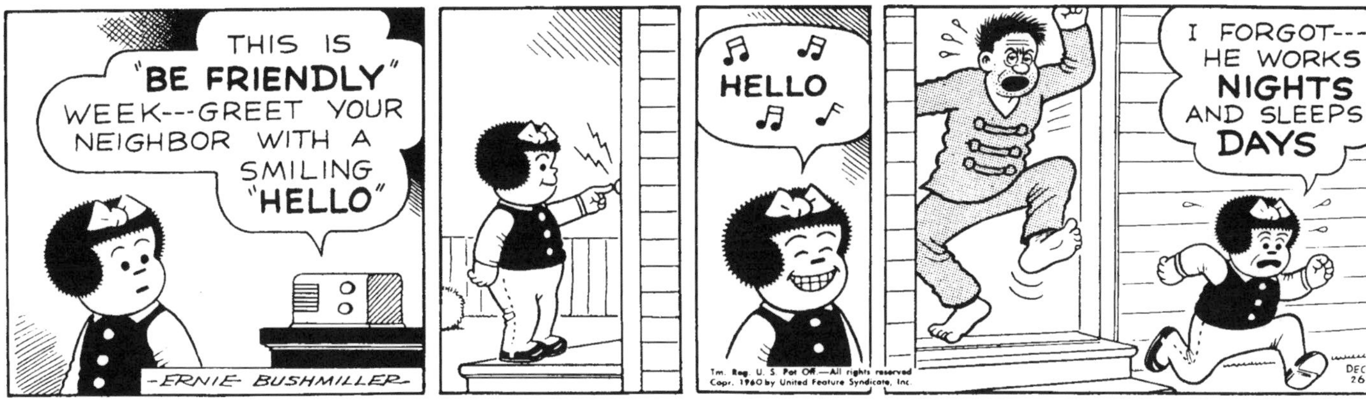
THIS IS "BE FRIENDLY" WEEK---GREET YOUR NEIGHBOR WITH A SMILING "HELLO"
-ERNIE BUSHMILLER
HELLO
Tm. Reg. U.S. Pat. Off.—All rights reserved Copr. 1960 by United Feature Syndicate, Inc.
I FORGOT--- HE WORKS NIGHTS AND SLEEPS DAYS
DEC-26-

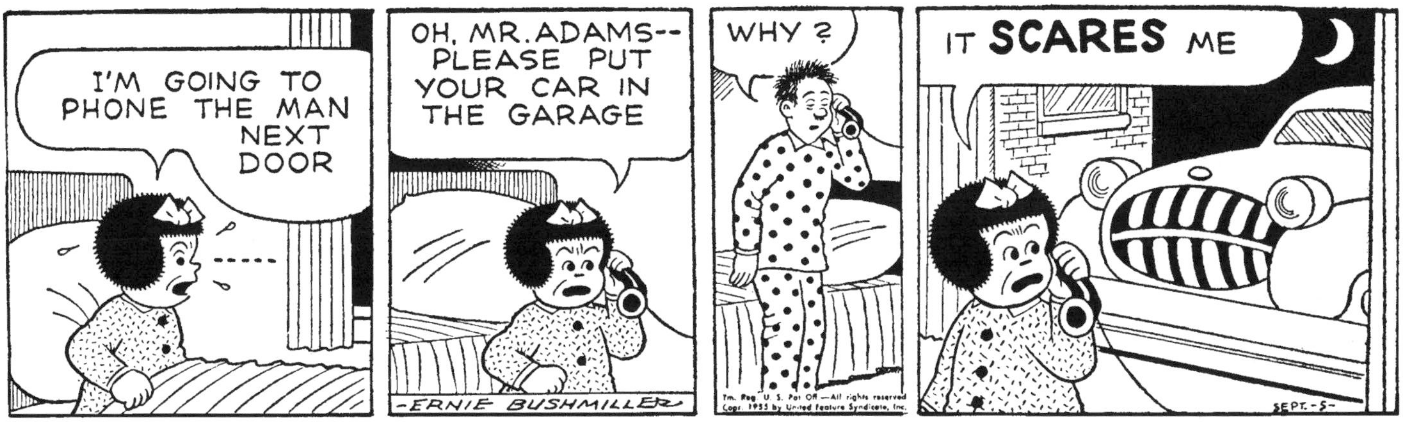
I'M GOING TO PHONE THE MAN NEXT DOOR
OH, MR. ADAMS-- PLEASE PUT YOUR CAR IN THE GARAGE
-ERNIE BUSHMILLER
WHY ?
Tm. Reg. U.S. Pat. Off.—All rights reserved Copr. 1955 by United Feature Syndicate, Inc.
IT SCARES ME
SEPT.-5-

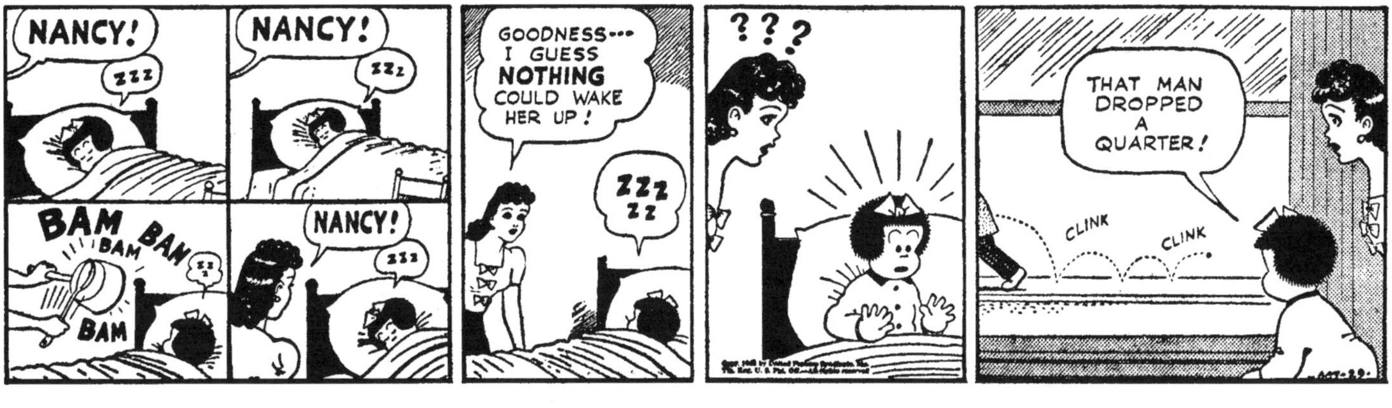
NANCY!
ZZZ
NANCY!
ZZZ
BAM BAM BAM BAM
ZZZ
NANCY!
ZZZ
GOODNESS--- I GUESS NOTHING COULD WAKE HER UP!
ZZZ ZZ
???
THAT MAN DROPPED A QUARTER!
CLINK
CLINK

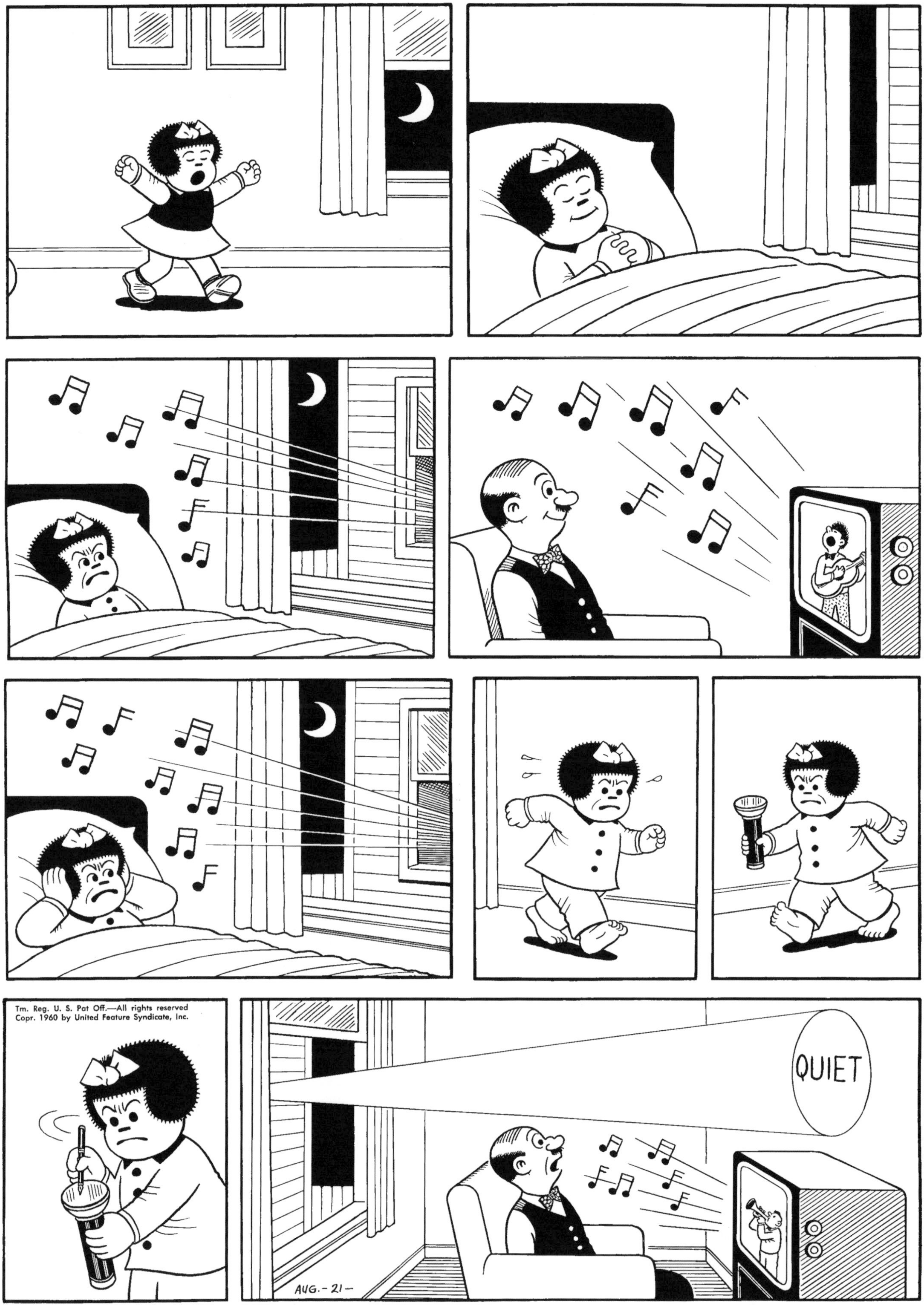
QUIET
AUG.-21-

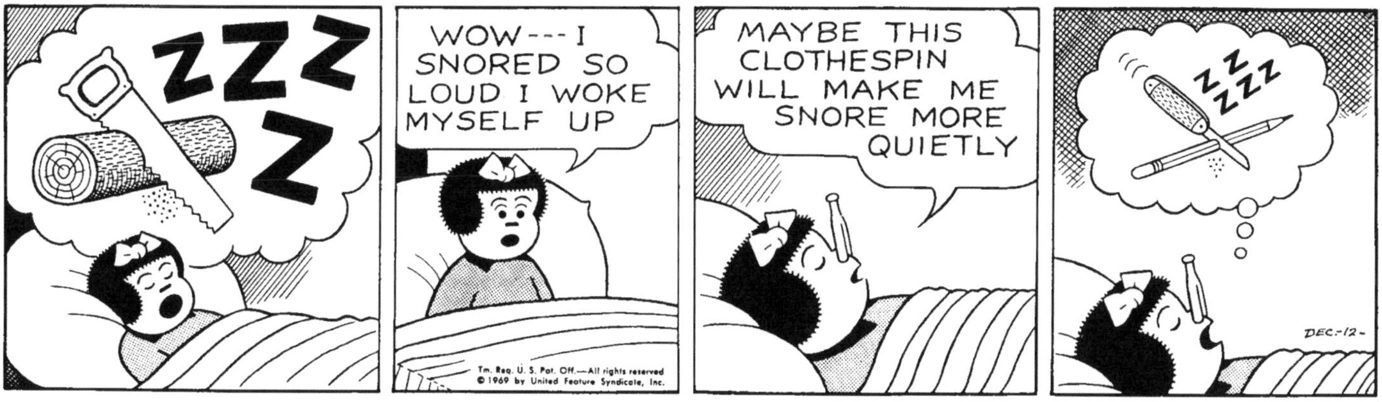
ZZZ
Z
WOW---I SNORED SO LOUD I WOKE MYSELF UP
Tm. Reg. U. S. Pat. Off.—All rights reserved © 1969 by United Feature Syndicate, Inc.
MAYBE THIS CLOTHESPIN WILL MAKE ME SNORE MORE QUIETLY
Z Z ZZZ
DEC.-12-

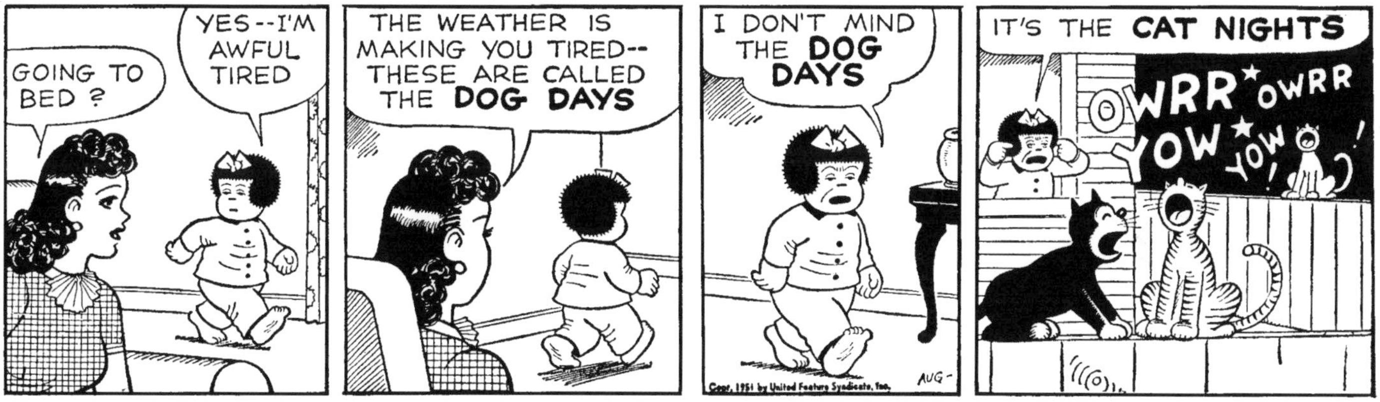
GOING TO BED ?
YES--I'M AWFUL TIRED
THE WEATHER IS MAKING YOU TIRED-- THESE ARE CALLED THE **DOG DAYS**
I DON'T MIND THE **DOG DAYS**
Copr. 1951 by United Feature Syndicate, Inc.
AUG-
IT'S THE **CAT NIGHTS**
OWRR OWRR
YOW YOW !
!

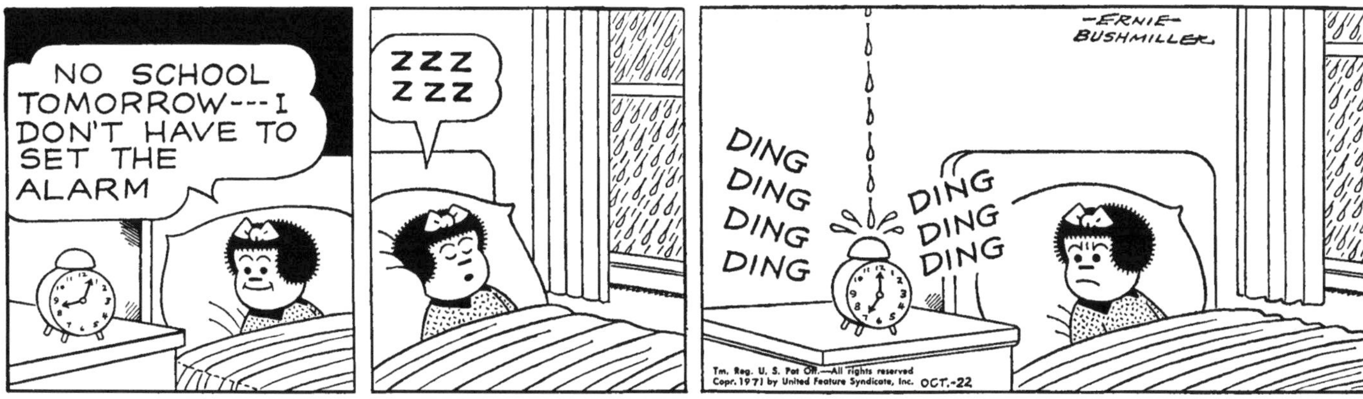
NO SCHOOL TOMORROW---I DON'T HAVE TO SET THE ALARM
ZZZ ZZZ
-ERNIE- BUSHMILLER
DING DING DING DING
DING DING DING
Tm. Reg. U. S. Pat. Off.—All rights reserved Copr. 1971 by United Feature Syndicate, Inc.
OCT.-22

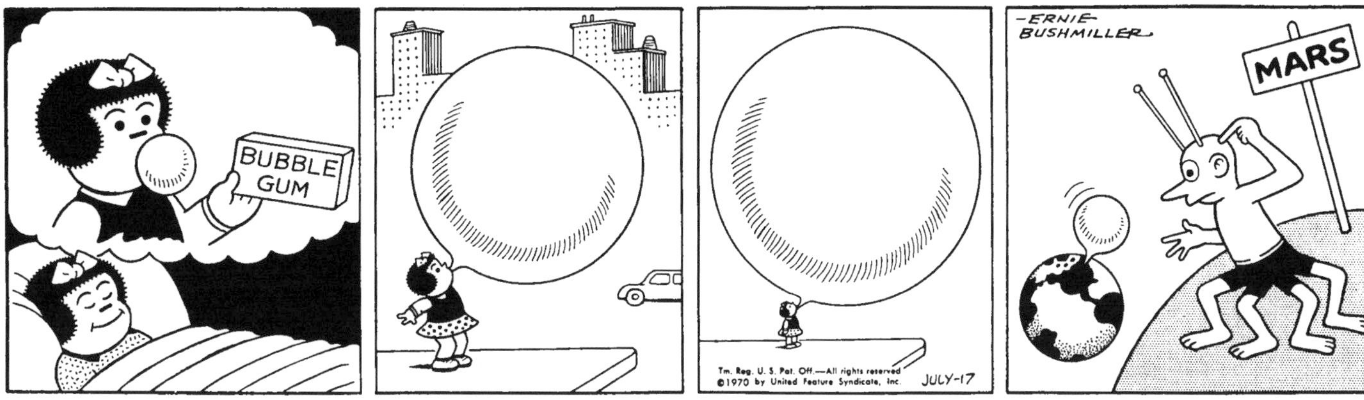
BUBBLE GUM
Tm. Reg. U. S. Pat. Off.—All rights reserved ©1970 by United Feature Syndicate, Inc.
JULY-17
-ERNIE- BUSHMILLER
MARS

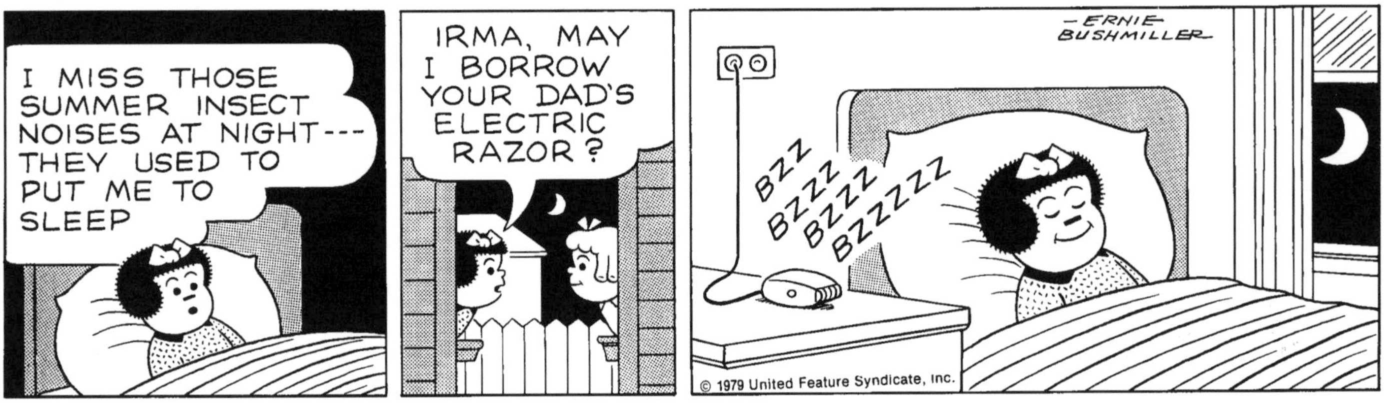
I MISS THOSE SUMMER INSECT NOISES AT NIGHT--- THEY USED TO PUT ME TO SLEEP
IRMA, MAY I BORROW YOUR DAD'S ELECTRIC RAZOR?
-ERNIE BUSHMILLER-
BZZ BZZZ BZZZ BZZZZZ
© 1979 United Feature Syndicate, Inc.

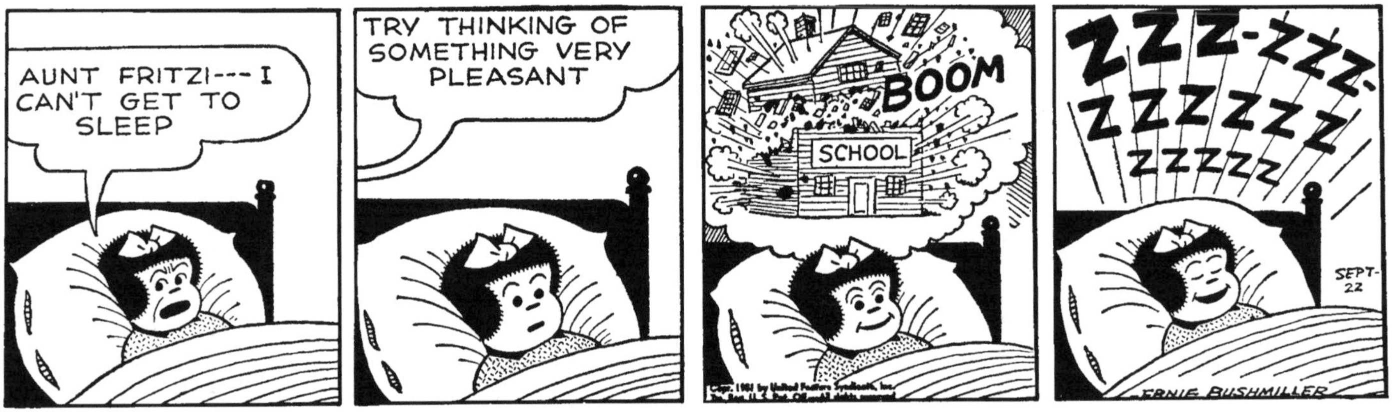
AUNT FRITZI--- I CAN'T GET TO SLEEP
TRY THINKING OF SOMETHING VERY PLEASANT
BOOM
SCHOOL
ZZZ-ZZZ-ZZZZZZZ ZZZZZ
SEPT-22
ERNIE BUSHMILLER

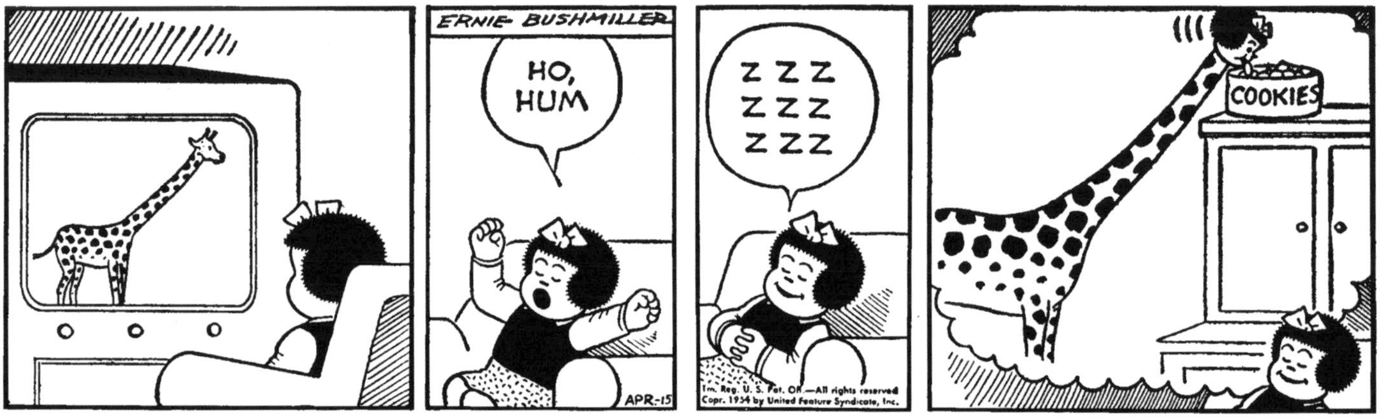
ERNIE BUSHMILLER
HO, HUM
APR-15
ZZZ ZZZ ZZZ
Tm. Reg. U. S. Pat. Off.—All rights reserved Copr. 1954 by United Feature Syndicate, Inc.
COOKIES

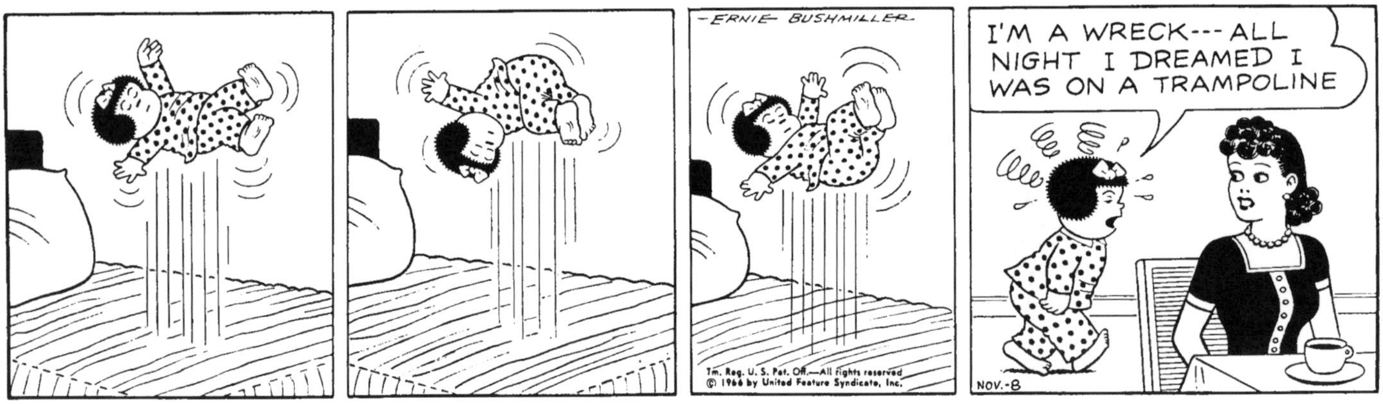
-ERNIE BUSHMILLER-
Tm. Reg. U. S. Pat. Off.—All rights reserved © 1966 by United Feature Syndicate, Inc.
I'M A WRECK--- ALL NIGHT I DREAMED I WAS ON A TRAMPOLINE
NOV.-8

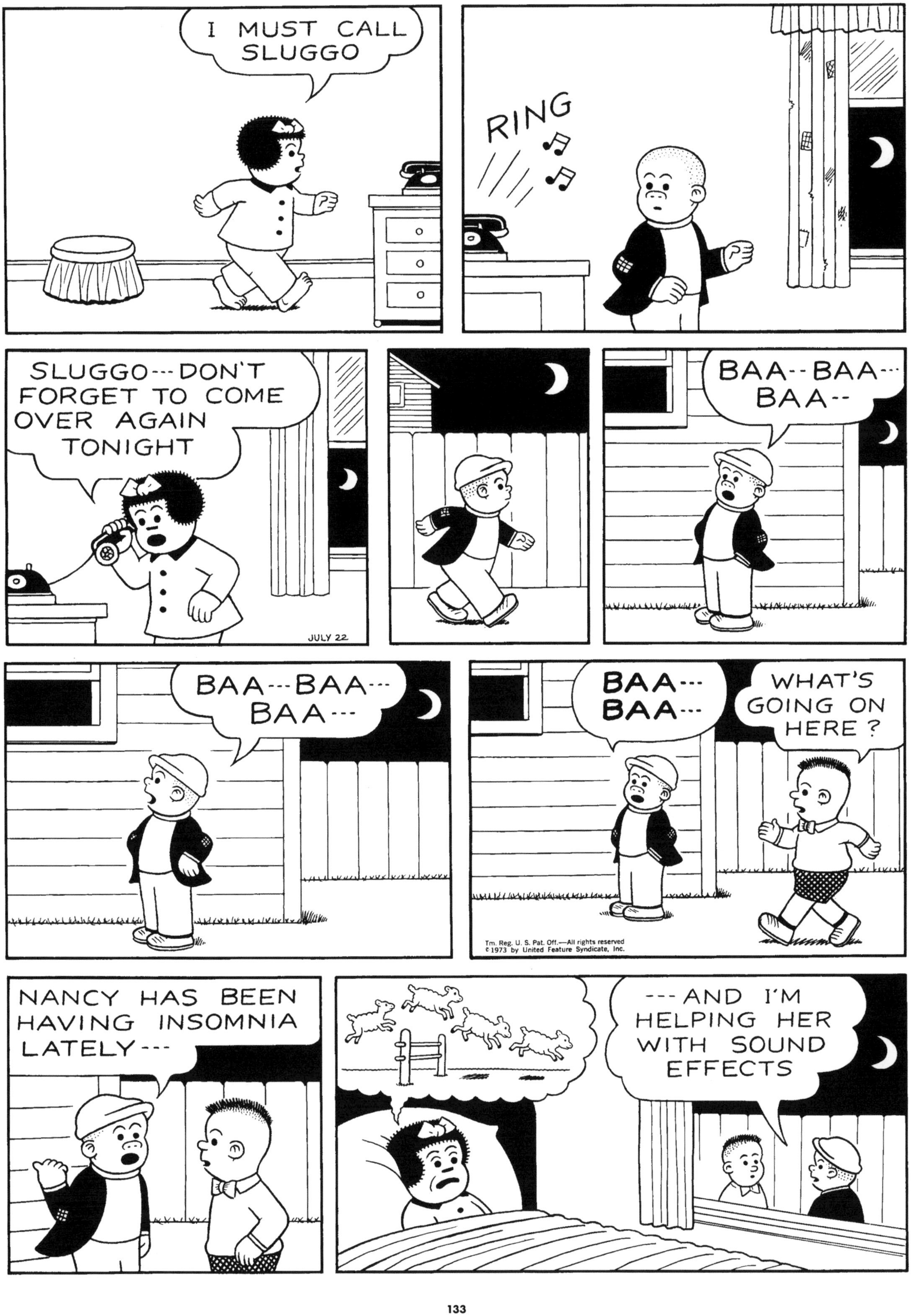
I MUST CALL SLUGGO
RING
SLUGGO---DON'T FORGET TO COME OVER AGAIN TONIGHT
JULY 22
BAA--BAA--- BAA--
BAA---BAA--- BAA---
BAA--- BAA---
WHAT'S GOING ON HERE?
Tm. Reg. U. S. Pat. Off.—All rights reserved
©1973 by United Feature Syndicate, Inc.
NANCY HAS BEEN HAVING INSOMNIA LATELY---
---AND I'M HELPING HER WITH SOUND EFFECTS

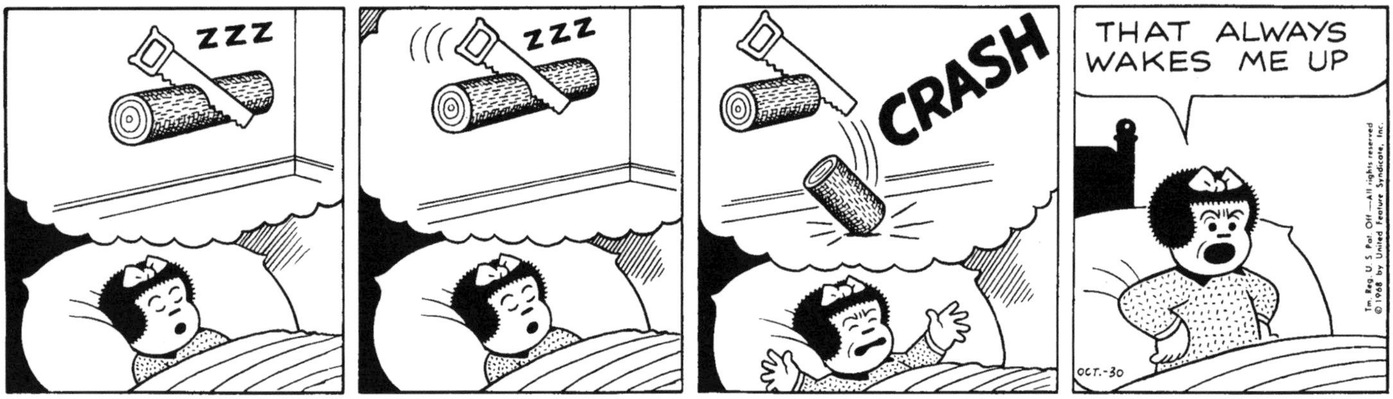
ZZZ
ZZZ
CRASH
THAT ALWAYS WAKES ME UP
Tm. Reg. U. S. Pat. Off.—All rights reserved © 1968 by United Feature Syndicate, Inc.
OCT.-30

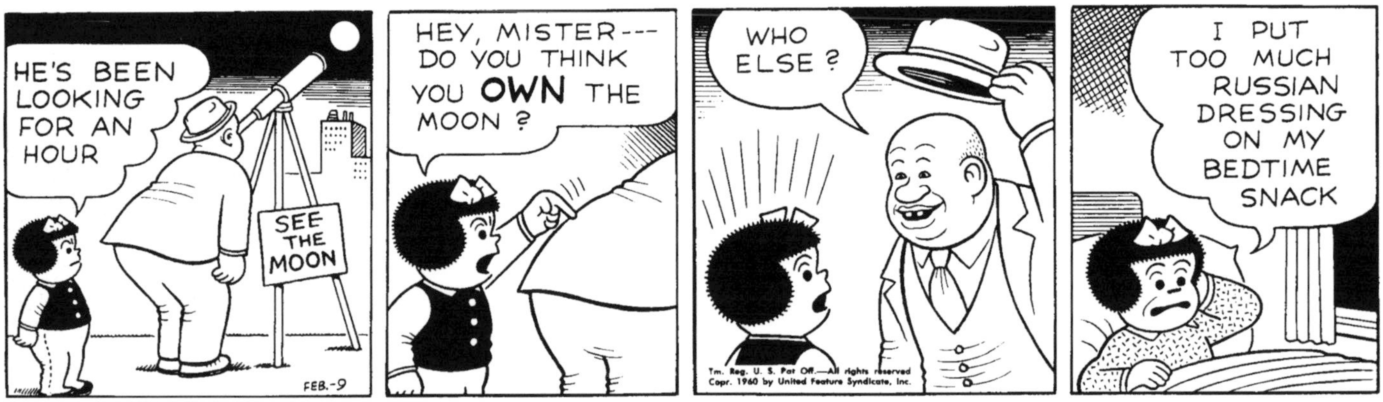
HE'S BEEN LOOKING FOR AN HOUR
SEE THE MOON
FEB.-9
HEY, MISTER--- DO YOU THINK YOU OWN THE MOON ?
WHO ELSE ?
Tm. Reg. U. S. Pat. Off.—All rights reserved Copr. 1960 by United Feature Syndicate, Inc.
I PUT TOO MUCH RUSSIAN DRESSING ON MY BEDTIME SNACK

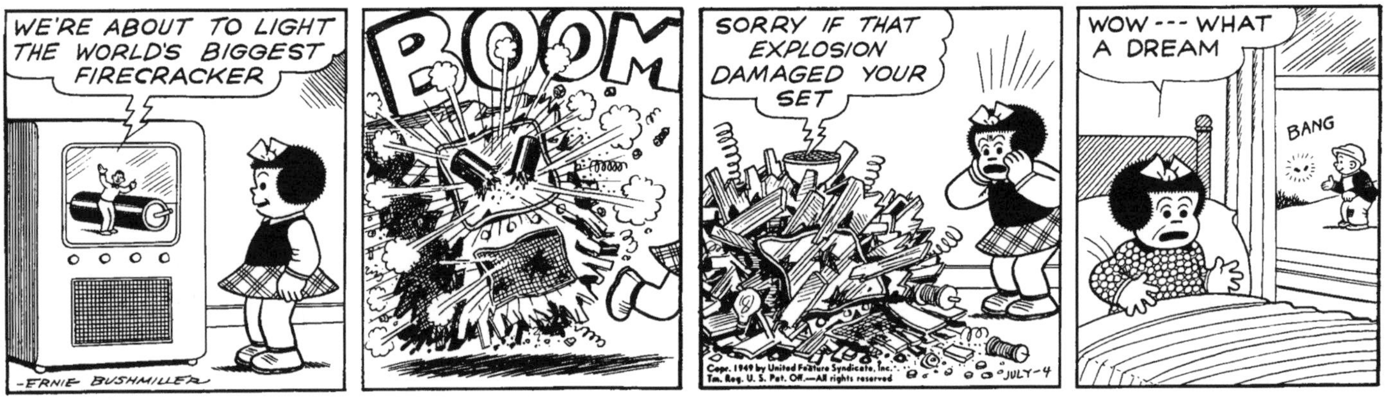
WE'RE ABOUT TO LIGHT THE WORLD'S BIGGEST FIRECRACKER
-ERNIE BUSHMILLER
BOOM
SORRY IF THAT EXPLOSION DAMAGED YOUR SET
Copr. 1949 by United Feature Syndicate, Inc. Tm. Reg. U. S. Pat. Off.—All rights reserved
JULY-4
WOW --- WHAT A DREAM
BANG

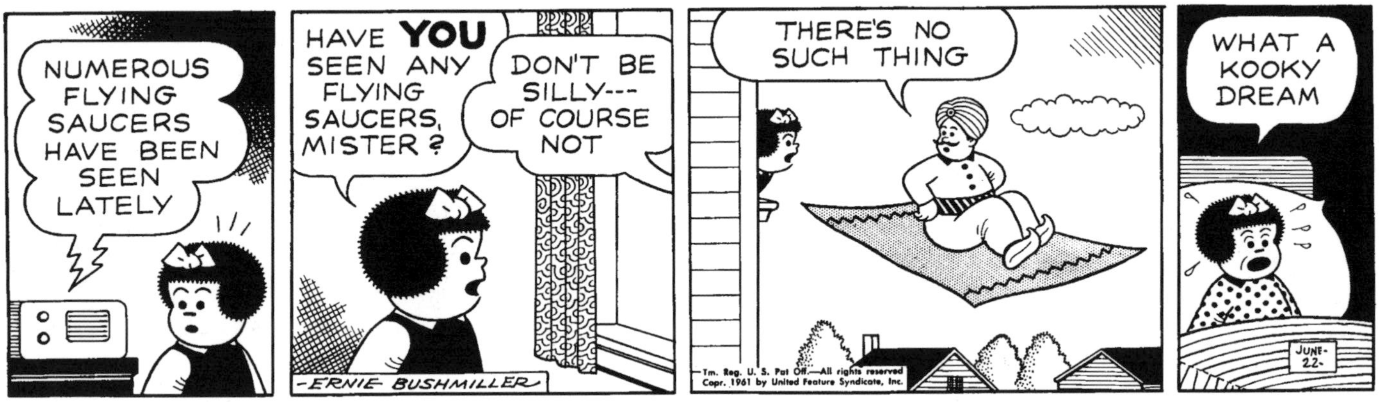
NUMEROUS FLYING SAUCERS HAVE BEEN SEEN LATELY
HAVE YOU SEEN ANY FLYING SAUCERS, MISTER ?
DON'T BE SILLY--- OF COURSE NOT
-ERNIE BUSHMILLER
THERE'S NO SUCH THING
Tm. Reg. U. S. Pat. Off.—All rights reserved Copr. 1961 by United Feature Syndicate, Inc.
WHAT A KOOKY DREAM
JUNE-22-

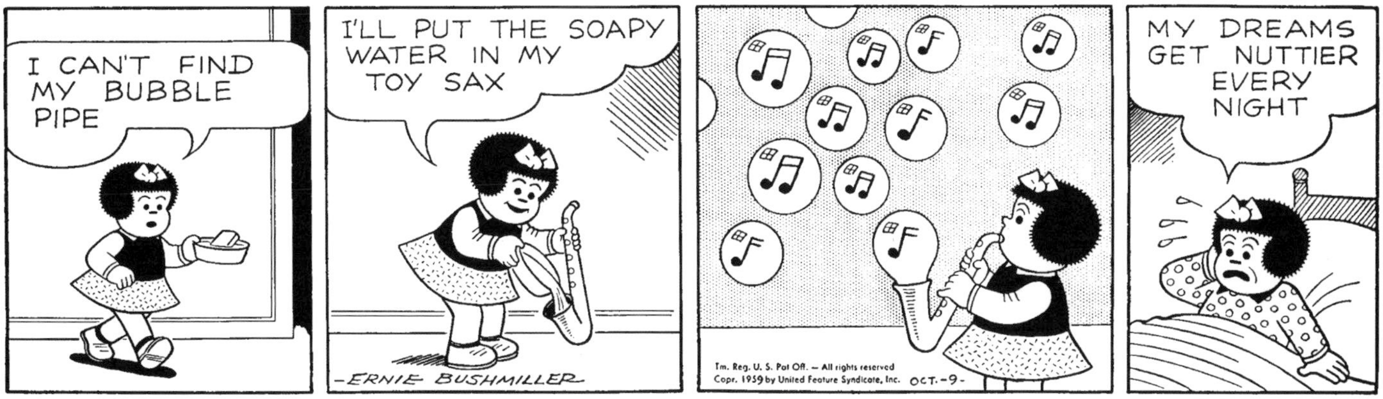
I CAN'T FIND MY BUBBLE PIPE
I'LL PUT THE SOAPY WATER IN MY TOY SAX
ERNIE BUSHMILLER
Tm. Reg. U. S. Pat Off. — All rights reserved
Copr. 1959 by United Feature Syndicate, Inc.
OCT.-9-
MY DREAMS GET NUTTIER EVERY NIGHT

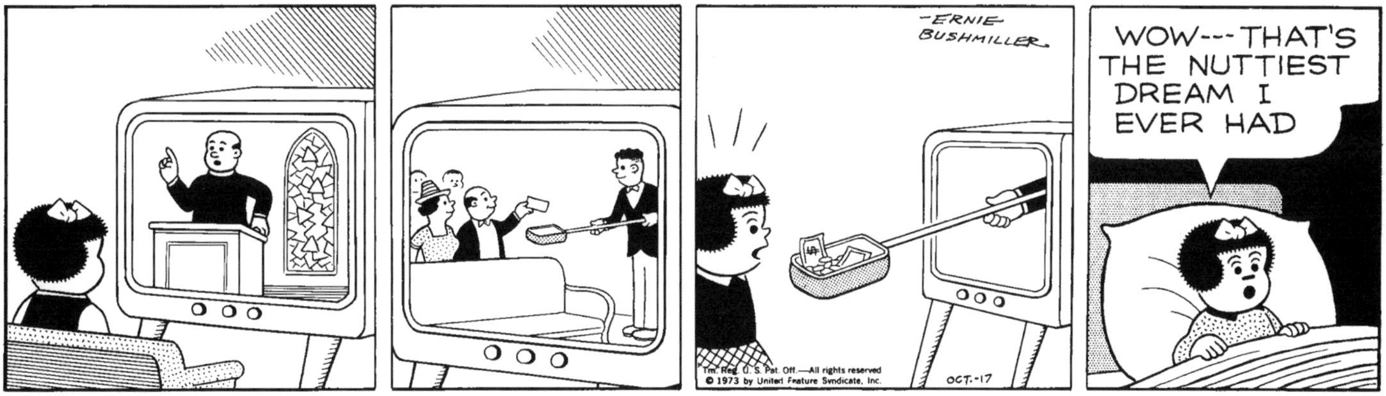
ERNIE BUSHMILLER
Tm. Reg. U. S. Pat. Off.—All rights reserved
© 1973 by United Feature Syndicate, Inc.
OCT.-17
WOW---THAT'S THE NUTTIEST DREAM I EVER HAD

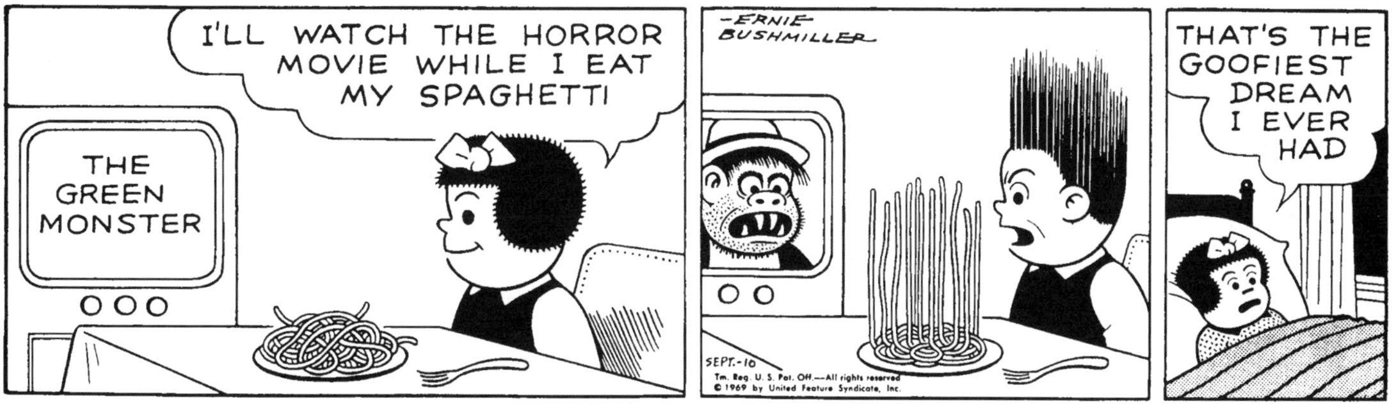
THE GREEN MONSTER
I'LL WATCH THE HORROR MOVIE WHILE I EAT MY SPAGHETTI
ERNIE BUSHMILLER
SEPT.-10
Tm. Reg. U. S. Pat. Off.—All rights reserved
© 1969 by United Feature Syndicate, Inc.
THAT'S THE GOOFIEST DREAM I EVER HAD

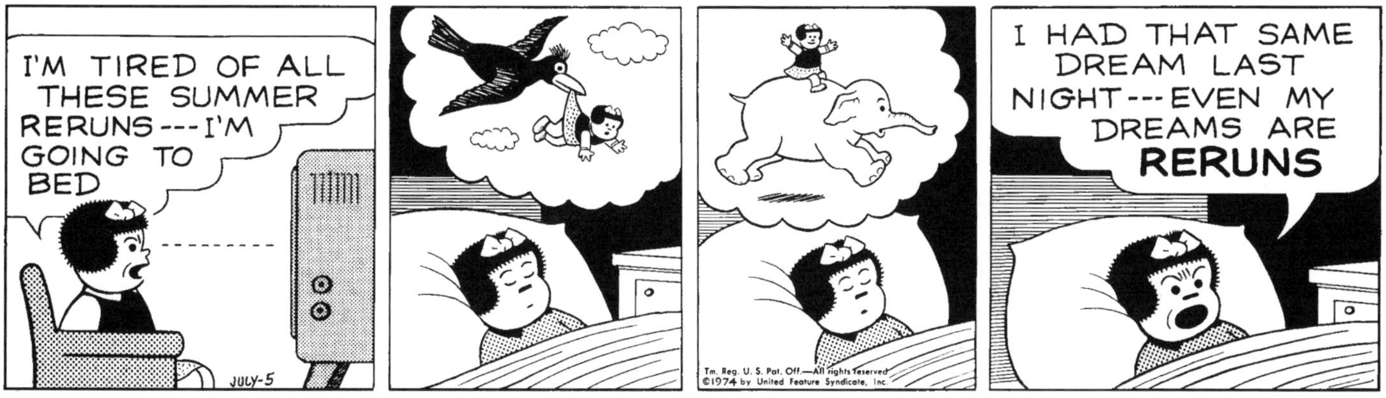
I'M TIRED OF ALL THESE SUMMER RERUNS---I'M GOING TO BED
JULY-5
Tm. Reg. U. S. Pat. Off.—All rights reserved
©1974 by United Feature Syndicate, Inc.
I HAD THAT SAME DREAM LAST NIGHT---EVEN MY DREAMS ARE **RERUNS**

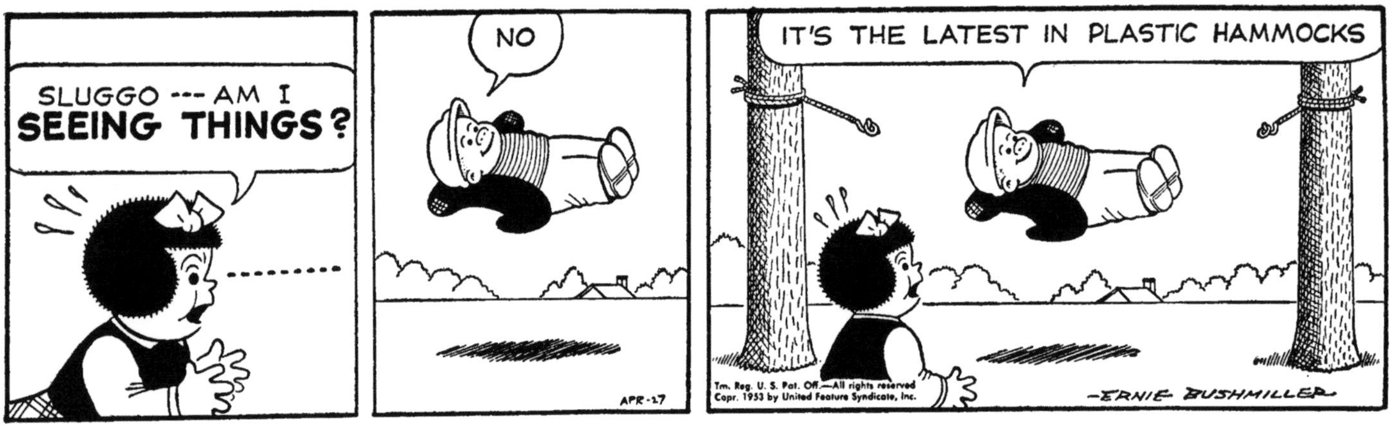
SLUGGO --- AM I SEEING THINGS?
NO
IT'S THE LATEST IN PLASTIC HAMMOCKS
APR-27
Tm. Reg. U. S. Pat. Off.—All rights reserved Copr. 1953 by United Feature Syndicate, Inc.
—ERNIE BUSHMILLER

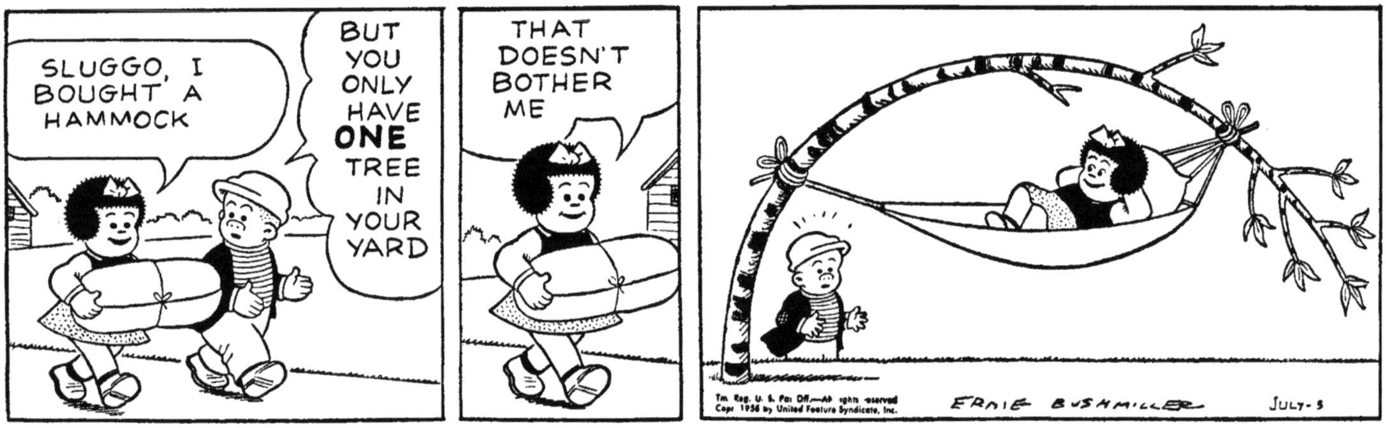
SLUGGO, I BOUGHT A HAMMOCK
BUT YOU ONLY HAVE ONE TREE IN YOUR YARD
THAT DOESN'T BOTHER ME
Copr. 1956 by United Feature Syndicate, Inc.
ERNIE BUSHMILLER
JULY-5

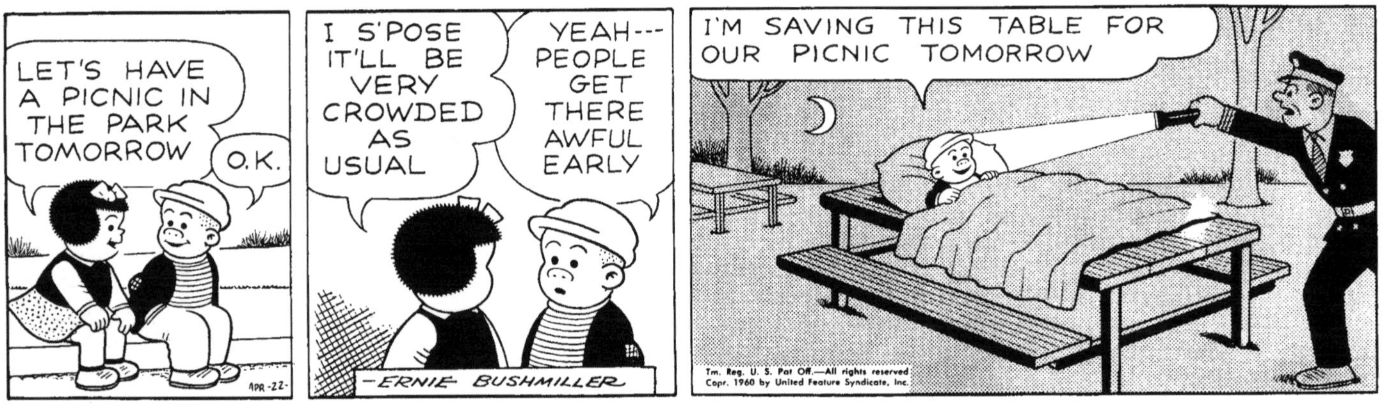
LET'S HAVE A PICNIC IN THE PARK TOMORROW
O.K.
APR-22-
I S'POSE IT'LL BE VERY CROWDED AS USUAL
YEAH--- PEOPLE GET THERE AWFUL EARLY
—ERNIE BUSHMILLER
I'M SAVING THIS TABLE FOR OUR PICNIC TOMORROW
Tm. Reg. U. S. Pat. Off.—All rights reserved Copr. 1960 by United Feature Syndicate, Inc.

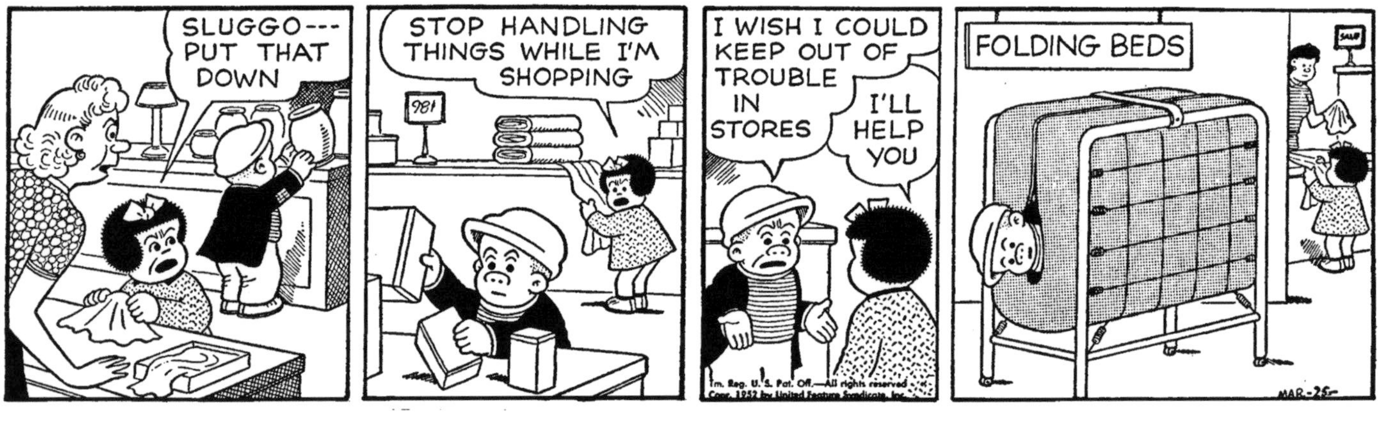
SLUGGO--- PUT THAT DOWN
STOP HANDLING THINGS WHILE I'M SHOPPING
98¢
I WISH I COULD KEEP OUT OF TROUBLE IN STORES
I'LL HELP YOU
FOLDING BEDS
SALE
MAR-25-

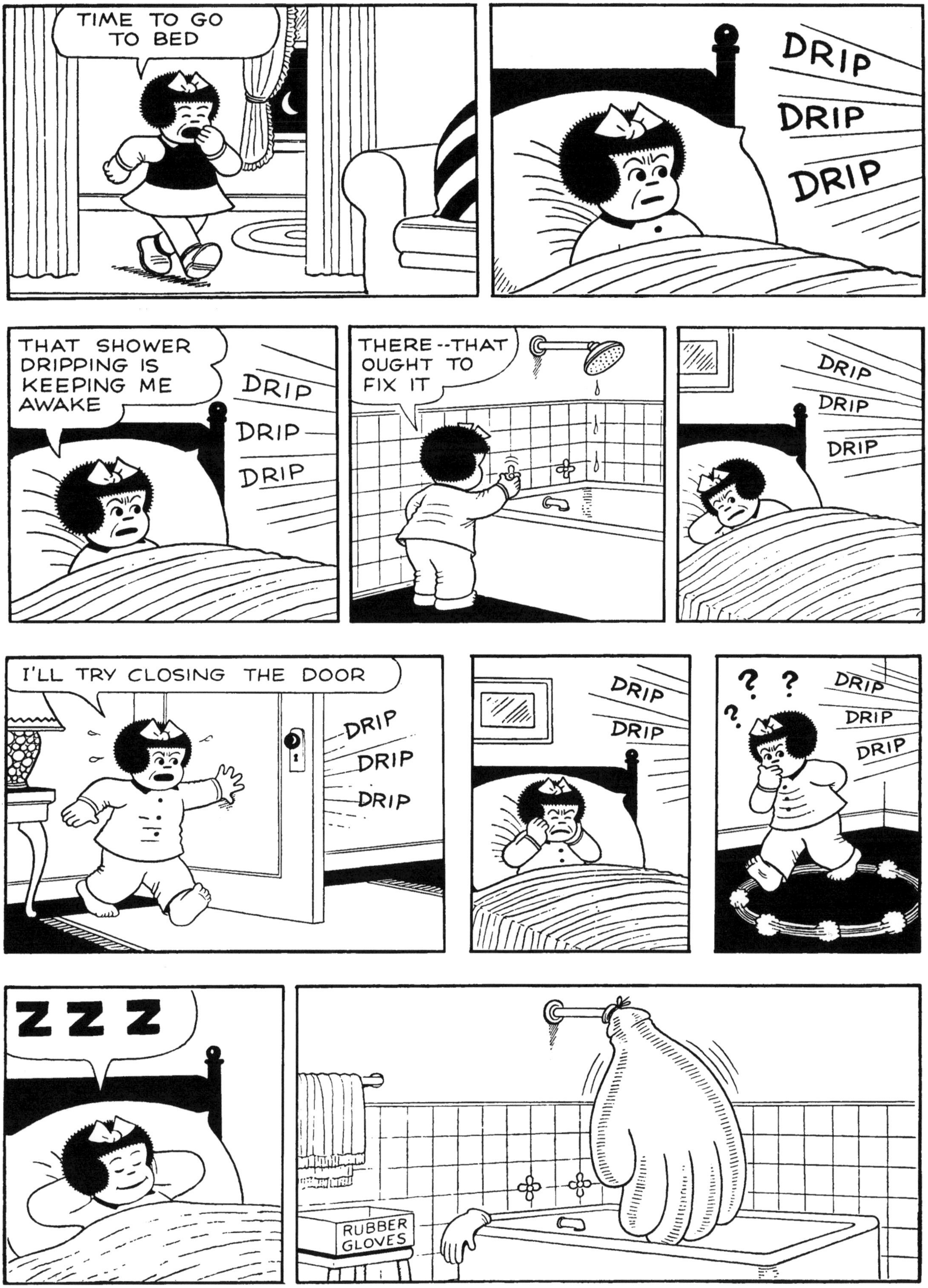

TIME TO GO TO BED
DRIP
DRIP
DRIP
THAT SHOWER DRIPPING IS KEEPING ME AWAKE
DRIP
DRIP
DRIP
THERE--THAT OUGHT TO FIX IT
DRIP
DRIP
DRIP
I'LL TRY CLOSING THE DOOR
DRIP
DRIP
DRIP
DRIP
DRIP
? ? ?
DRIP
DRIP
DRIP
Z Z Z
RUBBER GLOVES

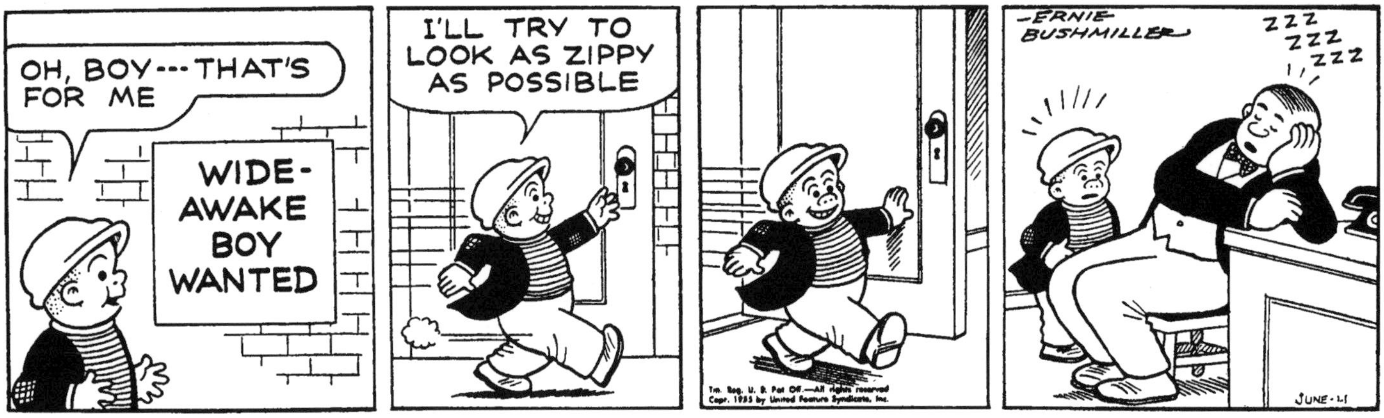
OH, BOY--- THAT'S FOR ME
WIDE-AWAKE BOY WANTED
I'LL TRY TO LOOK AS ZIPPY AS POSSIBLE
Tm. Reg. U. S. Pat. Off.—All rights reserved
Copr. 1955 by United Feature Syndicate, Inc.
-ERNIE BUSHMILLER
ZZZ ZZZ ZZZ

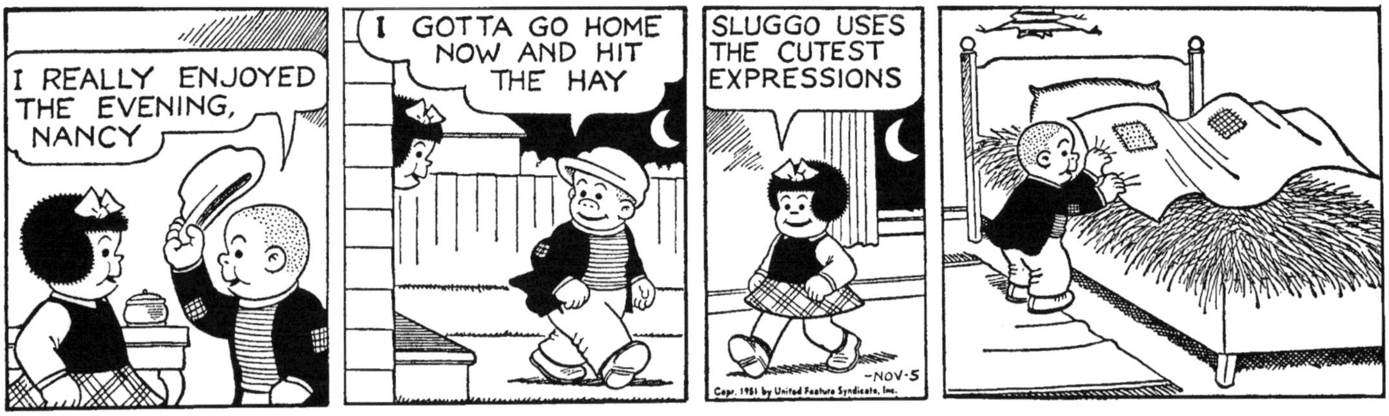
I REALLY ENJOYED THE EVENING, NANCY
I GOTTA GO HOME NOW AND HIT THE HAY
SLUGGO USES THE CUTEST EXPRESSIONS
-NOV-5
Copr. 1951 by United Feature Syndicate, Inc.

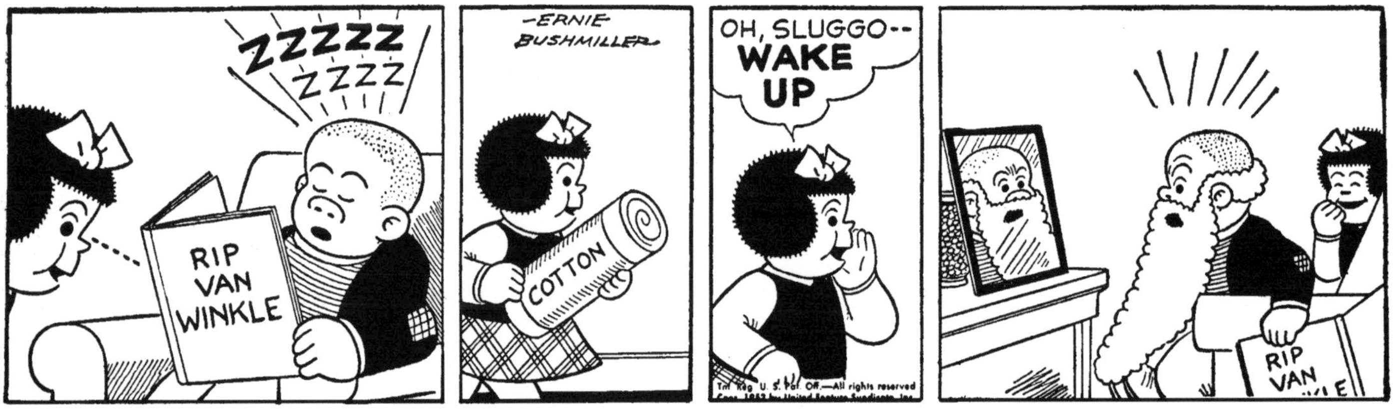
ZZZZZ ZZZZ
RIP VAN WINKLE
-ERNIE BUSHMILLER
COTTON
OH, SLUGGO-- WAKE UP
Tm. Reg. U. S. Pat. Off.—All rights reserved
RIP VAN

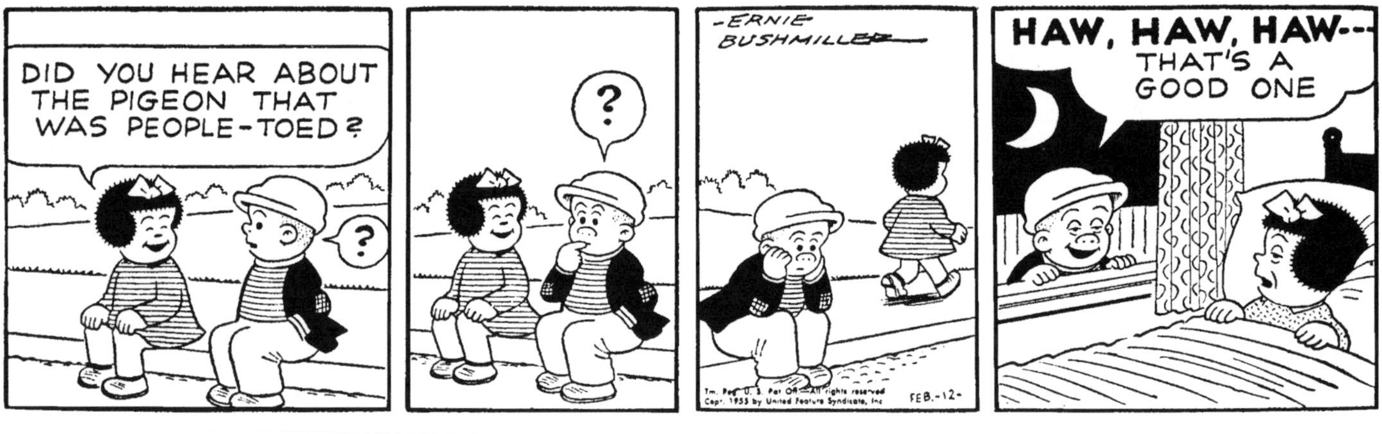
DID YOU HEAR ABOUT THE PIGEON THAT WAS PEOPLE-TOED?
?
?
-ERNIE BUSHMILLER
Tm. Reg. U. S. Pat. Off.—All rights reserved
Copr. 1955 by United Feature Syndicate, Inc
FEB.-12-
HAW, HAW, HAW--- THAT'S A GOOD ONE

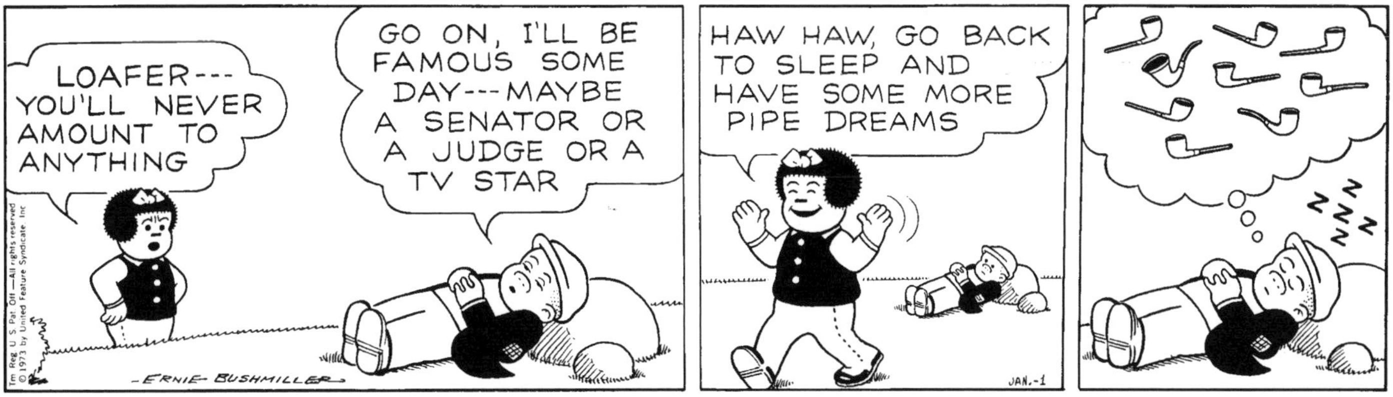
LOAFER--- YOU'LL NEVER AMOUNT TO ANYTHING
GO ON, I'LL BE FAMOUS SOME DAY---MAYBE A SENATOR OR A JUDGE OR A TV STAR
HAW HAW, GO BACK TO SLEEP AND HAVE SOME MORE PIPE DREAMS
Z Z Z
-ERNIE BUSHMILLER
JAN.-1
Tm Reg. U. S. Pat. Off.—All rights reserved © 1973 by United Feature Syndicate, Inc

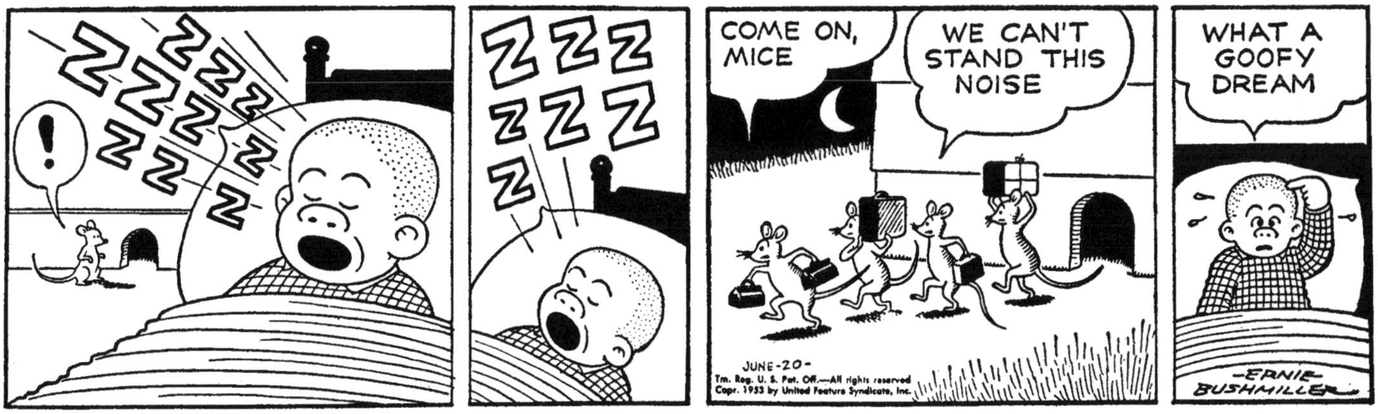
!
COME ON, MICE
WE CAN'T STAND THIS NOISE
WHAT A GOOFY DREAM
JUNE-20-
Tm. Reg. U. S. Pat. Off.—All rights reserved
Copr. 1953 by United Feature Syndicate, Inc.
-ERNIE BUSHMILLER

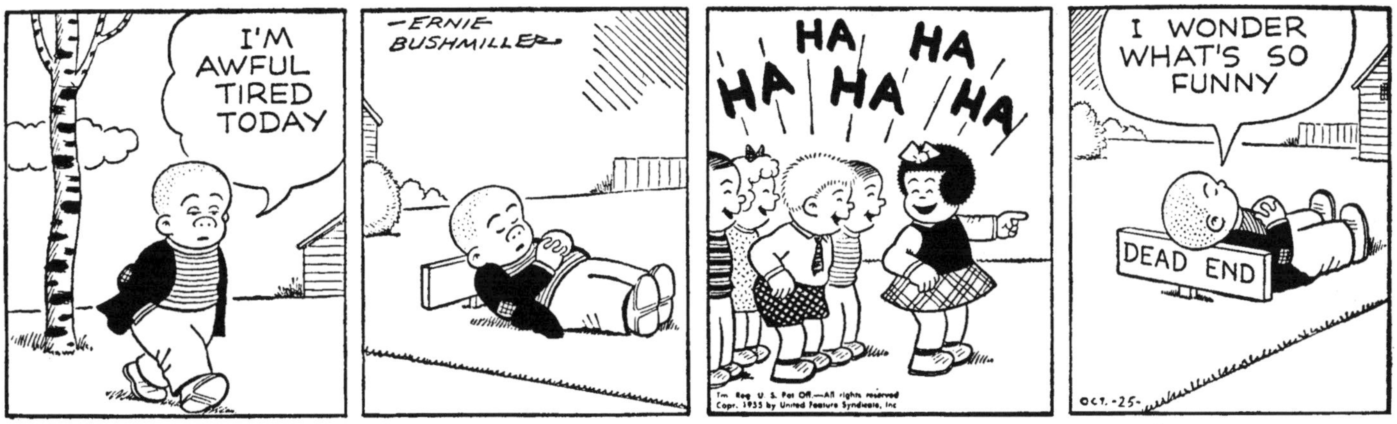
I'M AWFUL TIRED TODAY
-ERNIE BUSHMILLER
HA HA HA HA HA
I WONDER WHAT'S SO FUNNY
DEAD END
Tm Reg. U. S. Pat. Off.—All rights reserved
Copr. 1955 by United Feature Syndicate, Inc
OCT.-25-

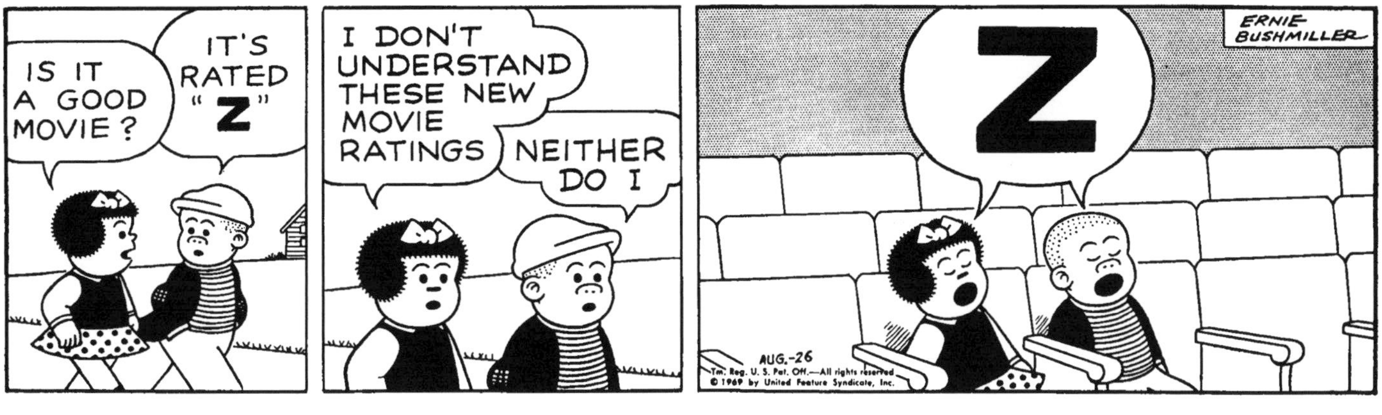
IS IT A GOOD MOVIE ?
IT'S RATED "Z"
I DON'T UNDERSTAND THESE NEW MOVIE RATINGS
NEITHER DO I
ERNIE BUSHMILLER
Z
AUG.-26
Tm. Reg. U. S. Pat. Off.—All rights reserved
© 1969 by United Feature Syndicate, Inc.

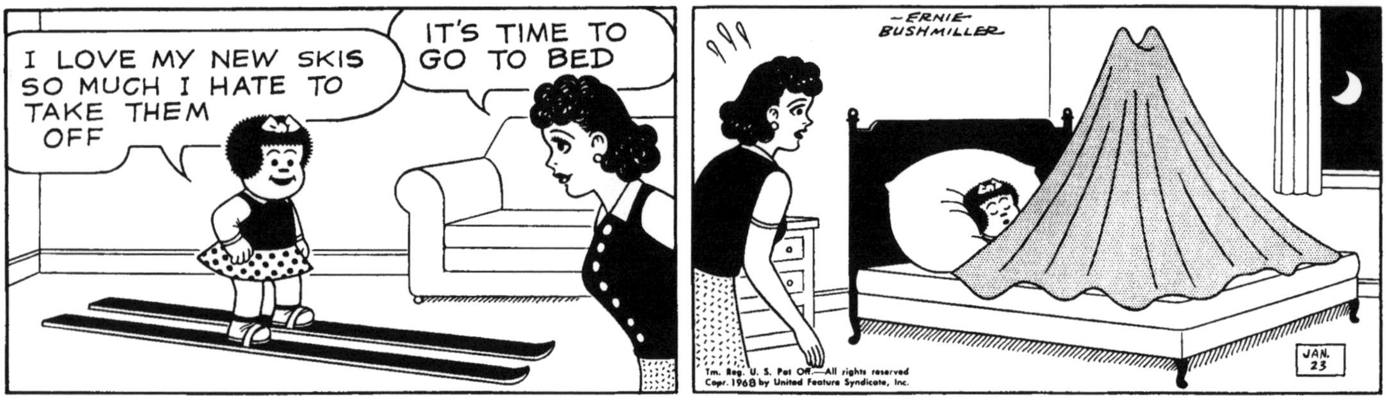
I LOVE MY NEW SKIS SO MUCH I HATE TO TAKE THEM OFF
IT'S TIME TO GO TO BED
-ERNIE BUSHMILLER
Tm. Reg. U. S. Pat. Off.—All rights reserved
Copr. 1968 by United Feature Syndicate, Inc.
JAN. 23

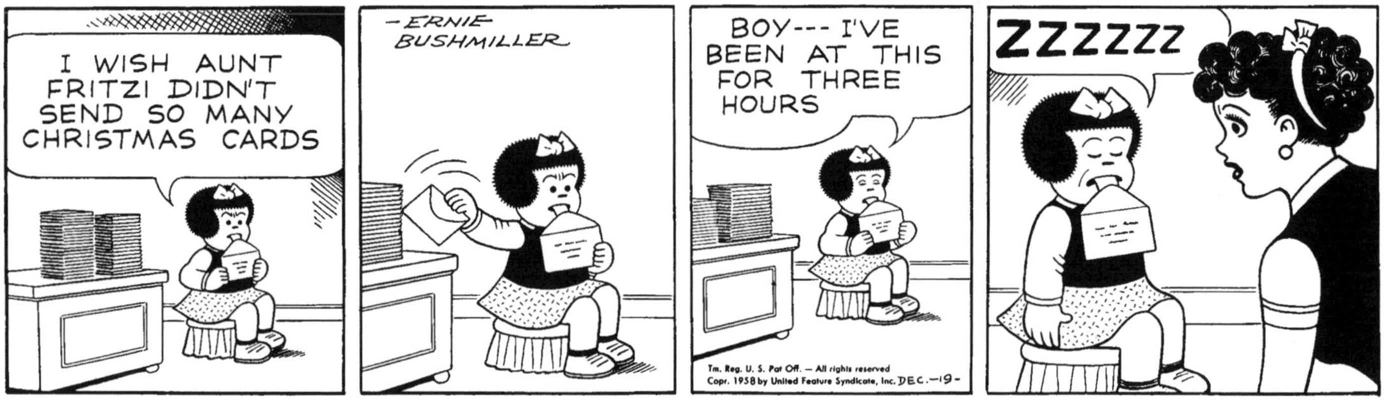
I WISH AUNT FRITZI DIDN'T SEND SO MANY CHRISTMAS CARDS
-ERNIE BUSHMILLER
BOY--- I'VE BEEN AT THIS FOR THREE HOURS
Tm. Reg. U. S. Pat. Off. — All rights reserved
Copr. 1958 by United Feature Syndicate, Inc. DEC.-19-
ZZZZZZ

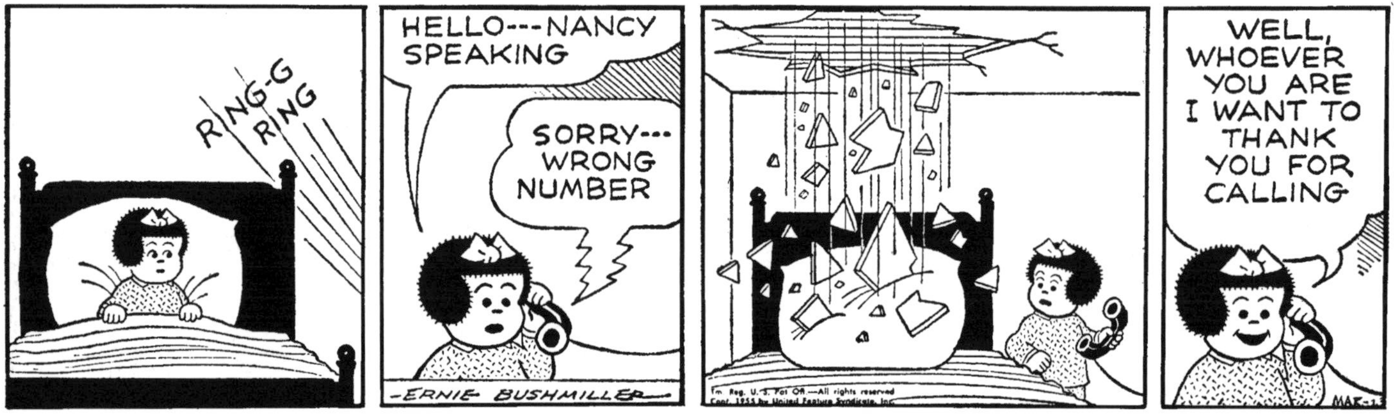
RING-G RING
HELLO---NANCY SPEAKING
SORRY--- WRONG NUMBER
-ERNIE BUSHMILLER
WELL, WHOEVER YOU ARE I WANT TO THANK YOU FOR CALLING

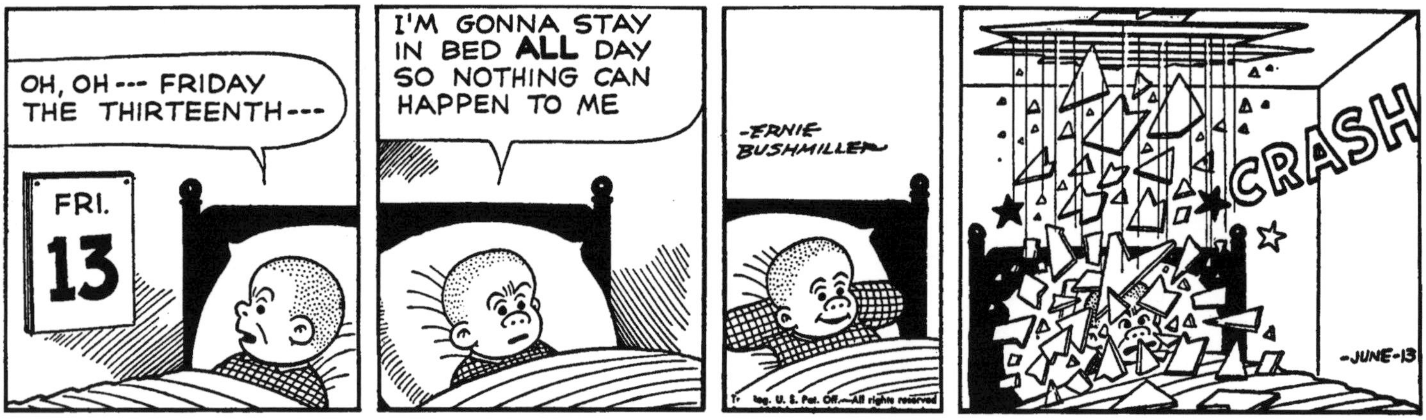
OH, OH --- FRIDAY THE THIRTEENTH---
FRI. 13
I'M GONNA STAY IN BED ALL DAY SO NOTHING CAN HAPPEN TO ME
-ERNIE BUSHMILLER
CRASH
-JUNE-13

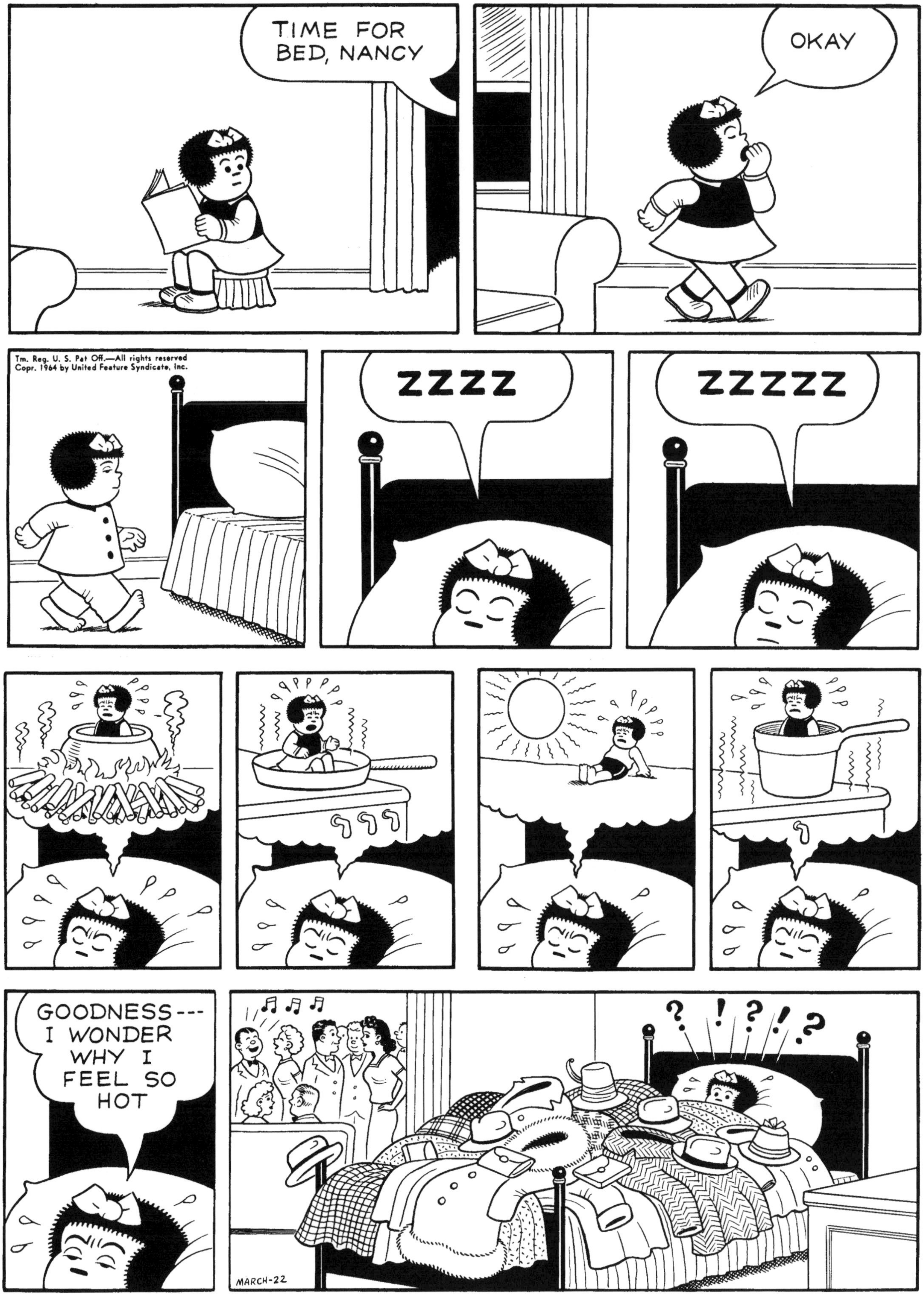
TIME FOR BED, NANCY
OKAY
Tm. Reg. U. S. Pat Off.—All rights reserved
Copr. 1964 by United Feature Syndicate, Inc.
ZZZZ
ZZZZZ
GOODNESS--- I WONDER WHY I FEEL SO HOT
? ! ? ! ?
MARCH-22

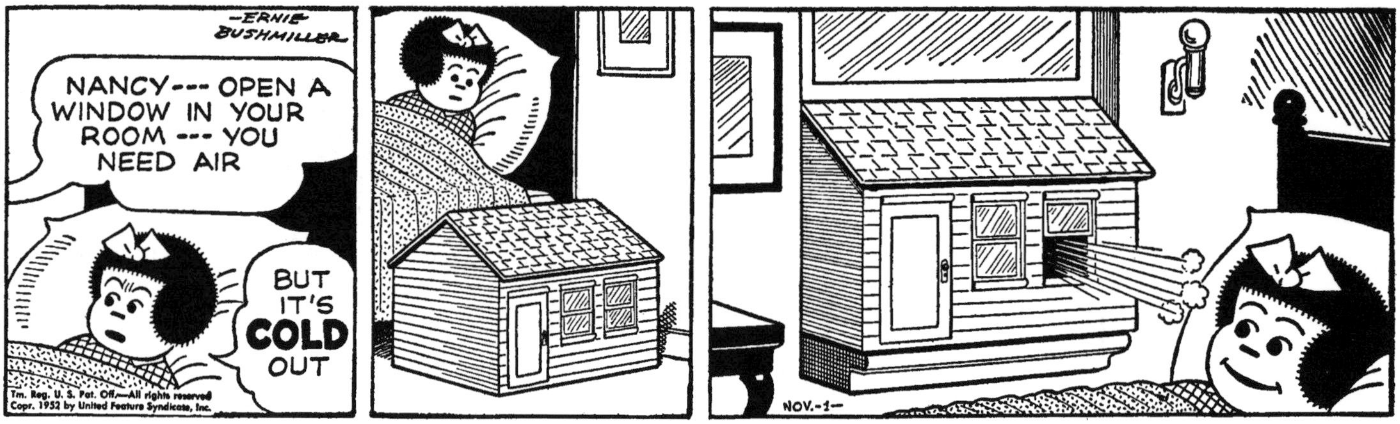

-ERNIE BUSHMILLER
NANCY--- OPEN A WINDOW IN YOUR ROOM --- YOU NEED AIR
BUT IT'S COLD OUT
Tm. Reg. U. S. Pat. Off.—All rights reserved
Copr. 1952 by United Feature Syndicate, Inc.
NOV.-1-

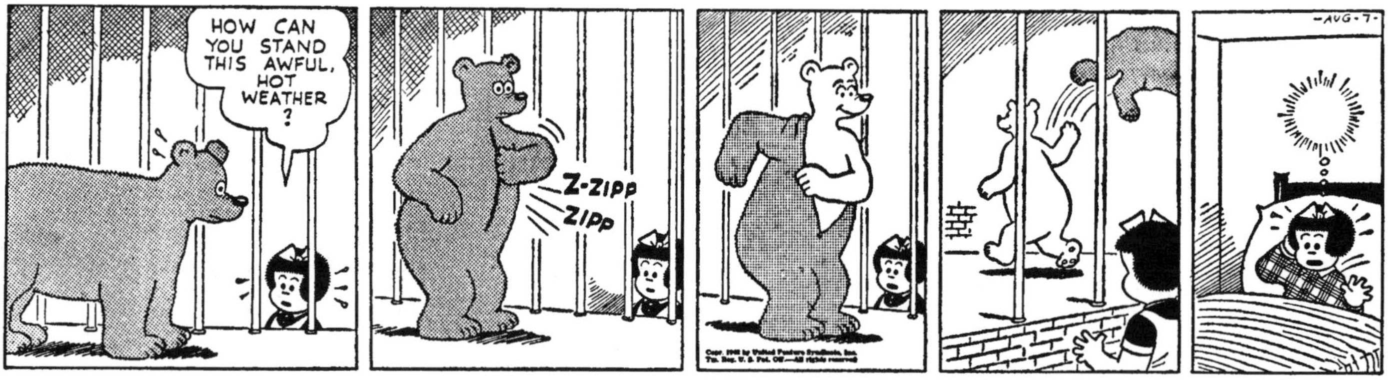

HOW CAN YOU STAND THIS AWFUL, HOT WEATHER ?
Z-ZIPP
ZIPP
-AUG-7-

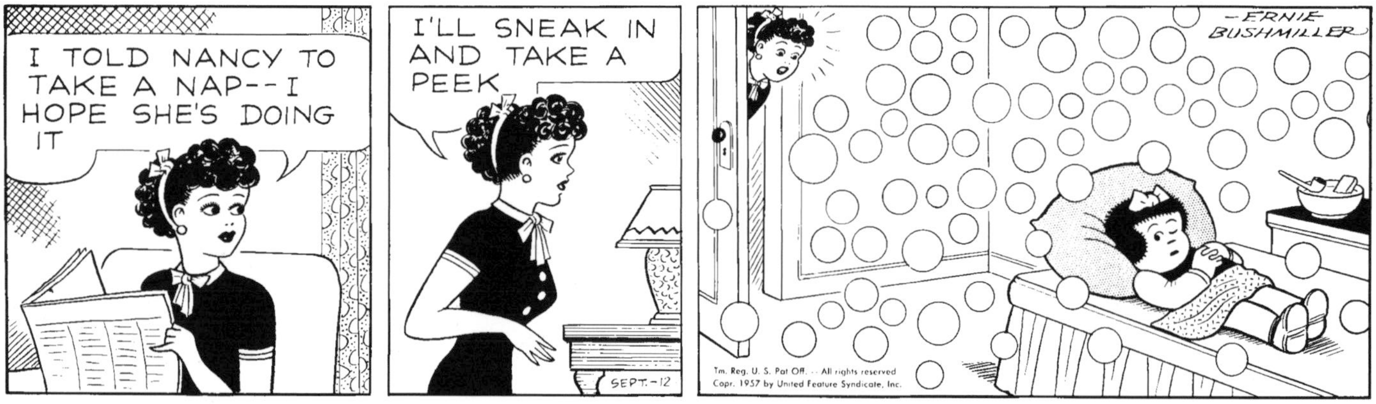

I TOLD NANCY TO TAKE A NAP--I HOPE SHE'S DOING IT
I'LL SNEAK IN AND TAKE A PEEK
SEPT.-12
-ERNIE BUSHMILLER
Tm. Reg. U. S. Pat. Off.--All rights reserved
Copr. 1957 by United Feature Syndicate, Inc.

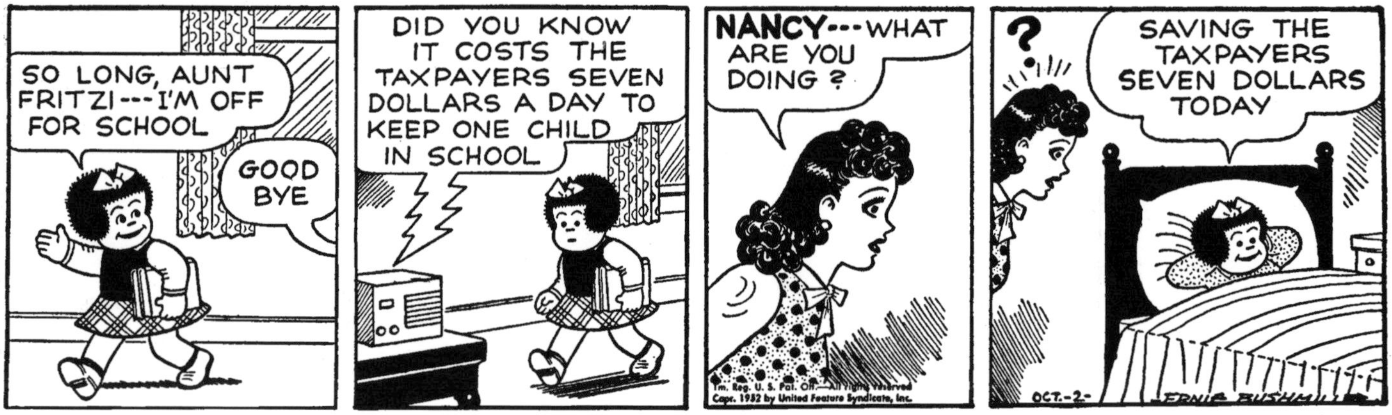

SO LONG, AUNT FRITZI---I'M OFF FOR SCHOOL
GOOD BYE
DID YOU KNOW IT COSTS THE TAXPAYERS SEVEN DOLLARS A DAY TO KEEP ONE CHILD IN SCHOOL
NANCY---WHAT ARE YOU DOING ?
Tm. Reg. U. S. Pat. Off.—All rights reserved
Copr. 1952 by United Feature Syndicate, Inc.
?
SAVING THE TAXPAYERS SEVEN DOLLARS TODAY
OCT.-2-
ERNIE BUSHMILLER

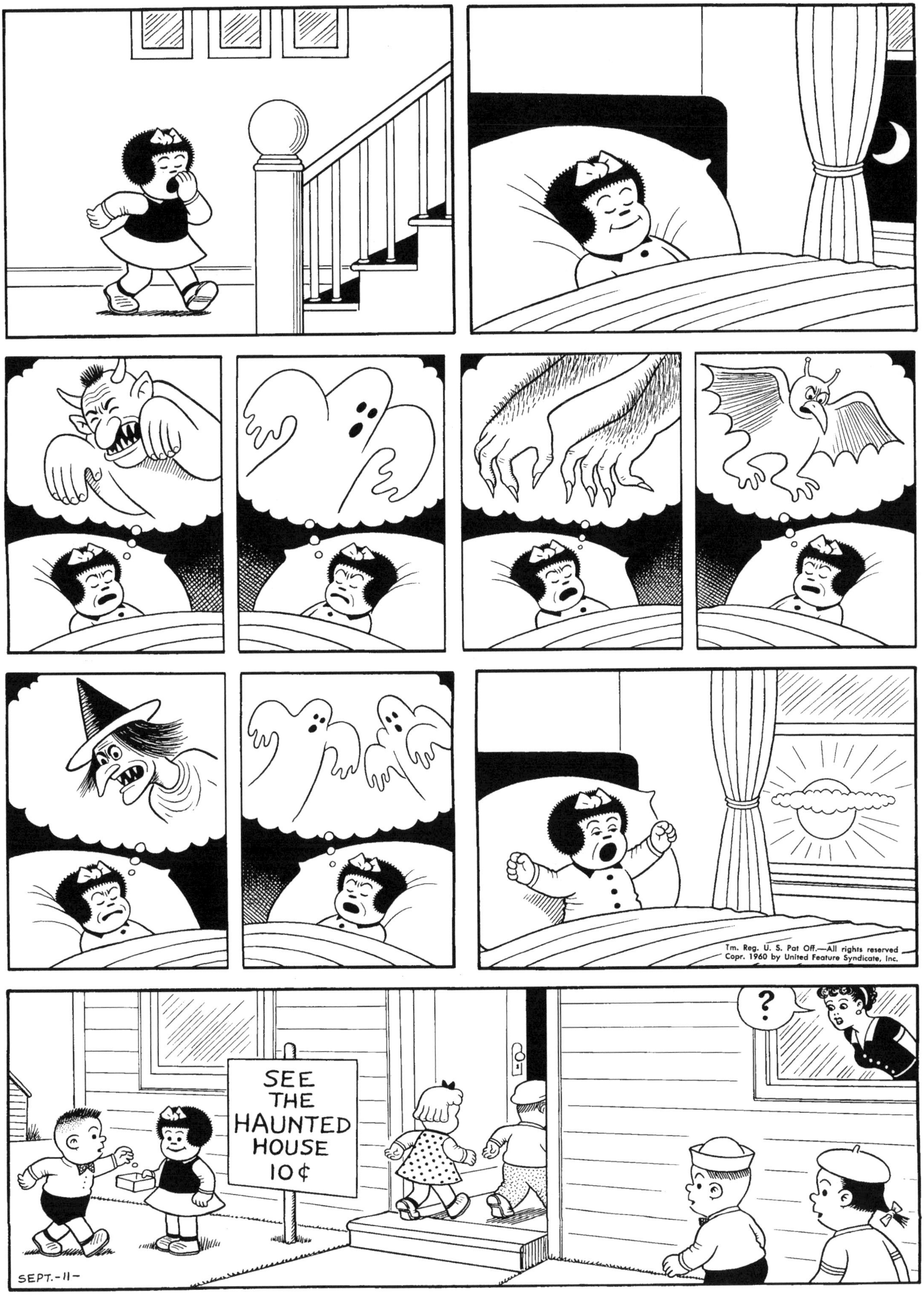

Tm. Reg. U. S. Pat Off.—All rights reserved
Copr. 1960 by United Feature Syndicate, Inc.
SEE THE HAUNTED HOUSE 10¢
?
SEPT.-11-

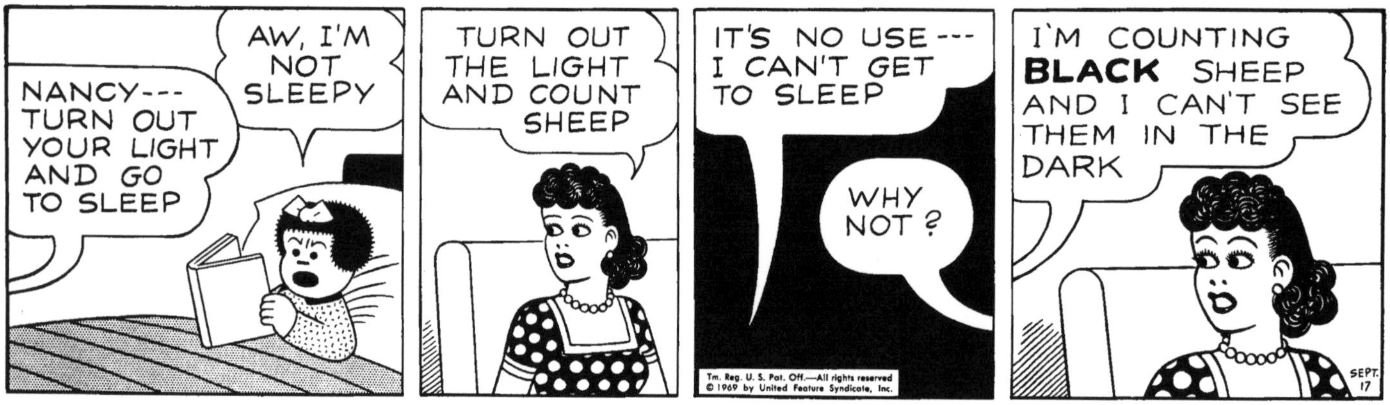
NANCY--- TURN OUT YOUR LIGHT AND GO TO SLEEP
AW, I'M NOT SLEEPY
TURN OUT THE LIGHT AND COUNT SHEEP
IT'S NO USE--- I CAN'T GET TO SLEEP
WHY NOT?
I'M COUNTING **BLACK** SHEEP AND I CAN'T SEE THEM IN THE DARK
Tm. Reg. U. S. Pat. Off.—All rights reserved © 1969 by United Feature Syndicate, Inc.
SEPT. 17

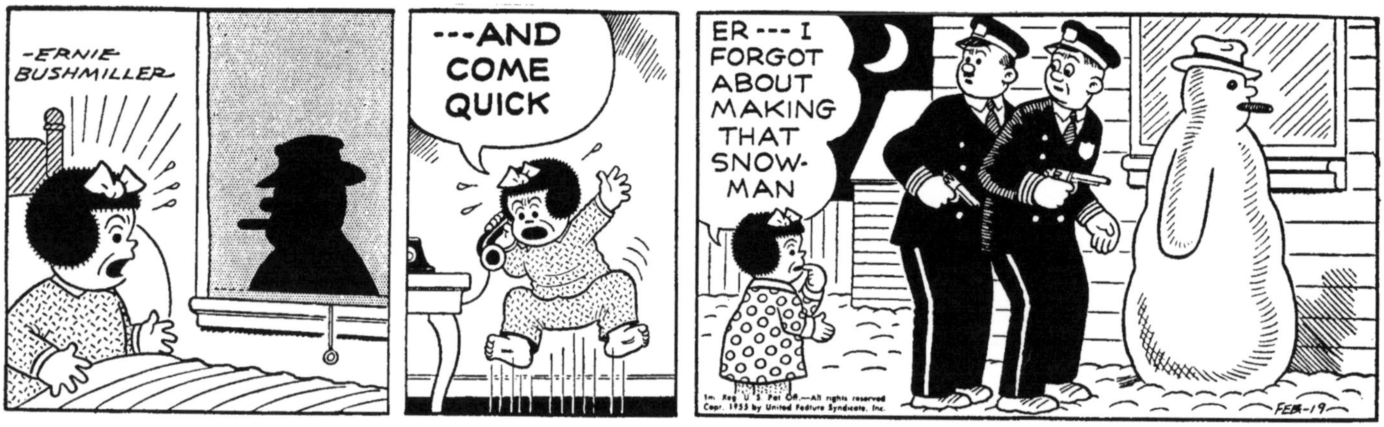
-ERNIE BUSHMILLER
---AND COME QUICK
ER--- I FORGOT ABOUT MAKING THAT SNOW-MAN
Tm. Reg. U. S. Pat. Off.—All rights reserved Copr. 1955 by United Feature Syndicate, Inc.
FEB-19-

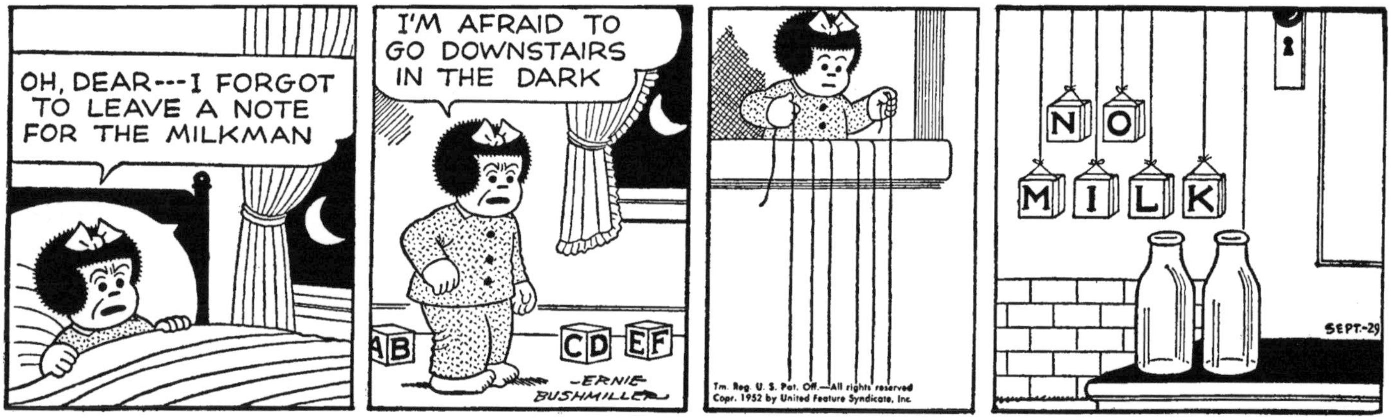
OH, DEAR---I FORGOT TO LEAVE A NOTE FOR THE MILKMAN
I'M AFRAID TO GO DOWNSTAIRS IN THE DARK
AB
CD EF
-ERNIE BUSHMILLER
Tm. Reg. U. S. Pat. Off.—All rights reserved Copr. 1952 by United Feature Syndicate, Inc.
NO
MILK
SEPT-29

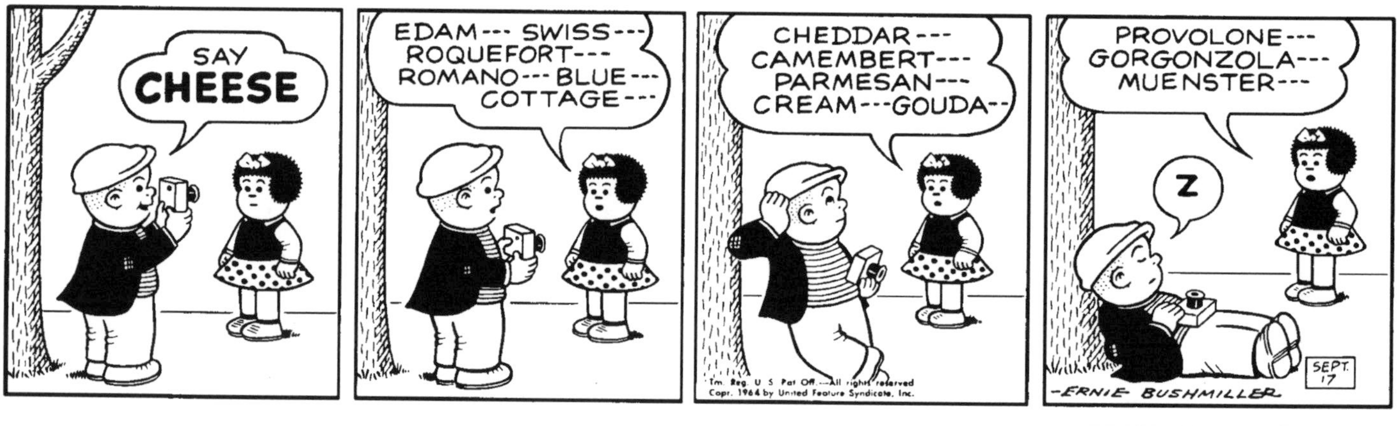
SAY **CHEESE**
EDAM--- SWISS--- ROQUEFORT--- ROMANO--- BLUE--- COTTAGE---
CHEDDAR--- CAMEMBERT--- PARMESAN--- CREAM---GOUDA--
Tm. Reg. U. S. Pat. Off.—All rights reserved Copr. 1964 by United Feature Syndicate, Inc.
PROVOLONE--- GORGONZOLA--- MUENSTER---
Z
SEPT. 17
-ERNIE BUSHMILLER

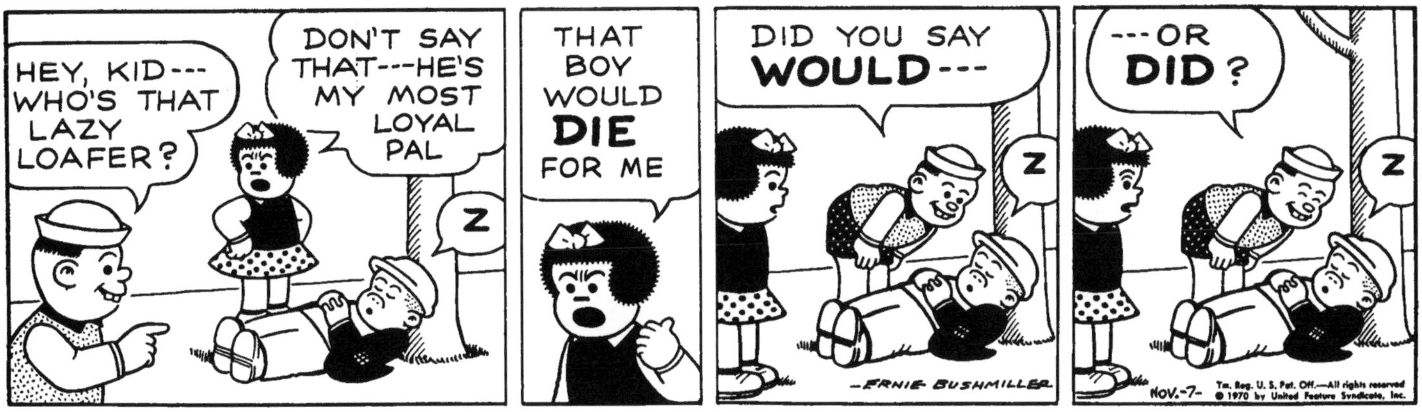
HEY, KID--- WHO'S THAT LAZY LOAFER?
DON'T SAY THAT---HE'S MY MOST LOYAL PAL
Z
THAT BOY WOULD DIE FOR ME
DID YOU SAY WOULD---
Z
-ERNIE BUSHMILLER
---OR DID?
Z
NOV.-7-
Tm. Reg. U. S. Pat. Off.—All rights reserved © 1970 by United Feature Syndicate, Inc.

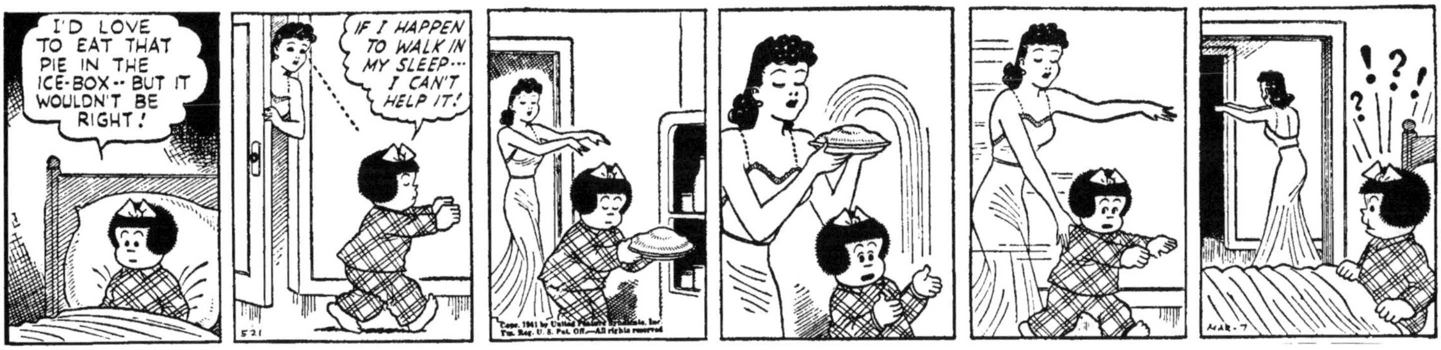
I'D LOVE TO EAT THAT PIE IN THE ICE-BOX-- BUT IT WOULDN'T BE RIGHT!
IF I HAPPEN TO WALK IN MY SLEEP--- I CAN'T HELP IT!
5-21
MAR-7

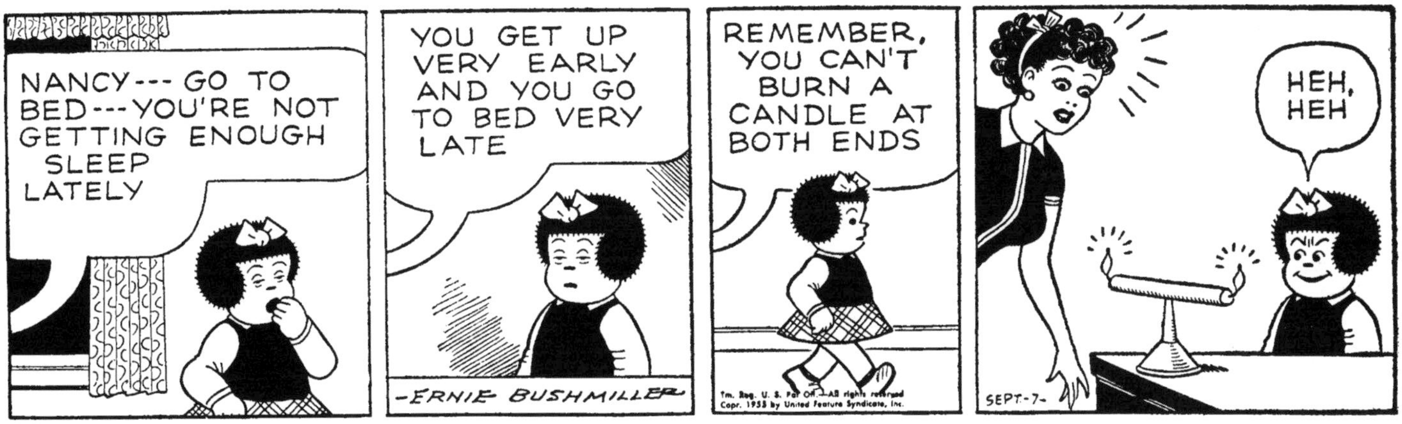
NANCY--- GO TO BED---YOU'RE NOT GETTING ENOUGH SLEEP LATELY
YOU GET UP VERY EARLY AND YOU GO TO BED VERY LATE
-ERNIE BUSHMILLER
REMEMBER, YOU CAN'T BURN A CANDLE AT BOTH ENDS
HEH, HEH
SEPT-7-

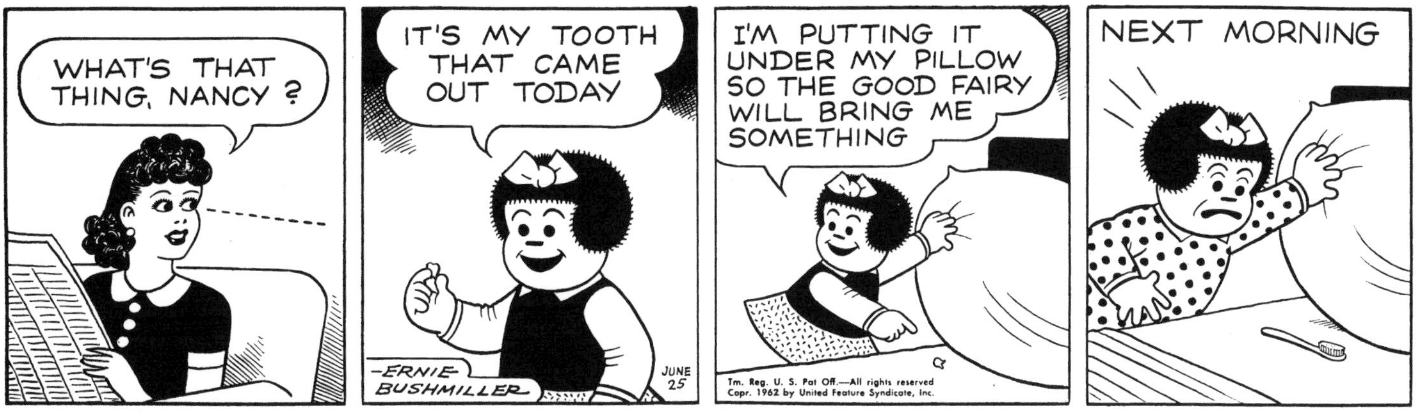
WHAT'S THAT THING, NANCY?
IT'S MY TOOTH THAT CAME OUT TODAY
-ERNIE BUSHMILLER
JUNE 25
I'M PUTTING IT UNDER MY PILLOW SO THE GOOD FAIRY WILL BRING ME SOMETHING
Tm. Reg. U. S. Pat Off.—All rights reserved Copr. 1962 by United Feature Syndicate, Inc.
NEXT MORNING

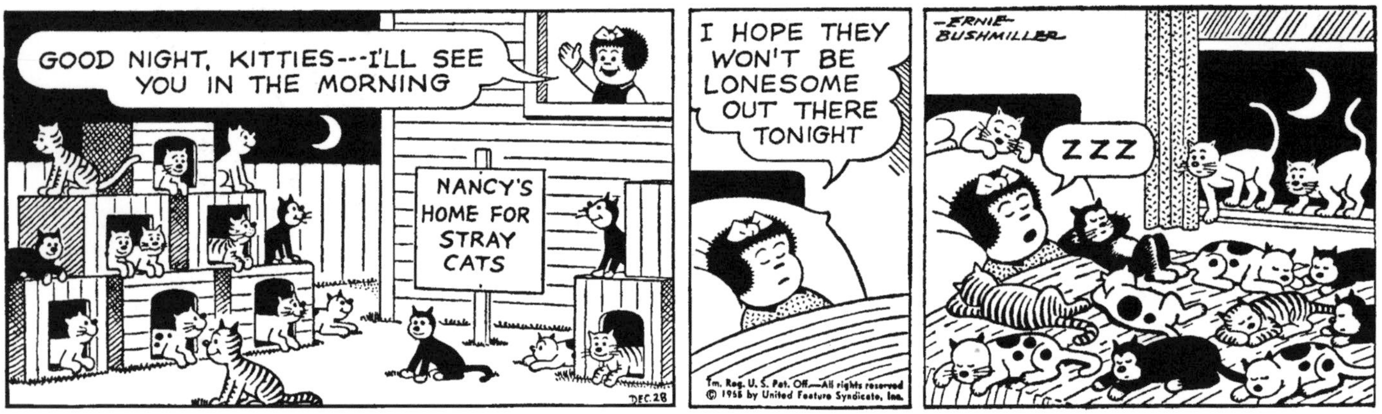
GOOD NIGHT, KITTIES---I'LL SEE YOU IN THE MORNING
NANCY'S HOME FOR STRAY CATS
DEC.28
I HOPE THEY WON'T BE LONESOME OUT THERE TONIGHT
Tm. Reg. U. S. Pat. Off.—All rights reserved © 1955 by United Feature Syndicate, Inc.
-ERNIE- BUSHMILLER
ZZZ

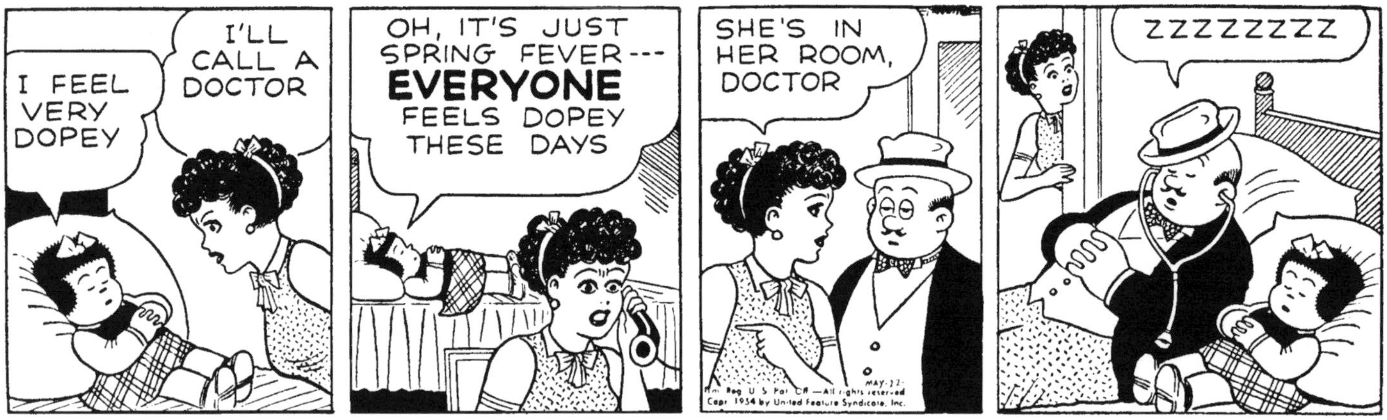
I FEEL VERY DOPEY
I'LL CALL A DOCTOR
OH, IT'S JUST SPRING FEVER---
EVERYONE
FEELS DOPEY THESE DAYS
SHE'S IN HER ROOM, DOCTOR
MAY-22-
Tm. Reg. U. S. Pat. Off.—All rights reserved Copr. 1954 by United Feature Syndicate, Inc.
ZZZZZZZZ

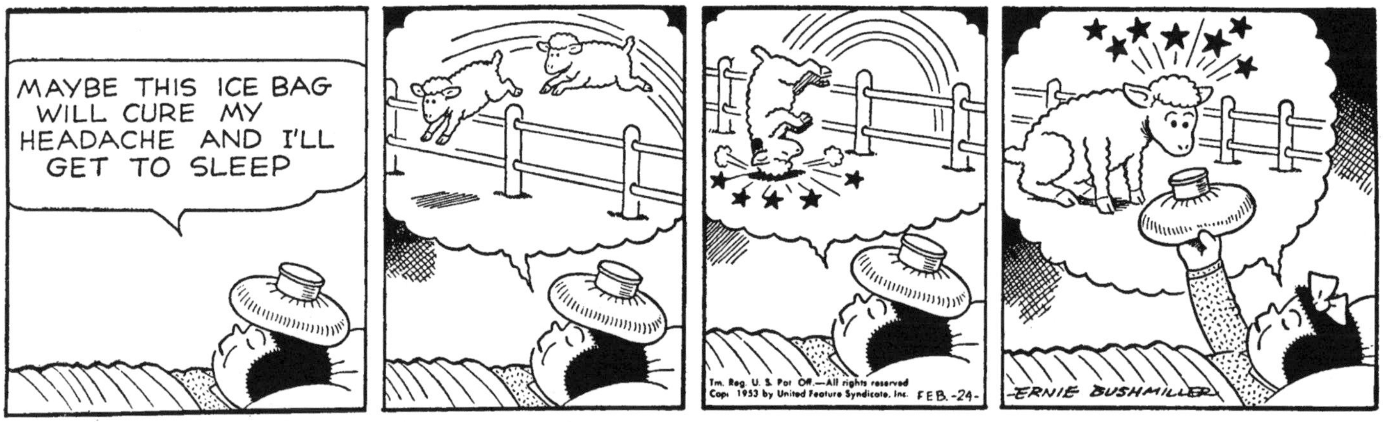
MAYBE THIS ICE BAG WILL CURE MY HEADACHE AND I'LL GET TO SLEEP
Tm. Reg. U. S. Pat. Off.—All rights reserved Copr. 1953 by United Feature Syndicate, Inc.
FEB.-24-
-ERNIE BUSHMILLER-

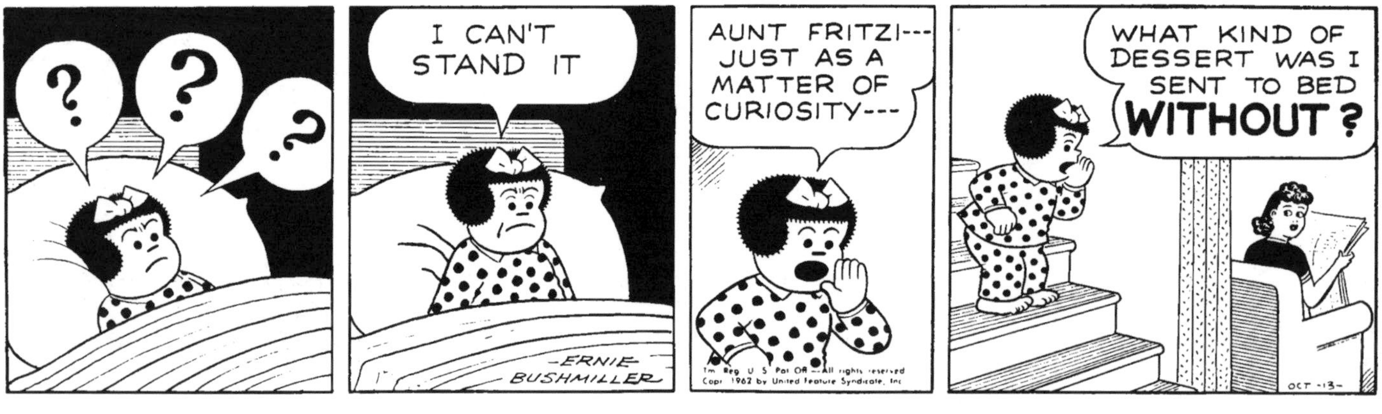
?
?
?
I CAN'T STAND IT
-ERNIE- BUSHMILLER
AUNT FRITZI--- JUST AS A MATTER OF CURIOSITY---
Tm. Reg. U. S. Pat. Off.—All rights reserved Copr. 1962 by United Feature Syndicate, Inc.
WHAT KIND OF DESSERT WAS I SENT TO BED
WITHOUT?
OCT-13-

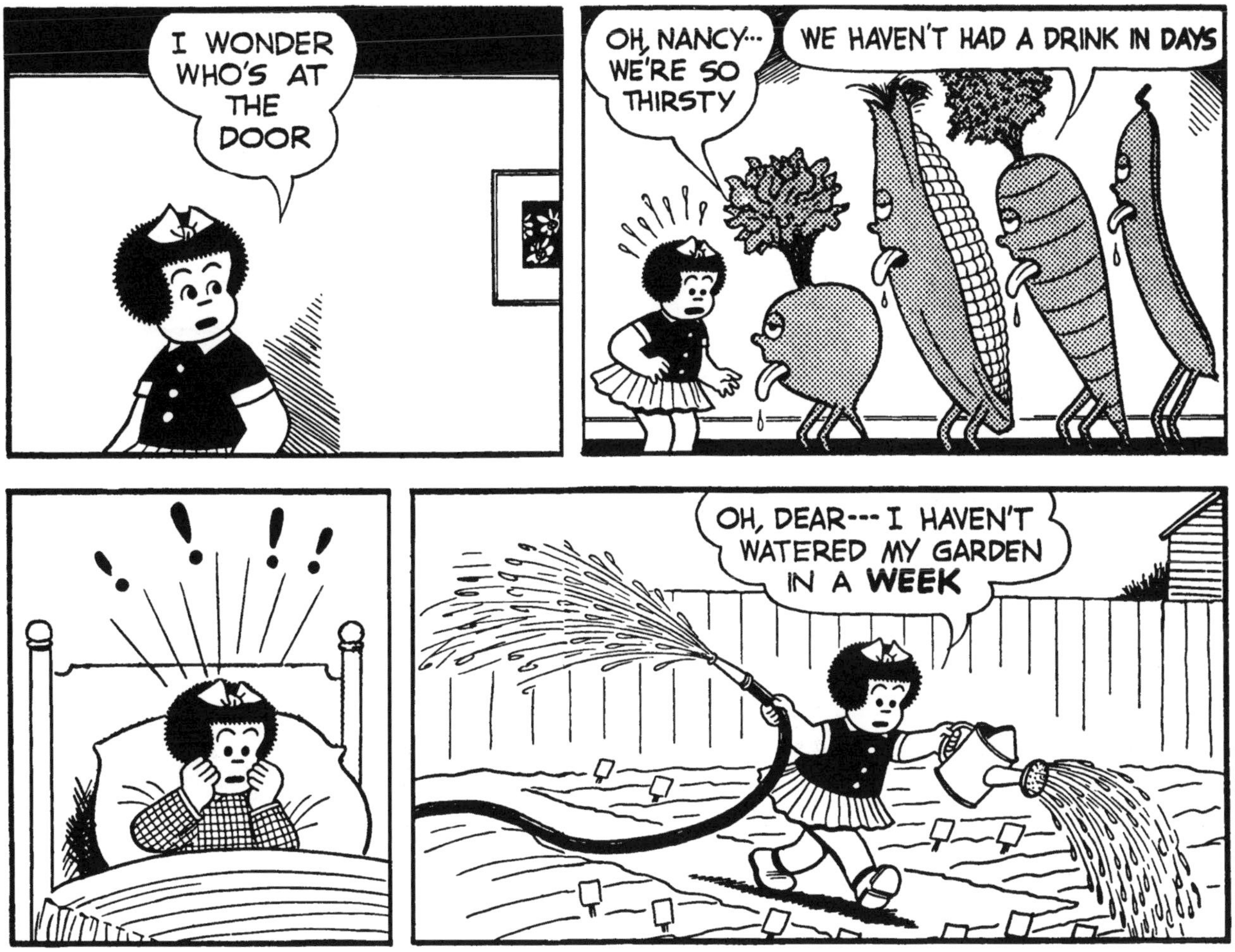
I WONDER WHO'S AT THE DOOR
OH, NANCY... WE'RE SO THIRSTY
WE HAVEN'T HAD A DRINK IN DAYS
OH, DEAR--- I HAVEN'T WATERED MY GARDEN IN A WEEK

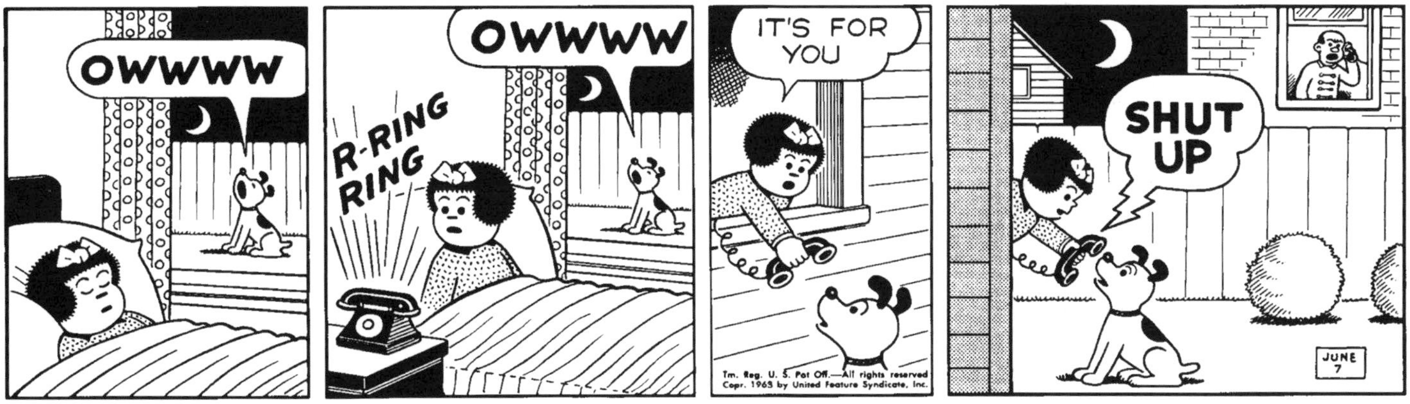
OWWWW
R-RING RING
OWWWW
IT'S FOR YOU
Tm. Reg. U. S. Pat. Off.—All rights reserved Copr. 1965 by United Feature Syndicate, Inc.
SHUT UP
JUNE 7

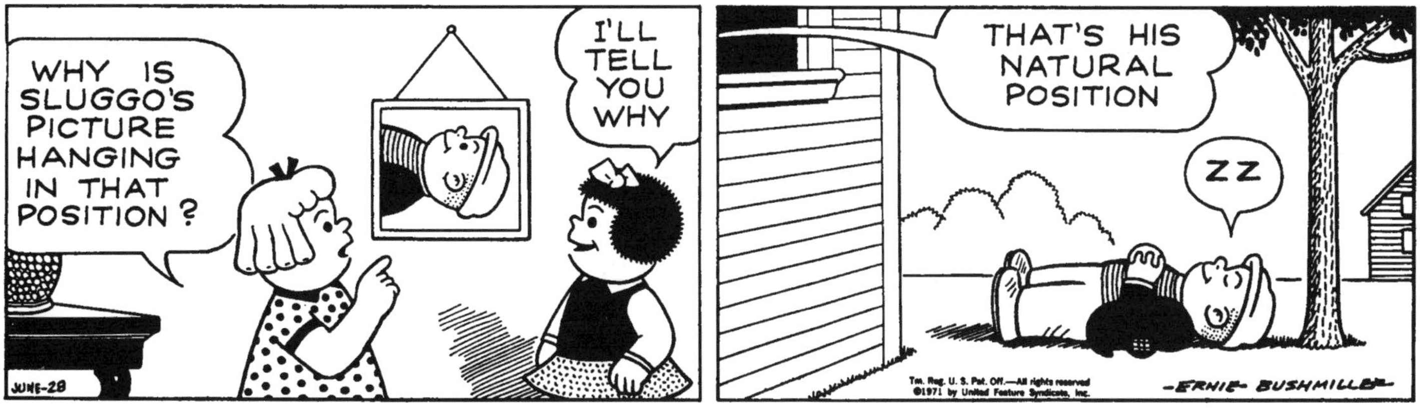
WHY IS SLUGGO'S PICTURE HANGING IN THAT POSITION ?
I'LL TELL YOU WHY
JUNE-28
THAT'S HIS NATURAL POSITION
ZZ
Tm. Reg. U. S. Pat. Off.—All rights reserved ©1971 by United Feature Syndicate, Inc.
ERNIE BUSHMILLER

ALSO AVAILABLE FROM NEW YORK REVIEW COMICS

YELLOW NEGROES AND OTHER IMAGINARY CREATURES Yvan Alagbé
PIERO Edmond Baudoin
ALMOST COMPLETELY BAXTER Glen Baxter
AGONY Mark Beyer
MITCHUM Blutch
PEPLUM Blutch
THE GREEN HAND AND OTHER STORIES Nicole Claveloux
WHAT AM I DOING HERE? Abner Dean
W THE WHORE Anke Feuchtenberger and Katrin de Vries
TROTS AND BONNIE Shary Flenniken
LETTER TO SURVIVORS Gébé
PRETENDING IS LYING Dominique Goblet
ALAY-OOP William Gropper
THE RULING CLAWSS Syd Hoff
BUNGLETON GREEN AND THE MYSTIC COMMANDOS Jay Jackson
ALL YOUR RACIAL PROBLEMS WILL SOON END Charles Johnson
THE GULL YETTIN Joe Kessler
SPIRAL AND OTHER STORIES Aidan Koch
MASTERS OF THE NEFARIOUS: MOLLUSK RAMPAGE Pierre La Police
VOICES IN THE DARK Ulli Lust
SOCIAL FICTION Chantal Montellier
IT'S LIFE AS I SEE IT: BLACK CARTOONISTS IN CHICAGO 1940–1980 Edited by Dan Nadel
JIMBO: ADVENTURES IN PARADISE Gary Panter
FATHER AND SON E.O. Plauen
SOFT CITY Pushwagner
THE NEW WORLD: COMICS FROM MAURETANIA Chris Reynolds
PITTSBURGH Frank Santoro
DISCIPLINE Dash Shaw
NINJA SARUTOBI SASUKE Sugiura Shigeru
MACDOODLE ST. Mark Alan Stamaty
POOR HELPLESS COMICS! Ed Subitzky
SLUM WOLF Tadao Tsuge
THE MAN WITHOUT TALENT Yoshiharu Tsuge
RETURN TO ROMANCE Ogden Whitney